# MOON HANDBOOKS

# ATLANTIC CANADA

D0034191

Lunenburg

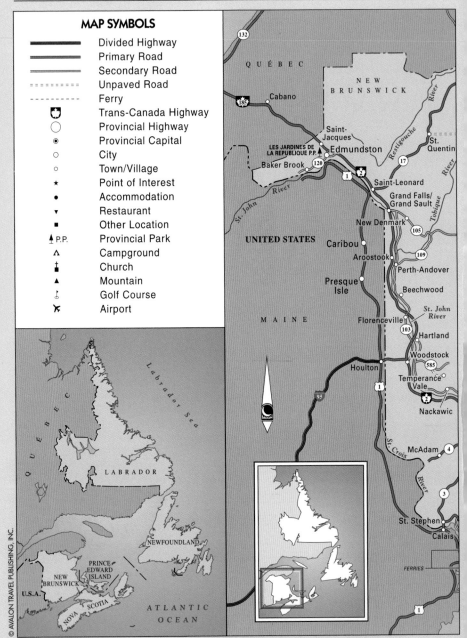

## MAP SYMBOLS

| | |
|---|---|
| | Divided Highway |
| | Primary Road |
| | Secondary Road |
| | Unpaved Road |
| | Ferry |
| | Trans-Canada Highway |
| ◯ | Provincial Highway |
| ⊙ | Provincial Capital |
| ○ | City |
| ∘ | Town/Village |
| ★ | Point of Interest |
| • | Accommodation |
| ▼ | Restaurant |
| ■ | Other Location |
| ▲ P.P. | Provincial Park |
| ∧ | Campground |
| ⛪ | Church |
| ▲ | Mountain |
| ⛳ | Golf Course |
| ✈ | Airport |

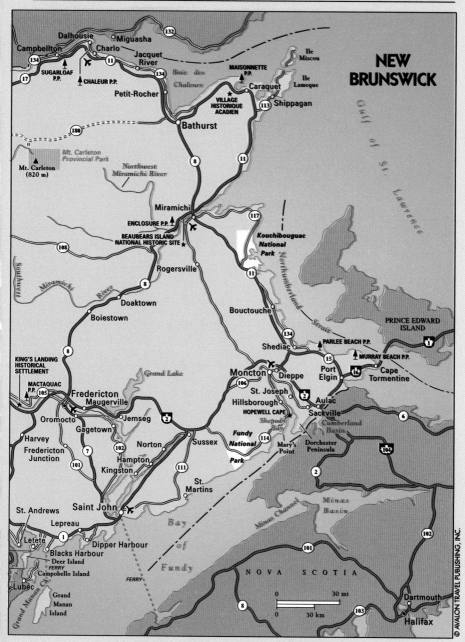

NEW
BRUNSWICK

Dalhousie
Miguasha
132
Campbellton
Charlo
134
Jacquet
River
11
SUGARLOAF
P.P.
17
134
CHALEUR P.P.
Petit-Rocher
Baie des
Chaleurs
Ile
Miscou
MAISONNETTE
P.P.
Ile
Lameque
Caraquet
VILLAGE
HISTORIQUE
ACADIEN
113
Shippagan
Bathurst
180
Mt. Carleton
Provincial Park
8
11
Mt. Carleton
(820 m)
Northwest
Miramichi River

Gulf of St. Lawrence

Miramichi
117
ENCLOSURE P.P.
BEAUBEARS ISLAND
NATIONAL HISTORIC SITE
Kouchibouguac
National
Park
108
Rogersville
11
Miramichi River
8
Doaktown
Bouctouche
Boiestown
134
PRINCE EDWARD
ISLAND
Shediac
PARLEE BEACH P.P.
KING'S LANDING
HISTORICAL
SETTLEMENT
8
Grand Lake
Moncton
15
MURRAY BEACH P.P.
Port
Elgin
16
Cape
Tormentine
1
MACTAQUAC
P.P.
105
Fredericton
Maugerville
106
Dieppe
St. Joseph
2
Aulac
Oromocto
Gagetown
Jemseg
Hillsborough
HOPEWELL CAPE
Sackville
6
Harvey
102
Norton
Shepody
Bay
Cumberland
Basin
Fredericton
Junction
7
Sussex
Fundy
National
Park
114
Dorchester
Peninsula
104
101
Hampton
Kingston
111
Mary's
Point
2
St. Andrews
Saint John
St.
Martins
Minas
Basin
Lepreau
1
Letete
Dipper Harbour
Bay
of
102
Blacks Harbour
Deer Island
FERRY
Campobello Island
Fundy
101
NOVA    SCOTIA
Dartmouth
Lubec
Grand
Manan
Island
FERRY
8
30 mi
0
30 km
103
Halifax

© AVALON TRAVEL PUBLISHING, INC.

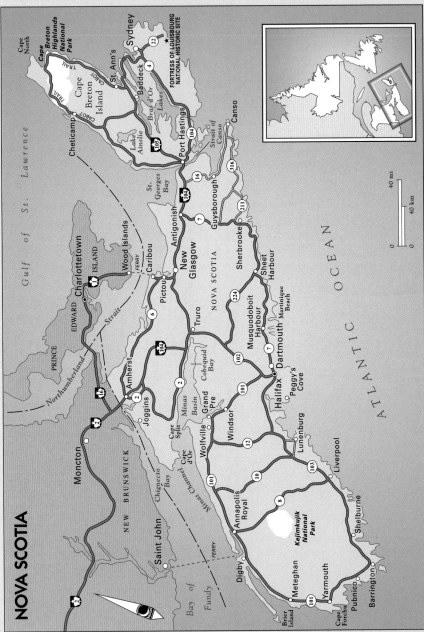

NOVA SCOTIA

© AVALON TRAVEL PUBLISHING, INC.

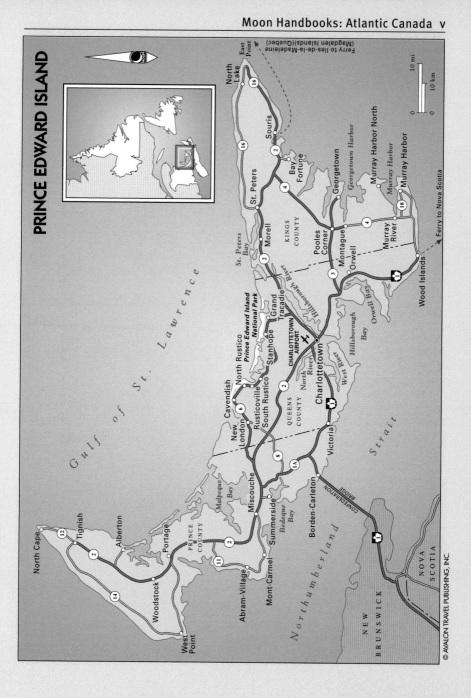

PRINCE EDWARD ISLAND

Ferry to Îles-de-la-Madeleine
(Magdalen Islands)(Quebec)

East Point
North Lake
Souris
North Cape
Tignish
Alberton
Portage
Woodstock
West Point
PRINCE COUNTY
Malpeque Bay
Abram-Village
Mont-Carmel
Summerside
Bedeque Bay
Miscouche
New London
Cavendish
North Rustico
Prince Edward Island National Park
Stanhope
Grand Tracadie
Rusticoville
South Rustico
QUEENS COUNTY
CHARLOTTETOWN AIRPORT
Charlottetown
North River
West River
Victoria
Borden-Carleton
CONFEDERATION BRIDGE
Northumberland Strait
NEW BRUNSWICK
NOVA SCOTIA
Gulf of St. Lawrence
St. Peters Bay
St. Peters
Morell
Bay Fortune
KINGS COUNTY
Pooles Corner
Montague
Orwell
Georgetown Harbor
Georgetown
Murray Harbor North
Murray Harbor
Murray River
Orwell Bay
Hillsborough Bay
Hillsborough River
Wood Islands
Ferry to Nova Scotia

10 mi
10 km

© AVALON TRAVEL PUBLISHING, INC.

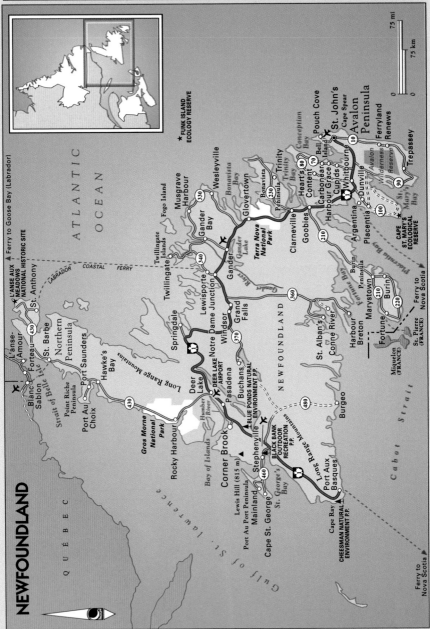

# NEWFOUNDLAND

**Q U É B E C**

ATLANTIC OCEAN

Ferry to Goose Bay (Labrador)

L'ANSE AUX MEADOWS NATIONAL HISTORIC SITE

St. Anthony

L'anse-Amour
Blanc Sablon
Forteau
St. Barbe
Strait of Belle Isle
Point Riche Peninsula
Port Au Choix
Port Saunders
Hawke's Bay
Northern Peninsula

LABRADOR COASTAL FERRY

Gros Morne National Park

Rocky Harbour

Bay of Islands
Humber River
Long Range Mountains

Springdale
Deer Lake
Pasadena
DEER LAKE AIRPORT
BLUE PONDS NATURAL ENVIRONMENT P.P.
Buchans
Corner Brook
Lewis Hill (815 m)
Stephenville
Mainland
Port Au Port Peninsula
St. George's Bay
Cape St. George

Gulf of St. Lawrence

460
430

BLACK BANK OUTDOOR RECREATION P.P.

Annieopsquotch Mountains

480

Burgeo

Long Range Mountains

Port Aux Basques
Cape Ray
CHEESMAN NATURAL ENVIRONMENT P.P.

Ferry to Nova Scotia

Cabot Strait

NEWFOUNDLAND

Gander River
Gander Lake
Gander
370
340
330
Lewisporte
Notre Dame Junction
Grand Falls
Windsor
Twillingate
Twillingate Islands
Fogo Island
Musgrave Harbour
Wesleyville
Gander Bay

360

St. Alban's
Conne River
Harbour Breton

Fortune
St. Pierre (FRANCE)
Miquelon (FRANCE)

Marystown
Burin
Burin Peninsula
210
220
Ferry to Nova Scotia

Bonavista Bay
Bonavista
Bonavista Peninsula
Glovertown
Terra Nova National Park
Clarenville
Goobies
230
210

Placentia Bay
Argentia
Placentia
100
CAPE ST. MARY'S ECOLOGICAL RESERVE

Trinity
Trinity Bay
Hear's Content
Harbour Grace
Carbonear
Cupids
Dunville
80
70
Bell Island
Conception Bay

Avalon Wilderness Reserve

90

St. Mary's Bay

Pouch Cove
St. John's
Cape Spear
10
Whitbourne
Avalon Peninsula
Ferryland
Renews
Trepassey

★ FUNK ISLAND ECOLOGY RESERVE

75 mi
75 km
0

© AVALON TRAVEL PUBLISHING, INC.

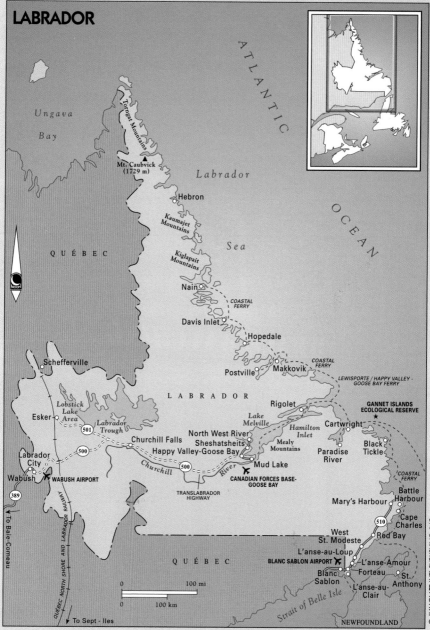

# LABRADOR

*Ungava Bay*

QUÉBEC

ATLANTIC OCEAN

Torngat Mountains

Mt. Caubvick
(1729 m)

*Labrador*

Hebron

Kaumajet Mountains

*Sea*

Kiglapait Mountains

Nain

COASTAL FERRY

Davis Inlet

Hopedale

Postville

Makkovik

COASTAL FERRY

LEWISPORTE / HAPPY VALLEY - GOOSE BAY FERRY

L A B R A D O R

Rigolet

Scheffervile

Lobstick Lake Area

Esker

Labrador Trough

Lake Melville

Hamilton Inlet

GANNET ISLANDS ECOLOGICAL RESERVE ★

Cartwright

Churchill Falls

North West River
Sheshatsheits

Happy Valley-Goose Bay

Mealy Mountains

Paradise River

Black Tickle

Labrador City

Wabush

WABUSH AIRPORT

Churchill River

Mud Lake

CANADIAN FORCES BASE-GOOSE BAY

COASTAL FERRY

To Baie-Comeau

389

500

501

TRANSLABRADOR HIGHWAY

Battle Harbour

Mary's Harbour

Cape Charles

510

QUÉBEC

West St. Modeste

Red Bay

L'anse-au-Loup

BLANC SABLON AIRPORT ✈

L'anse-Amour

Blanc Sablon

Forteau

St. Anthony

L'anse-au-Clair

0    100 mi

0    100 km

QUEBEC NORTH SHORE AND LABRADOR RAILWAY

To Sept - Iles

Strait of Belle Isle

NEWFOUNDLAND

WHALE WATCHING

St. Andrews, New Brunswick

# MOON HANDBOOKS

# ATLANTIC CANADA

## NEW BRUNSWICK, PRINCE EDWARD ISLAND, NOVA SCOTIA, NEWFOUNDLAND & LABRADOR

### THIRD EDITION

## MARK MORRIS & ANDREW HEMPSTEAD

AVALON
TRAVEL

Moon Handbooks: Atlantic Canada
New Brunswick, Prince Edward Island,
Nova Scotia, Newfoundland & Labrador
Third Edition

**Mark Morris and Andrew Hempstead**

Published by
Avalon Travel Publishing
5855 Beaudry St.
Emeryville, CA 94608, USA

Please send all comments, corrections,
additions, amendments, and critiques to:

**Moon Handbooks: Atlantic Canada**

AVALON TRAVEL PUBLISHING
5855 BEAUDRY ST.
EMERYVILLE, CA 94608, USA
email: atpfeedback@avalonpub.com
www.moon.com

Printing History
1st edition—1995
3rd edition—June 2002
5 4 3 2 1

ISBN: 1-56691-385-3
ISSN: 1538-6783

Editors: Ellen Cavalli, Kevin McLain
Series Manager: Erin Van Rheenen
Copy Editor: Peg Goldstein
Graphics Coordinator: Susan Mira Snyder
Production: Jacob Goolkasian, Karen Heithecker
Cover Design: Kari Gim
Interior Design: Kelly Pendragon, Amber Pirker, Alvaro Villanueva
Proofreader: Julie Leigh
Map Editors: Naomi Adler Dancis, Beth Polzin
Cartographers: Brian Bardwell, Bob Race, Chris Folks, Mike Morgenfeld, Kat Kalamaras
Indexer: Valerie Sellers Blanton

Front cover photo: © Andrew Hempstead

Distributed by Publishers Group West

Printed in the U.S.A. by R.R. Donnelley

# ABOUT THE AUTHORS
## Mark Morris

© BETH MORRIS

After seven years of working on travel guides from behind a desk as senior editor at Moon Publications, Mark Morris hit the trail to try his hand at writing a guidebook. The first edition of *Moon Handbooks: Atlantic Canada* was the result.

Mark has always found something profoundly alluring and sad about coastal places (he has also written guides to Ireland and the Oregon coast), and for him Atlantic Canada distills the essence of that feeling. His personal connections with the region date back to the early 19th century, when ancestors from Britain, Ireland, and France came to North America via the Maritimes.

Besides the great physical beauty of the land and sea, Mark is drawn to Atlantic Canada's rich cultural heritage—the legacy of the Irish, French, Scottish, English, and others who settled the provinces and have managed to resist (or have been overlooked by) modern homogenization just a little. The slower pace of life there is also particularly appealing. One of Mark's favorite pastimes in any town in Atlantic Canada is joining the locals—of all ages—as they come out for their after-dinner stroll on fine summer evenings. It's a priceless taste of simpler times that's getting hard to find elsewhere.

Mark is currently the managing editor at Expedia.com, the leading travel site on the Internet. He lives with his family near Seattle, where he can indulge his passions for steelhead, sailboats, and fiddle tunes.

# ABOUT THE AUTHORS
## Andrew Hempstead

On his first trip to Atlantic Canada, Andrew Hempstead made a beeline for the coast to photograph the legendary Nova Scotia sunrise. He then headed to the nearest local restaurant, and wearily ordered the daily breakfast special without bothering to check what it was: cod fried in pork fat, pickled beets, and a side of baked beans.

With this traditional (and unexpected) introduction to Canada's east coast, Andrew set off on a road trip that stretched the term "unlimited mileage" on his rental car to the limit. Teaming up with knowledgeable local, Ted Vautour, for part of the trip, Andrew traveled to the farthest corners of all four provinces.

Andrew has been travel writing since 1989, when, after leaving a well-established career in advertising, he took off for Alaska, linking up with veteran travel writer Deke Castleman to help research and update the fourth edition of *Moon Handbooks: Alaska-Yukon*. Andrew is now the author of books on British Columbia, Alberta, the Canadian Rockies, the Northwest Territories, and Nunavut, and has been a regular contributor to *Road Trip USA* and other guides. His writing and photographs have also appeared in a wide variety of magazines, including *National Geographic Traveler, Interval World,* and *Travesias*.

Farther afield, Andrew is coauthor of *Moon Handbooks: Australia* and has traveled to New Zealand multiple times on assignment to write and photograph for *Moon Handbooks: New Zealand*. He has also traveled purely for pleasure throughout most of the United States, Europe, the South Pacific, and India.

When not working on his books, Andrew enjoys hiking, fishing, golfing, camping, and the simple pleasures in life, such as skimming stones down on the river. He lives in Canmore, Alberta, with his wife, Dianne, and their two dogs.

The website www.westerncanadatravel.com showcases Andrew's work.

# Contents

**INTRODUCTION** . . . . . . . . . . . . . . . . . . . . . . . . . . . . . . . . . . . . . . . . . . . . . **1**

**THE LAND** . . . . . . . . . . . . . . . . . . . . . . . . . . . . . . . . . . . . . . . . . . . . . . . . . . 2
The Provinces (and the Départment); Climate; Flora; Fauna; Sea Life

**HISTORY** . . . . . . . . . . . . . . . . . . . . . . . . . . . . . . . . . . . . . . . . . . . . . . . . . . . 12
Beginnings; The Acadian Deportation; Toward Confederation

**GOVERNMENT AND ECONOMY** . . . . . . . . . . . . . . . . . . . . . . . . . . . . . . 18
Government; Economy

**PEOPLE** . . . . . . . . . . . . . . . . . . . . . . . . . . . . . . . . . . . . . . . . . . . . . . . . . . . . 22
Native Peoples and Métis; Provincial Distinctions; Language

**ON THE ROAD** . . . . . . . . . . . . . . . . . . . . . . . . . . . . . . . . . . . . . . . . . . . **28**

**PROVINCIAL HIGHLIGHTS** . . . . . . . . . . . . . . . . . . . . . . . . . . . . . . . . . 28
New Brunswick; Nova Scotia; Prince Edward Island; Newfoundland and
Labrador

**RECREATION AND ENTERTAINMENT** . . . . . . . . . . . . . . . . . . . . . . . 32
Outdoor Activities; Spectator Sports; Entertainment and Events; Shopping

**ACCOMMODATIONS AND FOOD** . . . . . . . . . . . . . . . . . . . . . . . . . . . . 35
Hotel, Motel, and Resort Groups; Hostelling International; Educational Stays;
Camping; Food and Drink

**GETTING THERE** . . . . . . . . . . . . . . . . . . . . . . . . . . . . . . . . . . . . . . . . . . 41
By Car; By Rail; By Air

**GETTING AROUND** . . . . . . . . . . . . . . . . . . . . . . . . . . . . . . . . . . . . . . . . 43
By Car; By Ferry; By Bus; By Air

**INFORMATION AND SERVICES** . . . . . . . . . . . . . . . . . . . . . . . . . . . . . 45
Visas and Officialdom; Health and Safety; Money; Communications; Media and
Maps; What to Take; Weights and Measures

**SPECIAL TOPICS**

Sightseeing Checklist . . . . . . . . . . . . . . . . . . . . .30
Lodging Reservations and Information Sources 36
Canada Select . . . . . . . . . . . . . . . . . . . . . . . .37
Cutting Flight Costs . . . . . . . . . . . . . . . . . . . .42
Confederation Bridge . . . . . . . . . . . . . . . . . .43
Provincial Tourism Offices . . . . . . . . . . . . . .45

# New Brunswick

**INTRODUCTION** . . . . . . . . . . . . . . . . . . . . . . . . . . . . . . . . . . . . . . . . . . . . **52**
Sightseeing Highlights; The Land; Climate; Flora and Fauna; History;
Government; Economy; The People; Parks and Recreation; Entertainment and
Events; Arts and Crafts; Accommodations and Camping; Food and Drink;
Information and Services; Getting There; Getting Around

## SPECIAL TOPIC

*Famous New Brunswickers* . . . . . . . . . . . . . . . . . . . . . . . . . . . . . . . . . . . . . . . . . . . . . . . . .*59*

# SAINT JOHN RIVER VALLEY . . . . . . . . . . . . . . . . . . . . . . . . . . . . . **66**

**FREDERICTON** . . . . . . . . . . . . . . . . . . . . . . . . . . . . . . . . . . . . . . . . . . . . . . . . . . . **.67**
History; Sights; Accommodations and Camping; Food; Entertainment and
Events; Recreation; Shopping; Information and Services; Transportation; Vicinity
of Fredericton
**UP THE SAINT JOHN RIVER** . . . . . . . . . . . . . . . . . . . . . . . . . . . . . . . . . . . . . . . . **.80**
Mactaquac and Vicinity; Kings Landing Historical Settlement; To Grand
Falls/Grand-Sault; Edmundston and Vicinity; Mount Carleton Provincial Park

## SPECIAL TOPICS

*By Any Other Name* . . . . . . . . . . . . . . . . . . .*70*   *République du Madawaska* . . . . . . . . . . . . . .*85*
*Houseboating the Saint John* . . . . . . . . . . . . .*81*

# FUNDY COAST . . . . . . . . . . . . . . . . . . . . . . . . . . . . . . . . . . . . . . . . . . . **87**

**INTRODUCTION** . . . . . . . . . . . . . . . . . . . . . . . . . . . . . . . . . . . . . . . . . . . . . . . . . . **.87**
History; Getting Around
**LOWER FUNDY COAST AND THE FUNDY ISLES** . . . . . . . . . . . . . . . . . . . . . . . **.91**
St. Andrews; St. George; Deer and Campobello Islands; Grand Manan Island;
East to Saint John
**SAINT JOHN AND VICINITY** . . . . . . . . . . . . . . . . . . . . . . . . . . . . . . . . . . . . . . . **.99**
History; Getting Oriented; Sights; Accommodations and Camping; Food;
Entertainment and Events; Recreation; Shopping; Information and Services;
Getting There; Getting Around
**UPPER FUNDY COAST** . . . . . . . . . . . . . . . . . . . . . . . . . . . . . . . . . . . . . . . . . . . **115**
Fundy National Park; Around Chignecto Bay; Sackville; Dorchester Peninsula
and Tantramar Marshes

## SPECIAL TOPIC

*Irving Nature Park* . . . . . . . . . . . . . . . . . . . . . . . . . . . . . . . . . . . . . . . . . . . . . . . . . . . .*111*

# ACADIAN COAST . . . . . . . . . . . . . . . . . . . . . . . . . . . . . . . . . . . . . . . **122**

**INTRODUCTION** . . . . . . . . . . . . . . . . . . . . . . . . . . . . . . . . . . . . . . . . . . . . . . . . . .122
History
**MONCTON AND VICINITY** . . . . . . . . . . . . . . . . . . . . . . . . . . . . . . . . . . . . . . . .126
Town Sights; Magnetic Hill; Accommodations; Food and Drink; Entertainment
and Events; Recreation; Shopping; Information and Services; Transportation;
Vicinity of Moncton
**THE STRAIT COAST** . . . . . . . . . . . . . . . . . . . . . . . . . . . . . . . . . . . . . . . . . . . . . .135
Cape Tormentine to Kouchibouguac; Kouchibouguac National Park

**MIRAMICHI RIVER** . . . . . . . . . . . . . . . . . . . . . . . . . . . . . . . . . . . . . . . . . . . . . .**138**
  Miramichi City; Up the River
**GULF COAST** . . . . . . . . . . . . . . . . . . . . . . . . . . . . . . . . . . . . . . . . . . . . . . . . . . .**141**
**BAIE DES CHALEURS** . . . . . . . . . . . . . . . . . . . . . . . . . . . . . . . . . . . . . . . . . . .**142**
  Caraquet and Vicinity; Bathurst to Campbellton

**SPECIAL TOPIC**

*Salmon Fishing on the Miramichi* . . . . . . . . . . . . . . . . . . . . . . . . . . . . . . . . . . . . . . . . . . . . . . *139*

# Nova Scotia

**INTRODUCTION** . . . . . . . . . . . . . . . . . . . . . . . . . . . . . . . . . . . . . . . . . . . . . **148**
  The Land; Climate; Flora and Fauna; History; Government; Economy; The
  People; Arts and Crafts; Entertainment and Events; Recreation; Accommodations
  and Camping; Food and Drink; Information and Services; Getting There;
  Getting Around

**SPECIAL TOPICS**

*Tracing Family Roots* . . . . . . . . . . . . . . . . . *155*    *A Photographer's Dream* . . . . . . . . . . . . . . . *161*
*Two Traditional Acadian Recipes* . . . . . . . . *158*

**CENTRAL NOVA SCOTIA** . . . . . . . . . . . . . . . . . . . . . . . . . . . . . . . . . . **164**
  History
**CUMBERLAND AND COLCHESTER COUNTIES** . . . . . . . . . . . . . . . . . . . . . . . .**167**
  Amherst; South of Amherst; North to the Strait Coast; Truro; North of Truro;
  Shubenacadie River
**HALIFAX** . . . . . . . . . . . . . . . . . . . . . . . . . . . . . . . . . . . . . . . . . . . . . . . . . . . . .**174**
  History; Getting Oriented; Downtown Sights; Sights South of Downtown; Sights
  In and Around Dartmouth; Parks; Accommodations; Food; Entertainment and
  Events; Recreation and Sports; Shopping; Information and Services; Getting
  There; Getting Around

**SPECIAL TOPICS**

*The Colossal Fundy Tides* . . . . . . . . . . . . . . *166*    *Sightseeing Tours* . . . . . . . . . . . . . . . . . . . . . *192*
*Halifax Harbour* . . . . . . . . . . . . . . . . . . . . . *176*

**SOUTHWESTERN NOVA SCOTIA** . . . . . . . . . . . . . . . . . . . . . . . . . . . . **196**
  History
**HALIFAX TO LUNENBURG** . . . . . . . . . . . . . . . . . . . . . . . . . . . . . . . . . . . . . .**198**
  Peggy's Cove; Chester and Vicinity; Mahone Bay
**LUNENBURG** . . . . . . . . . . . . . . . . . . . . . . . . . . . . . . . . . . . . . . . . . . . . . . . . . . .**202**
  Sights and Recreation; Accommodations and Camping; Food and Entertainment;
  Other Practicalities

**SOUTH SHORE** . . . . . . . . . . . . . . . . . . . . . . . . . . . . . . . . . . . . . . . . . . . . . . .207
Lunenburg to Shelburne; Shelburne; Shelburne to Yarmouth
**YARMOUTH AND LA CÔTE ACADIENNE** . . . . . . . . . . . . . . . . . . . . . . . . . .211
Yarmouth; La Côte Acadienne
**DIGBY AND VICINITY** . . . . . . . . . . . . . . . . . . . . . . . . . . . . . . . . . . . . . . . . . . .217
Digby; Kejimkujik National Park
**THE ANNAPOLIS VALLEY** . . . . . . . . . . . . . . . . . . . . . . . . . . . . . . . . . . . . . . .220
Annapolis Royal; Wolfville; Vicinity of Wolfville

SPECIAL TOPICS
*Captain Kidd's "Money Pit"* . . . . . . . . . . . .*200*      *Sailing Back in Time* . . . . . . . . . . . . . . . .*203*


**EASTERN NOVA SCOTIA** . . . . . . . . . . . . . . . . . . . . . . . . . . . . . . . . . . . . . .**226**
**THE STRAIT SHORE** . . . . . . . . . . . . . . . . . . . . . . . . . . . . . . . . . . . . . . . . . . . .**227**
Pictou and Vicinity; Antigonish
**THE EASTERN SHORE** . . . . . . . . . . . . . . . . . . . . . . . . . . . . . . . . . . . . . . . . . .**232**
Dartmouth to Sherbrooke; Sherbrooke and Vicinity; Canso

**CAPE BRETON ISLAND** . . . . . . . . . . . . . . . . . . . . . . . . . . . . . . . . . . . . . .**237**
**THE SOUTH** . . . . . . . . . . . . . . . . . . . . . . . . . . . . . . . . . . . . . . . . . . . . . . . . . . .**239**
Highway 4 to Sydney; Highway 19 to the Cabot Trail; Highway 105 to Baddeck;
Baddeck
**CABOT TRAIL** . . . . . . . . . . . . . . . . . . . . . . . . . . . . . . . . . . . . . . . . . . . . . . . . .**244**
Chéticamp; Cape Breton Highlands National Park; St. Ann's and Vicinity
**THE EAST** . . . . . . . . . . . . . . . . . . . . . . . . . . . . . . . . . . . . . . . . . . . . . . . . . . . . .**250**
Sydney and Vicinity; Fortress of Louisbourg

SPECIAL TOPIC
*Cape Breton Highlands National Park Campgrounds* . . . . . . . . . . . . . . . . . . . . . . . . . . . . . . . . . . . . . . .*246*

# Prince Edward Island

**INTRODUCTION** . . . . . . . . . . . . . . . . . . . . . . . . . . . . . . . . . . . . . . . . . . . . . . .**258**
The Land; Climate; Flora and Fauna; History; Government and Economy; The
People; Arts, Crafts, and Shopping; Entertainment and Events; Recreation;
Accommodations and Food; Information and Services; Getting There; Getting
Around

SPECIAL TOPIC
*Island Development Issues* . . . . . . . . . . . . . . . . . . . . . . . . . . . . . . . . . . . . . . . . . . . . . . . . . . . . . . . . . .*262*

# QUEENS COUNTY ...........................................**271**

## CHARLOTTETOWN AND VICINITY .........................272
History; Getting Oriented; Sights; Accommodations; Food; Entertainment and
Events; Recreation; Shopping; Information and Services; Transportation
## THE SOUTH SHORE ......................................284
Cornwall and Vicinity; Victoria; Borden-Carleton; East of Charlottetown
## THE NORTH SHORE ......................................289
The Eastern End; Prince Edward Island National Park; Around Rustico Bay;
Cavendish; Vicinity of Cavendish

### SPECIAL TOPIC
*Lucy Maud Montgomery* ...........................................*294*


# PRINCE COUNTY ..........................................**300**
Getting Around
## EASTERN PRINCE COUNTY ...............................302
Kensington and Vicinity; Summerside
## AROUND MALPEQUE BAY .................................306
Tyne Valley; Vicinity of Tyne Valley
## RÉGION ÉVANGÉLINE ....................................308
Miscouche; Mont-Carmel; Other Acadian Settlements
## WESTERN PRINCE COUNTY ..............................310
Mill River Provincial Park; O'Leary; The Strait Coast; Alberton and Vicinity;
Tignish and Vicinity


# KINGS COUNTY ...........................................**314**
History; Highways and Byways
## SOUTHERN KINGS COUNTY .............................317
Around Murray Harbour; Montague and Vicinity; Brudenell River Provincial
Park and Resort; Vicinity of Brudenell River Park
## NORTHERN KINGS COUNTY ............................320
Bay Fortune and Vicinity; Souris; The Eastern Corner; The Gulf Shore

### SPECIAL TOPIC
*Îles de la Madeleine* ...............................................*322*

# Newfoundland and Labrador

# INTRODUCTION ..........................................**326**
Sightseeing Highlights; The Land; Climate; Flora and Fauna; History; Government and
Economy; People; Crafts; Events and Entertainment; Recreation; Accommodations and
Camping; Food; Information and Services; Getting There; Getting Around

## SPECIAL TOPICS

The Bergs of Summer: Icebergs on Parade . . .329
The Newfoundland Dog and
   Labrador Retriever . . . . . . . . . . . . . . . .334
Newfoundland's Cod Industry: A Chronology . .336

Newfoundland's Role in Aviation History . . .340
A Few Favorite Local Foods . . . . . . . . . . . . .347
Caution: Moose on the Loose . . . . . . . . . . . .350


## NEWFOUNDLAND . . . . . . . . . . . . . . . . . . . . . . . . . . . . . . . . . . . . . . .352
Introduction
### ST. JOHN'S AND VICINITY . . . . . . . . . . . . . . . . . . . . . . . . . . . . . . . .353
History; Sights; Accommodations; Food; Entertainment and Events; Recreation;
Shopping; Information and Services; Getting There; Getting Around
### AVALON PENINSULA . . . . . . . . . . . . . . . . . . . . . . . . . . . . . . . . . . . .371
Northern Avalon; South of St. John's; The Cape Shore
### EASTERN NEWFOUNDLAND . . . . . . . . . . . . . . . . . . . . . . . . . . . . . .376
Burin Peninsula; St-Pierre and Miquelon; The South Coast; Bonavista Peninsula;
Terra Nova National Park; Gander to Twillingate; Grand Falls–Windsor
### WESTERN NEWFOUNDLAND . . . . . . . . . . . . . . . . . . . . . . . . . . . . .391
Gros Morne National Park; The Northern Peninsula; Corner Brook; Highway
450 West from Corner Brook; Corner Brook to Port Aux Basques

## SPECIAL TOPIC
The Fjords of Gros Morne . . . . . . . . . . . . . . . . . . . . . . . . . . . . . . . . . . . . . . . .394


## LABRADOR . . . . . . . . . . . . . . . . . . . . . . . . . . . . . . . . . . . . . . . . . . . . .407
### INTRODUCTION . . . . . . . . . . . . . . . . . . . . . . . . . . . . . . . . . . . . . . . . .407
The Land and People; History; Recreation; Transportation
### SOUTH AND CENTRAL LABRADOR . . . . . . . . . . . . . . . . . . . . . . . . .413
Happy Valley–Goose Bay and Vicinity; Labrador West; Labrador Straits;
Cartwright
### NORTH COAST . . . . . . . . . . . . . . . . . . . . . . . . . . . . . . . . . . . . . . . . . .421
Goose Bay to Nain; Nain and the Far North

## SPECIAL TOPICS
Laying Claim to Labrador . . . . . . . . . . . . . .408
The Grenfell Legend . . . . . . . . . . . . . . . . . .420


## RESOURCES . . . . . . . . . . . . . . . . . . . . . . . . . . . . . . . . . . . . . . . . . . . .423
### SUGGESTED READING . . . . . . . . . . . . . . . . . . . . . . . . . . . . . . . . . . .424
### INTERNET RESOURCES . . . . . . . . . . . . . . . . . . . . . . . . . . . . . . . . . . .432
### INDEX . . . . . . . . . . . . . . . . . . . . . . . . . . . . . . . . . . . . . . . . . . . . . . . . .434

# Abbreviations

B&B—bed-and-breakfast inn
C—Celsius
d—double occupancy
F—Fahrenheit
HST—Harmonized Sales Tax
Hwy.—highway
km—kilometers
kph—kilometers per hour
OW—one-way

PEI—Prince Edward Island
pop.—population
pp—per person
RCMP—Royal Canadian Mounted Police
RT—roundtrip
RV—recreational vehicle
s—single occupancy
WW I—World War I
WW II—World War II

# Keeping Current

Travel information changes constantly, and even the most diligent travel writer has a hard time keeping up with everything. We look to our readers to help keep us apprised of up-to-the-minute developments. Found a restaurant with the world's greatest goulash? The bed-and-breakfast of your dreams? That perfect deserted beach? Let us know. And if you find information in this book that is no longer valid, let us know about that, too, so we can make the appropriate changes in the next edition.

*Moon Handbooks: Atlantic Canada*
c/o Avalon Travel Publishing
5855 Beaudry St.
Emeryville, CA 94608, USA
atpfeedback@avalonpub.com

# Maps

New Brunswick  . . . . . . . . . . . . . .ii-iii
Nova Scotia  . . . . . . . . . . . . . . . . . .iv
Prince Edward Island  . . . . . . . . . . . .v
Newfoundland  . . . . . . . . . . . . . . . .vi
Labrador . . . . . . . . . . . . . . . . . . . .vii

## INTRODUCTION

Atlantic Canada . . . . . . . . . . . . . . . .3

# New Brunswick

## SAINT JOHN RIVER VALLEY

Fredericton Vicinity . . . . . . . . . . . . .67
Downtown Fredericton  . . . . . . . . . . .71
Downriver from Fredericton . . . . . . . .79
Upriver from Fredericton  . . . . . . . . . .83

## FUNDY COAST

Fundy Coast  . . . . . . . . . . . . . . . . . .88
St. Andrews . . . . . . . . . . . . . . . . . . .92
Saint John and Vicinity  . . . . . . . . . .100
Uptown Saint John  . . . . . . . . . . . . .103
Upper Fundy Coast  . . . . . . . . . . . . .118

## ACADIAN COAST

Acadian Coast  . . . . . . . . . . . . . . . .123
Moncton and Vicinity  . . . . . . . . . . .126
Downtown Moncton  . . . . . . . . . . . .127

# Nova Scotia

## CENTRAL NOVA SCOTIA

Central Nova Scotia . . . . . . . . . . . . .165
Amherst . . . . . . . . . . . . . . . . . . . . .167
Truro . . . . . . . . . . . . . . . . . . . . . . .171
Shubenacadie River  . . . . . . . . . . . . .173
Downtown Halifax . . . . . . . . . . . . . .177
Greater Halifax  . . . . . . . . . . . . . . . .181

## SOUTHWESTERN NOVA SCOTIA

Southwestern Nova Scotia  . . . . . . . .197
Halifax to Lunenburg . . . . . . . . . . . .198
Lunenburg . . . . . . . . . . . . . . . . . . .202
Shelburne  . . . . . . . . . . . . . . . . . . .208
Yarmouth  . . . . . . . . . . . . . . . . . . .211
La Côte Acadienne  . . . . . . . . . . . . .214
Digby  . . . . . . . . . . . . . . . . . . . . . .217
Wolfville . . . . . . . . . . . . . . . . . . . .222

## EASTERN NOVA SCOTIA

Eastern Nova Scotia . . . . . . . . . . . .227
Pictou . . . . . . . . . . . . . . . . . . . . . .228
The Eastern Shore . . . . . . . . . . . . . .233

## CAPE BRETON ISLAND

Cape Breton Island . . . . . . . . . . . . . .238
Sydney . . . . . . . . . . . . . . . . . . . . . .250

# Prince Edward Island

## QUEENS COUNTY

Charlottetown . . . . . . . . . . . . . . . .273
Central Charlottetown . . . . . . . . . . .275
Queens County . . . . . . . . . . . . . . . .285
Prince Edward Island National Park . .291
Lucy Maud Montgomery's
     Cavendish Landmarks . . . . . . . . . .296

## PRINCE COUNTY

Prince County . . . . . . . . . . . . . . . .301
Summerside . . . . . . . . . . . . . . . . . .303

## KINGS COUNTY

Kings County . . . . . . . . . . . . . . . . .315

# Newfoundland and Labrador

## NEWFOUNDLAND

Central St. John's . . . . . . . . . . . . . . .356
St. John's and Vicinity . . . . . . . . . . .358
Avalon Peninsula . . . . . . . . . . . . . . .372
St-Pierre and Miquelon . . . . . . . . . .378
St-Pierre . . . . . . . . . . . . . . . . . . . .379
The East Coast . . . . . . . . . . . . . . . .381
Trinity . . . . . . . . . . . . . . . . . . . . . .383
The Northeast . . . . . . . . . . . . . . . . .385
Twillingate Area . . . . . . . . . . . . . . .387
Grand Falls–Windsor . . . . . . . . . . . .389
Gros Morne National Park . . . . . . . .392
Corner Brook . . . . . . . . . . . . . . . . .399

## LABRADOR

Happy Valley–Goose Bay . . . . . . . . .414
Labrador Straits . . . . . . . . . . . . . . . .418

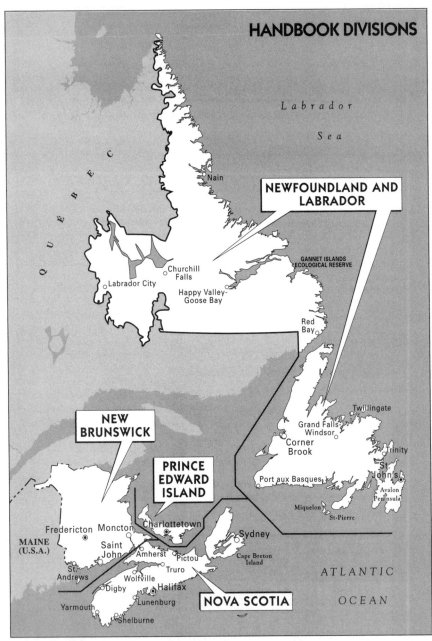

HANDBOOK DIVISIONS

Labrador Sea

NEWFOUNDLAND AND LABRADOR

GANNET ISLANDS ECOLOGICAL RESERVE

Nain

Churchill Falls

Labrador City

Happy Valley-Goose Bay

Red Bay

QUEBEC

Twillingate

Grand Falls-Windsor

Corner Brook

Trinity

St. John's

Port aux Basques

Avalon Peninsula

Miquelon

St-Pierre

NEW BRUNSWICK

PRINCE EDWARD ISLAND

Fredericton

Moncton

Charlottetown

Sydney

MAINE (U.S.A.)

Saint John

Amherst

Pictou

Cape Breton Island

ATLANTIC

St. Andrews

Truro

OCEAN

Wolfville

Digby

Halifax

NOVA SCOTIA

Yarmouth

Lunenburg

Shelburne

# Introduction

*They that go down to the sea in ships,*
*That do business in great waters,*
*These see the works of the Lord,*
*And his wonders in the deep.*

**Psalm 107**

Atlantic Canada—the sea-bound northeastern corner of North America—is a picture-book painting, a spacious canvas splashed with brightly colored seaports, red-clay roads, boulder-cluttered coasts, shadowy forests, and undulating fields of barley and potatoes, all of it framed by the variegated blues of the sky and surrounding seas.

This seacoast realm is an extraordinarily captivating place. Life in its hundreds of seaports has bred an insular culture. For centuries, the folk of Atlantic Canada have gone down to the sea in ships to ply their trade on the great waters. The hard seafaring life has given them what so much of the modern world has thoughtlessly let slip through its fingers: nearness to nature's honest rhythms, replete with the old values of kindness, thrift, and rugged self-reliance. In a world crowded with too many people and too much development, Atlantic Canada remains a refuge of sorts. This is not to imply that old-time values are bereft of sophistication. Rather, the people

©ANDREW HEMPSTEAD

Peggy's Cove, Nova Scotia

here embody the good life in a modern world too often prepackaged and bland.

Atlantic Canada makes a harmony out of contending elements, a fortuitous combination of place and people far from the maddening crowd and peaceful now after centuries of strife.

# The Land

Even among Canadians, there is sometimes confusion about the definition of the eastern Canada region. Atlantic Canada comprises the Maritime provinces, New Brunswick, Nova Scotia, and Prince Edward Island, together with Newfoundland and Labrador.

Atlantic Canada as a whole forms one-twentieth of the country's total area. The provinces, and the distances separating them, are far larger than they may seem at first glance, compared against the vastness of the whole of Canada. Nova Scotia, for example, is the country's second-smallest province, yet it will take you a long day to drive from Yarmouth, at the southwestern tip, to Cape Breton Highlands National Park, at the other end of the province. And from Cape Breton, it's a six-hour ferry ride to the next landfall—the island of Newfoundland—which itself lies nearer to Liverpool, England, than to Toronto.

More than any other region of Canada, the Atlantic provinces are defined by water, which divides and yet also unifies them. The planet's mightiest tides surge through the Bay of Fundy between New Brunswick and Nova Scotia. The

Cabot Strait separates Nova Scotia's Cape Breton and the island of Newfoundland's southern coastline. The unexpectedly warm Northumberland Strait, heated by the Gulf Stream, is a broad blue parenthesis dividing Prince Edward Island from Nova Scotia and New Brunswick. On the island's north side spreads the Gulf of St. Lawrence. The Baie des Chaleurs, its warmth owing to its shallow depth, lies between northeastern New Brunswick and Québec's Gaspé Peninsula.

Along Labrador's coast, currents from the chilly Labrador Sea move southward and fork into a channel known as the Strait of Belle Isle, which separates the island of Newfoundland from the mainland, while the rest of the current washes along Newfoundland's eastern coast.

If it were possible to walk the profoundly reticulated coastlines of the four provinces, following every cove, bay, point, and peninsula, the footsore traveler would eventually log some 25,000 miles before returning to his starting point.

Some of the finest landscapes Canada possesses are proudly displayed in the region's seven national parks. Each park is remarkable and unique in its own way, yet all share an intimate connection to water. Prince Edward Island National Park is a long ribbon of dunes, red sandstone cliffs, and salmon-pink beaches fronting the Gulf of St. Lawrence. East-central New Brunswick's Kouchibouguac National Park blends the coastal environment of the Northumberland Strait with salt marshes, bogs, and lagoons, as well as tidal rivers that permit canoe access deep into the park's interior. Fundy National Park, in southeastern New Brunswick, experiences 12-meter (40-foot) tides along Chignecto Bay. Kejimkujik National Park—although deep in the interior of southwestern Nova Scotia—nevertheless is 20 percent water, shot through as it is with lakes, rivers, and marsh. Cape Breton Highlands National Park,

© LISA COSTANTINO

**Terra Nova National Park**

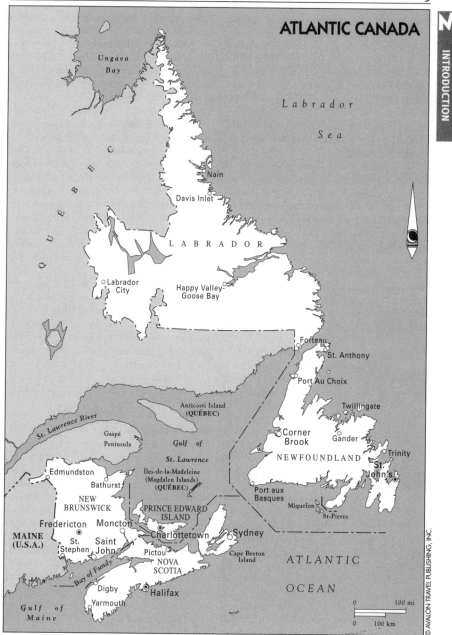

ATLANTIC CANADA

Ungava Bay

Labrador Sea

QUEBEC

Nain

Davis Inlet

LABRADOR

Labrador City

Happy Valley-Goose Bay

Forteau

St. Anthony

Port Au Choix

Twillingate

Anticosti Island (QUÉBEC)

St. Lawrence River

Gaspé Peninsula

Gulf of St. Lawrence

Corner Brook

Gander

NEWFOUNDLAND

Trinity

Edmundston

Bathurst

Iles-de-la-Madeleine (Magdalen Islands) (QUÉBEC)

Port aux Basques

St. John's

NEW BRUNSWICK

PRINCE EDWARD ISLAND

Miquelon

St-Pierre

MAINE (U.S.A.)

Fredericton

Moncton

Charlottetown

Sydney

St. Stephen

Saint John

Pictou

Cape Breton Island

ATLANTIC

Bay of Fundy

NOVA SCOTIA

Digby

Halifax

OCEAN

Yarmouth

Gulf of Maine

0    100 mi

0    100 km

© AVALON TRAVEL PUBLISHING, INC.

straddling the northern reaches of the island, faces two seas—the mountains sweep down to the relatively placid Gulf of St. Lawrence on the west and the raw Atlantic on the east. Gros Morne National Park also faces the gulf, where it is punctuated by four extraordinary landlocked fjords, known with characteristic Newfoundland understatement as "ponds." Water surrounds three sides of Terra Nova National Park, which rises in bold headlands from Bonavista Bay on Newfoundland's east coast.

The sea's pervasive presence is felt throughout the region, but the ties to the ocean are perhaps strongest in Nova Scotia and Newfoundland, whose outer coasts confront the open Atlantic. The waters off Newfoundland, in particular—the Gulf of St. Lawrence and the Grand Banks along the continental shelf—are among the most productive fisheries in the world, for five centuries an unbelievably rich resource for tuna, mackerel, herring, lobster, and cod.

Prince Edward Island, of course, is surrounded by water, so fishing is a major industry. But agriculture is an equally important component of the economy, the benevolent result of the last ice age, which blessed the land with a deep fertile loam. New Brunswick faces the sea on two sides and joins the mainland with a massive sweep of land rich in forests and ores, hence an economy comprised of fishing, forestry, and mining.

Nearly as ancient as the sea is the bedrock of the continent here. The Canadian Shield, a layer of tough Precambrian granite at least a billion years old, underlies nearly 5 million square km of eastern and central Canada, including much of Newfoundland and Labrador.

Six hundred million years ago, the collision of the North American and European continental plates pushed up the Appalachian Mountains. The range's ribs, starting far to the south in Alabama, extend through New England and the Maritime Provinces to the Gaspé Peninsula, whose highlands spread across Cape Breton and as far as Newfoundland. Geologists believe that the range was originally taller and more rugged than the modern Rockies. Glaciation and eons of erosion, however, have ground down the once-mammoth summits such that the rather modest

820-meter Mt. Carleton, in New Brunswick, is today the Maritimes' highest point. The highest peak in the Atlantic provinces, northern Labrador's desolate Mt. Caubvick, rises 1,729 meters above the Labrador Sea. Otherwise, great swaths of the region's terrain are mostly low and undulating, dipping and swelling in innumerable variations.

One of the reasons for this was glacial ice, uncountable trillions of tons of it, formed over the last four ice ages. Glaciers up to an estimated three km (two miles) thick weighed down on the elastic bedrock as recently as 14,000 years ago, submerging the coasts and counteracting the inexorable thrust of tectonic uplift.

Some 350 million years ago, as the tectonic plates shifted, a great slab of the earth's crust slumped, forming the valley that would be flooded by a rising sea to form the Bay of Fundy only 6,000 years ago.

For all the water without, in some places the region's interiors seem just as water-bound. Innumerable streams and rivers streak the landscape, pouring into copious bays and wide-mouthed estuaries at the seas. Uncounted thousands of lakes, another ice-age legacy, speckle the provinces' interiors.

# THE PROVINCES (AND THE DEPARTMENT)
## New Brunswick

New Brunswick is the largest (73,440 square km, pop. 720,000) of the Maritime provinces. Québec and Maine share its thick Appalachian woods, which cover almost 90 percent of the province. But New Brunswick is not just one endless forest; it has a 2,200-km coastline along the Bay of Fundy, Northumberland Strait, Gulf of St. Lawrence, and Baie des Chaleurs. It is here that the Maritimes reach their highest point, Mt. Carleton (820 m), the centerpiece of the provincial park of the same name in New Brunswick's north-central region.

Maine forms the province's border immediately to the west, and Prince Edward Island lies less than 16 km to the east. The province's coastal edges and the fertile Saint John River valley, which cuts a mammoth swath across the western woodlands, attract the most tourists.

## Nova Scotia

Nova Scotia (54,490 square km, pop. 900,000) typifies Atlantic Canada, with a dramatic, 7,459-km coastline notched with innumerable coves and bays holding scores of working seaports. The province is shaped like an abstract representation of a mammoth lobster, with Cape Breton Island forming the crustacean's claws, and the curving southwestern end around Yarmouth suggesting a plump tail.

Almost an island itself, mainland Nova Scotia is linked to the continent by the narrow Chignecto Isthmus at the New Brunswick border. Some 4,000 islands lie offshore; the largest of them is Cape Breton, which is nearly a quarter the size of the province's mainland.

Much of the terrain consists of low rolling hills, remnants of the ancient Appalachian Mountains. The land rises gradually from sea level at Yarmouth to finally peak at the rugged mountaintops of Cape Breton Highlands National Park in the northeast. The population is concentrated along the coasts. Much of the interior is thickly forested and sparsely inhabited.

## Prince Edward Island

Little Prince Edward Island can claim an armful of superlatives. PEI ranks as Canada's smallest province (5,656 square km, pop. 138,000), as well as its most densely populated, most cultivated, most ribboned with roads, and most bereft of original wilderness. The province also has the country's smallest provincial capital—Charlottetown, with just 16,000 inhabitants.

The land is gentle, with no point reaching over 152 meters in elevation. And it's fertile, thanks to mineral-rich soil deposited during the last ice age. Half the world's supply of potatoes originates from the island, and fields of grain and pasturelands support a large dairy industry. Some 10 million oysters (Canada's largest share) are harvested from the island's sheltered bays and estuaries each year.

The sea is visible most everywhere: a blue horizon seems to appear from atop every knoll and around every curve. No point on the island, in fact, is farther than 16 km from the shore.

## Newfoundland and Labrador

New Brunswick, Nova Scotia, and Prince Edward Island comprise the Maritimes, the triumvirate of provinces that lie at the region's south

Martinique Beach, north of Halifax, is Atlantic Canada's longest stretch of sand.

and southwestern rim. The inclusion of the province of Newfoundland and Labrador, three times the size of all the Maritimes put together, redefines the region as Atlantic Canada. The province is large (total area 405,720 square km, pop. 530,000)—larger, in fact, than Great Britain and Ireland combined. The province of Newfoundland includes the island of Newfoundland as well as Labrador on the mainland, which is three times the size of the island. (In December 2001, the province was renamed Newfoundland and Labrador. Before then, its official name was simply Newfoundland, which often led to confusion among outsiders.)

The Maritime Provinces share a kindred climate, history, and lineage, but Newfoundland is different. About half of the mountainous island is boreal forest, while much of the rest is rocky, barren, or boggy. Labrador is more heavily wooded, with a northern tundra. The province is sparsely populated, and the people in some ways seem generally more akin to their Irish or English forebears than culturally blended or archetypically Canadian.

The world at its most ancient is revealed at Gros Morne National Park, where, according to the plate-tectonics theory, the northwestern seacoast was formed of the earth's mantle and crust. Tossed asunder during primordial upheavals, the coastline today is an odd jumble of verdant meadows, volcanic formations, landlocked fjords, and moonlike canyons.

### Saint-Pierre and Miquelon

This geopolitical oddity, a little cluster of seven islands lying about 20 km west of Newfoundland's Burin Peninsula, is not part of Atlantic Canada but rather a *département* of France, retained when the Treaty of Paris in 1763 ceded all the rest of France's Canadian territory to the British. Today, this is the last toehold of France's once-vast holdings in North America. Saint-Pierre and the isthmus-linked Miquelon and Langlade are the archipelago's largest islands, which altogether cover 242 sq km. The population is about 6,400, and the culture is decidedly French.

## CLIMATE

Maritime weather varies from province to province, and from region to region within the provinces. As a rule, though, extremes are moderated by proximity to the sea. June through September are generally the most pleasant and popular months for visiting. The regions' landscapes and seascapes are recast by the changing

## SUMMER TEMPERATURES

| (in degrees Celsius) | JULY | | AUGUST | |
|---|---|---|---|---|
| | LOW | HIGH | LOW | HIGH |
| Charlottetown, PEI | 14 | 23 | 14 | 23 |
| Corner Brook, NF | 12 | 22 | 12 | 21 |
| Fredericton, NB | 10 | 23 | 12 | 25 |
| Halifax, NS | 14 | 23 | 14 | 23 |
| Happy Valley-Goose Bay, NF | 10 | 21 | 9 | 19 |
| Moncton, NB | 10 | 25 | 12 | 24 |
| Saint John, NB | 12 | 22 | 11 | 22 |
| St. John's, NF | 11 | 21 | 12 | 20 |
| Sydney, NS | 12 | 23 | 13 | 23 |
| Yarmouth, NS | 12 | 20 | 12 | 21 |

seasons. In springtime, occasional banks of thick fog blanket the coast from Yarmouth to St. John's. In summer, a pervasive balminess ripens the blueberry fields from Cumberland County in Nova Scotia to Newfoundland's Codroy Valley. Autumn brings the last burst of Indian summer, coloring the forests until winter's sea winds swirl in and send the leaves tumbling away to finish another year.

Below are overviews of the climate of each province; additional details are given in the Introduction to each chapter.

## New Brunswick

New Brunswick's continental climate contrasts hot summers with cold winters. Extremes are moderated by the surrounding seas, more so near the coast than in the interior. Summer means warm days and cool nights, with an average daytime high temperature of 23° C in June, 26° C in July, and 25° C in August. July is the sunniest month. September and October are pleasantly warm, with increasingly cool days toward November. Winter is cold.

Precipitation throughout the province averages 115.2 cm annually. The Bay of Fundy coast is steeped in dense fog about 70 days a year.

## Nova Scotia

The province has a pleasant, modified continental climate, moderated by air and water currents from the Gulf Stream and the arctic. Summers are warm and winters are mild. Cape Breton is subject to more extreme weather than the mainland. Precipitation province-wide averages 130 cm, falling mainly as rain during autumn and as snow in winter.

Spring high temperatures range from -2.5 to 9° C, though the days begin to warm up toward the end of March. Summer weather has a reputation for changing from day to day; daytime highs range up to 30° C, while nights are cool, averaging 12° C. Inland areas are generally 5° C warmer during the day. The coasts often bask in morning fog. Caribbean hurricanes, having spent their force farther south, limp through the region, bringing to the northwestern Atlantic short spells of rain and wind.

In autumn, the evenings start to cool, but pleasant days continue through September at up to 18° C. The days are cool to frosty October through mid-November. Winter lasts from late November through early March, with temperatures averaging -10 to 4° C.

## Prince Edward Island

The island basks in a typical maritime climate with one major exception: its growing season of 110–160 days is Atlantic Canada's longest. The island also gets more than its share of year-round breezes, pleasant and warm in summer but fiercer come fall. Spring is short, lasting from early to mid-May until mid-June. Summer temperatures peak in July and August, when temperatures range from 18 to 23° C; an unusually warm day can reach 35° C, while the other extreme can be quite cool at just 5° C. Autumn brings with it Atlantic Canada's brightest and most dramatic fall foliage. Winter temperatures can dip below 0° C in December and January.

Annual precipitation amounts to 106 cm, with half of that falling from May to October.

## Newfoundland

The climate is harsher and more extreme here than in the Maritimes. A sultry summer day can be interspersed with chilly breezes, brilliant sun, dark clouds, and showers from light to drenching. The island's eastern and southern seacoasts are often foggy due to the offshore melding of the warm Gulf Stream and cold Labrador current.

Overall, the island has cool, moist, maritime weather. Summer days average 16–21° C, dropping to 9–12° C at night, but hot spells are common, and the swimming season starts by late June. The island's low-lying interior and coastal areas are warmest and sunniest. Annual rainfall averages 105 cm. Frost begins by early October on the southern coast, earlier farther north. Snowfall averages 300 cm a year.

Winter high temperatures average -4 to 0° C, warm enough to turn snow to rain, while nighttime lows can tumble to -15° C. Expect year-round blustery winds along Marine Drive and nearby Cape Spear.

Conditions are severe in the Long Range Mountains' upper elevations; the peaks are snow-covered year-round, while winds can blow to gale force.

## Labrador

Labrador's climate is continental, and subject to great extremes. Summers are short, cool to sometimes hot, and brilliantly sunny with periodic showers. A July day averages 21° C, but temperatures have been known to rise to 38° C at Happy Valley–Goose Bay. Temperatures drop rapidly after mid-August. By November, daytime highs at Goose Bay fall to 0° C.

Winter is very cold and dry. Daytime high temperatures average -20° C in the subarctic, -18 to -21° C in the interior, and -51° C in the western area.

## FLORA

The receding glaciers of the last ice age scoured the land and left lifeless mud and rubble in their wake. Overall, the climate then was considerably cooler than it is today, and the first life forms to recolonize in the shadow of the glaciers were hardy mosses, lichens, and other cold-tolerant plants. Junipers and other shrubs later took root, and afterward came coniferous trees—hardy, fast-growing spruce and fir—which could thrive here despite the harsh climate and relatively brief growing season. In the boggy interiors sprouted moisture-loving willows and tamaracks. As the climate warmed and the soil grew richer, broadleaf, deciduous trees arrived, filling in the outlines of the forests still seen and enjoyed today.

### Forests

Maritime Canada's forests abound with ash, balsam fir, birch, beech, cedar, hemlock, maple, oak, pine, and spruce.

the lady's slipper, Prince Edward Island's provincial flower

Thick woodlands now blanket over 81 percent of Nova Scotia and 93 percent of New Brunswick, whose interior conifer forests in places resemble vast impenetrable fields of dark green wheat. Prince Edward Island, by contrast, is the country's least-forested province, with its land area about equally divided between farmlands and woodlands.

Newfoundland's forests are dominated by black spruce and balsam fir, with occasional stands of larch, pin cherry, pine, paper and white birch, aspen, red and mountain maple, and alder. In Newfoundland's alpine and coastal areas, you may encounter the formidable "tuckamore," a thicket composed of stunted, hopelessly entangled fir and spruce. Labrador's southern forests are cloaked with spruce, tamarack, juniper, and birch. White spruce 30 meters tall dominate the central area, while stunted black spruce, a mere meter tall, form a stubble along the timberline area. Farther north on the arctic tundra, dwarf birch and willow are common.

With so many provincial tree varieties, visitors may easily be confused. For a helpful general introduction, visit Odell Park Arboretum in Fredericton, New Brunswick, where a 2.8-km trail winds through woods made up of every tree native to the area.

### Wildflowers and Other Plants

Trees, of course, are only part of the picture. Along the forest margins, raspberry and blackberry thickets proliferate, among other benefits providing welcome snacks for summertime hikers. Throughout the spring and summer months, the Maritimes host magnificent wildflower shows that change subtly week by week. Common wildflowers throughout New Brunswick and Nova Scotia—seen especially along roadsides in summertime—include lupine, Queen Anne's lace, yarrow, pearly everlasting, and a variety of daisies. The showy spikes of purple loosestrife,

BOB RACE

a pretty but aggressive and unwelcome pest, can be seen everywhere.

Bayberries and wild rose bloom on the Chignecto Isthmus during June. The bayberry bush grows clusters of dimpled fruits close along woody stems and releases a pleasant spicy aroma popular in potpourris and Christmas candles. The yellow beach heather colors the Northumberland Strait dunes and sandy plains, and the rhodora (miniature rhododendron) brightens coastal marshes. Another dune resident, the beach plum, grows snowy white to pinkish flowers in June, which produce fruit welcomed by birds, beasts, and man in late summer and early fall. Nutrient-rich bogs in northeastern New Brunswick nurture plant exotica, especially at Laméque and Miscou Islands, where the wild cranberry and insectivorous pitcher plant and sundew grow among peat moss beds.

Prince Edward Island is like one large garden when late spring and summer's warm temperatures urge columbines, bachelor buttons, pansies, lilacs, wild roses, pink clover, and the delicate lady's slipper (the provincial flower) into blossom.

Across Newfoundland's marshes and bogs, you'll see white and yellow water lilies, rare orchid species, purple iris and goodwithy, and insectivorous plants (such as the pitcher plant, the provincial flower). Daisies, blue harebells, yellow goldenrod, pink wild roses, and deep pink fireweed thrive in the woodlands. Marsh marigolds, as brightly yellow as daffodils, are native to the western coast's Port au Port Peninsula. Low, dense mats of crowberry are common throughout Newfoundland and Labrador. The late-autumn crop of blue-black fruits is a favorite food of curlews, plovers, and other migrants preparing for their long flights to the Caribbean and South America.

Yellow poppies, heather buttercups, miniature purple rhododendrons, violets, and deep blue gentian, mixed among the white cotton grass, brighten Labrador's arctic tundra; farther south, the daisy-like arnica and purple saxifrage grow in plateau rock niches.

You may encounter poison ivy. Mushrooms are everywhere; be absolutely certain you know the species before sampling—the chanterelles are culinary prizes, but the amanitas are deadly poisonous.

## Along the Shore

Near the coasts, familiar plants—spruces, hardy cinnamon ferns, northern juniper—take on a stunted, gnarled look from contending with the unmitigated elements. It can take endurance and adaptation to survive here amid often harsh conditions. Trees and bushes lie cropped close to the ground or lean permanently swept back by the wind as if with a giant hairbrush.

Living on or near the beach requires specialization, too. Maram grass, also called American beach grass, is abundant all along the Atlantic coasts. Its extensive root systems help to stabilize the sand dunes on which it grows. Another important dune plant, the beach heather, grows in low mats that trap sand and keep the dunes in place. Small, abundant yellow flowers color large patches from May to July. Beach pea, seaside goldenrod, dusty miller, and sea rocket are a few of the other plants that can manage on the less-than-fertile soils just above the high-tide line. Lower down grow cord grass and glasswort, whose systems can tolerate regular soakings of salt water.

Within the intertidal zone, there's a different world altogether amidst the surging seawater and tide pools. The great disparities between high and low tides help to make the rocky coasts of the Maritimes among the richest and most varied anywhere in the world. Low tide exposes thick mats of tough, rubbery rockweed, or sea wrack, for a few hours each day. Farther out (or deeper down) is the lower intertidal zone of coral-pink to reddish brown Irish moss and brilliant green sea lettuce, which carpet the rocks and harbor populations of starfish, crabs, and sea urchins.

The deepest stratum of plant life is what marine biologists call the laminarian zone, typified by the giant brown kelps such as the common horsetail kelp. These algae attach to rocks at depths up to 40 meters and grow rapidly toward the surface, their broad leathery fans and air bladders lilting with the rise and fall of the swells. Storms can prune the upper extremities or tear entire plants from their moorings to wash ashore with populations of tiny mollusks, crustaceans, and other creatures that made their homes among the fronds.

## FAUNA

To a great extent, it was the land's animal resources—and the potential riches they represented—that attracted Europeans to Canada over the centuries. Since time immemorial, the wildlife had, of course, fed and clothed the Native peoples, who harvested only enough to sustain themselves. But the very abundance of the wildlife seemed to fuel the rapacity of the newcomers, driving them to a sort of madness of consumption—and hastening the exploration and settlement of the newfound continent.

Cod, flounder, mackerel, herring, and scores of other fish species in unbelievable numbers first lured brave seafarers across the Atlantic as early as the 15th century. The great whales, too, fell victim to widespread slaughter. Later, the fur-bearing mammals—mink, otter, ermine, beaver, and seals—became a currency of trade and the sine qua non of fashionable attire. Birds, too, by the millions in hundreds of species, represented money on the wing to the newcomers. Some, like the flightless great auk of the northeastern coast, were hunted to extinction.

But much remains, in sometimes astonishing abundance and variety, thanks to each species' own unique genius for survival, to blind luck, to the shifting vagaries of public tastes, and even to the occasional glimmer of human enlightenment.

### Birds

If you're an avid birder, Atlantic Canada's bird life may leave you breathless. In addition to hundreds of year-round resident species, the Atlantic migratory route stretches across part of the region, bringing in millions of seasonal visitors for spectacular and sometimes raucous displays.

Among the richest areas is the Bay of Fundy. In July, waterfowl, such as the American black duck and green-winged teal, and shorebirds, including the greater yellowlegs, descend on the Mary's Point mudflats at Shepody National Wildlife Area. Across Shepody Bay, 100,000 sandpipers stop at the Dorchester Peninsula to grow fat on their favorite food—tiny mud shrimp—before continuing on to South America. With over 300 species, Grand Manan Island is a prime bird-watching site. The show is thickest during September, when migrants arrive in force. Ornithologist-artist John James Audubon visited the island in 1833 and painted the arctic tern, gannet, black guillemot, and razorbill—annual visitors that can still be seen here.

Even greater numbers of seabirds, the region's densest concentrations, gather on the coastlines of Newfoundland's Avalon Peninsula, most notably at Cape St. Mary Sea Bird Sanctuary. Species found there include common and arctic terns, kittiwakes, great and double-crested cormorants, Leach's storm petrels, razorbills, guillemots, murres, gannets, and 95 percent of North America's breeding Atlantic puffins.

Each species has found its niche, and each is remarkable in its own way. The black-and-white murre, for example, is an expert diver who uses its wings as flippers to swim through the water chasing fish. This behavior can sometimes get the birds caught up with the fish in fishermen's nets. The murre's cousin, the comical-looking Atlantic puffin, borrows the penguin's tuxedo markings but is nicknamed the "sea parrot" for its distinctive triangular red and yellow bill. Puffins make Swiss cheese of the land, as they nest in burrows they've either dug out themselves or inherited from predecessors. In Labrador, ruffled and spruce grouse, woodpecker, raven, jay, chickadee, nuthatch, grouse, and ptarmigan are a few of the inland birds you may spot.

In New Brunswick's interior, crossbill, varied woodpecker species, boreal chickadee, and gray jay nest in the spruce and fir forests. Ibis, heron, and snowy egret wade among lagoons and marshes. Among Nova Scotia's 300 or so bird species, the best known is the bald eagle. About 250 pairs nest in the province, concentrated on Cape Breton—the second-largest population on North America's east coast, after Florida. The season for eagle watching is July and August. Other birds of prey include red-tailed, broad-winged, and other hawks; a variety of owls; and the gyrfalcon in Newfoundland and Labrador. Peregrine falcons were reintroduced to Fundy National Park in 1982. They nest in seaside cliffs, and attack their prey in "stoops," kamikaze dives in which the falcon can reach speeds of over 200 milers per hour.

The noisy blue jay, Prince Edward Island's official provincial bird, is at home throughout the province, but the island's showiest species is the enormous, stately great blue heron, which summers there from May to early August. The rare piping plover may be seen (but not disturbed) on the island's national park beaches, and arctic terns nest along the coast near Murray Harbour.

## Land Animals

Black bears, bobcats, red foxes, coyotes, white-tailed deer, porcupines, skunks, raccoons, and squirrels are widespread throughout all of Atlantic Canada's provinces, except diminutive Prince Edward Island, which supports less diversity. Kouchibouguac National Park, in northeastern New Brunswick, is also home to timber wolves and moose.

Newfoundland's wildlife also includes hares, beavers, otters, muskrats, martens, and mink. Labrador has populations of red wolf, wolverines, and, on the northern tundra coastline, polar bears. Moose, so naturally suited to Newfoundland's environment, are not native to the island. The estimated 150,000 or so that thrive in the province today are descended from a handful of individuals introduced in 1878 and 1904 as a source of meat.

# SEA LIFE

The fertile seas surrounding the Atlantic provinces nurture an astonishing abundance and variety of sea creatures, from tiny, uncounted single-celled organisms up through the convoluted links of the food chain to the earth's largest beings—the great whales.

Along the shores, the same conditions that provide for rich and diverse plant zones—rocky, indented coasts, dramatic tidal variations—also create ideal habitats for varied animal communities in the tidal zone. Between the highest and

lowest tides, the Maritime shore is divided into six zones, each determined by the amount of time it is exposed to air. The black zone, just above the highest high-water mark, gets its name from the dark band of primitive blue-green algae that grows here. The next zone is called the periwinkle zone, for the small marine snails that proliferate there. Able to survive prolonged exposure to air, the periwinkles can leave the water to graze on the algae. The barnacle zone, encrusted with the tenacious crustaceans, while also exposed several hours daily during low tides, receives the brutal pounding of breaking waves. Next is the rockweed zone—home to mussels, limpets, and hermit crabs (which commandeer the shells of dead periwinkles)—and the comparatively placid Irish moss zone, which shelters and feeds sea urchins, starfish, sea anemones, crabs, and myriad other animals familiar to anyone who has peered into the miniature world of a tide pool. Last is the laminarian zone, where lobsters, sponges, and fishes thrive in the forests of kelp growing in the deep, churning water.

Beyond these tidal life zones lie the waters of the continental shelf, and then the open sea. Flowing south from the arctic, the cold, oxygen-laden Labrador current also carries loads of silica, ground out of the continental granite by the glaciers and poured into the sea by coastal rivers. Oxygen and silica together create an ideal environment for the growth of diatoms, the microscopic, one-celled plants that form the bedrock of the ocean's food chain. In the sunlight of long summer days in these northern latitudes, the numbers of diatoms increase exponentially. They are the food source for shrimp and herring, which in turn support larger fish, such as mackerel, Atlantic salmon, and tuna.

The northeastern Atlantic fisheries have been the economic engine driving exploration and development of these coasts for centuries. In days past, codfish were said to carpet the sea floor of the shallow Grand Banks, and the men who caught them—first with lines from small dories, then with nets, and finally from great trawlers that scour the sea—have hauled in untold millions of tons of not only cod but also flounder, salmon, pollock, haddock, anchovies, and dozens of other species. But the fish are in serious trouble and so too, inexorably, are the people and communities whose lives have revolved around them.

## Marine Mammals

Not all the creatures that swim in the Maritime seas are cold-blooded. About 20 whale species cruise offshore. The so-called baleen or toothless whales—minke, humpback, beluga, and right whales—are lured by the massive food stocks of plankton and tiny shrimp called krill, which the whales strain from the water through their sievelike curtains of baleen. The toothed whales—a family that includes dolphins, orcas (killer whales), and fin and pilot whales—fed on the vast schools of smeltlike capelin, herring, and squid. In the last three decades, whaling has been halted by Canadian law and international moratoriums, and populations of these beleaguered mammals are undergoing very encouraging comebacks.

Today's lucrative whaling industry is based not on butchering but on simply bringing curious onlookers to observe the wonderful animals up close. Prime whale-watching areas are the Bay of Fundy—especially around Grand Manan Island and Brier Island—and off the shores of Cape Breton. Minke, pilot, finback, orca, and humpback whales are the most populous species. The whales that frequent Nova Scotia arrive from the Caribbean between June and mid-July and remain through October; the season peaks during August and September. On Newfoundland's western coast, fin, minke, humpback, and pilot whales are sighted off Gros Morne National Park.

Harp, gray, hooded, and harbor seals inhabit Maritime waters at various times of the year. Harp seals, after fattening themselves on fish off the Labrador and Greenland coasts, migrate to northern Newfoundland and the Gulf of St. Lawrence in January and February. The females arrive first, living on the ice and continuing to feed in the gulf, before giving birth to their pups. It's these snowy white, doe-eyed pups that became the poster children of the conservation movement in the 1970s. The slaughter of the young pups—carried out by sealers who bashed in their heads with clubs—galvanized protests against it and finally embarrassed the Canadian government into restricting the killing in the 1960s. The seal industry in Newfoundland and Labrador ended in 1981, finally succumbing to pressures by animal activists. But 30,000 seals are still legally culled by Native people each spring.

# History

## BEGINNINGS

Atlantic Canada's earliest inhabitants arrived in Labrador nearly 10,000 years ago. Archaeological research documents that these Maritime Archaic Indians hunted seals and whales along the Strait of Belle Isle, and hunted caribou inland, around 7500 B.C. They eventually crossed the strait to the island of Newfoundland's northern portion and established encampments such as Port au Choix, where their burial grounds and artifacts date to 2300 B.C. Around 1000 B.C., these people died out. A thousand years later, the Dorset people, ancestors of today's Inuit, arrived from the north. They survived until about A.D. 600. The Beothuk, called Red Indians

for their use of ocher in burial rituals, came to Newfoundland.

At the time of the European arrival, Labrador was inhabited by small clan-based bands of Eskimo (or, more properly, Inuit), linguistically and culturally related to the tundra and arctic dwellers of the northern continent as far west as Alaska. The island of Newfoundland was populated by Beothuk. The rest of Maritime Canada was inhabited by groups of Mi'kmaq, who shared Algonquian languages.

Brendan the Navigator, a fifth-century Irish monk, may have been the first European to explore the area; he sought Hy-Brazil, the "wonderful island of the saints," and later accounts of

**the last of the Beothuk people**

his voyage, recorded in the medieval best-seller *Navigatio Sancti Brendani,* describe a land with coastal topography similar to Newfoundland's.

Atlantic Canada's link to the Vikings is more certain. Driven out of Scandinavia, it's believed by overpopulation, Norse seafarers settled in Iceland and began to establish settlements in Greenland. Around A.D. 1000 they sailed in long, stout ships called *knorrs,* southwest from Greenland and down the Labrador coastline, and established a temporary settlement at L'Anse aux Meadows on Newfoundland's Northern Peninsula. There they built at least eight houses and two boatsheds of cut turf, and lived off the land. It is not known how long they lived here, but they stayed long enough to construct a forge for crafting implements from iron ore they dug and smelted here. It may have been hostilities with the Native people that drove them out. The remains of their settlement would remain unrecognized until the 1960s.

"Newfoundland" as a place-name originated with the Italian explorer Giovanni Caboto—better known today as John Cabot. Sailing westward from Bristol with a sanction to claim all lands hitherto "unknown to Christians," he sighted the "New Founde Lande" in 1497 and claimed it in the name of his employer, King Henry VII of England. His first landfall probably lay in the northern part of the island. He and his men explored the coast here, and also sighted Prince Edward Island and Nova Scotia, before returning to England. In the summer of 1997, celebrations in St. John's and across Newfoundland celebrated the 500-year anniversary of the event.

## The Fabulous Fisheries

So abundant were the cod fisheries of the Grand Banks, the shallow undersea plateaus south and east of Newfoundland, that John Cabot claimed that a man had only to lower a basket into the sea and haul it up full. His report exaggerated the truth only slightly. Although the specifics have not been documented, European fishermen are believed to have preceded Cabot by decades. Legends in Newfoundland describe the Basques as whale hunters in the Strait of Belle Isle as early as the 1470s. France's fishing exploits are better known. In the early 1500s, French fleets roamed the seas from the Grand Banks—where they caught cod and dried them on Newfoundland's beaches—to inland rivers such as the salmon-rich Miramichi in what is now New Brunswick. England's fishing fleets were equally active, leading one diplomat to describe Newfoundland as "a great ship moored near the Grand Banks for the convenience of English fishermen."

England also dabbled in other commercial interests in Newfoundland. A group of merchants from England's West Country settled Trinity in the mid-1500s. Cupids, England's first chartered colony on the island, began in 1610. In contrast, St. John's evolved independently and belonged to no nation; the port served as a haven and trading center for all of Europe's fishing fleets, and Signal Hill, the lofty promontory beside the harbor, dates as a lookout and signal peak from the early 1500s.

## French Interests

Ultimately, France was more interested in trading posts and settlements than in fishing. The French Crown granted Sieur de Monts a monopoly to develop the fur trade, and in 1604, the nobleman-merchant, with explorer Samuel de Champlain, led an exploratory party to the mouth of the Bay of Fundy. The expedition established a camp on an island in the St. Croix River (the river that now separates New Brunswick from Maine). The group barely survived the bitter first winter and relocated across the Bay of Fundy, establishing Port Royal as a fur-trading post in the Annapolis basin the following spring.

The grant was canceled, and while most of the expedition returned to France in 1607, a group of French settlers took their place at Port Royal in 1610. The French dubbed the area Acadia, or "Peaceful Land."

The French settlement and others like it ignited the fuse between England and France. John Cabot had claimed the region for England, but explorer Jacques Cartier also claimed many of the same coastlines for France several decades later. For France, the region was a choice piece of property, a potential New France in the New World. On the other hand, England's colonial aspirations centered farther south, where colonization had begun at Virginia and Massachusetts. England didn't *need* what is now Atlantic Canada, though the region offered much with its rich fisheries, but it was a place to confront the expansion of the French, England's most contentious enemy in Europe.

In terms of military strength, the British had the upper hand. An ocean separated France from its dream of settlement, while England's military forces and volunteer militias were located along the eastern seaboard. In 1613, a militia from Virginia plundered and burned the buildings at Port Royal. The French relocated the site to a more protected site farther up the Annapolis River, built another fort named Port Royal, and designated the setting as Acadia's colonial capital in 1635.

## France's Sphere Develops

The French Acadian settlements quickly spread beyond the Port Royal area to the Fundy and Minas Basin coastlines. The merchant Nicholas Denys, whose name is entwined with France's early exploration, established a fortified settlement on Cape Breton at St. Peters, and also at

Guysborough in 1653. So many Acadians settled at Grand-Pré that it became the largest settlement and hub of villages in the area. Other settlements were established across Acadia on Cape Breton, the Cobequid Bay and Cape Chignecto coastlines, and from the Restigouche Uplands to the Baie des Chaleurs in what's now northern New Brunswick.

France needed a military center and created it in the mid-1600s at Plaisance, one of the earliest and most important fishing ports on the Avalon Peninsula in Newfoundland. Here, they erected another tribute to the French Crown and named the new fortification Fort Royal.

British reprisals against the French increased. The British hammered Port Royal again and again, and in 1654, a militia from New England destroyed some of the Acadian settlements. In Newfoundland, France's presence at Plaisance prompted the British to counter by building forts around St. John's in 1675.

## The Treaty of Utrecht

Hostilities between England and France in the New World mirrored political events in Europe. Fighting ebbed and flowed across Atlantic Canada as the powers jockeyed for control on the European continent. Queen Anne's War (1701–13), the War of Austrian Secession (1745–48), and the Seven Years' War (1756–63) were all fought in Europe, but corresponding battles between the English and French took place in North America as well (where they were known collectively as the French and Indian Wars).

The Treaty of Utrecht in 1713 settled the Queen Anne's War in Europe. Under the terms of the treaty, England fell heir to all of French Acadia (though the borders were vague). In Newfoundland, Plaisance came into British hands and was renamed Castle Hill. The treaty awarded France the token settlements of the offshore Île Saint-Jean (Prince Edward Island) and Île Royale (Cape Breton). Acadia became an English colony. Nova Scotia (New Scotland) rose on the ashes of New France and the fallen Port Royal; the British took the fort in 1710, renamed it Fort Anne and renamed the settlement Annapolis Royal. The town was designated the colony's first capital until Halifax was established and became the capital in 1749.

The French military regrouped. They fled from the peninsula and began to build (and never finish) the Fortress of Louisbourg on Île Royale's Atlantic seacoast in 1719. Once again, the French envisioned the fortification as a New Paris and France's major naval base, port city, and trading center in North America. Simultaneously, they sent 300 fishermen and farmers across the Northumberland Strait to create a new settlement at Port la Joye; the enclave, at what is now Charlottetown's southwestern, outer edge, was intended to serve as the breadbasket for the Fortress of Louisbourg.

The British quickly responded. A fort at Grassy Island on Chedabucto Bay was their first effort, a site close enough to the Fortress of Louisbourg to watch the arrivals and departures of the French fleets. By 1745, Louisbourg represented a formidable threat to England, so the Brits seized the fortress and deported the inhabitants. But no sooner had they changed the flag than the French were moving back in again. The War of Austrian Succession in Europe ended with the Treaty of Aix-la-Chapelle in 1748, which, among other things, returned Louisbourg to France.

### Full-Fledged War

Peace was short-lived. Eight years later, in 1756, the Seven Years' War broke out in Europe, and once more both powers geared for confrontation in Atlantic Canada. Britain's Grassy Island fort was strategically located but too small a military base. In 1749, a British convoy sailed into Halifax Harbour, established England's military hub in the North Atlantic in the capacious harbor, and named Halifax the capital of Nova Scotia. Fort Edward near the Fundy seacoast went up in the midst of an Acadian area and guarded the overland route from Halifax. Fort Lawrence on the Chignecto Isthmus, between Nova Scotia and New Brunswick, was built to defend the route to the mainland. The fort defiantly faced two of France's most formidable forts: Fort Beauséjour and Fort Gaspéreau.

The stage was set for war, and the region's civilian inhabitants, the Acadian farmers, were trapped in the middle. Decades before, England had demanded but not enforced an oath of allegiance from the Acadians who lived under their jurisdiction. By the 1750s, however, the British decided to demand loyalty and also readied a plan to evict the Acadians from their land and replace noncompliant French inhabitants with Anglo settlers. In 1755, the British swept through the region and enforced the oath. In a show of force, more than 2,000 troops from Boston captured Fort Beauséjour and renamed it Fort Cumberland.

## THE ACADIAN DEPORTATION

England's actions unleashed chaos on the Acadians. Those who refused to sign the oath of allegiance were rounded up and deported, and their villages and farmlands were burned. By October, 1,100 Acadians had been deported, while others fought the British in guerrilla warfare or fled to the hinterlands of Cape Breton, New Brunswick, and Québec.

The Acadians being deported were herded onto ships bound for the English colonies on the eastern seaboard or anyplace that would accept them. Some ships docked in England, others in France, and others in France's colonies in the Caribbean. As the ports wearied of the human cargo, many of them refused the vessels entry, and the ships returned to the high seas to search for other ports willing to accept the Acadians. In one of the period's few favorable events, the Spanish government offered the refugees free land in Louisiana, and many settled there in 1784, where they became known as Cajuns.

Refugee camps, rife with disease and malnutrition, sprang up across the Maritimes. Beaubears Island, on New Brunswick's Miramichi River, began as a refugee center. About 3,500 Acadians fled from Nova Scotia to Île du Saint-Jean (Prince Edward Island); 700 lost their lives on two boats that sank on the journey. Many deported Acadians returned, only to be deported again, some as many as seven or eight times.

Exact deportation numbers are unknown. Historians speculate that 10,000 French inhabitants lived in Acadia in 1755; by the time the deportation had run its course in 1816, only 25 percent of them remained. The poet Longfellow distilled the tragedy in his *Evangeline,* a fictional story of two lovers divided by the events.

## England's Final Blow

In 1758, the British moved in for the kill. They seized the Fortress of Louisbourg and toppled Port la Joye, renaming it Fort Amherst. The French stronghold at Québec fell the next year. In the ultimate act of revenge, the British troops returned to Louisbourg in 1760 and demolished the fortress stone by stone so it would never rise again against England. New France was almost finished; bereft of a foothold in Atlantic Canada, the French launched a convoy from France and captured St. John's in 1762. The British quickly swooped in and regained the port at the Battle of Signal Hill, the final land battle of the Seven Years' War. Finally, the bitter French and Indian Wars were finished.

The Musee de Kent, in Bouctouche, New Brunswick, is one of many museums cataloging Acadian history.

© ANDREW HEMPSTEAD

## Postwar Developments

Atlantic Canada, as you see it now, then began to take shape. After the British had swept the Acadians from their land, prosperous "planters," gentlemen-farmers from New England, were lured to the lush Annapolis Valley with free land grants. Merchants settled Yarmouth in the 1760s, and other Anglo settlers went to Prince Edward Island. The island, formerly part of Nova Scotia, became an English colony in 1769.

Some of the Acadians had evaded capture, and settlements such as the Pubnico communities south of Yarmouth date to the pre-deportation period. But most of the region's surviving Acadian areas began after the refugees returned and settled marginal lands no one else wanted, such as the rocky seacoast of La Côte Acadienne (the Acadian Coast) in western Nova Scotia.

England lucked out. Even the inglorious defeat in the American Revolution benefited the British. Loyalists (Americans loyal to England) by the thousands poured into Nova Scotia and New Brunswick. The influx was so great in Saint John and Fredericton that New Brunswick, originally part of Nova Scotia, became an English colony, and Saint John became the first incorporated city in Canada.

## An Uneasy Peace

Even as peace settled across Atlantic Canada, the specter of war loomed again in Europe. Ever wary of their contentious enemy, the British feared a French invasion by Napoleon's navies in Atlantic Canada. In Halifax, the British built up the harbor's defenses at the Halifax Citadel and other sites. At St. John's, the British fortified Signal Hill with the Queen's Battery.

As if Britain didn't have enough problems with the Napoleonic Wars, at the same time the War of 1812 ensued as England and the United States wrangled over shipping rights on the high seas. More British fortifications went up, this time across the Bay of Fundy in New Brunswick with harbor defenses such as the Carleton Martello Tower at Saint John, the blockhouse at St. Andrews, and other strongholds at more than a dozen strategic places.

# TOWARD CONFEDERATION

The Napoleonic Wars ended in June 1815 with Napoleon's defeat at Waterloo. Atlantic Canada emerged unscathed. The war years had fostered shipping, and Halifax earned a questionable reputation as the home port of privateers who raided ships on the high seas and returned to port to auction the booty at the harbor. In Newfoundland, many ships had been lost on the treacherous shoals outside St. John's Harbour, prompting the British to build the lofty Cape Spear Lighthouse in 1836.

In 1864, a landmark event in Canada's history took place in Atlantic Canada. The **"Fathers of the Confederation"**—from New Brunswick, Nova Scotia, Prince Edward Island, Ontario, and Québec—met at Province House in Charlottetown. The small city owes its fame as the birthplace of Canada to the discussions of a potential joint dominion that followed. In 1867, England gave the union its blessing and signed the British North America Act (now known as the Constitution Act); the Dominion of Canada was born on July 1 as a confederation of Québec, Ontario, New Brunswick, and Nova Scotia united under a parliamentary government.

Under the leadership of its first prime minister, Sir John A. MacDonald, Canada expanded rapidly. The acquisition of Ruperts Land from the Hudson's Bay Company in 1869 increased it total land area sixfold. Manitoba and British Columbia joined the Confederation in 1870 and 1871, respectively. Prince Edward Island, having initially declined to become a Confederation member, joined the dominion in 1873. Alberta and Saskatchewan followed in 1905, and, nearly a half century later, in 1949, Newfoundland became Canada's tenth province.

As a condition of participation in the Confederation, British Columbia and New Brunswick insisted that the government build a railroad across Canada to facilitate trade, transport, and communication. Work on the daunting project

*In Atlantic Canada, attitudes toward separation are mixed; the general consensus, even in officially bilingual New Brunswick, seems to run in favor of continued Canadian unity.*

began in 1881, and in 1885, just four years later, the last spike was driven in the Canadian Pacific Railway. Linking Vancouver with Montréal, which in turn connected with regional lines in New Brunswick, Nova Scotia, and Prince Edward Island, the railroad united the country in a way no act of confederation could.

## World Wars and the Depression

Atlantic Canada became a hotbed of controversy during World War I, when the sensitive issue of Francophone rights was raised. The federal government had decided to initiate a military conscription, and French Canadians were afraid that the draft would decrease their already minority population. The measure was a failure, as both French- and English-speaking men of conscription age avoided the draft. By war's end, however, 63,000 Canadians had died in battle, and another 175,000 were wounded. During the war, the nation had supplied Britain with much of its food and also produced large quantities of munitions, ships, and planes—an experience that helped move Canada from a primarily agricultural economy to an industrial one. Afterward, Canada emerged stronger, more independent, and with a greater sense of self-confidence. The Atlantic provinces enjoyed a brief brush with prosperity as mining and manufacturing expanded.

But the Maritimes were not immune to the Great Depression of the 1930s, which hit Canada even harder than the United States. Many businesses collapsed under the financial crisis. When World War II erupted, Canada followed Britain's lead in joining the war against Hitler. Nearly one-tenth of the population of about 11.5 million served in the war effort. Atlantic Canada again took part in shipping much of the munitions and food supplies for the Allies, and the regional and national economies were again revived.

In 1959 the completion of the St. Lawrence Seaway, a project jointly undertaken by the United

States and Canada, opened a new sea lane between the Great Lakes and the Atlantic. Three years later, the new TransCanada Highway spanned the country from sea to sea. Linking Vancouver Island with St. John's, Newfoundland, the highway joined all 10 provinces along a single route and made the country just a little smaller.

## A Constitution and Autonomy

Starting in 1867, the British North America Act required the British Parliament's approval for any Canadian constitutional change. On November 5, 1981, Canada's federal government and the premiers of every province except Québec agreed on a Canadian Constitution and Charter of Rights and Freedoms. The Canada Act formally went into effect on April 17, 1982, removing the last vestiges of Parliament's control. Canada remains, however, a member of the Commonwealth.

## Old Divisions in Modern Times

The formation of the Parti Québecois in 1968

signaled a popular new militancy among French-speaking separatists in Québec, who desired a political and cultural divorce from the rest of Canada. The Official Languages Act recognized French as the country's second official language after English, but this act only bandaged over deep wounds. Referenda on the question of Québecois secession in the 1980s and '90s has failed to resolve the issue; a provincial vote on the question in 1995 saw the drive for separation defeated by a margin of barely 1 percent. It's difficult to predict which way the pendulum will swing, should there be another vote, but the Ottawa government, in any case, has indicated that it will honor the will of the Québecois. In Atlantic Canada, attitudes toward separation are mixed; the general consensus, even in officially bilingual New Brunswick, seems to run in favor of continued Canadian unity, but that consensus is undermined by a growing impatience with Québec's demands for what many Canadians see as preferential treatment from the federal government.

# Government and Economy

## GOVERNMENT

Canada is a constitutional monarchy. The federation of 10 provinces and two territories operates under a parliamentary democracy in which power is shared between the federal government, based in Ottawa, and the provincial governments. Canada's two non-provincial territories, Yukon and the Northwest Territories, exercise delegated—rather than constitutionally guaranteed—authority. The power to make, enforce, and interpret laws rests in the legislative, executive, and judicial branches of government, respectively.

## The Federal Government

Under Canada's constitutional monarchy, the formal head of state is the queen of England, who appoints a governor general to represent her for a five-year term. The governor general stays out of party politics and performs largely ceremonial duties such as opening and closing

parliamentary sessions, signing and approving state documents on the queen's behalf, and appointing a temporary replacement if the prime ministry is vacated without warning. The head of government is the prime minister, who is the leader of the majority party or party coalition in the House of Commons. In 1993 Jean Chretien of the Liberal Party became Canada's 20th prime minister. At publication, in 2002, he remains in office.

The country's legislative branch, the Parliament, is comprised of two houses. The House of Commons, with 295 members, is apportioned by provincial population and elected by plurality from the country's districts. The Senate comprises 104 members appointed by the governor general (formerly for a life term, though retirement is now mandatory at age 75) on the advice of the prime minister. Legislation must be passed by both houses and signed by the governor general to become law.

National elections are held whenever the majority party is voted down in the House of Commons or every five years, whichever comes first. Historically, it has been unusual for a government to last its full term.

## Provincial and Local Governments

Whereas the federal government has authority over defense, criminal law, trade, banking, and other affairs of national interest, Canada's 10 provincial governments bear responsibility for civil services, health, education, natural resources, and local government. Each of the nation's provincial Legislative Assemblies (in Newfoundland and Labrador, the body is called the House of Assembly) consists of a one-house legislative body with members elected every four years. The nominal head of the provincial government is the lieutenant governor, appointed by the governor general of Canada. Executive power, however, rests with the cabinet, headed by a premier, the leader of the majority party.

## The Judicial System

The basis of Canadian law is its constitution, one of the newest among the world's democracies. The constitution is defined by the Canada Constitution Act of 1982 as including the 1867 Constitution Act (formerly the British North America Act), the Canada Act of 1982 (which rescinded Great Britain's power to pass laws affecting Cana-

da), and a collection of common law, statutes, and legal conventions. A crucial element of the constitution is the Canadian Charter of Rights and Freedoms, which, like the U.S. Bill of Rights, guarantees basic rights and protections: freedom of speech, assembly, and religion; the right to due legal process and equality under the law; and so forth.

Canadian law has two main sources: legislation passed by the federal parliament and by the provincial and territorial legislatures; and case law, the outcome of legal decisions reached in federal and provincial courts.

At the provincial level, the judicial system consists of municipal and county courts at the lowest level, then provincial or territorial courts, then provincial/territorial courts of appeal. At the federal level, the Federal Court of Canada hears cases brought by or against the federal government. Presiding over the judicial system is the Supreme Court of Canada. The Supreme Court, in Ottawa, consists of nine judges (three of whom must come from Québec) and hears selected appeals from federal and provincial appeals courts in which legal issues of national interest are concerned.

# ECONOMY
## Fishing

Canada was once the world's largest fish-exporting country, but poor resource management and over-

fishing have destroyed its once-bounteous supplies. Even so, fisheries and fish processing still remain the third-biggest contributor to Nova Scotia's gross domestic product (GDP), and cod, haddock, herring, and lobster are caught inshore and off the Atlantic's Scotian Shelf. The province is Canada's largest lobster exporter.

New Brunswick's fisheries produce groundfish, lobster, crab, scallops, and herring. The newest

**processing codfish in the 16th century**

aquaculture developments are Atlantic salmon farms and blue mussel beds. Blacks Harbour,–area canneries on the Bay of Fundy rank first in Canada's sardine production.

Newfoundland and Labrador's fisheries, a chronic boom-or-bust industry, contribute some $500 million yearly to the economy with catches of mackerel, flounder, capelin, herring, squid, eel, fish roe, sole, salmon, perch, turbot, halibut, lobster, and farmed mussels and rainbow trout. Labrador also produces half of Canada's commercial char. Since the 1990s, when the cod industry came to a standstill, Newfoundland fisheries have diversified. Now scallops and shrimp make up a good percentage of the catch.

Prince Edward Island also has an important fishing industry, especially in lobster and shellfish such as farmed blue mussels.

## Natural Resources

Atlantic Canada's fisheries have declined as a consequence of modern fishing methods as well as foreign competition. As a result, the area has turned to its other resources: timber, coal, and other minerals. New Brunswick harbors Canada's largest silver, lead, and zinc reserves, and also mines potash, coal, and oil shale. Peat moss is collected in northeastern New Brunswick, especially from Lamèque and Miscou Islands— enough to make the province the world's second-largest exporter of this fuel.

Mining contributes $950 million to New Brunswick's economy and is the second-largest segment of Nova Scotia's. Over 30 mines and quarries in Nova Scotia are worked for their coal, limestone, and tin.

Nova Scotia's extensive forests supply a substantial lumber and paper industry; among the largest operators are Bowater (half owned by the *Washington Post*) on the South Shore and the Irving Forest Products pulp mills at Abercrombie Point, Point Tupper, Brooklyn, Hantsport, and East River.

Western Labrador's mines contribute about 80 percent of Canada's iron ore share. Other Newfoundland metals and minerals include copper, lead, zinc, gold, silver, chromium, limestone, gypsum, aluminum silicate, and as-

bestos. Newfoundland also holds Canada's sole commercial deposit of pyrophyllite, used in the production of ceramics. Newfoundland is economically on the bottom rung of Canada's per-capita income, yet the province is sitting on a gold mine when it comes to natural resources. Offshore oil fields started producing in 2000, and the extraction rate is 500,000 barrels per day.

## Agriculture

Agriculture contributes $220 million to New Brunswick's GDP; Victoria and Carleton Counties' seed potatoes make up 20 percent of Canada's total potato crop and are exported to Mexico, Portugal, and the United States. The benevolent spring floods wash the Saint John River valley with rich silt, helping to sustain a healthy mixed farming economy. The farms at Maugerville yield two crops each season. Other agricultural products include livestock (exported to France, England, Denmark, and the U.S.), dairy products, and berries.

Though just eight percent of Nova Scotia's land is arable, agriculture contributes heavily to the economy. The province produces fruits (including Annapolis Valley apples), dairy products, poultry, hogs, and Canada's largest share of blueberries.

Diminutive PEI ranks first in Canada's potato production. Half of the crop is grown in Prince County, and the remainder is produced by farms scattered across the province. Local farmers travel abroad to 32 nations to advise their foreign counterparts on varieties and farming methods. The province harvests 10 million oysters annually, and most are exported. The island's beauty may be attributed to its investments in agriculture, which contributes about 9.5 percent to the gross domestic product. The sector yields $120 million a year and employs 4,000 islanders on 2,200 farms, each of which averages 140 hectares. Grains, fruits, beef, pigs, sheep, and dairy products are other components of mixed farming production.

Agriculture in Labrador earns $20 million a year in hay, root crops, vegetables, berries, and mink farms.

## Power

Water is ubiquitous in the Atlantic provinces (one-third of all the world's freshwater is found in Canada), and hydroelectricity is a cheap, clean export. Québec Hydro alone sells over $1 billion worth of electricity a year to New England. The Mactaquac Generating Station, on the Saint John River near Fredericton, New Brunswick, is the Maritimes' largest hydroelectric station.

New Brunswick also built Atlantic Canada's first nuclear power generating plant at Point Lepreau.

The high ocean tides in the Bay of Fundy have been studied to ascertain the feasibility of harnessing that incredible power as well.

## Trade and Industry

Almost 70 percent of Atlantic Canada's export and import business is with the United States. With the latest Free Trade Agreement (1994), Canada has been made increasingly aware of this interdependence. The economies of the United States and Canada are so inextricably linked that America's car industry, for example, would quickly grind to a halt if it were not for the auto parts manufactured just across the border. Canadians are also major investors in the American economy, primarily as financial backers for urban development.

But trade continues to grease the Maritimes' economic wheels. Eleven of Nova Scotia's 267 harbors are major shipping ports, and Halifax, Sydney, and Point Tupper on the Strait of Canso rank as the busiest ports. A 36-hectare auto port, which handles 100,000 vehicles a year, is based at Dartmouth.

Saint John's merchant-shipping fleet ranks as Canada's largest, as does the city's sugar-refinery plant. Other industries include pulp mills, oil-refining plants, food-processing plants, and two breweries.

New Brunswick's annual gross domestic product is $17 billion. Manufacturing and shipping contribute two-thirds of this figure; products include food, beverages, fabricated metal products, plastics, chemicals, and forestry products.

In 2001 Nova Scotia's GDP was $13 billion. Manufacturing topped the list as the highest earner. Among the largest companies are Michelin Tire Canada, Volvo Canada, Crossley Karastan Carpet, and Pratt and Whitney. The province is also the region's federal civil service and military center. Halifax has served as a naval center since its founding in 1749 as headquarters for the Royal Navy. The city is now Maritime Command headquarters for the Canadian armed forces. Other military installations are at Shearwater, Cornwallis, and Greenwood; training stations are located at Barrington, Mill Cove, Shelburne, and Sydney.

Farming and fishing remain crucial to Prince Edward Island's economy, but it is slowly changing. In the late 1960s, after the request for a mainland fixed link collapsed, economic efforts were rechanneled to the **Comprehensive Development Plan,** aimed at education and industry. Optics and medical-component light industry formed the gist of new industrial parks. Unemployment measures 10–15 percent, due to the seasonal nature of fishing and farming.

*While the topography of this region—the dense forests, mountains, and rugged coastline—has tended to separate people and isolate them in scattered settlements, centuries of sometimes turbulent history have bound the Atlantic Canadians together.*

## Tourism

Tourism ranks as the fastest growing sector of the economy across Atlantic Canada, having doubled in worth over the last decade. Tourism contributes $1.3 billion to Nova Scotia's annual economy alone. Most visitors enter the region through New Brunswick, Atlantic Canada's land gateway, and arrive by car, RV, or tour bus. Only 25 percent fly in; air arrivals are increasing, however, as long-distance air links improve beyond Atlantic Canada. Most visitors (40 percent) are from the neighboring provinces, while central and western Canada contributes 25 percent, and the United States adds almost 25 percent. Together, these tourists contribute some $2.5 billion to the regional economy and support 90,000 jobs.

# People

While the topography of this region—the dense forests, mountains, and rugged coastline—has tended to separate people and isolate them in scattered settlements, centuries of sometimes turbulent history have bound the Atlantic Canadians together: the mutual grief of the early wars, the Acadian Deportation, immigration upheavals, and the abiding hardships common to resource-based economies. In the same sense, these and other factors have given each population an indisputable identity that makes it difficult to generalize about the diverse peoples of this part of Canada. Canadian Senator Eugene Forsey's observations on the country as a whole are equally applicable to Atlantic Canada: "I think our identity will have to be something which is partly British, partly French, partly American, partly derived from a variety of other influences which are too numerous even to catalogue."

A few statistics say much about the region. The entire population of the country numbers some 30 million—less than California's population. Atlantic Canada's four provinces make up less than a tenth of that figure, with a combined total of about 2 million. Nationally, almost 77 percent of the population is concentrated in cities, whereas in Atlantic Canada the urban-rural division is almost evenly split.

Like the United States, Canada is a nation of immigrants. In 2000, for example, the country accepted 240,000 immigrants, giving it one of the world's highest immigration rates. Sociologists have observed that immigrants to Canada tend to maintain their ethnic heritage and assimilate more slowly than their counterparts in the United States. The region's ethnic fabric is far richer than one might at first suspect—over 60 ethnic groups have been woven in.

Atlantic Canada's cultural diversity is also reflected in religion. Though Christian faiths have predominated since the first Europeans settled here, and despite Canada's less than sterling history of religious tolerance, the Maritime territories have offered sects and a variety of denominations—including oppressed minority groups such as Mennonites, Doukhobors, Eastern European and Russian Jews, and others—an opportunity to start anew. The domination of organized religions (primarily the Roman Catholic Church and various Protestant churches) over the lives of Canadians has waned substantially since the 1960s. Partly, this is due to the overall drop nationally in church membership over the past several decades, but it can also be an effect of Canada's increasingly multicultural population. In the Atlantic provinces, church affiliation is still high (see below), and the Catholic and Protestant churches, in particular, still play substantial roles in the lives and communities of people throughout the region.

In spite of diversity, the region still shares a common identity as a place apart from the rest of Canada. A foreign nation borders it to the southwest, and Atlantic Canada is separated from the body of its nation by the insular bastion of Québec Province. Though the country began in the east and was nourished by its resources for centuries, Canada's general prosperity has not been fully shared here. Atlantic Canada experiences higher unemployment, higher underemployment, and lower income than any of the other provinces. Unlike the rest of the country, the provinces of Atlantic Canada share economies that rise and fall largely on the vicissitudes of the fisheries and other natural resources.

## NATIVE PEOPLES AND MÉTIS

The first European explorers to reach North America found a land that was anything but uninhabited. Tribes or nations of aboriginals had been here for millennia, from coast to coast and up into the continent's subarctic and artic regions.

Prior to colonization and proselytizing, the Indian and Inuit populations practiced a kind of spiritual animism, deeply tied to the land. The trees, animals, and landforms were respected and blessed. Before food could be consumed or a tree felled, for example, it was appreciated for its life-sustaining sacrifice. Mythology also played an important part in spiritual life, along with rituals, shamanism, and potlatch ceremonies. Unfortunately, when the French and British arrived, they set about converting the natives.

In the intervening centuries, the experience of Canada's "First Nations" people has been depressingly similar to that of Native Americans in the United States—they have been persecuted and marginalized, robbed of their lands, heritage, and virtually all rights. Treatment of these native peoples has been a national tragedy. By the time of confederation, in 1867, their numbers had been reduced by half. Officially recognized Indians—so-called status or treaty Indians (a designation dating to the Indian Act of 1876)— were confined on more than 2,000 reserves across Canada and, until as recently as 1961, denied basic rights, including the right to vote in federal elections. Métis are the offspring of aboriginal and European people.

Today, the life expectancy for native people is 10 years less than for the average Canadian, while the infant-mortality rate is twice the national average. Native peoples suffer high rates of tuberculosis, pneumonia, lung cancer, and other ailments typical of the most impoverished Third World living standards. Alcohol and substance abuse are rampant. Beyond the fight for simple survival, native peoples continue to struggle to maintain pieces of their old way of life and religion. In the last three decades, they have made significant progress toward reclaiming lost rights, heritage, and the power of self-determination.

In 1991 the federal Department of Indian and Northern Affairs estimated the total population of native peoples nationwide at 802,852— about 3 percent of the country's population. This number had doubled in the preceding 25 years and continues to grow rapidly, indicating a birthrate that is about twice the Canadian average. Three main tribes survive in the Atlantic provinces: the Mi'kmaq, Maliseet, and Inuit.

## Mi'kmaq

When Europeans first arrived, perhaps 20,000 Mi'kmaq lived in the coastal areas of the Gaspé Peninsula and the Maritimes east of the Saint John River. The name Mi'kmaq (also Micmac) is thought to have derived from the word *nikmaq*, meaning "my kin-friends," which early French settlers used as a greeting for the tribe. The aboriginal Mi'kmaq fished and hunted, and became involved with the fur trade in the 18th century.

The Mi'kmaq historically had practiced little or no agriculture, and attempts by the British to convert them to farmers fared poorly. Later, they found employment building railways and roads and in lumbering and fisheries. Today the Mi'kmaq number an estimated 15,000 in the Maritime provinces, Newfoundland, and parts of New England.

## Maliseet

Culturally and linguistically related to the Mi'kmaq (both are members of the widespread Algonquian language group), the Maliseet (or Malicite) inhabited the Saint John River valley in New Brunswick and lands west to the St. Lawrence and what is now Maine. For the first century after contact, the Maliseet got on well with European fishers and traders, though Old World diseases greatly reduced their numbers.

As the fur trade dwindled, Maliseet women adopted agriculture, while the men continued to hunt and fish. Increasing white settlement along the Saint John, however, displaced the Maliseet from their traditional lands, eventually leaving them destitute. In the 19th century, the first Indian reserves were created for them, at Fredericton, Oromocto, Kingsclear, and other New Brunswick locations.

## Inuit

The Inuit (formerly known as Eskimos—a name many consider pejorative) inhabit the northern regions of Canada from Alaska to Greenland. Their ancestors arrived in the arctic in the 11th century, and today they number roughly 25,000 in eight main tribal groups. They share a common language—Inuktitut—with six dialects. Until the late 1930s, when a court ruled that their welfare was the responsibility of the federal government, the Inuit were largely ignored by Canada, principally because they occupied inhospitable lands in the far north that nobody else wanted.

In the late 18th century, Moravian missionaries in Labrador established the first lasting contact with the Inuit, followed by commercial whalers and explorers. The Europeans initiated cultural and technological changes in the traditional societies (including almost universal conversion to Christianity) that continue to this day. In the northern reaches of Labrador, the Inuit today live in small, remote settlements and still maintain some traditional practices: hunting seals, caribou, and whales, and other aspects of Inuit culture.

## Métis

The progeny of native people and Caucasians, the Métis (named for an old French word meaning "mixed") form a diverse and complex group throughout Canada. They date from the time of earliest European contact; in Atlantic Canada, unions between European fishermen and native women—sometimes casual, sometimes formal—produced Métis offspring by the early 1600s.

In the 17th century, the French government encouraged this mixing, seeing it as conducive to converting the native people to Christianity and to more speedily increasing the population of New France. Samuel de Champlain said, "Our young men will marry your daughters and we shall be one people." That policy had changed by the 1700s, however, and France then *discouraged* mixed unions, in part because of the increased availability of white women in North America. This policy led to the development of distinct Métis settlements, mainly around the Great Lakes (these settlements would later grow into cities such as Chicago, Milwaukee, Sault Ste. Marie, and Detroit).

Recent census figures estimate Métis numbers at about 60,000. Some identify themselves with the aboriginals, some with whites, while others consider themselves members of a society and culture distinct from both.

# PROVINCIAL DISTINCTIONS

## New Brunswick

Population: 720,000. The province is, in a sense, a miniature Canada, a provincial composite of Anglophones and Acadian Francophones who

Although each province has its own distinct characteristics, they all come together under one flag.

© ANDREW HEMPSTEAD

harmoniously coexist—the exception rather than the rule in a nation whose two dominant cultures are so often at odds. One suspects the harsh history that divided New Brunswick at its inception has run its course and mellowed. As Canada's only officially bilingual province, it steps to an agreeable duple beat.

The duality repeats itself in numerous ways. New Brunswick has an Anglophone region and another equally distinctive Acadian Francophone counterpart. The distinctions were set in stone centuries ago when the British evicted the Acadians from their original settlements and resettled the Loyalists. The Anglophone cities, towns, and settlements lie along the Fundy seacoast and throughout most of the Saint John River valley. The French-speaking Acadian region lies beyond, on the province's outer rim in the northwestern woodlands along the Saint John River and on the coastlines of the Baie des Chaleurs, the open gulf, and the sheltered strait. Today, English is the first language of about 65 percent of New Brunswickers, while French is the mother tongue for about 33 percent.

Historically, the Acadians have clung to a lean subsistence, while Anglos have prospered. The Acadians have traditionally been fishermen and loggers. Caraquet, on the Baie des Chaleurs, is Acadia's cultural heart and the center for seafaring families along the shores of the bay. Moncton is another Acadian stronghold, which has emerged today with nouveau-riche status and wealth as a light-industry, distribution, and educational center. Acadian loggers ended up in northwestern New Brunswick. Known as Brayons, their domain is the Madawaska Republic, centered at Edmundston on the upper Saint John River near the Maine border.

The Anglophones, meanwhile, steer the provincial ship of state from Saint John, New Brunswick's largest city, major port, and industrial center. The Anglo aristocracy, many with roots traceable to Loyalist times, is entrenched at Fredericton, the provincial capital and home campus of the University of New Brunswick.

About 4,100 Mi'kmaq and 3,300 Maliseet live in the province.

Roman Catholics, the majority of whom are Acadians, make up 54 percent of the population. Protestants, comprising about 43 percent of New Brunswickers, are spread among the Baptist, United Church of Canada, Anglican, Pentecostal, and Presbyterian sects. An evangelical "Bible Belt" runs strong through Carleton and Victoria Counties in the upper Saint John River valley and north of Moncton in Westmoreland County. Saint John also has a small Jewish population, well established in the city for more than a century.

## Nova Scotia

Population: 900,000. Nova Scotia cut its teeth as a genial host in Halifax's early years when Her Majesty's Royal Navy sailed into the harbor. The duke of Kent and his French mistress led the social scene during the late 1700s, and modern-day royalty still comes calling.

But the "commoners" created the backbone of the province. German, Swiss, and French "foreign Protestants" arrived in 1753. In 1760, England resettled the prime Fundy seacoast with 12 shiploads of farmers (New England "planters")

from its colonies farther south. For many visitors, the Scots of Nova Scotia typify the province: the first shipload of Scots docked at Pictou in 1773, and by 1830 there were 50,000 Scots in Pictou and Antigonish Counties.

After the American Revolution, 25,000 United Empire Loyalists poured into Nova Scotia. Several thousand African Americans arrived during the War of 1812, followed by Irish immigrants from 1815 to 1850. Recent worldwide immigration has added more than 50 other ethnic groups (including Caribbeans, Ethiopians, Greeks, Portuguese, Sri Lankans, and others) to the province's cultural milieu, making it the most cosmopolitan in the region. About 8,000 black people live in Nova Scotia today, many of them descendants of immigrants from colonial America. An estimated 5,800 Mi'kmaq also live in the province.

The population distribution is closely divided between urban and rural, with a full third of Nova Scotians concentrated in and around Halifax.

Protestants and Roman Catholics make up 58 and 37 percent of the mainland population, respectively, while on Cape Breton Catholics are in the majority. Anglicans account for almost 16 percent on the mainland and 10 percent on Cape Breton. Other denominations include the United Church of Canada and the Baptist and Presbyterian churches, as well as small populations of Jews, Buddhists, and Hindus, living mainly in Halifax.

## Prince Edward Island

Population: 138,000. Though it's anything but crowded, the province is Canada's most densely populated, with nearly 23 people per square km (50 per square mile). At the same time, Prince Edward Island is the most rural province, with fewer than two in five residents living in urban areas. PEI's people are also said to be Canada's most homogeneous. The province's ancestry is 80 percent Anglo—a third Irish and the remainder Scottish. Acadians represent 17 percent of the population (5 percent of them speak French). Southeast Asians, Germans, and a thriving population of about 500 Mi'kmaqs (most living on Lennos Island on the north shore and at

Scotchfort) together constitute about 2 percent of the population. PEI still lures immigrants, mainly from Ontario, Nova Scotia, New Brunswick, and Alberta.

Religious affiliations are important to islanders, who are overwhelmingly Christian. About half belong to Protestant denominations, mainly Presbyterian and Anglican, while 47 percent are Roman Catholic.

## Newfoundland and Labrador

Population: 530,000. In contrast to relatively crowded PEI, this province has less than 1.5 people per square km (3.6 per square mile). Ninety-five percent of the population is concentrated on the island of Newfoundland.

In Labrador, Inuits, Innu, and Anglo-Labradorians inhabit the sparsely settled eastern coastline and remote central interior. The people of the island of Newfoundland are an overwhelmingly Anglo and Celtic cultural mix (96 percent), whose psyche is linked to the sea and the Grand Banks fisheries. A small number of Mi'kmaq also live on the island.

An insular mentality still informs the provincial character, and 50 years after joining the Confederation, residents of the Rock may refer to their countrymen as "Canadians"—outsiders from another nation. They even inhabit their own time zone, Newfoundland time, a quirky half-hour ahead of Atlantic time.

Though a full-fledged province since 1949, Newfoundland was a colony of England's for centuries. This is why you'll still hear a clipped King's English accent in St. John's, a West Country dialect in some of the small, remote fishing villages (called outports), and a softly brushed Irish brogue on the Avalon Peninsula. Some 60 dialects and subdialects have been documented throughout the province, many of them incorporating colorful expressions and vocabulary that are unique to Newfoundland. In addition, the map of the province is decorated with one-of-

> *Residents of the Rock may refer to their countrymen as "Canadians"— outsiders from another nation. They even inhabit their own time zone, Newfoundland time, a quirky half-hour ahead of Atlantic time.*

a-kind place-names: Blow Me Down, Joe Batt's Arm, Happy Adventure, Jerry's Nose, and dozens of other toponymic oddities.

Less than 1 percent of the province's population claims French as a first language.

An economy long dependent on the fickle generosity of the sea and subject to chronic depression has made the Newfoundlanders a realistic and resourceful people. The collapse of the cod fishery in the 1990s has bitterly tested their mettle, as they struggle to survive without moving to the mainland, as so many have done.

The majority of Newfoundland's Irish and French are Roman Catholics (36 percent of the provincial population), while the English generally belong to the Anglican or United churches (63 percent together). Protestant evangelical denominations have strong followings and include the Pentecostals and Seventh-day Adventists. Labrador has a similar distribution, plus Moravians, members of the Church of the Nazarene, Plymouth Brethren, Baptists, and Methodists.

## LANGUAGE

Although Canada is constitutionally bilingual, English is the language of choice for most of the country and for the majority of Atlantic Canadians. (In 2000, French was the mother tongue of about 20 percent of Canadians, while the figure in Québec was 88 percent.) The Official Languages Acts of 1969 and 1988 established French and English as equal official languages and designated rights for minority language speakers throughout the country. Still, there has been no shortage of acrimony between Francophone Québec and the rest of the country over the issue of language (as well as broader cultural distinctions), which has led to constitutional crisis and nearly to the secession of Québec from the Confederation.

In Atlantic Canada, English is the first language for the majority. But in officially bilingual New Brunswick, French is the home tongue for a substantial portion of the population—about 28 percent—and the province's two languages and cultures have managed to coexist in reasonable harmony. Francophones are smaller minorities in Prince Edward Island (about 5 percent), Nova Scotia (4 percent), and Newfoundland (less than 1 percent).

The French spoken here is not a patois; it's closely tied to the language that was brought to the continent by the original settlers from France. Visitors who have studied standard Parisian French may have a little trouble with the accent, syntax, and vocabulary here (the differences are not unlike those between American and British English). Still, travelers who make an effort at speaking French will find the Francophones here patient and appreciative.

Some Dutch is spoken on Prince Edward Island, and, with the arrival of Asian immigrants starting around the 1960s, Chinese, Vietnamese, Punjabi, Hindi, Urdu, and other tongues can be overheard in urban areas. The Inuit of Labrador continue to speak Inuktitut, and the Mi'kmaq of the other provinces maintain their native language—with varying success.

Canadian English is subtly different from American English, not only in pronunciation but also in lexicon ("Eh?"). For instance, Canadians may say "serviette," "depot," and "chesterfield" where Americans would say "napkin," "station," and "couch." Spelling is a bit skewed as well, as Canadians have kept many British spellings—e.g., colour, centre. At the same time, Canadian English has been profoundly influenced by its neighbor to the south. Nevertheless, you'll find that language variations pose no serious threat to communication in Atlantic Canada.

# On the Road

## NEW BRUNSWICK

### Best Known For

The Bay of Fundy, with the world's most dramatic tides; picturesque covered bridges; the bizarrely eroded formations at Hope Cape; Roosevelt Campobello International Park on Campobello Island; bird-watching and whale-watching expeditions around Grand Manan Island; the warm beaches of the Northumberland Strait; world-class salmon fishing on the Miramichi River; Acadian Historical Village and Kings Landing Historical Settlement; the contrasting cultural legacies of Irish immigrants, United Empire Loyalists, and Acadians; vibrant weaving, quilting, pottery, and other craft industries.

### Most Interesting City Sights

In Fredericton, Officers' Square and the Beaverbrook Art Gallery; Moncton's Magnetic Hill, the Galerie d'Art et Musée Acadien at Université de Moncton; Saint John's historic Trinity Royal area, Old City Market, Partridge Island's poignant immigration landmarks, and Reversing Falls Rapids.

### Outstanding Lodgings

Fredericton's Lord Beaverbrook and the nearby Holiday Inn Fredericton upriver at the Mactaquac Dam; Moncton's Delta Beauséjour and Chateau Moncton; the Saint John Hilton, Delta Brunswick, and Parkerhouse Inn in Saint John; the Fairmont Algonquin the Inn on the Hiram Walker Estate in St. Andrews.

### Outdoor Highlights

Hiking to the summit of Mount Carleton; bicycle touring in the Saint John River Valley; houseboating on Grand Lake;

South Shore, Nova Scotia

canoeing on the Tobique, Kouchibouguac, and other rivers; swimming in the warm Northumberland Strait; sea-kayaking on the Baie des Chaleurs and Bay of Fundy; whale-watching off Grand Manan; bird-watching in the Tintamarre Marshes; fishing for Atlantic salmon, brook trout, shad, perch, bass, and other game fish.

## NOVA SCOTIA

### Best Known For

Centuries of seafaring tradition; Cape Breton's indelible Scottish heritage; the gorgeous rocky coastlines; the quintessential Atlantic fishing port of Peggy's Cove; photogenic lighthouses; the unforgettable roller coaster of the Cabot Trail scenic drive; Lunenburg's shipbuilding heritage and European-inspired architecture; the meticulously re-created Fortress of Louisbourg.

### Most Interesting City Sights

Halifax's Citadel and the harbor-front Historic Properties, the Art Gallery of Nova Scotia, the Nova Scotia Centre for Craft and Design, the Public Gardens; Cumberland County Museum at Amherst; Victoria Park at Truro; the Fisheries Museum of the Atlantic and the historic inns of Lunenburg; the Historic District at Shelburne; the Yarmouth County Museum in Yarmouth; the Acadia University Art Gallery at Wolfville; the waterfront Heritage Quay at Pictou; the Cossit House in Sydney; the fascinating Alexander Graham Bell National Historic Site.

### Outstanding Lodgings

Halifax's Sheraton Halifax; the Best Western Glengarry at Truro; the Brigantine Inn and Lunenburg Inn at Lunenburg; Cooper's Inn at Shelburne; the Pines Resort in Digby; the Tattingstone Inn in Wolfville; the Consulate Inn, Braeside Inn, and Pictou Lodge in Pictou; the high-rise Delta Sydney and Cambridge Suites Hotel in Sydney; the Keltic Lodge near Ingonish.

### Outdoor Highlights

Sailing the sheltered waters of Halifax Harbour, Mahone Bay, and Bras d'Or Lakes; hiking the varied trails of Cape Breton Highlands National Park; rafting the Fundy tidal bore on the Shubenacadie River; canoeing the extensive waterways of Kejimkujik National Park; fishing for trophy bluefins in St. George's Bay; golfing the world-class Cape Breton Highland Links at Ingonish Beach.

## PRINCE EDWARD ISLAND

### Best Known For

The settings of *Anne of Green Gables* and other Lucy Maud Montgomery landmarks; succulent Malpeque oysters and all-you-can-eat lobster suppers; family holidays and the touristy summer scene at Cavendish; the Prince Edward Island National Park coastal wilderness.

### Most Interesting City Sights

In Charlottetown, Founder's Hall, the rejuvenated interior of Province House, the Confederation Centre of the Arts exhibits, the murals at the All Souls' Chapel, the bookshop and archives at Beaconsfield, the Farmers' Market, Victoria Park, and the Royalty Oaks Woodlot; the Green Gables House in Cavendish.

### Outstanding Lodgings

Charlottetown's Great George Inn, Dundee Arms Inn, Elmwood Heritage Inn, and Rodd Charlottetown; the Silver Fox Inn and Loyalist Country Inn at Summerside; Dalvay by the Sea Hotel in Grand Tracadie; and Rodd Brudenell in Kings County.

### Outdoor Highlights

Hot-air ballooning over northern Queens County; bicycling the easygoing roads all over the island; seal-watching excursions in Murray Harbour; horseback riding at Brudenell River Provincial Park; camping and hiking in Prince Edward Island National Park; deep-sea fishing charters from Rustico Harbour.

## NEWFOUNDLAND AND LABRADOR

### Best Known For

The otherworldly fjords and mountains of Gros Morne National Park; naturalist excursions to watch

# SIGHTSEEING CHECKLIST

## New Brunswick

Acadian Historical Village (near Caraquet)—Marvelous living re-creation of Acadian life between 1780 and 1890 City Market (Saint John)—A lively indoor market for baked goods, seafood, produce, and people-watching

Fundy National Park (Upper Fundy Coast)—A dizzying cross section of environments, from sea and swamp to forest and mountains

Kings Landing Historical Settlement (26 km west of Fredericton)—Brings to life a typical Anglo settlement of the 19th century

Kouchibouguac National Park (the Acadian Strait Coast)—Good hiking, camping, and canoeing among lagoons, coastal rivers, and woodlands

Military Compound (Fredericton)—Restored complex of 19th-century buildings and public areas

New Brunswick Museum (Saint John)—A good introduction to the province's arts, culture, and natural history

St. Andrews—Attractive seaside town with lovingly preserved homes, gardens, and commercial buildings

## Nova Scotia

Art Gallery of Nova Scotia (Halifax)—Especially good for Maritime folk art and Canadian painting

Quilters demonstrate their craft at Acadian Historical Village, near Caraquet, New Brunswick.

© JAYME LYNES

*Bluenose II* (Halifax)—Replica of the famous schooner pictured on the Canadian dime

Halifax Citadel National Historic Site (Halifax)—Star-shaped 18th-century fortress overlooking the city

Maritime Museum of the Atlantic (Halifax)—Strong marine history collections, including exhibits on the *Titanic* and the age of sail

Fisheries Museum of the Atlantic (Southwestern Nova Scotia)—Excellent displays on Atlantic fishing, shipbuilding, and seafaring, including fishing craft (sometimes even the *Bluenose II*)

Lunenburg (Southwestern Nova Scotia)—Mid-18th-century fishing and shipbuilding town founded by German and Swiss Protestants, full of strikingly painted, well-preserved buildings

Alexander Graham Bell National Historic Site (Cape Breton Island)—Exceptionally absorbing museum preserving artifacts, photos, and memorabilia of this modern Renaissance man

Cabot Trail (Cape Breton Island)—Breathtaking 300-km scenic drive

Cape Breton Highlands National Park—Rugged mountains, fine beaches, and some of Cape Breton's loveliest landscapes

Fortress of Louisbourg (Cape Breton Island)—Magnificent reconstruction and re-creation of military and civilian life in 18th-century Nova Scotia

## Prince Edward Island

Confederation Centre of the Arts (Charlottetown)—The province's arts and performance headquarters, with four museums, an art gallery, and four theaters

Founders Hall—Tells the story of Canada in the city of confederation

Green Gables—Many sights connected to the writing of Lucy Maud Montgomery

Prince Edward Island National Park—Forty kilometers of red-sand beaches

## Newfoundland and Labrador

Gros Morne National Park—Extraordinary landscape of fjords, high cliffs, and thousands of acres of wilderness

L'Anse aux Meadows National Historic Site—Reconstruction of the only authenticated Viking settlement in North America

ON THE ROAD

**Waterfront dining is a highlight for many visitors to Halifax.**

whales, seabirds, and icebergs; outstanding fishing and hunting; knitted crafts; the Viking settlement at L'Anse aux Meadows; summer festivals or any excuse for music; and an abundance of moose.

## Most Interesting City Sights

In St. John's, the Newfoundland Museum, Signal Hill National Historic Site, Quidi Vidi Battery, Bowring Park, and the Newfoundland Freshwater Resource Centre (fluvarium) at C. A. Pippy Park, folk art at the Sticks and Stones House, the Historic Train at Corner Brook; and the Labrador Interpretation Centre outside Happy Valley-Goose Bay.

## Outstanding Lodgings

St. John's Prescott Inn Bed and Breakfast and Fairmont Newfoundland; the Glynmill Inn and Best Western Mamateek Inn in Corner Brook; and the Aurora Hotel at Happy Valley-Goose Bay.

## Outdoor Highlights

Iceberg-watching excursions around Twillingate; boat tours in the fjords of Gros Morne National Park; hiking in the Long Range Mountains; the seabird spectacles at Witless Bay and Cape St. Mary; the amazing light show of the aurora borealis; berry-picking outings in summertime; whale-watching off the east coast; salmon and arctic char fishing and big-game hunting in remote Labrador; whitewater canoeing and kayaking on the Upper Humber, Main, and Gander Rivers; scuba diving off the Avalon Peninsula; caribou- and polar bear-spotting flights in Labrador; ferry trip to Nain.

# Recreation and Entertainment

## OUTDOOR ACTIVITIES

In Atlantic Canada's great outdoors, just about every form of recreation is feasible and first-rate: bicycling and hiking, mountaineering, scuba diving, houseboating, river rafting and canoeing, ocean and river kayaking, sailing, windsurfing, rockhounding, bird-watching, hunting, fishing, hockey, tennis, golf—you name it. No matter what the temperature—35° C in summer or -15° C in winter—people can be found throughout the year enjoying some form of recreation.

The region's several national parks and scores of provincial parks come in a wide range of personalities, and offer an equally eclectic array of activities and facilities, from wilderness backpacking at New Brunswick's Mt. Carleton, say, to lounging in luxury at Cape Breton Highlands' Keltic Lodge resort. For more information on Atlantic Canada's national parks, contact Parks Canada, tel. 902/426-3436, www.parkscanada.gc.ca.

Spectator sports popular in the Atlantic provinces include minor-league professional ice hockey, harness racing, and rugby.

### Fishing and Hunting

For rural Maritimers, nature is the biggest playing field around. Hunting and fishing are year-round activities. Game selection depends on season, but hunters will find game birds and bigger game such as deer, moose, and bear.

Sportfishing here is legendary, especially for Atlantic salmon in Newfoundland, New Brunswick, and Cape Breton, and for tuna and other deep-sea species off Prince Edward Island and elsewhere. Ice-fishing is popular in the winter. See the travel chapters for specific suggestions.

Licenses are required for hunting or fishing. Visitors must purchase a nonresident license. Regulations vary from province to province; for more information, contact:

New Brunswick: Department of Natural Resources and Energy, Fish and Wildlife Branch, tel. 506/453-2440, www.gnb.ca.

Nova Scotia: Department of Agriculture and Fisheries, Inland Fisheries Division, tel. 902/485-5056, www.gov.ns.ca/nsaf.

Prince Edward Island: Department of Fisheries, Aquaculture and the Environment, Fish and Wildlife Branch, tel. 902/368-4683, www.gov.pe.ca.

Newfoundland and Labrador: Department of Natural Resources, Fish and Wildlife Division, tel. 709/729-2815, www.gov.nf.ca.

### Camping and Hiking

The hiking season in the Maritime provinces spans spring to autumn; hiking and camping in Newfoundland and Labrador is relegated for the most part to the height of summer, except for the hardiest adventurers. Coastal areas are generally free of pesky insects, but insect repellent is wise inland from May through September. Pets must be kept on a leash at all times in the national and provincial parks.

For specific information on backpacking, hiking, and recreational facilities, see the provincial travel chapters or contact the respective tourism bureaus: in New Brunswick, tel. 800/561-0123, www.tourismnbcanada.com; in Nova Scotia, tel. 800/565-0000, www.explore.gov.ns.ca; in Prince Edward Island, tel. 888/734-7529, www.peiplay.com; in Newfoundland and Labrador, tel. 800/563-6353, www.gov.nf.ca/tourism.

### Cycling

Reasonably good roads and gorgeous scenery make the Maritimes excellent bicycling territory. Except on main arteries, particularly the TransCanada Highway, car traffic is generally light. Cyclists, nonetheless, should remain vigilant: narrow lanes and shoulders are common, and, in some areas, drivers may be unaccustomed to sharing the road with bicycles.

In New Brunswick, following the Saint John River valley and the complex of lakes north of Saint John makes for pleasant touring. The narrow roads that slice through Prince Edward Island's gentle countryside are sublime avenues for biking. Touring opportunities, through a variety of terrains, are numerous in Nova Scotia; probably the ultimate trip is the five- to six-day trek around Cape Breton's Cabot Trail.

Many shops rent decent- to good-quality road and mountain bikes. But if you plan to do some serious riding, you'll probably want to bring your own; most airlines will let you bring a bike for little or no extra charge. Bike shops are also excellent resources for tips on local riding conditions and for information on cycling club rides you can join. For more details, see the specific travel chapters.

An outstanding information resource is **Atlantic Canada Cycling,** tel. 902/423-2453, www.atl-canadacycling.com. The organization publishes extensive information on cycling routes (including descriptions and ratings of highways and byways throughout Atlantic Canada), tours, races, clubs, and equipment, while its website has links to local operators and a message board.

**Freewheeling Adventures,** a Nova Scotia-based company, leads "pampered pedaling" cycling trips—agreeable arrangements of guided trips in small groups, each accompanied by a support van to carry the luggage and, if necessary, the weary biker. Owners Cathy and Philip Guest plan everything—snacks, picnics, and meals at restaurants en route, and overnights at country inns. If a bike malfunctions, they fix it promptly.

Expect to pay around $200–300 per person per day for an all-inclusive tour. You can bring your own wheels (ask what's best for the terrain) or rent a bike there. The trips start from each area's central gateway such as Halifax, Baddeck, Saint John, Charlottetown, Deer Lake, or Corner Brook, and head out into some of Atlantic Canada's prettiest, off-the-beaten-track countryside, including the Cabot Trail, the Annapolis Valley, Prince Edward Island, and Gros Morne National Park. For details, contact Freewheeling Adventures at 902/857-3600 or 800/672-0775, www.freewheeling.ca.

## Water Sports

With so much water surrounding and flowing through the provinces, **boating** opportunities

are nearly infinite. Sailing is popular in the Bay of Fundy, around Passamaquoddy Bay, and in spacious Halifax and Sydney harbors, as well as in protected inland areas such as Bras d'Or Lake and the extensive inland waterways of New Brunswick's Saint John River and Mactaquac Lake. Canoeing is extremely popular on the region's hundreds of lakes and streams. Coastal kayaking is another adventure, especially along Cape Breton's turbulent Atlantic or inland on the more placid Bras d'Or Lakes.

**Windsurfing** in the Maritimes has a growing legion of fans. Windsurfers exploit breezy waters everywhere, and flock in particular to the beaches on the Gulf Stream-warmed Northumberland Strait. New Brunswick's Chaleur Provincial Park east of Dalhousie is situated at a prime coastal windsurfing area and has a windsurfing school with board rentals. On Prince Edward Island, the winds are best in northern Queens County on the Gulf of St. Lawrence.

This sea-bound region has no shortage of beaches, and most waterside provincial parks have a supervised **swimming** area. Warmest beaches are found along the Baie des Chaleurs ("Bay of Warmth") and the Northumberland Strait. The Bay of Fundy and Atlantic shores tend to be somewhat cooler, though conditions vary considerably throughout the region.

## Winter Sports

Few visitors come to the Atlantic provinces outside of the prime travel season—late spring to early autumn. But you'll still find plenty to do should you arrive in winter. The national parks and many of the provincial parks stay open year-round. In winter, hiking routes are transformed by snow into excellent **cross-country ski** trails, and **snowmobilers** take to the woods and trails with a vengeance. Many city and regional parks, such as Halifax's Point Pleasant and Moncton's Centennial Park, also offer cross-country trails, along with frozen lakes for **ice-skating** and **hockey.** Downhill skiers head to Marble Mountain in Newfoundland, or Sugarloaf Provincial Park and Mont-Farlagne, both in northwestern New Brunswick.

# SPECTATOR SPORTS

Ice hockey, a Canadian invention, is the national sports obsession, and that applies in Atlantic Canada, too. Though the region is home to no National Hockey League teams, the exploits of the Toronto Maple Leafs, Montréal Canadiens, and other NHL franchises are passionately followed here. In the Atlantic Provinces, you can also see lively play from the Québec Major Junior Hockey League's Halifax Mooseheads and Moncton Wildcats; NHL farm teams in Fredericton, Saint John, and St. John's; and high-quality college and amateur teams in cities and towns throughout the region. The season runs October to March; check with local tourist-information offices for game schedules and ticket info.

# ENTERTAINMENT AND EVENTS

The Canada Council gives grants to theaters, dance troupes, orchestras, and arts councils to promote and keep the arts alive. Provincial tourism offices can tell you what's going on, or you can check out the local paper. See each travel chapter for specific listings detailing nightlife, theater, dance, and music options.

## Museums

With an ethnic heritage as varied as Atlantic Canada's, it's no wonder that museums are plentiful. Nova Scotia's 147 museums are among the region's best. Some museums are grand-scale provincial heritage sites, such as New Brunswick's King's Landing Historical Settlement—which re-creates early Anglo years with authentic buildings and demonstrations—and Nova Scotia's magnificently rebuilt Fortress of Louisbourg National Historic Site.

On a smaller scale, county and town museums document regional historic, cultural, and economic subjects. Municipal or privately operated museums in towns and villages put the emphasis on local history or specialties.

## Festivals

It's said that Nova Scotia is the land of 100,000 summer festivals; one might say the same about the whole of Atlantic Canada. Each province seems to have one sort of festival or event taking place somewhere just about every day of summer's peak travel season. But special events and performances are held throughout the year. Major events are listed in the introductions to every travel chapter, then detailed under specific locations within the text. Or you can stop by one of the tourism information offices found in just about every city, town, and village to get more complete listings.

# SHOPPING
## Arts and Crafts

Quilts, sweaters, hooked rugs, porcelains, and wooden carvings are deftly mixed among the watercolors, oils, and sculptures in many arts and crafts venues. The hand-woven tartans of Loomcrofters (the weavers who designed the New Brunswick provincial and Royal Canadian Air Force tartans) at Gagetown, New Brunswick, and the work of the Madawaska Weavers, in New Brunswick's Acadian northwest, are well known on the provincial fashion scene.

New Brunswick's craftspeople specialize in yarn portraits, glassblowing, pottery, wood sculptures, and pewter goods. The tourism department publishes the *Crafts Directory*, available at any tourism office. Antique buyers should head to Nova Scotia, where many historic sites and homes have been converted into antique shops. The Nova Scotia tourism department produces a buyer's guide, available at tourism offices. Newfoundland is known for a wide selection of labradorite jewelry as well as down jackets. The basketry work of the Mi'kmaqs of Lennox Island (Prince Edward Island) has received much attention. PEI shops also carry beadwork, leather goods, silver jewelry, pottery, handcrafted furniture, and woodcarvings.

> *It's said that Nova Scotia is the land of 100,000 summer festivals; one might say the same about the whole of Atlantic Canada.*

## NATIONAL HOLIDAYS

| | |
|---|---|
| New Year's Day | 1 January |
| Good Friday | late March to mid-April |
| Easter Monday | late March to mid-April |
| Victoria Day | third or fourth Monday in May |
| Canada Day | 1 July |
| Labour Day | first Monday in September |
| Thanksgiving Day | second Monday in October |
| Remembrance Day | 11 November |
| Christmas Day | 25 December |
| Boxing Day | 26 December |

### Export Details

Americans can bring $400 worth of duty-free goods back into the United States after a 48-hour stay in Canada; $25 is the duty-free limit following stays of less than 48 hours. Gifts sent by mail and worth a total of $50 or less are duty-free also.

If you are interested in shopping for exotic wares, such as whalebone carvings or bearskin rugs, beware of customs regulations prohibiting the export or import 87 of these items; hundreds of animals and their by-products are listed on the International Trade in Endangered Species (CITES) list. For a list of imports banned in your home country, contact your nearest customs office before departure.

Likewise, the export from Canada of certain items considered to be cultural property is restricted. Such items include fossils, archaeological artifacts, archival material, some fine and decorative art, and some old or rare books. For details or an export permit, contact the **Canadian Cultural Property Export Review Board,** tel. 800/622-6232, www.canada.gc.ca.

### Business Hours

Shopping hours are generally Mon.–Sat. 9 A.M.–6 P.M. Late shopping in most areas is available until 9 P.M. on Thursday and Friday, and supermarkets open 24 hours have begun to appear in a few towns. Generally, banks are open Mon.–Wed. 10 A.M.–4 P.M., Thurs.–Fri. 10 A.M.–5 P.M. A few banks may open on Saturday, but all are closed on Sunday.

# Accommodations and Food

### Lodging Reservations

Many large local, national, and international hotel, resort, and motel groups have properties in Atlantic Canada; if you want to make advance reservations at any of their lodgings, simply phone the toll-free reservation center or book online using their websites.

Reservations at many bed-and-breakfast and country inns can be made through a provincial reservations center. In Nova Scotia, most of the properties belong to Check In—the reservation service operated by the province—which has a toll-free phone line in North America. In New Brunswick, Dial-A-Night takes reservations at any of the provincial tourist offices at the border crossings.

Selected places to stay are detailed in the following chapters; the rates quoted are for a double

room unless noted otherwise. Many motels and hotels promote discounted weekend, off-season, and senior rates. Call individual lodgings directly to find out what discounts might be available at any given time.

## HOTEL, MOTEL, AND RESORT GROUPS

### Auberge Wandlyn Inns

This New Brunswick company started in its home province and now has 23 properties throughout the Maritimes. The chain emphasizes reasonable rates—ask about special weekend rates, supersavers, and senior Discounts. At each property guests enjoy dining facilities and the use of a heated pool and fitness room.

## LODGING RESERVATIONS AND INFORMATION SOURCES

**New Brunswick**
The province sponsors a free **Dial-A-Night** reservations system for all lodgings and privately operated campgrounds. Visitors may also make a reservation at any of the provincial tourist information centers situated at the entry points to New Brunswick. The provincial *Travel Planner* lists all lodgings, with prices included. Reservations can also be made online at www.tourism nbcanada.com.

**Nova Scotia**
More than 90 percent of the province's lodgings and campgrounds (they're all listed with details in the provincial *Travel Guide*) are affiliated with **Check In,** the province-sponsored, free reserva-

tion system. To make a reservation, call 902/425-5781 or 800/565-0000, or book online at www.checkinnovascotia.com.

**Prince Edward Island**
Hundreds of lodgings are listed and described in the provincial *Visitors Guide*. The Department of Tourism operates the **Vacancy Information Search** by phone (tel. 888/268-6667) and online (www.peiplay.com).

**Newfoundland and Labrador**
The province has no central reservation system. The properties are listed with details in the provincial *Travel Guide*, online at www.gov.nf.ca/tourism; for reservations, contact the lodgings directly.

For reservations, call 800/561-0000 or search out properties online at www.wandlyinns.com.

### Best Western
The world's largest motel chain has nine locations across Atlantic Canada. Each property is independently owned and operated, so services and standards vary greatly. Best Western has a worthwhile frequent traveler program and offers significant discounts for travelers aged 55 and over.

Locations include Dalhousie and Moncton, New Brunswick; Dartmouth, Kingston, North Sydney, Truro, and Yarmouth, Nova Scotia; Charlottetown, Prince Edward Island; and St. John's, Newfoundland.

The central reservations number for North America is 800/780-7234, www.bestwestern .com. The website www.bestwesternatlantic.com provides direct links to local properties.

### Choice Hotels Canada
This company owns 200 properties across the country. It operates seven brands, including Sleep, with smallish but clean, comfortable, and inexpensive rooms; Comfort, where guests enjoy a light breakfast and newspaper with a no-frills room; Quality, a notch up in quality with a

restaurant and lounge; and Econo Lodge, older properties that have been renovated to Choice's standard and often have a pool and restaurant.

For reservations, call 800/424-6423 or check www.choicehotels.ca.

### City Hotels
This brand comprises seven mid-priced properties in New Brunswick and Newfoundland. Locations include Saint John, Edmundston, Monton, Miramichi, St. John's (two locations), and Marystown.

Make reservations by calling 800/563-2489 or click through the links to make online reservations at www.cityhotels.ca.

### Country Inns and Suites
Part of the massive Carlson Hospitality Worldwide group, these well-designed motor hotels offer reasonably priced rooms decorated in pleasing country-style furnishings. Local calls and daily newspapers are complimentary, and kids under 18 stay free.

County Inns and Suites are located in 14 towns across Nova Scotia and New Brunswick. To check locations or make reservations, contact 800/456-4000 or www.countryinns.com.

## Delta Hotels and Resorts

This Canadian-owned company is a class operation; expect fine hotels with splendid facilities in notable settings. Locations include Saint John and Moncton, New Brunswick; Halifax and Sydney, Nova Scotia; and St. John's, Newfoundland.

Reservations can be made by calling 416/874-2000 or 800/268-1133, or online at www.deltahotels.com. Check the Delta website for package deals offered year-round.

## Fairmont Hotels and Resorts

Fairmont is the new name for **Canadian Pacific,** a company synonymous with high-quality, stunning hotels in major Canadian cities and resort towns such as Banff and Jasper. The company is represented in Atlantic Canada by the Fairmont Algonquin, a gorgeous, Tudor-style resort spread across manicured grounds and gardens at St. Andrews, New Brunswick. Besides the Algonquin, the group's only other Atlantic Canada property is in St. John's, Newfoundland.

For reservations, contact Fairmont at 506/863-6310 or 800/441-1414, www.fairmont.com.

## Hilton Worldwide

Luxurious trappings and superior facilities are the hallmarks of the Hilton company. Atlantic Canada is home to just one of 500 Hilton properties around the world. The hotel is on the waterfront in Saint John, tel. 506/693-8484 or 800/561-8282. Contact 800/744-1500 or www.hilton.com for central reservations for the Hilton chain.

## Holiday Inns

Under the umbrella of the Six Continents Hotels family, the ubiquitous Holiday Inn now has a variety of brands. Most of those in Atlantic Canada are regular inns, independently owned and operated but each a full-service property with recreational facilities, a business center, a restaurant with room service, and a lounge. At a Holiday Inn Express, rates include a light breakfast.

For reservations, call 800/238-8000 or search out properties online at www.holiday-inn.com. This company's frequent traveler program is well worth joining; it's free, and members enjoy benefits such as use of a private lounge.

## Keddy's Hotels and Inns

Atlantic Canadian–owned, Keddy properties range from landmark hotels like the high-rise Lord Beaverbrook Hotel in Fredericton to the

**ON THE ROAD**

## CANADA SELECT

Lodgings in Atlantic Canada are graded by a standard established by Canada Select, a nationwide grading system. The lodgings are grouped in four categories: hotels/motels; inns and bed and breakfasts; resorts (with recreational facilities); and sports lodges and cottages (fishing/hunting lodges, cottages, and cabins).

The gradings range from one to five stars. At a one-star property, expect basic, clean, and comfortable accommodations with no frills; a two-star lodging has the same basics with some amenities. The three-to five-star lodgings have better-to-deluxe accommodations with an increasing range of facilities and services. The provincial lodgings inspectors are *very* stringent in awarding star gradings; comparable properties (especially in the three- and four-star categories) in other parts of the world would rate higher grades.

The system is voluntary, but includes a majority of the lodgings. The provincial tourist offices emphasize the Canada Select program, and the provincial tourist guides include the star grades with the properties' details; the following chapters do not.

Rates more or less correspond with the star grades; the lowest grades are the least-expensive places to stay, and the hotels and resorts at the scale's higher end cost considerably more. Some of Atlantic Canada's top-grade hotels and resorts have not been rated as highly by Canada Select as their reputations would seem to justify. But the owners of these establishments know what their lodgings are worth according to world standards, and guests pay top dollar, regardless of Canada Select's rating.

newer, sprawling Bathurst Hotel, both in New Brunswick. The hotels feature comfortably appointed rooms, health centers with free facilities for guests, and dining rooms that serve some of the best food in town. Locations include Saint John, Fredericton, Moncton, and Bathurst, New Brunswick; Halifax (outskirts), Truro, and Port Hastings, Nova Scotia; and Summerside, Prince Edward Island. Keddy's has also taken on marketing for four **Howard Johnson,** www .hojo.com, properties in New Brunswick.

For reservations, call 800/561-7666 in Canada or the United States, or worldwide check out www.keddys.ca.

## Maritime Inns and Resorts

With package deals and locations in Pictou, Antigonish, Port Hawkesbury, and the Cape Breton resort town of Baddeck, these properties are popular with holidaying Maritimers. Generally, packages include meals and activities such as golfing for around $100 per person per day.

Reservations can be made at 888/662-7484 or online at www.maritimeinns.com.

## Rodd Hotels and Resorts

This locally owned hotel company is Prince Edward Island's lodgings standard bearer. The handsome Loyalist Country Inn at Summerside is the newest hotel, the Rodd Charlottetown in the capital is the oldest. Two full-facility resorts are situated within provincial-park settings at either end of the island; near Cardigan (Roseneath, Brudenell River Provincial Park), and O'Leary (Woodstock, Mill River Provincial Park).

Other Rodd locations include two more properties in Charlottetown; one in Moncton, New Brunswick; and two in Yarmouth, Nova Scotia. For reservations, call 902/892-7448 or 800/565-7633, www.rodd-hotels.ca.

## Signature Resorts

Nova Scotia's provincial government owns three stunning resorts. They appeal to the carriage trade—travelers who like the understated ambience of a resort lodge with a tony rustic setting and furnishings, gourmet dining, a remote location with manicured grounds, and the genteel sports of golf or fly-fishing.

© ANDREW HEMPSTEAD

**Many fine lodgings don't belong to a chain, including the Grand Barachois Country Inn, on New Brunswick's Acadian Coast.**

Provincial resorts in Nova Scotia are the Pines Resort at Digby; the Keltic Lodge at Ingonish Beach, Cape Breton; and Liscombe Lodge at Liscomb Mills.

The central reservations number is 877/375-6343, or book online at www .signatureresorts.com.

## HOSTELLING INTERNATIONAL

Formerly known as the Youth Hostel Association, this hostel operation maintains a network of budget-priced accommodations at over 4,000 locations in 60 countries. Hostelling International Canada operates nine hostels in Atlantic Canada, including in New Brunswick at Fredericton, Campbellton, and Alma (Fundy National Park); in Nova Scotia at Halifax, LaHave (near Lunenburg), South Milford (near Kejimkujik National Park), Wentworth, and Mabou; and in PEI at Charlottetown. For a dorm bed, members of Hostelling International pay $12–18 per night, nonmembers pay an extra $4.

### Membership

You don't *have* to be a member to stay in an affiliated hostel of Hostelling International, but membership pays for itself after only a few nights of discounted lodging. Aside from discounted rates, benefits of membership vary from country to country but often include discounted air, rail, and bus travel; discounts on car rental; and discounts on some attractions and commercial activities. For Canadians, the membership charge is $35 annually or $175 for a lifetime membership. For more information write Hostelling International, 400–205 Catherine St., Ottawa, ON K2P 1C3, tel. 613/237-7884, website www.hihostels.ca.

Joining the Hostelling International affiliate of your home country entitles you to reciprocal rights in Canada, as well around the world. In the United States the contact address is **Hostelling International-American Youth Hostels,** 733 15th St. N.W., Suite 840, Washington, DC 20005, tel. 202/783-6161, website www .hiayh.org; annual membership costs US$25 for adults and US$15 for seniors, or you can become a lifetime member for US$250. Other contact addresses include **YHA England and Wales,** Trevelyan House, St. Stephen's Hill, St. Albans, Herts. AL1 2DY, England, tel. 0170/870-8808, website www.yha.org.uk; **YHA Australia,** 422 Kent St., Sydney, NSW 2000, Australia, tel. 02/9261-1111, website www.yha.com; and **YHA New Zealand,** P.O. Box 436, Christchurch, tel. 03/379-9970, website www.yha.org.nz. For other countries, click through the links on the International Youth Hostel Federation website, www.iyhf.com.

## EDUCATIONAL STAYS

Several universities and colleges in the region offer short-term summer classes, most commonly in the arts and crafts fields (you're on your own to arrange for lodgings and meals).

**Elderhostel** has classes for older adults in a variety of subjects in conjunction with universities across Atlantic Canada. The subjects are often linked with the setting. For example, at Corner Brook, a class in geology explains the formation of nearby Gros Morne National Park, and day trips to the park form part of the program. At Fredericton, a class is oriented to tracing family roots, a subject of popular interest to many visitors who come to New Brunswick to research ancestral records.

Elderhostel's five- or six-day programs operate year-round; classes are held at the University of New Brunswick in Fredericton, Memorial University of Newfoundland in St. John's and Corner Brook, Dalhousie University in Halifax, and Acadia University at Wolfville in Nova Scotia, and the University of Prince Edward Island at Charlottetown. Expect to pay about $500 pp, all-inclusive. You must be at least 55 years old to participate.

The nonprofit organization publishes a free, quarterly *Elderhostel Catalog* with program details and a registration form. There's no charge to be added to the mailing list. Contact the organization at Avenue de LaFayette, Boston, MA 02111-1746, tel. 978/323-4141 or 877/426-2166, www.elderhostel.org.

ON THE ROAD

## CAMPING

Whenever possible, reservations for campsites—especially at the national parks and most popular provincial parks—should be made at least six weeks in advance. Most provincial parks, however, do not accept reservations, but instead assign sites on a first-come, first-served basis. At those parks, it's best to arrive before noon to assure yourself a spot. Most provincial parks are open mid-May to mid-October. Most privately owned campsites accept reservations, which are more likely to be held if you send a small deposit.

## FOOD AND DRINK

Maritime cuisine reflects its English and Acadian heritages, with some local specialties that reflect the character of the region and its available ingredients. The down-home dining is irresistible: a bountiful lobster feed in one of the community halls on Prince Edward Island; pickled Solomon Gundy herring sold from a roadside peddler's cart or planked Atlantic salmon cooked over an open fire at a resort in Nova Scotia; and seal-flipper pie, moose burgers, and roasted wild game—partridge, rabbit, and caribou—in Newfoundland.

Coastal dwellers nibble on dulse, a dried, iodine-rich, purple seaweed that thrives along the rocky shores of the Bay of Fundy; in the spring, they eat a cream soup made from ostrich fern fronds. Smelts are fried or baked. Vegetables and potatoes are stewed. Typical desserts include walnut toffee, trifle, homemade ice cream, or Ganong chocolates from St. Stephen.

While Anglo cuisine features red meats, Acadian fare is based on seafood. Common Acadian-style dishes include seafood chowder, shellfish (shrimp and queen crab), and fish (especially mackerel, herring, and cod). For variety, Acadian menus might offer chicken *fricot* (chicken stew),

> *For variety, Acadian menus might offer chicken* **fricot** *(chicken stew),* **poutine râpé,** *and desserts such as sugar pie, apple dumplings, or cinnamon buns. Acadian cooking may be terribly hard on the waistline, but it's delicious.*

*poutine râpé* (boiled or deep-fried pork and grated raw potatoes, rolled into a ball and dipped in corn or maple syrup or molasses), and desserts such as sugar pie, apple dumplings, or cinnamon buns. Acadian cooking may be terribly hard on the waistline, but it's delicious.

Save room for an Acadian culinary variation in Edmundston or another of the Madawaska area towns. Brayon cooking, as it's known, creates *les ployes*—buckwheat pancakes splashed with butter, molasses, or maple syrup or used as a wrapper for spicy pâté or seafood.

The Danes immigrated to Nova Scotia and New Brunswick in the late 19th century and still cling to Scandinavian ways at New Denmark in New Brunswick's upper Saint John River valley. A typical Danish meal may include homemade sausage, roast beef and red cabbage, ground beef patties, and apple cake.

### Alcohol

French imports and local wines from the Jost and Grand-Pré wineries are available at many fine restaurants. Regional and locally brewed beers are also popular; favorites include Schooner and Keith's. The Granite Brewery in Halifax produces a variety of brews, including stouts and seasonal specialties, but these beers may be scarce outside Nova Scotia.

As elsewhere in Canada, strict regulations govern alcohol consumption, though these were loosened somewhat in 1996. Licensed restaurants, dining rooms, and cocktail lounges serve liquor daily 11 A.M.–2 A.M. Beverage rooms with beer and wine are open Mon.–Wed. 10 A.M.–11 P.M., Thurs.–Sat. to midnight; lounge hours are Mon.–Sat. 11 A.M.–2 A.M.; and cabarets are open nightly 7 P.M.–3 A.M. Alcohol is sold at government liquor stores, open Mon.–Thurs. 10 A.M.—6 p.m., Fri. to 10 P.M., Sat. to 5 P.M. The minimum drinking age is 19.

# Getting There

## BY CAR

Drivers must possess a valid **driver's license** from their home state or country. If you bring your own car into Canada, you must also have the current **vehicle registration.** If you're driving a borrowed car, you should carry written permission from the legal owner authorizing you to use the vehicle in Canada.

Vehicle insurance ($200,000 minimum liability) is mandatory, and if there's an accident, the Royal Canadian Mounted Police (RCMP) will ask the drivers for proof of financial responsibility. Nonresident drivers can obtain such proof in the form of a **Canadian Non-Resident Inter-Provincial Motor Vehicle Liability Insurance Card,** available from insurance companies outside Canada.

Use of **seatbelts or infant car seats** is mandatory for drivers and passengers throughout Canada (except in the Yukon).

### Principal Routes into Atlantic Canada

The majority of visitors drive to Atlantic Canada. From the United States, Highway 9 heads east from Bangor, Maine, and enters New Brunswick—Atlantic Canada's principal land gateway—at St. Stephen, near the Fundy coast. The TransCanada Highway from central Canada (another main entry route) is more roundabout, following the St. Lawrence River through Québec Province to enter northwestern New Brunswick at Saint-Jacques near Edmundston. Once in New Brunswick, you can take the Confederation Bridge (see below) to Prince Edward Island or continue driving east into Nova Scotia.

From Cape Breton, you can get a car ferry to southwestern or southeastern Newfoundland. From northern Newfoundland, two car-ferry routes connect with Labrador. Labrador can also be reached from Québec Province on Hwy. 389, from Baie-Comeau, on the St. Lawrence River's northern bank. The 581-km drive takes nine hours; the two-lane road wends through the province's wilderness to enter western Labrador at Labrador City.

### Ferries

If you're passing through Maine on your way to Atlantic Canada, two ferry services provide a shortcut to Nova Scotia, saving a long drive along the Bay of Fundy. Both terminate at Yarmouth. The *Scotia Prince,* tel. 207/775-5616 or 800/341-7540, www.scotiaprince.com, takes 11 hours to reach Yarmouth from Nova Scotia. Peak season (mid-June to mid-September) one-way fare is US$86 for adults, US$43 for children, and US$105 for vehicles, with rates discounted to US$66, US$33, and US$85, respectively, outside peak season. Cabins range US$38–175 each way. Ferries leave Portland from the International Marine Terminal, 468 Commercial Street. *The Cat,* tel. 902/742-6800 or 888/249-7245, www.catferry.com, crosses between Bar Harbor and Yarmouth in 2.5 hours. It runs twice a day in each direction June–September, once a day in each direction in May and October. Peak season one-way fares (July and August) are adult US$55, senior US$50, child US$25, vehicle under 6.6 feet US$95, vehicle under 9.9 feet US$120, bicycle US$30.

## BY RAIL

**Amtrak,** tel. 800/872-8725, www.amtrak.com, has service from Seattle to Vancouver, from Chicago to Toronto, from New York to Toronto (via Buffalo), and from New York to Montréal.

Once you're in Canada, rail travel is handled by **VIA Rail,** tel. 416/236-2029 or 888/842-7245, www.viarail.ca. Best known for the transcontinental rail route, the spectacular journey from Vancouver to Toronto through the Rockies and central Canada's farmlands, VIA Rail has replicated the transcontinental route's deluxe trappings and service in Atlantic Canada with its Easterly Service. The service, begun in spring 1993, is featured on the **Montréal-to-Halifax**

## CUTTING FLIGHT COSTS

In today's topsy-turvy world of air travel, finding the cheapest fare and best-suited route can be a challenge. The Internet has changed the way many people shop for tickets, but even if you use this invaluable tool for preliminary research, having a travel agent that you are comfortable in dealing with—who takes the time to call around, does some research to get you the best fare, and helps you take advantage of any available special offers or promotional deals—is an invaluable asset in starting your travels off on the right foot.

In the first instance, though, to get an idea of what your agent should be able to come up with, call the airlines or check their websites and compare fares. Also look in the travel sections of major newspapers—particularly in weekend editions—where budget fares and package deals are frequently advertised.

Within Canada, **Travel Cuts,** website www.travelcuts.com, and **Flight Centre,** website www.flightcentre.ca, both with offices in all major cities, consistently offer the lowest airfares available with the latter guaranteeing the lowest. Flight Centre offers a similar guarantee from its U.S. offices (tel. 877/967-5347, website www.flightcenter.com), as well as those in Great Britain (tel. 08705-66-66-77, website www.flightcentre.co.uk), Australia (tel. 13-16-00, website www.flightcentre.com.au), and New Zealand (tel. 09-275-5423, website www.flightcentre.co.nz). In London, **Trailfinders,** 215 Kensington High St., Kensington, tel. 020/7937-5400, website www.trailfinders.com, always has good deals to Canada and other North American destinations. Reservations can be made directly through airline or travel agency websites, or use the services of an Internet-only company such as **Travelocity** (website www.travelocity.com).

Many cheaper tickets have strict restrictions regarding changes of flight dates, lengths of stay, and cancellations. A general rule: The cheaper the ticket, the more restrictions. Most travelers today fly on APEX (advance-purchase excursion) fares. These are usually the best value, though some (and, occasionally, many) restrictions apply. These might include minimum and maximum stays, and unchangeable itineraries (or hefty penalties for changes); tickets may also be nonrefundable once purchased.

When you have found the best fare, open a **frequent flyer** membership with the airline—**Air Canada,** part of the Star Alliance, has a popular program that makes rewards very obtainable.

---

routes aboard a vintage fleet of stainless-steel trains. The *Ocean* departs Montréal, follows the St. Lawrence River's southern shore to northern New Brunswick, cuts across the province to Moncton, speeds into Nova Scotia via Amherst and Truro, and finishes at Halifax.

Each of the revamped trains includes a domed car with three small salons (one of which is a replica of the transcontinental's mural lounge), a dining car with art-deco trappings, and a more informal car designed for lighter dining. Interiors on all the cars have been refurbished. VIA Rail promises home cooking, and dining-car meals are served all day instead of at specific sittings. A free continental breakfast is served in the dome car, and beverages are complimentary as well. Overnight accommodations include one-passenger roomettes and two-passenger bedroom compartments with a private toilet in the room or nearby. Each sleeping car also has a shower room.

### Canrailpass

This pass is an excellent value for those traveling extensivly by train. It offers unlimited travel anywhere on the VIA Rail system for 12 days within any 30-day period. During high season (June 1 to October 15), passes cost $658 for adults and $592 for seniors (over 60) and children, with extra days (up to three) costing $56 and $49 respectively. The rest of the year, adult passes cost $411; seniors and students pay $370, with extra days charged at $36 and $33 respectively. VIA Rail has cooperated with Amtrak to offer a North American Rail Pass, with all the same seasonal dates and discounts as the Canrailpass. The cost is $1,004 for adults; $892 for seniors and children; $702 and $632 respectively through the low season.

## BY AIR

Most long-haul international and domestic flights into eastern Canada set down at Toronto, Ottawa, or Montréal, with connecting or ongoing flights to Atlantic Canada. Halifax, the region's air gateway, also gets nonstop international flights from Bermuda, Glasgow, London, Boston, and Newark on Air Canada, tel. 888/247-2262, www.aircanada.ca.

Air Canada has a service agreement with **Con-** **tinental Airlines,** tel. 800/784-4444, www .continental.com, in the United States, making for easy connections from America cities. From any city served by Continental, you first fly to Newark International Airport, one of the airline's major hubs. From there you'll board Air Nova and be in Halifax in less than two hours. Another very workable connection is Continental's service from Houston to Toronto, connecting to Air Canada for the flight to Halifax or another major city in Atlantic Canada.

# Getting Around

## BY CAR

### TransCanada Highway

The TransCanada Highway is a godsend within Atlantic Canada. The high-speed highway slips across New Brunswick past Fredericton and Moncton, crosses the Chignecto Isthmus into Nova Scotia near Amherst, and speeds east to Cape Breton. The major road on Prince Edward Island is also designated as the TransCanada

## CONFEDERATION BRIDGE

In May 1997, the 13-km (8-mile) strait between New Brunswick's Cape Jourimain and the PEI coast at Borden-Carleton was spanned by the Confederation Bridge, a $900 million project undertaken four years earlier by an unusual public-private consortium. The bridge replaced a busy ferry route that had been in operation since 1832. Canada's longest bridge (and the world's longest continuous multispan bridge), the Confederation had been the subject of debate for decades, with passionate opinions running on both sides of the issue. Open now for a few years, there's little question that the link has increased traffic to the island. Whether the growing volume of visitors will dramatically alter the island's way of life, as opponents have warned, remains to be seen. In any case, crossing the bridge isn't cheap— tolls are $37.25 per vehicle. Check out the bridge at www.confederationbridge.com.

Highway, as is the major thoroughfare on the island of Newfoundland.

Scenic vistas are not, however, among the highway's greatest attributes, and long hours on the route can be awfully boring. Nonetheless, the benefits of direct routes and expressway speed outweigh the tedium in some cases.

### Rental Cars

All major car-rental companies have offices at airports and usually in the adjacent cities. Some have branches in other towns. Rentals can cost up to $70 per day if you just turn up at the desk. Always try to book in advance and use company websites to search out the best deals.

Rental companies represented in Atlantic Canada include **Alamo,** tel. 800/327-9633, www.alamo.com; **Avis,** tel. 800/879-2847, www.avis.com; **Budget,** tel. 800/268-8900, www.budget.com; **Discount,** tel. 800/263-2355, www.discountcar.com; **Dollar,** tel. 800/800-4000, www.dollar.com; **Enterprise,** tel. 800/325-8007, website www.enterprise.com; **Hertz,** tel. 800/263-0600, www.hertz.com; **National,** tel. 800/227-7368, www.nationalcar .com; **Rent-a-Wreck,** tel. 800/327-0116, website www.rentawreck.ca; and **Thrifty,** tel. 800/847-4389, www.thrifty.com.

## BY FERRY

The region is webbed with an efficient ferry service. **Bay Ferries** handles the important Bay of

Fundy crossing between Saint John, New Brunswick, and Digby, Nova Scotia, a shortcut that saves drivers hundreds of kilometers of highway miles between the two provinces. Operating year-round, one-way fares include adult $35, senior $30, child $15, vehicle $70. For ferry reservations and information, call Bay Ferries at 902/245-2116 or 888/249-7245, www.nfl-bay.com.

**Northumberland Ferries,** tel. 902/566-3838 or 800/565-0201, www.nfl-bay.com, operates between Caribou, Nova Scotia, and Wood Islands in eastern Prince Edward Island. The fare is $49 per vehicle, regardless of the number of passengers. You only pay when leaving the island, so take the ferry to PEI and return on the Confederation Bridge (see sidebar) to save a few bucks.

**Marine Atlantic** operates two routes between North Sydney, Nova Scotia, and Newfoundland. The shorter passage, to Port-aux-Basques, takes five to seven hours and costs $22 for adults, $20 for seniors, $11 for children, and $67 for vehicles each way. Summer-only sailings between North Sydney and Argentia take around 14 hours and cost $60 for adults, $55 for seniors, $30 for children, and from $135 for vehicles. Contact Marine Atlantic at 902/794-5254 or 800/341-7981, www.marine-atlantic.ca.

## BY BUS

The provinces are obliged by the government to provide relatively cheap, long-haul transportation. Government-funded or privately operated buses chug along on all the major highways and pull off to stop and pick up passengers at designated places in main towns.

A few cities, such as St. John's, also have commuter bus links with the outlying, smaller ports. If you have a day on your hands and no other plans, consider an early-morning bus to an unexplored area, and a late-afternoon or early-evening return to the city. Few outsiders do it, but mixing among the locals on a bus circuit is a terrific way to explore a province. Public transit in the cities is spottier: there's none in places like Charlottetown or Amherst where you might expect it, but more than enough in the larger communities such as Halifax, Sydney, and St. John's.

## BY AIR

Halifax International Airport, 35 km (21 miles) from Halifax, serves as Atlantic Canada's principal regional air hub. Other main provincial gateways are Saint John, Moncton, Bathurst, Yarmouth, Sydney, Charlottetown, and St. John's. **Air Nova/Air Canada,** tel. 888/247-2262, www.aircanada.ca, saturate the region with frequent flights. Air Nova's network includes Corner Brook, Gander, Happy Valley-Goose Bay, St. Anthony, St-Léonard, Stephenville, Sydney, and Wabush/Labrador City. Reservations and information are handled by Air Nova/Air Canada in Atlantic Canada and through Air Canada worldwide.

Air travel is the transportation mode of choice throughout the provinces. While the airlines haven't put bus or ferry travel (or trains, yet) out of business, the airports are usually crowded, and regional flights are often filled. Be sure to confirm your flights beforehand, and be at the airport 30 minutes before departure. Passengers not checked in 10 minutes before the flight may forfeit their seats to any stand-by passengers waiting to board.

# Information and Services

## VISAS AND OFFICIALDOM

Citizens and most permanent residents of the United States may enter Canada with a birth, baptismal, or voter-registration certificate. Naturalized citizens should carry a naturalization certificate, U.S. passport, or other citizenship evidence. Proof of residence may also be required; check with the nearest Canadian Consulate General office. A passport is the easiest such proof and will speed re entry into the United States.

Visitors from the United States with other citizenship status require special documents. Non-U.S. citizens who are permanent residents need a resident alien card, and U.S. residents with a temporary resident card or employment authorization card are required to carry a passport and in some cases a visitor's visa; for a visitor's visa, contact a Consulate General office *outside* Canada. For an update on required documents, or for other questions, contact the U.S. Immigration and Naturalization Service before departure.

Visitors from countries other than the United States must have a valid passport and may need a visa or visitor permit depending on their country of residence. At the time of publication, visas are not required for citizens of the British Commonwealth or Western Europe. Check with **Citizenship and Immigration Canada,** www .cic.gc.ca, for the latest requirements.

Foreigners entering Canada are allowed to stay for 180 days. For an extension, contact Citizenship and Immigration Canada, which has offices in all capital cities. You may be asked to show onward tickets or proof of sufficient funds to last through your intended stay. The Citizenship and Immigration Canada website, www.cic.gc.ca, has all the details.

## Clearing Customs

Visitors are allowed to bring in personal items that will be used during a visit, such as cameras, fishing tackle, and equipment for camping, golf, tennis, scuba diving, etc. The duty-free limits are: 1.1 liters of liquor or wine (19 years minimum age); 50 cigars, 200 cigarettes, and 400 grams of manufactured tobacco, plus 400 tobacco sticks (18 years minimum age); and gifts (not tobacco or alcohol) with a total value of $60 or less.

Firearms are strictly regulated. To bring a hunting rifle or shotgun into the country you must be at least 16 years old. Customs inspectors will not allow handguns, most pellet guns, or any firearm with no legitimate sporting or recreational use. A hunting rifle or shotgun is permitted but must be declared at entry.

If you are driving into Atlantic Canada, be sure you have the vehicle's registration. If the vehicle is rented or is registered to someone else, you'll need a rental contract or a letter from the owner that authorizes the vehicle's use. A valid driver's license from your home country is acceptable for driving in Canada. Wearing seat belts is mandatory in Canada, and studded tires are illegal except during winter.

If you're coming in by boat, you must contact Canada Customs or a regional customs office immediately after reaching port; if they're unavailable, get in touch with the RCMP.

## PROVINCIAL TOURISM OFFICES

**New Brunswick:** Tourism New Brunswick, P.O. Box 12345, Campbellton, NB E3N 1T6; tel. 800/561-0123; www.tourismnbcanada.com.
**Newfoundland and Labrador:** Department of Tourism, Culture, and Recreation, P.O. Box 8730, St. John's, NF A1B 4K2; tel. 709/729-2830 or 800/563-6353; www.gov.nf.ca/tourism
**Nova Scotia:** Department of Tourism and Culture, P.O. Box 456, Halifax, NS B3J 2R5, Canada; tel. 902/425-5781 or 800/565-0000; www.explore.gov.ns.ca
**Prince Edward Island:** Tourism PEI, P.O. Box 940, Charlottetown, PE C1A 7M5; tel. 902/368-5540 or 888/734-7529; www.gov.pe.ca

ON THE ROAD

## Employment and Study

Employment authorizations are not issued to foreigners if qualified Canadians or permanent Canadian residents are available for the job. Applications for work and study are available from all Canadian embassies and must be submitted with a nonrefundable processing fee. The **Citizenship and Immigration Canada** website, www.cic.gc.ca, has answers to all basic questions, as well as contact information for consulate offices around the world.

# HEALTH AND SAFETY

## Medical Care

No special health inoculations are needed before entering the country. Intra-provincial agreements cover the medical costs of Canadians traveling across the nation. For foreigners, however, medical care can be very expensive; a hospital's basic rate (without the physician's charge) can be up to $3,000 a day.

## Insurance

As a rule, the usual health-insurance plans do not include medical-care costs incurred while traveling; ask your insurance company or agent if supplemental health coverage is available, and if it is not, arrange for coverage with an independent carrier before departure.

## Outdoor Precautions

- Protect yourself from the sun. Pack plenty of sunscreen year-round; the sun's reflection on the snow can burn your skin more severely than direct sunlight.
- If you are visiting during the summer or spring months (mosquito season), bring insect repellent.
- Frostbite can occur in a matter of seconds if the temperature falls below freezing and if the wind is blowing. Layer your clothing for the best insulation against the cold, and don't forget gloves and, most important, a warm hat, which can offer the best protection against heat loss.

## Crime

The Atlantic provinces enjoy some of the country's lowest crime rates. Violent crimes are infrequent; the most common crime is petty theft. If you must leave valuable items in your car unattended, keep them out of sight, preferably locked in the vehicle's trunk. Women have few difficulties traveling alone throughout the region.

Halifax, St. John's, and Saint John are international ports with seamy (albeit interesting) bars and taverns at or near the working areas of the waterfronts; keep your wits about you here, especially late at night. Better yet, leave these night scenes to the sailors and others who frequent the areas.

Both possession and sale of illicit drugs are considered serious crimes and are punishable with jail time and/or severe fines. Furthermore, Canadians consider drinking while driving equally serious; the penalty upon the first conviction is jail and/or a heavy fine. A conviction here or in your home country can even be grounds for exclusion from Canada.

**RCMP:** The Royal Canadian Mounted Police, or Mounties, as ubiquitous a symbol of the country as the maple leaf, are similar to the highway patrol or state police in the United States. They operate throughout all the country's provinces and territories (except Ontario and Québec), complementing the work of local police. Despite the romantic image of the staid, red-jacketed officer on horseback, Mounties nowadays favor the squad car as their mount of choice and a less colorful uniform.

> *Despite the romantic image of the staid, red-jacketed officer on horseback, Mounties nowadays favor the squad car as their mount of choice and a less colorful uniform.*

# MONEY

Unless noted otherwise, **prices quoted in this book are in Canadian currency.** Canada's money is issued in notes ($5, $10, and $20 are the most common) and coins (1, 5, 10, and 25 cents; the $1 "loonie," so called because of the image of a loon embossed on it; and the $2 "toonie" ("two loonies").

Exchange rates vary from day to day, but as a rough guide the Canadian dollar generally trades at about 65 percent of the value of the U.S. dollar. The

## POST, TELEPHONE, AND TIME

### Postal Abbreviations

New Brunswick: NB

Newfoundland: NF

Nova Scotia: NS

Prince Edward Island: PE

To address a letter to Canada, use a five-line format: (1) name of addressee; (2) street address; (3) city and province; (4) postal code; (5) Canada. Ontario (ON) and Québec (PQ) provinces are mentioned in the text also.

### Telephone Area Codes

New Brunswick: (506)

Nova Scotia: (902)

Prince Edward Island: (902)

Newfoundland: (709)

### Time Zones

New Brunswick: AST

Newfoundland: AST and NST (see note below)

Nova Scotia: AST

Prince Edward Island: AST

Atlantic standard time (AST) is one hour ahead of eastern standard time (EST).

**Newfoundland standard time (NST),** 1.5 hours ahead of EST, is used on the island of Newfoundland and the southeastern Labrador communities on the Strait of Belle Isle; the rest of Labrador is on AST.

Daylight saving time starts throughout the Atlantic provinces the first Sunday in April, when the clocks are pushed ahead one hour; it ends on the last Sunday in October, when time reverts to standard time and the clocks go back one hour.

**ON THE ROAD**

most favorable exchange rates are given at banks. Many banks charge an extra fee (usually $2–2.50) to convert traveler's checks to cash. It helps to arrive with a small amount of Canadian funds for tips, airport-to-hotel taxi fare, and so forth. Banks are generally open Monday through Friday 9 A.M. to 3 or 5 P.M.; a few banks are open Saturday mornings.

U.S. and English currencies are readily accepted in the larger cities, but the exchange rates are often less than favorable. All the major credit cards are accepted, Visa most widely. But many of the smaller, privately operated lodgings and dining places want cash.

**Service charges and tips** are *not* usually added to the dining tab. It's customary to add a 15 percent gratuity for meals and drinks, 20 percent if the service is extraordinarily good.

### Harmonized Sales Tax (HST)

In the spring of 1997, the Harmonized Sales Tax, a 15 percent tax levied on most goods and services, supplanted the mishmash of "goods and services" and provincial sales taxes in effect in the various provinces. All residents must pay the tax, as must visitors. However, foreigners with sufficient

amounts of patience and a minimum of $100 in purchase receipts are eligible for **refunds.**

Items not eligible for refunds are: meals and beverages, alcohol, tobacco, transportation (including plane or train tickets, or fuel costs for cars), services like auto repair or entertainment, goods consumed in Canada, some goods worth $2,000 or more (such as paintings, jewelry, and rare books), and accommodations such as a rented campsite, houseboat, tent, recreational vehicle, or trailer.

A Visitor Rebate Program refunds the tax on accommodations for less than one month's stay and also for goods taken home. In 2001 the refund process was made more complicated. You must now produce all goods upon demand when leaving Canada and have the =orresponding receipt stamped as proof that the items have left the country with you. Rebates can be claimed any time within one year of the date of purchase. You'll need to include with your claim stamped receipts that prove the GST was paid. Most visitors apply for the rebate at duty-free shops (also called Visitor Rebate Centres) when exiting the country. The duty-free shops can rebate up to $500 on the spot. For rebates over $500, you'll need to mail your completed GST rebate form directly to Visitor Rebate Program, Summerside Tax Centre, Canada Customs and Revenue Agency, 275 Pope Rd., Suite 104, Summerside, PE C1N 6C6, Canada. For more information, call toll-free from anywhere in Canada: 800/668-4748; from outside Canada call 902/432-5608 or visit www.ccra-adrc.gc.ca/visitors.

## COMMUNICATIONS

### Post

**Canada Post** issues postage stamps that must be used on all mail posted in Canada. First-class letters and postcards travel for $.48 within Canada, $.60 to the United States, and $1.15 to foreign destinations. Prices increase along with the weight of the mailing. You can buy stamps at post offices, automatic vending machines, most hotel lobbies, railway stations, airports, bus terminals, many retail outlets, and some newsstands.

### Phone

The country code for Canada is 1, the same as the United States. Public phones accept 5-, 10-, and 25-cent coins; local calls cost $.35, and most long-distance calls cost at least $2.50 for the first minute.

### Internet

If your Internet provider doesn't allow you to access your email away from your home computer, open an email account with **Hotmail** (www.hotmail.com) or **Yahoo** (www.yahoo.com). Although there are restrictions to the size and number of emails you can store, and junk mail can be a problem, these services are handy for traveling and, best of all, are free.

Public Internet access is available throughout Atlantic Canada. Many hotels in larger cities have high-speed access from guest rooms. Those that don't—usually mid- and lower-priced properties—often have an Internet booth in the lobby. You'll also find Internet booths in many cafés, in some McDonald's restaurants, and in public areas such as bus depots. Aside from a lack of privacy, the downside to these public access points is the lack of a mouse at most terminals—you must move around the screen using a touch pad.

## MEDIA AND MAPS

Atlantic Canada is too expansive and diverse to be well covered by one newspaper, but plenty of regional and big-city papers are available. The *Globe and Mail* and *National Post* are distributed throughout the Atlantic provinces, and Halifax's *Chronicle Herald, Mail-Star,* and *Daily News* are found throughout Nova Scotia. Publications for the other provinces are listed under each specific province.

Canada's best-selling and most respected news magazine is *Maclean's. L'Actualité* is the French counterpart. *Newsweek, Time,* and other big American publications are available at drugstores, bookstores, and corner groceries.

### Maps

Map offices and some bookstores and other shops stock general, topographic, and hydrographic maps. Some of the best are produced by **Map Art Publishing,** www.mapart.com, an Ontario-based company that publishes the excellent *Atlantic Canada Road Atlas* as well as many regional maps.

The **Centre for Topographical Information** and the **Canada Map Office** produce topographical and aerial maps sold through 900 offi-

© ANDREW HEMPSTEAD

**the perfect spot to catch up on the latest news**

cial dealers across Canada. The website www.nrcan.gc.ca provides a catalog of maps and links to dealers. One such dealer is **World of Maps,** 1235 Wellington St., Ottawa, Ontario, tel. 613/724-6776 or 800/214-8524, www .worldofmaps.com.

Nautical maps are handled by the **Canada Hydrographic Service,** a division of Fisheries and Oceans Canada, but they don't sell directly to the public. To request a map catalog and a list of dealers, call 613/995-4413 or check www .chs-shc.dfo-mps.gc.ca. This department also distributes *Sailing Directions,* a composite of general navigational information, port facility descriptions, and sailing conditions (in English or French) for Nova Scotia, the Gulf of St. Lawrence, and Newfoundland. Also, a *Small Craft Guide* is available for the Saint John River in New Brunswick, plus the *Tides, Currents and Water Level Information* (English only) for the Atlantic Coast and Bay of Fundy (Vol. 1) and the Gulf of St. Lawrence (Vol. 2).

## WHAT TO TAKE

If the Atlantic provinces are your first stop in Canada, it helps to arrive with some Canadian currency for taxi rides and incidental expenses. For the best exchange rates, convert foreign currency at the local banks, rather than at the airport.

No special inoculations or other health precautions are required. But if you plan on camping or other outdoor activities out in the countryside, you'll be wanting insect repellent; the mosquitoes and biting black flies can be merciless.

### Clothing

The season and itinerary determine clothing. Late spring to autumn visitors should pack comfortable, informal clothing, including a lightweight to heavy sweater or jacket depending on the month, dressier garb for dinnertime, and comfortable walking shoes. Shorts and T-shirts and other cool clothing are called for during the hottest summer days and evenings. For winter travel, you'll want a rainproof jacket, down wear, gloves, hat, warm boots, and thermals. For breezy coastal sightseeing, a sweater or windbreaker, hat, sunscreen, and comfortable shoes with rubber soles will come in handy.

For inland trekking, bring hiking shoes or boots and heavy cotton or woolen socks, and be prepared to dress like an onion with several layers to peel to accommodate changing temperatures. Even in summer, an umbrella or some kind of rainwear is good insurance in the event of sudden showers.

Don't fret too much about clothing you've forgotten to pack—consider it an opportunity to shop for some of Atlantic Canada's most attractive and skillfully made apparel at local crafts shops. See the travel chapters for additional suggestions.

### Photographic Supplies

The weather is variable, with days of both blinding sun and lead-gray overcast. Bring film of various light speeds, and bring enough of it—film is expensive in Canada. Include a telephoto lens for catching distant whales, icebergs, and seabirds. A water-resistant camera cover can also come in handy. And pack your film in a zinc-lined film bag that protects the rolls during the airport X-ray process. If photography is an important part of your visit, bring two cameras; the cities have the best-equipped camera shops, but if your camera malfunctions and can't be fixed on the spot, the only recourse may be to send it to another province.

## WEIGHTS AND MEASURES

Canada uses the metric system, with temperature measured in degrees Celsius, liquid measurements in liters, solid weights in kilograms and metric tons, land areas in hectares, and distances in kilometers, meters, and centimeters. (See the back of this book for a handy metric conversion table.) This newfangled system hasn't completely taken hold everywhere, and many Atlantic Canadians still think in terms of the imperial system; expect to hear a lobster described in pounds, local distances given in miles, and the temperature expressed in Fahrenheit degrees.

The electrical voltage is 120 volts. The standard electrical plug configuration is the same as that used in the United States: two flat blades, often with a round third pin for grounding.

# New Brunswick

# Introduction

Canada meets the Atlantic at New Brunswick, the largest (73,440 square km, pop. 720,000) and most accessible of the Maritime provinces. Dense Appalachian forests spill across the borders of Québec and Maine and blanket almost 90 percent of the province. Beyond the forests, a coastline over 2,200 km long lies along the Bay of Fundy, Northumberland Strait, Gulf of St. Lawrence, and Baie des Chaleurs. The adjacent provinces of Nova Scotia and Québec are accessible by land, as is the state of Maine, immediately to the west. The province of Prince Edward Island, separated from New Brunswick by Northumberland Strait, is just a quick drive away across Confederation Bridge. A web of regional air service via Halifax, Nova Scotia, also connects New Brunswick with its neighbors.

The tourist's New Brunswick lies mainly around the province's coastal edges and along the fertile Saint John River valley, which cuts a mammoth swath across the western woodlands. The sparsely populated interior is immensely rich in minerals and forestry products, the source of New Brunswick's dominant industrial status within Atlantic Canada.

Old Bend Museum, Riverbend

# SIGHTSEEING HIGHLIGHTS

Canada's only bilingual province, New Brunswick combines Anglos (two-thirds) and French Acadians (one-third) in a generally harmonious cultural blend. Cultural differences flare occasionally, and new political parties from time to time spring forth spouting old notions of ancestral "superiority." But on the whole, the two vastly different cultures interact amicably. In fact, Canada's popular *Chatelaine* magazine cited Moncton as one of the best Canadian cities for its "enviable secret" of harmony between the Anglophones and Francophones.

Historic and natural sites are recognized nationally and internationally. The St. Croix River's Douchet's Island, eight km from St. Andrews on Highway 127, is an international historic site marking the location of explorer Samuel de Champlain's first New World settlement in 1604. On Campobello Island, one of the Bay of Fundy islands, Franklin Delano Roosevelt's former summer compound is now an international park.

Some museums are grand-scale provincial heritage sites, such as the **Kings Landing Historical Settlement** west of Fredericton, which re-creates early Anglo years with authentic buildings, demonstrations, and events. The **Acadian Historical Village** near Caraquet is the expansive Acadian counterpart.

The teeming waters off neighboring Deer Island, just off the Maine coast, have been proposed as Canada's first marine national park. A dozen-plus national historic sites are scattered across the province, and Saint John's rejuvenated Prince William Street ranks as a national historic "streetscape."

And nowhere else in Atlantic Canada can you put together an itinerary wending from one covered bridge to another. The province's 73 covered bridges are a necessity rather than a picturesque whim. Rain and sun will rot an uncovered wooden bridge in 10–20 years; covered, a bridge's life span can increase to 80 years. You'll find the world's longest covered bridge at Hartland, where the 391-meter bridge spans the upper Saint John River above Woodstock.

Hundreds of hiking trails probe the interior and rim the seacoasts. You can go canoeing on rapid or placid waters and find abundant opportunities for sea kayaking and sailing. The province's scores of rivers, most notably the Miramichi, brim with Atlantic salmon. Bear, deer, small mammals, and birds attract both naturalists and hunters. And prime 18-hole golf courses stretch across the province from border to shore.

# THE LAND

New Brunswick is about the size of Ireland and almost as large as neighboring Maine. Northeastern North America reaches land's end in this gently undulating province with its back to the mainland and three sides facing the sea. Just 9 percent of the land is cleared for towns and agriculture, while nearly all the rest lies under woodlands.

## Regional Distinctions

Despite its ubiquitous forests, New Brunswick is a collection of distinct geographic and cultural regions, defined largely by rivers and coastlines.

The Miramichi Basin is the vast valley through which the Miramichi River and its tributaries flow. These waterways drain much of the province's interior and empty into the Gulf of St. Lawrence at Miramichi City. North and east of the basin, the Acadian Coast, notched with French-speaking communities and seaports, rims the Northumberland Strait and the Baie des Chaleurs. The Restigouche Uplands, named for the Restigouche River, lies northwest of the basin and forms the province's northwestern corner, rising in the interior to peak at 820-meter-high Mt. Carleton, highest point in the Maritimes.

While the Miramichi Basin is New Brunswick's geographic center, the Saint John River valley forms the province's spiritual heart. New Brunswickers have dubbed the river the "Rhine of North America"; it originates in Maine, winds 724 km across the province, and empties into the Bay of Fundy at the city of Saint John.

The Fundy tidal coast, a naturalist's dream, encompasses almost all of the southern coastline. The world's highest tides surge in twice daily—flooding the land's edge and floating fishing fleets off the mud—and then retreat six hours later, leaving gifts of seashells and marine flora. The Fundy tides rise and fall an average of eight meters (26 feet), and have been measured at 16 meters (52 feet) at Chignecto Bay, off southeastern New Brunswick.

The province's eastern corner fronts the upper Fundy on one seacoast and the Northumberland Strait on the other. New Brunswick's summertime beach scene is focused along the Strait, where the waters are as warm and tranquil as the Fundy's are chilly and turbulent.

## CLIMATE

New Brunswick has hot summers and cold winters, both moderated somewhat by the surrounding seas. For **weather conditions** and forecasts anywhere in the province, call 506/446-6240 or check the Environment Canada website, www.weatheroffice.com.

Summer high temperatures average 23° C in June, 26° C in July, and 25° C in August; nights are cool. July is the sunniest month. September and October are pleasantly warm, with increasingly cool days. Winter is cold, with temperatures frequently dipping well below freezing.

The province's growing season—about 125 days—spans May to September. Precipitation throughout the province averages 115.2 cm annually. Rainfall is greatest on the Fundy coast, with 120–140 cm typical at Grand Manan and Sackville; Saint John gets an average of 115 cm a year.

Fredericton has a moderate climate, with hot summers and moderate to very cold winters. The capital's average summer temperature is 26° C, with 8.5 centimeters of rain a month. In spring and summer, Saint John and the Fundy coast are periodically steeped in fog, with visibility under a kilometer about 70 days a year. Fog occasionally closes the airport, so travelers flying in or out of the city may find themselves rerouted.

The seas are chilly most of the summer, but in places they warm to bathtub temperatures by August. The warmest waters are at Maisonnette

Provincial Park, on a two-km-long sandy beach at Caraquet. The Baie des Chaleurs here heats to 30° C. Kouchibouguac National Park is another warmish gem and has a 17-km beach on a sheltered lagoon. Other noteworthy (and very popular) places for pleasant saltwater swims are the supervised beaches at Shediac's Parlee Beach Provincial Park (19–24° C) and Charlo's Eel River Bar (15–24° C). The water along the Fundy coast tends to be colder, though it's nonetheless inviting and very refreshing on a hot summer day.

## FLORA AND FAUNA
### Flowers

The province hosts magnificent wildflower shows. Early spring's purple violet (the provincial flower) is one of some 200 wildflower species in New Brunswick. Many of these wildflowers are rare, endangered varieties, such as the Furbish's lousewort, a native of the upper Saint John River valley.

The tall-stalked lupine blooms with a profusion of blue, pink, white, or cream flowers during late June to mid-July, from Saint John to Blacks Harbour and Fundy Isles. The red cardinal flower thrives along southwestern riverbanks and lakes.

The bayberry bush and wild rose bloom on the Chignecto Isthmus during June. The yellow beach heather colors the strait and gulf dunes and sandy plains, and the rhodora (miniature rhododendron) brightens eastern coastal marshes. Farther northeast, nutrient-rich bogs nurture plant exotica; at Lamèque and Miscou islands at the extreme northeastern tip, wild cranberries and insect-eating pitcher plants and sundews grow among the peat moss beds.

Other common wildflowers, seen especially along roadsides in summertime, are Queen Anne's lace, yarrow, pearly everlasting, and a variety of daisies.

### Woodlands

The significance of New Brunswick's timber resources was recognized in 1991, when the Canadian Forestry Association named Nackawic, west of Fredericton, as Forestry Capital of Canada. Provincial forests abound with balsam fir (the provincial tree), spruce, and pine (without rival for strong, white paper products), as well as black spruce, birch, beech, cedar, hemlock, ash, and oak.

With so many provincial tree varieties, visitors to the province may see the forests, rather than the trees. For a manageable introduction, visit Fredericton's Odell Park Aboretum, where a 2.8-km trail winds through woods made up of every tree native to the province.

The provincial Clean Environment Act regulates New Brunswick's natural resources and development, especially the dominant forestry industry. Critics warn that the forest is vanishing, and debate continues on how best to maintain the forests while supplying demand. Environmentalists advocate selective forest cutting. The paper-and-pulp industry counters that taking only the biggest and best trees is both difficult and costly. The industry favors cheaper clear-cut methods, leveling forests wholesale and replanting seedlings.

## Animals

The highlands, deep valleys, and swampy lowlands of Fundy National Park are protected habitat for bobcats, snowshoe hares, porcupines, and large white-tailed deer. Farther north, at Kouchibouguac National Park, local fauna includes the timber wolf, coyote, red fox, black bear, lynx, bobcat, deer, moose, and many small mammals.

Since the last confirmed cougar (*Felis concolor*) sighting in New Brunswick in 1938, 20 or so sightings are reported each year, including one by wildlife officers in 1994. Officially, though, the species is classified as extinct in the province.

New Brunswick's prime whale-watching region lies off Grand Manan Island. Minke, pilot, finback, and humpback whales are the most numerous species; the season peaks during August and September.

## Birds

New Brunswick's varied ecosystems and climatic differences make it a haven for all sorts of birds. Over 350 resident and migrant species find some corner of the province to their liking. The chickadee is the provincial bird.

New Brunswickers are active birdwatchers,

and many birders belong to **New Brunswick Federation of Naturalists,** a private group based at the New Brunswick Museum in Saint John. The museum publishes a free provincial bird list that describes range areas and population densities of the many indigenous species; for details, write to New Brunswick Museum, Natural Sciences Division, 277 Douglas Ave., Saint John, NB E2K 1E5.

The crossbill, various woodpecker species, the boreal chickadee, and gray jay nest in New Brunswick's interior spruce and fir forests. The crossbill likes the Appalachian uplands and Mt. Carleton's spruce forests. The ibis, heron, and snowy egret wade among lagoons and marshes. The Baie des Chaleurs coastline lures the gannet, and the northeastern tip's Île Miscou is the piping plover's nesting ground.

In March, many songbirds fly south—their numbers peak in late May. In late July, seabirds descend on the Mary's Point mudflats at Shepody National Wildlife Area. On Shepody Bay's opposite side, 100,000 sandpipers, en route to South America, stop at the Dorchester Peninsula during July's last two weeks.

An awesome bird-watching show takes place in spring and early autumn at Grand Manan Island in the Bay of Fundy. This was the haunt of John James Audubon, the ornithologist and artist, who visited in 1833 and painted the arctic tern, gannet, black guillemot, and razorbill. Birding is still the island's claim to fame, and over 300 species have been sighted on wet heath, woods, ponds, and sedge reserves. The bird show is thickest during September, when migratory seabirds—including auks, puffins, razorbills, murres, guillemots, phalaropes, gannets, storm-petrels, and kittiwakes—can be spotted. Grand Manan is also the gateway for boat tours to the Atlantic puffin rookery at Machias Seal Island, a rocky outcrop in the Fundy.

## HISTORY

The Malecite (or Maliseet, as New Brunswickers spell the word) and Mi'kmaq Indian settlements date back to 2000 B.C. on the interior's Miramichi

River, and to 1000 B.C. at the Fundy's Passamaquoddy Bay.

In 1534, the explorer Jacques Cartier claimed the northeastern seacoast for France and named the waters off the northern coast the Baie des Chaleurs ("Bay of Warmth").

In 1604, Samuel de Chaplain and Sieur de Monts attempted to reinforce France's claim by establishing the first settlement in the New World north of Florida on a St. Croix River island. A harsh winter devastated the population and sent the survivors fleeing across the Fundy to establish Port Royal in Nova Scotia as Acadia's hub in 1605.

The French influence in the New World radiated from Port Royal. The French Crown sold land grants to competitive developers, who established fortified trading posts. Eventually, a French presence returned to New Brunswick. French settlers arrived and carved out farmlands spreading from the Chignecto Isthmus marshes to the Restigouche Uplands.

War erupted between France and Britain in 1689, and eastern regions of Canada were pulled into the conflict. The 1713 Treaty of Utrecht favored the English, granting them what is now New Brunswick. But the vagueness of boundaries north of the Bay of Fundy left much of the area in controversy, and fighting continued sporadically for another five years. Acadians fleeing Nova Scotia settled Saint-Anne's Point (Fredericton) in 1732. To counter the expanding British presence in Nova Scotia, France bolstered its position in New Brunswick with fortifications at the mouth of the Saint John River, plus the forts Gaspéreau and Beauséjour, which guarded the route across narrow Chignecto Isthmus into northern Acadia.

## England Triumphs

Territorial disputes flared again into war in 1755. Acadians deported from British territories poured into New Brunswick and settled the northern and gulf coasts. Over the ensuing years, the French military sustained several defeats. Decades of war wound down to a military whimper at Baie des Chaleurs near Campbellton. There England vanquished the French at the Battle of Restigouche—the final naval battle of the Seven Years' War—in 1763.

The Peace of Paris awarded the plums of victory to England, and Anglo migration increased. The New England planters (the influential and rich "farmers" from England's original 13 colonies farther south) arrived in waves from 1760 to 1775 and were followed by the immigrant Scottish Highlanders through 1815.

Loyalists fleeing the American Revolution made the most significant impact. Though historians still argue about the exact numbers, it's estimated that 40,000 Loyalists fled to eastern Canada. The first influx of 3,000 refugees to New Brunswick (then part of Nova Scotia) arrived in Saint John from New York in 1783. Before the great refugee wave finished that year, 14,000 Loyalists had settled that port, as well as other parts of the Fundy coastline. They also sailed up the Saint John River and settled Saint-Anne's Point, naming the town Fredericton for George III's son.

Almost overnight, Saint John was transformed from village to city, and was incorporated as Canada's first city in 1785. Flexing its population strength, the colony petitioned England for separate colonial status and cut the tie with Nova Scotia the same year. New Brunswick took its name from Germany's duchy of Brunswick (Braunschweig), ruled also by England's King George III.

Fighting between England and France erupted again during the Napoleonic Wars and the hostilities spilled over to North America in the war of 1812. The British fortified St. Andrews with a blockhouse and added the Carleton Martello Tower at Saint John to defend against U.S. invasion. Timber prices shot up, and New Brunswick rode to riches with shipbuilding and trade. Saint John was dubbed North America's Liverpool and ranked fifth in registered tonnage worldwide.

## The Thriving Colony

The good years continued. King's College, now the University of New Brunswick, opened at

Fredericton in 1785, and the Collège de Saint-Joseph at Saint-Joseph-de-Memramcook started in 1864 as the colony's first Acadian college. The colony's population soared from 25,000 in 1809 to 200,000 in the 1850s. Irish immigrants, fleeing religious and political persecution as well as the potato famine, settled at Saint John and transformed the port into Canada's most Irish city.

Shipbuilding made New Brunswick rich. The *Marco Polo* was launched at Saint John in 1851. The ship flew like the wind on a route from Liverpool, England, to Melbourne, Australia, in 76 days and made history as the first vessel to circumnavigate the globe in less than six months.

## Confederation: A Mixed Blessing

New Brunswick fared poorly initially with confederation. High tariffs favored internal trade but discouraged international shipping. Provincial trade declined, and the population took a tumble as out-of-work New Brunswickers immigrated to the "Boston States" (Massachusetts and neighboring states).

One of the promises of confederation, however, was a railroad, and when it was built the economy rebounded quickly. It funneled the Dominion's manufactured wares to Saint John for shipping, and brought with it vacationers. The entrepreneurial spirit thrived. On the Fundy coast, St. Andrews emerged as a resort town with the opening of the first Algonquin Hotel in 1880. At Saint John, Susanna Oland started the brewery that became Moosehead Beer, and A. D. Ganong developed the first chocolate bar in 1906, founding the Ganong Chocolatier factory at St. Stephen.

The economy faltered in the early 1900s. The Bank of Nova Scotia took over the Bank of New Brunswick in 1913. The province prospered briefly during World War I, but the economy took another tumble during the 1920s, and the Great Depression worsened the bleak conditions. By the 1940s, New Brunswick's illiteracy and infant-mortality rates were Canada's highest.

The federal government sent assistance. Loomcrofters, the famed crafts center at Gage-town, began as a federally sponsored youth-training program. Canadian Forces Base Gagetown opened north of Oromocto in the 1950s and went on to become the British Commonwealth's largest military training base. Hinterland New Brunswickers began to migrate to the cities. The province's population, predominantly rural in 1941, was predominantly urban just 30 years later.

## The Contemporary Province

The 1960s inaugurated a decade of self-appraisal. The cumbersome provincial government was redesigned in 1963. The Official Languages Act put Anglos and Acadians on equal linguistic footing, and New Brunswick became Canada's first (and only) bilingual province. Education received top priority. The Université de Moncton opened and is the only French-speaking university east of Québec City. The University of New Brunswick added a Saint John campus. The province now has four universities, nine community colleges, and 38 research centers.

In the 1970s and '80s, Saint John was revitalized with high-speed highways and a harbor bridge. The port's historic harbor-front warehouses were transformed into Market Square, with shops, restaurants, and an adjacent convention center and hotel.

# GOVERNMENT

New Brunswick is governed by a lieutenant governor, an executive council dominated by the ruling party, and a 58-member legislative assembly with a five-year mandate. The province sends 10 senators and 10 House of Commons members to Ottawa.

In 1999, the Progressive Conservative Party swept to power over the ruling Liberals. Today, the Liberal Party stands as the official opposition, with fringe parties such as the New Democrats and Confederation of Regions holding a few seats between them. The Confederation of Regions Party had its heyday in the mid-1990s, as a strong political newcomer opposing bilingualism.

## ECONOMY

New Brunswick harbors Canada's largest share of silver, lead, and zinc reserves. Zinc deposits near Bathurst are among the world's largest supply. The province built Atlantic Canada's first nuclear power plant at Point Lepreau between Saint John and Blacks Harbour. The Mactaquac Generating Station, on the Saint John River near Fredericton, is the Maritimes' largest hydroelectric station.

Saint John's claim to fame is industry and shipping. The city's merchant shipping fleet ranks as Canada's largest, as does the city's sugar refinery. Other industries include pulp mills, oil refineries, food-processing plants, and two breweries.

The province's annual gross domestic product (GDP) is $15 billion. Manufacturing—of food products, beverages, fabricated metal products, plastics, chemicals, and forestry products—and shipping contribute two-thirds of this. Saint John's Forest Products Terminal, Canada's largest forestry port facility, annually ships 800,000 metric tons of paper, lumber, and other forest products, as well as another 1.5 million metric tons in potash and salt. Moncton, located at the Maritimes' geographic center, serves as a distribution center for ports up and down the coast.

Mining contributes $900 million to the economy. In addition to the large silver, lead, and zinc deposits south of Bathurst, other mineral resources include potash in Sussex, coal in the Grand Lake area, oil shales in Westmoreland County, and gold in veins along parts of the Fundy's coastline. Peat moss collected in the northeast, especially from Lamèque and Miscou islands, makes the province the world's second-largest exporter of the fuel.

About 80 percent of the 1.5 million tourists who visit the Maritimes annually enter the region through New Brunswick, Atlantic Canada's land gateway. Tourism brings in about $800 million in revenues annually.

Agriculture contributes $270 million to the GDP. Victoria and Carleton Counties' seed potatoes make up 20 percent of Canada's total production and are exported to Mexico, Portugal, and the United States. The benevolent spring floods, with their ensuing silt, enrich the Saint John River valley's mixed farming picture, and the farms at Maugerville yield two crops each season. Other agricultural products include livestock (exported to France, England, Denmark, and the U.S.), dairy products, and berries.

New Brunswick's fisheries produce $140 million annually in ground fish, lobster, crab, scallops, and herring. The newest aquaculture developments are Atlantic salmon farms and blue mussel beds. Black Harbour–area canneries rank first in Canada's sardine production.

## THE PEOPLE

The province's 720,000 residents are divided almost evenly between urban and rural populations. Anglos, comprising about two-thirds of the population, live along the lower Saint John River valley and Fundy coast. About a quarter-million Acadians form the other third of the population and are concentrated in the northwest and along the northern and eastern coastlines; Caraquet is considered Acadia's cultural heart, while Moncton is its educational and commercial center.

The Mi'kmaq and Malecite Indians, both eastern Algonquin tribes, are spread among 13 reserves. Other minority groups include Germans, Dutch, Scandinavians, Asians, Italians, and Eastern Europeans.

"There is a New Brunswick character," wrote Michael Collie in his reflective *New Brunswick,* "a personality, which is at first difficult to fathom: proud yet hospitable, somewhat dour yet essentially warm-hearted, independent in spirit yet with the virtues of neighbourliness. . . This distinctiveness that is the New Brunswick character derives in large measure from the ruggedness of the life and the ruggedness of the stock."

Some say the friendly, affable New Brunswickers have Atlantic Canada's best sense of humor. A strong sense of tolerance prevails above propriety, and no one raises an eyebrow if a visitor uses the wrong fork at dinner.

The crime level here is Atlantic Canada's lowest. Commonest infractions are petty theft and

## FAMOUS NEW BRUNSWICKERS

New Brunswickers, who are less than modest about their famous native-born compatriots, say the legend of **Paul Bunyan** originated with 19th-century Acadians who worked as lumbermen in northwestern New Brunswick's Edmundston area. The Ontario-born **William Maxwell Aitken,** better known as Lord Beaverbrook, grew up in Newcastle as the son of a Presbyterian minister and became Great Britain's minister of aircraft production under Winston Churchill during World War II. This millionaire financier, politician, and publisher lavished gifts worth millions of dollars on his beloved adopted province. The provincial capital at Fredericton was among the major recipients: Lord Beaverbrook funded the Theatre New Brunswick's start, and gave the Beaverbrook Art Gallery to the city. **Joseph Cunard,** the brother of Samuel Cunard (of the famed Cunard shipping empire that began in Halifax), carried on the family's tradition at his own shipyards on the Miramichi River. **Andrew Bonar Law,** Great Britain's only prime minister to be born out-

side the British Isles, came from New Brunswick. **Dr. Abraham Gesner,** kerosene's inventor, was born in Saint John, as were Hollywood movie mogul **Louis B. Mayer** and actors **Walter Pidgeon** and **Donald Sutherland.** Hollywood makeup artist **Anthony Clavet** came from Edmundston, and **Antonine Maillet,** the well-known author, was born in Bouctouche on the Acadian Coast. From Bouctouche also came the entrepreneurial industrialist **Kenneth Colin Irving,** born there in 1899. Before he died in 1992, he left an indelible mark on New Brunswick's economy. Irving began with a pre–World War I gas station and by 1924 had formed the Irving Oil Company, whose holdings now include shipbuilding concerns, oil tankers and cargo vessels, forestry-product plants, four provincial newspapers, TV stations in Saint John and Moncton, bus lines, and numerous small companies, including the ubiquitous Irving service stations, all now managed by family members. *Forbes* magazine has ranked the elder Irving among the world's 10 richest men.

NEW BRUNSWICK

burglary. Women can generally travel alone without problems. As general tourist precautions, roll up car windows and lock car doors, take cameras and other valuables with you, and keep luggage in the trunk or otherwise out of sight.

### Language and Religion
The province is equally tuned to English and French, and in most parts of New Brunswick the locals are fluent in both languages. Some Acadians in remote Acadian towns and seaports speak only French, and la République du Madawaska has its own dialect.

In religious followings, Roman Catholics dominate at 52 percent; the majority of them are Acadians. Protestants are spread among Baptist, United Church of Canada, Anglican, Pentecostal, and Presbyterian sects. The evangelical "Bible Belt" runs strong through Carleton and Victoria Counties in the upper Saint John River valley and north of Moncton in Westmoreland County. Saint John has a small Jewish population whose antecedents date to the mid-19th century.

### Tracing Family History
Genealogical searches start at the **Provincial Archives of New Brunswick,** the province's most complete heritage records. The more information you already have about your ancestors, the better. The archive also publishes county genealogy guides to help family researchers; for details, contact or visit the archives at the Bonar Law-Bennett Building, University of New Brunswick, 23 Dineen Dr., Fredericton; tel. 506/453-2122; www.gov.nb.ca/archives.

Acadian lineage records are kept at the **Centre d'études Acadiennes,** University of Moncton, tel. 506/858-4085, www.umoncton.ca.

## PARKS AND RECREATION
### "Adventure Capitalism"
In recent years, most of New Brunswick's provincial parks have been privatized to some extent, and the pleasant and familiar "provincial park" label has given way as the parks have been, in the words of the parks people, "rebranded." In an

effort to coordinate marketing for both the privatized parks and all the outdoor-outings tour operators in New Brunswick, the province has come up with the Marketing Plan from Hell. Its cumbersome, bizarre nomenclature now includes such technolinguistic phenomena as "Day Adventure Centres," "Day Adventure Outlets," and "Day Adventure Stations."

True, the province's *Day Adventures* catalog pulls together in one place information on a wide array of commercial outings providers, but in the process it comes off like some unsavory menu offering a good time with Mother Nature—anything your heart desires, for a price. It concentrates exclusively on matters of commerce, neglecting to provide the reader a sense of the beauty of the place or a sense of why he or she would *want* to shell out the loonies for the activities being sold. John Muir must be rolling over in his grave.

In any case, you can request a copy of the *Day Adventures* catalog—which includes information on commercial hiking, cycling, whale-watching, sailing, houseboating, canoeing, kayaking, scuba diving, birding, rock-climbing, horseback riding, caving, water-parking, fishing, jet-skiing, jet-boating, goat farming, and the high adventure of coffee roasting—by calling 800/561-0123 or visiting www.tourismnbcanada.com.

## Provincial Parks and National Parks

When you get to one of the province-approved sites formerly known as provincial parks, you'll find all the usual facilities you'd expect, but in most cases the facility will be operated and maintained by a private concessionaire.

Among the larger parks are **Mactaquac,** a 567-hectare spread with a lodge, hiking trails, campgrounds, and an 18-hole golf course alongside the Saint John River near Fredericton; **Les Jardins de la Republique,** with a theater and tennis and canoeing facilities at Edmundston; **Sugarloaf,** with a lodge, hiking trails, tennis courts, and a chair lift near Campbellton; and **Mt. Carleton,** the wilderness domain southeast of Saint-Quentin.

Smaller parks include **Chaleur Park,** east of Dalhousie, situated at a prime coastal windsurf-

ing area; **Enclosure Park,** in a historical setting of French, Acadian, and English settlements near Miramichi and featuring ongoing archaeological digs; **Parlee Beach,** near Shediac, which boasts a long warm-water beach and summertime sports tournaments; and two prime bird-watching parks—**Murray Beach,** near Cape Tormentine, and **The Anchorage** on Grand Manan.

New Brunswick's *national parks* include 206-square-km **Fundy National Park** and 238-square-km **Kouchibouguac National Park;** both have coastal campgrounds.

## Hiking and Biking

A number of trails splice through the national parks and "provincial" parks. Mt. Carleton is a favorite destination for wilderness hiking. Tourism New Brunswick provides detailed trail information and small locator maps for some areas. Another excellent resource, describing over 100 trails, is the *Hiking Guide to New Brunswick,* published by Goose Lane Editions, tel. 506/450-4251, www.gooselane.com.

Bicyclists should have a look at another Goose Lane publication, *Biking to Blissville,* which outlines a number of provincial cycling routes. Except on main arteries, particularly the TransCanada Highway, car traffic is generally light and the roads are safe for cyclists. Following the Saint John River valley past the complex of lakes north of Saint John makes for pleasant touring; along the Fundy and Northumberland Strait coasts, scores of local highways loop off the main routes to take cyclists even closer to the sea.

## Water Sports

**Houseboats,** with space enough for 6 to 10 passengers, roam the lower Saint John River and Grand Lake and rent for $800–1,700 a week. Inland, **canoeing** is extremely popular on numerous rivers, such as the 137-km Tobique River, which feeds into the upper Saint John River. **Windsurfers** exploit breezy waters everywhere, from Shediac on the strait to the interior's Saint John and Kennebecasis Rivers.

**Kayakers** like the contrasting Baie des Chaleurs and the Bay of Fundy. The two seas also lure **scuba divers.** The Baie des Chaleurs, from Caraquet to Bathurst, offers good visibility and fascinating shipwrecks, while the western Bay of Fundy is especially rich in marine life and has excellent visibility before July's plankton blooms. **Whale-watching** off Grand Manan makes for a popular day trip. A number of companies offer tours. More than 20 whale species frequent the Bay of Fundy; most commonly seen are finbacks, minkes, humpbacks, and North Atlantic right whales, in addition to Atlantic white-sided dolphins and harbor porpoises.

**Eastern Outdoors,** 39 King St., Saint John, tel. 506/634-1530, www.easternoutdoors.com, is one of several outfits offering year-round introductory and advanced **sea and white-water kayaking** classes; they charge $245 per person for a weekend trip; more for three- to five-day trips.

humpback whale

BOB RACE

## Hunting and Fishing

The woodlands and fields teem with white-tailed deer, black bear, moose, rabbit, ruffled grouse, geese, woodcock, partridge, and other game. Hunting licenses are required, and hunters must also obtain a Federal Migratory Game Bird Permit for ducks, geese, woodcock, and snipe.

Bass fishing, in the fast-running streams and rivers in the northwestern hinterlands and in the lakes in southwestern New Brunswick, is among Atlantic Canada's best. The season runs from mid-April through September. Other inland game fish include brook trout, shad, perch, and pickerel. And New Brunswick, of course, is famous worldwide for its Atlantic salmon fishing, particularly on the revered Miramichi—considered by many to be the premier salmon-fishing river anywhere. Fly-fishing is the only allowed method for taking salmon; nonresidents are also required to hire a guide. Inland fishing requires a license, and fishing in the national parks requires a federal angling license, available at the parks.

Details on hunting and fishing seasons and regulations are available from the Department of Natural Resources and Energy, Fish and Wildlife, tel. 506/453-2440, www.gnb.ca. Ask for the booklets *New Brunswick Hunting Summary* and *New Brunswick Angling Summary.* The province is thick with **outfitters and guides** who can arrange both fishing and hunting expeditions. They're detailed in Tourism New Brunswick's free *Aim & Angle Guide.*

## Photography Seminars

Some of the best photography seminars in the province are led by Freeman Patterson, whose professional skills are known far beyond New Brunswick. The seminars are held in photogenic places such as the Kingston Peninsula. Workshops are offered in summer and fall and cost around $1,500 per person for six days, including lodging and meals. Call 506/763-2189 or visit www.freemanpatterson.com.

# ENTERTAINMENT AND EVENTS
## Holidays and Festivals

Everything shuts down on national holidays and on **New Brunswick Day,** the province's natal celebration on August's first Monday.

Summer in New Brunswick brings sheaves of annual festivals, many of them conceived as celebrations of ethnic or historical heritage. These are listed in the travel chapters; a few of the biggest are described here.

The **Loyalist Days** festival in Saint John recalls the Loyalists who settled New Brunswick. The event gives Anglos (and everyone else) reason to celebrate with costumed parades, street casinos, and general merriment for seven days in mid-July. Caraquet's **Acadian Festival,** the French Acadian version, reportedly ranks as Canada's largest Acadian event, with theater, concerts, food, and cabaret entertainment through the first two weeks of August. Edmundston's **Foire Brayonne** celebrates the heritage of the Madawas-

NEW BRUNSWICK

ka Republic—an Acadian cultural offshoot—and showcases arts, crafts, sports, and culinary delights in early August.

The province is at its best in concert festivals. The 11-day **International Festival of Baroque Music** has had astonishing success as a setting for international musicians who perform in the acoustically perfect de-Petite-Rivière church on remote Île Lamèque in late July. Farther south down the gulf coast, Miramichi City's **Irish Festival** (mid-July) and the **Miramichi Folksong Festival** (July and August) are outstanding showcases for traditional music expressing the Miramichi Basin's Celtic musical soul. Saint John's **Festival by the Sea** is another top winner and includes 10 days of performing arts and concerts in early to mid-August.

Love of good food drives the **Shediac Lobster Festival** for six days in early July. The **Chocolate Festival** at St. Stephen, where Ganong's chocolate factory reigns, celebrates its raison d'etre for five days in early August.

## Nightlife

Except in university towns like Moncton and Fredericton, the provincial night scene is low-key. New Brunswickers like intimate small bars, lounges, and watering holes. Bars are open Mon.–Sat. to 2 A.M.; beverage rooms serve alcohol Mon.–Sat. 9 A.M.–1 A.M. Nothing much happens on Sunday nights.

## ARTS AND CRAFTS

Crafts here are varied, abundant, and carefully handmade. The province boasts 800 artisans who work in 125 studios and crafts shops. The **New Brunswick College of Craft and Design** in Fredericton deserves much credit for the quality and profusion. The school is Canada's sole postsecondary school that grants degrees to artisans,

*Certain places are known for specific crafts. Kings County's Sussex, Norton, and Hampton excel in hand-woven tweeds. Sussex also has a reputation for fine silver jewelry, and Hampton shops stock some of the best provincial quilts and woodworking wares.*

and many of New Brunswick's best craftspeople are alumni.

Certain places are known for specific crafts. Kings County's Sussex, Norton, and Hampton, for example, excel in hand-woven tweeds. Sussex also has a reputation for fine silver jewelry, and Hampton shops stock some of the best provincial quilts and woodworking wares. Grand Manan knitters embellish apparel with seagull and whale motifs. Fredericton is the provincial pewter center.

The *New Brunswick Craft Directory,* published by Tourism New Brunswick, is free and lists craftspeople and their locations and telephone numbers; it's available from the provincial tourism office and also at tourist centers and some shops. Crafts studios have varying hours, so it's wise to call ahead.

## ACCOMMODATIONS AND CAMPING

The province's wide spectrum of lodgings includes hotels and motels, inns, resorts, bed-and-breakfasts, farmhouses, sport lodges, and cottages. Some accommodations are awarded one to five stars in a voluntary lodging evaluation system; absence of grading stars carries no weight, however.

Lodgings and campgrounds are exhaustively listed by towns and cities in Tourism New Brunswick's two guides, the *Travel Planner* and the *Touring Guide.* Free reservations can be made online (www.tourismnbcanada.com) and at all provincial visitor information centers. To make a reservation, you'll need the date, day, number of people, and arrival time; reservations are held until 6 P.M. unless guaranteed. Lodgings can also be phoned directly.

**Note:** The prices included in the following lodgings coverage are for one room during high season. Rates listed do not include the 15 percent harmonized sales tax (HST), which is added to most accommodations.

For a memorable splurge, consider staying at one of the province's historic inns, many of which were once grandiose private residences. A select number are members of **New Brunswick Heritage Inns,** a private group of innkeepers whose lodgings meet special standards and were built before the 1930s. The group publishes a folder depicting and describing the member inns; provincial and municipal tourist offices have copies.

**Hostelling International,** tel. 506/454-9326, www.hihostels.ca, has affiliated hostels in Campbellton, Fredericton, and Fundy National Park. Rates range $12–16 for members, a bit higher for nonmembers.

## Camping

The season at the majority of parks spans mid-June to early Sept., though some operate May-Oct., and a few stay open year-round. Camping fees average around $15 per site, with a discount for stays of seven or more days. (Many of the more popular parks charge a day-use fee of $2–5.) At the national parks, camping fees range from $9 for a barebones backpacker site to up to $19 with full amenities (plus a day-use fee of $3.50 per adult, or a four-day pass for $10.50 per adult). The maximum stay for campers is 14 days.

Reservations are accepted at many parks; additional details on specific parks are given in the following travel chapters. In addition to the former provincial parks and the national parks, New Brunswick has some 125 or so private campgrounds; the majority are concentrated along the coasts and along the Saint John River. The campgrounds can be anything from simply a grassy field with the barest essentials to cushy resorts with all the amenities. Tent sites generally run $10–15 a night, while sites with two- and three-way hookups can cost anywhere from $15 to $28.

## FOOD AND DRINK

New Brunswick cuisine reflects its English and Acadian heritages, with some local specialties. New Brunswickers nibble year-round on salty,

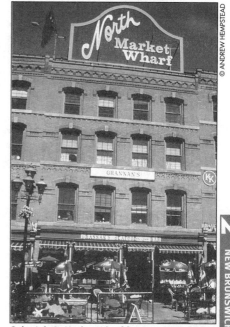

**Saint John's Market Wharf features lots of local delicacies in a refurbished waterfront building.**

chewy dulse, a purple, iodine-rich Fundy seaweed that's dried in the sun and sold in little bags. Spring is celebrated with "fiddleheads," an ostrich fern's unopened fronds that are served boiled as a vegetable or in cream soup. Smelts are fried or baked. Vegetables and potatoes are often melded as hodgepodge, a nutritious stew served by the steaming bowlful. Dessert favorites include walnut toffee, trifle, homemade ice cream, or Ganong chocolates from St. Stephen.

Acadian cooking may be terribly hard on the waistline, but it's delicious. *Poutine râpé* combines boiled or deep-fried pork and grated raw potatoes, and it's customary to dip the ball in corn or maple syrup or molasses. A well-rounded Acadian meal includes seafood chowder, shellfish (shrimp and crab), fish (especially mackerel, herring, and cod), poultry (usually in the form of chicken stew), and, for dessert, sugar pie, apple dumplings, or cinnamon buns.

Save room for an Acadian culinary variation in Edmundston or another of the Madawaska area towns. Brayon cooking, as it's known, features buckwheat pancakes, *les ployes,* splashed with butter, molasses, or maple syrup, or wrapped around spicy pâté or seafood.

The Danes immigrated to the province in the late 19th century and still cling to Scandinavian ways at New Denmark in the upper Saint John valley. If you're interested in Danish cuisine, try the town's Valhalla Restaurant for homemade sausage, roast beef and red cabbage, ground beef patties, and Danish apple cake.

### Drink

New Brunswickers are wine drinkers, and you'll find an ample assortment of national and imported brands. For a decent martini or a mixed-drink variation, any place in Saint John, Fredericton, or Moncton will do. In the hinterlands, ask for the local specialty or limit your imbibing to whiskey and water. Moosehead and Labatt's are the beers of choice. Provincial liquor stores are open 9 A.M.–9 P.M. or 10 A.M.–10 P.M., Sat. 9:30 A.M.–6 P.M. The legal drinking age is 19.

## INFORMATION AND SERVICES

### Tourist Information

Extremely helpful **Tourism New Brunswick** answers questions and distributes piles of provincial literature, including the provincial *Travel Planner.* The guide describes attractions, travel routes, accommodations, and events. Tourism NB also offers maps and more specific booklets on fishing and hunting, outdoor recreation, crafts producers, and other topics. Call 800/561-0123 from Canada or the continental United States, or write to New Brunswick Department of Economic Development and Tourism, P.O. Box 12345, Campbellton, NB E3N 1T6. You can also find the department on the Web at www.tourismnbcanada.com.

If you're looking for tourist information during your stay in the province, check out any of the local provincial and municipal tourist offices; most places stock the same general provin-

cial literature, with additional local and regional information. **Provincial Visitor Information Centres** are located at Aulac (tel. 506/364-4090), Saint-Jacques (tel. 506/735-2747), Woodstock (tel. 506/325-4427), St. Stephen (tel. 506/466-7390), Cape Jourimain (tel. 506/538-2133), and Campbellton (tel. 506/789-2367); all are open mid-May to mid-October. Fredericton, Saint John, Moncton, Edmundston, Sackville, and another 50 towns operate **municipal visitor information offices** with varying hours.

### Communications and Media

New Brunswick's area code is **506.**

**Canada Post** offices are open Mon.–Fri. 8:15 A.M.–5 P.M. **Retail post offices** augment the postal system; mall locations are open Mon.–Sat. 10 A.M.–10 P.M. Tourist information centers also sell stamps.

**Newspapers** flourish with dailies like Saint John's *Telegraph-Journal* and *Times-Globe* and Fredericton's *Daily Gleaner.* Twenty-seven weeklies cover towns and counties throughout the province.

## GETTING THERE

### By Air

**Air Canada/Air Nova,** tel. 888/247-2262, flies from Toronto to Moncton, Saint John, and Fredericton; from Ottawa to Saint John; from Halifax to Moncton; and from Montreal to Fredericton and Saint John.

### By Land

Main U.S. border crossings are at Edmundston, Woodstock, Campobello, Saint-Léonard, and St. Stephen. From Québec, the TransCanada Highway enters at Saint-Jacques near Edmundston, and Highway 132 enters at Campbellton. Aulac, in southeastern New Brunswick, is where the TransCanada Highway crosses into and out of Nova Scotia.

**VIA Rail** enters the province from Québec at Campbellton and makes its way south and east to Halifax, Nova Scotia, via Charlo, Jacquet River,

Petit-Rocher, Bathurst, Miramichi, Rogersville, Moncton, Sackville, Amherst, Springhill Junction, and Truro. Call 800/561-3952 or check the website www.viarail.ca.

### By Sea

**Bay Ferries,** tel. 506/649-7777 or 888/249-7245, www.nfl-bay.com, sails the *Princess of Acadia* between Saint John and Digby, Nova Scotia, year-round, with trips up to three times daily each way in peak summer season, twice daily in the late-spring and early-fall shoulder seasons, and once daily the rest of the year. In summer season (June 21 to September 12), the one-way fare is adults $35, seniors $30, children $15, and vehicles $70. The fare for transporting a vehicle remains the same year-round, but outside of summer, passenger fares are discounted to adults $20, seniors $17.50, and children $10.

Car ferry service crosses the Baie des Chaleurs' western end from Miguasha, Québec, to Dalhousie ($5 per person; $16 per vehicle). It operates daily mid-June to mid-September, 8:30 A.M.–8:30 P.M.

## GETTING AROUND

### By Car

Speed limits are 80 kph (50 mph) on highways and 50 kph (30 mph) in cities and towns, unless posted otherwise. In urban areas, vehicles yield to pedestrians at crosswalks, and cars are permitted to turn right on a red light after a full stop unless otherwise posted. Seat belts are required for driver and passengers; children under five years old or under 18 kg (40 pounds) must be in an infant carrier or approved child restraint. Helmets are required for motorcyclists and their passengers.

Minimum vehicle insurance coverage is $200,000, and if there's an accident involving damage over $1,000 or injury or death, it must be reported immediately to the local police or RCMP. Drinking while driving and "impaired driving" carry severe penalties.

Be particularly careful driving the provincial roads at early morning and dusk, when deer and moose roam woodlands and cross roads. Annually, about 1,000 deer and 100 moose are hit by cars. Watch out too for slow-moving porcupines, especially at night.

Highways are classified by numbers; for example, high-speed, principal highways are distinguished with single-digit numbers. Secondary highways, either paved or unpaved, have low-number triple digits, and local highways are marked with high-number triple digits. Local roads are unnumbered. The **Maritime Automobile Association,** tel. 506/652-3300, provides daily 24-hour emergency road service for members.

### Public Transportation

**SMT** bus service, tel. 506/859-5060 or 800/567-5151, www.smtbus.com, serves the province with terminals in Saint John, Fredericton, Moncton, Bathurst, Campbellton, Edmundston, Miramichi, St. Stephen, Sussex, and Woodstock. Buses connect with Greyhound buses from across Canada, Nova Scotia's Acadian Line, Québec's Voyageur, and Maine's Concord Trailways. If you plan on extensive bus travel, consider a SMT pass (seven days unlimited travel for $175; 10 days for $235; 14 days for $330).

**VIA Rail,** 800/561-3952 in the Maritimes, 800/561-9181 from the United States, is another good alternative if you're heading north or south along the east side of the province. The route serves Sackville, Moncton, Rogersville, Miramichi, Bathurst, Petit-Rocher, Jacquet River, Charlo, and Campbellton.

Major **car rental** companies have locations in the larger cities and airports. All rental charges are subject to the 15 percent sales tax.

**Ferries** are a fun way to get around. Free cable ferries connect many riverbanks in the lower Saint John River valley and along the Kennebecasis River. Other toll ferries run from the mainland to Deer Island, from Blacks Harbour to Grand Manan, and from Deer Island to Campobello Island, all in the southern corner of the province.

# Saint John River Valley

The Saint John River's original name was the Woolastook, an Indian word that translates aptly as the goodly (or godly) river. The French explorer Samuel de Champlain christened it the Saint John to mark his arrival at the river's mouth on Saint John's feast day in 1604. Other French explorers followed and tracked the river's circuitous route 724 km north from the Bay of Fundy to the forested interior. This watery highway, dubbed the "Rhine of North America," was mapped before any other part of New Brunswick.

The great river originates in remote northern Maine near the Québec border and enters New Brunswick's northwestern corner alongside Hwy. 205, a backcountry road used more by loggers than sightseers. The young river tumbles along, over riverbed boulders and through glistening pools frequented by moose and white-tailed deer. It flows through Edmundston and then curves southeast through the French-flavored towns and villages of Madawaska until it's squeezed into a spuming torrent at the stony gorge at Grand Falls.

The rest of the river's journey grows increasingly placid. It's tamed by hydro dams at Beechwood and Mactaquac, spanned by the world's longest covered bridge at Hartland, and

Fredericton and the Saint John River

flows gently through the capital city of Fredericton and finally on to Saint John—a pretty stretch houseboaters love to explore. The following coverage starts in Fredericton, then moves upriver.

Mount Carleton Provincial Park, though deep in the northern interior and far from the Saint John River, is accessible by two routes off the TransCanada Highway, and so is included in this chapter.

## Fredericton

Fredericton (pop. 45,000), in the southwestern heart of the province, is New Brunswick's legislative, cultural, and educational center, and one of the country's oldest settlements. The city is the exception to the usual rule of thumb that a province's busiest and largest city is the logical choice for the capital. Fredericton is hardly a metropolis. Rather, it's of modest size, elegant, pic-

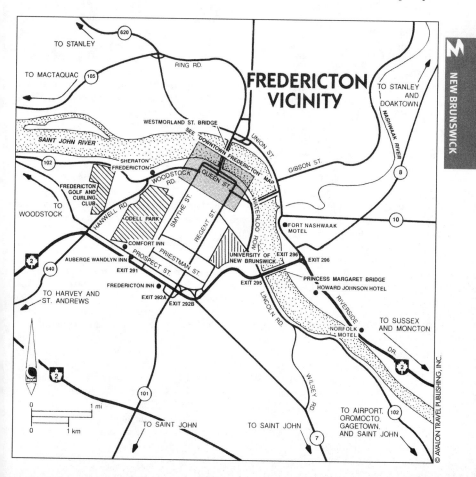

ture-book pretty, and very Anglo in tone and shape. "There is something subtle and elusive about it," Michael Collie wrote of Fredericton, "like a person who has had long sessions of psychoanalysis and has become more sophisticated and charming in the course of them."

Visitors flying in to New Brunswick will find Fredericton makes a good introduction to the province and a good sightseeing base. Roads lead from here to every part of the province. St. Andrews and Saint John on the Fundy are each about a two-hour drive south, and Moncton is another hour to the east. And it's always nice to return to Fredericton, the province's quintessential hometown.

## HISTORY

Fredericton is one of North America's oldest cities, though early attempts at settlement were short-lived. The French tried settlements in the late 1600s. Joseph Robineau de Villebon, Acadia's governor, built a fur-trading fort on the northern bank of the Saint John River, at the mouth of the Nashwaak River. Heavy winter ice wrecked the fortification, and the inhabitants fled to Port Royal across the Bay of Fundy. In 1713, the Treaty of Utrecht awarded mainland Nova Scotia to the British, and Acadians fled back across the Fundy and founded Saint-Anne's Point (now site of Fredericton's historic area). The British demolished the village after the Acadian Deportation. Malecite Indians camped along what is now Woodstock Road, but moved upriver to the Kingsclear area before the Loyalists arrived in the late 18th century.

### The Capital's Fortuitous Beginning

The situation that created Fredericton as provincial capital was an interesting one. After the American Revolution, Loyalists by the thousands poured into New Brunswick at Saint John. England directed the mass exodus from New York, but military forces at Saint John were unprepared for the onslaught.

Arriving Loyalists and families, finding limited food and no housing, rioted. Stung by the backlash, the British directed subsequent emigrants 103 km upriver to Saint-Anne's Point. The Loyalists arrived in the wilderness, founded a new settlement as a "haven for the King's friends," and named it Frederick's Town in honor of King George III's second son. Two years later, in 1785, provincial governor Thomas Carleton designated the little river town the colonial capital, and the people of Saint John were permanently miffed.

England had great plans for Fredericton. Surveyor Charles Morris drew up the first street grid between University Avenue and Wilsey Road. By 1786, the population center had shifted, and central Fredericton as you see it today was redrawn by another surveyor and extended from riverfront to George Street, bounded by University Avenue and Smythe Street.

Priorities were established. Space was set aside for the Church of England sanctuary and King's College, now the University of New Brunswick. Public commons were marked off between riverfront and Queen Street, except for two blocks earmarked for the British Army garrison.

The first winters were brutal, and Loyalists buried their dead at Salamanca on Waterloo Row. Wooden boardwalks were laid as sidewalks along muddy streets, and sewage was funneled into the river. The colonial government began at Government House in 1787, and New Brunswick's first assembly met the next year at a coffeehouse.

### Expansion

The infamous Benedict Arnold lived awhile in Fredericton—and was burned in effigy at Saint John. Jonathan Odell, an influential Loyalist politician whose former estate land is now Odell Park, acted as negotiator between Arnold and England. American artist and naturalist John James Audubon visited Fredericton in 1830 and painted the *Pine Finch,* one of his best-known works, during his stay at Government House.

By 1800, wharves lined the riverfront from Waterloo Row to Smthye Street, and sloops, schooners, and brigantines sped between the capital and Saint John. Shipping lumber was a profitable early business, and Fredericton added foundry products, processed leather, carriages, and wagons to its economy in the 1800s.

Fredericton and Christ Church Cathedral had a tightly woven beginning. The town was barely three generations old when Queen Victoria got wind of the cathedral's construction. But with fewer than 10,000 inhabitants, the settlement was hardly the proper setting for the foundation of the first Anglican cathedral to be built on British soil since the Reformation. Royalty, of course, can do anything it wants, and Queen Victoria remedied the hitch. She elevated little Fredericton to the official "city" status required for an Anglican cathedral's setting. The city was incorporated in 1848, and in 1873 the city limits were extended to nearby towns, doubling the population. The city hall opened three years later.

**Benedict Arnold**

## Fires and Floods

Fredericton had its share of scourges. At various times, flames consumed even the sturdiest stone buildings, from Government House to the Military Compound's Guard House. Great conflagrations leveled 300 downtown buildings in 1849, destroyed 46 houses and stores in 1854, and took the first Christ Church Cathedral's steeple in 1911. Even the Westmorland Street Bridge was vulnerable, and the first bridge, built in 1885, burned in 1905.

River floods were equally devastating: Queen Street was frequently under water during spring's ice melt. Floods in 1887 and 1923 swamped the capital. The upriver Mactaquac Dam was built to divert the river's impact, but floods again threatened the capital during 1973–74.

## The Town Evolves

England's plan for Fredericton as a miniature London was never fulfilled. Shipping and manufacturing diminished in the early 1900s, and Fredericton settled in as a prosperous, genteel government town, university center, and haunt of the Anglo establishment. The **New Brunswick College of Craft and Design** started up in the 1940s and relocated to the renovated Military Compound in the 1980s. The **University of New Brunswick,** with 7,500 engineering, arts, education, business, and science students, overlooks the city from a steep hilltop and shares the campus with **St. Thomas University,** a Roman Catholic institution with 1,200 liberal-arts students.

William Maxwell Aitken, better known as Lord Beaverbrook, paved the way for Fredericton's cultural accomplishments. The **Beaverbrook Art Gallery** was a gift to the city in 1959, and **Lord Beaverbrook Playhouse** across the street followed in 1964. It became the home of Theatre New Brunswick, Atlantic Canada's only provincial repertory touring company.

City planners wisely avoided commercial saturation and set most of the city's dozen shopping malls and its motel row beyond the residential area on the outskirts on Prospect St., which parallels the TransCanada Highway.

## SIGHTS

The tourist's Fredericton is easy to understand and very manageable. The town started at the riverfront with Queen, King, Brunswick, George, and Charlotte streets, and everything important lies adjacent or nearby. For most sightseeing, follow Queen Street, a block inland from the river. At riverfront, walking paths weave through **The Green,** a slender, five-km promenade that encompasses the whole curving riverbank from Princess Margaret Bridge to the Sheraton. Queen Street also forms the shopping area's edge, and the city's notable crafts shops lie along Regent and other cross streets. From there, tree-lined streets feed back to shady, quiet residential areas of historic oversize houses with

**NEW BRUNSWICK**

# BY ANY OTHER NAME

Fredericton is known by many names. New Brunswickers have dubbed the city "North America's Last Surviving Hometown." You could debate the claim, perhaps, but it nonetheless does sum up local priorities.

The naming trend goes back to the 1800s when locals ruefully joked that the city had a fire every Saturday night, and dubbed it the "City of Fires." In 1911 one such fire destroyed the Christ Church Cathedral. The sanctuary was quickly rebuilt, its grandiose silhouette on the skyline leading to the moniker "Cathedral City."

Another Fredericton nickname, "City of Stately Elms," is a testa-

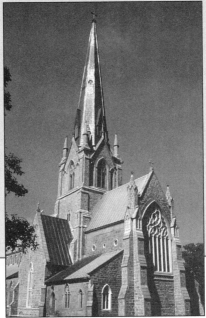

**Christ Church Cathedral**

ment to Fredericton's leafy ambience. The quiet streets are lined mainly with elms, a choice that goes back to founding Loyalist times. They've survived centuries, even beating Dutch elm disease, which the city quelled in the 1960s and '70s.

Fredericton's reputation as "Canada's Poets' Corner" is a tribute to native sons Bliss Carmen, Sir Charles G. D. Roberts, and Francis Joseph Sherman. And finally, the nickname "Canada's Pewtersmith Capital" singles out the city's preeminent craft, developed here first by pewtersmith Ivan Crowell in the 18th century.

© ANDREW HEMPSTEAD

open porches, bay windows, and gardens of pearl-colored peonies and scarlet poppies.

Metered parking is plentiful in parking lots behind sites and curbside on Queen, King, upper York, Carleton, Regent, and Saint John streets. The city provides free three-day parking passes for out-of-province visitors; the passes are available at city hall and the Legislative Assembly building, both on Queen Street.

## City Hall

The brick city hall, as pretty as a gingerbread house, anchors one end of the downtown sightseeing district. The elegant building, at the corner of Queen and York streets, began in 1876 as city offices, jail, farmers' market, and opera house. Its high tower houses the city's copper clock, and the decorative fountain in front—crowned by the figurine that Frederictonians have dubbed

"Freddie, the little nude dude"—was added in 1885.

The building was used as an opera house into the 1940s. Today it's mainly city offices. The **Council Chamber** is adorned with a series of 27 locally produced tapestries depicting the city's history. The tapestries were woven for Fredericton's bicentennial. The **Fredericton Visitors Bureau,** tel. 506/460-2129, in the building's front vestibule, conducts daily chamber tours mid-May to early October, 8:15 A.M.–7:30 P.M. The rest of the year, tours are available by appointment, weekdays 8:15 A.M.–4:30 P.M. Free one-hour **guided walking tours,** led by informative, entertaining, and period-dressed members of the Calithumpians—the city's theatrical troupe—start from here in July and August. They leave daily at 9:30 A.M. and 3:30 P.M. For details, ask at the bureau desk.

## Military Compound: Heart of the City

The Military Compound, a national historic site, begins across York Street from city hall at the imposing Justice Building (tours unavailable) and spreads across two blocks between Regent, Queen, and York Streets. It is distinguished by the curlicue, wrought-iron black fence enclosing the expanse. The complex, as old as Fredericton itself, began as England's defensive base for guarding New Brunswick's interior. It was staffed with British Army and subsequent Canadian regiments until 1914.

At the corner of Queen and Carleton Streets, the stone **Soldiers' Barracks** and the **Guard House** are restored rooms harking back to the 1820s to 1860s; open June through early September, daily 10 A.M.–6 P.M.; by appointment the rest of the year. Admission is free.

On the opposite corner, the John Thurston Clark Memorial Building peers over the compound from an impressive 1881 Second Empire French Revival edifice that once served as customs house and post office. The building holds the **New Brunswick Sports Hall of Fame,** tel. 506/453-3747, with exhibits on provincial sports history. The center is open June to early Sep-

tember, daily 10 A.M.–6 P.M. and all other months Mon.–Fri. noon–4 P.M. or by appointment.

Facing the greensward of the old Parade Square, the **York-Sunbury Historical Society Museum,** tel. 506/455-6041, is housed within the former Officers' Quarters (1825), a three-story stone building unusually styled with a ground-level colonnade of white pillars and an iron handrail, designed by the Royal Engineers. The museum is devoted to provincial history from early Malecite and Mi'kmaq Indians to contemporary events. The unlikely surprise is the **Coleman Frog,** a 17-kilogram, 1.6-meter-long amphibian stuffed for posterity and squatting inside a glass showcase on the second floor. The believe-it-or-not frog was found a century ago by local Fred Coleman, who developed a friendship with the mammoth frog and fattened it up by feeding it rum pudding and June bugs in honey sauce. The museum is open year-round: daily from May 1 to early September; Tues.–Sat. from early September to early October; Monday, Wednesday, Friday the rest of the year. Hours vary. Admission is $2 adults, $1 students, $4 families.

DOWNTOWN FREDERICTON

NEW BRUNSWICK

© AVALON TRAVEL PUBLISHING, INC.

**Officers' Square,** once the regimental parade ground and now the grassy center of everything happening in Fredericton, lies alongside the museum. A changing-of-the-guard ceremony takes place July–August, Tues.–Sat. at 11 A.M. and 7 P.M. The 1832 **Militia Arms Store,** the only surviving wooden building in the complex, is now used for offices and is closed to visitors.

## Historic Cemeteries

The **Old Burial Ground** is bounded by Regent, Brunswick, George, and Sunbury Streets. The site—spliced with walkways beneath tall trees—is one of two historic burial grounds in town. This spread of greenery was the final resting place for Loyalist notables. The **Loyalist Cemetery** (formerly the Salamanca graveyard), on an unmarked gravel road off Waterloo Row at riverfront, is simpler and marks the final resting place of the founding Loyalists who died in that first winter of 1783–84.

## Fredericton Lighthouse

Walking back up Regent Street to The Green at riverfront will bring you to this privately operated lighthouse, tel. 506/459-2515, which still guides river traffic. The tower's interior consists of 13 separate landings exhibiting shipping and river-sailing artifacts The top level commands a magnificent riverfront view. At ground level, you'll find a gift shop and summertime outdoor cafe serving light lunches. The lighthouse is open May–June, Mon.–Fri. 10 A.M.–4 P.M., Sat.–Sun. noon–4 P.M., and July to early September, daily 10 A.M.–9 P.M. Admission is $2 adults, $1 children.

## Beaverbrook Art Gallery

Take any of the short streets back into town to the Beaverbrook Art Gallery, 703 Queen St., tel. 506/458-8545, which was given to the city in 1959 by New Brunswick art maven Lord Beaverbrook, also known as William Maxwell Aitken. The gallery boasts an impressive 2,000-piece collection—the most extensive British fine-arts collection in Atlantic Canada, if not the nation. Among the British painters represented are Thomas Gainsborough, Sir Joshua Reynolds, John Constable, and Walter Richard Sickert. You'll find Graham Sutherland's sketches of Winston Churchill—drawn in preparation for Churchill's official portrait—and works by Atlantic Canada's Miller Brittain, Alex Colville, and Jack Humphrey. Also central to the collection are the oils of Cornelius Krieghoff, depicting social and domestic scenes of early life in Acadia. Lord Beaverbrook could not resist the European masters—Salvador Dali's large-scale *Santiago El Grande* and Botticelli's *Resurrection* are prominently displayed.

The gallery and gift shop are open June through September, Mon.–Fri. 9 A.M.–6 P.M. and Sat.–Sun. 10 A.M.–5 P.M.; the rest of the year, hours are Tues.–Fri. 9 A.M.–5 P.M., Saturday 10 A.M.–5 P.M., and Sunday noon–5 P.M. Guided tours depart the lobby daily at 11 A.M. Admission is $5 adults, $4 seniors, $2 students, $10 families.

## Legislative Assembly Building

The splendidly regal legislative building lies kitty-corner from the gallery on Queen Street, tel. 506/453-2527. The sandstone French Revival building spreads across a manicured lawn, its massive wings pierced with high, arched windows, and the upper floor and tower rotunda washed in glistening white.

The building was completed in 1882 at a cost of $120,000, including construction and furnishings. The front portico entrance opens into an interior decorated in high Victorian style—the apex of expensive taste at the time. Glinting Waterford prisms are set in brass chandeliers, and the spacious rooms are wallpapered in an oriental design. The interior's pièce de résistance is the **Assembly Chamber,** centered around an ornate throne set on a dais and sheltered with a canopy.

John James Audubon's *Birds of America* is kept in the **Legislative Library.** One of four volumes is on display in a climate-controlled exhibit, and pages are periodically turned to show the meticulous paintings. Each of the building's nooks and corners has a story, which tour guides are eager to relate.

Tours are offered through summer, daily 8:30 A.M.–6:30 P.M. Legislative sessions (Feb.–May, October) are open to the public.

## Christ Church Cathedral

Gothic-styled cathedrals were designed to soar grandiosely toward heaven, and this storied stone cathedral is no exception. With a lofty, copper-clad central spire and elegant linear stone tracery, the cathedral rises from a grassy city block at Church and Brunswick streets. Begun in 1845 and consecrated in 1853, this was the first entirely new cathedral founded on British soil since the Norman Conquest way back in 1066. It was rebuilt after a fire in 1911 and is still the place where the city's nabobs go to pay their respects to the benevolent powers that be. It's open year-round, and free guided tours of the cathedral are given mid-June to Labour Day, Mon.–Fri. 10 A.M.–6 P.M. Recitals take place Mon.–Fri. 12:10–12:50 P.M. Contact the church at 506/450-8500.

## City Parks

Of the 355 hectares of lush parkland throughout the city, **Odell Park** alongside Smythe Street, tel. 506/460-2038, is the choice spread, holding 16 km of trails, formal lawns, duck ponds, a deer pen, barbecue pits, and picnic tables. The park is Fredericton's largest, covering 175 hectares (388 acres). It is best known for an arboretum holding every tree species in the province; a 2.8-km walking trail divided in three loops wanders through the shady expanse. The park is open dawn to dusk.

## Photogenic Vistas

If you're interested in capturing a scene of the river rimming the town, start with the red-and-white-striped Fredericton Lighthouse near the Regent Street Wharf. A trudge up the lighthouse's interior steps to the top opens up sweeping views of the Saint John River as it curves around the historic area. Get another encompassing view a few blocks inland, at the University of New Brunswick; the campus edge on a steep hilltop peers across the city and river.

The most memorable angle, though, is from across the river. The Saint John flows alongside Fredericton like a long looking glass, and scenes of stately old houses set back on green lawns reflect across the water's surface.

# ACCOMMODATIONS AND CAMPING

## Budget

**Fredericton International Hostel** is centrally located in Rosary Hall at 621 Churchill Row (at Regent Street), tel. 506/450-4417, www.hihostels .ca. It's a Hostelling International hostel with 40 beds (members pay $16 per night; nonmembers $20), laundry, and kitchen facilities. Single and family rooms are available.

The **UNB-Tourist Hotel** on Bailey Drive at the University of New Brunswick, tel. 506/453-4800, www.unb.ca/housing, is the campus's official name for dormitory rooms that the school rents out after students go home for the summer. They're open July to mid-August. Students pay around $18 per day for a single room; $15 per day each to share a double room. Non-students pay $28.40 s, $41.50 d. Weekly and monthly rates are available. Bring your own towels.

## Inns and B&Bs

The three-story, Queen Anne Revival **Carriage House Inn** at 230 University Avenue, tel. 506/452-9924 or 800/267-6068, has 11 guest rooms furnished with antiques ($75 single, $80 double with full breakfast). Facilities include a solarium and laundry. The highly rated **Fowler House,** 2785 Woodstock Rd., tel. 506/459-7766, offers three guest rooms ($85 single, $89 double) in an 1820s farmhouse. The 10-hectare grounds hold a swimming pool and gardens. Equally well regarded is **The Very Best. . . A Victorian B&B,** 806 George St., tel. 506/451-1499, which offers three rooms ($99 single or double), a heated pool, and a sauna.

## Motels and Hotels

Lodgings are concentrated along Prospect Street, which parallels the TransCanada Highway (Highway 2) about three km southwest of the town center. The **Auberge Wandlyn Inn** at 958 Prospect Street West, tel. 506/462-4444 or 800/561-000, www.wandlyn.com, has 100 rooms and suites (from $95 single, $99 double), a restaurant, swimming pools, a hot tub, a sauna, and an exercise room. The **Fredericton**

**Inn,** 1315 Regent St., tel. 506/455-1430 or 800/561-8777, is a good-looking lodging near Prospect Street between the Regent and Fredericton shopping malls. It has 200 guest rooms, a dining room, lounge, pool, and whirlpool. Summer rates are quoted at $129 single or double, discounted to as low as $79 the rest of the year. In the vicinity, the **Comfort Inn** at 797 Prospect Street, tel. 506/453-0800 or 800/228-5150, www.choicehotels.ca, has 59 basic, clean rooms ($105 single, $115 double) with no frills.

One of Fredericton's better lodgings is the **Lord Beaverbrook Hotel,** 659 Queen St., tel. 506/455-3371 or 800/561-7666, www .keddys.ca, which puts you within quick striking distance of downtown sightseeing and has 165 spacious rooms ($129 single, $139 double; request a riverfront room for terrific views), dining rooms, a sauna, indoor pool, and exercise room.

The four-star **Sheraton Fredericton Hotel,** 225 Woodstock Rd., tel. 506/457-7000 or 800/325-3535, www.sheraton.com, hugs the Saint John River several blocks west of downtown in a splendid architectural statement. It has 223 rooms ($145–225 single or double, discounted to under $100 through winter), indoor and outdoor pools, a hot tub, sauna, exercise facilities, restaurants, and a lounge.

Across the river from downtown, the **Fort Nashwaak Motel,** 15 Riverside Dr., tel. 506/472-4411 or 800/684-8999, charges $58 single and $64 double for a basic room. Downstream four km from the Fort Nashwaak Motel, the **Norfolk Motel** on Highway 2 East, tel. 506/472-3278 or 800/686-8555,

*Fredericton has a reputation for so-so dining. Don't believe it. You can sample virtually all the capital's fare without a qualm, and your dining dollar will go a long way, too.*

is even more basic, charging just $44 for a single, $50 for a double. In between the two, the **Howard Johnson Hotel,** 480 Riverside Dr., tel. 506/460-5500, www.hojofred.com, holds 116 rooms ($99 single, $109 double), a dining room, an indoor tennis and fitness center, a pool (with poolside bar), a hot tub, and a sauna.

## Camping

The closest camping to Fredericton is at **Hartt Island Campground,** about seven km west of town on the TransCanada Highway, tel. 506/462-9400. It's open May to October, and its 100 sites cost $15–24 per night. Self-contained motor homes and trailers can park free overnight in the lot behind the Justice Building.

# FOOD

Fredericton has a reputation for so-so dining. Don't believe it. True, you won't find tony dining rooms by the dozens, and aside from at a few fine restaurants, the cooking is less than fancy. Nonetheless, you can sample virtually all the capital's fare without a qualm, and your dining dollar will go a long way, too.

The **Hilltop Grill,** 1034 Prospect St., tel. 506/458-9057 or 450-2739, specializes in aged charbroiled beef. The **Lobster Hut,** 1216 Regent St., tel. 506/455-4413, is City Motel–Sequoia's claim to fame. They boil, broil, stuff, fry, or serve cold the best lobsters in town, starting at $16—and the largest available lobsters (more expensive) can be requested with an advance phone call. Other entrees run $6–25.

The **Lunar Rogue** at 625 King St., tel. 506/450-2065, one of Fredericton's most popular pubs, offers dining indoors or alfresco. The breakfasts are cheap and filling, and the Rogue serves lunches and worthy light dinners (Cornish pasties, stir-fry chicken, sirloin strip, and pub-grub specials such as barbecued chicken wings; $8–15.50) as well. The beer selection is excellent. Across the street and a block down, **Mexicali Rosa's,** 546 King St., tel. 506/451-0686, is a popular spot for reasonably priced fajitas, enchiladas, and daily lunch specials. It's a long way from Mexico, but the recipes nonetheless come off quite well. Margaritas and cold *cerveza* are available. Anyone hankering for pizza can step right next door to **Brew Bakers,** 546 King St., tel. 506/459-0067, where the pies are baked in a wood-fired oven and accompanied by pastas and salads.

The dining rooms at the major hotels are good bets for fancier fare. At the Auberge Wandlyn Inn, 958 Prospect St. W., tel. 506/462-4444, the moderately priced **958 Prospect** offers buffets and an à la carte menu with some good seafood selections. At the Lord Beaverbrook Hotel, 659 Queen St., tel. 506/451-1804, the **Terrace Room** offers buffets and basic dinners at moderate prices, while the **Governor's Room** serves a more upscale menu of French fare and nouvelle cuisine. Reservations required. At the Sheraton Fredericton Hotel, 225 Woodstock Rd., **Bruno's Seafood Cafe,** tel. 506/457-7919, lures crowds for fare such as chicken saltimbocca—a sautéed stuffed chicken breast basted with white wine and served on linguine—and seafood, beef, and pasta. Look for moderately priced dinners and Sunday brunch, as well as an inexpensive weekday lunch buffet. It's open 6:30 A.M.–11 P.M. daily. Also at the Sheraton is **The Dip,** tel. 506/457-7000, a poolside bar and grill open for inexpensive lunch and dinner daily in summer, weather permitting.

## Light Fare and Food Stores

You'll find plenty of fast food along Regent St. and across the river on Main Street. If you're planning a picnic, the **J M & T Deli** at 66 Regent St., tel. 506/458-9068, has a tempting assortment of cold cuts, breads, muffins, bagels, and carrot cake. The **Boyce Farmers' Market,** 665 George St. (between Regent and Saint John Streets), tel. 506/451-1815, lures *everybody* with stalls heaped with baked goods, homemade German sausage, other local delicacies, and crafts. It's open year-round, Sat. 6 A.M.–1 P.M. **Sobey's,** on Prospect St., is the largest supermarket, open Mon.–Sat. 24 hours a day.

Provincial **liquor stores** are at the Fredericton Mall on Prospect St.; at 225 King Street; at the Devon Shopping Plaza on Union St.; and at the Brookside Mall on Brookside Drive.

# ENTERTAINMENT AND EVENTS

## Theater and Cinema

Fredericton specializes in entertaining summertime visitors. Festivities center around the Military Compound's Officers' Square, where the **Calithumpians,** the city's theatrical troupe, take to the boards July to early September. Their humorous and historical productions take place weekdays at 12:15 P.M. and weekends at 2 P.M. Local pipe bands and folk, country, and bluegrass groups also entertain at the same location, July–August, Tues. and Thurs. at 7:30 P.M. For more information call 506/457-1975.

The **Theatre New Brunswick,** the province's only professional English-speaking theater company, operates full-tilt during the autumn-to-spring theater season at the Lord Beaverbrook Playhouse on Queen Street. Past presentations have included *A Streetcar Named Desire* and *Shirley Valentine.* The playhouse presents several shows in summer; for details, call the box office at 506/458-8344. **Symphony New Brunswick** also call the Playhouse home.

**Empire Theatres** at Regent Mall, tel. 506/458-9704, is an eight-screen multiplex offering first-run film choices nightly, as well as weekend matinees. The **Nashwaaksis Twin Cinemas** has two screens at the Nashwaaksis Plaza, 15 Ferry Ave., tel. 506/457-0286.

## Nightlife

Touring rock groups and big bands head for **Sweetwaters** at 339 King St., tel. 506/444-0121, where admission costs $8–20. Featuring five bars and two dance floors, venue presents pulsating, high-energy rock to 2 A.M., Thurs.–Saturday.

Otherwise, the locals like their pubs. The **Lunar Rogue** at 625 King St., tel. 506/450-2065, heads the list with English pub ambience, Canadian and British draft beer, and live music— usually with a Celtic flavor—several nights a week. The **Hilltop Grill,** 1034 Prospect St., tel. 506/458-9057, is another choice pub and spreads out with nooks and corners on several levels.

A cluster of pubs surrounds Pipers' Lane, an alley that connects the 300 blocks of King and

Queen Streets. Among the offerings here you'll find **Dolan's Pub,** 349 King St., tel. 506/454-7474, which offers an excellent menu of pub-grub and slightly fancier fare, as well as Beamish on tap and live entertainment Thurs.–Saturday. The **Upperdeck Sports Bar,** 375 King St., tel. 506/457-1475, offers a deck out in the sun and look out on the comings and goings in Pipers' Lane, three bars, pool tables, and bands on weekends.

Country-and-western fans should head to **Rockin' Rodeo,** 546 King St., tel. 506/444-0122. The Sheraton Inn Fredericton devotes a spacious corner without music to **D. J. Purdy's Lounge** (named for an old-time local riverboat), where it serves deftly mixed drinks in pleasant riverside surroundings.

### Events

The **Festival Francophone,** for three days late in May, celebrates Acadian language and culture with concerts, dancing, and children's activities. The festivities take place at Le Centre Communautaire Sainte-Anne, 715 Priestman St. near Regent St., tel. 506/453-2731.

On Tuesday and Thursday evenings from mid-June to early September, the **Outdoor Summer Music Series,** tel. 506/460-2129, brings a wide range of musical entertainment to Officers' Square. Starting at 7:30 P.M., bring your lawn chairs or picnic blankets to these free concerts and expect to enjoy everything from jazz and blues to bagpipes.

The **Highland Games and Scottish Festival,** a local three-day Celtic tribute featuring pipe bands, Highland dancing, Gaelic singing, clan booths, and more, takes over the city the last weekend of July. For more information, call 506/452-9244.

**New Brunswick Day,** the first Monday in August, brings parades, street-food vendors, and fireworks to the Military Compound. Later in August, look for the New Brunswick Summer Music Festival—a series of chamber music concerts featuring renowned classical musicians.

Fredericton had its first fall fair in 1825, and the tradition continues at the **Fredericton Exhibition,** tel. 506/458-9819, with six days of country-fair trappings, including harness racing

and stage shows, at the Fredericton Exhibition Grounds during early September. The season finishes in a clamor of music, as the outdoor **Harvest Jazz and Blues Festival** takes over the downtown streets in mid-September. It's billed as the biggest jazz and blues fest east of Montréal, and it features musicians from all over North America. For more information call 454-2583 or 888/622-5837.

## RECREATION

The **Fredericton Small Craft Aquatic Center,** located along the riverfront off Woodstock Rd., tel. 506/460-2260, rents recreational rowing shells, canoes, and kayaks and gives lessons. It's open mid-May to early October; July–Aug., daily 9 A.M.–1 P.M. and 4–9:30 P.M., Sat.–Sun. 10 A.M.–4 P.M., shorter hours in early and late season.

The **Fredericton Golf and Curling Club,** tel. 506/458-1003, has user-friendly links (aside from the 18th hole—known as "Cardiac Hill"). The course lies beyond the Sheraton Fredericton Hotel on Woodstock Road's inland side and is open May–September. Greens fee is $55 for non-members. Rental carts and clubs are available.

**The Radical Edge,** 386 Queen St., tel. 506/459-3478, rents bikes for around $5 per hour, $20 per day.

## SHOPPING

Shopping areas are concentrated downtown, mainly along Regent, Queen, York, King, and the adjacent side streets, plus on Woodstock Road and at the malls. Largest mall in town is Regent Mall on upper Regent Street, on the south side of the TransCanada Highway. It holds 95 stores including Wal-Mart, Sears, Toys "R" Us, and Empire Theatres. Other malls include the 70-store Fredericton Mall, on Prospect Street near Regent, just north of the TransCanada Highway; and Kings Place, 440 King St., right downtown, open Mon.–Wed. 9 A.M.–5:30 P.M., Thurs.–Fri. 9 A.M.–9 P.M., Saturday 9 A.M.–5 P.M.

### Craft Shops

Several shops are known for craft specialties.

Open daily, **Aitkens Pewter** at 65 Regent St., tel. 506/453-9474, stocks handcrafted pewter hollowware, jewelry, and decorative ware. **Cultures Boutique,** 383 Mazzuca's Lane (off York Street between King and Queen Streets), tel. 506/462-3088, is a nonprofit operation featuring crafts produced by Third World artisans. For porcelain and stoneware, check out **Garden Creek Pottery** at 1538 Woodstock Rd., tel. 506/455-7631. At Kings Place Mall, **Table for Two,** tel. 506/455-1401, specializes in the crafts of New Brunswick.

## Art Galleries and Artists

The **Gallery Connexion,** 453 Queen St. (at York St.), tel. 506/454-1433, is a nonprofit artists' outlet with an eminent reputation for provincial arts; open Tues.–Fri. noon–4 P.M. For local artists' works, check out **Capital Art Gallery,** 126 Queen St., tel. 506/458-8192. **Print Gallery** at Kings Place Mall, tel. 506/459-7493, has a nice selection of Fredericton sketches. **Gallery 78,** 796 Queen St. (at Church St.), tel. 506/454-5192, is the oldest commercial art gallery in New Brunswick and stocks a collection of art from all over Canada.

Several **local artists** are well known. Cathy Ross has established a fine reputation for prints, as has David Mackay, who works in egg tempera. Bruno Bobak is known for provincial scenic paintings, and no one does wildflower renderings like Molly Lamb.

# INFORMATION AND SERVICES

## Visitor Information

The friendly staff at the **Fredericton Visitors Bureau** stocks literature about the city; the office is in the front vestibule of City Hall, 397 Queen St. (at York St.). It's open mid-May to mid-June, daily 8 A.M.–5 P.M.; mid-June to early September, daily 8 A.M.–8 P.M.; early Sept. to early October, daily 8 A.M.–5 P.M.; the rest of the year, Mon.–Fri. 8:15 A.M.–4:30 P.M. For advance information, contact **Fredericton Tourism,** tel. 506/460-2129 or 888/888-4768, www.city.fredericton.nb.ca.

The **New Brunswick Geographic Information Corp.,** 527 King St., stocks provincial topo-graphical maps for 120 areas, as well as a Saint John River canoe map, and other detailed, local renditions.

## Books, Bookstores, and Archives

Stocking around 80,000 titles and newspapers from around the world, the **Fredericton Public Library** is at 12 Carleton Street alongside the Military Compound, tel. 506/460-2800. It's open July–August, Mon.–Tues. and Thurs. 10 A.M.–5 P.M., Wed. and Fri. to 9 P.M.; the rest of the year it has longer weekday hours and is open on Saturdays. The library also has public Internet access.

**Coles The Book People** at Regent Mall shopping center, tel. 506/458-8994, stocks the city's most extensive book assortment, and there are a dozen other bookstores in town. The **Reading Corner,** at 259 Main Street, tel. 506/458-9680, is nearby and has a trove of used books and paperbacks.

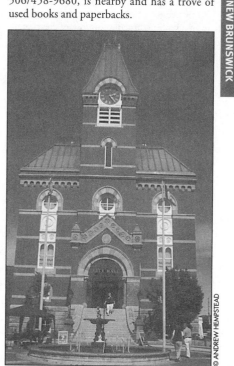

© ANDREW HEMPSTEAD

**Start your city exploration at City Hall, where you'll find the main information center.**

The **Provincial Archives of New Brunswick,** tel. 506/453-2122, www.gov.nb.ca/archives, stock provincial ancestral records. To get there, take University Avenue to the end and turn right to Dineen Drive. The archives are in the Bonar Law-Bennett Building on the UNB campus and are open year-round, Mon.–Fri. 10 A.M.–5 P.M., Sat. 8:30 A.M.–5 P.M.

### Environmental Organization

Lacking heavy industry, Fredericton boasts clear air and few problems. The Saint John River is clean within city limits, but conditions vary up- and downriver. The privately operated **Conservation Council of New Brunswick,** 180 Saint John St., tel. 506/458-8747, keeps abreast of ecological issues throughout New Brunswick. Their efforts publicizing underground oil spills from storage tanks in Fredericton brought about city intervention. The group has also worked to oppose nuclear-energy projects and clear-cutting, and is currently engaged in bringing attention to reducing greenhouse gas emissions.

### Services

In an emergency, call 911. The **RCMP** is at 1445 Regent Street, tel. 506/452-3400. The **Dr. Everett Chalmers Hospital** is on Priestman Street, tel. 506/452-5400, and the **Fredericton Medical Clinic** is at 1015 Regent Street, tel. 506/458-0200.

Hours of operation among the city's eight major banks and numerous branches vary; generally they open between 9 and 10 A.M. and close at 4 or 5 P.M., Mon.–Friday. Closing times are often later on Thursday and Friday. The Prospect Street branch of **Toronto-Dominion Bank** is open Saturday 9 A.M.–3 P.M.

Hours at the **Canada Post** at 570 Queen Street, tel. 506/444-8602, are Mon.–Fri. 8 A.M.–5 P.M.; the retail outlets at Kings Place and Fredericton Mall shopping centers have longer hours and are open Saturday.

**Spin & Grin** launderette is at 516 Smythe Street, tel. 506/459-5552. It's open daily to 9:30 P.M. If you arrive with luggage to stash, you can leave it in a locker at the **SMT** bus terminal, 101 Regent St., tel. 506/458-6009.

## TRANSPORTATION
### Getting There

The Fredericton Airport is 14 km (a 30-minute drive) from downtown Fredericton and lies off Highway 102 alongside the Saint John River; taxis ($17 to downtown) wait outside during arrivals. **Avis, Hertz, Budget,** and **National** car-rental counters are near the baggage carousels.

The airport is served by **Air Canada** and its inter-Maritimes affiliate, **Air Nova,** tel. 506/458-8561 or 888/247-2262, for both. Flights are offered to Montréal, Toronto, and Ottawa.

**SMT** at 101 Regent St., tel. 506/458-6009, offers frequent bus service to all parts of the province at low prices (Fredericton-Edmundston, for example, costs $45 one-way). The terminal is open 8 A.M.–8:30 P.M.; storage lockers are available for $1 per day.

### Getting Around

**Fredericton Transit,** tel. 506/460-2200 or 454-6287, has a web of bus routes connecting downtown with outlying areas. Fare is $1.25. The buses run daily except Sunday.

The city is saturated with **taxis** that cruise downtown city streets, wait at hotels, and are on-call. Rates are based on city zones, and tips— 50 cents to $1 for a basic fare—are expected, although optional. **Trius Taxi,** tel. 506/454-4444, is among the largest outfits and charges $3–12 within the city.

**Car rental** firms are plentiful. Chains in town include **Avis,** tel. 506/446-6006; **Budget,** tel. 506/452-1107; **Hertz,** tel. 506/446-9079; and **National,** tel. 506/453-1700.

## VICINITY OF FREDERICTON

The Saint John River below Fredericton is dotted with islands, around which a skein of twisting channels is braided. In the beautiful countryside between Upper Gagetown and Saint John, a series of free car ferries link the two sides of the river,

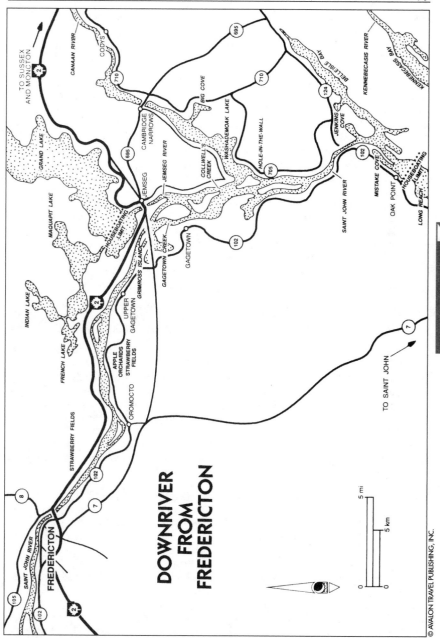

DOWNRIVER FROM FREDERICTON

NEW BRUNSWICK

making it easy to get around the scenic tangle of waterways.

## Oromocto

This riverfront town's raison d'etre is the Canadian Forces Base Gagetown, the military training installation located near town center off Broad Road. The **CFB Gagetown Military Museum,** tel. 506/422-1304, has exhibits on the past and present of the Canadian armed forces since the late 18th century—weapons, uniforms, and other memorabilia. The museum is open year-round: July–Aug., Mon.–Fri. 8 A.M.–4 P.M., Sat.–Sun., holidays 10 A.M.–4 P.M.; the rest of the year, Mon.–Fri. noon–4 P.M. Admission is free.

## Gagetown

Highway 102 follows the river to the pretty riverfront town of Gagetown, an hour from Fredericton. The handful of lanes here are lined with craft shops, small restaurants, and inns.

Quite a bit goes on in this little town of 600 over the course of the season. Look for the late-May Apple Blossom Festival, the Village of Gagetown Craft Festival at the fairgrounds in late June, and the four-day Queens County Fair in mid-September.

The **Queens County Museum** is also on Front St., tel. 506/488-2966. A national historic site, the handsome white wooden house was the birthplace of Sir Leonard Tilley, one of the "Fathers of Confederation." The first floor is dutifully furnished with Loyalist antiques, and upstairs there are vintage county exhibits. It's open June to mid-Sept., daily 10 A.M.–5 P.M. Admission is $2.

**Steamers Stop Inn,** 74 Front St., tel. 506/488-2903 or 877/991-9922, is a heritage inn with six guest rooms ($95), a screened patio overlooking the river, and a well-known dining room that caters to guests of the inn, as well as to boaters who tie up at the Gagetown Creek pier out back. It's open year-round.

# Up the Saint John River

## MACTAQUAC AND VICINITY

Once navigable from end to end, the Saint John River's course was first stemmed by the dam at Grand Falls/Grand-Sault. The hydroelectric dam at Beechwood near Bath came next. The **Mactaquac Dam,** some 20 km west of Fredericton, was completed in 1968. The dam rerouted the river and raised the water level 60 meters, flooding the valley and creating Mactaquac Lake Basin. Historic buildings from the flooded area found a new home at the Kings Landing Historical Settlement, a provincial heritage park that opened in 1974.

Not all New Brunswickers were pleased with this massive river alteration (it's the Maritimes' largest hydroelectric scheme), the abundant and cheap electrical power notwithstanding. The province sweetened the project with benefits, including an Atlantic salmon hatchery near the dam (visitors can tour the hatchery grounds), and 567-hectare Mactaquac Provincial Park, which opened in 1969.

The **Mactaquac Generating Station,** on the river's southern bank and just off the TransCanada Highway, offers free guided tours mid-May to early September, daily 9 A.M.–4 P.M.; call 462-3800 for details. Below the dam, the **Mactaquac Visitor Interpretation Centre,** tel. 506/363-3021, releases 300,000 salmon fry annually. It's open mid-May to August, daily 9 A.M.–4 P.M.; guided tours are offered in July and August.

## Mactaquac Provincial Park

This provincial park showpiece, 24 km upriver from Fredericton on Highway 105, tel. 506/363-4747 or 506/363-4926, was created from prime forest and farmland. The wooded campground has 305 sites ($17 unserviced, $19.50 with electrical hookups) with kitchen shelters, hot showers, a launderette, and a campers' store fronting the Mactaquac Lake Basin. There's also a restaurant, supervised beaches, hiking trails, bike rentals, picnic areas, and fishing streams. Marinas are available for both motorboats and sailboats. The park

# HOUSEBOATING THE SAINT JOHN

Boating on the Saint John River's historic waters is an idyllic and popular pastime, and houseboating is a pleasant and memorable way to do it. As you glide down the Saint John, you'll pass fields of strawberries and apple orchards along the banks, and small islands in midstream—inhabited only by occasional cows and horses barged over by riverfront farmers to graze.

### Where to Boat

Lope along anywhere for 300 km between Fredericton and Oak Point. Secluded coves and offshoot waterways abound. The aroma of apple blossoms drifts over the river late May and early June. During June, Fredericton celebrates the **River Jubilee,** and Gagetown has a **Craft Festival** late in the month. Barbecues and food vendors are part of Oak Point's **Fun Days** in mid-August. At Gagetown during mid-September, country-fair fixings are the highlights of the **Queens County Fair.** Gagetown Creek ambles off the main river; you can tie up at the public marina or at the backyard pier of Steamers Stop Inn. At **Middle Island** near Fredericton, the beach on a peninsula is lapped by shallow, warm water, and ospreys, bald eagles, and blue herons soar overhead. **Grimross Island,** above Gagetown, is populated by goats; you'll hear them bleating as your houseboat glides past.

Houseboat operators will outline areas that are off limits, including **Grand Lake,** where sudden, strong storms and high waves can engulf a boat,

and the river stretch below **Oak Point,** another treacherous area for houseboats.

### Renting a Houseboat

Tidy, compact houseboats have all the trappings and comforts of home in a scaled-down package. In general, the main deck has a forecabin equipped with one or more foldaway beds. Heading aft, you'll typically find a galley with a fridge, stove, oven, small sink, and cupboards stocked with cooking and dining utensils. Next comes the head with a hot shower, sink, and flush toilet. The sitting room brings up the rear with couches that convert to foldaway beds. Upstairs, a railed sundeck with chairs and space to sunbathe extends the houseboat's full length.

Expect to pay around $1,400–1,800 a week during July and August, and from $1,200 a week in June and September. Advance reservations are wise, especially during peak summer season. A 20–25 percent deposit is required, with the balance to be paid upon picking up the boat. Renting a houseboat is like renting a car. You'll get a full tank of gasoline to start and refill along the way. Marinas with **fuel stops** are at Fredericton, Oromocto, Jemseg, Cambridge-Narrows, Codys, and Gagetown.

The river's two rental companies are **Pioneer Princess Houseboat Rentals,** tel. 506/459-2515, and **Bayshore Houseboat Vacations,** tel. 506/757-8759.

is open mid-May to mid-October. There's a $4-per-vehicle day-use fee to enter the park.

The setting's pièce de résistance is the challenging 18-hole **Mactaquac Provincial Park Golf Course.** Ranked as one of Canada's top 10 public courses, greens fee is a reasonable $42 on weekends and holidays, $36 on weekdays, and $22 at twilight. For reservations call 506/363-4926.

The nearby **Holiday Inn Fredericton,** 35 Mactaquac Rd. (a stone's throw from exit 274 off the TransCanada Highway), tel. 506/363-5111 or 800/561-5111, www.holidayinnfredericton.com, has 82 rooms and suites ($79–209 single or

double), with some nonsmoking, housekeeping units available, a dining room with lounge, and a health center with a heated indoor pool, hot tub, and exercise deck. Six higher-priced two-bedroom chalets are also on the manicured grounds.

## KINGS LANDING HISTORICAL SETTLEMENT

A marvelous counterpoint to Caraquet's Acadian Historical Village, this grand-scale provincial heritage site meticulously re-creates a typical 19th-century Anglo settlement with authentic buildings, demonstrations, and events. Bring

BOB RACE

**old sawmill at Kings Landing**

comfortable walking shoes, as the site spreads across 121 hectares (299 acres) with 60 vintage houses and buildings in a beautiful setting alongside the Saint John River, 35 km west of Fredericton (take exit 253 from Highway 2). The mood is easy and down-home, and if you'd like to dress the part, the staff can provide costumes; ask at the main gate or call the costume department at 506/363-5090.

At each of the authentically detailed buildings—among them a sawmill, farmhouses, a school, forge, and printing office—informative costumed "residents" depict rural New Brunswick life as it was lived in the 1800s. Demonstrations include horse shoeing, metal forging, cloth spinning and weaving, and farming. Special events include an Agricultural Fair in late August, the Provincial Town Criers' Competition in early September, and a Harvest Festival in early October to close out the season.

The Kings Head Inn restaurant here, tel. 506/363-4950, serves hearty 19th-century fare and offers summer dinner-theatre Fri.–Sun. (around $35 per person; call 363-4999 for reservations). Fast food is available at a cafeteria at the Visitor Reception Centre.

Kings Landing is open late May/early June to mid-October, daily 10 A.M.–5 P.M.; it's also open some dates off-season for special events, such as Christmas in the Valley in early December and Victoria Day weekend in late May. Admission is $12 adults, $10 seniors, $7 for ages 6–16, $30 for a family. For more information, call 506/363-4999.

## TO GRAND FALLS/ GRAND-SAULT

West from Kings Landing, the TransCanada Highway and Highway 105 follow the river along one of its loveliest stretches. Tourism New Brunswick refers to this stretch of highway as the **River Valley Scenic Drive.** The Saint John is wide and blue, bounded by green fields and forests of maple and hemlock. Handsome, elm-shaded **Woodstock** is an agricultural service center for this rich potato-producing region. North of Woodstock at **Hartland,** Highway 103 crosses the Saint John River on the **world's longest covered bridge.** Completed in 1901, the bridge measures 391 meters (1,283 feet).

### Grand Falls

The otherwise placid Saint John River becomes a frothing white torrent when it plunges 23 meters over the stony cataract which gave Grand Falls, or Grand-Sault, its name. Below the falls, which have been harnessed to produce hydroelectric power, the tremendous force of the river has worn a two-km-long, horse-shoe-shaped gorge through 70-meter-high rock walls. Here, the river is at its narrowest, and the gorge's bottleneck impedes the water's force. The river pushes through the narrows in tumultuous rapids, like pent-up champagne bursting from the bottle. The erosive power of flowing water and gravel have also combined to scoop out the "Wells-in-Rocks," circular potholes up to nine meters deep.

In town, **Malabeam Reception Centre,** off Front Street, tel. 506/475-7767, makes a convenient starting point. From the center's rear windows, you'll see the thundering cataracts tumbling through the gorge. The bridge that extends east from Broadway and crosses the gorge is another good vantage point from which to view the falls; paths lead down to the river from there. If you're lucky, you'll also see a rainbow hovering over the falls.

From there, follow a series of two-km-long footpaths alongside the gorge to **La Rochelle,** the second visitor center at riverfront Centennial Park on Chapel Street. Here, a rock staircase leads down to the cataract edge, where the agitated river swirls in the rocky wells. Locals say the scene was far more impressive in the 1920s, before the province diverted the river's force for a hydroelectric plant and dam. Regardless, don't expect impressive, year-round waterfall shows; the river level is lowest during late summer and highest between March and early June.

The gorge's footpaths and staircases are walkable year-round (be careful when it's wet); the visitor centers are open daily 9 A.M.–9 P.M. from early June to early Sept., then to 5 P.M. until early October.

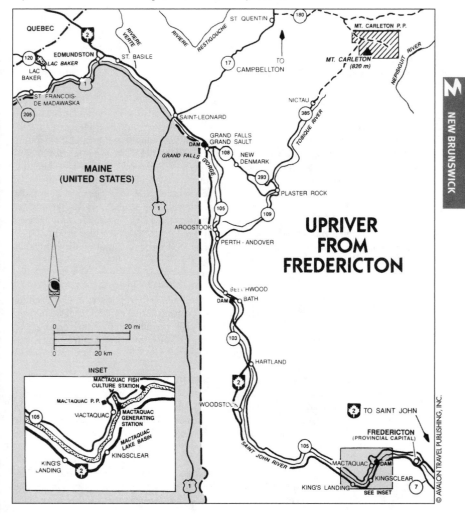

NEW BRUNSWICK

© AVALON TRAVEL PUBLISHING, INC.

In late June or early July, Grand Falls celebrates the area's economic mainstay with the **Potato Festival.**

Several well-priced lodgings in Grand Falls make the town all the more appealing for overnight stays. The best choice is **Auberge Pres du Lac Inn** on the TransCanada Highway, tel. 506/473-1300 or 888/473-1300, www.presdulac.com, featuring 100 rooms ($90 single, $95 double), an indoor pool, a small fitness room, a sauna, and a manmade pond with pedal boats. Save a few bucks and stay at **Coté Bed and Breakfast,** centrally located at 575 Broadway Boulevard, tel. 506/473-1415 or 877/444-2683, which charges from $65 for a single, $75 for a double, including breakfast that includes delicious homemade jams.

# EDMUNDSTON AND VICINITY

Edmundston, considered the "capital" of Madawaska, was by far the largest town hereabout before amalgamating with Saint-Basile and adjoining hamlets into a single municipal entity in 1998. The town's population now numbers around 12,000. Originally settled by Acadian refugees on the site of a Malecite Indian Village, it was first called Petit Sault for the rapids here at the confluence of the Saint John and Madawaska rivers. The town was renamed after a visit in 1850 by Sir Edmund Head, the provincial governor.

## Sights and Recreation

For an insight into the area's checkered history, stop in at the **Madawaska Historical Museum,** 195 Blvd. Hébert (at the junction with the TransCanada Highway, exit 18), tel. 506/737-5282. It's open daily 9 A.M.–8 P.M. in summer; the rest of the year, Wed.–Thurs. 7–10 P.M., Sunday 1–5 P.M. Admission is $1. But to truly experience Madawaska's Acadian-flavored culture, come for the five-day **la Foire Brayonne,** the weekend closest to August 1. Over 100,000 people show up for the celebration of Brayon foods, music, dance, sports, and other entertainment. Call 506/739-6608 for more information.

In summer, golf is popular at the 18-hole **Edmundston Golf Club,** 579 Victoria (accessed via Highway 2, exits 15A or 18), tel. 506/735-7266. **Petit Témis Linear Interprovincial Park** follows the bank of the Madawaska River and connects Edmundston, Saint-Jacques, the New Brunswick Botanical Garden (see below), and Cabano (Québec) with a 62-km bicycle trail. You can rent bicycles from **Jessome's La Source du Sport,** 12 D'Amours St., tel. 506/735-6292.

## Accommodations and Food

The ritziest hotel in town is the large **Howard Johnson Hotel & Convention Centre,** 100 Rice St., tel. 506/739-7321 or 800/654-2000, www.hojo.com. It has an indoor pool, hot tub, sauna, laundry facilities, restaurant, lounge, and 103 rooms ($80 single, $85 double). Other large hotels include **Hotel République,** 919 Canada Rd., tel. 506/735-5525 or 800/563-2489, www.cityhotels.ca, offering 133 rooms ($80–88 single or double) along with a restaurant, nightclub, game room, indoor pool, hot tub, and sauna; and **Comfort Inn,** 5 Bateman Ave., tel. 506/739-8361 or 800/668-4200, www.choicehotels.ca, with 81 rooms for $94 single, $98 double.

For a taste of the local French cuisine and a good selection of seafood, try **La Terrasse,** at 100 Rice St., tel. 506/739-7321, in the Howard Johnson Hotel. Dinner entrees run $13–22.

Fast food and shopping are available right off the TransCanada Highway (exit 18) at **Brunswick Shopping Centre,** 180 Blvd. Hébert, tel. 506/739-9379. In and around the mall you'll find a Shoppers Drug Mart, several clothing stores, a bank, gift store, McDonald's, Subway, KFC, and the ubiquitous Tim Horton's. The town's **Visitor Information Centre** is just across the parking lot.

## Saint-Jacques

North of Edmundston, about halfway to the Québec border, is Saint-Jacques, home of **Les Jardins de la République Provincial Park,** Rue Principale, tel. 506/735-2541. To get there, take Highway 2 for eight km north of Edmundston, exit 8. The park offers an eclectic mix of sights, including the **New Brunswick Botanical Garden,** tel. 506/737-5383. If you've admired the flower-filled setting at the Montréal Botanical

# RÉPUBLIQUE DU MADAWASKA

War is hell, and often it spawns subsequent conflicts, like red hot coals that tumble from a central conflagration and flare up anew. The République du Madawaska, the independent Acadian republic based in Edmundston alongside the Maine border, had such an origin.

The republic owes its creation (in a roundabout way, you might say) to the American Revolution. The rebellious Americans won the war, and England lost the Eastern Seaboard colonies. But a few loose ends remained. A few international boundaries between Canada and the U.S. remained hazy, one of which was the border between New Brunswick and Maine.

### No Border, No Peace

Border delineation was a slow process that took a toll among settlers. Pity the Acadians. First they had been forced to resettle by the Acadian Deportation. Some fled to New Brunswick's remote forested northwestern corner where they worked as lumberjacks and hoped to find peace. But by 1839, disputes over contested lumber rights pitted the Acadian lumberjacks against Maine loggers, and once again the Acadians found themselves in confrontations with the Anglos. Fistfights ensued. As the dispute picked up steam, it became known as the **Pork and Beans War,** named ironically for the lumbermen's ubiquitous main meal. Neither Canada nor the U.S. officially recognized the dispute. At least, not until an Anglo lumberman named John Baker, from Baker Brook near Edmundston, set the boundaries of the jutting thumb of land that pokes oddly into Maine and proclaimed the area the "American Republic of Madawaska." High treason, cried the British, who jailed him for several months.

### England Takes a Hand

Treason or not, Baker's outrageous deed riveted England's interest on the area—not particularly in the remote western hinterlands, but rather on the upper Saint John River valley from Grand Falls/Grand-Sault to Woodstock. Loyalists had settled the richly fertile riverbanks, and believed they resided in Canada. But rumors assigned the area to Maine.

England's honor was at stake. Years before, the British had lost face at Castine, Maine, south of Bangor. Fleeing Loyalists had settled there as the Revolutionary War wound down, but were soon forced to relocate to St. Andrews—some 200 kilometers farther up the coast—when the international border between New Brunswick and Maine was officially set at the St. Croix River.

The Pork and Beans War dragged on unmercifully, and by 1842 it had turned into the larger international Aroostook War, named for the Aroostook River (which originates in Maine and empties into the Saint John River near Perth-Andover).

Both nations were ready for war. Troops for both sides were mounted at Aroostook. England's Sir John Harvey and American Gen. Winfield Scott drew up a hasty truce, and the **Webster-Ashburton Treaty** settled the boundary issue. The U.S. gained more than half of the contested land, but New Brunswick won the Saint John River valley with a few kilometers to spare on the western bank. Baker's American Republic of Madawaska dropped out of sight and reemerged as the Acadians' République du Madawaska, named for New Brunswick's major players in the issue. Regardless, the oddly shaped wedge of land between Québec Province and the Saint John River remained part of New Brunswick.

### The République Lives On

Madawaska as a mythical republic and political oddity still thrives. The republic flies its own flag (an eagle on a white background, overhung by six red stars representing the republic's six founding ethnic groups), and the titular governor, who doubles as Edmundston's mayor, rules the area. The regional culture evolved as an amalgamation of several Acadian groups (collectively known as the Brayons) with a distinct dialect and lifestyle. Summertime's Foire Brayonne festival at Edmundston sums up the area's heritage flavor; the event has been so successful that the tourists arriving from throughout North America and even Europe outnumber by a wide margin the illustrious Brayons.

Garden in Montréal, you will see a resemblance here. The formal garden complex on 17 hectares was designed by the same skilled Michel Marceau. The garden brims with 60,000 plants of 1,500 species. Roses, perennials, and rhododendrons bloom among the prolific posies in nine gardens, all orchestrated with classical music in a romantic vein. Admission is $5 adults, $4.50 seniors and students, $2.50 children 7–12, $12.50 families. It's open May–Sept., daily 9 A.M.–dusk.

Also at the park is the **Antique Automobile Museum,** tel. 506/735-2525, a fascinating collection of vintage and rare cars including a primitive 1905 Russell, a 1933 Rolls-Royce Phantom, and one of the only 2,880 Bricklins that were manufactured during New Brunswick's brief experiment with auto production. Admission is adults $3, children $1.50; open year-round.

Nearby, **Camping Panoramique,** tel. 506/739-6544, has 150 sites at $16–18, open May through October.

The provincial **Visitor Information Centre,** tel. 506/735-2747, is located on the TransCanada Highway.

## Lac-Baker

Lac-Baker is in New Brunswick's remote northwestern corner, near where the Saint John River flows into the province from the northern reaches of Maine. Here you'll find all the quiet woodlands you could ever want, as well as the rustic **Camping RJ Belanger,** off Highway 120 at 510 Church Road, tel. 506/992-2136. The lakeshore complex lies several kilometers north of the river and has eight cabins (from $50 single or double, serviced campsites ($13–15), a dining room and canteen, and swimming, canoeing, and kayaking.

## MOUNT CARLETON PROVINCIAL PARK

From Perth-Andover on the Saint John River, Highway 109 branches off northeast into the interior to Plaster Rock. From there, Highway 385 continues another 84 km northeast to 17,000-hectare Mount Carleton Provincial Park. The park can also be reached off Highway 17, which runs between the TransCanada Highway at Saint-Léonard and Campbellton on the Baie des Chaleurs (take Highway 180 east from St.-Quentin).

This provincial park, surrounding the Maritimes' highest mountain, encompasses a lot of wilderness and takes some determination to reach. Count on a two- to three-hour drive to reach the park entrance from either the Trans-Canada Highway or Campbellton.

If you're interested in climbing the mountain (elev. 820 meters/2,700 feet), wear sturdy shoes, and bring a jacket to combat the winds. The easiest, marked ascent goes up a 4.4-km trail through a spruce, fir, and yellow birch forest. The mountain's peak rises above the tree line and the view is marvelous, overlooking the adjacent mountains and lakes from a summit strewn with mountain cranberries and wild blueberries. Other trails in the 62-km network include a 300-meter path to Williams Falls.

Incidentally, Mt. Carleton's peak divides the provincial watershed. The waters on the summit's western side drain into the Saint John and Tobique Rivers and eventually reach the Bay of Fundy; on the peak's east side, the waters drain to the Nepisiguit River and the Baie des Chaleurs.

The park's main campground has 88 campsites ($15), toilets, showers, kitchen shelters, a dump station for RVs, a playground, boat-launching ramp, and unsupervised swimming on Nictau Lake. Other campgrounds include a group camp, two primitive walk-in campgrounds of eight to nine sites (also along the lakeshore), and a four-site backcountry campground.

The park is open year-round; winter activities include snowmobiling and cross-country skiing. For more information, call the ranger office at 506/235-0793.

# Fundy Coast

## Introduction

The natural beauty of New Brunswick's Fundy coast is sublime. Sea breezes bathe the shore in crisp, salt air, and the sun illuminates the seascape colors with a clarity that defies a painter's palette. Wildflowers bloom with abandon, nourished by the moist coastal air. And fog, thick as cotton, sometimes envelopes the region during the summer. Yet despite the luxuriant growth, there's a notable absence of ragweed. Visitors who suffer from hay fever are among the coast's most frequent vacationers. (Anything below 1.00 on the ragweed index translates as easy breathing; here, the index registers just 0.23.)

### Fundy Tides

Imagine the scene. An unearthly stillness pervades. Seabirds wheel and dart across the horizon.

Suddenly, the birds cry out in a chorus as the incoming tide approaches. The tidal surge, which began halfway around the world in the southern Indian Ocean, quietly and relentlessly pours into the Fundy's mouth, creating the highest tides on the planet. Fishing boats are lifted from the muddy sea floor, and whales in pursuit of silvery herring hurry along the summertime currents, their mammoth hulks buoyed by the 100 billion tons of seawater that gush into the long bay between New Brunswick and Nova Scotia.

The cycle from low to high tide takes a mere six hours. The tide peaks, in places high enough to swamp a four-story building, and then begins to retreat. As the sea level drops, coastal peninsulas and rocky islets emerge from the froth, veiled in seaweed. The sea floor reappears, shiny as shellac and littered with sea urchins, periwinkles,

© ANDREW HEMPSTEAD

Fundy fishing boat

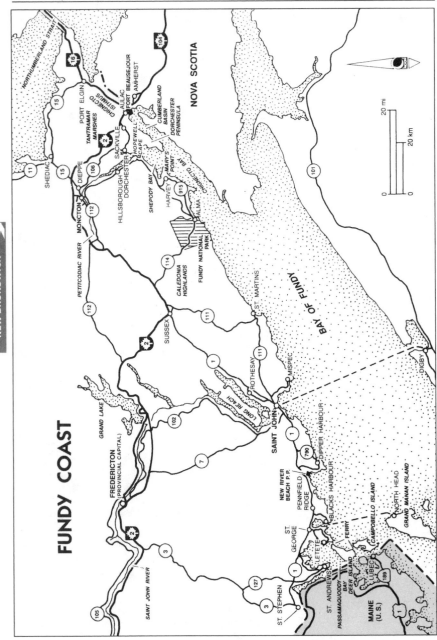

# FUNDY COAST

NEW BRUNSWICK

and shells. Where no one walked just hours ago, local children run and skip on the beaches, pausing to retrieve tidal treasures. New Brunswickers take the Fundy tides for granted. For visitors, it's an astounding show.

The incoming sea first smacks against the Fundy Isles at the entrance to the bay, creating riptides, big waves, and swirling currents. At peak tide, the world's second-largest whirlpool, dubbed the Old Sow, swirls here just off Deer Island. The high tide lashes at the mainland, foaming against granite headlands and low-lying peninsulas from St. Stephen up to Saint John. Beyond Saint John, the bay narrows, and the high tide's relentless pounding of the coastline has carved caves at St. Martins. At Alma, near Fundy National Park, the tide floods the beach, rising a vertical distance of 14 meters. At Hopewell Rocks off Highway 114, the sea rises 16 meters and has sculpted massive, bizarrely shaped pillars crowned with miniature forests.

**Warning:** High tide arrives every 12.5 hours, and the quickly rising sea is *always* treacherous. Tidal times are posted everywhere and warn sightseers away from the seacoast at peak times. Incoming tides are especially formidable during new- and full-moon phases, when the Fundy peaks 20 percent higher than normal. So be aware of tidal schedules and pay careful attention along the seashore to avoid unpleasant surprises.

### Sightseeing Highlights

Many visitors come to New Brunswick's 250-km-long tidal coast to take advantage of the diverse outdoor-recreation possibilities it provides. Kayakers enjoy the complex fringe of bays and inlets. Scuba divers explore the sea depths, which are enriched by the sea's turbulence. Hikers follow the coastline for some of the province's most challenging trekking. Birdwatchers come to the region for its abundance of migratory birds, which soar through the province's Atlantic flyway from Mary's Point to Grand Manan.

**Saint John** has the Fundy coast's best supply of lodgings, shopping, and nightlife. **St. Andrews** and **Sackville** anchor opposite ends of the coastline and add a rural aristocratic flavor with quality accommodations, meals, and historical ambience. The Fundy Isles settlements offer smaller shares of creature comforts; advance reservations are a must, especially on **Grand Manan,** the province's foremost naturalist destination. In between are small coastal towns, seaports, and **Fundy National Park.**

## HISTORY
### Early French Settlement

In 1604, a French exploration party led by Samuel de Champlain sailed into the Bay of Fundy and named the Saint John River. After rejecting the site of the present city of Saint John as a proper spot for a settlement, the group spent the bitterly cold winter of 1604–05 on Douchet's Island in the St. Croix River. Champlain complained in his diary: "Winter in this country lasts six months." The encampment barely survived; hunger and scurvy claimed 35 lives. (Douchet's Island can be seen from the highway about nine km northwest of St. Andrews.) The following spring, they packed up and headed for Nova Scotia's more agreeable side of the Fundy. There they established Port Royal, the early hub of "Acadia," the name they gave this part of eastern Canada.

From the Port Royal base, Champlain explored the bay and named Grand Manan and Campobello islands. Acadia's development followed. The merchant Charles de la Tour set up a trading post at Saint John Harbour's northern end. French settlers, who knew the Bay of Fundy

Samuel de Champlain

BOB RACE

as the Baie Française, founded settlements along the coast from the Sackville area to Campobello Island. In the upper Fundy, sea marshes were reclaimed as fertile farmland with *aboideaux*, a system of dikes that opened at low tide, allowing river water to drain, and closed at high tide, shutting the sea out.

## Strategic Chignecto Isthmus

Acadian settlements were densest on the Chignecto Isthmus. A hundred French families (ancestors of today's Maritime Acadian population) reclaimed 207 square km of land across the Tantramar Marshes. Tantramar is a corruption of *tintamarre* (hubbub), the early settlers' description of the ceaseless racket raised by the local wildfowl. More Acadians fled into the area after the Treaty of Utrecht awarded most of the Nova Scotia peninsula to England in 1713. The British dominated Nova Scotia, and the Acadians found life safer across the Fundy.

The French tried to prevent the British from crossing the Chignecto Isthmus corridor with Forts Gaspéreau and Beauséjour, which faced England's Fort Lawrence on the isthmus. France's defense might have worked had it not been for Thomas Pichon, the secretary to the Abbé le Loutre at Fort Beauséjour, who passed military strategies on to the British. In 1755, the British sailed into Chignecto Bay with 2,000 troops. The French forts quickly fell; Fort Beauséjour was renamed Fort Cumberland, and Fort Gaspéreau was demolished (its ruins still lie at the end of Fort Street in the town of Port Elgin).

## Resettling the Anglos

The British quickly reinforced the mouth of the Saint John River on the Fundy with Fort Frederick, situated near an earlier French trading post. Advertisements for pro-Crown settlers were posted in the colonies farther south, and New England planters immigrated north to Campobello Island, St. Andrews, and Sackville. Other immigrant convoys landed at St. Stephen, Grand Manan Island, and Dorchester. A Loyalist infusion to St. Andrews arrived from Castine, Maine, after international conflicts forced their resettlement farther up the Fundy coast.

Simultaneously, insurrection stirred in England's colonies on the eastern seaboard. In a flare of pre-Revolutionary defiance, patriot privateers from the rebellious New England colonies attacked Saint John and destroyed Fort Frederick. Fort Howe replaced the demolished fort three years later.

At Sackville, the New England planters and Yorkshire immigrants took the place of the expelled Acadians. The town's Mount Allison University, begun as an academy in 1843, grew to a full-fledged university by 1886. The New Englanders also settled the shipbuilding communities of Alma and St. Martins.

At St. Andrews, shipbuilding and trade with the West Indies greased the economic wheels until 1850. When the era of wooden ships ended, the town made an easy transition into a resort center. The Shiretown Inn opened in 1881; the first Algonquin Hotel burned and was rebuilt in 1915.

# GETTING AROUND

The Fundy coast is a paradox: it's at once the most- and least-developed part of the province. Saint John—the province's largest city and major port—sits at the midpoint. To either side, the coastline is remotely settled and wonderfully wild.

The region is best considered as two distinct areas, with Saint John interposed between them. The **Lower Fundy,** situated at the bay's southwestern end, includes St. Andrews—the province's definitive resort town on sheltered Passamaquoddy Bay—and the Fundy Isles, the archipelago (made up of Grand Manan, Deer, and Campobello islands) that dangles into the sea alongside Maine's northernmost coast. The **Upper Fundy** area, situated at the coast's northeastern end, takes in Fundy National Park, Sackville, and several coastal bird sanctuaries.

If you're driving, you'll probably enter Saint John via the TransCanada Highway (Highway 2), then Highway 1; from St. Stephen at the U.S. border; on Highway 7 from Fredericton; or on one of the expressways from Moncton. If you're traveling the 125 km from Fredericton to St. Stephen via Highway 3, be forewarned that gas stations and other services thin out quickly after you leave the TransCanada Highway.

The Saint John area is spliced with an excellent road system; beyond city limits, traffic moves on narrower, two-lane roads. If time is a consideration, use the TransCanada Highway whenever possible, especially as a high-speed access route to the bird sanctuaries on the Chignecto Isthmus.

If you have the time, by all means leave the main highway and amble down the scenic local roads that loop along the shoreline. Note that between St. Martins and Fundy National Park, no roads access the coast. Transportation is forced far inland, with the most expedient route being along Highway 1 and the TransCanada Highway (Highway 2).

# Lower Fundy Coast and the Fundy Isles

## ST. ANDREWS

An immensely attractive seaside town, St. Andrews (pop. 1,800), the province's first—and now definitive—resort town, sits at the end of a peninsula dangling into tranquil Passamaquoddy Bay, sheltered from the tumultuous Fundy by Deer Island and Letang Peninsula. The resort crowd revels in St. Andrews's version of old-time, velvet-glove Canadiana, especially visible at the Algonquin Hotel.

The seaport rivals Grand Manan Island as the area's major destination. Naturalists come for ecological programs sponsored by the Sunbury Shores, a private environmental group, and tourists enjoy the picturesque lodgings and the plethora of crafts shops and small dining places.

### History

The town has a special, almost sacred historic status among New Brunswickers. It was founded by Loyalists who sailed into the Fundy and followed the coastal curve to the peninsula's tip in 1783. The courageous journey was a technical wonder. The settlers, originally from England's former colonies farther south, had moved to what they believed was Canada at Castine, Maine. But a subsequent international boundary decision forced them to relocate once again. The pro-Crown settlers reloaded convoys with all their possessions, disassembled houses and reloaded the structures on barges, and set sail for a safe homeland.

St. Andrews was their creation. Most every street is named for George III or one of his kin. A few Loyalist houses remain and sit cheek-to-jowl

with similar New England-style houses fronting narrow residential streets.

### Historic Buildings

St. Andrews is a historic gem. Nearly half the buildings in the town core date back 100 years or more, and most have been maintained or restored to mint condition. Water Street is the main avenue, following the bay shore through the five-block commercial district. Pick up a copy of *A Guide to Historic St. Andrews* (25 cents) at one of the tourist information offices. The guide details a walking tour with over 30 buildings of historical or architectural significance.

The **St. Andrews Blockhouse National Historic Site,** tel. 506/529-4270 or 887-6000, lies along Joe's Point Road, a western extension of Water Street. The fortification, the last survivor of 12 similar structures, was intended to protect the town from attack in the War of 1812, but nary a shot was fired in battle at this site. The interior depicts the War of 1812 era with re-created soldiers' quarters. The site is open June through August daily, 9 A.M.–8 P.M., and the first half of September daily, 9 A.M.– 5 P.M. Admission is $1 for adults, free for children. The adjacent **Centennial Park** is a pleasant spot for a picnic.

In the town's center, the **Sheriff Andrews House Historic Site,** 63 King St., tel. 506/529-5080, offers an attractive visual insight into the early Loyalist era. Costumed guides will show you around the county sheriff's Georgian-style 1820 house, which is simply but elegantly furnished in local period style. The house is open late

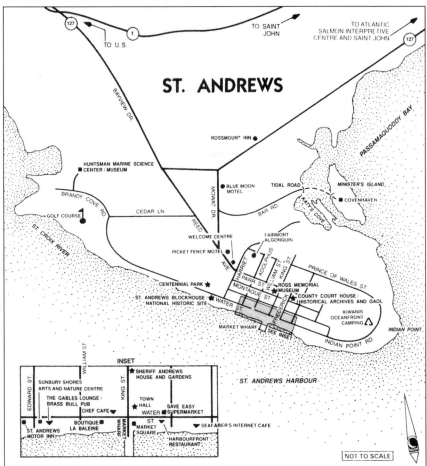

June to early September, Mon.–Sat. 9:30 A.M.–4:30 P.M., Sun. 1–4:30 P.M. Admission is free, though donations are appreciated.

Another national historic site, the white-painted **Charlotte County Court House** on Frederick Street, tel. 506/529-3843, dates to 1840 and is thought to be the country's oldest courthouse in continuous use. It's open July–August, Mon.–Sat. 9:30 A.M.–noon and 1–4:30 P.M. The adjacent gaol (jail), built in 1832, houses the Charlotte County Archives.

The **Ross Memorial Museum,** 188 Montague St., tel. 506/529-5124, in an early-19th-

century neoclassical brick home, preserves the furniture, porcelains, rugs, mirrors, paintings, and other items of Henry and Sarah Ross, discerning collectors of antiques and objets d'art. It's open Mon.–Sat. 10 A.M.–4:30 P.M. in summer, Tues.–Sat. 10 A.M.–noon and 1–4:30 P.M. in fall. Free guided tours are offered.

**Minister's Island Historic Site,** in Passamaquoddy Bay, was where Canadian Pacific Railway magnate William Van Horne built his summer retreat, **Covenhoven.** Completed in 1903, the modest 50-room home was built of locally quarried sandstone. The island is accessi-

ble by a sandbar that's drivable at low tide. Call
506/529-5081 to arrange a tour.

## Tide Watching

St. Andrews not only offers a splendid historical
setting but is also the area's naturalist hub. The
town is a prime place for Fundy watching; for the
best times, check out the high-tide schedules
posted in the shop windows. Then take a seat at
the end of the pier off Water Street and wait for
the show. The tide plows into Passamaquoddy
Bay like water filling a bathtub. On a quiet
evening, you may even *hear* it, gurgling over
rocks and filling in small depressions. And then
the tidal rise ceases, idles for a time, and flows
back out to start all over again.

For an impressive low-tide scene, check out
the beachfront at the St. Andrews Blockhouse,
where the retreating tide bares the sea floor to
reveal a rocky peninsula and pools that had been
fully submerged during high tide. Beachcombers
strolling the shores around St. Andrews may
come across bits of coral and pebbles of polished
flint, neither of which occurs naturally here. Both
were carried as ballast by 18th- and 19th-cen-
tury merchant ships, which loaded themselves
with flint from Dover, England, and coral from
the Caribbean, and then jettisoned these loads
here when they arrived to collect their cargoes
of fish and timber.

## Whale-Watching and Boat Tours

Whale-watching is a popular activity here, and
several companies offer cruises in search of finback, minke, and humpback whales. The *Quod-
dy Link,* tel. 506/529-2600, is a power
catamaran taking visitors on three-hour natu-
ralist-narrated cruises. Light snacks and beverages, and use of binoculars and foul-weather
gear, are included in the price: $46 adults, $40
seniors, $23 kids 14 and under. **Fundy Tide
Runners,** tel. 506/529-4481, offers two-hour
tours four times daily in a 24-foot rigid-hulled
Zodiac. Prices are adults $48, youths 5–13 $23.

Visitors who would rather sail than motor
can book a whale-watching excursion aboard
the tall ship **S/V Cory,** a 72-foot gaff-rigged cut-
ter. You're invited to help hoist the sails or take

the helm as you head out in search of minke,
finback, or humpback whales. Prices are adults
$52, seniors $42, children 3–14 $35, under 3
free. Call 506/529-8116 for information and
reservations. All of the these companies are based
at Market Wharf.

## Activities and Classes

At the **Sunbury Shores Arts and Nature Centre,** 139 Water St., tel. 506/529-3386, displays
watercolors and sculptures for sale. The center
also hosts films, lectures, workshops, concerts,
and other activities focused on arts, crafts, and
natural history. Painting classes, special programs for kids, and free, guided nature walks
are popular. The center is open daily 9 A.M.–5
P.M. May–September.

The **Huntsman Marine Science Centre and
Aquarium,** three km northwest of town center
on Brandy Cove Road, tel. 506/529-1202, is a
nonprofit marine-biology study center that draws
researchers from far and wide. The aquarium is
stocked with hundreds of local fish, crustaceans,
mollusks, and marine plant species. A touch tank
gives children gentle access to intertidal animals,
while seals cavort in the outdoor pool. The facility
is open mid-May to late October; 10 A.M.–6 P.M.
in July and August, shorter hours the rest of the
season. Admission is $5 adults, $3.50 for ages
4–17. The center also offers environmental classes with guest lecturers and field/lab work (around
$700 per week) and scuba sessions in July
($800–950 per week). Contact the center's Pub-
lic Education Department, Brandy Cove, St. Andrews, NB E0G 2X0, tel. 506/529-1220.

## Water Sports

**Seascape Kayak Tours,** based at Market Wharf
at the foot of King Street, tel. 506/529-4866,
offers a variety of sea-kayak classes and guided expeditions around Passamaquoddy Bay. A one-
day introductory skills course costs $95. Tour
packages include a sunset paddle ($35); a half-day
tour ($58); and a four-day, three-night expedition
($420 with meals).

**Katy's Cove,** tel. 506/529-8823, is a privately operated saltwater swimming area with a good
sandy beach at the end of Acadia Drive, close to

© ANDREW HEMPSTEAD

**Fairmont Algonquin**

the Algonquin. The day-use fee is $2 adults, $1 children. Swimming is free at Indian Point, east of downtown, and nearby on the sandy tidal bar leading out to Minister's Island.

## Fairmont Algonquin

In a class by itself among the town's lodgings is the Tudor-style Algonquin, 184 Adolphus St., tel. 506/529-8823 or 800/441-1414, www.fairmont.com, whose expansive, manicured grounds dominate the hill above St. Andrews.

Here are visions of old-time, velvet-glove Canadiana: golfers ambling across the fairways, the tinkling of crystal in the hotel's dining room, and young couples in tennis whites leisurely sipping cool drinks on the veranda. The tony Algonquin and everything about it bespeak gentility and class. Verdant lawns are everywhere, and the hotel is fronted by deftly designed flowerbeds. Within, the public and guest rooms are arrayed with overstuffed furniture, oriental carpets, and gleaming dark furniture. The resort's image is very proper, and so are the members of the staff, who are snappily attired in Scottish ceremonial-style garb, replete with kilts.

The older, main hotel has 184 spacious rooms with large, old-time windows and comfortable period furnishings. Another 54 units (with kitchenettes—perfect for families) are situated in a similarly styled recent addition and are connected by a second-floor walkway to the main hotel. In summer, room rates start at $269 single or double, with suites starting at $349. The resort is open year-round, with off-season rates starting at $149 single or double.

The facilities include dining rooms and lounges, an outdoor pool, tennis courts, a health spa, and squash/racquetball courts. Between the baronial estate and Passamaquoddy Bay is the **Fairmont Algonquin Golf Course,** which was redesigned and practically rebuilt in 2000 to include a string of holes along the water and a new clubhouse. Green fees are $115 for resort guests, $125 for others. For tee times call 506/529-7142.

To get to the Algonquin, turn onto Harriet Street from Reed Avenue (the continuation of Highway 127/Bayview Drive) and watch for Adolphus Street.

## Other Accommodations

In addition to the Algonquin, the town has a splendid assortment of comfortable lodgings, many of them just a short stroll from the historical town center.

The least expensive options are on the access roads into town. These include the **Picket Fence Motel,** 102 Reed Ave., tel. 506/529-8985 ($55 single, $65 double) and, further out toward Saint John, the **Blue Moon Motel,** 310 Mount Dr., tel. 506/529-3245 or 877/534-5271 ($59 single, $69 double).

The **Rossmount Inn,** a provincial heritage inn six km northeast of St. Andrews on Highway 127, tel. 506/529-3351 or 877/529-3351, reflects historic St. Andrews at the town's sumptuous best. Within the three-story mansion are a dining room, lounge, and 18 guest rooms (from $95 single, $125 double) furnished with Victorian antiques. Outdoors, guests congregate on the patio or use the walking trails to explore the expansive, 35-hectare grounds.

Right on the edge of the bay and 200 meters from the heart of the village, **St. Andrews Motor Inn,** 111 Water St., tel. 506/529-4571, is a neat two-story lodging charging $125 single or double, discounted to well under $100 outside summer.

A member of the prestigious Relais & Chateaux group, the **Kingsbrae Arms,** 219 King St., tel. 506/529-1187, www.kingsbrae.com, features nine comfortable guest rooms, all with fireplaces, marble baths, and great bay views. In July and August, a three-night minimum applies, with the rate of $600 for two people including meals.

St. Andrews' most luxurious accommodation is the **Inn on the Hiram Walker Estate,** set on four hectares at 109 Reed Avenue, tel. 506/529-4210 or 800/470-4088, www.walkerestate.com. Once owned by Edward Chandler Walker of Hiram Walker Distillery fame, the chateau-style mansion features nine luxurious guest rooms, a heated outdoor pool, a hot tub, and ocean views. Rates start at US$175, rising to US$275 for the magnificent personal suite once used by Walker. This lodging is one of the few in Atlantic Canada that earns five stars from Canada Select.

Area B&Bs include **Garden Gate Bed and Breakfast,** 364 Montague St., tel. 506/529-4453, fax 506/529-1115, where you can enjoy a non-smoking environment within a lovely late 19th

century home ($79 single, $89 double); **Harris Hatch Inn,** 142 Queen St., tel. 506/529-4713, which occupies a beautiful restored brick home built in 1840 ($85 single, $95 double); or perhaps the **Pansy Patch,** 59 Carleton St., tel. 506/529-3834 or 888/726-7972, www .pansypatch.com, a Canadian heritage property where the nine plush rooms go for $165–250 single or double, including breakfast and afternoon tea.

### Campground

Camping is available close in at **Kiwanis Oceanfront Camping** on Indian Point Road east of town center, tel. 506/529-3439. The unserviced tent sites are $19, while the serviced sites are $23–30. The campground is just a short walk to the beach.

### Food

The **Gables Restaurant,** 143 Water St., tel. 506/529-3440, occupies a choice spot right on the bay. The seafood specials get high marks,

Seafood is a local specialty in St. Andrews.

**NEW BRUNSWICK**

and the wooden deck out back couldn't be more romantic—a great spot for sipping an after-dinner cognac and watching the lights shimmer across the water. The **Historic Chef's Cafe,** 180 Water St., tel. 506/529-8888, dishes up the best breakfasts in town. The atmosphere is casual, with a few tables set on the sidewalk. Continuing east along the waterfront, **Market Square Grill,** 211 Water St., tel. 9506) 529-8241, has a simple, country-style atmosphere. Lunches range $7.50–12; dinners run $13–23. The **Harbourfront Restaurant** at 225 Water Street, tel. 506/529-4887, is a massive eatery, with halibut, sole, and two scallop dishes, all under $20. At the other end of the price spectrum, **Waterfront Takeout,** 40 King St., tel. 506/529-4228, gets rave reviews for its fried clams.

You don't need to be a guest at the Fairmont Algonquin, tel. 506/529-8823, to take advantage of its various eating options, including the **Passamaquoddy Room,** open in summer only for buffet breakfasts, lunches, and dinners. The resort's **Library Lounge** has a casual yet elegant atmosphere and opens to the terrace.

If you'd rather do it yourself, you can pick up groceries at the **Save Easy Supermarket** in the center of town at the corner of Water and Frederick.

### Services and Information

Craft and gift shops abound. Whether you're looking for sweaters, souvenir T-shirts, locally produced pottery, or what-have-you, one of the de rigueur activities in St. Andrews is strolling along Water Street and drifting in and out of the shops. One of the nicest is **Boutique la Baleine,** 173 Water St., tel. 506/529-3926. Across the street, **Cockburn's Corner Drug Store,** 192 Water St., tel. 506/529-3113, carries magazines and the local newspapers.

Entering town from the west, the **St. Andrews Welcome Centre** is at 46 Reed Avenue (hidden in the trees to the left, just beyond the Picket Fence Motel), tel. 506/529-3556. It's open in summer daily, 9 A.M.–6 P.M. Check your email at **Seafarer's Internet Café,** 233 Water St., tel. 506/529-4610, where you'll find high-speed access, coffee and cakes, and friendly owners. It's open daily 9 A.M.–10 P.M.

## ST. GEORGE

The most impressive sight at St. George, 32 km east of St. Andrews, is the thundering granite gorge of **Magaguadavic Falls.** Visitors can park and walk down a staircase beside the falls to watch salmon swimming upstream past a viewing window. The specialty at **Oven Head Salmon Smokers** is Atlantic salmon, smoked to perfection over hickory and oak chips. The smokehouse wholesales to culinary notables such as the Fairmont Algonquin Hotel. If you're interested in picnic ingredients, stop at the retail outlet on Highway 1, open Mon.–Sat. 8 A.M.–5 P.M.

St. George is also the place to turn off Highway 1 for the short drive to the Deer Island ferry terminus at Letete. Highways 772 and 776 lead to Black Bay, picturesque **Blacks Harbour** (terminus for the Grand Manan Island ferry), and a welter of other islets. If you find yourself in Blacks Harbour in early September, don't miss the North American Sardine Packing Championship. Only in the Maritimes!

## DEER AND CAMPOBELLO ISLANDS

The sea swirls mightily around Grand Manan but diminishes in intensity as the currents spin off around the coast of Maine to Deer and Campobello Islands. These two islands hug the neighboring United States so closely that their sovereignty was disputed for decades after the American Revolution; a treaty gave the islands to New Brunswick in the 1840s.

### Getting to the Islands

A free year-round ferry connects Letete, New Brunswick, with Deer Island.

**East Coast Ferries,** tel. 506/747-2159, www.eastcoastferries.nb.ca, schedules hourly crossings 9 A.M.–6 P.M. between Deer and Campobello Islands. The fare for vehicle and driver is $13, plus $2 per passenger (to a maximum of $18 per car).

East Coast Ferries also operates regular crossings June–September, linking Eastport, Maine, with Deer Island. Ferries depart hourly 9 A.M.–6 P.M., with an extra evening crossing (7 P.M.) in July and August. The rate for vehicle and driver is $10; $2 per passenger (maximum $15 per car).

Campobello Island is also accessible by a bridge from Lubec, Maine.

## Deer Island

Wilder and with a lower profile than Campobello, Deer Island is nevertheless reached first from the New Brunswick mainland. It's devoted to fishing and is encircled with herring weirs (stabilized seine nets); other nets create the "world's largest lobster pounds." The **Old Sow,** the largest tidal whirlpool in the Western Hemisphere, can be viewed three hours before high tide from **Deer Island Point Park** at the island's south end.

**Cline Marine Tours,** tel. 506/747-0114 or 800/567-5880, offers three-hour whale-watching cruises departing from Richardson Wharf, Deer Island, mid-June to October. The fare is $45, $22.50 for children 6–12, free for ages 5 and under.

**Gardner House** in Lambert's Cove, tel. 506/747-2462, combines a three-room B&B ($40 single, $50 double) with a steak-and-seafood dining room. In Fairhaven, on the island's west side, **Clam Cove Farm Bed and Breakfast,** tel. 506/747-2025, charges $70 single or double for each of its two suites.

## Campobello Island

Campobello, cloaked in granite, slate, and sandstone, was a favorite retreat of President Franklin Delano Roosevelt. The shingled, green and bell-pepper-red family vacation home is now the main attraction at the **Roosevelt Campobello International Park** on Highway 774 at Welshpool, tel. 506/752-2922. The 34-room interior is furnished with authentic family trappings, made somehow all the more poignant as FDR was stricken with polio while on vacation here. The house is open late May to mid-October, daily 10 A.M.–6 P.M. Admission to the house and grounds is free.

At Herring Cove, near the island's south end, you'll find hiking trails, a two-km-long beach,

**Roosevelt cottage**

BOB RACE

a golf course, and **Herring Cove Provincial Park,** tel. 506/752-7010, with 40 serviced ($21.50) and 35 unserviced ($24) sites; open May to October.

# GRAND MANAN ISLAND

As the Fundy Isles' largest and most southerly island, Grand Manan (pop. 2,600) gets the brunt of the mighty Fundy high tide. Pity the centuries of ships that have been caught in the currents during malevolent storms; near the island, shipwrecks litter the sea floor and pay homage to the tide's merciless power. Four lighthouses atop the island's lofty headland ceaselessly illuminate the sea-lanes and warn ships off the island's shoals.

Apart from the surging tide, Grand Manan is blissfully peaceful. White, pink, and purple lupines and dusty pink wild roses nod with the summer breezes. Windswept spruce, fir, and birch shade the woodland pockets. Amethyst and agate are mixed with pebbles on the beaches at **Whale Cove, Red Point,** and **White Head Island** offshore. Dulse, a nutritious purple seaweed rich in iodine and iron, washes in at **Dark Harbour** on the western coast, and islanders dry and package the briny snack for worldwide consumption.

Offshore, every species of marine life known to the Bay of Fundy congregates in the bay's nutrient-rich mouth. Whales in pursuit of herring schools swim in on incoming currents—the right, finback, humpback, and minke whales cavort in the tempestuous seas. They're at their most numerous when the plankton blooms, mid-July through September.

## Outings

Space is limited (and is always in demand) on the scheduled land and boat tours; always make reservations beforehand.

One of the finest, most well-established sightseeing outfits in town is **Sea Watch Tours** in North Head, tel. 506/662-8552, which runs sightseeing boat tours ($45 for a six-hour trip) to Machias Seal Island, mid-June to early August. Whale-watching tours are scheduled August–September. Also in North Head, **Island Coast Whale Tours,** tel. 506/662-8181, runs four- to five-hour whale-watching/sightseeing cruises twice daily July to September 15. Rates are $45; $42 for seniors, $24 for kids 12 and under.

For sea kayaking, talk to the folks at **Adventure High** in North Head, tel. 506/662-3563 or 800/732-5492. They organize a variety of kayaking, cycling, and hiking trips.

## Bird-Watching

Birds of almost 350 species flutter everywhere in season, and each species has a place on this rock in the sea. Seabirds and waterfowl nest at the **Castalia Marsh** on the island's eastern side. Ducks and geese by the thousands inhabit the **Anchorage Beach** area, where a wet-heath bird sanctuary is speckled with ponds. Expect to see bald eagles and other raptors on the southern cliffs from mid-August through November. The eider, storm petrel, and Atlantic puffin prefer offshore islets.

Bird populations are thickest early April through June and late summer to autumn. A great way to see the birds is by hiking one of the 18 trails totaling 70 km that crisscross the headland. Many wind through bird sanctuaries. Another incredible place for bird-watching is **Machias Seal Island,** the outermost bird-sanctuary island. Boat tours, restricted to a limited number of passengers, depart Grand Manan to see the archipelago's highest concentration of exotic bird species, including razorbill auks, arctic terns, and 900 pairs of nesting Atlantic puffins.

## Accommodations and Camping

Though lodgings have blossomed across the island during recent years, it's smart to book ahead. Among the island's best is the **Compass Rose,** tel. 506/662-8570, a provincial heritage inn atop a lofty, headland edge in North Head with seven guest rooms, each with a private bath ($115 single, $125 double, including full breakfast). The inn is open May to October. Other commendable properties in North Head are the **Surfside Motel,** tel. 506/662-8156 or 877/662-8156, with 28 rooms ($69 single, $73 double), open year-round; and the **Marathon Inn,** tel. 506/662-8144, a historic inn that's been taking in guests since 1871. It has 15 rooms ($64–99 single or double), a dining room, a heated outdoor pool, and a tennis court. It's open May to October.

The **Shorecrest Lodge Country Inn** at North Head, tel. 506/662-3216, accommodates birdwatchers for the late August through September migratory pelagic-bird season. They charge $65–99 single or double for an overnight with continental breakfast; the services of a birding guide cost extra. It's open April–November.

**The Anchorage** at Seal Cove, tel. 506/662-7022, offers 100 serviced ($21.50) or unserviced ($24) campsites with toilets, hot showers, and kitchen shelters; it's open May to October. Reservations are not accepted, so it's wise to call ahead to check on availability.

## Food

For a quick pizza or burger, try the **Fundy House Takeout** in Seal Cove, tel. 506/662-3144; open seven days a week till 11 P.M. In North Head, the **Griff-Inn Restaurant,** tel. 506/662-8360, specializes in seafood and sea views.

For groceries, the **Newton Store** in Grand Harbour is open daily; **High Tide Groceries** in Seal Cove and **Grand Manan IGA** in Woodward's Cove are both closed Sundays.

## Getting There

**Coastal Transport Ltd.,** tel. 506/662-3724, operates a ferry line between Blacks Harbour and Grand Manan's North Head. The 27-km crossing takes about 90 minutes. The car/passenger ferries sail daily year-round. Up to 12 daily departures are scheduled late June to early September; as few as three in the off-season. Toll rates are adults $8.75, children $4.40, vehicles $26.20, bicycles $3, vehicles with trailers or motor homes $6.55 per meter. Expect at least a half-hour wait in line at both ends. If the car ferry fills up quickly, you'll have to keep your place in line for the next one.

## EAST TO SAINT JOHN

In addition to the intrinsic beauty of the coast—with thick forests growing right down to the rocky shoreline—several detours spice up the drive eastward to Saint John.

At **Pennfield Ridge,** a few kilometers northeast of Blacks Harbour, blueberry farms offer roadside stands or fields for do-it-yourself picking.

A good-value accommodation along this stretch of highway is the **Clipper Ship Beach Motel,** tel. 506/755-2211, in a stunning water-front location at Pocologan. The rooms are basic, but at $53 for a single and $58 for a double, it's the location you pay for. Open March–November. A few kilometers beyond, **New River Beach Provincial Park,** tel. 506/755-4042, lies alongside the highway and has picnic tables, a long, curving sandy beach, hiking trails through bogs and spruce woodlands, and boat-launching facilities. The 100 campsites are open May to October; there's a day-use fee for access to the beach.

Continuing toward Saint John, **Point Lepreau Nuclear Generating Station** is off Highway 790 at the end of a broad peninsula jutting into the Fundy. It opened in 1980 as Canada's first nuclear-power station. Now supplying New Brunswick with 30 percent of its power needs, the facility is slated for a massive refurbishment in the next few years. Call the public affairs office at 506/659-2220, ext. 6433, for tour details. A three-km, wheelchair-accessible nature trail starts at the information center.

## Saint John and Vicinity

Saint John (pop. 68,000) ranks as New Brunswick's largest city, its major port, and its principal industrial center. It is also Canada's largest city in terms of area, sprawling across 321 square km. The city perches on steep hills, laid out southwest to northeast across two peninsulas that almost mesh, like two hands about to meet in a handshake. The setting is among Atlantic Canada's most unusual—Saint John looks east across the spacious Saint John Harbour to the Bay of Fundy and is backed on the west by the confluence of the Saint John River and Kennebecasis Bay. You may recognize parts of Saint John and neighboring communities from the movie *Children of a Lesser God,* which was filmed here in the summer and fall of 1985.

Saint John began as a collection of small Loyalist settlements. Today these settlements maintain their identities in the form of neighborhoods within greater Saint John. This accounts for numerous street-name duplications, a confusing fact of life you will have to deal with as you sightsee across the oddly laid-out city. For example, one Charlotte Street runs through the city's historic part, while another Charlotte Street may be found in western Saint John. It helps to keep a map handy, or just ask: the locals are sympathetic to the visitor's confusion.

The city today doesn't exude much vitality. With the local economy in a slump, much of the downtown area is beginning to feel like a ghost town. Though the Market Square/King Square corridor is buffed up for tourists, a few blocks outside this core area you'll find streets and buildings curiously devoid of activity; modern restaurants nearly empty; struggling all-ages nightclubs relying on kids as their primary clientele. It seems as if most of the adults have packed up and gone elsewhere.

## HISTORY

On June 24, 1604, the feast day of St. John the Baptist, French explorer Samuel de Champlain sailed into the harbor area and named the river in the saint's honor. He dismissed the site, however,

NEW BRUNSWICK

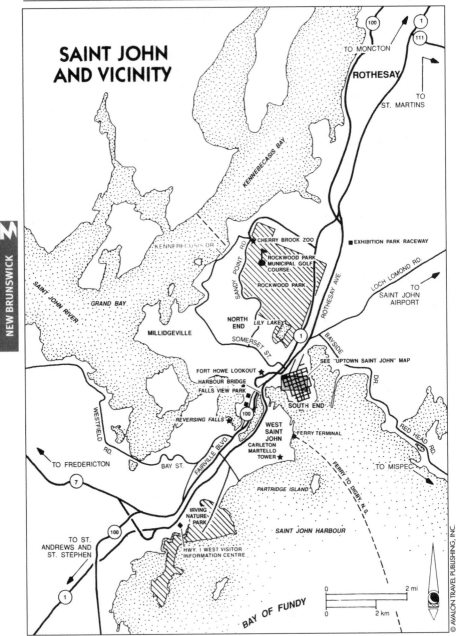

## SAINT JOHN AND VICINITY

NEW BRUNSWICK

TO MONCTON

ROTHESAY

TO ST. MARTINS

KENNEBECASIS BAY

KENNEBECASIS DR.

CHERRY BROOK ZOO

EXHIBITION PARK RACEWAY

ROCKWOOD PARK MUNICIPAL GOLF COURSE

ROCKWOOD PARK

SANDY POINT RD.

ROTHESAY AVE.

LOCH LOMOND RD.

TO SAINT JOHN AIRPORT

SAINT JOHN RIVER

GRAND BAY

MILLIDGEVILLE

NORTH END

LILY LAKE

SOMERSET ST.

BAYSIDE

SEE "UPTOWN SAINT JOHN" MAP

FORT HOWE LOOKOUT

HARBOUR BRIDGE

FALLS VIEW PARK

SOUTH END

RED HEAD RD.

WESTFIELD RD.

REVERSING FALLS

WEST SAINT JOHN

CARLETON MARTELLO TOWER

FERRY TERMINAL

TO MISPEC

TO FREDERICTON

BAY ST.

FAIRVILLE BLVD.

PARTRIDGE ISLAND

FERRY TO DIGBY, N.S.

TO ST. ANDREWS AND ST. STEPHEN

IRVING NATURE PARK

HWY. 1 WEST VISITOR INFORMATION CENTRE

SAINT JOHN HARBOUR

BAY OF FUNDY

0   2 mi

0   2 km

© AVALON TRAVEL PUBLISHING, INC.

as unsuitable for settlement, and continued on to a disastrous winter farther west on the St. Croix River near St. Andrews.

Saint John as an Anglo settlement began with 14,000 Loyalists, who arrived by ship in 1783. The refugees quickly settled the fledgling town and spread out to create Carleton west of the harbor and Parrtown to the east. The city was incorporated in 1785, making it Canada's oldest. The port was an immediate economic success, and the **Carleton Martello Tower** was built to guard the harbor's shipping approaches during the War of 1812.

The city's next great wave of immigrants brought the Irish, who were fleeing poverty and persecution at home. Saint John's reputation as Canada's most Irish city began with a trickle of Irish in 1815; before the wave subsided in 1850, the city's 150,000 Irish outnumbered the Loyalists, and Saint John's religious complexion changed from Protestant to Roman Catholic. The clash between religious factions led to the York Point Riot in 1849, which left 12 dead.

Many of the Irish immigrants arrived sick with cholera, typhus, and smallpox. The city earmarked **Partridge Island** in the harbor for a quarantine station with 13 hospitals (and six graveyards).

## The Liverpool of America

Despite its early social woes, Saint John strode ahead economically and became known as the Liverpool of America. The *Marco Polo*, the world's fastest ship in its heyday, was launched in 1852 during an era when the port ranked third worldwide as a wooden ship builder. After steel-hulled steam vessels began to replace the great sailing ships in the 1860s, the city plunged into a decline, which was deepened by the Great Fire of 1877. The fire at the Market Square area raged for nine hours and left 18 people dead and another 13,000 homeless.

The blaze cost the city $28 million but, undaunted, Saint John replaced the damage with more elaborate, sturdier, brick and stone buildings designed in the ornate Victorian style. The economic surge continued after New Brunswick joined the Confederation of Canada in 1867 and the nation's new railroads transported goods to Saint John for shipping. In an ironic twist, the new Confederation bypassed Saint John as the dominion's official winter port, in favor of Portland, Maine. Saint John's officials argued that the choice was illogical, as Saint John Harbour is ice-free. In 1894, Ottawa recognized its error and transferred federal shipping operations to Saint John two years later.

## Architectural Additions

The decades have imbued Saint John with a wealth of landmarks. The old **New Brunswick Museum** was begun in 1842 by Dr. Abraham Gesner, the inventor of kerosene. The **Aitken Bicentennial Exhibition Centre** was built with funding from Andrew Carnegie, the U.S. billionaire. Other early grandiose sites were **Rockwood Park,** the 870-hectare (2,150-acre) expanse of woodland and lakes on the city's outskirts, which opened in 1894; and the 1913 **Imperial Theatre,** the imposing vaudeville showplace-cum-performing arts center on King's Square South.

Saint John thrived during World War I as a shipping center for munitions, food, and troops bound for the Allied offensive in Europe. The port took an economic plunge during the Depression, further worsened by another devastating fire that destroyed port facilities. Prosperity returned during World War II; the fortifications at Fort Dufferin, Partridge Island, Fort Mispec, and Carleton Martello Tower guarded the nation's shipping lifeline as German submarines roamed the Bay of Fundy.

## A New City Emerges

Saint John modernized after the war. New Brunswick's native-son billionaire, K. C. Irving, diversified his petroleum empire with the acquisition and expansion of the Saint John Shipbuilding facilities. The **University of New Brunswick** opened a campus at the city's north end; enrollment today is 1,150 full-time and 1,500 part-time students.

Canada's Confederation centennial launched Saint John's rejuvenation in 1967. **Barbour's**

**General Store,** an authentic country store, was restored and moved to harbor as a museum and tourist center. Close by, the historic brick warehouses were transformed into **Market Square,** with shops, restaurants, and a trade and convention center. In 1982, the remarkably preserved South End was renamed **Trinity Royal Heritage Preservation Area.** The downtown area also gained the **Canada Games Aquatic Center** for the national sports competitions that convened in Saint John in 1985.

The city serves as headquarters for the Moosehead Brewery, Labatt's New Brunswick Brewery, Canada's largest sugar and oil refineries, and K. C. Irving's 300 companies.

## GETTING ORIENTED

On a map, Saint John looks large and somewhat unmanageable, almost intimidating. Forget about Saint John's unusual shape and the soaring bridges that connect the city's parts. Rather, concentrate on the main highways: the closely aligned Highway 1 and Highway 100, which parallel each other in most parts, are often the best route for getting from one section of the city to another.

Tackle Saint John by areas. Most sightseeing is located on the eastern peninsula in **uptown Saint John.** Access here is easiest from Highway 1's exits 112 or 111; the access roads peel down into the heart of downtown, centered on Market Square. The surrounding area is **Trinity Royal,** a National Heritage Preservation Area protecting the original 20 blocks laid out by the Loyalists. You'll also know you've arrived by the street names: the early Loyalists called the area Parrtown, and the avenues were royally named as King, Princess, Queen, Prince William, and Charlotte Streets. This precinct is easily identified by distinctive blue and gold street signs.

**Northern Saint John** (the North End) lies on the highways' other side. **Rockwood Park,** one of Canada's largest municipal parks, dominates the area with 870 wooded hectares speckled with lakes and an 18-hole golf course; numerous roads off Highway 1 feed into the

park. This part of the city is also known for the Saint John Harbour's best views; for a sublime overview, drive up to the **Fort Howe Lookout,** where timber blockhouses perch atop a rocky outcrop on Highway 1's northern side. Worthy hotels are nearby.

**Western Saint John,** the city's newly developing area, lies across the highway bridges on the western peninsula. Here you'll find some of the newer motels and shopping malls alongside Highway 100, the area's commercial row, while Highway 1 widens as the Saint John Thruway on its way west to St. Stephen. The residential area, with several interesting bed-and-breakfasts, spreads out closer to the water, while the Bay Ferries ferry terminal (with service to Digby, Nova Scotia) is at the harbor's edge.

### Tours

Taking a guided tour can be a good way to become familiar with the city in a short time. The **Saint John Transit Commission,** tel. 506/658-4700, covers the whole city with three-hour bus tours ($15). The tours depart from Barbour's General Store at the Market Slip, mid-June to early October, daily at 12:30 P.M. The **Saint John Visitor and Convention Bureau** operates free guided walking tours of the historic areas departing from Barbour's General Store July–Aug. twice daily. For do-it-yourself walking tours through the city's historic areas, ask at the tourist office at Market Square for the three free self-guided walking tour maps. **Saint John Department of Recreation and Parks** sponsors free **Walks 'n' Talks,**

Barbour's General Store

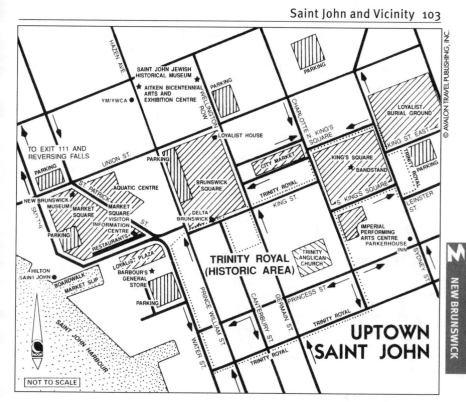

© AVALON TRAVEL PUBLISHING, INC.

**UPTOWN SAINT JOHN**

NOT TO SCALE

NEW BRUNSWICK

insightful walking tours designed for locals (but visitors are welcome, too). The tours are given year-round, but the schedule varies. For details, call 506/672-8601.

## SIGHTS

### New Brunswick Museum

The province's prime resource for fine arts and natural-history lore is this museum inside the Market Square development, tel. 506/643-2300. One of Canada's oldest museums, it's now in a new three-story building and packed with elegant ship models, shipbuilding tools, war memorabilia, stuffed birds and beasts, agricultural and domestic implements, you name it. There's a hands-on Discovery Centre for kids and a bookstore that stocks books about the province. It's open year-round; summer hours are Mon.–Sat. 9 A.M.–5 P.M. (Thursday until 9 P.M.), Sunday and

holidays noon–5 P.M. Off-season hours vary; call ahead. Admission is $6 adults, $4.75 seniors, $3.25 students and youths, $13 families, free for toddlers three and under. The museum also operates a library and archives at 277 Douglas Avenue, tel. 506/643-2322.

### Barbour's General Store

At the foot of steep King Street, opposite Market Square, the essence of old-time New Brunswick is re-created at this restored country store-cummuseum, formerly upriver at Sheffield. Inside are 2,000 artifacts typical of the period from 1840 to 1940, as well as a restored turn-of-thecentury barbershop in the back room. It's open mid-May to mid-October, daily 9 A.M.–6 P.M., mid-June to September to 7 P.M.; tel. 506/658-2939. Free guided walking tours of the historical town center depart from here twice daily in July and August.

Germain Street is lined with historic commercial buildings.

## Prince William and Germain Streets

A block up from Market Square, these two parallel streets delineate the commercial heart of old Saint John. Following the devastating fire of June 1877, the city hurried to rebuild itself in even grander style. The stone and brick edifices along Prince William Street are a splendid farrago of architectural styles, incorporating Italianate facades, Corinthian columns, Queen Anne Revival elements, scowling gargoyles, and other decorative details. One of the country's finest surviving examples of 19th-century streetscape, this was the first "national historic street" in Canada. Some good art galleries and craft shops are ensconced here among the other businesses. Two blocks east, Germain Street is the more residential counterpoint, with a number of opulent townhouses.

For a brief history and description of each of the magnificent buildings, pick up a copy of *Prince William's Walk* at any tourist information office.

## Loyalist House National Historic Site

This simple, white clapboard Georgian-style house was built between 1810 and 1817 by pioneer David Merrit, and it remained in his family for five generations. Having survived the 1877 fire and now meticulously restored, it's the oldest unaltered building in the city.

The original front door with brass knocker opens into an authentic evocation of the early Loyalist years, furnished with Sheraton, Empire, and Duncan Phyfe antiques. The house is at 120 Union Street at the corner of Germain, tel. 506/652-3590. It's open Mon.–Fri. 10 A.M.–5 P.M. in June and daily 10 A.M.–7 P.M. July to Labour Day; by appointment the rest of the year. Admission is $3 adults, $1 for ages 4–18.

## Jewish Historical Museum

Half a block up the hill, this modest museum at 29 Wellington Row, tel. 506/633-1833, has a functioning Hebrew school, chapel, and *mikvah,* sacred and secular artifacts, and exhibits about the city's small Jewish community, which dates its arrival to 1858. The museum is open May–September Mon.–Fri. 10 A.M.–4 P.M., plus Sunday 1–4 P.M. during July and August. Admission is free, and a free guided tour is offered.

## Aitken Bicentennial Exhibition Centre

The grandiose former Carnegie Library (known locally as the ABEC), tel. 506/633-4870, fronts 20 Hazen Avenue (at Carleton Street), two blocks west of Wellington Row. Inside are six galleries (including the City of Saint John Gallery) holding frequently changing fine arts, photography, and science exhibits. ScienceScape is a permanent interactive science gallery for children. ABEC is open year-round: June to early September, daily 10 A.M.–5 P.M.; the rest of the year Tues.–Sun. 11:30 A.M.–4:30 P.M. Admission is free.

## Saint John City Market

For a visual and culinary treat, spend some time at Saint John's Old City Market, 47 Charlotte St., tel. 506/658-2820, which spans a whole city block between Charlotte and Germain Streets. The national and provincial historic site is open year-round, Mon.–Thurs. 7:30 A.M.–6 P.M., Fri. to 7 P.M., Sat. to 5 P.M.

*Everyone* shops at City Market. It's a great venue for people-watching, and for sampling freshly baked goods, cheeses, seafood, meat, and produce. If you haven't yet tried dulse, a leather-tough purple seaweed that's harvested from the Bay of Fundy, dried, and sold in little packages for a dollar or two, here's your chance. Antiques and splendid, reasonably priced crafts have a sizable niche here, too.

The setting is impressive. The original ornate iron gates stand at each entrance, and there's usually a busker or two working the crowd. Inside the airy stone building, local shipbuilders framed the expansive ceiling in the form of an inverted ship's hull. "Market Street," the market's central, widest aisle, divides the space in half; alongside the adjacent aisles, the bustling stalls stand cheek-to-jowl, their tables groaning with wares. Notice the building's pitched floor, a convenient arrangement on the slanted hillside that makes hosing the floor (a tradition since 1876, when the building opened) easier after the market closes each day.

The founding Loyalists started the first farmers' market at Market Square in 1785, a tradition (though transplanted to the present city market) that makes Saint John's market Canada's oldest Common Law Market (it was chartered by George III). The first market outgrew the original site and relocated to the present site a year before the Great Fire destroyed the harborfront; Saint John was rebuilt around it.

## King's Square and the Loyalist Burial Ground

Across Charlotte Street from the City Market are two maple-shaded, vest-pocket green spaces situated on separate, kitty-corner blocks. At King's Square, the walkways are laid out like the stripes on the British Union Jack, radiating from the 1908 bandstand, the site of summertime concerts.

Across Sydney St. is the Loyalist Burial Ground, a surprisingly cheerful place with benches and flower gardens, scattered with old-style headstones dating back to 1784.

As busy as the square and burial ground are—alive with schoolchildren on field trips, bantering pensioners, and mums with strollers—**Queen's Square,** three blocks south, is virtually deserted.

## Trinity Anglican Church

A victim of the city's historic fires, this handsome Loyalist church at 115 Charlotte Street, tel. 506/693-8558, was built in 1791, rebuilt in 1856, and rebuilt again in 1880 after the Great Fire. The sanctuary's famed treasure is the House of Hanover Royal Coat of Arms from the reign of George I, which had been rescued by fleeing Loyalists from the Boston Council Chamber in 1783 and rescued again from the 1877 runaway fire. Guided tours of this National Historic Site are available Mon.–Fri. 9 A.M.–3 P.M.

## Reversing Falls

If ever there were a contest for Most Overhyped Tourist Attraction, this site would win grand prize. Tour buses and out-of-province license plates pack the parking lot, disgorging gaggles of camera-toting visitors to see. . . what? At low tide, the Bay of Fundy lies 4.4 meters (14.5 feet) below the Saint John River, and the river flows out to sea across a small falls (more like a rapids) here. During the slack tide, the sea and the river levels are equal and the rapids disappear. Then, as the slack tide grows to high tide, the waters of the rising sea enter Saint John Harbour, muscling the river inland for 100 km and creating some turbulent currents (no falls). It's an unspectacular sight, and even the minimal physical-science interest can't be appreciated unless you're willing to hang around for 12 hours and watch the tide go through a full cycle. Nevertheless, throngs of visitors line up here for the requisite photo opportunity.

What all the hype does accomplish, however, is to draw all those tourists in to the friendly and helpful **Reversing Falls Tourist Bureau,** Bridge Road West (Highway 100), tel. 506/658-2937, which is probably as good a place as any to get information about the area. If you're interested in a capsule version of the sea and river encounter, check out the movie ($1.25 admission) inside the bureau complex. The building also holds **The Falls Restaurant,** tel. 506/635-1999, and a souvenir shop. Open mid-June to Labour Day, daily 8 A.M.–8 P.M., then 8 A.M.–7 P.M. until mid-October.

For a reverse angle on Reversing Falls, go to **Falls View Park,** which overlooks the spectacle from the east side of the river, off Douglas Avenue near the New Brunswick Museum.

### Fort Howe National Historic Site

The blockhouse of 1777 did double duty as harbor defense and city jail. The structure itself is now closed, but the rocky promontory site on Magazine Street nonetheless offers an excellent panoramic view of the city and harbor. It's about a five-minute drive from the historic area. Get there by following St. Patrick Street north, then turn left (west) on Main Street.

### Rockwood Park

This huge woodland park, speckled with 13 lakes and laced with foot and horse trails, is a real gem just a short distance from central Saint John. In spring, yellow lady's slipper and colorful wild orchid varieties bloom on the forest floor, and the gardens and arboretum are in full glory. Activities in summer include fishing, boating, swimming, bird-watching, hiking, horseback riding, golfing at the 18-hole course, picnicking at lakeside tables, and camping (see below). In winter, the ice-skaters come out and the trails are taken over by cross-country skiers. The park is open year-round, daily dawn to dusk. Entry to the park is free. For general information, call 506/658-2883.

The **Cherry Brook Zoo,** 901 Foster Thurston Rd., tel. 506/634-1440, at the park's northern end off Sandy Point Road, is stocked with lions, leopards, zebras, and other exotic animals. Admission prices: adults $4, seniors $3, children $2.50. It's open year-round, daily 10 A.M. to dusk.

### Carleton Martello Tower National Historic Site

The massive circular stone tower on Fundy Drive at Whipple Street in western Saint John has served as a harbor defense outpost since 1812. The superstructure above it was a military intelligence center during World War II. Within,

stone staircases connect the restored quarters and powder magazine. The observation decks provide splendid views of the harbor. The site is open June to mid-September, daily 9 A.M.–5 P.M., then daily 1–5 P.M. until October 1. Admission prices are $2.50 adults, $2 seniors, $1.50 children, $6.25 families. For more information call 506/636-4011.

### Partridge Island

This island near the mouth of Saint John Harbour, a national and provincial historic site and now a coast guard light station, was formerly a quarantine station for almost a million arriving immigrants during the 19th and 20th centuries. Some 2,000 newcomers who never made it any farther are buried here in six graveyards. A Celtic cross was erected for the Irish refugees, and a memorial stone commemorates Jewish immigrants. From the early 1800s up to 1947, the island was used as a military fortification. The site serves as a memorial to the new settlers' courage, and has a museum devoted to them and to the island's history.

## ACCOMMODATIONS AND CAMPING

Ideally, you'll want to be within walking distance of historic old Saint John and the harbor. The area's bed-and-breakfasts often provide sumptuous accommodations for lower cost than many hotels. Lodgings beyond walking distance include the Fort Howe–area hotels, with great harbor vistas at reasonable prices; and the many budget choices on Rothesay Avenue northeast of uptown Saint John, and along motel row—Fairville/Manawagonish/Ocean Westway—in western Saint John.

### Uptown and Near Harborfront

The **Saint John YM/YWCA,** 19–25 Hazen Ave., tel. 506/634-7720, is mainly a resident lodging but is equipped with 16 single rooms for men and another 5 single rooms for women. Rooms cost $24, plus a refundable $10 key charge. Facilities include a pool, saunas, steam rooms, and a racquet court.

Pretty bed-and-breakfast lodgings cluster near King's Square. The **Earle of Leinster Inn,** 96 Leinster St., tel. 506/652-3275, is an excellent choice with congenial hosts and a very central location just a couple blocks from King's Square. This gracious brick Victorian townhouse has seven rooms with private baths ($61 single, $71 double, including a full breakfast). One of the rooms is a family suite. Amenities include laundry facilities, a game room with pool table, a courtyard, and a fax machine and photocopier for use by business guests. Open year-round.

The top-notch **Parkerhouse Inn,** 71 Sydney St., tel. 506/652-5054 or 888/457-2520, www.parkerhouseinn.net, occupies an oversize Victorian townhouse with all the elements of grand style. Within the three-story mansion are stained-glass windows, a curved staircase, fireplaces, a solarium, and a terrace. The nine guest rooms ($109 single, $139 double), some non-smoking, are furnished with antiques.

Canada Select gives its ultimate five-star rating to **Homeport Historic Bed & Breakfast,** 80 Douglas Ave., tel. 506/672-7255 or 888/678-7678, www.homeport.nb.ca, which overlooks the harbor from a restored shipbuilder's mansion built in 1858. Rates of $85–165 single or double include a full gourmet breakfast.

Several hotels also enjoy great harbor views. The avant-garde high-rise **Delta Brunswick,** 39 King St., tel. 506/648-1981 or 800/268-1133, www.deltahotels.com, forms part of the Brunswick Square Mall one block from the harbor and has 112 rooms ($125–170 single or double), a restaurant and lounge, and an indoor pool and saunas. The hotel is connected by a pedestrian walkway to the nearby Market Square complex and Aquatic Centre.

The **Hilton Saint John,** Market Square, tel. 506/693-8484 or 800/561-8282, www.Hilton .com, commands great views of the harbor and is also linked by the pedway to the adjacent malls. It offers 197 rooms and suites (from $220), a restaurant and lounge, and a health center with an indoor pool, saunas, a whirlpool, and an exercise room. Kids under 18 stay free in the same room as their parents.

## Farther Afield

Not far from the historic area, the hotels near Fort Howe overlook the harbor from the city's North End. The eight-story **Coastal Inn Saint John,** 10 Portland St. (at Main), tel. 506/657-7320 or 800/943-0033, www.coastalinns.com, shares the same view as the fort and has 135 rooms and suites (from $99; ask for a room with a view), rooftop dining, lounges, and a health center with an indoor heated pool, saunas, and a whirlpool.

The **Howard Johnson Hotel,** 400 Main St. (at Chesley Dr./Hwy. 100), tel. 506/642-2622 or 800/475-4656, www.hojo.com, has 100 rooms ($115 single, $125 double) and a health center with an indoor heated pool, whirlpool, sauna, and exercise room.

A few motels are strung along Rothesay Avenue (Highway 100) east of central Saint John, which is convenient if you're flying into town at night. The **Park Plaza Motel,** 607 Rothesay Ave., tel. 506/633-4100 or 800/561-9022, has 79 rooms, some nonsmoking, for $58 single, $64 double. **Fundy Line Motel,** 532 Rothesay Ave., tel. 506/633-7733, is clean, comfortable, and generic, with 76 rooms at similar rates.

## Western Saint John

In western Saint John, the **Five Chimneys Bed and Breakfast,** 238 Charlotte St. W., tel. 506/635-1888, has three guest rooms ($80–90 with a cooked breakfast) in historic 1850s quarters. Nearby, the **Dufferin Inn,** 357 Dufferin Row, tel. 506/635-5968, was the former provincial premier's residence and has been re-created as a pleasant lodging with five guest rooms ($80 per person) and a creative restaurant.

Motel Row—handy if you're arriving on the night ferry from Nova Scotia—lies north of the residential area along Highway 100 (Fairville Boulevard, Manawagonish Avenue, and Ocean Westway). The **Comfort Inn,** 1155 Fairville Blvd., tel. 506/674-1873 or 800/228-5150, www .choicehotels.ca, has 59 basic rooms ($90–100). The **Country Inn and Suites,** 1011 Fairville Blvd., tel. 506/635-0400 or 800/456-4000, www.countryinns.com, boasts fancier trappings with larger rooms and suites and space enough for families ($95–105 with a light breakfast).

The **Hillcrest Motel,** 1315 Manawagonish Ave., tel. 506/672-5310, is spacious and offers Fundy views; rooms with cable TV run $42 single, $46 double. Farther west is the **Regent Motel,** 2121 Ocean Westway, tel. 506/672-8273, which offers 10 rooms at $50 single, $58 double.

## Camping

A five-minute drive from downtown, **Rockwood Park,** tel. 506/652-4050, has over 200 sites ($15–20), most with electricity and water; the facilities include toilets, kitchen shelters, fireplaces, hot showers, and a campers' canteen. Available recreation includes golfing at the nearby course, swimming, boating at the lake, and hiking on trails around the lake. The park is just a five-minute drive from city center. The easiest way to get there is to take Highway 1 exit 111 or 113 and follow the signs north. The campground is open May–September on a first-come, first-served basis; no reservations are taken.

# FOOD

Saint John has limited dining choices for a high-style dinner out—a tribute to the locals' culinary skills at home but an inconvenience for visitors looking for formal dining. What's available represents the city's *very* special places, fine enough to lure the locals out of the kitchen. Most everyone eats out at noontime, and there's a spectrum of choices.

## Dinners

Market Square is the most obvious and convenient choice for visitors looking for a meal. A string of restaurants lines the bottom floor; outdoor tables at all of them look out on the comings and goings of the well-traveled strip. Restaurants at Market Square include **Don Cherry's Grapevine Restaurant,** tel. 506/635-7870, serving varied Canadian fare and seafood; **Keystone Kelly's,** tel. 506/634-0616, also with a wide-ranging menu; and **Grannan's Seafood Restaurant and Oyster Bar,** tel. 506/634-1555, where you'll enjoy lavish servings of salmon, halibut,

oysters, scallops, shrimp, clams, and the ubiquitous lobster prepared in numerous variations. Reservations are wise.

The dining rooms in the major hotels are also safe bets, though pricier. **Shucker's,** the Delta Brunswick's seafood dining room, 39 King St., tel. 506/648-1981, offers tempting selections such as grilled Fundy Bay salmon fillet splashed with lemon butter or served with capers and cream. An alternative "Heart Smart" menu features low-fat poultry, seafood, and fruit-salad dishes. Shucker's is open daily for breakfast, lunch (buffet-style on weekdays), and dinner.

**Top of the Town,** 10 Portland St., tel. 506/657-7320, is a casual restaurant atop the Coastal Inn Saint John. It matches exquisite views with sumptuous steak and seafood selections. The emphasis is on beef with porterhouse, strip, and sirloin steaks prepared tableside. Seafood choices include scallops, lobster, shrimp, halibut, and salmon. The Coastal Inn also has a street-level café.

The Saint John Hilton's **Turn of the Tide,** Market Square, tel. 506/632-8564, is right on the waterfront, with awesome views and a seafood and beef menu to match. Try the pan-fried Atlantic salmon served with stewed tomatoes and fiddleheads or one of the tenderloin steak variations.

Just a block off King Street, the city hustle and bustle drops off dramatically. Small, casual, and nonsmoking **Taco Pica,** 96 Germain St., tel. 506/633-8492, is a real find on a quiet side street in the Trinity Royal historic area, away from the tourist traffic. The Guatemalan proprietor offers a mouthwatering menu of recipes from his homeland, as well as dishes from Mexico and Spain. Try the *pepian* (a spicy Guatemalan beef stew) or Spanish paella, washed down with a Mexican beer. Outstanding and reasonably priced, it's open Mon.–Sat. 10 A.M.–10 P.M.

## Light Meals

**City Market** offers an array of places to get a good lunch or between-meal snack. **Jeremiah's Delicatessen,** tel. 506/658-0188, is one of several delis in the market. It offers smoked meats, cheeses, salads, and creamy coleslaw.

For the best variety of dining options, head to the waterfront and Market Square.

© ANDREW HEMPSTEAD

NEW BRUNSWICK

Up the hill a little way from City Market, **Reggie's** at 26 Germain Street, tel. 506/657-6270, is a great old-fashioned diner in a historic building. It serves commendable homemade chowders, lobster rolls, corned beef hash, and a huge menu of breakfast specials, sandwiches, and burgers, all at good prices.

For soup, sandwich or quiche, and a rich dessert, check out **Incredible Edibles** at 42 Princess Street, tel. 506/633-7554. **Mexicali Rosa's,** a few doors up at 88 Prince William Street, tel. 506/652-5252, is a popular hangout that serves Mexican food, margaritas, and imported beers.

**Mother Nature's Pita Bakery and Restaurant** has soups, sandwiches, stuffed pita pockets, and salads. It's located at 20 Charlotte Street, tel. 506/642-2808, and at Brunswick Square, tel. 506/634-0955. **Winning Ways** at Brunswick Square, tel. 506/634-1155, is the place for nondairy hard and soft ice cream and yogurt cones. The shop also carries food supplements, organic foods, and other health wares. It's open Mon.–Wed. and Sat. 10 A.M.–5:30 P.M., Thurs.–Fri. to 9 P.M.

If hunger strikes while you're out shopping, you'll find food courts with virtually infinite meal choices at Brunswick Square's **Courtyard** and at **Market Square.** Out at Reversing Falls, you may want to combine sightseeing with a sandwich or daily meal special ($6–17) at **The Falls Restaurant,** 200 Bridge St., tel. 506/635-1999; open May–September.

## Groceries

For a picnic or snack fixings, make **City Market** your first stop. Beyond the historic area, **Sobey's** supermarkets has six locations in the city, all with extensive delicatessens, bakeries, and produce sections. Hours are Mon.–Sat. 9 A.M.–10 P.M. The store at 149 Landsdowne Avenue near Fort Howe is closest to the historic district. Otherwise, the city is peppered with Green Gables and other convenience and corner grocery stores.

Provincial **liquor stores** are located at 75 King Street, tel. 506/633-3942, open 9 A.M.–10 P.M., and at Prince Edward Square, tel. 506/693-4128, open 10 A.M.–10 P.M.

## ENTERTAINMENT AND EVENTS

### Nightlife

Much of the city's nightlife is concentrated around the harbor boardwalk. Most places stay open till 2 A.M. **Grannan's Seafood Restaurant** in Market Square, tel. 506/634-1555, forms a hub for the many nearby bars of many moods (with little or no cover charges). The restaurant's own **Grannan's Bar** has an inviting pub ambience, while **Spirit's** has the upscale action with bands on Monday and Tuesday, karaoke on Wednesday, and something special Thursday.

The **Brigantine Lounge** in the Saint John Hilton, Market Square, tel. 506/632-8564, is less pretentious than you may expect. It's open daily from 11 A.M. and offers basic food.

The Historic Trinity Royal area, bounded by Prince William, Princess, King, and Germain Streets, is another nightlife center, with nightclubs, pubs, lounges, and sports bars. Locals and tourists like **O'Leary's** at 46 Princess Street, tel. 506/634-7135, which has two bars with draft beer and Irish and Cape Breton music Thursday–Saturday.

For sports events, locals get together to bend elbows at **Callahan's Sports Bar,** 122 Prince William St., tel. 506/634-0366, or **Rocky's Sports Bar,** across the street from Market Square.

### Performing Arts

The city's pride and joy is the immaculately restored 1913 **Imperial Theatre,** 24 King Square S., tel. 506/674-4100 or 800/323-7469. In its heyday, the theater hosted performances by the likes of Ethel Barrymore, John Philip Sousa, and Harry Houdini. After closing in the 1950s, it was reopened and used by the Full Gospel Assembly Pentecostal Church for 25 years. In 1994, decade-long renovations to restore the theater to its former glory were completed. Today it's once again the star venue of Saint John's performing-arts scene, hosting concerts by Symphony New Brunswick, stage productions of Theatre New Brunswick, and a variety of touring performers (who recently have included Montréal Danse, The Royal Winnipeg Ballet, and Steve Allen). For a sched-

ule of upcoming performances, call the box office at 506/674-4100.

**Saint John Department of Recreation and Parks** sponsors varied concerts; for details call 506/658-2893. It also handles the rock, blues, piping bands, and country concerts that take place at King's Square, mid-June to the start of July's Loyalist Days, at noon and 7 P.M. Another offshoot is the classical concert series at the Centenary Square United Church at Wentworth and Princess Streets, held late May to August, Tuesdays at 8 P.M.

### Events

The city awakens from its annual winter hibernation with a blowout **St. Patrick's Week** celebration in March, tel. 506/634-7919. That's followed in late April by the **New Brunswick Competitive Festival of Music,** which features performers from across the province. Locations and times vary; call 506/672-3082 or check at the tourist information offices for details. Summer opens with the six-day **Saint John YM/YWCA Quilt Fair** at the Aitken Bicentennial Exhibition Centre, 20 Hazen Ave., held late May to early June.

July and August are the big festivals months in town. Look for the **Saint John Jazz and Blues Festival,** tel. 506/648-3490, the second weekend of July. The third week of the month brings the weeklong **Loyalist City Heritage Festival,** tel. 506/632-0096. It's one of the summer's biggest hoedowns, emphasizing the contributions of the province's Loyalist, Acadian, Celtic, and Aboriginal communities. Highlights include parades, street vendors, music and dance events, arts and crafts exhibits, and costumed New Brunswickers. Around the same time, the **Buskers Festival,** tel. 506/658-3600, draws street performers from around the province for impromptu fun at Market Square's boardwalk.

Canadian and international performers join forces at the **Festival by the Sea** for 10 days in August. Activities include free daily stage shows, evening concerts, a children's festival, and more. Call 506/632-0086 for details. Acadia Day (August 15) caps the three-day **Festival Acadien,** tel. 506/658-4600, which brings out the city's

# IRVING NATURE PARK

Irving Nature Park occupies an unlikely setting. The remote reserve encompasses an entire peninsula dangling into Saint John Harbour, the province's busiest port. At the harbor's northeastern corner rises the skyline of New Brunswick's largest city. Across the harbor's center, oceangoing vessels enter and leave the port. Yet at the harbor's northwestern corner, this speck of natural terrain remains blissfully remote and as undeveloped as it was when the city's founding Loyalists arrived centuries ago.

To get there, take Hwy. 1 out of the city to western Saint John and watch for the Sand Cove Road turnoff (Exit 107). The narrow road angles south off the highway, takes a jog to the right (west), descends through a residential area then lopes across an undeveloped marshland to the 225-hectare reserve. A sandy beach backed by the Saints Rest Marsh heralds the park's entrance. Many visitors park at the bottom of the hill and continue on foot. It also possible to continue by road into the park, to a parking lot 500 meters from the beach, or to follow a one-way road that encircles the entire headland. Trails probe the park's interior and also wander off to parallel the water.

The reserve's mixed ecosystem offers interesting trekking terrain and draws songbirds, waterfowl, and migratory seabirds. More than 240 bird species are seen regularly; 365 species have been sighted over the past 20 years. Rare red crossbills and peregrine falcons are occasionally spotted in the marsh. Eastern North America's largest cormorant colony lies offshore on Manawagonish Island. Semipalmated plovers like the reserve's quiet beaches and tidal flats. You can count on sandpiper varieties on the beach in July, greater shearwaters and Wilson's stormy petrels gliding across the water during summer, and a spectacular show of loons, grebes, and scoters during the autumn migration along the Atlantic flyway.

Birds are the most noticeable, but by no means the only, wildlife to be found here. Deer, porcupines, red squirrels, and snowshoe hares inhabit the reserve. And starfish and sea urchins laze in the tidal pools.

© ANDREW HEMPSTEAD

George Rocks, Irving Nature Park

Francophones for a celebration of Acadian culture. The seven-day **Atlantic National Exhibition** finishes the summer with a super-size county fair geared to families. It runs from late August to early September at the Exhibition Grounds on McAllister Drive, tel. 506/633-2020.

For up-to-the-minute information on events taking place during your visit, contact the City of Saint John, tel. 506/649-6040, www.city .saint-john.nb.ca.

## RECREATION
### Water Sports
The **Dive Shack,** 70 Saint James St. off Charlotte St., tel. 506/634-8265, is the city's prime source for dive trips to the Bay of Fundy. The shop also rents dive outfits and can provide a dive guide. Hours are Mon.–Wed. 9 A.M.–5:30 P.M., Thurs.–Fri. to 9 P.M., Sat. to 5 P.M.

For canoes and sea kayaks, check out **Fundy Yachts Sales and Charters** at Brunswick Square, tel. 506/634-1530. They're open Mon.–Thurs. 9:30 A.M.–5:30 P.M., Fri. to 9:30 P.M., Sat. 11

NEW BRUNSWICK

A.M.–5 P.M. The company also leads two- and three-day sea kayaking and whale-watching tours ($400 per person and up), departing Saint John for Grand Manan, June to early October.

**A to Z Rentals** at 535 Rothesay Avenue, tel. 506/633-1919, also rents canoes equipped with life jackets and paddles at $25 per day (credit-card deposit required). They're experts on local canoeing and can recommend appropriate beginner-to-expert inland routes. Hours are Mon.–Fri. 7:30 A.M.–5:30 P.M., Sat. 8 A.M.–4 P.M.

The top-notch facilities at the **Canada Games Aquatic Centre**, 50 Union St. near Market Square, tel. 506/658-4715, include a 50-meter pool with five diving boards, two shallower pools, two water slides, whirlpools, saunas, a weight room, and a cafeteria. The center is open daily; call for the long but irregular hours. A day-use pass to the pool and fitness center costs $9; for the pool alone it's $5.

Public beaches are another option for a hot summer day. You'll find supervised swimming at Fisher Lake in **Rockwood Park,** at **Dominion Park** in western Saint John, and at **Little River Reservoir** off Loch Lomond Road in the city's eastern area. The parks are open dawn to dusk.

**Mispec Beach** at Saint John Harbour's eastern edge is unsupervised and the water is cold, but it's a nice spot on a warm day and provides close-up views of ships from around the world entering and leaving the harbor. To get there, take Union Street to the causeway to eastern Saint John; there, take the sharp right turn to Bayside Drive, which turns into Red Head Road.

### Golf
The 18-hole **Rockwood Park Golf Course,** tel. 506/634-0090, is a challenging, narrow terrain bordered with pastoral woodlands. The greens fee is $25 adults, $21 seniors and students. The course is open mid-May to mid-October; rental clubs and pull carts are available.

### Other Activities
The **Saint John YM/YWCA,** 19–25 Hazen Ave., tel. 506/634-7720, admits guests. A day-use pass to the facility's pool, sauna, steam room, and racquet courts costs $10. As at most Ys, grubby

road warriors can also just get a shower here. The cost is $2.50.

Harness-racing takes place every now and then at **Exhibition Park Raceway** on McAllister Drive, tel. 506/633-2020.

## SHOPPING
The city's main shopping district lies along Charlotte, Union, Princess, Germain, and Prince William Streets. Business hours are typically Mon.–Wed. and Sat. 9:30 A.M.–5:30 P.M., Thurs.–Fri. to 9 P.M. Some **Market Square** shops nearby are also open Sunday noon–6 P.M.

### Arts and Crafts
The province boasts an excellent reputation for crafts, profusely available at many shops around the city. The local penchant for high-quality weaving and handmade apparel is particularly evident. In addition, woodworking and furniture are outstanding, thanks in part to New Brunswick's plentiful native oak, pine, and birch, as well as the skill of local craftspeople. A preeminent selection of fine-arts galleries gets rave reviews by visitors, due mainly to the wide array of multimedia works displayed by well-known provincial artists like Jack Humphrey, Miller Brittain, Fred Ross, Herzl Kashetsky, and Robert Percival.

The **Rocking Chair** at 104 Prince William Street, tel. 506/634-3800, is awash in fine-quality furniture, pottery, and the Madawaska Weavers' domestic linens and clothing, while the **Country Treasures** shop at 91 Prince William Street, tel. 506/642-3509, carries an equally laudable stock of folk art, furniture, and hand-woven domestic linens. Saint John is Canada's most Irish city, and Celtic wares are abundant. The **House of Tara** at 72 Prince William Street, tel. 506/634-8272, is stuffed with Irish imports, including plentiful jewelry and clothing (the tweeds are particularly attractive). **Handworks Gallery,** 12 King St., tel. 506/652-9787, offers a mix of New Brunswick crafts and fine art.

### Books and Bookstores
**Saint John Central Library** is in the downtown Market Square complex. It holds a good selection

of New Brunswick titles, including all those listed in the back of this book under Recommended Reading. It's open Mon.–Fri. 9 A.M.–5 P.M. (Thursday until 9 P.M.)

To purchase books about the province's natural, human, and cultural history, head for the **New Brunswick Museum,** right by the library in Market Square, tel. 506/643-2350 or 506/643-2300. Also in Market Square is **Canterbury Tales,** tel. 506/652-8253, with a good selection of fiction and nonfiction titles. Other worthy book sources are **Coles The Book People** at the shopping centers at Brunswick Square, tel. 506/658-9114; Lancaster Mall, tel. 506/672-7670; and McAllister Place, tel. 506/633-1810; and **Book Mart** at Parkway Mall, tel. 506/658-0368, and the Loch Lomond Mall, tel. 506/634-7625.

Used and antiquarian books are sold at the **Book Trellis,** across from the Delta at 15 Canterbury Street, tel. 506/633-7584, and at the **Scholar's Den,** 105 Prince Edward St., tel. 506/657-2665.

## INFORMATION AND SERVICES
### Tourist Information
**Market Square Visitor Information Centre** is at the eastern (Water Street) entrance to Market Square, tel. 506/658-2855. It's open daily year-round. Approaching the city from the west (St. Andrews) on Highway 1, you're better off stopping at the much larger **Highway 1 West Visitor Information Centre,** overlooking Irving Nature Park and the Bay of Fundy, tel. 506/658-2940. Contact the **Saint John Visitor and Convention Bureau** directly by calling 506/658-2990 or 888/364-4444 or visiting www.city.saint-john.nb.ca.

### Health and Safety
**Saint John Regional Hospital** is at 400 University Avenue near Rockwood Park, tel. 506/648-6000 (for quick help, tel. 506/648-6900). The hospital has a kidney-dialysis unit. **St. Joseph's Hospital** is at 130 Bayard Drive, tel. 506/632-5555. For the police or other emergencies, call 911.

### Banks
You can change foreign currency everywhere, but the city's nine major banks with many branch outlets have the most favorable exchange rates. Most are open Mon.–Wed. 10 A.M.–4 P.M., Thurs.–Fri. to 5 P.M. The **Bank of Nova Scotia,** the city's largest bank operation, does not charge to convert foreign currency to Canadian dollars, but you'll pay $2 extra to cash a traveler's check.

Banks are concentrated in uptown Saint John. Opposite King's Square are a Bank of Nova Scotia and a Royal Bank. Along King Street are another Bank of Nova Scotia, a Bank of Montréal, Toronto Dominion Bank, and others.

### Other Services
**Canada Post** is at 125 Rothesay Avenue, tel. 506/636-4781. It's open Mon.–Fri. 8 A.M.–5:15 P.M. For philatelic services, go to **Postal Station B** at 41 Church Street in western Saint John, tel. 506/672-6704. It's open 8 A.M.–3 P.M. and to 5 P.M. for other postal services. **Lawton's Drugs** at Brunswick Square, tel. 506/634-1422, serves as one of the city's numerous retail postal outlets and has longer hours. **Shoppers Drug Stores** also have postal service outlets.

## GETTING THERE
### By Air
**Saint John International Airport** is 16 km east of downtown. The airport is served by **Air Canada/Air Nova,** tel. 506/632-1500 or 888/247-2262, from Ottawa, Toronto, and Montréal.

Taxis wait outside the airport during flight arrivals; the 25-minute cab ride to Market Square costs about $26. Car rentals from **National, Hertz, Avis, Delta,** and **Budget** are also available at the airport.

### By Sea
**Bay Ferries,** tel. 506/649-7777 or 888/249-7245, www.nfl-bay.com, sails the *Princess of Acadia* between Saint John and Digby, Nova Scotia, year-round. It runs up to three times daily each way in peak summer season, twice daily in the late-spring and early fall shoulder seasons, once daily the rest of the year. Mid-

June to mid-September, the one-way fare is adults $35, seniors $30, children $15, vehicles $70. The rest of the year, the fares are adults $20, seniors $17.50, children $10 (the fare for a vehicle remains at $70 year-round). The terminal is at the foot of Lancaster Street, across Saint John Harbour from downtown.

### By Land

**SMT Eastern Ltd.,** 300 Union St., tel. 506/648-3500 or 800/567-5151, has frequent bus service throughout the province. The terminal is open daily 7:30 A.M.–9 P.M.

## GETTING AROUND



Saint John is a walking town in the historic area, but beyond there you'll need wheels. Highway 1 serves as the city's high-speed expressway and routes east-west traffic through Saint John from St. Stephen and Moncton. Highway 100 is the city's local traffic route, and it serves as a feeder route for Highway 7 to and from Fredericton. Driving is slow going most everywhere in Saint John but it's worst during the 7–9 A.M. and 4:30–6 P.M. rush hours.

### Public Transportation

**Saint John Transit,** tel. 506/658-4700, operates public buses ($1.50 a ride) throughout the city; buses operate Mon.–Fri. 6 A.M.–midnight, with limited service on weekends. The company also offers two-hour guided bus tours of Saint John twice daily (at 10 A.M. and 1 P.M.) from late June to early October. The price is $14; $5 for children 6–15, children under 6 ride free. Tours pick up passengers at various points around town; call for more information.

**Taxi cabs** wait at the hotels and also cruise the Market Square and Brunswick Square areas. The fares are based on 14 city zones; expect to pay around $5 from Market Square to Fort Howe (most passengers tip the driver 50 cents and up). **Vet's Taxi,** tel. 506/658-2020, has 24-hour service.

### Downtown Parking

Parking garages and lots in the historic area are plentiful and inexpensive. Outdoor lots cost 75 cents an hour, indoor lots are $1.10 an hour. All-day and overnight rates are available. The most central lots are located behind Market Square off Smythe Street; behind the Barbour General Store on Water Street; off Chipman Hill at Brunswick Square; beside the Trinity Church on Charlotte Street; and opposite the Loyalist Burial Ground on Sydney Street. Summertime **RV parking** is free at the lot at the south end of Water Street. Meters downtown cost $1 per hour.

# Upper Fundy Coast

The impact of high tide is extraordinarily dramatic on the Upper Fundy's coastline. The sea floods into the bay and piles up on itself, ravaging the shore at Mispec—where it has clawed into the land's edge to reveal gold veins—and pocking the coastline with spectacular caves at St. Martins. St. Martins also marks the starting point for the region's most challenging trek—to Fundy National Park. The backpacking trip involves just 40 km, but expect to spend three to five days. In places the high tide washes out all beach access and forces hikers back inland.

Beyond the national park, the tide's strength increases as the bay forks into the narrow Chignecto Bay and Cumberland Basin. No place is safe during an incoming tide, especially the remote seacoast from Saint John to Hopewell Cape. At Alma, the village at the park's eastern edge, the sea rises waist-high in a half hour and continues rising to a height of 14 meters.

The Fundy orchestrates its final swan song at Hopewell Cape. Beyond the cape, its tidal impact is exhausted; some of the sea moves inland as a tidal bore and flows up the Petitcodiac River to Moncton, and the remainder washes Dorchester Peninsula's coastal marsh edges.

## Bird-Watching

Here where the Fundy peaks and dissipates, the setting belongs to a few remote villages and one of North America's most spectacular shows of migratory birds. The American bittern, Virginia rail, short-eared owl, marsh wren, and hundreds of other species soar across the wide stage.

Several bird sanctuaries are found in the sizable area extending from upper Chignecto Bay's western coast across Shepody Bay to the Dorchester Peninsula and the Chignecto Isthmus. The bird-watching season varies according to

species, but is generally late March to late May and August through September.

Most of the sanctuaries are owned or managed by the **Canadian Wildlife Service** (CWS) and the province. **Ducks Unlimited (Canada),** www.ducks.ca, a private environmental group, owns additional protected hectares; they've endeared themselves to hikers with sanctuaries threaded with trails and dikes—making for far easier bird-watching terrain than the usual muddy lanes.

The sanctuaries are easily bypassed. Signs are often obscure, and numbered roads may be the only landmarks. The reserves are often known locally by other than the official names, a situation that may further confuse the visitor. If you need help, contact the Canadian Wildlife Service at the Atlantic Canada head office, handily located on the Fundy Coast in Sackville at the waterfowl park, tel. 506/364-5044, www.cws-scf.ec.gc.ca.

## St. Martins

St. Martins, founded in 1783 as Quaco, became one of the busiest shipbuilding centers in the Maritimes in the 1800s, turning out more than 500 ships over the course of the 19th century. Today the handsome little village is a fishing port, as evidenced by the stacks of lobster traps on the quay. At the harbor, two covered wooden bridges stand within a stone's throw of one another. The local tourist information office is housed in the lighthouse close by.

Some of the great attractions in the vicinity are the seaside caves scooped out of the red sandstone cliffs by the Fundy tides. The caves can be explored at low tide.

**Fundy Hiking and Nature Tours,** tel. 506/833-2534 or 800/563-8639, operates a great variety of hiking and bird-watching

Virginia rail

BOB RACE

NEW BRUNSWICK

tours, June to early October. Options range from a two-hour guided hike from the St. Martins base for $10 per person to a weeklong, all-inclusive tour for around $1,500.

The historic **Quaco Inn,** 16 Beach St., tel. 506/833-4772 or 888/833-2531, has comfortable beach house quarters with 12 guest rooms ($95–150), a dining room, a hot tub housed outdoors in a gazebo, and bicycles for rent.

Overlooking the Fundy, the Victorian Gothic **St. Martins Country Inn,** tel. 506/833-4534 or 800/565-5257, former home of one of the seaport's most prosperous shipbuilding families, has aptly been dubbed the Castle by locals. The 12 antique-furnished rooms, each with private bath, run $85–145. The inn is open year-round and has a dining room on the premises.

## Sussex

The **New Brunswick Agricultural Museum,** 28 Perry St. in Princess Louise Park, tel. 506/433-6799, is open mid-May to mid-September, Mon.–Sat. 10 A.M.–5 P.M.; Sun. from noon. Admission is $2.

# FUNDY NATIONAL PARK

This magnificent park is a bit out of the way but well worth the effort to get to. The 206-square-km park encompasses a cross section of Fundy environments and landforms: highlands, deeply cut valleys, swampy lowlands, dense forests of red and sugar maple, yellow birch, beech, red spruce, and balsam fir, and a shoreline of dizzying cliffs and sand and shingle beaches.

From Saint John, Highway 1 feeds into the TransCanada Highway, and the backcountry Highway 114 branches off east of Sussex, peels over the Caledonia Highlands, and plummets through woodlands to sea level. Thick woods rise on one side and conceal the park's deep valleys sewn with rivers and waterfalls. Glimpses of the sea, cradled by beaches, appear on the road's other side; most of the 13-km shoreline is wrapped with formidably steep sandstone cliffs.

For all its wilderness, though, Fundy National Park has a surprising number of civilized comforts, including rustic housekeeping chalets, a motel, a restaurant, and a golf course.

The park is open year-round, though full services operate (and entry fees are charged) only mid-May to mid-October. A one-day entrance pass costs $3.50 adults, $2.75 seniors, $1.75 children, $7 families. A four-day pass costs $10.50 for adults, $8.25 for seniors, $5.25 for children, and $21 for families.

## Hiking

Two dozen hiking trails wander the coastline or reach up into the highlands. The highlands hikes are easy-to-moderate treks, while the toughest trails lie along the coast, impeded with cliffs, ridges, fern glades, and thick forests.

Shorter, easier trails include the **Caribou Plain,** a 3.4-km loop on flat terrain through forest and bog, and **Dickson Falls,** a 1.5-km loop that offers views above and below the waterfall via a system of boardwalks and stairs. The moderately difficult **Goose River Trail** is 7.9 km each way, along an old cart track to a wilderness campground at the mouth of Goose River in the park's southwestern corner. The 10-km (each way) **Coastal Trail** is graded as difficult, but the rewards include lush fern glades and forest and great ridge-top views over the bay and coastal sea stacks. You can get more detailed information at park headquarters or the Wolfe Lake information center, both of which sell the useful *Fundy National Park Trail Guide.*

## Other Recreation

The **golf course's** nine holes tumble down the hillside near the administration building and slice through the coastal forest like a green velvet glove whose fingers reach into the woodlands. The greens fee is $11.50 for nine holes, or you can play all day for $22. Call the pro shop at 506/887-2970 to reserve a tee time. The course is open mid-May to mid-October.

Near park headquarters, a path nearby leads across the highway to the seaside **pool** filled with heated seawater piped in from the Fundy. It's open 11 A.M.–7 P.M. Admission is $2 for adults, $1.50 for children, $5 for families.

The park's lakes are open to nonmotorized

**boats.** Sailboats, canoes, kayaks, and rowboats can be rented at Bennett Lake for $6–8 per hour. There are **tennis courts** and **lawn bowling courts** in the headquarters area; rental equipment is available at the pro shop.

**Fishing** is good for the plentiful trout found in the lakes and rivers; a national park fishing license, available at either visitor center, is required ($4.50 per day; $6.50 per week).

## Accommodations and Food

Four **campgrounds** in the park offer a total of 600 sites: **Wolfe Lake** near the northwest park entrance; **Point Wolfe** near the beach; and **Chignecto** and **Headquarters** close to the southeast entrance near Alma. Unserviced sites cost $12 ($10 at primitive Wolfe Lake campground), serviced sites $17–19. Hike-in **wilderness camping** is available at Goose River, Marven Lake, Tracey Lake, Foster Brook, and Upper Salmon River campsites. To use these, you must register in advance at the visitor center, Pointe Wolfe Campground, or Wolfe Lake Information Centre. Sites cost $3 per person per night. For campsite reservations, call 800/213-7275. For wilderness-site reservations call 506/887-6000.

For roughing it in style, the **Fundy Park Chalets,** tel. 506/887-2808, has 29 housekeeping units at $65–78 single or double; open May to October. **Caledonia Highlands Inn and Chalets,** tel. 506/887-2930, offers 44 housekeeping units; from $75 for up to four people. **Fundy National Park Hostel** is open to Hostelling International members and nonmembers. It's on Devil's Half Acre Road west of the visitor center, tel. 506/887-2216; open June to Labour Day. Rates are $13 for members, $18 for nonmembers. **Seawinds Restaurant and Takeout,** overlooking the golf course, tel. 506/887-2098, is the only restaurant within the park.

In the village of **Alma,** just outside the park's eastern entrance, you'll find nearly a dozen motels, inns, and B&Bs. The seaside **Alpine Motor Inn,** tel. 506/887-2052, has 40 rooms and housekeeping units at $65–75 single or double, a swimming pool, and a dairy bar. Also overlooking the bay, the **Parkland Village Inn,** tel.

506/887-2313, has rooms at $55–65 and a dining room and lounge on the premises.

Across the street, the **Harbour View Restaurant,** tel. (506/887-2450, serves breakfast, lunch, and dinner; it's open daily 7:30 A.M.–10 P.M. For locally harvested seafood to take back and cook at your campsite, **Butland's,** tel. 506/887-2190, sells live and cooked lobster, scallops, salmon, and haddock.

## Information

The main **Park Information Center,** tel. 506/887-6000, is across the river from the village of Alma, at the park's eastern edge and within walking distance of the Headquarters Campground. In addition to handing out general park information, the center is home to various natural history displays and holds a large bookstore. It's open in summer, daily 8 A.M.–10 P.M.; reduced hours the rest of the year. Entering from the northwest, you'll find a small visitor center beside picturesque Wolfe Lake, tel. 506/432-6026. It's open mid-June to August, daily 10 A.M.–6 P.M.

For more information, contact the park administration at P.O. Box 1001, Alma, NB E4H 1B4, tel. 506/887-6000, www.parkscanada.gc.ca/fundy.

# AROUND CHIGNECTO BAY

## Shepody National Wildlife Area

Shepody National Wildlife Area—New Brunswick's stellar bird-watching sanctuary—is made up of three different habitat areas. You'll approach the first on Highway 114, the narrow, coastal road from Fundy National Park to Hopewell Cape.

The **Germantown/Beaver Brook Marshes,** situated 14.7 km beyond Alma, is the reserve's only inland area and spreads out on 686 hectares on Highway 114's east side. As you approach the area, look for Midway Road, the reserve's southern boundary. Turn right on Midway, cross the covered bridge, and park beyond at the second path. The nine-km trail follows the marsh's edge alongside woodlands and fields rich with ducks and herons.

The 185-hectare **New Horton Marsh** attracts

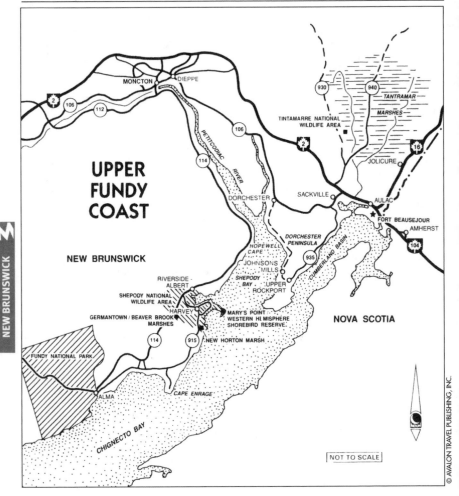

UPPER
FUNDY
COAST

NEW BRUNSWICK

NOVA SCOTIA

NOT TO SCALE

ducks and herons to a coastal setting. At Alma, take coastal Highway 915 for a 30-km drive to the mudflats. The reserve's northern tip is situated where the road divides; one branch leads to inland Riverside-Albert, the other to Mary's Point Road farther out on the coast. A four-km trek through the marsh starts on a dike off the latter road. **Be wary of the tides:** the mudflats reach almost to the sea and quickly flood.

A few kilometers beyond New Horton Marsh, Mary's Point Road leads to **Mary's Point,** Cana-

da's only shorebird reserve. Shorebirds by the hundreds of thousands set down on the 109-hectare coastal reserve, their numbers peaking mid-July through mid-August. Among the onslaught are about 9,000 blue herons and an uncountable number of cormorants, all of which swarm over the intertidal zone.

Be very aware of high tide at Mary's Point. The road ends at a remote loop on the reserve's edge, where you'll be surrounded on three sides by the Fundy and a long way from any help. Inland, a main trail edges the marsh, and a few subsidiary paths angle off the road and probe the reserve's interior; landmarks are few, and it's easy to get lost. To play it safe, stay close to the road and observe the exquisite wildlife through binoculars.

## Harvey

Halfway between Alma and Hopewell Cape, the lush setting of **Florentine Manor** tel. 506/882-2271 or 800/665-2271, is an especially welcome bit of civilization in the heart of pastoral Albert County. The heritage inn offers nine nonsmoking guest rooms ($50 single, $85 double, including full breakfast), just a short sprint from the Fundy seacoast. It's open year-round.

## Hopewell Cape

The great Fundy tides have created a curiously compelling scene below Hopewell Cape, known as the **Hopewell Rocks**. You'll arrive at the parking lot, leave your vehicle, and descend a railed stone staircase to the damp tidelands. At the staircase's first landing, you overlook an otherworldly collection of giant natural arches and mushroom-shaped pillars jutting up from the sea floor. New Brunswickers call the formations "flowerpots," a poetic way of describing the sea-sculpted red shale and conglomerate sea stacks that have been separated from the mainland cliffs by the abrasive tide. Many of the flowerpots are "planted" with stunted black spruce and balsam fir, looking somewhat like clipped haircuts stuck atop the stacks.

At low tide, sightseers—dwarfed by the enormous pillars—roam the beach and retrieve seashells left by the tide. Be careful of falling rocks; the pillars and cliffs are continually eroding, and there's always a chance that rocks will loosen and tumble. Also, pay special attention to the time-to-go clock at the stairwell's top. **The seabed is safe only from three hours before low tide to two hours after.**

Catch the scene again at high tide and you'll understand why. The tide rises 16 meters here, fully flooding the area. All you'll see are the pillars' tree-covered crowns.

The entrance fee to Hopewell Rocks is a worthwhile $5 for adults, $4 for seniors, $3 for children five and up, and $12 for families. The gates are open mid-May to early October, daily 9 A.M.–6 P.M. (in July and August until 8 P.M.). For information, call 506/734-3534.

**Hopewell Rocks Motel,** near the access road, tel. 506/734-2975 or 888/759-7070, www .hopewellrocksmotel.com, has 33 rooms ($75 single, $85 double), a restaurant, a café, and an outdoor pool.

# SACKVILLE

The 17th-century French settlers who founded Sackville originally called the town Tintamarre, from the French word for a noisy commotion. They were referring to the din produced by the geese and other birds that inhabit the surrounding wetlands. The name was later anglicized to Tantramar, a name that today refers to the entire marsh system of the area.

These first settlers had emigrated from around the estuaries of western France, so they were experienced in wresting tidelands from the sea. By creating an extensive system of dikes called *aboideaux,* they reclaimed thousands of acres of Chignecto Isthmus marsh and brought the extremely fertile alluvial lands into agricultural production. Their raised dikes can be seen around Sackville and into Nova Scotia, and are occasionally signposted along the highway, with a date given to indicate their antiquity.

Mount Allison Academy (later University) was founded here in 1843; 11 years later, a "Female Branch" was opened. In 1875, the university gained the distinction of being the first in the British Empire to grant a college degree to a woman.

The beautiful campus is still at the heart of this town, surrounded by stately houses and tree-shaded streets. A number of artists have chosen Sackville as their home, and one of the best places to see their work is at Mount Allison University's **Owens Art Gallery** on York Street (at the campus's edge near downtown), tel. 506/364-2574. The Owens ranks as one of the major galleries in the province and emphasizes avant-garde work by local, regional, and national artists. It's open Mon.–Fri. 10 A.M.–5 P.M., Sat.–Sun. 1–5 P.M., and Tues. nights 7–10 P.M.

## Sackville Waterfowl Park

If you're short on time and can stop at only one of the area's several wildlife sanctuaries, make it the Sackville Waterfowl Park—it's an idyllic, vest-pocket tribute to the Tantramar Marshes. The site, a few blocks from downtown and owned mainly by Mount Allison University, was restored as a marsh with flooding in 1988; a trail and boardwalks were added the following year to maximize access.

The main entrance is easy to miss. It's along Waterfowl Lane between exit 544 of Highway 2 and downtown (at the bottom of the dip in the road, marked by a small green and gold sign). Here you'll find the **Wildlife Interpretation Centre,** tel. 506/364-4967, filled with interesting park displays.

From the center, the 22-hectare sanctuary spreads out with trails routed through bushes, and bleached wooden walkways crossing wet areas. The university town's bustle lies just outside the reserve, yet the stillness here is penetrating. Ring-tailed ducks paddle through the waters. Pie-billed grebes surface and dive. Coots dabble here and there. Bitterns chase frogs. Summer breezes rustle among cattails and bulrushes. Is this heaven or what?

In mid-August, the three-day Atlantic Waterfowl Celebration acknowledges the wealth of wildlife and the rich wetlands habitat of the surrounding area. The event features arts and crafts and tours of the waterfowl park. For information, call 506/364-8080.

### Accommodations

For a place to stay, the **Marshlands Inn,** 55 Bridge St., tel. 506/536-0170, www.marshlands.nb.ca, is among the town's finest lodgings. The inn, built in the 1850s, got its name from an early owner, who named the mansion in honor of the adjacent Tantramar Marshes. The resplendent white wooden heritage inn sits back from the road under shady trees and offers 20 guest rooms ($69–95) furnished with antiques and a dining room of local renown. Open daily for guests and non-guests, the dining room is smart and elegant, with many steak and seafood choices ($18–24), as well as a dish of roast duck glazed in cranberry sauce ($23).

## DORCHESTER PENINSULA AND TANTRAMAR MARSHES

Another prime birding site is not far from Sackville. From Dorchester, 14 km west of Sackville on Highway 106, turn off on Highway 935. The backcountry gravel road loops south around the Dorchester Peninsula—the digit of land separating Shepody Bay from the Cumberland Basin.

Some 50,000 semipalmated sandpipers nest from mid-July to mid-September between Johnson Mills and Upper Rockport, as the road loops back toward Sackville. Roosting sites lie along pebble beaches and mudflats, and the birds are most lively at feeding time at low tide. Smaller flocks of dunlins, white-rumped sandpipers, and sanderlings inhabit the area late September to October.

Continuing on Highway 935, the road follows the peninsula's coast alongside the Cumberland Basin and ends at Highway 106, a few kilometers from the TransCanada Highway. (Highway 2). Be prepared to deal with the fast-moving TransCanada Highway traffic, with drivers more intent on speeding to Aulac, the province's land gateway to Nova Scotia, than the slow-moving, idyllic pastime of bird-watching.

Speeding cars notwithstanding, this area across the Chignecto Isthmus forms an entree into the Tantramar Marshes, an incredibly fertile habitat so rich in waterfowl and birds that the early Acadian settlers described the area as a *tintamarre* ("ceaseless din"). A few roads haphazardly thread through the marshes, and there's no official approach to bird-watching here. Head off the TransCanada Highway anywhere and wander; you can't go wrong on any of the backcountry roads from the Sackville area to the province's border crossing.

### Fort Beauséjour

Eight km east of Sackville, a signpost marks the turnoff from the TransCanada Highway to the Fort Beauséjour National Historic Site, located on the Cumberland Basin just west of the Nova

Scotia border. Continue on the road to the fort ruins, which mark France's last-ditch military struggle against the British, who threatened Acadia centuries ago. France lost the fort in 1755 after a two-week siege. The Brits renamed it Fort Cumberland, and used it in 1776 to repel an attack by American revolutionaries. The fort stood ready for action in the War of 1812, though no enemy appeared. Fort Cumberland was abandoned in the 1830s, and nature soon reclaimed the site.

Some of the ruins have since been restored. Facilities include a picnic area and a museum/visitor center with exhibits on what life was like in the old days. The fort is open June to mid-October, daily 9 A.M.–5 P.M. Admission is $2.50 adults, $2 seniors, $1.50 youth, $6.25 families. For more information, call 506/364-5080.

The setting is also prime bird-watching terrain. Keep an eye out and you'll be rewarded with sightings of the sharp-tailed sparrow or one of the other species that nest in the tall grasses rimming the ruins.

## The Tintamarre Sanctuary

The Tintamarre National Wildlife Area fans out beyond the fort ruins. To get there, get back on the TransCanada Highway for a short drive toward the Nova Scotia border and turn off at Highway 16, the highway's spur that turns northeast at Aulac to Cape Tormentine. Continue on Highway 16 for about 10 km to Jolicure, a village at the reserve's edge. No trails penetrate the 1,990-hectare mix of marshes, uplands, old fields, forests, and lakes. A few dikes provide steady ground through some of the terrain, but you are asked to stay on the roads encircling the area to do your bird-watching.

Amid the cattails, sedges, and bulrushes, sightings include migratory mallards, grebes, red-winged blackbirds, yellow warblers, swamp swallows, common snipes, black ducks, Virginia rails, and bitterns; short-eared owls take wing at dusk.

Bring binoculars—and insect repellent. The area is thick with mosquitoes. For more information on the area, call 506/364-5044.

# Acadian Coast

## Introduction

Along the eastern edge of New Brunswick are the Acadian Coasts—a French-flavored realm of seaports, barrier beaches, sand dunes, salt marshes, sandy pine-clad shores, and rocky coastlines shaped by three seas.

The Northumberland Strait is the shallow, narrow sea strip between New Brunswick's southeastern coast and Prince Edward Island. Here the coastline attracts summertime sunbathers, swimmers, and windsurfers to welcoming beaches and waters warmed by the Gulf Stream.

Farther north, the warm sea mixes with the cooler Gulf of St. Lawrence. Here the Labrador Current swirls in the open gulf, and the swift currents arrive ashore with low rolls of surf. Offshore, barrier islands hold sheltered seaports.

Farthest north, the Baie des Chaleurs ("Bay of Warmth") is the shallow sea pocket between northern New Brunswick and Québec's Gaspé Peninsula. It was named by early French explorer Jacques Cartier, who sailed into the bay in 1534 and was impressed by the surprisingly tepid waters.

The essence of French-speaking Acadia is entwined in its dining and festivals. To understand the region's cultural roots, visit the Acadian Historical Village at Caraquet, where early Acadian life has been re-created with authentic buildings and costumed animators. In the south, Moncton, Acadia's trendy urban commercial and educational center, is Caraquet's bustling modern counterpoint—a very successful Acadia of the 1990s.

Acadian pride runs high, and everywhere in the region the Acadian flag—the red, white, and blue French tricolor with a single gold star—is

© ANDREW HEMPSTEAD

Kouchibouguac National Park

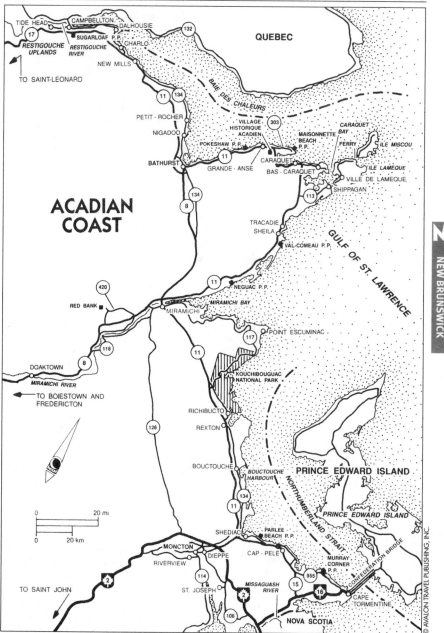

ACADIAN
COAST

© AVALON TRAVEL PUBLISHING, INC.

displayed prominently. But other ethnic groups are represented here as well. Canada's Irish Festival has been held every July since 1984 at Miramichi City. And throughout the year you can find the local Irish community celebrating its cultural roots with dancers, pipe bands, food, films, workshops, lectures, and, of course, a St. Patrick's Day parade.

Stretched-out distances notwithstanding, getting around is easy and very manageable. Highway 11 lopes along most of the three coasts from seaport to seaport, with the sea almost always within view. End to end, it's an easygoing, 10-hour drive one way between Campbellton and Shediac, if you take your time. But by all means, take the side roads branching off the main route and amble even closer to the seas to explore the seaports and scenery. For example, Highway 11 diverges from the coast and cuts an uninteresting bee line between Miramichi and Bouctouche. Coastal Highway 117 is far more scenic, running through Kouchibouguac National Park and curling out to remote Point Escuminac—a lofty shale plateau at Miramichi Bay's southeastern tip, frequented, in season, by thousands of migratory seabirds.

## HISTORY

From earliest times, the Mi'kmaq Indians camped on the seacoasts during their journeys from the Saint John River valley to summertime hunting and fishing grounds on Prince Edward Island. In the 1500s, French and Basque fishermen ventured into the area to catch salmon offshore and on the Miramichi River.

Cartier claimed the land for France in 1534, and a century later the explorer-merchant Nicolas Denys built a fort on Île Miscou, started a settlement in the Bathurst area, and scouted the Miramichi River.

Early French settlements spread up the coast all the way to the Restigouche area at Baie des Chaleurs' western end. By 1739, the region's population reached 8,000, swelled by Acadians who fled mainland Nova Scotia as the British established military dominance there.

## The Acadian Deportation

In the mid-1700s, decades of war between England and France were winding down in England's favor. The British demanded unqualified oaths of allegiance from the Acadians, who refused and claimed neutrality. Instead, they fled Nova Scotia for Acadia's more peaceful north. The British followed, burning villages and crops as they went. The Acadian deportation began in 1755, when about 1,100 Acadians were deported to England's other colonies in South Carolina, Georgia, and Pennsylvania. Guerrilla warfare raged as the Acadians fought for their lives and then fled to the hinterlands.

Refugee camps sprang up, the most famous of which were Beaubears Island, now a national historic site on the Miramichi River, and the nearby swatch of land today home to Enclosure Park (at Derby Junction, five km west of Miramichi), one of the province's most important archaeological sites. Many Acadians died of scurvy and starvation.

The Peace of Paris in 1763 ushered in an uneasy truce. France surrendered its mainland possessions, but during the ensuing decades about 3,800 Acadians returned to the region. The deportation officially finished in 1816.

## Early Post-Deportation Settlements

England swept the lower Saint John River valley as far north as Saint-Anne's Point (now Fredericton) and evicted the Acadians. The French settlers' intense love of the land prevailed, however, and they fled north to the remote Baie des Chaleurs: Caraquet began in 1758, Campbellton in 1773, Cap-Pelé in 1780, and Tracadie in 1785.

The British resettled Anglo immigrants and others who were more amenable to the English Crown on the vacated land. Moncton began as Monckton, named for the British officer who had led the Acadian deportation north of the Missaguash River; Germans from Pennsylvania, lured with free land grants, founded the settlement in 1766. Scots, Loyalists, and Irish poured into the region and carved settlements in the Miramichi River forests. Their descendants moved on to the Restigouche Uplands and the Baie des Chaleurs' western end.

The sea shaped the early economy. Bathurst and Monckton shipyards began operations in the early 1800s, and in the Miramichi area, Joseph Cunard (the brother of Samuel Cunard, who launched the Cunard shipping empire at Halifax) started his own shipyard in 1825.

## Moncton Emerges as an Economic Kingpin

As shipbuilding petered out in the 1870s, Moncton tumbled into bankruptcy. But the town revived quickly when the Intercolonial Railway chugged into New Brunswick and designated the town as the railroad's Atlantic hub. (Note Moncton's new spelling; the provincial legislature misspelled its official name in 1855.) By 1885, the city was an industrial center with a tannery, soap factory, cotton mill, brass works, sugar refinery, foundries, lumberyards, and riverside wharves.

In the hinterlands, the Great Miramichi Fire charred 15,500 square km of forests and almost destroyed Newcastle (now called Miramichi West) in 1825. And while the name of Max Aitken (Lord Beaverbrook) is traditionally linked to Fredericton, the philanthropic industrialist's earliest years began at Newcastle when his father, a Presbyterian minister, moved the family from Ontario to the town on the Miramichi River in 1880. Max, youngest of six children, arrived as an infant and grew up in the stately house with the black mansard roof on Mary Street, a provincial heritage site that now serves as the town's public library.

## The Contemporary Region

The region dozed through the first half of the 20th century. In the early 1950s, Bathurst developed as an industrial center when zinc, lead, silver, and copper were discovered 35 km south of the city. Since 1964, Brunswick Mining and Smelting has mined the ore body, which is 975 meters deep and said to be among the world's largest. Moncton has maintained its economic edge through the decades. The city has thrived as the geographic center of the Maritimes, an enormous shipping and distribution advantage. The Université de Moncton, which began with a single building, now spreads across a large campus with an enrollment of 4,000 students. It is Atlantic Canada's sole French-speaking university and grants degrees in business, fine arts, science, education, nursing, and law.

Though development in the rest of the region is more low-key, the towns on the Baie des Chaleurs have added lodgings and restaurants as visitor demand has increased. On the gulf, Kouchibouguac National Park is so popular it's run out of campground space, and there's talk of expansion.

# Moncton and Vicinity

Moncton (population 65,000) is a bustling small city involved in a renaissance of arts, commerce, and physical expansion. The economy hums, fueled by the city's advantageous position as the Maritimes' geographic center and distribution hub. Lodgings and shops are plentiful. Local restaurants offer some of New Brunswick's best cooking. The city also works nicely as a sightseeing base for drives to the strait.

You can't help but sense the city's vitality and energy. The *Commercial News,* Atlantic Canada's monthly business and economic magazine, summed up its essence by calling Moncton "the Renaissance City"; and a 1994 *New York Times* article described it as one of the most attractive cities in North America for business.

Moncton has maintained its economic edge through the decades, and the wealth has spilled over into the suburbs of Dieppe and Riverview. Riverview keeps a low profile. Dieppe is another story. After World War II, returning soldiers renamed the town, formerly Leger Corner, to honor their fallen comrades who died on the beaches at Dieppe, France. The suburb now rivals Moncton in economic importance and is the site of the Moncton Airport; the Palais Crystal, Atlantic Canada's largest amusement center; and Champlain Place, a large shopping mall. The Magic Mountain Water Park, a large theme park close to Magnetic Hill on Moncton's northwestern outskirts, attracts 120,000 visitors a year.

The city is officially bilingual. About 30 percent of the population speaks French as a first language. So while most everyone also speaks English, a knowledge of French will help the visitor.

## TOWN SIGHTS
### Getting Oriented
Moncton started at "The Bend," a sharp turn in the Petitcodiac River, and developed outward. Rejuvenated, historic **Main Street,** a block in from the river, has new brick sidewalks, old-time lampposts, and park benches beneath fledgling

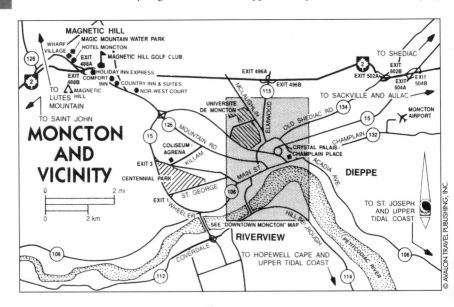

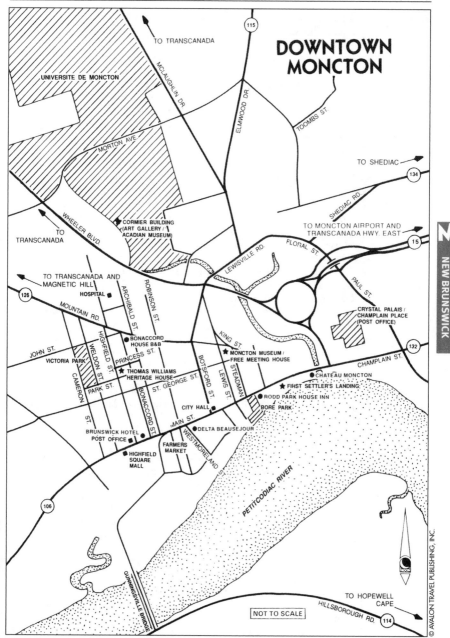

DOWNTOWN MONCTON

NEW BRUNSWICK

NOT TO SCALE

© AVALON TRAVEL PUBLISHING, INC.

trees. This is the place for people-watching; Acadia at its most chic passes this way.

The rest of the city spreads out in the shape of a fan. The adjacent suburb of Dieppe lies on Moncton's eastern side; **Highway 15,** a fast-moving expressway, rims the western side; the **Trans-Canada Highway** wraps around the city's north side and has well-marked exits.

**Mountain Road,** the city's commercial and fast-food stretch, starts four blocks inland from Main Street and works its way across town to the northwestern corner and the Magnetic Hill theme-park area. The **Université de Moncton** lies north of the city center off Wheeler Boulevard.

Moncton's interior is a confusing maze of mainly residential streets; it helps to keep a map handy. Wheeler Boulevard makes a big loop around the town, connecting at its west and east ends with Main Street, so if you can find Wheeler it'll eventually take you back into the town center.

The following sights are located at the riverfront and outward. There's no parking on Main Street. Instead, use one of the adjacent side streets and plug a loonie ($1 coin) for an hour into a metered parking slot, or park in one of the nearby lots.

## Bore Park

The Fundy's tidal bore, a lead wave up to 60 centimeters high, pulses up the Petitcodiac River twice daily as the tide rises on the Bay of Fundy. Within an hour or so, the muddy bed of the Petitcodiac—locally dubbed the "Chocolate River"—will be drowned under some 7.5 meters of water. The tourist information center on Main Street can provide a tidal schedule. While the Moncton tourism folks put watching the tidal bore on their list of must-see attractions, many locals call it the Total Bore. In any case, the sight is most impressive at those times of the month when the tides are highest—around the full and new moons.

The best place to witness the tidal phenomenon is off Main Street at Bore Park, which is dotted with shade trees and park benches. Founding settlers landed here, too, and the site is marked with a cairn. On weekdays in July and August, free outdoor concerts are offered at the park; times vary, so check at the tourist information center for a schedule.

## Moncton Museum

Artifacts from the city's history—from the age of the Mi'kmaqs to World War II—and touring national exhibits are displayed at the former city hall. When the building was modernized, the city architect concocted an interesting arrangement that combined the building's original native-sandstone facade with an updated interior. The museum is at 20 Mountain Road, tel. 506/856-4383. It's open July–August, daily 9 A.M.–5 P.M.; Sept.–June, Mon.–Sat. 9 A.M.–4:30 P.M., Sun. 1–5 P.M. Donations requested.

Adjacent to the Moncton Museum, the tidy, small **Free Meeting House** (Moncton's oldest building) dates to 1821 and served as a sanctuary for religious groups as diverse as Anglicans, Adventists, Jews, and Christian Scientists. If you're interested in seeing the interior, ask at the museum.

## Thomas Williams Heritage House

A century ago, the Intercolonial Railroad brought the movers and shakers to town. Among them was Thomas Williams, the railroad's former treasurer. His 12-room Second Empire–style mansion, 103 Park St., tel. 506/857-0590, was built in 1883 and is now open to the public. Elegantly furnished with period pieces, it's a showpiece of the good old days. It's open May and September, Monday, Wednesday, and Friday 10 A.M.–3 P.M.; June, Tues.–Sat. 9 A.M.–5 P.M., Sun. 1–5 P.M.; July–August, Mon.–Sat. 9 A.M.–5 P.M., Sun. 1–5 P.M. The Verandah Tea Room serves tea, coffee, and muffins in summer. Admission to the house is free, though donations are requested.

## Galerie d'Art et Musée Acadien

The Acadian region is as creatively avant-garde as it is historic. At the Université de Moncton, in the Clément Cormier Building, this gallery and museum touch upon numerous aspects of Acadian culture in the combined exhibits—a foretaste of the excellent Acadian Historical Village near Caraquet. The gallery and museum are open June–September, Mon.–Fri. 10 A.M.–5 P.M., Sat.–Sun. 1–5 P.M.; tel. 506/858-4088. Admission is $2.

## Centennial Park

At the western side of town, the 180-hectare spread of greenery off St. George Boulevard makes a pleasant place to picnic and relax amid woodlands with hiking trails and a lake with a sandy beach. Summer activities include lawn bowling, swimming, tennis, and canoeing or paddling on the lake. In winter, lighted trails invite cross-country skiers, ice-skaters, and hockey players to take to the frozen lake. The park is open year-round, 9 A.M.–11 P.M. A day-use fee is charged to visit the beach: adults $3, discounts for youngsters. For more information, call 506/853-3516.

## Lutz Mountain Heritage Museum

Exhibits on the founding settlers and artifacts fill this former Baptist church at 3143 Mountain Road (Highway 126 beyond Magnetic Hill), tel. 506/384-7719. It's open July–August, Mon.–Sat. 10 A.M.–6 P.M.

# MAGNETIC HILL

This area on Moncton's northern outskirts (exit 488 off the TransCanada Highway) comprises a whole complex of entertainment venues that draw the tourist hordes. First, there's **Magnetic Hill** itself. It's just a hill, but if you believe your eyes, you'll agree it's one of the world's oddest. Is Magnetic Hill magnetic? It must be. The unassuming dirt road, which seems to defy the rule of logic, is said to be Canada's third-most-popular natural tourist attraction, behind Niagara Falls and the Canadian Rockies.

The hill's slope plays tricks on anything with wheels. Set your car at the hill's "bottom," shift into neutral, and release the brake. The car appears to coast backward *up* the hill. Cars aren't the only things that defy gravity here. A stream alongside the road seems to flow uphill, too.

The illusion baffled Monctonians for decades. Before the 1900s, the local farmers fought the

incline when they tried to haul wagons "down" the hill. Several decades later, reporters from Saint John discovered Magnetic Hill. Their newspaper coverage of the "natural phenomenon" brought a slew of spectators, and the stream of nonbelievers hasn't stopped since.

So many tourists arrived to observe the illogical hill that local Muriel Lutes (whose ancestors named nearby Lutes Mountain) opened a gift shop and restaurant for visitors. In 1974, Stan Steeves, another Monctonian, bought the operation and began serving as the hill's unofficial host. His favorite story involves a Japanese film crew that plied the hill with a plastic hose, beach ball, and a bicycle built for two. As expected, the hose's water current, the ball, and the bike riders coasted backward up the hill.

If you think a strange and otherworldly force powers Magnetic Hill, think again. For the record, the whole countryside hereabouts is tilted. Magnetic Hill forms the southern flank of 150-meter-high Lutes Mountain northwest of Moncton. The hill is an optical illusion, and believe it or not, the hill's top crest is lower than where the hill's "bottom" starts. Try to walk the hill with your eyes closed. Your other senses will tell you that you are traveling down rather than up.

The unpaved country road on Magnetic Hill looks the same as it did decades ago. The city of Moncton bought the hill in the 1980s and preserved Magnetic Hill Road as the central point in a park. There's a $3 charge to try out the hill in your car. The site is open mid-May to Labour Day, 8 A.M. to 8 P.M. For more information on Magnetic Hill, call 506/853-3540

## Commercial Attractions

Magnetic Hill is dotted with family-oriented attractions. **Magnetic Hill Zoo**, tel. 506/384-2350, bills itself as the largest zoo in Atlantic Canada. It houses some 80 animal species, including zebras, reindeer, tigers, camels, wolves, and gibbons. A petting zoo entertains

*Is Magnetic Hill magnetic? It must be. The unassuming dirt road, which seems to defy the rule of logic, is said to be Canada's third-most-popular natural tourist attraction, behind Niagara Falls and the Canadian Rockies.*

the wee ones. The zoo is open mid-June to early September, daily 9 A.M.–8 P.M., Mon.–Fri. 10 A.M.–6 P.M., Sat.–Sun. 9 A.M.–7 P.M. until November 1. Admission is $6 for adults, $5 for seniors and youths, $3.75 for children, and $15 for a family of two adults and two kids.

**Magic Mountain Water Park,** tel. 800/331-9283 or 506/857-9283, has a wave pool, numerous chutes, tube rides, and mini-golf. (No, the water here does not run uphill.) Hours are 10 A.M.–8 P.M. daily, mid-June to mid-August, then until 6 P.M. through early September. Admission is a stiff $19.50; $14 for kids 4–11 and seniors 65 and up and $59 for a family of four. Afternoon rates are $12; $11 for children and seniors.

**The Boardwalk,** tel. 506/852-9406, offers go-cart rides, mini-golf, batting cages, a driving range (open 9 A.M.–dusk), and a playground. It's open 10 A.M.–10 P.M. **Wharf Village,** tel. 506/858-8841, is a shopping area featuring arts and crafts and a family-style restaurant. **Magnetic Hill Golf & Country Club,** tel. 506/858-1611, offers a golf course for the grown-ups; $32 for 18 holes.

## ACCOMMODATIONS

Lodgings are conveniently concentrated in three areas. The Université de Moncton, whose campus spreads out between downtown Moncton and the TransCanada Highway, offers a trove of seasonal campus rooms. At the city's northwestern corner near Magnetic Hill and Magic Mountain, motels line the TransCanada Highway and upper Mountain Road. The best-located lodgings are downtown in the Main Street area, where the splendid variety is a bonus. There you'll find the city's most attractive bed-and-breakfasts (convivial places to meet other visitors), hotels, and motels. But no matter what the location, Moncton's accommodations are better than average.

### Campus Housing

When the students leave for the summer, the **Université de Moncton,** tel. 506/858-4008, rents out dorm rooms in two residence halls to travelers. The rooms are available May–August (except one week in July and another in August)

and rent for $30 for a single room and $42 for a double room. For details, ask at the registration office at the Taillon Building on Archibald Street.

### Downtown

**Bonaccord House Bed and Breakfast,** 250 Bonaccord St., tel. 506/388-1535, is a charming meld of Victoriana with five nonsmoking rooms ($55 single, $60 double, with breakfast), a balcony, and a veranda, located in a tree-shaded residential area. The **Park View Bed and Breakfast,** 254 Cameron St., tel. 506/382-4504, overlooks Victoria Park nearby. It is an art deco charmer with three nonsmoking rooms; $55 single, $60 double, with full breakfast.

The five-story **Rodd Park House Inn,** 434 Main St., tel. 506/382-1664 or 800/565-7633, www.rodd-hotels.ca, overlooks Bore Park with 97 elegant rooms ($105–145; the highest rate gets you a room with views) and a restaurant, lounge, and pool.

On the edge of downtown, the **Chateau Moncton,** 100 Main St., tel. 506/870-4444 or 800/576-4040, www.chateau-moncton.nb.ca, is a distinctive red-roofed, chateau-style lodging overlooking the tidal bore. Guests enjoy modern and spacious rooms with high-speed Internet access, an exercise room, voice messaging, free local calls, and daily newspapers. The hotel also has a riverside deck, restaurant, and piano bar. Rates are $109–129.

**Brunswick Hotel,** 1005 Main St., tel. 506/854-6340 or 800/561-7666, www.keddys.ca, peers over bustling downtown with 191 high-rise rooms and suites ($139 single, $149 double), restaurants, an indoor heated pool, and a sauna, whirlpool, and exercise room.

**Delta Beauséjour,** 750 Main St., tel. 506/854-4344 or 800/268-1133, www.deltahotels.com, is *the* best in Moncton. One side of the hotel overlooks the river. It has 310 well-appointed, large rooms and suites (from $169), three restaurants, a piano bar, and an indoor pool.

### Lodgings Near Magnetic Hill

The **Hotel Moncton,** 2779 Mountain Rd., tel. 506/384-3554 or 800/563-2489, is close to Magnetic Hill off Highway 126 and TransCanada's exit 488B. It has 81 basic rooms ($70 single, $80 double), a restaurant, a lounge, and an outdoor heated pool. The nearby **Holiday Inn Express,** tel. 506/384-1050 or 800/595-4656, spreads out on the northern side of Highway 126, exit 488B. It has 101 simply decorated rooms ($99), plus an indoor pool, restaurant, lounge, hot tub, sauna, and business center. Some nonsmoking rooms are available, as are rooms specially equipped to accommodate guests with disabilities. **Comfort Inn,** 2495 Mountain Rd., tel. 506/384-3175 or 800/228-5150, www .choicehotels.ca, offers 59 rooms ($95–120 including continental breakfast), some of which are nonsmoking.

**Nor-West Court,** 1325 Mountain Rd., tel. 506/384-1222 or 800/561-7904, is another low-slung motel spread with 33 rooms ($75 single, $80 double), a restaurant, and some facilities for visitors with disabilities. **Country Inn and Suites,** 2475 Mountain Rd., tel. 506/852-7000 or 800/456-4000, www.countryinns.com, has 77 spacious, nicely appointed suites ($90 single, $105 double, including continental breakfast) with VCRs and free videos; some nonsmoking suites are available.

**Magnetic Hill Campground,** 1380 Mountain Rd. (behind PetroCanada), tel. 506/384-0191, lies within walking distance of Magnetic Hill. It has 120 serviced and unserviced sites ($16–18), kitchen shelters, a canteen, showers, and a launderette. It's open May to October.

## FOOD AND DRINK

You might stumble on a few Acadian dishes, but the city's most sophisticated chefs tilt toward continental cooking, with an emphasis on nouvelle cuisine ingredients and presentation. California culinary variations are new and encompass a trove of healthy foods such as fruit sauces, mixed-grain breads, salad sprouts, and legume variations. Otherwise, Moncton is a steak-and-seafood town—expect unadorned, hearty basics and a side dish or two of salad and fries.

**Boomerang's Steakhouse,** 130 Westmoreland (at Main St.), tel. 506/857-8325 (reservations are advised), also caters to a beef-eating clientele. It opens at 4 P.M. daily and serves the best western Canadian beef prepared any way you like it. Boomerang's is also proud of its seafood and features the freshest catches, especially shrimp and scallops from Cape Enrage served *en brochette.* The setting is among the prettiest in Moncton, and the building features old-time architectural elegance throughout its three dining rooms.

Local hotels also provide good choices. The **Park Bench** at the Rodd Park House Inn, 434 Main St., tel. 506/382-1664, overlooks the river. The mixed menu is strong in beef, especially filet mignon. Sunday brunch is an excellent buy. The restaurant is open 9 A.M.–2 P.M. The **Top Deck** atop the Brunswick Hotel at 1005 Main Street, tel. 506/854-8991, offers incredible views and fine dining to match. The menu is mixed with beef (especially prime rib) and seafood.

The **Windjammer,** at Delta Beauséjour, 750 Main St., tel. 506/854-4344 (reservations required), has all the creative trappings of dining excellence in a plush, intimate setting. The inventive chef introduced California-style dining to Moncton. Selections include Atlantic salmon sautéed in pecan butter and lobster awash in mango sauce served over pasta.

**Kramer's Corner,** 720 Main St., tel. 506/857-9118, offers a full lunch and dinner menu and declares itself home to "Moncton's largest selection of imported beer."

### Magnetic Hill Dining

Overlooking the pond at Wharf Village is **Wharf Village Restaurant,** tel. 506/859-1812, which does a fine job feeding theme-park visitors with seafood family fare at good value for the dollar (daily specials cost around $7). Seating is outside on a covered deck or inside with basic decor. On the right side of the restaurant is a self-service counter with soup and sandwiches to go. The restaurant is open May to October, daily to 8 P.M.

The **Riverboat Restaurant,** Magic Mountain Water Park, tel. 506/857-9282, serves basic seafood and daily specials. It's open mid-July to early September, daily 5–8 P.M.

**NEW BRUNSWICK**

## Groceries

For picnic ingredients, stop at **Sobey's,** which has a deli corner and bakery. The supermarkets are located at the downtown Highfield Square shopping center, at the Moncton Mall at 1380 Mountain Road near Magnetic Hill, and at Champlain Place shopping center, 477 Paul Street in Dieppe. All are open Mon.–Fri. 9 A.M.–9 P.M., Sat. to 6 P.M. Smaller **Green Gables** corner groceries are scattered throughout the city. **Emily's Bakery,** 34 King St., tel. 06/857-0966, serves a delightful selection of European-style breads, pastries, and cakes. It's open Tues.–Sat.

# ENTERTAINMENT AND EVENTS

## Nightlife

Moncton's steamy night scene—dancing, drinking, and people-watching extraordinaire—is concentrated on Main Street. Local favorite **Club Cosmopolitan,** 700 Main St., tel. 506/857-9117, better known as the Cosmo, has a dance floor and excels in jazz. It's open nightly to 2 A.M.; disc jockeys fill in between the live shows. Cover charges vary. The **Atrium,** 720 Main St., tel. 506/858-5005, lures crowds with more of the same. **Ziggy's,** 730 Main St., tel. 506/858-8844, features bands and stand-up comedy for a small cover charge. The club also has pool tables, video games, and big-screen TV.

Elsewhere, **Club Mystique,** 939 Mountain Rd., tel. 506/858-5861, features two separate clubs—one for bands and the other for DJ dancing. The **Press Box,** 834 Mountain Rd., tel. 506/389-2977, pours draft beer and has big-screen sports television. For dim lights and mixed drinks, slink into the cocktail lounges at the Rodd Park House Inn or the Brunswick Hotel.

## Theaters

The **Capitol Theatre** at 811 Main Street reopened in 1993. This lovely old grande dame, ornately decorated with frescoes and murals, began as a vaudeville venue in the 1920s and glitters again thanks to a $1.5 million rejuvenation. Concerts, ballets, shows, and film festivals

come to the theater on a regular basis. For what's on, call 506/856-4379.

For movies, try **Crystal Palace Cinemas** in Dieppe, tel. 506/853-8433, or **Famous Players,** 125 Trinity Dr., tel. 506/854-3456.

## Festivals and Events

Early to mid-August brings the **Victoria Park Craft Fair,** tel. 506/386-1200, one of the province's top art events (admission $2 adults, $1 students and seniors). Also in August look for the **Acadien Festival** celebrating Acadian culture and heritage; tel. 506/877-7950. In fall, the two-day **Harvest Festival,** sponsored by the New Brunswick Arts and Crafts Association, brings an arts and crafts fair to town; call 506/382-9944 for dates. And mid-September features the **Festival international du cinéma francophone en Acadie,** a major French-language film festival, tel. 506/855-6050. In mid-November, look for the **World Wine Festival,** tel. 800/258-5684, where you can sample from among some 250 different wines.

# RECREATION

Locals like golf, and six 18-hole courses in Greater Moncton serve them. The best of these is **Royal Oaks,** a challenging links-style course that plays to over 7,100 yards from the back markers. It's located at 401 Royal Oaks Boulevard off Highway 115 North (exit 496), tel. 506/384-3330 or 866/769-6257. Green fees are $55–65. **Magnetic Hill Golf & Country Club,** a public course, is known for having the most challenging terrain; its 18 holes lie among rough hills, and one hole sits across a pond. The greens fee is $32, and you can rent carts and clubs. For reservations, call 506/858-1611. The **Lakeside Golf and Country Club,** 1896 Shediac Rd. (Rte. 134), tel. 506/861-9441, is more user-friendly ($20 greens fee). It's semiprivate, and members play first.

The city's **Centennial Park,** off St. George Boulevard, has a sandy beach and a public pool; it's open daily 10 A.M.–8 P.M. Keddy's Brunswick Hotel allows non-guests use of its fitness facilities (pool, hot tub, sauna, and weight machine) with a $5.75 day-use pass; open daily 7 A.M.–midnight.

## SHOPPING

Major shopping malls in the area include Dieppe's **Champlain Place,** Paul and Champlain Sts., tel. 506/855-6255, with a Sears, Wal Mart, Sobeys, and over 150 other shops; **Highfield Square,** Highfield and Main Sts., tel. 506/857-4914, which has 60 shops including Eaton's and Sobeys; **Moncton Mall,** 1380 Mountain Rd. (at Wheeler Blvd.), tel. 506/858-1380, offering 24 shops including Zellers; and **Riverview Mall,** 720 Coverdale Rd., tel. 506/387-7171, with 30-some stores. Mall hours are generally Mon.–Sat. 9:30 A.M.–9:30 P.M.

The local flair for arts and crafts surfaces at a trove of local shops. Craft shop and studio hours vary, and it's wise to call ahead for an appointment. Artisans market wares at the **Farmers' Market** on Robinson Street; open year-round, Sat. 7 A.M.–1 P.M. Check out **Fiddlehead Fleece,** 2420 Hwy. 115 off the TransCanada Hwy., tel. 506/856-6881, for knitted wares (also sold at the Craft Gallery in Sackville). For glassware try **Schella Glass Studio,** 330 Cameron St., tel. 506/856-7070. **Gifts Galore,** 569 Main St., tel. 506/857-9179, carries a little bit of everything—glass, pottery, pewter, T-shirts, and more.

It helps to speak French at some shops, such as **Galerie Sans Nom,** 140 Botsford St., Suite 16, tel. 506/854-5381, a local arts and crafts cooperative. Other art galleries include **Hudson Van-Loo Gallery,** 3083 Mountain Rd., tel. 506/384-8426, and **Lighthouse Gallery,** 587 Main St., tel. 506/855-9255.

### Sundries

**Ivan's Camera** stocks basic film and equipment at 181 Saint George, tel. 506/857-4018, as does **Black's Photography** in Champlain Place Shopping Center, tel. 506/857-0480.

**Attic Owl Bookshop,** 885 Main St., tel. 506/855-4913, stocks secondhand and rare books about New Brunswick. It's open Mon.–Fri. 10 A.M.–6 P.M., Sat. 10 A.M.–5 P.M.

## INFORMATION AND SERVICES
### Visitor Information

The city's main **Tourist Information Centre** is at City Hall, 655 Main St., tel. 506/853-3590 or 800/363-4558. It's open Mon.–Fri. 8:30 A.M.–6:30 P.M. mid-May to early September, and 9 A.M.–5 P.M. the rest of the year. A second center at Magnetic Hill's Wharf Village Shoppes, tel. 506/853-3540, is open late May to mid-October, daily 8 A.M.–8 P.M.

The **Greater Moncton Chamber of Commerce,** tel. 506/857-2883, www.gomoncton.com, is another source for information.

For recorded **weather updates** for the Moncton area, call 506/851-6600.

### Media, Books, and Maps

The *Times-Transcript* is the local six-day daily anglophone newspaper, while *L'Acadie Nouvelle* is the local Francophone paper. **Reid's Newsstand,** 985 Main St., tel. 506/382-1824, has a good selection of local newspapers and magazines and Canadian, British, and U.S. dailies. **Coles The Book People** stocks new books and an assortment of New Brunswick literature at Highfield Square, tel. 506/854-7540, and Champlain Place, tel. 506/854-7397. And if you're looking for French-language reading material, **Librairie Acadienne** has it at the Université de Moncton's Taillon Building on Archibald Street, tel. 506/858-4140, or at Champlain Place, tel. 506/858-4101.

The **public library** is at Blue Cross Centre, 644 Main Street, tel. 506/869-6000. It's open in summer, Mon. and Fri. 9 A.M.–5 P.M., Tues.–Thurs. 9 A.M.–8:30 P.M.; the rest of the year, Tues.–Thurs. 9 A.M.–8:30 P.M., Fri.–Sat. 9 A.M.–5 P.M. **New Brunswick Geological Information Centre/Land Information Centre** stocks the best assortment of topographical maps and nautical charts in town. The center is in the twin towers connected to City Hall, 633 Main St., third floor, tel. 506/856-2322; open Mon.–Fri. 8:30 A.M.–4:15 P.M.

### Environmental Organization

**ECO Action,** a citizens' environmental group, works in the forefront of local ecological concerns.

NEW BRUNSWICK

Major issues include preserving Petitcodiac River wetlands, local marshlands, and other environmentally sensitive terrain. For details, contact the group at P.O. Box 66, Moncton, NB E1C 8R9, tel. 506/859-0618.

## Services

**Moncton Hospital** is at 135 MacBeath Avenue near Mountain Road, tel. 506/857-5111. **Hôpital Dr. Georges L. Dumont,** the French hospital, is at 330 University Avenue, tel. 506/862-4000. For the RCMP/police, call 506/857-2400.

The **Bank of Nova Scotia,** 780 Main St., tel. 506/857-3636, changes U.S. and British currency to Canadian dollars without an extra fee but adds $1 for each traveler's check; open Mon.–Fri. 10 A.M.–5 P.M.

**Canada Post** has branches at 281 St. George Street (at Highfield Street), tel. 506/857-7240, open Mon.–Fri. 8 A.M.–5:30 P.M.; and at 19 Katherine Avenue off Mountain Road. The St. George Street branch has a philatelic counter. A retail post office in Moncton Mall is open longer hours.

The VIA Rail terminal behind Highfield Square on Main Street has **storage lockers,** as does the SMT bus terminal at 961 Main Street. **St. George Laundromat** at 66 St. George Boulevard is open daily 8:30 A.M.–9 P.M.

# TRANSPORTATION
## By Air

**Moncton Airport** is 10 km from downtown Moncton on Champlain Street/Highway 132 (a continuation of Main Street in Moncton) in adjacent Dieppe, and 30 km from Shediac. The airport has a basic layout with no frills, and it's easy-in, easy-out. Air passengers from Saint John occasionally jam the facility when fog closes Saint John Airport. A taxi ride to Main Street in Moncton costs about $13 one-way.

The airport is served by **Air Canada** (from Toronto) and affiliated **Air Nova** (frequent flights to and from Halifax). For all flight details and reservations call 506/857-1021 or 888/247-2262.

**Avis, Hertz, Thrifty,** and **National** car rentals operate at or near the airport.

## By Land

Moncton is served by **VIA Rail,** tel. 506/857-9830 or 800/561-3952; the terminal is behind Highfield Square on Main Street. Trains depart town heading northwest toward Campbellton and southeast toward Halifax, Nova Scotia.

Buses from throughout the province arrive at the **SMT terminal** at 961 Main Street (open 7:30 A.M.–8:30 P.M.), tel. 506/859-5060.

## Getting Around

**Codiac Transit,** tel. 506/857-2008, operates local bus service Mon.–Sat. 6:20 A.M.–7 P.M., Thurs.–Fri. to 10:15 P.M. Taxis are metered. **Air Cab,** tel. 506/857-2000, charges $2.15 to start and about $1 per kilometer. Visitors with disabilities can use the services of **Ability Transit;** call 506/853-3055 for schedules and information.

A riverfront trail leads beyond downtown along the Petitcodiac River. Consult a tidal chart (at the information center) to catch the incoming bore as it covers the dry river bed.

## VICINITY OF MONCTON

### Dieppe

A short, narrow river tributary separates Moncton from adjacent Dieppe, where you'll find **Palais Crystal** (Crystal Palace) aside the Highway 15 rotary. This complex, at Paul and Champlain Streets, is an architectural wonder, a geodesic dome of angled glass walls with the Crystal Palace Amusement Park ($15 for 20 tickets), tel. 506/859-4386, and a science center located within. **Champlain Place,** Atlantic Canada's largest one-level shopping mall is next door. And the **Best Western Crystal Palace Hotel,** tel. 506/858-8584 or 800/528-1234, www .bestwestern.com, takes up the rest of the complex's space. It holds 115 rooms ($90) and suites ($140–170), a dozen of which are gussied-up fantasies—one is a sultan's tent, another employs a rock 'n' roll theme (the bed's a pink Cadillac), and so on. Facilities include an indoor pool, whirlpool, sauna, and McGinnis Landing restaurant. Some rooms are nonsmoking and some are adapted for guests with disabilities.

If you're heading to dinner in Dieppe, try **Fisherman's Paradise,** 375 Dieppe Blvd., tel. 506/859-4388, serving a great menu of seafood and steaks. Don't miss the lobster.

### Saint-Joseph-de-Memramcook

A half hour southeast of Moncton off Highway 106, **Monument-Lefebvre National Historic Site,** 488 Centrale St., tel. 506/758-9808, is dedicated to the memory of Father Camille Lefebvre, founder of Canada's first French-language university. Within the historic Monument-Lefebvre building on the Memramcook Institute campus, **Acadian Odyssey** explains Acadian survival with a series of exhibits and displays. The site is open June to mid-October, daily 9 A.M.–5 P.M. Admission is $2 adults, $1.50 seniors, $1 children, $5 families.

# The Strait Coast

## CAPE TORMENTINE TO KOUCHIBOUGUAC

Cape Tormentine, the easternmost extremity of New Brunswick, is near the terminus of the **Confederation Bridge** to Prince Edward Island. PEI is clearly visible from here, just 14 km away across the Northumberland Strait. Overlooking the strait and close to the beach, **Hilltop Bed and Breakfast,** 89 Main St., tel. 506/538-7702, is a comfortable and convenient place to overnight before heading over to PEI. Its three rooms cost $40 for a single, $50 for a double, and there's a hot tub.

### Jourimain Nature Centre

Nestled below the southern end of the Confederation Bridge, this interpretive center sits at the gateway to a 675-hectare sanctuary, home to a reported 170 species of birds. The center has varying ecology exhibits and is the starting point for an 11-km trail system. It's open late June to early October, daily 9 A.M.–8 P.M. Admission is adults $4.50, seniors $4, children $3, families $10.

### Continuing West

Continuing west on coastal Highway 955, you'll find **Murray Beach Park,** tel. 506/538-2628, with 110 campsites on a bluff above the shore; open May–September.

A few fine, quiet beaches dot the **Cap-Pelé** area, farther west on Highway 15. At Gagnon Beach, **Gagnon Beach Camping,** tel. 506/577-2519 or 800/658-2828, has 208 sites with full hookups plus a separate wooded tenting area, while at Aboiteau Beach, **Chalets de l'Aboiteau,** tel. 506/577-2005 or 888/366-5555, offers a complex of 40 modern beachfront cottages along with showers and washrooms, a restaurant, and a patio overlooking the ocean. Rates are $85–125.

The **Grand Barachois Country Inn,** 1204 Hwy. 133, Grand Barachois (four km east of Shediac), tel. 506/532-1140 or 800/355-2122, www.grandbarachois.com, is backed by a huge grassed area that slopes down to Northumberland Strait. The inn itself boasts 10 comfortable rooms; $75 for a single, $85 for a double.

## Shediac

The self-proclaimed "lobster capital of the world," 20 km east of Moncton, Shediac backs up its claim with the "world's largest lobster"—an 11-meter-long, cast-iron crustacean sitting beside the road into town. For the real stuff, head for the town's restaurants, which have a reputation for some of the province's best lobster dinners.

The little town can be crowded on weekends—this is *the* beach getaway for Moncton residents—and it's packed during the early July Lobster Festival. Another big event is the week-long Festival Baie Jazz and Blues in mid-July; call 506/382-6464 for details. **Parlee Beach Provincial Park,** tel. 506/532-1188, at Shediac's eastern edge, is one of the main attractions here. Its placid, three-km-long beach is popular for the warmth of the water, which reaches 24° C in summer; day-use fee for the beach is $3. The park's 165 camping spaces fill up fast and reservations are not accepted, so plan accordingly; $24 per night.

The beautiful white **Auberge Belcourt Inn,** tel. 506/532-6098, boasts special provincial status as a heritage inn. The inn sits back at 112 Main Street beneath stately trees, with seven rooms ($79–115) and a dining room. It's near the western edge of town, just a quick stroll from the beach. Closed January.

If you can't make it to the lobster fest, stop in at **Fisherman's Paradise** on Main Street, tel.

This 11-meter-long cast-iron crustacean marks the entrance to Shediac, the "lobster capital of the world."

© JAYME LYNES

506/532-6811. Yes, it's the same outfit as in Dieppe, offering *homard* on its own or in sandwiches, salads, stews, and chowders. It's open daily for lunch and dinner. Or head out to Pointe-de-Chêne Marina (turn off the highway on the east side of town), where you'll find **Captain Dan's,** tel. 506/532-0010, a super-casual, and perennially crowded bar and grill with a beachin' atmosphere and great food. Hang loose, watch the boats, and feel your blood pressure drop. Highly recommended.

## Bouctouche

North of Shediac, Highway 11 zips through a wooded corridor, sacrificing scenery for efficiency. For a taste of the slower pace of rural, coastal Acadia, strike out on any of the local highways (such as 530, 475, or 505) to the east, which hug the coast and lead to quiet beaches at Saint-Thomas, Saint-Edouard-de-Kent, and Cap-Lumière.

The literary world learned about the often lean Acadian life during the Depression from the novels of Antonine Maillet, the famed writer who grew up in this small seaport north of Shediac. Maillet's fictional settings have been re-created at **Le Pays de la Sagouine,** 57 Acadie St., Bouctouche, tel. 800/561-9188 or 506/743-1400, situated on a peninsula and islet with a hamlet of houses and other buildings, a reception center, and a crafts shop. Evening dinner-theater (in French) is the site's big draw; you'll have a choice of seafood, Canadian, or—the best bet—traditional Acadian fare. And your meal will be accompanied by Acadian music, which might be in any number of styles. Admission to the park is $8 adults; the evening dinner theaters vary in price but run around $35 per person. The theme park is open June–August, daily 10 A.M.–8 P.M., September to 6 P.M. Dinner theater runs 7–10 P.M. To get there, take Highway 134 off Highway 11 and follow the signs to the waterfront site.

Also at Bouctouche, in a restored 1880 convent two km east of downtown, is **Le Musée de Kent,** which catalogs Acadian life through the last two centuries. Admission is adults $3, seniors $2, children $1. Open July–August, Mon.–Sat. 9 A.M.–5:30 P.M.

Further east is the **Irving Eco-Centre,** tel. 506/743-2600, which preserves the ecosystem surrounding a 12-km-long sand dune along Bouctouche Bay. A public-relations gesture created by New Brunswick mega-corporation J. D. Irving Ltd. (petroleum, logging, you name it), the center offers a two-km wheelchair-accessible boardwalk from which to observe the dune environment. Other trails lead through forest and marshland. Naturalists work on-site May–November, doing ecology research and leading school field trips and such. Bird-watchers will spot great blue herons, piping plovers, and long-winged terns, among other species.

### Rexton

This anglophone enclave near the mouth of the Richibucto River prospered as a shipyard in the 19th century. The town was the birthplace of Bonar Law, the only British prime minister in history born outside the British Isles. He was elected in 1922. **Bonar Law Historic Site,** aside Highway 116, tel. 506/523-7615, preserves Law's 1870s-era ancestral homestead and farm. Costumed guides take you around the house and outbuildings. The park is open late June to early September, daily 9:30 A.M.–4:30 P.M. Admission is by donation.

## KOUCHIBOUGUAC NATIONAL PARK

The Northumberland Strait coast ends at Kouchibouguac National Park, tel. 506/876-2443, a 238-square-km gem of a park that takes its name from the Mi'kmaq Indian word for "river of the long tides"—a reference to the waterway that meanders through the midsection of the low-lying park. Some pronounce it "KOOSH-e-buh-gwack," others say "Kee-gee-boo-QUACK," Parks Canada says it's "Koo-she-boo-gwack," and you'll hear many other variations.

Slender barrier islands and white beaches and dunes, laced with marram grass and false heather, face the gulf along a 25-km front. A gray seal colony occupies one of the offshore islands. In the park's interior, boardwalks ribbon the mudflats, freshwater marshes, and bogs, and nature trails probe the woodlands and old fields.

The park is open year-round; some campgrounds are seasonal (see below). Make your first stop the **Visitor Centre,** one km inside the main entrance off Highway 134; open daily 9 A.M.–5 P.M. mid-May to mid-October, until 8 P.M. mid-June to early September. For a memorable introduction, be sure to see the 20-minute slide presentation, *Kouchibouguac,* which takes the viewer on a seasonal trip through the park's sublime beauty and changing moods. Campsite registration is handled at the center, and information on activities, outdoor presentations, and evening programs is posted here, too. Another good information source is the website www.parkscanada.gc.ca/kouchibouguac.

Entry fees are charged mid-May to mid-October. A one-day pass costs $3.50 adults, $2.75 seniors, $1.75 children, $7 families. A four-day pass goes for $10.50 adults, $8.25 seniors, $5.25 children, $21 families. Fishing in the national park also requires a license: $4.50 daily, $6.50 weekly, $14 for the season, plus an additional license/fee for taking salmon.

### Camping

**South Kouchibouguac Campground** offers 265 unserviced sites ($16.25 in summer, $13 in late spring and fall) and 46 sites with electricity hookups ($22 in summer, $18 in spring and fall). The campground's civilized comforts include showers, flush toilets, kitchen shelters, firewood ($4 per bundle), launderettes, and a campers' store near the beach. It's open May to October. In summer, campers outnumber sites available, and people line up in droves. Site occupancies change most frequently on Sunday and Monday, so put your name on the waiting list, take a number, be patient, and wait for the week's exodus.

**La Côte-à-Fabien Campground** has 32 unserviced wilderness sites ($14) with toilets, trails, and a supervised beach; open late June to early September. The Côte-à-Fabien Group Campground has five sites for up to 25 people per site (at $2.50 per person per night); open mid-May to mid-October.

Primitive campgrounds at **Petit-Large** (accessible by foot or bicycle, open year-round), **Sipu** (accessible on foot or by canoe), and **Pointe-à-Maxime** (accessible by canoe only) charge $10 a night for the first two persons, and $2 a night for each additional person.

For campground reservations call 506/876-2443.

### Recreation

The land and coast are environmentally sensitive; park officials prefer that you stay on the trails and boardwalks or use a bike to get around on the 30 km of bike trails. Naturalist-led programs and outings are organized throughout summer. Check at the visitor information center for schedules.

Trails that explore the park's varied ecosystems include the short **Kelly's Beach Boardwalk,** the **Pines** and **Salt Marsh** trails, and the 1.8-km **Bog** trail. You can take longer hikes on the **Clair-Fontaine** (3.4 km), **Osprey** (5.1 km), and **Kouchibouguac** (14 km—allow five hours) trails.

The Black, St. Louis, Kouchibouguac, and other rivers that weave through the park are wonderful to explore by canoe, kayak, rowboat, or paddleboat. Those watercrafts, as well as fishing equipment and bicycles, are available at **Ryan's Rental Centre,** tel. 506/876-3733; open daily 8 A.M.–9 P.M., mid-June to early September. In winter, cross-country skiers take over the 30-km bicycle trails. Tobogganing and snowshoeing are also popular.

**Swimming** is supervised at Kelly's Beach in summer; swimming at Callander's and other beaches is unsupervised.

## Miramichi River

The gorgeous Miramichi ("meer-ma-SHEE") River and its myriad tributaries drain much of the interior of eastern New Brunswick. The river enjoys a wide reputation as one of the best (if not *the* best) Atlantic salmon waters in the world. In the early 17th century, Nicolas Denys, visiting the Miramichi estuary, wrote of the salmon, saying: "So large a quantity of them enters into this river that at night one is unable to sleep, so great is the noise they make in falling upon the water after having thrown or darted themselves into the air."

Leaving the conurbation of Miramichi City near the river's mouth, Highway 8 follows the river valley southwest for most of its length. Most of the valley is lightly populated.

### MIRAMICHI CITY

Don't get too confused if that old road map of New Brunswick you're using doesn't seem to jibe with the signs you're seeing out the car window. No, the cities of Chatham and Newcastle didn't disappear; in 1995 they amalgamated into a single municipal entity called Miramichi. The former Chatham is now Miramichi East, and the former Newcastle is Miramichi West.

Old French maps of this area show the Miramichi River as the Rivière des Barques, the "River of Ships." From as early as the last quarter of the 18th century, the locally abundant timber and the deepwater estuary has made this an excellent location for the shipbuilding industry. The Cunard brothers began their lucrative shipbuilding empire at Chatham in 1826 and built some of the finest vessels of their day. The industry thrived for half a century and then faltered and faded, leaving no physical evidence—outside of museums—that it ever existed. Ritchie Wharf, the old shipbuilding center, is now a family fun park with a visitor information center.

### Events

In the mid-19th century, Middle Island, a river island just east of town, was the destination of thousands of Irish emigrants, many of them fleeing the catastrophic potato famine of the 1840s. Their descendants are still here, and since 1984 the area has celebrated its Irish heritage with the **Irish Festival.** The four-day event in mid-July includes concerts, dances, a parade, lectures and music workshops, booths selling Irish mementos and books, and the consumption of a good deal of beer. Main events take place at Lord Beaverbrook Arena on University Avenue in Miramichi East and at the Civic Centre and Beaverbrook Kin Centre in Miramichi West. The evening concerts tend to sell out, so it's wise to buy tickets in advance. For more information, call 506/778-8810.

In late July and early August, the **Miramichi Folksong Festival** brings a shindig of traditional and contemporary singing, dancing, and fiddling; it's been going strong since 1958. The Civic Centre and Beaverbrook Kin Centre, downtown Miramichi West, are the main venues. For information and reservations, call 506/623-2150.

## Accommodations, Camping, and Food

During festival weekends, lodging can be scarce, so book ahead if you plan to be here during those times.

The **Wharf Inn,** 1 Jane St., tel. 506/622-0302, www.cityhotels.ca, spreads out at the riverfront with over 100 spacious rooms ($65–85), a restaurant, and a pool. **Country Inn and Suites,** 333 King George Hwy., tel. 506/622-1215, www.countryinns.com, offers 60 rooms for $84–106. At the upper end of the price range is the **Rodd Miramichi River,** 1809 Water St., Miramichi East, tel. 506/773-3111 or 800/565-7633, www.rodd-hotels.ca, which boasts an indoor pool and a restaurant with river views. Decorated in warm heritage colors, its rooms rent from $90. For B&B accommodations try **Sunny**

**Side Inn,** 65 Henderson St., tel. 506/773-4232, which offers four rooms in a restored 1870s home for $58 single, $68 double, including breakfast.

**Enclosure Campground** on Highways 8 and 420 at Derby Junction, five km west of Miramichi, tel. 506/622-8638, has 100 campsites ($19 unserviced or $21–24 with full hookups), boat-launching facilities, hiking trails, a beach, a heated pool and spa, kitchen shelters, a canteen, and a playground. It's open year-round; reservations are accepted.

The **Cunard Restaurant,** 32 Cunard St. (Miramichi East), tel. 506/773-7107, serves Canadian and Chinese food. For groceries and sundries, the biggest stores around are the **Sobey's** markets—you'll find one on Chapel Road in Miramichi East and another at Northumberland Square on Highway 8.

## Information

The **Miramichi Visitor Centre** is located at the south end of town (opposite the airport), tel. 506/778-8444 or 800/459-3131. It's open mid-June to early September, Mon.–Fri. 9 A.M.–6 P.M., Sat.–Sun. 10 A.M.–6 P.M.

# UP THE RIVER

## Enclosure Park

Ongoing digs at this site have yielded post-Deportation Acadian artifacts, including the

---

# SALMON FISHING ON THE MIRAMICHI

Fly-fishing is the only method allowed for taking Atlantic salmon. Fish in the 13- to 18-kilogram range are not unusual; occasionally, anglers land specimens weighing up to 22 kg. The salmon season runs from 8 June to 15 October. Nonresidents are required to hire guides, who are plentiful hereabouts.

Riverside fishing resorts, which let you drop a line in rustic elegance, are a popular way to enjoy the piscatorial experience. They're not cheap, however. **Pond's Resort,** Porter Cove Rd., Sillikers, tel. 506/369-2612 or 877/971-7663, www.pondsresort.com, charges $100 pp per day in-

cluding meals, and then around $300 per day for fishing and guide service.

**Upper Oxbow Outdoor Adventures,** near Trout Brook, further upstream, tel. 506/622-8834 or 888/227-6100, www.upperoxbow.com, starts at $300 per person per day for lodging with all meals and fishing. The company also offers guided fishing without lodging for $225 per day, including equipment, license, and lunch. Also ask about their canoeing, tubing, and hiking packages. For a listing of outfitters, check the Tourism New Brunswick website, www.tourismnbcanada.com.

© ANDREW HEMPSTEAD

The Woodmen's Museum, at Boiestown, is a worthwhile stop along Highway 8.

remains of the communal fire pit from the site's refugee-camp days (1756–1761). Acadian house ruins and artifacts from later British settlers have also been found. The site is open late June–August, Tues.–Sat. 8 A.M.–4:15 P.M.; archaeologists work amid the visitors. A 100-site, full-service campground at the park charges $17–19 a night.

### Red Bank

On Highway 420, 15 km west of Miramichi, the **Red Bank Indian Band,** one of 15 First Nations bands in the province, welcomes visitors and sells handicrafts at the band office; open weekdays 9 A.M.–noon and 1–4 P.M. For details and directions, call 506/836-2366.

### Doaktown

Crossing through the deep interior of the province, Highway 8 runs alongside the famed salmon-rich Miramichi River to Doaktown, 86 km southwest of Miramichi. Squire Robert Doak from Scotland founded the town and gave it a boom start with paper and gristmills in the early 1800s.

The squire's white wooden house with some original furnishings and nearby barn aside the road miraculously survived the 1825 Great Fire that leveled vast tracts of the Miramichi Basin. **Doak Historic Site,** tel. 506/365-4363, spreads out in a verdant setting. It's open late June to early September, Mon.–Sat. 9:30 A.M.–4:30 P.M., Sun. 1–4:30 P.M. Admission by donation.

The **Miramichi Salmon Museum,** on Highway 8, tel. 506/365-7787, will be especially interesting to kids. Exhibits depict the lifecycle and habitat of this king of game fish, as well as the history of the art of catching it (including a collection of rods, reels, and gaudily attractive flies). Live salmon specimens at various stages of development swim in the aquariums. The museum is open June–September, daily 9 A.M.–5 P.M.; adults $4, seniors and children 6–12 $3, families $8.

### Boiestown and Vicinity

Another well-conceived museum is the **Central New Brunswick Woodmen's Museum,** tel. 506/369-7214, which spreads over 15 acres along Highway 8 near Boiestown. The museum's exhibits explain forestry's past and present. Among the buildings are replicas of a sawmill, blacksmith shop, wheelwright shop, trapper's cabin, bunkhouse, and cookhouse. A Forestry Hall of Fame remembers the Paul Bunyans of New Brunswick's timber industry, and a miniature train makes a 15-minute loop through the grounds ($2 adults, $1 children). Hours are May–September, daily 9:30 A.M.–5:30 P.M.; admission is $5 adults, $4 seniors, $2 children, $12 families. Camping is available for $7 a night unserviced, $8.50 with electricity.

# Gulf Coast

North of Miramichi Bay, the Acadian peninsula juts northeast into the Gulf of St. Lawrence. One side of the peninsula faces the gulf, while the other side fronts the Baie des Chaleurs. The gulf coast from Miramichi City to Miscou Island is a wild shore where the sea rolls in with a tumultuous surf.

## Bartibog Bridge

It's a 20-minute drive on Highway 11 from Miramichi to this bayside town, where the **MacDonald Farm Historic Site,** tel. 506/778-6085, re-creates a Scottish settler's life in 1784. Guides take visitors through the two-story manor house, fields, orchards, and outbuildings. The site is open late June to early September, daily 9:30 A.M.–4:30 P.M.; adults $2.50, seniors and ages 6–18 $1.50, families $7.

## Neguac and Val-Comeau Parks

These remote parks northeast of Miramichi are backed by lush sphagnum bogs, formed when the last ice sheet melted and pooled without a place to drain on the flat terrain. Seabirds inhabit the nutrient-rich marshes; both parks are known for bird-watching, and Val-Comeau has an observation tower for good views. Val-Comeau also offers a campground, tel. 506/393-7150, with 55 sites (unserviced $16, serviced $21), boat-launching facilities, swimming areas, and a playground.

## Shippagan

New Brunswick's largest commercial fishing fleet is based in this sheltered bay at the tip of the Acadian Peninsula. Nearby, the **Aquarium and Marine Centre** on Highway 113, tel. 506/336-3013, opens up the world of gulf fishing with exhibits and viewing and touch tanks holding 125 native fish species; admission is $7 adults, $4.50 seniors, $3.50 kids 6–18, $12 families. The center is open mid-May to early September, daily 10 A.M.–6 P.M.

**Camping Shippagan,** four km west of town, tel. 506/336-3960, enjoys a great location, right on the water with a nice beach. Its 153 basic campsites cost $13 with no electricity, $17 with electricity, $25 with full hookups. The sunsets are free. Amenities include firewood, showers and washrooms, a licensed restaurant, kitchen shelters, a picnic area, Laundromat, and organized activities. Open June through the end of September.

## The Remote Islands

Offshore of Shippagan, two islands nose out into the gulf one after the other to form the prow of the peninsula. **Île Lamèque** is best known as a venue for early-music concerts, as unlikely as that may seem out here among the peat bogs and fishing villages. Since 1975, the island has hosted the annual **Lamèque International Baroque Music Festival,** which attracts a stellar roster of musicians and singers in late July for performances of music from the Baroque period (1600–1760). The setting is superb—almost divine—within the acoustically perfect Petite-Rivière-de-l'Île Church. For details and tickets, contact the festival office at 506/344-5846 or 800/320-2276, www.festivalbaroque.acadie.net. The audiences have increased yearly since the series began, so make sure you book an area lodging beforehand.

Fanciest digs on the island are at **Auberge des Compagnons,** 11 rue Principale, tel. 506/344-7766. The inn offers 16 rooms with bay views ($100–175).

Connected to Lamèque by a bridge, **Île Miscou** is a blissfully remote gem barely touched by the modern world. The island marks New Brunswick's extreme northeastern tip, where the open gulf pounds the island's eastern side, and the Baie des Chaleurs laps peacefully on the other side. Point Miscou Lighthouse, New Brunswick's oldest, has peered out to sea from the island's northern tip since 1856, and is one of Canada's few remaining manned lighthouses.

The island changes with the seasons: spring brings a splendid show of wildflowers; summer brings wild blueberries ripening on the barrens; autumn transforms the landscape to a burnished red. The spruce trees here are bent and dwarfed by the relentless sea winds, but oysters, moon snails, blue mussels, and jackknife clams thrive along the beautiful white, sandy beaches.

**Camping Île Miscou,** tel. 506/344-8638, offers 56 serviced sites at $15–17 and four very basic housekeeping units at $35; open June–September. **Plage Miscou,** tel. 506/344-1015, has unserviced sites for $12, serviced sites for $17, and six cabins for $70.

# Baie des Chaleurs

In contrast to the wild Gulf of St. Lawrence, the shallower Baie des Chaleurs is warm and calm. Busy seaports dot the eastern coast of the bay—the region's commercial fishing fleets lie anchored at Bas-Caraquet, Caraquet, and Grande-Anse. Interspersed between the picturesque harbors are equally beautiful peninsulas, coves, and beaches. Swimming is especially pleasant along the sheltered beaches, where the shallow sea heats up to bathtub warmth in summer. Across the bay, Québec's Gaspé Peninsula is usually visible, sometimes with startling clarity when conditions are right. From Bathurst west, the fishing villages give way to industrial towns.

## CARAQUET AND VICINITY

Highway 11 lopes into town and turns into a boulevard lined with shops, lodgings, and sights. Established in 1758, picturesque Caraquet (pop. 4,200) is northern New Brunswick's oldest French settlement and is known as Acadia's cultural heart. The town lives up to its promise with the **Musée Acadien de Caraquet,** 15 St-Pierre Blvd. (the main street), tel. 506/726-2682. Within, exhibits and artifacts depict Acadian history. The museum is open May, June, and September, Mon.–Sat. 10 A.M.–6 P.M., Sun. 1–6 P.M., July and August, Mon.–Sat. 10 A.M.–8 P.M., Sun. 1–6 P.M. Adults $3, seniors 60 and up $2, students $1,

under 15 free. If you can budget only so much time for Acadiana, hold out for the Acadian Historical Village (see below).

The museum is adjacent to the **Carrefour de la Mer,** 51 Blvd. Sainte-Pierre Est, tel. 506/726-2688 or 506/726-2689, a complex that also includes the tourist information office (tel. 506/726-2676), La Poisson d'Or restaurant (tel. 506/727-0004), a playground, mini-golf, and the boarding point for day trips out to nearby Caraquet Island.

The town is also the place to be for early August's two-week **Acadian Festival,** one of the province's best-attended events. It includes the blessing of the huge fishing fleet by the local Roman Catholic clergy; jazz, pop, and classical music concerts; live theater; food and drink; and the Tintamarre, a massive street celebration on Acadia Day (August 15). For more information call 506/727-6515.

Small sailboats and kayaks are available for rent at the Plage Centre-Ville. Swimming in the placid bay is supervised and safe for small children.

Caraquet's fishing fleet is based at **Bas-Caraquet,** a 10-minute drive east on Highway 145 toward Île Laméque. In the other direction on Caraquet's western outskirts, the **Ste.-Anne-du-Bocage Shrine** honors early Acadian settlers with a 200-year-old church set on tree-studded grounds at the waterfront.

© JAYME LYNES

Craftspeople at Acadian Historical Village demonstrate the traditional method of dyeing yarn.

## Accommodations

**Auberge de la Baie,** 139 St-Pierre Blvd., tel. 506/727-3485, is a sprawling modern complex of 54 motel rooms ($79–109) and a restaurant. The distinctive three-story, red and green **Hotel Paulin,** St-Pierre Blvd., tel. 506/727-9981, has eight comfortable rooms for $90–125 single, $95–150 double, as well as a restaurant open to the public. The hotel is open May to October.

## Acadian Historical Village

Ten km west of Caraquet, the Village Historique Acadien (Acadian Historical Village) provides a sensory journey through early Acadia. To re-create the period from 1780 to 1890, more than 40 rustic houses and other authentic buildings were transported to this 1,133-hectare site and restored. The buildings—including a church, smithy, farmhouses, school, printing shop, carpenter's shop, gristmill, and others—are spread across woods and fields along the North River. You walk the dusty lanes or hop aboard a horse-drawn wagon to get from one building to the next, where informative, costumed "residents" describe their daily lives, their jobs, and surroundings, in French and English. A marvelous experience.

Out in the park, two "post houses" serve sandwiches, snacks, and drinks. At the reception center are a cafeteria and the Table des Ancêtres Restaurant, which serves typical Acadian dishes and offers Acadian dinner theater Wed.–Sun. evenings in summer ($38 per person; call 506/726-2623 for reservations). Acadian Historical Village, 14311 Route 11, Rivière du Nord, tel. 506/726-2600, is open early June to mid-September, daily 10 A.M.–6 P.M. Admission to the village is adults $9.50, seniors $8, college students $6, youths ages 6–18 $5, families $24.

## Grande-Anse

Highway 11 continues to the coast, where it takes a turn west to Grande-Anse. For a swim in the warm bay, take Highway 320, the narrow road that diverges to the right, to **Maisonnette Beach Park,** an exquisite spread of beach overlooking Caraquet across Baie Caraquet. The warm-water beach is a favorite, especially when the tide retreats to reveal sand dune fingers washed by shallow, sun-heated waters. Seabirds are everywhere here: you'll see them in large numbers on nearby, aptly named Bird Island, where the long bluffs at **Pokeshaw Community Park** overlook rookeries of squawking cormorants.

In town, the **Musée des Papes** ("Popes Museum"), 140 Acadie St., tel. 506/732-3003, commemorates the visit of Pope John Paul II to New Brunswick in 1985. Exhibits include vestments, chalices, and other ecclesiastical paraphernalia, plus a detailed scale replica of St. Peter's Basilica. The museum also has a dining room and picnic area. It's open daily 10 A.M.–6 P.M., mid-June to September. Admission is $5, with discounts for seniors and children.

## BATHURST TO CAMPBELLTON

### Bathurst and Vicinity

The town of Bathurst (pop. 13,000) sits by its own fine natural harbor at the vertex of Nepisiguit Bay, a broad gulf on the Baie des Chaleurs. Behind the town, seemingly limitless forests spread as far as the eye can see.

**Daly Point Wildlife Reserve** spreads across 40 hectares of salt marshes, woodlands, and fields northeast of town; an observation tower provides views of nesting ospreys, as well as various seabirds and songbirds. To get there, take Bridge Street (the Acadian Coastal Drive) east from Bathurst, then turn left on Carron Drive. Bring insect repellent.

**Gowan Brae Golf Course,** Youghall Dr., tel. 506/546-2707, enjoys a beautiful location and town views on Bathurst Harbor's northwest side. At the end of the road, at the harbor mouth, is **Youghall Beach Park,** with supervised swimming at one of the area's nicest strands.

**Le Château Bathurst,** 80 Main St., tel. 506/546-6691 or 800/561-7666, www.keddys.ca, has a central location overlooking the harbor, plus an indoor swimming pool and hot tub. Its glass-walled café is a pleasant spot for Sunday brunch. Other amenities include a sports bar and fitness center. The 136 rooms start at $74.

**Chez Luc,** 555 Murray Ave., tel. 506/546-5322, serves a varied board of seafood, meats, and poultry, complemented with a wide selection of wines. It's open for dinner daily, 5–10 P.M. Most of the town's fast-food joints and grocery stores are concentrated nearby along St. Peter Avenue.

The **visitor center** off Highway 11 at Vanier Boulevard west of town, tel. 506/548-0418, is well stocked with information on Bathurst and the rest of the Baie des Chaleurs area.

### West to Campbellton

Highway 11 stays inland for the scenically dull 85-km stretch between Bathurst and Charlo. Far preferable is the coastal Highway 134, which runs through the fishing villages of Nigadoo, Petit-Rocher, Pointe-Verte, and Jacquet River. The coast between Bathurst and Dalhousie is famed for

sightings of a "phantom ship." Numerous witnesses over the years have described a ship under full sail engulfed in flames on the bay; sometimes the vision includes a crew frantically scurrying across the deck. Some say the vision dates from the Battle of Restigouche (1760)—the last naval engagement between France and England in this part of eastern Canada—when France's fleet was destroyed by the British.

**La Fine Grobe Sur-Mer,** 289 Principale (Highway 134) in Nigadoo, tel. 506/783-3138, enjoys a delightful setting on the beach, separated from the main road by a small but lovely wood. The little inn's dining room is worth a stop in itself for fine French cuisine and fine wines. But to make the most of the great setting and food, stay the night in one of the inn's two guest rooms, each with private bath ($69, including breakfast). The staff is exceptionally friendly.

Down the street (Highway 134) in Petit-Rocher, the **Mines & Minerals Interpretation Centre,** 397 Principale, tel. 506/542-2672, has exhibits detailing the industry's past and present with a simulated mine shaft. It's open June through August, daily 10 A.M.–6 P.M. Admission is adults $5, seniors $4, students $3, families $12. Kids under 6 get in free.

Farther northwest, in New Mills, the **Auberge Blue Heron,** tel. 506/237-5560, has eight comfortable guest rooms ($50–69 single, $55–79 double) furnished with antiques. Set back from the road in an oversized former farmhouse opposite Heron Island, it's open May to October in a setting worthy of Provincial Heritage Inn status.

**Eel River Bar,** south of Dalhousie, is one of the world's longest sandbars. With freshwater on one side and saltwater on the other, it's a popular spot for windsurfing and swimming.

### Campbellton and Vicinity

At the head of the Baie des Chaleurs, the New Brunswick and Gaspé coastlines meet near Campbellton, the area's largest town. A bridge here spans the broad mouth of the Restigouche River to connect with Québec's Highway 132.

Campbellton (pop. 8,700) was originally settled by Scots, who founded the local salmon industry. Later, farming, lumbering, and shipbuilding developed, and in the 1870s, the railroad came. The Scottish legacy remains, in place-names such as Glen Livet, Dundee, and Balmoral. After a devastating fire in 1910, the town began to rebuild itself in brick. "Cambellton is not the ugliest town in Canada," Michael Collie wrote in the 1970s, "but it must be one of the most accidental in appearance, because of the medley of wooden and brick houses."

**Galerie Restigouche,** 39 Andrew St., tel. 506/753-5750, is a public art gallery displaying works by local, national, and international artists, as well as natural history and science exhibits. It's open year-round; free admission.

**Sugarloaf Mountain Provincial Park,** outside Campbellton off Highway 11, tel. 506/789-2366, overlooks the whole region and has a year-round chairlift with views to the 283-meter, gumdrop-shaped peak. The park has 76 campsites ($15–20) open May to October, lighted tennis courts, hiking trails, and supervised swimming. In winter, the park is popular for snowmobiling, ice-skating, and cross-country skiing.

The **Auberge Maritime Inn,** 26 Duke St., tel. 506/753-7606 or 800/953-5005, www.maritimeinninc.com, is downtown and has a pool and dining room.

Its 58 rooms run $60–80. Other chain lodgings include the **Howard Johnson Hotel,** 157 Water St., tel. 506/753-4133 or 800/909-4656, with 66 rooms for $80 single, $84 double; and the **Comfort Inn,** 11 Val d'Amour Rd., tel. 506/753-4121 or 800/228-5150, www.choicehotels.ca, with 60 rooms at $90 single, $110 double. Hostelling International's **Campbellton Lighthouse Youth Hostel** occupies a lighthouse alongside the Restigouche River. It's located at 1 Ritchie Street, tel. 506/759-7044, www.hihostels.ca, and offers 20 beds for $12–15 a night. Open mid-June to late August.

Tide Head, a small town at the river's mouth, is known for fiddleheads—fern fronds served as a springtime culinary delicacy. Here, **Sanfar Cottages** on Restigouche Drive, tel. 506/753-4287, has tidy housekeeping units for ($42 single, $47 double), plus a licensed dining room.

From Campbellton, Highway 134 connects with Québec's Highway 132 at Matapédia. Highway 17 plunges deep into the virtually unpopulated interior, across the region known as the Restigouche Uplands. It's 92 km to Saint-Quentin, where you can veer east to Mt. Carleton Provincial Park or continue another 80 km to join the Saint John River valley at Saint-Léonard.

# Nova Scotia

# Introduction

Beautiful Nova Scotia is almost an island, encircled completely by water except at its slender, 15-km-long border with New Brunswick. As a consequence, the province's land and the culture of its people are profoundly defined by the surrounding seas. The 7,459-km-long coastline is etched by the Atlantic Ocean, Bay of Fundy, Northumberland Strait, and Gulf of St. Lawrence, and is speckled with almost 4,000 rocky outcroppings and islands, the best known and by far the largest of which is Cape Breton, which is about one-third the size of Nova Scotia's mainland portion. The province's interior of farmland and thick boreal forest is only lightly inhabited; most Nova Scotians live close to the sea, in coastal towns and in hundreds of little seaports on the sheltered coves, harbors, and bays notching the shore.

Canada's second-smallest province (55,490 square km/21,425 square miles), Nova Scotia nevertheless offers visitors some of the region's best museums, as well as abundant opportunities for recreation, including bicycling and hiking, inland canoeing and ocean kayaking, deep-sea diving, river rafting, rockhounding, sailing, hunting, fishing, and golf, just for starters.

Events here are another draw. Hundreds of happenings of one kind or another are scheduled annually, most during the summer, which has led some wags to switch the province's nickname from Land of a Hundred Thousand Welcomes to Land of a Hundred Thousand Summer Festivals. Many events are linked to the Maritime's seafaring tradition and feature lobster bakes and sailboat races, while others celebrate agricultural harvests, music, and the arts.

© ANDREW HEMPSTEAD

Ingonish Beach, Cape Breton

Among the most colorful festivals are those that tap into the ethnic spirit. The province's Scottish heritage (Nova Scotia translates from Latin as New Scotland) is held in such high esteem by its Highland cousins that the annual International Gathering of the Clans festival alternates between Scotland and the province (where it's scheduled for odd-numbered years).

But after centuries of immigration, Nova Scotia's heritage draws together more than 50 diverse ethnic and cultural threads from all corners of the world. Ancestry is important and well documented here; numerous genealogical centers are geared to assist visitors with roots searches.

## THE LAND

The province is predominantly rocky and thinly covered with soil, making it less conducive to farmland than to forests. Consequently, thick woodlands blanket over 80 percent of the province. The Atlantic coast is rugged, edged with granite, and flanked with sandy beaches, salt marshes, and bogs. The Fundy coast, from Yarmouth to Cape Split, is rimmed by basalt bedrock mixed with tidal flats. Along this coast, Annapolis Valley, famed for its fruit orchards, is a geological oddity; scoured out by glaciers at the end of the Ice Age, the valley is sheltered by mountains north and south, creating a hothouse of warmth and humidity. Along the Northumberland Strait seacoast, rolling terrain with fertile farmlands rises to picturesque high hills and plateaus in Pictou and Antigonish Counties.

Cape Breton Island is joined to mainland Nova Scotia by the 1.4-km Canso Causeway. Cape Breton's smaller, eastern portion consists of lowlands and rolling hills, with deeply indented Sydney Harbour on its northern coast. The western part of the island rises gradually from sea level to soaring headlands and highlands culminating at Cape Breton Highlands National Park near the northern tip. Much of the island's center is taken up by the expansive saltwater Bras d'Or Lake.

Another island also falls within the province's domain. Sable Island lies 285 km east from Hal-

Enormous pressures deep beneath the earth's surface have created varied geological formations across the province, including these sea cliffs in Cape Breton Highlands National Park.

ifax and is now the site of natural gas and oil exploration. The arc-shaped sand spit is inhabited only by wild horses dropped off by European ships centuries ago. Known as the Graveyard of the Atlantic, the province's shores and treacherous shoals are littered with scores of shipwrecks.

### In the Beginning

The region was under a shallow sea until 500 million years ago. Then pressurized sand and clay oozed to the surface where it cooled and hardened to create the first landscape of sandstone, quartzite, and slate. Molten granite later emerged the same way, heaved, and broke apart. You can see these primordial extrusions at Peggy's Cove near Halifax, where the coast is strewn with oddly placed mammoth boulders.

The earth's surface heaved and shuddered, and

the land contours and seacoasts were formed. Between 405 and 190 million years ago, the turbulent earth devoured its own creations; evidence is visible at Joggins on the upper Fundy's Chignecto Bay, where upright trees were enfolded into cliff edges. Archaeologists date these fossils at 280 to 345 million years old.

The last ice sheet retreated and took what remained of prehistory with it. The ice had scoured the earth's surface as it raked back and forth, and this too can be seen at Peggy's Cove, where the ancient scratches are etched in the granite boulders.

As the ice sheet moved, it bulldozed glacial debris into drumlins, large islands of fine soil piled up in places on the predominantly rocky land. The best known of these drumlins is the steep hill upon which the Halifax Citadel sits. Many of the province's most fertile farmlands are situated on the pulverized, mineral-rich soil of drumlins.

### National Parks

Parks Canada, www.parkscanada.gc.ca, oversees two national parks and 14 national historic sites in Nova Scotia. Nova Scotians dote on **Kejimkujik National Park** (kedgie-muh-KOO-jick), which combines interesting ice-age topography and gold-mining history with an interior network of lakes ideal for canoeing. But it is **Cape Breton Highlands National Park** that ranks as the showstopper among Atlantic Canada's national parks. It's more than twice as large as Kejimkujik, and whereas that park can be hot during summer, the Highlands park with its high elevations can range from balmy to downright cool during peak summer months. Park entry fees range up to $5 per person per day, making the annual pass (adults $30, seniors $22.50, children $15, families $75), good for entry to all 11 Atlantic Canada national parks, the best deal.

### Provincial Parks

Of Nova Scotia's 122 provincial parks, 98 are scenic day-use parks with picnic facilities and often hiking trails and beaches for clam digging and swimming; another four day-use sites are wildlife parks with indigenous flora and fauna.

The **day-use parks,** open mid-May to mid-October, daily 9 A.M.–7 P.M., often boast sensational views; Blomidon Provincial Park, for example, north of Wolfville, provides access to a hiking trail atop steep sandstone cliffs that jut out into the Bay of Fundy and overlook the foaming sea. In addition, some of Nova Scotia's best beach scenes are found at the day-use parks; some have lifeguards, but otherwise facilities are limited. The best of these are **Risser's Beach** near Lunenburg; **Clam Harbour** northeast of Halifax, which often has sand-sculpture contests; and **Sand Hills** near Barrington, where the Atlantic water warms among sandbars. Naturalists go for **Martinique Beach** near Musquodoboit Harbour because of its dunes, salt marshes, and the nearby bird sanctuary; and **Taylors Head** near Spry Bay, which has boardwalk-laced dunes, a beach, and peninsula hiking trails.

**Wildlife parks** include the Shubenacadie park southwest of Truro; Upper Clements near the theme park near Annapolis Royal; Two Rivers park at Marion Bridge, Cape Breton; and the newly developed park at Goshen south of Antigonish. This quartet features indigenous small mammals, birds of prey, and waterfowl in open or enclosed settings, hiking trails outside the animal area, and picnic tables.

Provincial parks are detailed in the annual *Doers and Dreamers* travel guide, available at all information centers as well as on the government website, www.gov.ns.ca.

## CLIMATE

Nova Scotia's climate is similar to the rest of Atlantic Canada. The seasons are distinct, with mild winters and cool summers. Mainland Nova Scotia's climate differs noticeably from Cape Breton's, where more extreme weather patterns occur. Average precipitation amounts to 130 centimeters, falling mainly as rain during autumn and as snow in winter. Frost-free periods range from 120 days on Cape Breton to 145 days in the sheltered Annapolis Valley.

**Spring** arrives late, with temperatures ranging from -2.5 to 9° C. **Summer** weather varies. Daytime temperatures average up to 30° C.

Nights are usually cool at around 12° C, but can dip to 5° C in late summer. Inland areas are generally five degrees warmer. The coasts often bask in morning fog, which is later dispersed by sea breezes and the warming sun. Late in the season, Caribbean hurricanes, having spent their force farther south, limp through the region, bringing to the northwestern Atlantic short spells of rain and wind.

In **autumn,** the evenings start to cool, but warm days continue until the end of September at up to 18° C. The days are cool to frosty October through mid-November. **Winter** lasts from late November through early March, with high temperatures averaging -10 to 4° C.

**Environment Canada** has updated weather forecasts; contact 902/426-9090 or www.weatheroffice.com.

## Water Temperatures

Atlantic Canadians know that Nova Scotia is famed for its swimming and surfing. The seas are not bathtub hot, but water temperatures in some areas can be pleasantly warm. Conditions vary on the four seas and in each region. The warmest seas during August are found around Cape Breton's northern tip and along the Northumberland Strait—in both places temperatures reach 18° C. The Atlantic is a cool 10–15° C at Mahone Bay and warms a bit as you head up the coast to the northeast, hence the popularity of surfing at Martinique and Lawrencetown beaches. Generally, Cape Breton's coastal waters range 14–17° C. The Bay of Fundy is always cool to cold, although it becomes bearable at Mavillete Beach above Yarmouth, where low tide leaves shallow pools that warm up.

## FLORA AND FAUNA

In the 1970s, environmentalists were alarmed by the rapid rate of deforestation in the province, as woodlands were felled for their timber and to make room for expanding farmland. In the following decades, however, protective measures were enacted, and today over 80 percent of Nova Scotia is thickly blanketed by typical Acadian forest of mixed hardwoods and conifers. Common trees include hemlock, spruce, balsam fir, yellow and paper birches, cedar, maple, ash, and oak. In autumn, the brilliant hues of the changing leaves are one of the province's most cherished attractions.

The province has set aside large tracts at Kejimkujik and Cape Breton Highlands national parks, which protect areas of unique plant habitat. In the Cape Breton Highlands, for example, stands of 300-year-old maples (believed to be the oldest in the country) have survived, and unusual wild orchid species thrive there as well. In the Highlands' highest elevations, the stunted taiga and alpine-arctic plant communities have been included in an international biological preserve. Bogs in the national parks nourish insectivorous pitcher plants, more orchids, and other specially adapted species.

Common wildflowers throughout Nova Scotia—easily seen along roadsides in summertime—include lupine, Queen Anne's lace, yarrow, pearly everlasting, and a variety of daisies. Everywhere, the showy spikes of purple loosestrife, a pretty but aggressive and unwelcome pest, flourishes. Bayberry bushes and wild roses bloom on the Chignecto Isthmus during June. The provincial flower is the trailing arbutus (mayflower), which blooms in early spring in woodlands and barrens.

## Fauna

Some 260 bird species have been reported in Nova Scotia. The province is best known for its bald eagles; about 250 pairs nest here, the second-largest population on North America's east coast after Florida. The season for eagle watching is July and August. Some of the prime viewing areas are the Lake Ainslie and St. Ann's Bay coastlines; the village of Iona, where Bras d'Or Lake meets St. Andrews Channel on Cape Breton; and the St. George's Bay coastline. Ospreys nest on McNab's Island in Halifax Harbour. Other raptors may be seen at Brier Island on the Bay of Fundy.

As Nova Scotia lies on the Atlantic flyway, many migratory species can be spotted including common and arctic terns, kittiwakes, great and double-crested cormorants, Leach's storm petrels, Atlantic puffins, guillemots, and various gulls, ducks, and geese.

The **whales** that frequent Nova Scotia arrive from the Caribbean between June and mid-July and remain through October. Watching the whales cavort is one of summer's great visitor delights; whale-watching boats leave from Brier Island on the Bay of Fundy and Cape Breton's Chéticamp. The Fundy is especially rich in whales, and the fast incoming tides bring in the mammoth mammals in pursuit of herring schools. Among the 20 species that summer offshore, the most frequently sighted are minkes, pilots, fins, orcas, humpbacks, and the rare right whale.

Other mammals found in the province are black bear, bobcat, lynx, red fox, coyote, whitetailed deer, and moose.

## HISTORY

The earliest evidence of human habitation in the region dates from about 8600 B.C. and is found at the present site of Debert, inland from the Minas Basin's northern coast. The Vikings may have visited about A.D. 1000; a boulder inscribed with what may be Nordic runes was found near Cape Forchu, where, some believe, Leif Eriksson and his men put ashore. (The boulder is now on display at the Yarmouth County Museum in Yarmouth.)

### Early European Settlement

Nova Scotia's tie to Europe began in 1497, when the explorer John Cabot sighted Cape Breton and claimed it for England. England's claim notwithstanding, France eyed the area for colonization and dispatched explorer Samuel de Champlain to the region in 1604. Champlain's expedition first wintered (and almost perished) at a settlement on the St. Croix River, which now forms the New Brunswick–Maine border. In 1605, the encampment moved across the Bay of Fundy, where the fortified **Port Royal,** one of the earliest European settlements in Canada, was established near what is now Annapolis Royal. The French named the region—encompassing what is now Nova Scotia, New

Brunswick, PEI, and part of Maine—Acadia ("Peaceful Land"). Not to be outdone, England's James I named the same region Nova Scotia— New Scotland—and granted it to Sir William Alexander in 1621. The British burned Port Royal in 1613. Scottish settlers arrived in 1629 and staked out the same area, but left within three years.

A 1632 peace treaty forced England to surrender Nova Scotia to the French. Bitter military confrontations began and flared through the mid-1700s. The two powers had different strategies: France first built settlements, then used its military to defend them. England, boasting a superior military savvy, fought its battles first, then used settlements to stabilize areas. As it turned out, Britain had the edge, and it was upon this advantage that Maritime history frequently turned over the following century and a half.

### Expansion

From their Port Royal hub, the French explored the Fundy coast and the Atlantic seacoast as far south as LaHave. By 1632, 45 Acadian villages rimmed the upper Fundy's marshes. The villagers cultivated grains and forage crops on wetlands reclaimed by dikes, and farther southwest planted the region's first orchards. By 1650, merchant-explorer Nicolas Denys had established fortified settlements at Guysborough on Chedabucto Bay and St. Peters on the southern tip of Île Royale. Grand-Pré, just east of Wolfville, was a major Acadian town from 1675 to 1755.

In 1705, France's original Port Royal was relocated to the Annapolis River's other side. Five years later, the British swooped in and took the fort, renaming it Fort Anne in honor of their queen. They also rechristened the town as Annapolis Royal, which served as Nova Scotia's first capital (Halifax took over the role in 1749).

The 1713 Treaty of Utrecht awarded the region to England. The French military fled to Île Royale (Cape Breton Island) where they began construction of the Fortress of Louisbourg and Acadian seacoast settlements. England countered with a fort on Grassy Island in Chedabucto Bay, captured Louisbourg in 1745, again in 1758, and finally demolished the site in 1760.

England had deported 10,000 Acadians from Fort Edward near Windsor in 1755. Some had fled to the Île Royale hinterlands—St. Ann's, Chéticamp, Isle Madame—and to other remote areas. But within a few years, the resilient Acadians started to return to the mainland, settling along the Côte Acadienne (Acadian Coast), on the lower Bay of Fundy.

The British began peopling the territory with less fractious, pro-Crown settlers. Lunenburg began with 2,000 German, Swiss, and French "foreign Protestants" in 1753. In 1760, England resettled the prime Fundy seacoast once farmed by the Acadians with 12 shiploads of farmers (New England planters) from its colonies farther south. The Crown officially regained the region, including Île Royale, with the Peace of Paris in 1763. The first shipload of Scots fleeing Scotland's infamous land clearances docked at Pictou in 1773. In 1830, a census counted 50,000 Scots in Pictou and Antigonish Counties.

After the American Revolution, 25,000 British Loyalists poured into Nova Scotia. Several thousand American blacks arrived during the War of 1812, followed by Irish immigrants from 1815 to 1850.

## Nova Scotia Takes Shape

In the late 18th century, Prince Edward Island and New Brunswick were defined as distinct colonies. Cape Breton, for a while a separate colony, was reannexed to Nova Scotia in 1820. Responsibility for government was granted in 1848.

The province became a founding member of the Dominion of Canada in 1867. Confederation was unpopular, but it offered economic inducements, including the rail connections to eastern Canada that Nova Scotia wanted. By 1876, the Intercolonial Railway had service as far as Ontario, and rail service within the province linked major towns by 1881.

Fortunes were founded on trade. Halifax's Samuel Cunard started a shipping empire based on steamship service to England in 1839. During the Great Age of Sail, shipbuilding seaports thrived. In 1878, Yarmouth ranked as Canada's second-largest port. Coal mining began in 1872 at Springhill, near Amherst, where the 1,220-meter shaft was Canada's deepest.

The luster faded by the 1900s. Shipbuilding's heyday was over. Nova Scotians looking for work migrated to the United States, and farms were abandoned. On April 15, 1913, the *Titanic* sank in the chilly waters of the North Atlantic east of Newfoundland. Many unidentified victims were buried in Halifax cemeteries. Four years later, during the height of World War I, two ships collided in Halifax Harbour. The explosion blew out 1,600 buildings, killed 2,000 Haligonians, and injured an estimated 9,000 more.

## Famous Nova Scotians

Prominent personalities emerged with the prosperous times. **Alfred Fuller** was born at Annapolis Royal, lived for a while in Yarmouth, and later moved to the United States, where he made a fortune with Fuller Brushes. **Alexander Graham Bell,** the Scottish inventor whose business interests were in the United States, created a retreat at Cape Breton's Baddeck, where he conducted tireless research and among other achievements helped launch the first airplane flight in the British Empire in 1909.

**Anna Leonowens,** later immortalized as the prim governess in Broadway's *The King and I,* joined relatives in Halifax and started an arts school, which evolved into the Nova Scotia College of Art and Design. The 1800s finished as **Joshua Slocum** of Westport sailed around the world and set a record as the first man to do so alone. Among the province's more famous expatriates are singer Anne Murray and television's Robert MacNeil.

Famous Nova Scotian author Thomas Chandler Haliburton

BOB RACE

NOVA SCOTIA

## The *Bluenose*

The famous schooner *Bluenose* was launched from Lunenburg in 1921. The schooner won every racing competition it entered and served also as a Grand Banks and Scotian Shelf fishing craft. Sold eventually to foreign investors, the vessel sank off Haiti during World War II. The original *Bluenose,* whose image is on the back of the Canadian dime, was re-created in 1963 as the *Bluenose II* at Lunenburg, where it is now permanently berthed.

**Bluenose II under full sail**

BOB RACE

## GOVERNMENT

The Progressive Conservatives dominate the 52-member provincial Legislative Assembly, with the New Democrats forming the official opposition. The Liberal Party has historically been the strongest, having held power for more than 100 years in total since confederation, but the party was badly defeated in 1999. On the federal level, Nova Scotia sends 10 senators to the Upper House and 11 to the House of Commons.

Sixty-six municipalities make up the province, and Halifax is the capital.

## ECONOMY

In 2001, Nova Scotia's gross domestic product (GDP) was a little over $13 billion, with manufacturing generating the largest segment ($1.6 billion). Among the largest manufacturers here are Michelin Tire Canada, Volvo Canada, Crossley Karastan Carpet, and Pratt and Whitney. Governments are usually better at spending money than earning it, but are officially listed as having contributed $1.3 billion to the provincial economy. Tourism ranks third, generating $1.2 billion. Most visitors (38 percent) are from the neighboring provinces, while the rest of Canada contributes 30 percent, and the United States adds almost 25 percent. Of the 1.6 million people who arrive annually, more than three-quarters are returning vis-

itors. Traditional stalwarts of the economy have recently decreased in importance dollar-wise. Fisheries and fish processing are tenth in economic importance—cod, haddock, herring, and lobster are caught inshore and off the Atlantic's Scotian Shelf. (The province is the world's largest lobster exporter.)

Though just 8 percent of Nova Scotia's land is arable, agriculture contributes heavily to the economy, producing fruits (including Annapolis Valley apples), dairy products, poultry, hogs, and the world's largest share of blueberries. The province's extensive forests support substantial lumber and paper industries; among the largest are Bowater (half owned by the *Washington Post*) on the south shore and the Irving Forest Products pulp mills at Abercrombie Point, Point Tupper, Brooklyn, Hantsport, and East River.

The province is also the region's federal civil service and military center. Halifax has served as a naval center since its founding in 1749 as headquarters for the Royal Navy. The city is now Maritime Command headquarters for the Canadian armed forces. Other military installations are at Shearwater, Cornwallis, and Greenwood; training stations are located at Barrington, Mill Cove, Shelburne, and Sydney.

And trade still greases the economic wheels here. Eleven of the province's 267 harbors are major shipping ports, and Halifax, Sydney, and Point Tupper on the Strait of Canso rank as the busiest ports. Dartmouth has a 36-hectare auto port that handles 100,000 vehicles a year.

## THE PEOPLE

Nova Scotia's population of about 900,000 is dominated by persons of English ancestry; four of five Nova Scotians trace their lineage to the British Isles. Some 49 original Scottish families, from Archibald to Yuill, are still on the rolls of the Scottish Societies Association of Nova Scotia, which does genealogical surveys. After the American Revolution, Loyalists came here from New York, New Jersey, Connecticut, Rhode Island, and Massachusetts.

The other 20 percent of the population is a mix of ethnicities. Descendants of the original Acadians now number 35,000, a 4.5 percent minority. About 25,000 Mi'kmaq Indians lived in the region when the Europeans arrived; the Mi'kmaqs now number 6,305 on 16 reservations. And the province has more than 50 other minority ethnic groups, including Poles, Ukrainians, Germans, Swiss, Africans, and Lebanese.

The province has a youthful population, with 40 percent of the people under 25 years old. And they're well educated: Nova Scotia has the highest college and university attendance rate of any Canadian province. Population density is about 17 people per square kilometer.

### Language and Religion

Nova Scotians speak with an eastern Canadian lilt derived from British and Gaelic, ending each sentence on a high note, as though a question had been asked. English is spoken by 94 percent of Nova Scotians, while 7.4 percent are bilingual. French has gained appeal as a second language, and one in four primary schoolchildren in Halifax is enrolled in French immersion classes.

## TRACING FAMILY ROOTS

If you are interested in tracing family ties, the place to start is with **Nova Scotia Archives & Records Management,** 6016 University Ave., Halifax, tel. 902/424-6060, www.gov.ns.ca /nsarm. The facility is open to the public Mon.–Fri. 8:30 A.M.–4:30 P.M., as well on Saturday (with limited services) 9 A.M.–5 P.M. It's possible to take advantage of the departments resources without visiting in person. Their website is an excellent starting point—helpful for everyone from those searching out long lost relatives to professional genealogists.

Ancestries originating on Cape Breton can be traced at the **Beaton Institute,** University College of Cape Breton, Glace Bay (near Sydney), tel. 902/563-1329, www.uccb.ns.ca/archive.

Roman Catholics predominate at 37 percent on the mainland and 62 percent on Cape Breton. Anglicans account for almost 16 percent on the mainland and 10 percent on Cape Breton. Other Protestant denominations include the United Church of Canada, Baptist, and Presbyterian.

## ARTS AND CRAFTS

Arts and crafts shopping opportunities are numerous in Nova Scotia. About 60 major art galleries are scattered across the province. The farmers' markets are a source for local crafts; the major market is in Halifax, while another 16 summer markets are held at major towns and seaports from Annapolis Royal to Tatamagouche.

For a distilled taste of the province's fine arts and crafts, spend several hours at the **Art Gallery of Nova Scotia** in Halifax. Quilts, porcelains, and wooden folk carvings are deftly mixed among the watercolors, oils, and sculptures in the spacious galleries on Hollis Street, and the cream of provincial creativity is stocked at the museum's gift shop. The newest crafts developments are nurtured by the **Nova Scotia Centre for Craft and Design** on Barrington Street. The center opened in 1990 in Halifax, and its gallery includes weaving, wood, and jewelry exhibits.

The **Nova Scotia College of Art and Design,** 1891 Granville, is an accredited college in the avant-garde of the fine art world. The college's Anna Leonowens Gallery provides insight into the artists' direction.

Other homegrown products include the furniture of Bass River Chairs, with its factory and an outlet at Bass River west of Truro; and Grohmann Knives, which sells its cutlery at its factory outlet in Pictou near the Caribou ferry. Nova Scotia is also the place for things Scottish. Tartans in innumerable clan variations are available by the yard in wool or blends; tartan apparel is stocked at shops in Halifax, Yarmouth, and Cape Breton's South Gut St. Ann's.

*Studio Map* is a handy shopping guide. The free paperback book divides crafts producers by regions and towns, and an index lists the producers by medium. It's available at information centers, listed outlets, and online at www.studiorally.ca.

## ENTERTAINMENT AND EVENTS

Halifax attracts concerts and major events to the Halifax Metro Centre near the harbor. Farther up the hillside, the Neptune Theatre hosts year-round repertory theater, as does Dalhousie University's Rebecca Cohn Auditorium, which doubles as the home of the Symphony of Nova Scotia. Dozens of nightclubs and other venues around the capital city showcase established and up-and-coming local bands, such as Sloan, which are earning the province, and especially Halifax, a reputation as an influential breeding ground for pop, rock, and alternative music.

Cape Breton is renowned for its contributions to folk music. Not surprisingly, Scottish and Irish fiddle tunes form much of the source material, but Cape Breton musicians have taken that extremely rich foundation and made something with a uniquely Maritime flavor: frisky jigs and reels for dancing, as well as ballads, often centering on the theme of fishing and the ubiquitous sea. The more mainstream of these acts, such as the Rankins and Natalie MacMaster, draw huge crowds across Canada, as does the precocious and often eccentric Ashley MacIsaac. Cape Breton Island is also home to Rita MacNeil, whose rich and emotional songs are a source of inspiration worldwide.

### Events

Nova Scotia bills itself as "Canada's Official Festival Province"—something's almost always going on from spring through fall. Summers are particularly busy; a visitor could easily attend a different festival almost daily from June through August without a spare day.

Early season events provide a warm-up for the busy summer ahead. The **Apple Blossom Festival** is a showstopper when Annapolis Valley's apple trees are drenched in white blossoms during late May and early June.

As the weather heats up, so does the festival schedule. Some events take place over the whole summer. If your ancestral roots are Scottish (and even if they aren't), the **International Gathering of the Clans** will win you to the tartan fold with 80 festivals from Annapolis Royal to Cape Breton spaced over nine summertime weeks. Crustacean-cuisine connoisseurs will appreciate the **lobster bakes** that take place all summer in the towns of Pictou, River John, and Wallace on the Northumberland Strait.

Befitting its status as Canada's Maritime Command naval center, Halifax hosts the razzle-dazzle **Nova Scotia International Tattoo** over two weeks of festivals in late June or early July. The tattoo's events unfold in military precision. Crowds cheer as competing national naval reserve units take apart and reassemble an 1812 cannon in the Naval Gun Run. Bands play, military units compete in other contests of skill, and 10,000 spectators crowd the Metro Centre each night.

Named for a famed Canadian singer, the **Stan Rogers Folk Festival** draws thousands of music fans to the tiny fishing community of Canso the first weekend of July. Celtic merriment comes to nearby Antigonish in mid-July with the three-day **Highland Games,** featuring Highland dancing, pipe bands, piping competitions, concerts, and sports competitions. In late July, the two-day **Journées Acadienne de Grand-Pré** remembers the Acadian deportation at Grand-Pré. Life is seemingly a party year-round for Cape Bretoners, and their Celtic music can be heard at summer get-togethers throughout the island. One official event is **Festival de l'Escaouette,** an Acadian gathering held in Cheticamp late in July.

Events by the hundreds are listed with dates and sites in the *Doers and Dreamers* tourist guide, available online at www.explore.gov.ns.ca. The province observes federal holidays like the four-day Good Friday to Easter Monday weekend, plus Boxing Day and Christmas. The province adds its own Natal Day, and shops and public offices close the first Monday in August.

## RECREATION

The province boasts a fully developed sports scene, from the pedestrian to the exotic, and you can dabble in tennis or bird-watching, canoeing, deep-sea diving, hiking, and bicycling for starters. Many outfitters around the province rent bicycles, boats, and other equipment, and can equip you for wilderness expeditions and all sorts of other activities.

## Hiking

Hiking is popular throughout the province, including the two national parks, Kejimkujik and Cape Breton. The latter is showcased by an extensive trail system that traverses some of the world's most spectacular coastal scenery. The parks are managed by Parks Canada, www.parkscanada.gc.ca. Nova Scotia's 126 provincial parks generally lack long trails, but short walks often lead to local natural landmarks. Brochures on these walking trails are widely available at information centers, or check the Department of Natural Resources website, www.gov.ns.ca. Among the best of many books on the subject is *Hiking Trails of Nova Scotia,* available from the Nova Scotia Government Bookstore in Halifax. The hiking season spans spring to autumn; coastal areas are free of insects, but insect repellent is wise inland from mid-May through August.

## Biking

Getting around Nova Scotia by bike is easy. **Bicycle Nova Scotia,** www.bicycle.ns.ca, handles cycling information and publishes *Nova Scotia by Bicycle,* detailing 4,000 km of roads along 20 detailed routes. Halifax-based **Atlantic Canada Cycling,** tel. 902/423-2453, www.atl-canadacycling.com, promotes cycling throughout the region. Its website includes tips, a message board, and links to commercial operators.

Numerous outfits rent bikes and provide guided bike tours. **Freewheeling Adventures,** tel. 902/857-3600 or 800/672-0775, www.freewheeling.ca, leads tours emphasizing secondary roads and wooded trails, with accommodations arranged at country inns. In addition to set itineraries, the company is flexible, giving you the option to travel unguided, to combine biking with hiking and kayaking, or to design your own itinerary. Well-respected **Vermont Bike Tours,** tel. 802/453-4811 or 800/245-3868, website www.vbt.com, offers a seven-tour circuit from Halifax that hits all the hot spots including Lunenburg and the Annapolis Valley, with the option to ride as much or as little as you like between overnight stops at historic accommodations.

## Water Sports

Falling under the umbrella of Sport Nova Scotia, **Canoe Kayak Nova Scotia** provides information on all types of paddling, including lists of accredited instructors and commercial operators; write 5516 Spring Garden Rd., P.O. Box 3010, Halifax, NS B3J 3G6 or contact 902/425-5450, www.sportnovascotia.com.

The **Nova Scotia Underwater Council** handles deep-sea diving, and you will need a valid certification card to buy air. Only advanced divers should attempt the area, as ocean currents are swift and conditions change rapidly; divers must assume responsibility for checking out conditions before starting. The council can provide details on the province's dive clubs and dive sites (including 3,000 offshore wrecks). Contact the council at 902/425-5450 or through www.sportnovascotia.com.

Commercial operators run rafts and motorized Zodiacs on the tidal bore as the incoming Fundy high tide pushes inland up the Shubenacadie River.

Surfing has a small, dedicated following along the east coast. The best spots lie northeast of Halifax, including at Lawrencetown Beach.

## Fishing

Freshwater and anadromous fish varieties include Atlantic salmon, trout, shad, and bass. Salmon fishing with artificial flies or lures is the genteel passion here. Deep-sea fishing's star attraction is the giant bluefin tuna, which runs September–November. In 1979, a bluefin weighing a record 679 kilograms was caught off St. Georges Bay. The bay ranks as the top tuna area, while the Fundy coast off Yarmouth from Cape St. Mary to Wedgeport is another prime fishing area. Expect to pay $125–300 per person per day for a tuna charter. In addition to tuna, other deep-sea catches include pollock, mackerel, striped bass, sea trout, and bottom dwellers like haddock, cod, and halibut.

Anglers must purchase a license to fish inland waters and for salmon. For species other than salmon, no license is required for fishing in tidal waters, but seasons and bag limits are in effect. A seven-day general fishing license costs $23 for nonresidents. An annual general fishing license

# TWO TRADITIONAL ACADIAN RECIPES

**Rappie Pie**

This traditional recipe is unique for the texture of the potato filling, one succulent bite will make you a convert. (For best results, read recipe clear through before starting.)

5–6 lbs. chicken
6 large onions
2 tsp. salt (or 2 tbsp. salted onions)
1 tsp. pepper
1 pail of big potatoes

**1)** Cut chicken in pieces, place in large pot, and cover with water. Bring to boil. Add three large chopped onions, salt, and pepper. (While chicken is cooking, continue with following steps.) When chicken is cooked, remove it from the pot, remove meat from bones, and break pieces into desired size. Keep broth simmering to be used later.

**2)** Chop the remaining onions and sauté in butter or margarine until tender but not brown. Set aside to be used later.

**3)** Peel, rinse, and grate potatoes in a large bowl. Take note of how much grated potato you have, because later you will use this same large bowl to scald the potatoes after they are squeezed and you should have the same amount of potato mixture then as you have grated potatoes now.

**4)** Squeeze potatoes (about two cups at a time) in a fine cotton bag or cloth until quite dry. Place the squeezed potatoes in a second bowl as you go, and transfer them back into the large bowl when done. Add the sautéed onions.

---

costs $46 ($17.25 for Nova Scotia residents). If you have salmon fishing in mind, you'll need a different license; residents pay $28.75 for an annual license, nonresidents pay $46 for a seven-day license and $120.75 for an annual license. The regulatory authority is the Inland Fisheries Division of the Department of Agriculture and Fisheries, tel. 902/485-5056. Contact this office for a copy of the annual *Angling Regulations* booklet, or download it from www.gov.ns.ca/nsaf.

## Other Activities

The province has over 75 golf courses, a dozen within an hour's drive of Halifax. The best-known course in the province, considered one of Canada's finest, is **Cape Breton Highland Links** at Ingonish Beach within Cape Breton National Park. The provincial governing body is the **Nova Scotia Golf Association**, tel. 902/798-2532, www.nsga.ns.ca, which provides a listing of all courses with contact numbers and fees. The website www.golfin-gns.com holds similar information.

**Magnam Outfitters** leads guided outdoor-photography tours to backcountry areas with photogenic vistas of hills, vales, canyons scooped

like gigantic cups, and isolated headlands overlooking precipitous cliffs. For more information, write to P.O. Box 1001, Halifax, NS B3J 2X1 or call 902/685-2967.

The **Nova Scotia Bird Society** can put you onto prime birding sites and answer even the most esoteric questions about the province's 298 species. It also publishes the quarterly *Nova Scotia Birds* magazine and updates a birding hotline (tel. 902/852-2428). The group is based at the Nova Scotia Museum, 1747 Summer St., Halifax, NS B3H 3A6.

## ACCOMMODATIONS AND CAMPING

Nova Scotia has lodgings by the hundreds: historic inns in silk-stocking towns and salty seaports, sleek hotels in Halifax, and cabins and lodges in the hinterlands.

Hotels and motels range from deluxe high-rise towers and stately buildings to modest properties in the country. All major chains are represented, with details given in the travel chapters. Inns and bed-and-breakfasts are often his-

5) Scald the squeezed potatoes by adding the boiling chicken broth gradually and stirring constantly. Remember, you must end up with the same amount of scalded-potato mixture in this bowl as you had grated potatoes before. If you do not have enough broth, add boiling water. When you're through scalding, the mixture should be slightly thicker and darker. Add salt and pepper to taste.

6) Grease 17-by-12-inch pan and dust with flour. Spread half of the potato mixture in the pan. Spread chicken meat evenly over this. Cover with other half of potato mixture. Bake at 400° F for 2.5 hours. It should come out brown, crusty, and delicious! The more often you make it, the better it gets!

**Chicken Fricot**
A cross between a soup and a stew, this dish is especially appreciated on a cold winter evening.

2 lbs. chicken (meat cut in small pieces)
2 large onions, diced
2 tsp. salted onions (or 1 tsp. salt)
1/2 tsp. pepper
8 medium-sized potatoes, diced and rinsed
2 medium sized potatoes, grated

In a soup pot put chicken pieces, diced onions, salted onions, and pepper. Add 12 cups of water and bring to a boil. Cook for 30 minutes on medium heat. Add diced potatoes and continue to boil until cooked. To thicken fricot, lower heat to simmer and add grated potatoes. Cook a few minutes more. Serve hot in bowls.

*Courtesy of Imelda Chiasson, lifetime resident of Nova Scotia, from the village of Concessions, Municipality of Clare*

toric lodgings, and at their best are heritage properties furnished with antiques. Many market themselves under an umbrella organization, such as the **Nova Scotia Association of Unique Country Inns,** www.uniquecountryinns.com. Resorts are often geared to sports and recreational facilities. Three are operated by the province itself: the Pines Resort at Digby; Liscombe Lodge at Liscomb Mills; and Keltic Lodge within Cape Breton National Park; click on the individual links at www.signatureresorts.com for details.

Hostelling International, www.hihostels.ca, operates hostels in Halifax, LaHave (near Lunenburg), South Milford (near Kejimkujik National Park), Wentworth (between Amherst and Truro), and Mabou River (Cape Breton Island).

### Reservations
Reservations (up to a month in advance) at all lodgings are wise during July and August. During June and from September to October, reservations a day or two beforehand should be sufficient. Most lodgings accept credit cards, although bed-and-breakfasts may ask for cash or traveler's checks.

All reputable lodgings—hotels and motels,

B&Bs, lodges, and resorts—belong to the provincially operated **Check In** reservation system, tel. 902/425-5781 or 800/565-0000, www.checkinnovascotia.com. The system works well, but always confirm your booking and arrival time directly with the accommodation. The government's tourism website, www.explore.gov.ns.ca, provides links to all registered accommodations and is divided into helpful categories such as price range and region.

### Campgrounds
Dozens of commercial campgrounds dot the province, but often the best-located campgrounds are found in national and provincial parks. Campsites in the two national parks range $14–21 a night, depending on services. Most national park campgrounds have hiking trails and access to swimming and fishing, while some have hot showers, washrooms, and laundry sinks. Make reservations through Parks Canada at tel. 800/414-6765, www.parkscanada.gc.ca.

In addition to the day-use parks, 21 provincial parks are equipped with unserviced, basic **campgrounds** with potable water, cooking shelters and grills, washrooms, pay showers, inexpensive bundled wood, and often hiking trails, playgrounds, and beaches. They're open mid-May to early September. Sites cost $9–14. Check the *Doers and Dreamers* guide for details, or click through to the Provincial Parks link at www.gov.ns.ca.

## FOOD AND DRINK

Nova Scotian cooking is so distinctive that one of the best souvenirs is a cookbook with some of the culinary secrets. The style varies and is often on the sweet side. Locals shun hot spices and go lightly on other condiments. Dining in Halifax offers sophisticated cuisines from continental to nouvelle cuisine. Country-style cooking embodies the essence of provincial style in the smaller towns and seaports. Some wines are produced locally, and berries and fruits for mouthwatering desserts are harvested in the province.

Nova Scotians have been enjoying beer from Alexander Keith's Brewery for almost 200 years.

Seafood, meat, and produce abound here. Local lamb originates in Pictou County. Fruits and vegetables are fresh and are often picked from backyard inn and restaurant gardens. Local delicacies include wild chanterelle mushrooms, smoked mackerel pâté, and seafood from lobster to locally caught Digby scallops and pickled Solomon Gundy herring. Preserves are generally homemade. Soups range from lobster chowder thickened with whipped cream to pea soup brimming with corned beef chunks.

Salmon is often cooked on a board plank before an open fire, as the Mi'kmaq historically prepared it. Desserts know no limit and range from trifles rich with raspberry jam and sherry, to cheesecakes concocted of local cheese and cream, to molded flans embellished with fruit toppings.

Acadian cooking is another provincial variation. Acadian chicken *fricot* melds meat, onions, and potatoes in a soup as thick as stew. The *chiard* stew has its base in beef. *Rappie pie*, the best-known regional Acadian dish, mixes clams or chicken with grated potatoes as translucent as pearls.

If you travel on your stomach, look for the Taste of Nova Scotia emblem affixed to restaurant front windows or doors. The emblem is awarded to dining places judged noteworthy by the province; a booklet of the same name costs $1 and is available from tourist information centers.

### Drink

Locals like wine, especially French imports and local wines from the Jost and Grand-Pré wineries. Regional and locally brewed beers are quite popular, too. Nova Scotia favorites include Schooner and Keith's. The Granite Brewery in Halifax produces a variety of local brews, including stouts and seasonal specialties.

As elsewhere in Canada, strict regulations govern alcohol consumption. Licensed restaurants, dining rooms, and cocktail lounges serve liquor daily 11 A.M.–2 A.M. Beverage rooms with beer and wine are open Mon–Wed. 10 A.M.–11 P.M., Thurs.–Sat. to midnight. Lounge hours are Mon.–Sat. 11 A.M.–2 A.M.; cabarets are open nightly 7 P.M.–3 A.M. Alcohol is sold at govern-

# A PHOTOGRAPHER'S DREAM

Nova Scotia has incredible light for photography. The sky turns from a Wedgwood color to sapphire blue—a beautiful background for seacoast photographs. Rise at dawn to take advantage of the first rays of sunlight hitting picturesque east coast villages like popular **Peggy's Cove** (home to the "world's most photographed lighthouse") and **Fisherman's Cove,** both within an hour's drive of Halifax, as well as delightful seaside gems such as **Blue Rocks,** beyond Lunenberg. The town of Lunenberg itself attracts photographers for its harborfront panorama of colorful buildings. While

photography is best when the weather is favorable—and that's more often than not—don't pass up a morning basking in thick mist, as bright sun illuminates the sky behind the thick clouds. The fog breaks apart gradually, and when it does, the sun radiates like a spotlight, illuminating the sparkling dampness that clings briefly to the landscape.

© ANDREW HEMPSTEAD

**the oft-photographed Peggy's Cove, south of Halifax**

ment liquor stores, open Mon.–Thurs. 10 A.M.–6 P.M., Fri. to 10 P.M., Sat. to 5 P.M. The minimum drinking age is 19.

## INFORMATION AND SERVICES
### Visitor Information
In the first instance, contact the **Department of Tourism and Culture,** P.O. Box 456, Halifax, NS B3J 2R5; tel. 902/425-5781 or 800/565-0000; www.explore.gov.ns.ca. This office distributes numerous publications, including the information-packed *Doers and Dreamers* guide, updated annually, as well as guides to golfing, fishing, festivals and events, and accommodations. Order by mail, phone, or online. The province also operates 11 **visitor information centers.** Locations include the International Visitor Centre at 1595 Barrington Street in Halifax, the Halifax International Airport, and gateway cities such as Amherst, Pictou, Yarmouth, Digby, Portland (Maine), and Bar Harbour (Maine).

### Visitors with Disabilities
The **Nova Scotia League for Equal Opportunities** acts as an information source for the handicapped and compiles updated lists of lodgings and other places equipped with wheelchair access and special facilities like telephones with amplifying devices. For more information call 902/455-6942 or 866/696-7536. The league's website, www.nsnet.org/leo, is another excellent source of information.

### Communications
The area code for all Nova Scotia is **902.**

City and town post offices are open Mon.–Fri. 8:15 A.M.–5:15 P.M., while rural outlets have varying hours and some are open Saturdays.

**Public Internet access** is a breeze in Nova Scotia. The Community Access Program (CAP) consists of 300 locations across the province with public Internet access. Its brochure, available at information centers, gives addresses, but it's easier to print out the list in advance from www.nsaccess.ns.ca/cap.

NOVA SCOTIA

# GETTING THERE

The TransCanada Highway links Nova Scotia and New Brunswick with an easy travel corridor that funnels visitors into and out of the province; in fact, more visitors arrive at Amherst near the border than anyplace else. Frequent air service connects Nova Scotia with neighboring provinces, the States, and Europe. Ferry service links the province with Prince Edward Island, New Brunswick, Newfoundland, and the state of Maine.

## By Air

Halifax International Airport, 902/873-1233, is served by **Air Canada** and its regional connector **Air Nova,** tel. 888/247-2262, www.aircanada.ca, from throughout all Canadian provinces as well as Boston, Newark, and London. Other airlines serving Halifax include **Air Labrador,** tel. 800/563-3042; **Air St. Pierre,** tel. 902/873-3566; **Continental,** tel. 800/784-4444; and **Icelandair,** tel. 800/223-5500.

Smaller airports at Yarmouth and Sydney handle provincial and regional air traffic.

## By Land

The TransCanada routes visitors into the province at Amherst near the New Brunswick border. By **bus,** Voyageur from Montréal and Greyhound from the United States connect with SMT, whose buses run throughout Atlantic Canada under various regional names, including Acadian Lines in Nova Scotia, tel. 800/567-5151, www.smtbus.com

**VIA Rail,** tel. 800/561-3952, www.viarail.ca, has frequent service from Montréal via New Brunswick and stops at Amherst, Truro, and Halifax.

## By Sea

Nova Scotia is linked to the United States by two ferry routes, both originating in Maine. *The Cat,* tel. 902/742-6800 or 888/249-7245, www.cat-ferry.com, makes the 167-km (100-mile) crossing between Bar Harbor and Yarmouth at speeds of up to 90 kph (55 mph) and in an astonishing 2.5 hours. The space-age Aussie-built vessel is as big as a football field—but infinitely faster. The

*Cat* runs twice a day in each direction June through September, once a day in each direction in May and October. The peak season one-way fare (July and August) is adults US$55, seniors US$50, children US$25, vehicles under 6.6 feet US$95, vehicles under 9.9 feet US$120, and bicycles US$30. Walk-on passengers returning to their point of origin on the same day as departure pay only the one-way fare. The longer option is the 11-hour trip between Yarmouth and Portland aboard the *Scotia Prince,* tel. 207/775-5616 or 800/341-7540, www.scotiaprince.com. Peak season (mid-June to mid-September) one-way fare is adults US$86, children US$43, vehicles US$105; discounted to US$66, US$33, and US$85, respectively, outside peak season. Cabins range US$38–175 each way. Ferries leave Portland from the International Marine Terminal at 468 Commercial Street.

Ferries also link Nova Scotia to all three neighboring Atlantic Canada provinces. **Bay Ferries,** tel. 902/245-2116 or 888/249-7245, www.nfl-bay.com, sails the *Princess of Acadia* between Saint John and Digby, Nova Scotia, year-round. Boats leave up to three times daily each way in peak summer season, twice daily in the late spring and early fall shoulder seasons, once daily the rest of the year. In summer season (late June to mid-October), the one-way fare is adults $35, seniors $30, children $15, vehicles $70. The rest of the year, the fares are discounted to $20, $17.50, and $10, but the vehicle fare remains at $70. This 2.5-hour, 72-km crossing saves you many hundreds of kilometers if you're traveling from the southern end of New Brunswick to Nova Scotia.

Ferry routes to Prince Edward Island have been cut since the opening of the Confederation Bridge to the mainland, but one important sailing remains. It's between Wood Islands, 62 km east of Charlottetown, and Caribou, 25 km north of Pictou. One-way fares are $49 per vehicle including passengers, walk-on passengers $11, bicycles $20, motorcycles $25, and motor homes, campers, and cars with trailers $61–74. You pay only for leaving the island—the trip over is free. The service is operated by **Northumberland Ferries Ltd.**

(NFL), tel. 902/566-3838 or 800/565-0201, www.nfl-bay.com. The 75-minute crossing operates May to mid-December, with up to nine crossings in each direction daily during peak summer season.

Marine Atlantic, tel. 902/794-5254 or 800/341-7981, www.marine-atlantic.ca, operates vessels along two routes from North Sydney on Cape Breton Island to Newfoundland. The North Sydney–Port aux Basques ferry takes 5–7 hours, depending on the season, with up to 16 crossings per week year-round. The one-way fare is adults $22, seniors $20, children $11. Vehicles up to six meters long are charged $67. The North Sydney–Argentia service ferry runs mid-June through September only, with two 14-hour crossings per week. One-way fare is adults $60, seniors $55, children $30, vehicles up to six meters long $135.

## GETTING AROUND

Forget about taking in the whole province on a quick driving circuit. Nova Scotia boasts more sightseeing than a visitor can digest in a lifetime of short visits. Itinerary planning beforehand is essential.

The province consists of the capital at Halifax and three main regions. The **central region** includes the cities of Amherst—where the Trans-Canada enters the province—and **Truro,** where another expressway (Hwy. 102) heads south to Halifax. The **southwest region** encompasses the mainland peninsula's southwestern end and includes the Atlantic shore southwest of Halifax, Yarmouth and the Acadian coast, and the Annapolis Valley. The **eastern region** extends northeast beyond Halifax and Truro to Cape Breton's tip; the area includes the Atlantic shore northeast of Halifax, the Northumberland Strait coast, and **Cape Breton Island,** which is treated in this guide as a separate section.

### Roads and Driving

Long distances notwithstanding, the province has a superb system of roads, classified by numbers. For example, the TransCanada (Highway 104) enters at Amherst, zips east across the mainland, and finishes at North Sydney. The highway is one of the new 100-series roads designed for rapid transit. Similar highways connect major towns in the central region and rim the heavily traveled southwest region's seacoast along the Fundy.

The highways numbered 1–99 often parallel the 100-series expressways and connect major cities and towns. Roads numbered 200–399 are paved, rambling, two-lane routes that take visitors to all the interesting out-of-the-way places. These roads often work as diversionary routes off major sightseeing highways such as Highway 316, which departs the eastern shore's Highway 7 and meanders through Canso and Guysborough on its way to the Canso Strait.

The Cabot Trail around western Cape Breton is the exception. It is unnumbered and ranks as a special scenic highway.

The province is strict about driving regulations. Seat belts must be worn. The minimum fine for speeding is $50. Drinking while driving carries a $2,000 fine, six months in jail, or both.

### Bus

The major bus companies are based in Halifax. **Acadian Lines,** the province's largest bus service, has routes throughout the province. **Zinck Bus** serves towns along the eastern shore to Sherbrooke.

Halifax, Dartmouth, Sydney, Yarmouth, and Pictou have local public transit systems. Otherwise, be prepared to hoof it, as people in smaller communities rely on private transportation.

### Rental Cars

**Avis,** tel. 902/429-0963; **Budget,** tel. 902/492-7500; **Dollar,** tel. 902/860-0203; **Hertz,** tel. 902/873-3700; **National,** tel. 902/873-3505; and **Thrifty,** tel. 902/424-1515, rent cars at Halifax International Airport. Avis and Budget also have rentals at the Yarmouth and Sydney airports.

# Central Nova Scotia

Central Nova Scotia was once the realm of Glooscap, the Mi'kmaq Indian god who roamed this part of Nova Scotia as a man as large as Gulliver among the Lilliputians. A legend relates that Glooscap slept stretched out over the region's northern portion and used Prince Edward Island as his pillow.

This region is at once the most traveled and least known part of the province. The provincial highway system here is, you might say, too efficient. The TransCanada Highway. (Highway 104 here) enters the province from New Brunswick and breezes past Amherst near the border. From there it slices across the region's northern hinterlands and jogs south to Truro, getting you there in two quick hours. At Truro, the TransCanada turns east on the way to Sydney, Cape Breton—a six-hour drive. Truro also marks the place where Highway 102 peels off to Halifax, 100 km southwest.

Sightseers on a fast track see central Nova Scotia as a flash of landscape. But why hurry? The region is refreshingly off the beaten tourist track. Lodgings and dining places are plentiful at Amherst, Truro, and innumerable villages. The area's sightseeing is worth several days, more if you have such eclectic interests as geology, archaeology, wine-tasting, Fundy watching, or river rafting.

The summer climate is pleasant. Beaches on the strait are bathtub-warm. Vineyards flourish in the

Halifax waterfront

temperate climate, and the area revels in berries. Strawberries ripen in June, and blueberries are ready in August. Both harvests beget summertime events.

## HISTORY

Nova Scotia's first man lived 10,000 years ago in a Stone Age village at Debert northwest of Truro. The site's archaeological dig yielded 4,000 artifacts; arrowhead reproductions are on exhibit at the Debert Development Office near exit 13 on the TransCanada. The first Europeans to find their way here were French. Champlain established Port Royal in 1605 and made an exploratory sweep of the upper Fundy in 1607. French farmers subsequently settled along the coastlines.

England's Acadian Deportation recast the region with an Anglo complexion. The Acadians had settled Les Planches in 1675, but the village became Amherst when New England planters settled it in 1764. The Acadians' village of Cobequid changed to Truro in 1759, when it was settled with immigrants from northern Ireland. Amherst gained Yorkshire settlers in the 1780s, and the Scots and more Irish arrived in the northern region in the early 1800s.

Sandstone quarried from Wallace on the strait built some of Canada's finest buildings, such as Ottawa's Parliament Buildings and the province houses in both Halifax and PEI's Charlottetown. Canada's largest wooden ship was built and launched by Maitland shipbuilding magnate W. D. Lawrence in 1874.

The region's importance as a travel corridor goes back centuries. Dirt roads first traversed the southern area during colonial times. The Shubenacadie Canal project was the next great projected route. The scheme was funded in 1797

## THE COLOSSAL FUNDY TIDES

The world's highest tides rise in the upper Bay of Fundy—up to a 17-meter vertical gain at the head of the bay. The Fundy and its numerous branches hereabouts have as many place-names as the bay has moods. The upper Fundy is split into two arms by Cape Chignecto, the wedge-shaped point that angles into the bay. On one side, Chignecto Bay with its raw, lonesome coastline penetrates inland and finishes at Cumberland Basin near Amherst. On the cape's other side, the bay compresses itself first into the Minas Channel. Cape Split blocks high tide's route with a hook-shaped peninsula that reaches north almost to the opposite shore.

The tides work on roughly a six-hour cycle, and each peak or low arrives 50 minutes later each day. Twice daily, six hours after high tide, the bay is empty, but then the Fundy surges onward and water pours into Minas Basin like a restrained tidal wave. The force finishes in Cobequid Bay, not as a whimper but as an upright tidal bore (lead wave) that rides inland up the area's rivers. The arriving wave can be a dainty, ankle-high ripple or an upright wall of knee-high water, depending on the tide. During the highest tides, rafters ride the advancing bores upstream.

Due to the convoluted coastline, viewing the phenomena is possible at dozens of points around the bay, including near Truro, along the Shubenacadie River, around Minas Basin, on Cape Chignecto, and across the border in downtown Moncton (New Brunswick). Tide tables are posted in shops and storefronts everywhere. Tides are highest around the full or new moon.

**Warning:** The Bay of Fundy at low tide can be perilously alluring, when the coastal sea floor looks tranquilly bare, and mudflats glisten like glass. High tide's arrival is subtle and hardly noticeable. The distant tidal stirrings alert sea birds, and they cry out and wheel and turn across the sky. But then the sea moves in relentlessly, swelling and pushing forward into the bay at six knots an hour—and up to 13 knots in tidal rips. The incoming sea can wash across the empty bay faster than a person can swiftly walk. Only a foolhardy sightseer walks the mudflats. The high tide stops for nothing.

17 METERS = 55.77'

and begun in 1826, but the emergence of quicker, cheaper railroad shipping caused its demise in 1870. A century later, the province restored some canal locks in the most picturesque places. Locks 6, 7, and 8 now form the backdrops for picnicking visitors in the Enfield area near Halifax International Airport.

The region has a diverse economy. Manufacturing and light industry are based at Amherst and Truro. Farming, forestry, and quarrying operations lie across the interior, and fishing and fish processing are centered at seaports on Northumberland Strait.

Among the region's better-known sons and daughters are Simon Newcomb, the scientist and astronomer born at Wallace in 1835, and country music singer Anne Murray, whose life is depicted at Anne Murray Centre in her hometown of Springhill.

# Cumberland and Colchester Counties

## AMHERST

Amherst (pop. 9,000) is built on high ground above Amherst Marsh—part of the larger, 200-square-km Tantramar Marshes—on the isthmus joining Nova Scotia to the mainland. The fertile marshes were first diked and farmed by the Acadians in the 1600s, and are still productive today, mainly as hayfields.

Amherst was named for Jeffrey Amherst, who led the British victory over the French at Louis-bourg in 1758. Four Fathers of the Confederation were born in the town, and the Cumberland County Museum is in the spacious former homestead cottage of Robert Dickey, one of the distinguished quartet. As the geographic center of the Maritimes, the town accrued its initial wealth as "Busy Amherst," the hub of textile, piano, and shoe production in the late 1800s.

Amherst is easy to bypass, as expressways with fast-moving traffic encircle but do not enter the town. The TransCanada's initial loop

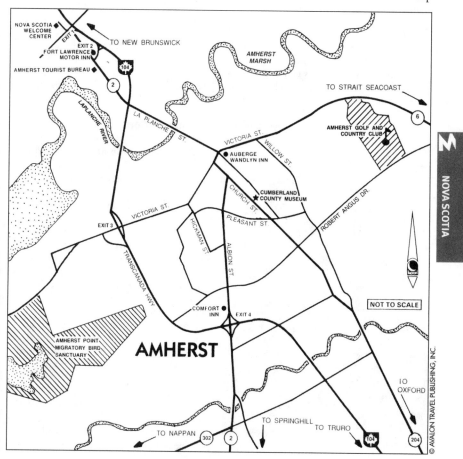

NOVA SCOTIA

around Amherst comes up quickly at exit 2, which leads to Laplanche Street. The highway's next exit to Victoria Street is situated on another fast-moving curve, and the following exit is almost beyond town.

None of which helps Amherst, though the town is certainly worth a stop. The historic district is along Victoria Street's eastern end. Laplanche Street is motel row. The town's two shopping malls are on the outskirts on Albion Street. The main streets form routes that lead out of town. Victoria Street turns into Highway 6 and heads for the strait seacoast, while Albion Street changes to Highway 2 and becomes the scenic backcountry road to Springhill.

## Sights

Amherst is at its architectural best along Victoria Street, where the profits of industry and trade were translated into gracious houses and commercial buildings garnished in Tudor, Gothic, Queen Anne Revival, and other ornate styles. Royal Bank of Canada occupies a historic sandstone showpiece built in 1903. Its windows are embellished with arches, peaks, and Corinthian pillars. The nearby Bank of Nova Scotia is in another sandstone beauty built in 1887. A few blocks south of the historic district, **Cumberland County Museum,** 150 Church St., tel. 902/667-2561, is in the 1838 home of early provincial legislator Robert McGowan Dickey. The museum does an impressive job of tracking the past with exhibits on early Acadian settlements, Amherst's Anglo background, and spicy tidbits relating to Russian revolutionary Leon Trotsky, who was interned in an Amherst POW camp in 1917. The museum is open year-round; May–September, Mon.–Sat. 9 A.M.–5 P.M., Sun. 2–5 P.M. Admission is $1 for adults.

**Amherst Point Migratory Bird Sanctuary,** a few kilometers from town at the end of Victoria, spreads out over 190 hectares with trails through woodlands, fields, and marshes, and around ponds. The sediment-rich Cumberland Basin lures 200 bird species, including Eurasian kestrels, bald eagles, hawks, and snowy owls.

## Accommodations

If you're coming across from New Brunswick, the **Fort Lawrence Motor Inn** on La Planche Street, tel. 902/667-3881, is a convenient choice on the western outskirts of Amherst. It charges $55–85 for a basic motel room and has a restaurant, lounge, and laundry facilities. To get there, take the Nova Scotia Welcome Centre exit and continue east along La Planche Street for a few hundred meters. **Auberge Wandlyn Inn** on Victoria Street off Highway 104 at exit 3, tel. 902/667-3331 or 800/561-0000, www.wandlyn.com, the town's largest lodging, has 88 rooms (from $70), a dining room and lounge, a heated indoor pool, saunas, and a whirlpool. **Comfort Inn,** 143 S. Albion St., tel. 902/667-0404 or 800/228-5150, www.choicehotels.ca, has 61 rooms and includes the morning newspaper and coffee in its rates of $95–110.

## Food

**David A's Café,** 125 Victoria St., tel. 902/661-0760, has a surprisingly varied menu for a small-town restaurant, with local produce and seafood prominent in most dishes. It's open Mon.–Sat.

Amherst mural

for lunch and dinner. On the next downtown block, the **Helm Restaurant,** 85 Victoria St., tel. 902/667-8871, may lack the atmosphere of David A's but offers good value, nightly specials, and a Friday night beef buffet for $10. The dining room at the Auberge Wandlyn Inn, tel. 902/667-3331, has inspired offerings by a creative chef who likes flamed steak with shrimp sauce and Caesar salad tossed at the table. Entrées range $14–28.

Supermarkets and other food stores are at **Cumberland Mall,** 147 S. Albion, tel. 902/667-1030, and **Amherst Centre Mall,** 142 S. Albion, tel. 902/667-2435. **Jacob's Larder,** 127 Victoria St., tel. 902/667-4848, stocks natural foods.

### Entertainment and Recreation

Amherst is *quiet.* Locals roll up the sidewalks on Sunday and turn in early other nights. **Paramount Theatre,** 47 Church St., tel. 902/667-2098, has shows nightly. **Teazer's** on Gerard Avenue reigns as the local beer joint; it's liveliest on Friday and Saturday nights with occasional music. The lounge in the **Auberge Wandlyn Inn** has dim lights, comfortable trappings, and a bartender who knows how to mix his drinks.

Eighteen-hole **Amherst Golf and Country Club** on John Black Road, tel. 902/667-8730, is a 6,100-yard course that challenges golfers with ravine hazards.

### Shopping

Check out the **farmers' market** on Maple Street for local flavor, baked goods, and crafts. It's open May–December, Friday 10 A.M.–2 P.M. The local source for oils, watercolors, graphics, and other media is **Art Connection,** 81 Victoria St. E., open Tues.–Sat. 10 A.M.–4 P.M.

### Information and Services

The **Nova Scotia Welcome Centre,** tel. 902/667-8429, is a large complex west of downtown on the TransCanada Highway. It's open year-round, daily 8:30 A.M.–4:30 P.M., May–September 8 A.M.–8 P.M. Adjacent is a promenade describing driving routes through the province, with picnic tables overlooking Tantramar Marshes. On the same side of town, the **Amherst**

**Tourist Bureau** is located in a railroad car at 51 La Planche Street, tel. 902/667-0696; open May–August, Mon.–Sat. 10 A.M.–6 P.M.

**Highland View Regional Hospital** is located at 110 Pleasant Street East (at Townshend), off Church Street on the town outskirts. Call Amherst **police** at 902/667-8600 or the **RCMP,** tel. 902/667-3859. In emergencies call 911.

### Transportation

**D & J Taxi,** tel. 902/667-8288, is one of two local taxi outfits and charges a flat $3.75 rate anywhere in Amherst. Outside town, ask for a rate estimate. Expect to pay $28.75 one-way to Joggins.

**Acadian Lines,** tel. 902/667-8435, offers bus service to Truro and Halifax from 213 South Albion Street. The **VIA Rail** station on Station Street, tel. 902/667-1059, is open when trains stop at Amherst on the Montréal-Moncton-Halifax route.

## SOUTH OF AMHERST
### Nappan

Just 10 minutes southwest of Amherst on Highway 302, the **Canada Department of Agriculture Experimental Farm,** tel. 902/667-3826, provides a look at the latest federal research efforts in cattle feed and fertilizers. Grazing cattle and sheep provide a bucolic backdrop for a picnic; picnic tables are on the grounds. The farm is open year-round, Mon.–Fri. 8:30 A.M.–3:30 P.M. Admission is free.

### Joggins

This town on the Chignecto Bay seacoast is 40 km southwest from Amherst. The **Joggins Fossil Centre,** 30 Main St., off Hwy. 302, tel. 902/251-2727 (call for directions or ask around locally), exhibits 300-million-year-old fossils excavated from the surrounding area. Daily two-hour guided tours are offered ($7) to the fossil-rich Joggins-area cliffs, where ancient trees and other plants were frozen in time eons ago. The facility is open June–September, daily 9 A.M.–6:30 P.M. Admission is $3.50 adults, $3 seniors, $2 children.

## Springhill

The **Anne Murray Centre,** 36 Main St., tel. 902/597-8614, pays tribute to the beloved local warbler who hit the Top 40 in the 1970s with "Snow Bird" and is still going strong. Exhibits include photos, clothing, and other memorabilia, and an audio-visual display catalogs her career. The center is open mid-May to mid-October, daily 10 A.M.–5 P.M.. Admission: adults $5, seniors $4, children $2.

The **Springhill Miners' Museum,** 145 Black River Rd. off Hwy. 2, tel. 902/597-3449, is all that remains of the former coal industry whose hazards claimed hundreds of miners' lives between 1872, when coal mining began here, and 1958, when the mines shut down. Former miners lead tours of the mine; exhibits document the good and bad times and offer visitors the opportunity to try their hand at digging coal. The museum is open mid-May to late October, daily 9 A.M.–5 P.M. Admission ranges $2.50–4.50, and a tour costs an extra $3.

## Parrsboro

The sea's erosive force has opened a window on the ancient world along the coastlines of Chignecto Bay and Minas Basin. The world's largest discrete fossil find was at Parrsboro on the basin's northern coast. *National Geographic* joined with the province on archaeological digs, which yielded 100,000 fossilized bone fragments of ancient dinosaurs, crocodiles, lizards, sharks, and primitive fishes. The famous digs spanned a decade. By 1980 unrestricted fossil digs by amateur collectors were declared illegal by the province; for permission to dig in restricted areas, you will need a Heritage Research Permit from the Nova Scotia Museum, 1747 Summer St., tel. 902/424-7353.

In Parrsboro center off Highway 2, **Fundy Geological Museum,** 6 Two Islands Rd., tel. 902/254-3814, exhibits fossils, minerals, and gems and sells topographic maps. It's open June to mid-October, daily 9:30 A.M.–5:30 P.M. Admission is $3.50 adults, $2.75 seniors and students over 18, $2.50 youth (6–17), $8.50 families. **Parrsboro Rock and Mineral Shop and Museum,** 39 Whitehall Rd., tel. 902/254-2981, is famed local geologist Eldon George's pride. The museum displays dinosaur, reptile, and amphibian footprint fossils. The shop stocks fossil and gem specimens, rock hound supplies, books, and maps. It's open May–December, Mon.–Sat. 9 A.M.–9 P.M., Sun. 9 A.M.–5 P.M.

# NORTH TO THE STRAIT COAST

## Linden

**Heather Beach Provincial Park,** on Highway 366, eight km east of East Linden, is the most popular beach in this area of the strait seacoast. If its small parking lot is filled, try **Northport Beach Provincial Park,** on Highway 366 three km east of Northport, for warm seas among the sandbars.

## Malagash

**Jost Vineyards** off Route 6, tel. 902/257-2636 or 800/565-4567, is the creation of the Jost family from Europe's Rhineland. Their 18-hectare vineyard produces some of the province's finest white wines. Guided tours are given daily in summer at noon and 3 P.M., a deli is stocked with picnic treats, and a restaurant serves up lunch. The vineyards are open year-round; mid-June to mid-September hours are Mon.–Sat. 9 A.M.–6 P.M., Sun. noon–6 P.M.

# TRURO

Situated at the convergence of the province's major expressways and served by VIA Rail, Truro (pop. 12,000) is called the hub of Nova Scotia. It is the province's third-largest town, with an economy based on shipping, dairy

Fossilized bones of the *sphenodontid* were uncovered near Parrsboro.

DAVID KIEFER

NOVA SCOTIA

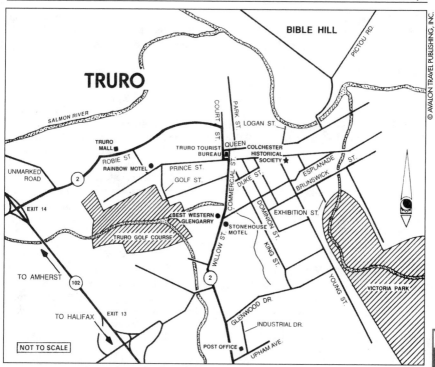

TRURO

BIBLE HILL

SALMON RIVER

TRURO MALL

TRURO TOURIST BUREAU

COLCHESTER HISTORICAL SOCIETY

ROBIE ST.
RAINBOW MOTEL

PRINCE ST.

GOLF ST.

UNMARKED ROAD

2

EXIT 14

BEST WESTERN GLENGARRY

STONEHOUSE MOTEL

TRURO GOLF COURSE

TO AMHERST

102

TO HALIFAX

EXIT 13

NOT TO SCALE

LOGAN ST.

QUEEN

COURT ST.
PARK ST.

COMMERCIAL ST.

DUKE ST.

DOMINION ST.

WILLOW ST.

KING ST.

EXHIBITION ST.

ESPLANADE
BRUNSWICK ST.

YOUNG ST.

VICTORIA PARK

2

GLENWOOD DR.

INDUSTRIAL DR.

POST OFFICE

UPHAM AVE.

PICTOU RD.

MOOR

© AVALON TRAVEL PUBLISHING, INC.

NOVA SCOTIA

products, and the manufacture of clothing, carpets, plastic products, and wines. Truro's academic side includes a teachers' college in town and an agricultural college on the outskirts.

Due to the expressways, Truro, like Amherst, is easy to bypass. The TransCanada's exit 15 feeds into Highway 102, the highway to Halifax, and skirts past Truro Golf Course on the town's western side. Highway 102's exits 14A to 13A peel off in quick succession as the expressway rushes beyond Truro.

The highway's prime access into town is exit 14, which turns into Robie Street, which leads shortly into central Truro. Robie ends at Commercial Street, which turns into Willow Street, the town's motel row, a few blocks farther south.

## Sights

Truro makes an excellent base for watching the Fundy tides and the **tidal bore.** The town has a prime location on Cobequid Bay at the inner-

most end of the sea pocket. The twice-daily high tides spill over into the Shubenacadie and other rivers emptying into the Cobequid Bay. At Truro, the lead wave travels up the Salmon River as it flows toward town beneath the Highway 102 overpass. If you want a close-up look at the tidal bore, take Robie Street west out of town toward Highway 102 and turn off on one of the roads leading to the river. Tidal-bore arrival times are listed in the *Truro Daily News* and at the town's tourist office, tel. 902/893-2922.

**Colchester Historical Society Museum,** 29 Young St., tel. 902/895-6284, does a fine job entwining exhibits on Fundy eccentricities, the area's natural history, and local genealogy. It's open year-round; June–September, Tues.–Fri. 10 A.M.–5 P.M., Sat.–Sun. 2–5 P.M. (shorter off-season hours). Admission is adults $2, children 50 cents.

**Victoria Park,** at Brunswick Street and Park Road, showcases stands of Norway spruce, hemlock, and white pine. The 400-hectare park is thickly forested and spliced with hiking trails that lead along a deep canyon and past two waterfalls. The park is open all year during daylight hours.

## Accommodations

Lodgings in Truro are plentiful and reasonably priced. Occupying a prime site for watching the tidal bore, the **Palliser Motel** is west of downtown off Robie Street (Highway 2), or take exit 14 from Highway 102; tel. 902/893-8951 or 800/565-000. It's on the banks of the Salmon River, and the bore-watching area is lit at night. Rooms run $44–59. The motel is open May to October. Closer to downtown, but away from the excitement of the tidal bore, another inexpensive option is the **Rainbow Motel,** 341 Prince St., tel. 902/893-9438, an unassuming, well-located motel with 34 rooms ($46–70), a restaurant of local renown, and an outdoor pool.

A step up in quality is offered at the **Stonehouse Motel,** 165 Willow St., tel. 902/893-9413 or 800/660-6638. Rooms start at $70; $90 with a kitchen. Diagonally opposite, **Best Western Glengarry,** 150 Willow St., tel. 902/893-4311 or 800/567-4276, www.bwglengarry.com, comprises 112 spacious rooms ($75–120), a restaurant, lounge, and piano bar, indoor and outdoor pools, a sauna, and a whirlpool.

## Food

In a nondescript strip mall near the heart of downtown, **Murphy's** on the Esplanade, tel. 902/895-1275, serves up some of the best-priced seafood anywhere in this part of the province. I had the deep-fried haddock and chips—cooked to perfection— for just $7. A variety of fish is offered—pan-fried, poached, or "Texas style"— amid bright, nautical-themed decor. Murphy's is open daily 11 A.M.–8 P.M. Another favorite is the **Wooden Hog,** 627 Prince St., tel. 902/895-0779, open Mon.–Sat. 9 A.M.–10 P.M. While locals often stop by just for coffee and one of the many delicious pastries, the lunch and dinner menu provides good value, with all dinner mains under $15 (including poached salmon smothered in hollandaise sauce for $11).

All four accommodations detailed above have in-house dining rooms. You can combine dining with tidal bore watching at the riverside restaurant in the **Palliser Motel,** tel. 902/893-8951. The **Glengarry Dining Room,** at the Best Western Glengarry, 150 Willow St., tel. 902/893-4311, has a busy weekday evening buffet heaped with casseroles and desserts, while the **Rainbow Dining Room** at the Rainbow Motel, 341 Prince St., tel. 902/893-9438, offers a buffet with lots of seafood. The **Stonehouse Restaurant** in the motel of the same name at 165 Willow Street, tel. 902/893-9413, is known locally for its home-style cooking. Especially tasty are the daily roast beef, turkey, and pork specials.

Supermarkets are located at Truro Mall near Robie Street and Highway 102's exit 14; **IGA** is open Mon.–Sat. 9:30 A.M.–9:30 P.M. **Sun Spun Natural Foods** is located at 583 Prince Street, tel. 902/895-7177.

## Information and Services

The **Truro Tourist Bureau,** at Victoria Square alongside Court Street, tel. 902/893-2922, stocks literature about the town and area. It's open daily 8 A.M.–9 P.M. from late May to mid-October.

For a line of books about Truro and the province, check out the **Colchester Historical Society Museum bookstore,** 29 Young St., tel. 902/895-6284. **Colchester-East Hants Regional Library,** 754 Prince St., tel. 902/895-4183, is open Tues., Wed., and Sat. 10 A.M.–5 P.M., Thurs.–Fri. to 9 P.M.

**Canada Post** is on Industrial Avenue in the Truro Industrial Park; open Mon.–Fri. 8 A.M.–5:15 P.M. **Colchester Regional Hospital** is at 207 Willow Street, tel. 902/893-4321 or 893-5507 (emergencies). Call the **police** at 902/895-5351 and the **RCMP** at 902/893-1323. Call 911 in emergencies.

## Transportation

Truro has several taxi companies. **Layton's Taxi,** 42 Outram, tel. 902/895-4471 or 895-4472, charges $3 for each mile (not kilometer). A ride to the Bible Hill track costs about $4; Truro to Halifax International Airport costs about $50 one-way.

**VIA Rail,** 104 Esplanade, offers twice-daily service to Halifax; call 902/895-0189 for a quick taped recording, 902/429-8421 for a human being. **Acadian Lines,** 280 Willow St., tel. 902/895-3833, operates seven buses daily to Halifax and three daily departures to Sydney.

## NORTH OF TRURO

North of Truro, the land dips and sweeps in manicured farmlands as far as the Northumberland Strait coastline. The villages are small; the backcountry roads are scenic. This is rural Nova Scotia at its best. Balmoral Mills is a 40-minute drive north of Truro, and Denmark lies another 10 minutes beyond that.

### Balmoral Mills

Best known for its gristmill, this village lies 38 km north of Truro along Highway 311. **Balmoral Grist Mill Museum,** 660 Matheson Brook Rd., tel. 902/657-3016, is a photographer's ideal setting. The barn-red mill fronts a fast-running river and is nestled in a verdant, wooded gorge. Wheat, oats, and barley are still ground using 19th-century methods at this historic gristmill-cum-museum built in 1874. A picnic ground is across the river. The site is open June to mid-October, Mon.–Sat. 9:30 A.M.–5:30 P.M., Sun. 1–5:30 P.M., with milling demonstrations at 10 A.M. and 2 P.M. The mill is busiest the first Sunday in October—an Open Day with all sorts of family activities drawing a crowd of hundreds. Admission is by donation.

### Denmark

The **Sutherland Steam Mill Museum** on Highway 326, tel. 902/657-3365, provides another look at old-time rural technology. The restored woodworking mill that once made carriages and sleighs was powered by a steam boiler, and the mill is periodically put into operation. The site is open June to mid-October, Mon.–Sat. 9:30 A.M.–5:30 P.M., Sun. 1–5:30 P.M. Admission is by donation.

## SHUBENACADIE RIVER

This river, draining into the Bay of Fundy west of Truro, is not just a good place to view the tidal

bore but also to *ride* it! **Tidal Bore Rafting Park** on Highway 215 between South Maitland and Highway 102 (exit 10), tel. 902/758-4032 or 800/565-7238, operates two-hour Zodiac raft excursions mid-May to August. You board the rafts at low tide and head downstream, just in time to catch the tidal bore back upriver. Three levels of white-water excitement are offered, at rates ranging $50–65, inclusive of hot drinks and a barbecue. The park also offers accommodations in one- and two-bedroom cottages (from $55).

Further upstream, five km south of Highway 102 (Halifax—Truro), families will enjoy **Shubenacadie Wildlife Park & Environmental Centre,** tel. 902/758-2040, which has indigenous animals on 20 wooded hectares. It's open mid-May to mid-October, 9 A.M.–7 P.M.; admission is $3 adults, $1 ages 6–17, $7.50 families.

### Maitland

If you're planning on heading along the Bay of Fundy from Truro, the most direct route is Highway 14 west from Highway 102 at Milford. The longer alternative is Highway 215 (Glooscap Trail), which begins by following the Shubenacadie River

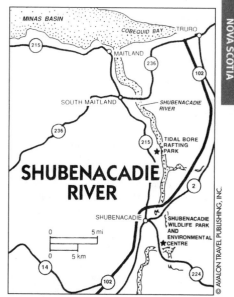

© AVALON TRAVEL PUBLISHING, INC.

to its mouth at Maitland. Canada's largest wooden ship, the three-masted *William D. Lawrence*, was built at this seacost village. Documentaries, ship portraits, and memorabilia are kept at the shipbuilder's former homestead, the **Lawrence House Museum**, which overlooks Cobequid Bay from 8660 Highway 215, tel. 902/261-2628. It's open June to mid-October, Mon.–Sat. 9:30 A.M.–5:30 P.M., with a tea party each Sunday afternoon at 1 P.M.–5:30 P.M. The actual 1874 launching is commemorated on the middle Saturday of each September with a parade of period-dressed locals, a symbolic launch, and seafood suppers hosted throughout the village.

# Halifax

Halifax (pop. 110,000), the 250-year-old provincial capital, presents Nova Scotia's strikingly modern face, wrapped around a historic heart. It's one of the most vibrant cities in Canada, with an exuberant cultural life and cosmopolitan population. The tourist's Halifax is tidily compact, concentrated on the manageable, boot-shaped peninsula the city inhabits. Its prettiest parts are clustered between the bustling waterfront and the short, steep hillside that the early British developed two centuries ago. In these areas you'll find handsomely historic old districts meshed with stylishly chic new glass-sheathed buildings.

Halifax's sister city, Dartmouth (pop. 67,800), is a 10-minute ferry ride or quick drive across the harbor. Its harbor-front sightseeing and dining district is studded with shipyards and light industry.

## HISTORY
### Founding
The French learned about the area in the early 1700s, when local Mi'kmaq Indians escorted the French governor on a tour of what they called Chebooctook, the "Great Long Harbor," and adjacent waterways. But it was the British who saw the site's potential; in 1749 Colonel Edward Cornwallis arrived with about 2,500 settlers on 13 ships, and founded Halifax along what is now Barrington Street. The settlement was named for Lord Halifax, then president of Britain's Board of Trade and Plantations.

Early Halifax was a stockaded settlement backed by the Grand Parade, the town green where the militia drilled. The first of four citadels was built on the hilltop. St. Paul's Church, the garrison church at Grand Parade's edge, opened in 1750, making it Canada's first Anglican sanctuary. It was a gift from King George III. More English settlers arrived in 1750 and founded Dartmouth across the harbor. By 1752, the two towns were linked by a ferry system, the oldest saltwater ferry system in North America. Nova Scotia was granted representative government in 1758.

### The Royal Military
The completion of Her Majesty's Royal Dockyard in 1760 was the prelude to Louisbourg's absolute destruction the same year. The harbor's defensibility was ensured by a ring of batteries at McNab's Island, North West Arm, Point Pleasant with its Martello Tower, and the forts at George's Island and York Redoubt. In 1783, the settlement got another massive Anglo infusion with the arrival of thousands of Loyalists from America. Among them was John Wentworth, New Hampshire's former governor. He received a baronet title for his opposition to the revolution in the American colonies, and was appointed Nova Scotia's lieutenant governor. Sir John and Lady Wentworth led the Halifax social scene, hobnobbing with Prince Edward (the Maritimes' military commander-in-chief, who would later sire Queen Victoria) and his French paramour Julie St. Laurent (to the chagrin of propriety-minded local society).

### Prosperous Times
The seaport thrived in the 1800s. Halifax became a center of higher education in 1802 with the establishment of Saint Mary's University. By

1807, the city's population topped 60,000 and more schools opened. Dalhousie University, modeled after the University of Edinburgh, began instruction in 1818. A proper government setting—the sandstone Colonial Building (now Province House)—opened in 1819. Other academic institutions followed: University of King's College, Nova Scotia College of Art and Design, Technical University of Nova Scotia, Atlantic School of Theology, and Naropa Institute of Canada.

In 1835, a landmark precedent in British law was established in Halifax when Joseph Howe, a newspaper editor and politician, successfully defended himself against a charge of criminal libel. The decision broadened freedom of the press throughout the British Empire.

The harbor front—which during the War of 1812 served as a black-market trade center for Halifax privateers—acquired commercial legitimacy when native Haligonian Samuel Cunard, rich from lumbering, whaling, and banking, turned his interests to shipping. By 1838, the Cunard Steamship Company handled the British and North American Royal Mail, and by 1840 Cunard's four ships provided the first regular transport between the two continents.

The seaport's incorporation in 1841 ushered in a prosperous mercantile era. Granville Street, with its stylish shops, became in its day Atlantic Canada's Fifth Avenue. Less stylish brothels and taverns lined Brunswick, Market, and Barrack Streets, and the military police swept through the area often, breaking up drunken fistfights and reestablishing order.

## Tragedies Strike

The early 1900s brought tragedies. The *Titanic* sank northeast of Nova Scotia in 1912, and many of its victims are buried at Fairview, Olivett, and Baron de Hirsch cemeteries, with their graves marked by small black headstones.

On the morning of Thursday, December 6, 1917, the harbor was busy with warships transporting troops, munitions, and other supplies bound for the war in Europe. A French ship, the *Mont Blanc,* stuffed to the gunwales with explosives—including 400,000 pounds of TNT—

was heading through the narrows toward the harbor mouth when it was struck by a larger vessel, the *Imo,* which was steaming in the opposite direction, and caught fire. The terrified crew of the *Mont Blanc* took immediately to the lifeboats, as the burning ship drifted close to the Halifax shore.

About 20 minutes later, at 9:05 A.M., the *Mont Blanc* cargo blew up, instantly killing an estimated 2,000 people, wounding another 9,000, and obliterating some 130 hectares of northern Halifax. So colossal was the explosion that windows were shattered 80 km away, and the shock wave rocked Sydney, Cape Breton, 430 km northeast. The barrel of one of the *Mont Blanc's* cannons was hurled five and a half km, while its half-ton anchor shank landed over three kilometers away in the opposite direction. It was then the largest manmade explosion in history, unrivaled until the detonation of the first atomic bomb.

With a massive international relief effort, the city quickly rebuilt. Near the site of the explosion, Fort Needham, overlooking Halifax's side of the Narrows, serves as a memorial to the tragic events.

## The Modern Era

By the 1960s, Halifax looked like a hoary victim of the centuries, somewhat the worse for wear. Massive federal, provincial, and private investment, however, restored the harbor to its early luster, with its warehouses groomed as the handsome **Historic Properties.** During the late 1960s and '70s, an infusion of upscale hotels added sorely needed lodgings.

The city continued to polish its image, as sandblasting renewed the exterior of architectural treasures like Province House. The Art Gallery of Nova Scotia moved from cramped quarters near the Public Archives and settled within the stunningly renovated former Dominion Building. Municipal guidelines sought to control the city's growth. The unobstructed view on George Street between the harbor and the Citadel was secured with a municipal mandate, and the height of the hillside's high-rise buildings was also restricted to preserve the cityscape.

# HALIFAX HARBOUR

Halifax is more than a city, more than a seaport, and more than a provincial capital. Halifax is a harbor with a city attached, as the Haligonians say. Events in the harbor have shaped Nova Scotia's history. The savvy British military immediately grasped its potential when they first sailed in centuries ago. In fact, Halifax's founding as a settlement in 1749 was incidental to the harbor's development.

From the first, the British used the 26-km-long harbor as a watery warehouse of almost unlimited ship-holding capacity. The ships that defeated the French at Louisbourg in 1758—and ultimately conquered this part of Atlantic Canada—were launched from Halifax Harbour. A few years later, the Royal Navy sped from the harbor to harass the rebellious colonies on the eastern seaboard during the American Revolution. Ships from Halifax ran the blockades on the South's side during the American Civil War. And during World Wars I and II, the harbor bulged with troop convoys destined for Europe.

From a maritime standpoint, Halifax Harbour is a jewel, the world's second-largest natural harbor (after Sydney, Australia). High rocky bluffs notched with coves rim the wide entrance where the harbor meets the frothy Atlantic. **McNab's Island** is spread across the harbor's mouth, and is so large that it almost clogs the entrance. Many an unwary ship has foundered on the island's shallow, treacherous Eastern Passage coastline.

On the western side of McNab's Island, the harbor is split in two by Halifax's peninsula. The North West Arm, a fjordlike sliver of sea, cuts off to one side and wraps around the city's back side. Along its banks are the long lawns of parks, estates, yacht clubs, and several university campuses. The main channel continues inland, shouldered by uptown Halifax on one side and its sister city of Dartmouth on the other.

## The Tourist's Harbour

The harbor puts on its best show where the cities almost face each other. White-hulled cruise ships nose into port and dock alongside Halifax's **Point Pleasant Park** at the peninsula's southern tip. Freighters, tugs, tour boats, and sailboats skim the choppy waters, and ferries cut through the sea traffic, scurrying back and forth between the two cities with their loads of commuters and sightseers.

The scene has a transfixing quality about it. Tourist season unofficially starts and ends when the harborfront Halifax Sheraton hotel sets tables and chairs for alfresco dining on the waterfront promenade. Stiff summer breezes usually accompany lunch, but the view is worth it. Less hardy diners jostle for tables with a harbor view at **Salty's,** the nearby restaurant with its enviable, wide-windowed dining room overlooking the same scene.

Beyond the tourist's realm and the two cities' harborfronts, the spacious harbor compresses itself into **The Narrows.** Two high-flung steel expressways—the **MacDonald** and **MacKay bridges** (75 cents toll)—cross the Narrows at either end. The MacDonald bridge permits pedestrians, and provides an aerial view of the **Maritime Command** and **Her Majesty's Canadian Dockyard** along the Halifax side.

The slender Narrows then opens into 40-square-km **Bedford Basin,** 16 km long and as capacious as a small inland sea. Sailboats cruise its waters now, but the expanse has seen a parade of ships cross its waters over the years—from the white-sailed British warships of centuries ago to the steel-hulled vessels of the Allies during both World Wars.

## The Harbour from Varied Angles

Halifax Harbour reveals itself in different views. Its pulse can be probed from one of the ferries or from harborfront in either city. The approach from the Atlantic can be seen best from the historic fort at **York Redoubt** on Purcells Cove Road. And you get a good view of North West Arm's ritzy estate and university scene from Fleming Park's **Memorial Tower** on the same road. **Seaview Park** beneath the MacKay Bridge overlooks the Narrows where that slender strait meets Bedford Basin.

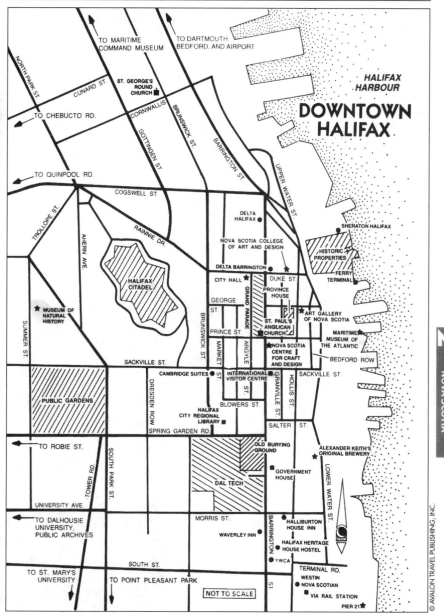

NOVA SCOTIA

## GETTING ORIENTED

The layout of Halifax is easy to grasp. Lower and Upper Water Streets and Barrington Street rim the harbor. A series of short streets rise like ramps from the waterfront, past the grassy Grand Parade and up Citadel Hill. Around the hill, parks, playgrounds, and gardens cut a great swath of green across the heart of the city. Beyond the hilltop's Citadel, to the south, is the city's academic area, site of Dalhousie University, University of King's College, St. Mary's University, and the Atlantic School of Theology.

From Historic Properties' wharves at the waterfront, sightseeing boats explore the harbour. The splendid Maritime Museum and Art Gallery of Nova Scotia are close by, while the Nova Scotia Museum of Natural History and the Sports Heritage Museum are a few blocks inland. Nova Scotia's finest hotels are set cheek by jowl along the narrow streets. Shopping is more urbane than out in the province; the city's art galleries, bookstores, and crafts shops are especially tempting.

## DOWNTOWN SIGHTS

The following sights begin at the harbour, proceed up and over the hilltop, and then spread out from there to include outlying areas. Parking is scarce in Halifax, especially near the waterfront. If you're driving, look for a parking spot a few blocks inland and walk from there.

### Historic Properties

Canada's oldest surviving group of waterfront warehouses lies in a three-block expanse on Upper and Lower Water Streets known as the Historic Properties. The wooden and stone warehouses, chandleries, and buildings once used by shipping interests and privateers have been restored. They now house restaurants, shops, and other sites impressively styled with Victorian and Italianate facades. The history of the precinct is catalogued halfway along the Privateer Wharf building (on the inside) with interpretive panels.

### Maritime Museum of the Atlantic

The seaport's store of nautical memorabilia lies within this sleek, burnished-red museum at 1675 Lower Water Street, tel. 902/424-7490. The museum is one of the crowning achievements of the city's Waterfront Development Project. Exhibits include *Titanic* artifacts, a Shipwrecks of Nova Scotia display, Queen Victoria's barge, a riveting documentary from the 1917 Halifax explosion, and various historic small craft. ***Titanic 3D,*** a National Geographic documentary created from footage taken from the wreck, shows continuously.

The museum is open year-round, Mon.–Sat. 9:30 A.M.–5:30 P.M. (Tues. until 8 P.M.), Sun. 1–5:30 P.M. In summer, admission is adults $6, seniors $5, children $2, families $15; the rest of year, prices are cut by half.

Outside, two historic vessels are tied up at the wharf. One of these, the **CSS *Acadia,*** spent its

CSS *Acadia* tied up out front of the Maritime Museum

© ANDREW HEMPSTEAD

NOVA SCOTIA

life as Canada's first hydrographic vessel, its crew surveying the east coast using sextants and graphing shoreline features. The other, **HMCS Sackville,** is the last remaining Canadian World War II convoy escort corvette. Both are open Mon.–Sat. 9:30 A.M.–5 P.M., Sun. 1–5:30 P.M. Admission is $1 to each, or free with proof of admission to the maritime museum.

## Art Gallery of Nova Scotia

Atlantic Canada's largest and finest art collection is housed in the refurbished and expanded former Dominion Building at 1741 Hollis Street, tel. 902/424-7542. The building was completed in 1868 of brown sandstone quarried from Pictou and Cumberland Counties. Some 2,000 works in oils, watercolors, stone, wood, and other media are exhibited throughout its four floors of spacious galleries. The permanent collections give priority to current and former Nova Scotia residents, and include works by Mary Pratt, Arthur Lismer, Carol Fraser, and Alex Colville. The mezzanine-level regional folk-art collection is a particular delight. The ground-floor Gallery Shop trades in the cream of provincial arts and crafts and sells books, cards, and gifts.

The museum is open year-round, Tues.–Fri. 10 A.M.–6 P.M., Sat.–Sun. noon–5 P.M. General admission is charged, but visit on Tuesday and pay what you wish.

## Nova Scotia Centre for Craft and Design

Provincial crafts development and innovation are nurtured at this tidy workshop geared to weaving, woodworking, metal, and multimedia production. Its galleries, 1683 Barrington St. (at Prince St.), tel. 902/424-4062, showcase the center's newest creations. The center is open year-round, Mon.–Sat. 9 A.M.–4 P.M. Admission is free.

## St. Paul's Anglican Church

This stately white wooden church at 1749 Argyle Street, tel. 902/429-2240, was built in 1749, making it the oldest surviving building in Halifax and the first Anglican church in Canada. The interior is full of memorials to Halifax's early res-

idents. Notice the bit of metal embedded above the door in the north wall; it's a piece of shrapnel hurled from the exploding *Mont Blanc,* two km away. The church is between Barrington and Argyle Streets at the edge of the Grand Parade; look for the square belfry topped by an octagonal cupola. It's open year-round.

## Province House

The seat of the provincial government, Province House, 1726 Hollis St. (at Prince St.), tel. 902/424-4661, was completed in 1819. It's the smallest and oldest provincial capitol in the country and features a fine Georgian exterior and splendid interior, resembling a rural English mansion more than an official residence. On his visit to modest but dignified Province House in 1842, author Charles Dickens remarked, "It was like looking at Westminster through the wrong end of a telescope. . . a gem of Georgian architecture."

Look closely for interesting details such as the decapitated stone falcons, beheaded by a 19th-century official who said the raptors too closely resembled the symbolic eagle of the United States. The building is open July and August, Mon.–Fri. 9 A.M.–5 P.M., Sat.–Sun. 10 A.M.–4 P.M.; the rest of the year, Mon.–Fri. 9 A.M.–4 P.M. The spring legislative sessions are open to the public. Admission is free.

## Old Burying Ground

Designated a national historic site in 1991, this cemetery sits opposite Government House at Barrington Street and Spring Garden Road. Its history goes back to the city's founding. The first customer, so to speak, was interred just one day after the arrival of Cornwallis and the original convoy of English settlers in 1749. Also among the thicket of age-darkened, hand-carved, old-fashioned headstones is the 1754 grave of John Connor, the settlement's first ferry captain. The most recent burial took place over 150 years ago, in 1844. The grounds are open June–September, daily 9 A.M.–5 P.M.; literature with details on the site and gravestones is available at St. Paul's Anglican Church, Grand Parade, tel. 902/429-2240.

## Alexander Keith's Original Brewery

Behind Government House and across from the waterfront, Keith's is North America's oldest operating brewery. Keith arrived in Halifax in 1795, bringing with him brewing techniques from his English homeland and finding a ready market among the soldiers and sailors living in the city. The brewery of today, an impressive stone and granite edifice extending along an entire block, dates to 1834. Tours led by costumed guides depart daily 10 A.M.–10 P.M. (Sunday until 6 P.M.) and cost adults $8, seniors and children $6. The brewery is on Lower Water Street, tel. 902/455-1474.

## Pier 21

Continuing south along Lower Water Street from the brewery, the waterfront is dominated by Halifax's massive cruise ship terminal. This 3,900-square-meter structure has a long and colorful history of welcoming foreigners in its original capacity as an "immigration shed," where more than a million immigrants, refugees, and war brides first set foot on Canadian soil between 1928 and 1971. It was also the main departure point for 500,000 Canadians who fought in World War II. The building displays firsthand accounts from some of those who passed through and interactive exhibits that draw visitors back to the days of departing troops. Don't miss *Oceans of Hope*, a 30-minute film narrated by a fictional immigration officer. The terminal is located at 1055 Marginal Road, tel. 902/425-7770. It's open year-round.

## Halifax Citadel National Historic Site

Halifax's premier landmark is also the most visited national historic site in Canada. The Citadel crowns the hill at the top of George Street, commanding the strategic high ground above the city and harbor, with magnificent views of the entire area. This star-shaped, dressed-granite fortress, the fourth military works built on this site, was completed in 1856. In its heyday, the Citadel represented the pinnacle of defensive military technology, though its design was never tested by an attack.

In summer, students in period uniforms portray soldiers of the 78th Highlanders and the Royal Artillery, demonstrating military drills, powder magazine operation, changing of the sentries, and piping. At the stroke of noon each day, they load and fire a cannon with due military precision and ceremony, a shot heard round the city. Most of the fortress is open for exploration; exhibits include a museum, barrack rooms, a powder magazine, and a 50-minute audiovisual presentation on the fort's history.

Guided tours are available. Friends of the Citadel, a volunteer group, operates a shop and restaurant within the fortress. The Citadel is open mid-May to mid-October, daily 9 A.M.–5 P.M. (until 6 P.M. June 15 through August); the grounds are open year-round. Admission through summer is adults $6, seniors $4.50, and children $3; discounted in the off-season. For more information, call 902/426-5080.

On the harbor side of Citadel Hill stands the green-domed **Old Town Clock,** itself as much a symbol of Halifax as the Citadel. The four-faced clock tower, which could be seen from every corner of the town, was completed in 1803 by order of the compulsively punctual Prince Edward.

## Museum of Natural History

One of Atlantic Canada's finest natural history museums, this spacious, modern building holds a trove of dinosaur relics, gem specimens, Mi'kmaq artifacts, and plant and animal exhibits. One of the centerpieces is a huge whale skeleton.

A few minutes' walk from the Citadel, the museum is at 1747 Summer Street, tel. 902/424-7353. It's open year-round. From June to mid-October, hours are Mon.–Sat. 9:30 A.M.–5:30 P.M. (Wed. to 8 P.M.), Sun. 1–5:30 P.M. In summer, admission is $3.50 for adults, $3 for seniors, $1 for children, and $8 for families. The rest of the year, hours are shorter and admission is free.

## St. George's Round Church

Architect William Hughes designed this unusual and charming church, which at once accommo-

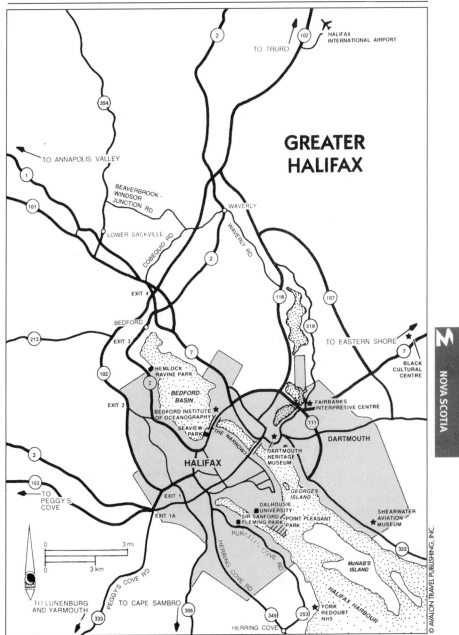

GREATER HALIFAX

NOVA SCOTIA

dated the overflow of parishioners from the nearby Dutch Church on Brunswick Street and satisfied Prince Edward's penchant for round buildings. The cornerstone was laid in 1800, and the chancel and front porch were added later. St. George's is located a few blocks north of the Citadel at Brunswick and Cornwallis Streets. The church is open year-round by appointment; call 902/423-1059 or 902/425-3658.

## Maritime Command Museum

The Georgian-styled Admiralty House, tel. 902/427-0550, ext. 8250, exhibits photos, uniforms, ship models and other artifacts relating to the history of the Canadian Maritime Military Forces. Now a national historic site, the museum is five blocks north of Citadel Hill (a 10-minute walk) at Gottingen at Almon Streets. It's open year-round, Mon.–Fri. 10 A.M.–3:30 P.M. Admission is free.

## SIGHTS SOUTH OF DOWNTOWN

### York Redoubt National Historic Site

Set on a bluff with impressive views of the harbor entrance, this park is six km south of Halifax off Purcells Cove Road. The setting draws visitors with hiking paths and picnic tables near the strategic fortifications, which were used from 1793 through World War II. The site, tel. 902/426-5080, is open year-round, 10 A.M.–dusk, and it is staffed mid-June to mid-September, daily 10 A.M.–6 P.M. Admission free.

### McNab's Island

The five-km-long wooded island at Halifax Harbour's entrance was first fortified as part of the early defensive ring created by the British. Toward the southern end of the island, Fort McNab, now a national historic site, dates to 1888. It was Halifax's first battery designed to hold breech-loading guns. The island has been popular with day-visitors since the 1870s, when several "pleasure grounds" were established. Activities today on the bucolic parcel include exploring the fort ruins, hiking, bird-watching (look for ospreys), and swimming.

Year-round access to the island is provided by McNab's Island Ferry, at Fisherman's Cove in Eastern Passage on the Dartmouth side of the harbor, tel. 902/465-4563 or 800/326-4563. Round-trip fare is $10 adults, $8 seniors and children; no extra charge for bringing bicycles.

The other island in the harbor, **Georges Island,** is being made into a historic park and will eventually be opened to the public.

## SIGHTS IN AND AROUND DARTMOUTH

Dartmouth is a large residential, commercial, and industrial area across the harbor from Halifax. The two cities are joined by bridge and by a ferry between Cable Wharf on the Halifax side and the Dartmouth waterfront; $1.75 each way.

The **Dartmouth Heritage Museum,** an easy walk from the ferry dock at 100 Wyse Road, tel. 902/464-2300, explains the natural, historic, and cultural heritage of Halifax's sister city with artifacts and exhibits. At the same location, the Dartmouth Art Gallery displays the work of local artists. Both are open through summer, Mon.–Sat. 10 A.M.–5 P.M.; the rest of the year Wed.–Sat. 1:30–5 P.M. Admission is $2.

For a look at Canada's latest deep-sea exploration technology, visit the **Bedford Institute of Oceanography** off the Shannon Park exit on Dartmouth's side of the MacKay Bridge, tel. 902/426-4306. Self-guided tours explain the institute's fisheries science, oceanography, and hydrography programs. The institute is open year-round, Mon.–Fri. 9 A.M.–4 P.M. Admission is free.

In 1858, navigation began on a canal system that linked Halifax Harbour with the Bay of Fundy via Dartmouth's lakes and the Shubenacadie River. The canal was abandoned just 12 years later. Today, two sections of the canal have been restored. On Dartmouth's northern outskirts, the **Fairbanks Interpretive Centre,** Hwy. 318 at Shubie Park, tel. 902/462-1826, has working canal locks, working models, and other displays; open late May to early September, Mon.–Fri. 9 A.M.–8 P.M., Sat.–Sun. 1–5 P.M. Admission is free.

**Shearwater Aviation Museum,** 13 Bonaventure St., tel. 902/460-1083, documents Canadian maritime military aviation history. It's open June–August, Tues.–Fri. 10 A.M.–5 P.M., Sat.–Sun. noon–4 P.M.; September–November, Tues.–Thurs. 10 A.M.–5 P.M., Saturday noon–4 P.M.; December–March, by appointment; April–May, Tues.–Thurs. 10 A.M.–5 P.M., Sat. noon–4 P.M. Admission is free.

## Westphal

The **Black Cultural Centre for Nova Scotia,** 1149 Main St. (Rte. 7), tel. 902/434-6223 or 800/465-0767, on Dartmouth's eastern outskirts, documents local black history, starting in the 1600s, and includes a library and exhibit rooms. It's open year-round, Mon.–Fri. 9 A.M.–5 P.M., and Sat. 10 A.M.–4 P.M. June–September. Admission is $5 adults, $3 seniors and students, $2 children under 12.

## Bedford Basin Area

**Hemlock Ravine Park,** on Kent Avenue off Highway 2, showcases 75 hectares of hemlocks, once the romantic retreat of Prince Edward and Julie St. Laurent, his French mistress. The park is open year-round dawn to dusk. At the town of Bedford, at the head of the basin, **Mount Saint Vincent University Art Gallery,** at Seton Academic Centre on Highway 2, tel. 902/457-6160, concentrates on fine arts and crafts produced mainly by women. It's open year-round, Mon.–Fri. 11 A.M.–5 P.M., Sat.–Sun. 1–5 P.M. Admission is free.

# PARKS

## Public Gardens

South across Sackville Street from the Citadel grounds, the Public Gardens are an irresistibly attractive oasis spread over seven hectares in the heart of the city. Bordered by Spring Garden Road, South Park Street, Summer Street, and Sackville Street, this is considered one of the loveliest formal gardens in North America and is reminiscent of the handsome parks of Europe, such as Dublin's St. Stephen's Green.

Inside the wrought-iron fence (main entrance at the corner of South Park Street and Spring Garden Road), the setting revels in roses, lilacs, dahlias, and exotic and native trees, as well as lily ponds and fountains, gravel walkways, and benches. The ornate bandstand dates from Queen Victoria's Golden Jubilee and is the site of free Sunday afternoon concerts in July and August. Also during the summer months, vendors of arts and crafts hawk their wares outside the gardens along Spring Garden Road. The gardens are open May to mid-October, 8 A.M.–dusk.

## Seaview Park

Halifax's peninsula is bookended by a pair of expansive green spaces. Seaview Park is at the north end, overlooking Bedford Basin from the foot of the A. Murray McKay Bridge. This was once the site of Africville, a community of black Haligonians established in the 1840s but since demolished. George Dixon, holder of three world boxing titles, was born here in 1870.

## Point Pleasant Park

This park at the peninsula's southern tip (at the end of Young Avenue) spreads out on 75 hectares of harbor-front greenery, with terns, gulls, and ospreys winging overhead. A field of heather (rare hereabouts) was seeded from a Scottish soldier's split mattress in the 1800s. The park's Quarry Point has interesting ice-age striations. Forty km of trails here allow for hiking, jogging, and cross-country skiing in winter. A bit of real-estate trivia: the park is still rented from the British government, on a 999-year lease, for one shilling per year.

Point Pleasant's military significance is evidenced by the Prince of Wales Martello Tower (ordered built by Prince Edward in 1796) and Fort Ogilvie, built in 1862, both part of the Halifax's defensive system. The thick-walled round tower, based on those the British were building at the time to repel Napoleon's forces, was the first of its kind to be built in North America. The park is open year-round during daylight hours; the tower is open July to early September, daily 10 A.M.–6 P.M. Admission is free.

## Sir Sandford Fleming Park

A 38-hectare grassy spread off Purcells Cove Road, across the North West Arm from Dalhousie

University, this park attracts hikers with one trail that encircles picturesque Frog Pond and another that leads to a lookout. It's open year-round, 8 A.M.–dusk. The land was donated by the Scottish-born Fleming, who lived in Halifax from the 1880s until his death in 1915.

Square stone **Dingle Tower,** erected at Fleming's suggestion in the early 1900s to commemorate the 150th anniversary of Nova Scotia's first legislative assembly, provides a great view; open June–August, daily 9 A.M.–5 P.M. Admission is free.

The enterprising Sir Sandford, by the way, also gets credit for devising standard time zones, designing Canada's first stamp, and surveying the route of the first trans-Canadian railway.

## ACCOMMODATIONS

Halifax has the province's widest lodgings variety, with over 3,000 rooms. Location largely determines cost. Many of the choicest properties are at the harbor, and prices decrease from there up the hillside. A plentiful supply of low-cost lodgings at local universities offsets the city's otherwise high-priced hotels. The budget-priced hostel, YWCA, YMCA, and university settings are informal—good places for meeting other travelers.

### Budget Overnights

The **Halifax Heritage House Hostel,** 1253 Barrington St., tel. 902/422-3863, www.hihostels.ca, has standard hostel lodgings (73 beds total) in dorm rooms at $18 for HI members, $22 for nonmembers and in private rooms for $40 single, $47 double. Facilities include a kitchen, laundry room, television in the common room, and a storeroom for bikes. Some good restaurants are in the neighborhood, and it's just a 15-minute stroll to the Citadel or historic harbor front.

Next door, the **YWCA,** 1239 Barrington St., tel. 902/423-6162, has rooms for women ($32 for a single room, $46 for a double). Amenities include a kitchen, exercise equipment, and sauna. The **YMCA,** 1565 S. Park St., tel. 902/423-9622, charges $28 for a single room and has exercise equipment available.

In summer (May through August), **Dalhousie University,** tel. 902/494-8840, www.dal.ca /confserv, offers both standard residence hall rooms and two- and three-bedroom apartments to students and non-students alike. Students (with valid student IDs) can rent single dorm rooms for $26 per night and double rooms for $42 per night, including breakfast, linen, towels, and unlimited use of the Dal-Plex recreation facility. Non-students pay $36 for a single room, $54 for a double, and those rates also include maid service and parking. The apartments are downtown and rent for $58 per night for the two-bedroom units, $78 per night for the three-bedroom units; breakfast is not included (the apartments have kitchenettes), and parking is $5 per day.

Other university lodgings, available mid- to late May through mid- to late August, can be found at **Saint Mary's University,** 923 Robie St., tel. 902/420-5486 or 888/347-5555, www.stmarys.ca, and **Mount Saint Vincent University,** 166 Bedford Hwy. on the outskirts of Halifax, tel. 902/457-6286, www.msvu.ca.

### B&Bs and Inns

Oscar Wilde and P. T. Barnum both slept (not together) at the 1866 **Waverley Inn,** centrally located at 1266 Barrington Street, tel. 902/423-9346, www.waverleyinn.com. Rates for the 32 rooms ($95–125) include breakfast; complimentary tea, coffee, and snacks are offered all day and evening in the hospitality suite. Rooms are furnished with Victorian-era antiques, and deluxe rooms contain whirlpool tubs and featherbeds.

Around the corner, the plush **Halliburton House Inn,** 5184 Morris St., tel. 902/420-0658, www.halliburton.ns.ca, is a beautiful heritage property with 29 antiques-furnished rooms (from $110), each with private bath. Two suites have fireplaces. Amenities include a complimentary continental breakfast, a library, a garden courtyard, and an acclaimed dining room.

Further out, prices begin to drop. **Fresh Start Bed and Breakfast,** 2720 Gottingen St., tel. 902/453-6616 or 888/453-6616, occupies a Victorian mansion facing the Maritime Command Museum and has eight nonsmoking rooms ($65

**Waverley Inn**

single, $70 double with full breakfast), some with private baths. Laundry service is available. Not far from the Public Gardens. **Virginia Kinfolks,** 1722 Robie, tel. 800/668-7829 or tel. 902/423-6687, has three antiques-furnished suites ($100 single, $175 double, with full breakfast) and is open year-round.

In Dartmouth, **Caroline's Bed and Breakfast,** 134 Victoria Rd., tel. 902/469-4665, has a convenient location close to the town center, Dartmouth Common, and the cross-harbor ferry. The two rooms ($40 single, $50 double, with continental breakfast) are available May through October.

## Hotels

North of Citadel Hill, the **King Edward Inn,** 5780-88 West St., tel. 902/422-3266 or 800/565-5464, www.kingedward.com, has some nonsmoking units among its 45 rooms and suites ($79–149). Some suites are equipped with Jacuzzis.

Further out still, **Keddy's Halifax Hotel,** 20 St. Margaret's Bay Rd., tel. 902/477-5611 or 800/561-7666, www.keddys.ca, matches good

value with 135 spacious rooms and suites ($52–93), a dining room, lounge, outside decks, an indoor pool, whirlpool, sauna, fitness center, and a small lake for swimming.

Expect to pay for a downtown location. The following are the best of many choices. **Cambridge Suites** at 1583 Brunswick St., tel. 902/420-0555 or 888/417-8483, cabridgesuiteshotel.com, has 200 suites ($139–189), a morning dining room (serving complimentary continental breakfast), a whirlpool and sauna, a rooftop fitness center, laundry facilities, and guest parking within a handsome brick structure.

The **Delta Barrington** at 1875 Barrington St., tel. 902/429-7410 or 800/268-1133, www.deltahotels.com, shares space with Barrington Place Mall in the historic area and has 201 impressively furnished rooms. Rates range from $89 in winter to $159 in summer; check the Delta website for deals year-round. Its McNab's Restaurant offers formal dining, and the hotel also has a bistro, health club with pool, and shopping arcade.

On the same street as its sister property is the **Delta Halifax,** at 1990 Barrington St., tel.

902/425-6700 or 800/268-1133, www.deltahotels.
com. Built by the Canadian Pacific Railway, this
was the first of the city's grande dame hotels,
and the old girl's still a handsome dowager among
Halifax's accommodations. Its 300 rooms (from
$149 single, $159 double) and suites (from $279)
are outfitted with lavish carpeting and comfortable furniture. The Bluenose Room offers Sunday
brunch, the Crown Bistro formal dining, and
Sam Slick's Lounge is the venue for a quiet cocktail. The hotel also has a health club with pool
and is adjacent to shopping at Scotia Square.

The **Sheraton Halifax,** 1919 Upper Water
St., tel. 902/421-1700 or 800/325-3535,
www.sheratonhalifax.com, was designed to resemble the garrison that once occupied the waterfront, then underwent renovations and
expansions that were finally completed in 2001.
The impressive stone hotel is graced with a
pitched copper-covered roof and dormer windows that peer across Historic Properties and
Halifax Harbour. Its 356 rooms (from $189)
mirror each other in space and furnishing. Ask for
a room facing the harbor for incredible views.
The hotel's dining room sets the city's pace for
hotel dining. Other facilities include cafés,
lounges, a health club with indoor pool, and a
shopping arcade. The hotel's second-floor bar is
the place to see and be seen, especially early Friday evening as the weekend merriment com-
mences—it's a nice place to meet people.

The **Westin Nova Scotian,** at 1181 Hollis
St., tel. 902/421-1000 or 877/993-7846,
www.westin.ns.ca, adjacent to the VIA Rail terminal, has been lushly and extensively refurbished from top to bottom. Featuring over 300
rooms, a restaurant, fitness center with an indoor pool, tennis court, and shopping arcade,
rack rates are published at $250–400, but deals
are usually offered, especially through the cooler months.

# FOOD

Haligonians expect and get good cooking—lots
of it. The town is crowded with all sorts of eateries: cafés, pubs, bistros, and restaurants, including
the province's widest selection of ethnic cuisine.

## Dinner Houses

At most of the nicer, fine-dining restaurants in
town, plan on paying $15–30 for your entrée.

**McKelvie's,** at 1680 Lower Water Street, tel.
902/421-6161, does a commendable job with
every kind of seafood. Try the Crunchy Halibut or Haddock—it's rolled in crushed cereal
and almonds, fried, and served with creamy
barbecue sauce. The restaurant is in a refurbished historic former firehouse overlooking
Historic Properties.

**Salty's,** 1869 Lower Water St. at Historic Properties' waterfront, tel. 902/423-6818, mixes
seafood with succulent meat dishes in a sublime
setting. But first, kick back with a margarita and
watch the boats sail in and out of the harbor.
Then sit indoors or out to enjoy some of the
city's best food in a casual atmosphere. And don't
miss the scrumptious desserts.

Just north of Salty's, diners at **Murphy's,** 1751
Lower Water St., tel. 902/420-1015, also enjoy
panoramic harbor views. This restaurant fills a
converted warehouse, with a few outside tables
right at the end of the pier. Naturally, the emphasis is on seafood, with lunches starting at
around $9 and rising to $16 for a lobster sandwich. Dinner mains range $16–30, but there's no
need to spend a fortune, with dishes such as the
Taste of Nova Scotia for $15 the perfect starter to
share and the delicious Seafood Medley main
just $18.95.

**Five Fishermen,** 1740 Argyle St., tel. 902/422-
4421, occupies one of Halifax's oldest buildings—it was built in 1816 and once used by
famed governess Anna Leonowens (of *Anna and
the King of Siam* fame) for her Victorian School of
Art and Design. The restaurant is popular with
seafood-loving Haligonians for its 68-dish menu,
which includes swordfish, Louisiana shrimp,
Malpeque oysters, and Digby scallops, as well as
chicken and Alberta steaks. All entrées come
with complimentary all-you-can-eat mussels,
steamed clams, and salad bar.

**O'Carroll's** at 1860 Upper Water Street, tel.
902/423-4405, features such culinary specialties as steak and kidney pie, duck à l'orange, lobster thermidor, and roast beef. Closed Sunday.
**Halliburton House Inn,** 5184 Morris St., tel.

902/420-0658, is the dining room at the heritage lodging of the same name. Specialties include seafood and local and imported game. Open for dinner daily year-round.

The **Upper Deck,** Historic Properties, tel. 902/422-1289, is the upstairs dining room at Privateers Warehouse. The setting is soothingly refined, and the European-inspired menu balances seafood and red meats. Appetizers are all under $10, while mains, such as a mixed seafood grill, average $25–30.

On Spring Garden Rd., you'll find a couple of other popular choices. **Duffy's Steakhouse,** upstairs at Dresden Row, 5640 Spring Garden, tel. 902/421-1116, has earned an admirable dining reputation with dishes like scallops in Pernod sauce. Its local fame rests on its prime beef—cut, weighed, and charbroiled or sizzled on hot rocks. It's open for lunch Mon.–Sat. and for dinner daily.

**Your Father's Moustache,** 5686 Spring Garden, tel. 902/423-6766, is a casual favorite with a reasonably priced menu of seafood, steaks, and pasta. Open year-round, for lunch and dinner daily, and a poplar brunch served Sunday 11 A.M.–3 P.M.

## Lighter Meals

For a casual lunch, head for the **Harbourside Market** at the waterfront end of the Privateers Warehouse. Various food outlets surround the seating area, including a coffee bar, a bakery, a deli, a fish and chip shop, and an outlet specializing in Cajun cuisine. At the seafood outlet, expect to pay around $8 for fish and chips, $2 per pound for mussels, $11 per pound for scallops, and a reasonable $12 per pound for lobster (cooked lobster is slightly higher).

**Le Bistro,** 1333 South Park St., tel. 902/423-8428, offers informal Global cuisine and often a weekend guitarist. It has an open-air patio and live entertainment Thurs.–Sun. evenings.

The **Granite Brewery,** 1222 Barrington St., tel. 902/423-5660, is in a historic building and has a lively pub ambience. Its own excellent beers are brewed on-site, and complement lunch specials and a Saturday brunch of steak and eggs or creamed smoked fish.

© ANDREW HEMPSTEAD

**Sweet Basil Bistro, Historic Properties**

NOVA SCOTIA

The **Lower Deck,** tel. 902/425-1501, and **Crawdad's,** tel. 902/422-5200, in the Historic Properties' Privateers Warehouse, both take a comfortable approach to casual dining. The Lower Deck's chili is heartily spiced, burgers are oversized, and the fried seafood is ample and tasty—no one goes away hungry. Crawdad's specializes in New Orleans–style dishes in a matching atmosphere.

**Sweet Basil Bistro,** in the Historic Properties, 1866 Upper Water St., tel. 902/425-2133, serves homemade hot and cold pasta, salads, and great desserts. It's a nonsmoking establishment.

## Vegetarian and Ethnic

Some of the best vegetarian fare in town is at **Satisfaction Feast,** 1581 Grafton St., tel. 902/422-3540, where curry enlivens the casseroles, and carrot juice is the favorite beverage. Two highly recommended Japanese restaurants are **Dharma-Sushi,** 1576 Argyle, tel. 902/425-7785, and **Maki Maki,** 5974 Spring Garden Rd., tel. 902/422-3818. The later draws the biggest crowds Mon.–Wed., when a 2-for-1 sushi dinner is offered.

**Curry Village,** 5677 Brenton Place off Spring Garden Rd., tel. 902/429-5010, serves chicken tandoor, biryanis, lamb vindaloo, and other Indian dishes, including vegetarian options. It's open Mon.–Sat. for lunch, daily for dinner. **Chicken Tandoor,** 6285 Quinpool Rd., tel. 902/423-7725, specializes in East Indian cuisine but also offers a few Thai dishes; reservations recommended on weekends.

Try the **Hungry Hungarian,** 5215 Blowers St., tel. 902/423-4364, for authentic goulashes and other Eastern European fare, as well as seafood and sandwiches. **Mexicali Rosa's,** 5680 Spring Garden Rd., tel. 902/422-7672, serves up California-style Mexican cuisine for lunch and dinner year-round.

## Supermarkets

**IGA** is the largest food chain and has nine supermarkets in Metro Halifax. Small groceries like the **Green Gables Food Stores** are everywhere.

**European Pantry,** 6516 Chebucto Rd., tel. 902/422-5679, is among the most interesting smaller places, carrying Greek, Italian, and Lebanese foods. Its deli has picnic ingredients. The lower level at the **Spring Garden Place Mall,** 5640 Spring Garden Rd., offers more appetizing ingredients for quick meals and picnics at various bakery, butcher, dairy, and dessert shops.

# ENTERTAINMENT AND EVENTS

## Cinemas

When it comes to movies, cosmopolite, college-going Haligonians tend to favor avant-garde, foreign, and other art-house fare. Dalhousie University's **Rebecca Cohn Auditorium,** 6101 University Ave., tel. 902/494-3820 or 494-7081, is the venue for such fare.

Recently released mainstream movies are shown at numerous multiple-screen theaters: the **Famous Players Cinemas,** in Park Lane Mall, 5657 Spring Garden Rd., tel. 902/423-5866; **Empire 6 Dartmouth Cinemas,** Superstore Mall, 650 Portland St., Dartmouth, tel. 902/434-4200; **Oxford Theatre,** 6408 Quinpool Rd. at Oxford, tel. 902/423-7488.

At Bayer Industrial Park on the outskirts of the city, the **Empire IMAX Theatre,** 190 Chain Lake Dr., tel. 902/876-IMAX, holds an IMAX theater as well as numerous standard-size screening rooms. To get there, take Highway 102 toward Truro and get off at the Lacewood Drive exit, by Costco.

## Theater and Shows

Haligonians have a sweet and sometimes bittersweet Canadian sense of humor (somewhat like the British), and local theater revels in their brand of fun. A $30 admission will get you into dinner-theater musical productions at **Grafton Street Theatre,** 1741 Grafton St., tel. 902/425-1961, or **Halifax Feast Dinner Theatre,** in the Maritime Centre on Barrington, tel. 902/420-1840, which offers a lighthearted look at the city's past.

At the **Neptune Theatre,** 1593 Argyle St., tel. 902/429-7070, private companies like Legends of Broadway take to the boards during summer with musicals and Gilbert and Sullivan shows. The regular theater season runs September–May.

## Bars, Nightclubs, and Live Music

If you're going to have just one beer in Halifax, make it at the **Stag's Head Tavern,** part of the Keith's Brewery complex on Lower Water Street, tel. 902/455-1474. Best known as North America's oldest working brewery, Keith's still uses traditional British brewing techniques. Its famous India Pale Ale is widely available on draught and bottled across the province, but best enjoyed in the Stag's Head, surrounded by convivial atmosphere and with traditional Maritime music in the background.

Walk the hillside on Friday and Saturday evenings to experience Atlantic Canada's best and most concentrated music, entertainment, and drinking scene.

**Your Father's Moustache,** 5686 Spring Garden Rd., tel. 902/423-6766, puts on excellent live, usually local, music most evenings. On Saturday afternoon, they host their popular Blues Matinee. A few doors down, the **Thirsty Duck,** 5472 Spring Garden Rd., tel. 902/422-1548, doesn't usually have entertainment but it's a popular hangout nonetheless. The open, rooftop deck is a great spot for whiling away an afternoon, sipping a quiet beer or two.

**Maxwell's Plum Tavern,** 1600 Grafton St., tel. 902/423-5090, has an excellent selection of imported draft beers (notably, Beamish Irish Stout, John Courage, and Newcastle Brown Ale) and single-malt scotches. That alone may be reason enough to visit there, but it's also a good venue for straight-ahead jazz, including Sunday afternoon jam sessions.

The local hipoisie mix and dance at **Lawrence of Oregano,** 1726 Argyle St., tel. 902/425-8077, where bands play six nights a week. **Cheers,** 1743 Grafton St., also has live entertainment Tues.–Sat. nights; expect to pay a $3–5 cover. Popular nightspots include **The Attic,** 1741 Grafton St., tel. 902/423-0909, **Iniome,** 1581 Barrington St., tel. 902/423-7186, and **New Palace,** 1721 Brunswick St., tel. 902/429-5959, all of which appeal to the college-aged crowd.

Quieter evenings can be had along the harbor. A drink or two starting at 6 P.M. at the Sheraton Halifax's **Fife & Drum Bar,** 1919 Upper Water St., tel. 902/428-7805, starts the Haligonian weekend. **O'Carroll's,** an Irish-style pub at 1860 Water St., tel. 902/423-4405, has Saturday afternoon and weeknight sing-alongs, followed by Cape Breton, Newfoundland, and Irish folk music. **Granite Brewery,** 1222 Barrington St., is a favorite stop for its English-style beers, including the ever-popular Ringwood Ale. **Stayner's Bar & Grill,** 5075 George St., tel. 902/492-1800, is in the heart of the tourist district, but as it's away from the water, the casual visitor often misses this quiet, elegant bar.

### Events

Nothing reflects Halifax's long military heritage better than the **Nova Scotia International Tattoo,** which presents a week of performances in early July. A Nova Scotian "tattoo" is an outdoor military exercise presented as entertainment. Here it involves competitions, military bands, dancers, gymnasts, and choirs. Tickets (around $20) may be ordered by mail as early as December; by April, they're available by telephone from

Metro Centre Box Office, tel. 902/451-1221, or online at www.nstattoo.ca. For general event information, call 902/420-1114.

Noon concerts bring crowds to the Grand Parade July–August, and to the Public Gardens July–September. During July, the Mayor of Halifax hosts **Weekday Tea** for visitors at City Hall at the Grand Parade's edge, Mon.–Fri. 2–3 P.M.

The city celebrates **Natal Day** for four days in early August, with live music, entertainment, parades, and fireworks. The **Buskers** arrive for 10 days in mid-August, and you'll find street performers everywhere on the hillside, especially throughout Historic Properties. Summer finishes with the five-day **Atlantic Fringe Theatre Festival,** featuring 200 shows at various downtown venues through the first week of September.

The city's newest major event, **Snow Jam,** has grown quickly in popularity. Thousands of tons of snow are dumped on Citadel Hill for boarders and skiers to demonstrate their skills many months before winter arrives. The action takes the middle weekend of September. Also in mid-September is the **Atlantic Film Festival,** tel. 902/422-6965, www.atlanticfilm.com, showcasing over 200 films, many Canadian in origin.

Numerous other summertime one-day festivals and family clan gatherings are scheduled; the *Doers and Dreamers* travel guide lists many of them.

## RECREATION AND SPORTS

For jogging, tennis, baseball, Frisbee, soccer, or just about anything else you can do outdoors, head for Central Common and adjacent Halifax Commons—spacious, grassy parks off Cogswell Street just northwest of Citadel Hill.

### Workouts

The **YMCA** is centrally located in Halifax at 1565 South Park Street, tel. 902/423-9622; another is in Dartmouth at 26 Brookdale Court, tel. 902/469-9622. The Halifax **YWCA** is at 1239 Barrington Street, tel. 902/423-6162.

NOVA SCOTIA

Saint Mary's University's **Tower Fitness and Recreation Facility,** 920 Tower Rd., tel. 902/420-5555, is the city's preeminent fitness center, and facilities are augmented with tennis and squash courts. A day-use pass costs $7. It's open weekdays 7 A.M.–10:30 P.M., weekends 8 A.M.–5:30 P.M.

Many of the city's hotels have splendid health-club facilities. Two of the best can be found at the **Sheraton Halifax,** 1919 Upper Water St., tel. 902/421-1700, and the **Delta Halifax,** 1990 Barrington St., tel. 902/425-6214; non-guests can use these facilities for around $15 per visit.

### Water Sports

Municipal pools are open to visitors ($3) at **Centennial Pool,** 1970 Gottingen St.; **Northcliffe Pool,** 111 Clayton Park Dr.; and **Needham Pool,** 3372 Devonshire Street. The pools are open Mon. and Wed.–Fri. for noontime adult dips, and Tues. and Sat. 4–6 P.M.

The City of Halifax Recreation Department's **Saint Mary's Boat Club,** tel. 902/490-4538 or 490-4607 (November–March), offers canoe rentals and lessons on the Northwest Arm, the harbor channel behind central Halifax.

The coastal waters off Nova Scotia are well known among divers for numerous shipwrecks, and local dive shops do a brisk business. A dozen shops rent equipment in Metro Halifax, and most run charters. Try **Divers World,** in Lakeside Industrial Park, tel. 902/876-0555 or 800/616-3483, or **Torpedo Ray's Scuba Adventures,** 1440 Bedford Hwy., Bedford, tel. 902/835-4800.

**Crystal Crescent Beach Provincial Park** lies a half hour south of Halifax off Highway 349 and is the locals' favorite Atlantic beach. Its sand is fine, and the sea is usually cold, but summer crowds heat up the action. Nature lovers will enjoy the 10-km trail to remote Pennant Point.

### Cycling

Halifax and vicinity, with its many lakes and harborside coves, is a great area for exploring by bike. Be careful where you park, and be sure to use a lock—there's a lively trade in stolen bicycles here. A centrally located source for rentals and advice is **Harbour Bike & Sea Rentals,** 1781 Lower Water St., tel. 902/423-1185. Standard bikes cost $8 per hour or $38 for a full day.

*Halifax and vicinity, with its many lakes and harborside coves, is a great area for exploring by bike. Be careful where you park, and be sure to use a lock—there's a lively trade in stolen bicycles here.*

### Golf

Half a dozen public golf courses lie within just a 15-km radius of Halifax and Dartmouth. For starters, there's the **Briarwood Golf Club** south of Halifax along Herring Cove Rd., tel. 902/477-4677; it's an easy but enjoyable layout, with plenty of available tee times. One of the region's best courses is **Granite Springs,** west of downtown off Highway 333 at 4441 Prospect Road, Bayside, tel. 902/852-4653. The challenging layout winds through 120 hectares of mature forest, with distant ocean views. Green fees are $55 ($35 twilight), club rentals $20–35, power cart $30.

### Winter Sports

In winter, walking paths become **cross-country ski trails** at Point Pleasant Park, Sir Sandford Fleming Park, and Hemlock Ravine (north of Halifax). For outdoor **ice-skating** conditions, call the Halifax-Dartmouth Recreation Department at tel. 902/490-4685 or 490-7240. Dartmouth maintains groomed surfaces at Lake Charles, and several lakes in Halifax are great for skating.

## SHOPPING

Halifax has numerous shopping malls on Spring Garden Rd. and elsewhere on the hillside; open Mon.–Wed. and Sat. 9:30 A.M.–5:30 P.M., Thurs.–Fri. to 9 P.M. **Eaton's,** the largest department store, is in the Halifax Shopping Centre on Mumford Road.

### Arts and Crafts

The city's art galleries are superb. The newest fine arts trends are on exhibit at Nova Scotia

College of Art and Design's **Anna Leonowens Gallery,** 1891 Granville St., tel. 902/494-8223; open Tues.–Fri. 11 A.M.–5 P.M., Sat. noon–5 P.M. (The college's Granville Street facade may appear familiar—the college uses a line drawing of the historic storefront row in its literature and catalogs.)

Hundreds of clan fabrics and tartans in kilts, skirts, vests, ties, and other apparel are stocked at **Celtic Traditions,** 5640 Spring Garden Rd., tel. 902/492-3390, and **Plaid Place,** 1903 Barrington St., tel. 902/429-6872. More of the same is for sale at **Bounty Boutique,** in the Privateers Warehouse, tel. 902/425-1200.

Upscale quilted apparel by Vicki Lynn Bardon is sold throughout Atlantic Canada and is available at **Suttles and Seawinds,** 1869 Upper Water St., tel. 902/423-9077. **Studio 21,** 1223 Lower Water St., tel. 902/420-1852, is a good source of contemporary paintings by local artists. The capital's definitive crafts source is **Jennifer's of Nova Scotia,** 5635 Spring Garden Rd., tel. 902/425-3119, an outlet for 120 provincial producers.

The **Halifax City Market** is another crafts source, and crafts vendors are part of the scene at Alexander Keith's Brewery on Lower Water Street; open year-round, Sat. 7 A.M.–3 P.M.

## Bookstores

The **Nova Scotia Government Bookstore,** 1700 Granville St., tel. 902/424-7580 or 800/670-4357 (in Nova Scotia), has a trove of titles covering everything from provincial heritage to natural history, hiking, food, and other subjects.

The **Book Room,** 1546 Barrington St., tel. 902/423-8271, is the oldest trade bookstore in Canada, founded in 1839. In addition to a broad general selection, this excellent shop specializes in books on Nova Scotia and Canadiana, Native studies, and genealogy. Upstairs in the Spring Garden Place Mall, **Frog Hollow Book,** 5640 Spring Garden Rd., tel. 902/429-3318, is a comfortable store which occasionally hosts visiting literati.

For used books and rare editions, try **Schooner Books,** 5378 Inglis St., tel. 902/423-8419; **Back Pages,** 1526 Queen St., tel. 902/423-4750; or **Attic Owl Bookshop,** 5802 South St., tel. 902/422-2433.

## Photography

Fast-processing photography shops are plentiful. **Camera Repair Centre** at 2342 Hunter St., tel. 902/423-6450, handles repairs. It's open Mon.–Fri. 9 A.M.–5 P.M. Reliable equipment and hard-to-find film speeds are stocked at **Carsand-Mosher Photographic,** 1559 Barrington St. (at Blowers St.), tel. 902/421-1980.

# INFORMATION AND SERVICES

## Visitor Information

Make your first stop the **International Visitor Centre,** in the heart of downtown at 1595 Barrington Street, tel. 902/490-5946. This excellent facility in the heart of downtown holds racks stuffed filled with information for the city and all of Nova Scotia. Along two walls are a series of boards and computer terminals each devoted to a different area of the province while scattered through the center of the room are manned desks, where staff hand out personalized information and have access to a computerized reservation system for local accommodations. The visitor center also holds a tour-booking desk, a gift shop, and washrooms. It's open through summer, daily 8:30 A.M.–7 P.M., the rest of the year daily, but shorter hours.

Other year-round information centers include at **Halifax International Airport** (beyond the Hertz desk), tel. 902/873-1223; the **Red Store Visitor Information Centre** in the Historic Properties, tel. 902/424-4248; and at **Alderney Landing,** Dartmouth, tel. 902/490-4433.

**Tourism Halifax** also maintains the excellent website, www.halifaxinfo.com. The government website, www.explore.gov.ns.ca, is another good source of trip-planning information.

Numerous free tourist magazines circulate, such as *The Greater Halifax Visitor Guide,* and *Where: Halifax.* Pick them up at the tourist offices.

## Maps and Media

Map sources are plentiful. **Halifax Land Information Centre,** 1551 Terminal Rd., tel. 902/424-2735, sells topographic maps of provincial regions ($8); it's open weekdays 8:30 A.M.–4:15 P.M. **Trail Shop** is another source at

# SIGHTSEEING TOURS

Halifax is an enjoyable city to explore on foot, but taking one of the following tours is a great way to see a wide range of sights while enjoying a knowledgeable commentary.

### The Harbour Hopper

Harbour Hopper Tours, tel. 902/490-8687, has pick-up points from three booths along Lower Water St. for a quick trip around the historic streets of Halifax, and then the fun really starts, as the company's distinctive green and yellow amphibious vehicles plunge into the water for a cruise around the harbor. The trip lasts around one hour, with up to 15 departures daily.

### Other Harbour Cruises

The harborfront's premier attraction, the magnificent schooner *Bluenose II,* divides her time between Halifax, her home port Lunenburg, and goodwill tours to other Canadian ports. When in Halifax, two-hour harbor tours are available twice daily from the Maritime Museum's wharf; adult $20. Each sailing has 75 spots—40 spots can be reserved in advance by calling 902/634-1963 or 800/763-1963, with the remaining 35 going on sale 90 minutes prior to departure. Without a reservation, expect to line up for a spot.

Many other sightseeing craft also offer harbor tours. Murphy's on the Water, Cable Wharf, 1751 Lower Water St., tel. 902/420-1015, operates several vessels, through a sailing season that runs from mid-May to late October. The 23-meter sailing ketch *Mar II* makes daily lunch cruises ($12.95–17.95) and cocktail cruises from its Nathan Green Square moorage. The *Harbour Queen I* is a 200-passenger paddlewheeler offering a narrated harbor cruise ($15.95) and a variety of lunch and dinner cruises (from $19.95). The *Haligonian III* takes passengers on two-hour nature cruises of the harbor and North West Arm ($24.95). The latter two vessels depart from Cable Wharf. Murphy's also arranges

6210 Quinpool Rd., tel. 902/423-8736, open Mon.–Wed. 9 A.M.–5 P.M., Thurs.–Fri. to 9 P.M. **Binnacle** at 15 Purcell's Cove Rd., tel. 902/423-6464, sells nautical charts. Another prime map source is the provincial Novia Scotia Government Bookstore (see above). The daily *Halifax Herald* circulates throughout the province while *Coast* is a free arts and entertainment weekly.

## Libraries

**Halifax City Regional Library** is at 5381 Spring Garden Rd., tel. 902/490-5700; open Tues.–Fri. 10 A.M.–9 P.M., Sat. to 6 P.M., Sun. 2–5 P.M. In addition to a large stock of local fiction and nonfiction, it holds a good selection of newspapers from around the world, magazines from around North America. Library visitors also enjoy free Internet access. A branch library is at 2285 Gottingen Street, tel. 902/490-5723; same hours.

## Health and Safety

The city's hospital services are coordinated under the auspices of the **Queen Elizabeth II Health Sciences Centre,** tel. 902/473-2700.

Municipal **police** are assigned to Halifax and Dartmouth; in emergencies, dial 911, and for non-emergency business call 902/490-5026. The **RCMP** can be reached by calling 911 or 902/426-3611.

## Banks

As Atlantic Canada's banking center, Halifax has banks by the dozens. Shopping around for the best exchange rate is worth it. **Bank of Nova Scotia** has nine city branches and does not charge to convert foreign currency to Canadian dollars. The fee for cashing traveler's checks is $2, so it pays to convert several checks at one time. The bank is open Mon., Tues., Wed., and Sat. 10 A.M.–3 P.M., Thurs. and Fri. to 8 P.M.

**Hong Kong Bank of Canada** likewise charges no transaction fee. Its three branches are open weekdays, 9 A.M.–4:30 P.M. Other banks in the downtown core include **Bank of Montréal, Canadian Imperial Bank of Commerce, National Bank of Canada,** and **Royal Bank.**

Hotel desks also exchange currency, but rates are more favorable at the banks.

whalewatching trips, fishing charters, and visits to McNab's Island. *The Ladyhawk,* tel. 902/420-9713, is a small hovercraft with darts about the harbor on regular 30-minute tours departing from its berth between Cable Wharf and the ferry terminal; adult $25, child $16.

### Land-based Tours

On land, city-sponsored bilingual sightseeing tours are free and depart Grand Parade at City Hall to 30 sites, July–Aug., weekdays at 9:30 A.M. and 2 P.M. The **Pavement Pounders,** all university students, work stints as rickshaw haulers and take sightseers

Harbour Hopper

on guided tours along harborfront streets mid-June through September; a 20-minute ride costs about $10.

Commercial tours are also plentiful. **Double Decker Tours,** tel. 902/420-1155, runs 90-minute tours on red double-decker buses daily, mid-June to mid-October. The tours depart from Historic Properties and from the Halifax Sheraton daily at 10:30 A.M. and 12:30 P.M., taking in over 100 spots of interest. Fare is adult $20, senior $16, child $7. Like most cities across the country, **Grayline,** tel. 902/425-9999, has a strong presence, with various tours departing from the front of the Maritime Museum of the Atlantic. These include a three-hour trolley bus tour (departs 9 A.M. and 1 P.M.; adult $25.25, senior $24.35, child $5.20) and a 1.5-hour double-decker bus tour (departs four times daily; adult $19.15, senior $17.40, child $2.60).

## Post and Internet

The city has three post offices, open Mon.–Fri. 8 A.M.–5 P.M. The General Post Office is at 1680 Bedford Row, tel. 902/494-4734; branches are at 6175 Almon Street and 1969 Upper Water Street. Retail postal outlets are at the Scotia Square mall and at IGA food stores; weekday hours vary, but the outlets are open Sat. 8 A.M.–6 P.M.

Public Internet access is free at **Halifax City Regional Library,** 5381 Spring Garden Rd., tel. 902/490-5700, or pay $2 for 10 minutes, $9 per hour, at **Ceilidh Connection,** 1672 Barrington St., tel. 902/422-9800. It's open Mon.–Fri. 10 A.M.–10 P.M., Sat.–Sun. noon–8 P.M.

## Laundries and Lockers

Coin-operated laundries are located beyond Halifax's hillside. **Agricola Laundromat,** at 2454 Agricola Street, tel. 902/429-2829, is open Mon.–Fri. and Sun. 7 A.M.–9 P.M., Sat. to 7 P.M. **Bluenose Laundromat,** 2198 Windsor St., tel. 902/422-7098, will wash, dry, and fold your clothes with same-day service. It's open Mon.–Sat. 7:30 A.M.–7:30 P.M.

Lockers for stashing luggage are at the **Acadian Lines** terminal, 6040 Almon St. **VIA Rail's** CN Station has limited capacity and stores luggage in baggage storage; the charge is $1.50 a day for each piece.

## GETTING THERE
### By Air

**Air Canada** and **Air Nova,** combine to serve all major Atlantic Canada airports with flights to and from Halifax. Contacts are tel. 888/247-2262, www.aircanada.ca. Air Canada also flies directly to Halifax from throughout Canada, Boston, and Newark. From other U.S. cities, flights to Halifax are routed through Toronto or Montreal. Also flying to Halifax is **Air Labrador,** tel. 800/563-3042;

Air St. Pierre, tel. 902/873-3566; Canada 3000, tel. 902/873-3555; Continental, tel. 800/784-4444; Icelandair, tel. 800/223-5500; and Northwest, tel. 800/225-2525.

Halifax International Airport is at Elmsdale, 38 km north of Halifax. The only facilities in the arrivals area are rental car desks and small information booth. Continue beyond the information booth to access a food court, bar, duty-free shops, a currency exchange counter open 7 A.M.–9 P.M., and a bookstore.

The Airbus, tel. 902/873-2091, runs between the airport and major downtown hotels ($12 one-way; $20 round trip) six to eight times daily. A cab runs around $35.

Airport parking costs $1.35 per hour to a maximum of $7.50 per day and $32.50 per week.

## By Land

The Halifax bus terminal is at 6040 Almon Street, tel. 902/454-9321. Acadian Lines operates bus routes throughout the province. Its Halifax–Yarmouth bus departs the terminal daily at 8 A.M. and 6 P.M.; the Halifax–Sydney route has thrice-daily departures. Zinck Bus, tel. 902/468-4342, operates along the eastern shore; the four-hour Halifax to Sherbrooke ride leaves daily at 5:30 P.M.

VIA Rail enters the province from New Brunswick, stops at Amherst and Truro, and finishes at Halifax's CN Station, Barrington at Cornwallis streets, tel. 902/494-7900 or 800/561-3952.

## By Yacht

Three yacht clubs welcome visiting yachts and will contact customs officials to clear the vessel after you disembark. Armdale Yacht Club, North West Arm, tel. 902/477-4617, opens its facilities (showers, meal service) to visitors; the overnight mooring fee is charged by the boat's length. For more info contact them at P.O. Box 40, Armdale, Halifax, NS B30 4J7. Similar facilities and rates are offered at the Royal Nova Scotia Yacht Squadron, 376 Purcells Cove Rd., tel. 902/477-5653, and Bedford Basin Yacht Club, 73 Shore Dr., Bedford, tel. 902/835-3729.

# GETTING AROUND

## Driving Logistics

Haligonians are painstakingly careful and slow drivers—a wise way to go as hillside streets are steep, and many roads are posted for one-way traffic. Pedestrians have the right-of-way on crosswalks. Two bridges link Halifax and Dartmouth, the A. Murray MacKay and the Angus L. MacDonald; toll is 75 cents one-way for cars, free for bicyclists and pedestrians.

Parking is scarce. Commuters clog the hillside streets 7:30–9 A.M. and 4–5:30 P.M., and the university areas are crowded weekdays. Some lodgings, such as the Halifax Sheraton, Cambridge Suites, and the Citadel Inn Halifax, have guest parking. Public parking garages and lots are located on Granville, Upper and Lower Water, Barrington, and Duke streets, plus Spring Garden Road. All charge about $1.50 an hour.

## Pedestrian Walkways

Lofty pedestrian walkways ("pedways") connect many stores, hotels, and other buildings in downtown Halifax. Pedways are quicker than weaving through traffic and are especially helpful during summer showers and winter flurries. The pedway system connects the Sheraton Halifax, Delta Halifax, Scotia Square Mall, Delta Barrington, and a few other places in between. An underground tunnel beneath George St. links the World Trade and Convention Centre to Prince George Hotel.

## Buses and Taxis

Metro Transit buses saturate city streets, charge $1.65 (exact change only) with free transfers, and operate daily 6 A.M. to midnight. Main bus stops are on Water, Barrington, Cornwallis, Cogswell, and Duke Streets, Spring Garden Road, and Gottingen Street, with service to Quinpool Road and Bayers Street. For route information, call 902/490-6600.

Fred (an acronym for Free Rides Everywhere Downtown), tel. 902/423-3848, is a free, summer-only bus service that makes 18 stops on a circuit which begins northbound along Lower

Water Street, then heads along Barrington Street and Spring Garden Road before returning to Water Street on South Street.

Taxis cruise or wait at hotels and bus and rail terminals. Rides are metered (the rate card is on the back of the front seat); flag fare is $2.60, then around $1.25 per km. To the airport costs around $35. **Ace-Y Taxi** is one of the largest outfits, with 200 cabs; tel. 902/429-4444 or 902/422-4433.

## Rental Cars
Each of the major car rental companies is represented at the airport and downtown. As always, book as far in advance as possible, and use the Internet to find the best deals. Local contact numbers include: **Avis,** tel. 902/429-0963; **Budget,** tel. 902/492-7500; **Dollar,** tel. 902/860-0203; **Hertz,** tel. 902/873-3700; **National,** tel. 902/873-3505; and **Thrifty,** tel. 902/424-1515

## Ferries
The **Halifax–Dartmouth ferry** (terminals at the foot of George Street in Halifax and at Alderney Drive and Ochterloney Street in Dartmouth) carries pedestrians and bikes on the 15-minute crossing, year-round, Mon.–Sat. 6:30 A.M.–midnight, and June–September on Sun., same hours. The one-way fare is adults $1.75, children $1.20.

The ferry to Woodside (south Dartmouth) departs the same Halifax-side terminal, year-round, Mon.–Fri. peak hours only.

# Southwestern Nova Scotia

Nova Scotians must have had the southwest region in mind when they coined the province's motto, "So Much to Sea." The crashing Atlantic lays itself out in foaming breakers for 300 km along the southern coast, while the formidable Bay of Fundy—site of the world's highest tides—advances and retreats along the northern coast. The seaports and towns along both coastlines follow one another, like a series of glossy, life-size picture postcards.

The region comprises the southwestern half of the Nova Scotian peninsula, and most sightseeing is concentrated around the coastal edges. The highway network consists of a coastline system of efficient expressways and parallel scenic roads. Highway 103 and its continuation as Highway 101 speed travel between destinations. But if time allows, route yourself onto the secondary scenic roads meandering through ports and overlooking the Atlantic and Bay of Fundy.

You can skirt the region in a day, driving nonstop. More realistically, plan a day in each place that interests you. As elsewhere in Nova Scotia, dining at its best is superb, and the region's specialty is its abundance of top-notch country inns with public dining rooms. Museums with well-conceived historical exhibits are everywhere. Many lodgings are in historic houses and mansions converted to country inns and in categories best described as better, best, and beautiful.

## HISTORY

To a great extent, the history of the province's southwest region is the story of all of Nova

Lunenburg

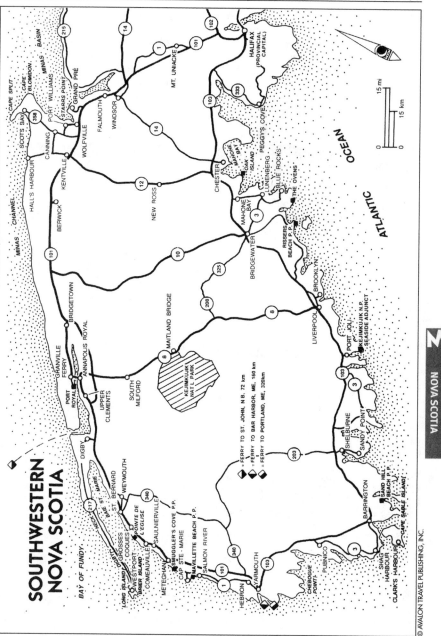

SOUTHWESTERN NOVA SCOTIA

NOVA SCOTIA

= FERRY TO ST. JOHN, N.B. 72 km
= FERRY TO BAR HARBOR, ME. 160 km
= FERRY TO PORTLAND, ME. 320km

Scotia. France's colonial ambitions began at Port Royal and clashed head-on with England's quest for New World dominance. England prevailed. In 1753, a convoy of 1,453 German, Swiss, and French Huguenot "foreign Protestants" arrived in Lunenburg. New England planters settled Liverpool in 1759, while Shelburne was the destination of 16,000 Loyalists in 1783.

Of the 10,000 or more Acadians who had been deported in 1755, some of the original settlers returned after the peace treaty between England and France in 1763. La Côte Acadienne's 8,000 Acadians are the descendants of the survivors of those troubled times. Some Acadians in remote areas eluded the deportation; the Pubnico villages southeast of Yarmouth are Nova Scotia's oldest Acadian area.

## Halifax to Lunenburg

From downtown Halifax, it's 103 km along Highway 103 to Lunenburg, but for the most scenic views and interesting insights, forget the expressway and drive the secondary coastal routes. Make your first stop Peggy's Cove, then continue along the coastal route to the wealthy towns of Chester and Mahone Bay, overlooking crescent-shaped Mahone Bay and its islands. One of these,

Oak Island, looms large in the world of treasure-hunting legends—pirates are believed to have buried incalculable booty on it in the 1500s.

### PEGGY'S COVE

Atlantic Canada's most photographed site is a 40-minute drive along Highway 333 southwest

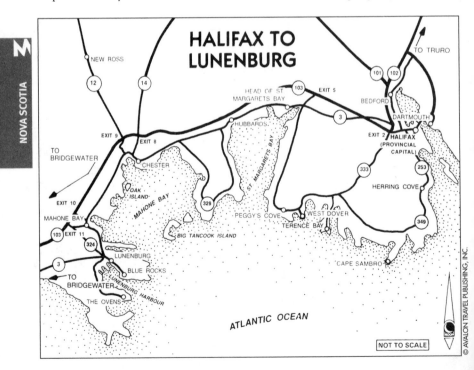

© ANDREW HEMPSTEAD

seaside Chester

from Halifax—the place is everything its fans say it is. With the houses of the tiny fishing village clinging like mussels to the weathered granite shelf at the edge of Margaret's Bay, the Atlantic lathering against the boulder-bound coast, the fishing boats moored in the small cove, and the white, octagonal lighthouse overlooking it all, the scene is the quintessence of the Nova Scotia coast. Sightseers clog the site during the daytime, wandering across the rocky expanse around the photogenic lighthouse, which serves as a post office in summer. (Wear rubber-soled shoes on the slippery surfaces.) To miss the crowds, get there before 8:30 A.M. or after 5 P.M.

Also at Peggy's Cove, **William E. deGarthe Memorial Provincial Park** is easily bypassed as the seaport's road curves toward the lighthouse, but it's worth seeking out. DeGarthe sculpted a 30-meter-long frieze on a granite outcropping, depicting 32 of the seaside village's fishermen and families.

On a sad note, the town received worldwide attention in September 1998, when a Swissair MD-11 jetliner bound from New York City to Geneva crashed in shallow waters off the coast here, killing all 229 people aboard. A small memorial overlooks the ocean along Highway 333, two km west of the village.

## Practicalities

Two bed-and-breakfasts offer a total of six rooms in Peggy's Cove, so book ahead if you'd like to stay overnight in this delightful village. The **Breakwater Inn,** tel. 902/823-2440, has three rooms sharing a bathroom for $90 single or double, including a light breakfast. At the head of the actual cove, **Peggy's Cove B&B,** tel. 902/823-2265 or 800/725-8732, has rooms of a similar standard, with guests also enjoying the use of an outdoor hot tub and a full breakfast (from $90 single, $100 double).

The road through the village ends at the **Sou'wester,** tel. 902/823-2561, a large restaurant open daily for breakfast, lunch, and dinner. The menu is designed to appeal to the tourist crowd, but does have a distinct maritime flavor, with dishes such as fish cakes, pickled beets, and eggs offered in the morning.

If you don't have your own transportation, consider the **Gray Line,** tel. 902/425-9999, Breakfast in Peggy's Cove tour, which departs Halifax hotels daily at 8 A.M. and lasts around three hours; adults $25.25, seniors $23.50, children $7.85.

## CHESTER AND VICINITY

The bayside town of Chester, first settled by New Englanders in 1759, lies at the northern head of

NOVA SCOTIA

Mahone Bay, just off Highway 103 (take exit 8). Its first hotel was built in 1827, and the town, with its ideal sailing conditions and many vacation homes, has been a popular summer retreat ever since. Visitors come for the beaches, sailing, golfing, and easy access to Tancook Island, as well as the downtown shopping.

The **Chester Playhouse,** 22 Pleasant St., tel. 902/275-3933 or 800/363-7529, hosts some form of live entertainment weekly between April and December. Its Chester Theatre Festival draws professional talents in July and August. Past seasons have included musicals, Broadway-style revues, comedy improv, puppet shows, and children's programs. **Race Week,** Atlantic Canada's largest sailing regatta, takes place in mid-August and attracts folks from up and down the coast.

## Accommodations and Food

Chester has several noteworthy inns and B&Bs. **Captain's House Inn,** 129 Central St., tel. 902/275-3501, occupies a restored 19th-century lodging and is open year-round. Continental breakfast is included in the rates ($90–105), and other meals are available; the inn's dining room has an excellent reputation. **Haddon Hall Inn,** 67 Haddon Hill Rd., tel. 902/275-3577, www.haddonhillinn.com, enjoys sweeping views from its hilltop perch. Amenities include a heated pool, tennis court, and complimentary use of mountain bikes and other recreation gear. All of the 10 guest rooms have a distinct character (heritage, nautical, etc.), some have whirlpool tubs, and a few have fireplaces. Open April–December; rates range $300–500, including all meals.

Seafood restaurants abound, serving everything from quiet lunches to huge lobster dinners. Locally recommended is **Seaside Shanty Restaurant,** in the Chester Basin, tel. 902/275-2246. The restaurant features great waterfront ambience and patio dining. It's open for lunch and dinner year-round.

For a light breakfast or lunch in town, follow your nose to **Julien's Pastry Shop, Bakery, and Tea Room,** 43 Queen St., tel. 902/275-2324, where you'll find delectable fresh breads, pastries, and desserts.

## New Ross

In 1816, Captain William Ross began clearing 23 hectares of fertile land for a homestead, 26 km inland from Chester along Highway 10. It would remain in his family for five generations. The **Ross Farm Living Museum of Agriculture** on Highway 12, exit 9, tel. 902/689-2210, com-

## CAPTAIN KIDD'S "MONEY PIT"

Legend holds that the Scottish pirate "Captain" William Kidd (circa 1645–1701) buried a trove of treasure on a secluded island somewhere east of Boston. In 1795, on Oak Island, near Chester off the south coast of Nova Scotia, young explorer Daniel McGinnis came upon an area where the forest had been cut away. Besides the stumps, he found a large forked limb with an old tackle block and a "treenail," and the ground nearby was sunken in a pit about 13 feet in diameter. Lending credence to his suspicion that this was the spot, LaHave, 15 miles south of Oak Island at the entrance to Mahone Bay, was once a well-known depot for pirates.

After hours of digging, McGinnis and two farmer friends reached a depth of 10 feet and hit wood. It turned out, however, to be not the rotted lid of a treasure chest but rather a platform of logs. So the men pressed on, convinced that the treasure lay just below. At the depth of 25 feet, digging became difficult and they halted. Before leaving, the three men drove wooden sticks into the sides of the pit and covered it with trees and brush.

It is believed that the three men made a pact not to reveal anything about the Money Pit until they could safely finance a dig, so the story remains an unsolved mystery.

About 1,000 feet across at its northwest section, the island today is linked to the mainland by a narrow causeway constructed in 1965 to transport digging equipment. The Money Pit, as the spot is now known, lies near the top of a tall hill on the east end of the island.

© ANDREW HEMPSTEAD

Mahone Bay

memorates the rural lifestyle of a bygone age. Activities include butter and cheese making, coopering and blacksmithing, and historical farming demonstrations. The museum is open June to mid-October, daily 9:30 A.M.–5:30 P.M.; open January–March for weekend sleigh rides. Admission is $5 adults, $1 ages 6–17, $10.50 families.

## MAHONE BAY

The town of Mahone Bay (pop. 1,100), on the island-speckled bay of the same name, was settled in the mid-1700s by German, French, and Swiss Protestants, who were enticed here by the British government's offer of free land, farm equipment, and a year's "victuals." The little town is known for its gingerbread houses and its arts and crafts galleries selling pewter, pottery, quilts, hooked rugs, and other wares made by local artisans. The distinctive bayside quartet of 19th-century churches—three with pointed spires, the fourth with a crenellated square belfry, all reflected in the still water—has become one of the most photographed scenes in Nova Scotia.

From 1850 to the early part of this century, shipbuilding thrived in a dozen shipyards along

the waterfront. The town's prosperity was mirrored in its architecture, with Gothic Revival, Classic Revival, and Italianate styles in evidence. Many of these buildings have been converted to B&Bs, restaurants, and shops. The visitor information center, 165 Edgewater St., tel. 902/624-6151, with a very friendly and helpful staff, provides a walking-tour brochure outlining the town's architectural highlights.

Mahone Bay's annual July (last weekend) **Wooden Boat Festival** at Government Wharf celebrates the town's boat-building heritage. Activities include coracle- and canoe-building demonstrations, children's workshops and treasure hunts, displays of lovingly handcrafted skiffs and other small boats, races, live entertainment, and refreshments. For more information, contact the visitor information center, or call 902/624-8443.

The **Settlers Museum,** located in a 150-year-old house at 578 Main Street, tel. 902/624-6263, is open year-round with exhibits on topics ranging from boat building to ceramics and furniture dating from the mid-1700s. Open mid-May to 30 September, Tues.–Fri. 10 A.M.–5 P.M., Sat.–Sun. 1–5 P.M. Admission is by donation.

### Accommodations and Food

Like nearby Chester, Mahone Bay is well equipped with genteel bed-and-breakfast inns, convivial cafés, and interesting shops. Opposite Government Wharf, **Fairmont House B&B,** 654 Main St., tel. 902/624-8089, is an 1850s Victorian home with three guest rooms furnished with antiques ($70, with full breakfast). **Mahone Bay B&B** also enjoys a prime downtown location, across from the water at 558 Main Street, tel. 902/624-1121. Each of the four guest rooms has a private bathroom, and rates of $70–115 include a full breakfast in a dining room overlooking the bay. **Manse at Mahone Bay Country Inn,** 88 Orchard St., tel. 902/624-1121, offers four rooms in a renovated 1860s mansion and carriage house. It's open year-round, and a full breakfast is included in the rates of $90–105.

**Ocean Trail Retreat,** Hwy. 3 at Mader's Cove, tel. 902/624-8824 or 888/624-8824, www

NOVA SCOTIA

.oceantrailretreat.com, offers 17 motel-style rooms ($75–85) and three two-bedroom chalets ($120), all with private baths. Amenities include horseback riding and sailing (from the retreat's private dock and anchorage).

Of the many places to eat in the village, the **Saltspray Café,** a few hundred meters toward Lunenburg from the main intersection at 621 Main Street, stands out for value and quality. Set in a waterfront building with a large deck out back, the caféé offers breakfasts for under $5, *including* bottomless cups of coffee. As you'd imagine, the Saltspray is perpetually busy. Another popular spot is the **Innlet Cafe,** 249 Edgewater St., tel. 902/624-6363, which has received national attention from culinary critics. It's open for lunch and dinner daily. The **Mug and Anchor,** 643 Main St. at Mader's Wharf, tel. 902/624-6378, is an English-style pub serving locally brewed ales, with live music on occasion.

# Lunenburg

Lunenburg (pop. 2,800) lies about equidistant between Halifax and Shelburne off Highway 103. Sited on a hilly peninsula between two harbors, this is one of the most attractive towns in Nova Scotia, with a wealth of beautiful homes painted in a crayon box of bold primary colors. In 1991, Lunenburg's Old Town was designated a national historic district, and in December 1995, the town received the ultimate honor when UN-ESCO designated it a world heritage site—one of only two cities in North America to enjoy that status. In May 1998, the town was featured in *Architectural Digest* magazine.

## History

To understand what the fuss is all about, you have to go back in time a couple of centuries. Protestant German, Swiss, and French immi-

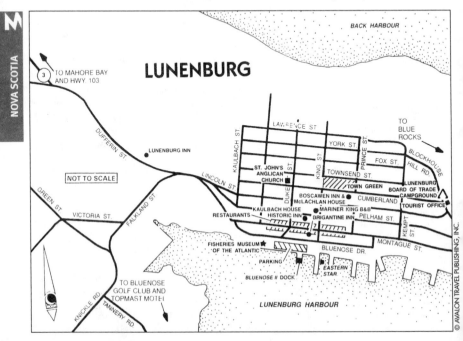

## SAILING BACK IN TIME

Lunenburg is a wooden-ships kind of town, and what better way to tour the harbor than aboard one? The two ships detailed below aren't glitzy so much as utilitarian. Rather than separating you from the maritime experience with cushy reclining seats, Plexiglas windows, and a cocktail lounge, these boats take you to sea as a sailor. Cruising out of the harbor under a fresh breeze—the sails snapping taught and the hull slicing through the chilly waters—you'll begin to understand, to actually feel the history and lifeblood of Lunenberg.

### Bluenose II

In 1942, the era of the sail-powered fishing industry was giving way to that of modern steel-hulled trawlers. The great *Bluenose* was sold to carry freight in the West Indies. Four years later, she foundered and was lost on a Haitian reef. In July of 1963, however, the *Bluenose II* was re-created from the plans of the original and launched at Lunenburg. Some of the same craftspeople who had built the

first *Bluenose* even participated in its construction. When not in Halifax or visiting other Canadian ports, the *Bluenose II* can be found here at her home berth, outside the Fisheries Museum. When in Lunenburg she departs June–Sept. at 9:30 A.M. and 1 P.M. for a two-hour harbor cruise; adult $20, child $10. Call 902/634-1963 or 800/763-1963 for her sailing schedule and reservations.

### Eastern Star

The *Eastern Star,* tel. 902/634-3535, is a character-imbued 48-foot wooden ketch lovingly tended by an amiable and knowledgeable crew passionately intent on perpetuating the seafaring tradition that put Lunenburg on the map. The *Eastern Star* makes four cruises a day June–Oct., with a sunset cruise added in July and August. Standard fare is $20 adults, $14 students, $12 children, $50 families. Sunset tours are $22 adults, $15 students, $12 children, $50 families. The ticket booth is at the east end of Fisheries Museum Wharf.

grants, recruited by the British to help stabilize their new dominion, settled the town in 1753; their influence is still apparent in the town's architectural details. With its excellent harbor—a protected inner arm of the Atlantic embraced by two long, curving peninsulas—Lunenburg became one of Nova Scotia's premier fishing ports and shipbuilding centers in the 19th century. In 1921, the famous schooner *Bluenose* was built here. The 49-meter fishing vessel won the International Fisherman's Trophy race that same year, and over the next 18 years it remained the undefeated champion of the Atlantic fleets. The ship has become the proud symbol of the province, and its image is embossed on the back of the Canadian dime.

Today, the fishing industry that fostered the town's growth and boat-building reputation is comatose, and the Atlantic fisheries are mere shadows of their former selves. But here in Lunenburg, the townspeople carry on the ship-building and shipfitting skills of their ancestors. The port is still known as a tall ship mecca, and big multi-masted sailing ships, old and new

alike from around the world, continue to put in here for repairs, shipfitting, or provisions—whatever excuse the owners can come up with. Underneath the tourist glitz, the community pride in this tradition runs strong and deep, and the town's international reputation among mariners remains formidable. Strike up a conversation with a local about sailing ships and see what happens.

## SIGHTS AND RECREATION

The port's oldest part is set on the hillside overlooking the harbor. The nine blocks of Old Town rise steeply from the water, and the village green spreads across the center. Bluenose Drive, the narrow lane along the harbor, and Montague Street, a block uphill, define the main sightseeing area. A mesh of one-way streets connects Old Town with the newer area built with shipbuilding profits. One of the pleasures of Lunenburg is strolling the residential and commercial streets, admiring the town's many meticulously preserved architectural gems.

NOVA SCOTIA

© ANDREW HEMPSTEAD

The Lunenburg Inn is one of many historic lodgings in town.

## Fisheries Museum of the Atlantic

This spacious, bright red museum at 68 Bluenose Drive, tel. 902/634-4794, boasts a trove of artifacts and exhibits on shipbuilding, seafaring, rum-running, and marine biology. This thoroughly fascinating museum engages the visitor with demonstrations on fish filleting, lobster-trap construction, dory building, net mending, and other maritime arts. Inside are aquariums, tanks with touchable marine life, a gallery of ship models, full-size fishing vessels from around Atlantic Canada, a theater, restaurant, and gift shop. Tied up at the wharf outside are the fishing schooner *Theresa E. Connor*, built in Lunenburg in 1938; the steel-hulled trawler *Cape Sable*, an example of the sort of vessel that made the former obsolete; the *Royal Wave*, a Digby scallop dragger; and, when it's in its home port, the *Bluenose II*. All the vessels may be boarded and explored. The museum is open mid-May to mid-October, daily 9:30 A.M.–5:30 P.M.; the rest of the year, Mon.–Fri. 8:30 A.M.–4:30 P.M. Admission is $7 adults, $5.50 seniors, $2 children, $17 families.

## St. John's Anglican Church

This church at Cumberland and Cornwallis Streets, tel. 902/634-4994, was built in 1759 and is the second-oldest church in Canada. The white clapboard Carpenter Gothic church was a gift of the British Crown; it's open mid-June to mid-September, Mon.–Sat. 10 A.M.–5 P.M., Sunday noon–7 P.M.

## Blue Rocks

Follow any of Lunenburg's downtown streets eastbound to link with a road that leads eight km to Blue Rocks, toward the end of the peninsula. The coast around the little hamlet of Blue Rocks is wrapped with blue-gray slate and sandstone, and the combination of color and texture will inspire photographers. The scenery rivals Peggy's Cove for beauty, but lacks the crowds.

## Recreation

Several other activities are also available down at the waterfront in the heart of the tourist district. **Lunenburg Whale Watching,** tel. 902/527-7175, offers whale- and bird-watching excursions May to October. In summer, boats leave three times a day, wind and weather permitting.

**Trot in Time Buggy Rides,** tel. 902/634-8917, offers 30-minute narrated tours around town in a horse-drawn buggy. The price is $12 adults, $6 children, free for ages five and under.

You'll find them down at the wharf, near the Fisheries Museum.

The nine-hole **Bluenose Golf Club** spreads out across 2,370 meters in a handsome setting overlooking the seaport from the opposite peninsula edge. Handcarts, rental clubs, and lunch are available; for details, call 902/634-4260.

## ACCOMMODATIONS AND CAMPING
### Historic Inns
Right downtown, above the excellent Grand Banker Restaurant, the tidy **Brigantine Inn,** 82 Montague St., tel. 902/634-3300 or 800/360-1181, www.brigantineinn.com, offers seven nautically themed rooms, each with a private bathroom and named for a famous sailing ship. Summer rates start at a reasonable $69, with rooms from $105 having water views. Rates include a light breakfast. The inn is open year-round, with harbor view rooms for well under $100 outside of summer.

**Kaulbach House Historic Inn,** 75 Pelham St., tel. 902/634-8818 or 800/568-8818, www.kaulbachhouse.com, is one of Lunenburg's many historic treasures (circa 1880) converted to an inn. Overlooking the harbor, it features seven antiques-filled rooms ($70–120 with full breakfast), six of them with a private bath. It's open mid-March to mid-December.

The ornately detailed **Mariner King B&B,** 15 King St., tel. 902/634-8509 or 800/565-8509, built circa 1830, has four cozy rooms (from $75 single, $80 double, with full breakfast), an outdoor patio garden, a well-stocked library, and a lounge. Open year-round.

Incorporating two registered heritage properties (circa 1888 and 1905), the **Boscawen Inn & McLachlan House,** 150 Cumberland St., tel. 902/634-3325 or 800/354-5009, is a European-style hotel with a scenic perch above the harbor. Each of its 20 rooms has a private bath, and breakfast is included in the rates of $95–175 single, $100–180 double. Other amenities include a licensed dining room and an outdoor sundeck open to the public. Closed February.

Away from the waterfront, but still within easy walking distance, the **Lunenburg Inn,** 26 Dufferin St., tel. 902/634-3963 or 800/565-3963, www.lunenburginn.com, has a covered veranda, seven rooms ($117–150 with full breakfast), two suites with whirlpool tubs, a dining room, and a sitting room with fireplace, books, and TV. A Registered Heritage Inn, it was built circa 1893 and features Victorian-era furnishings. Open April through October.

### Motel
There's really no reason not to stay in one of the historic lodgings detailed above, but other options do exist. The **Topmast Motel,** Mason's Beach Rd., tel. 902/634-4661 or 877/525-3222, www.topmastmotel.com, overlooks the harbor with outdoor decks adjoining 15 rooms ($75–95); housekeeping units are available. It's open year-round.

### Campground
The **Lunenburg Board of Trade Campground** at Blockhouse Hill Road on Blockhouse Hill, tel. 902/634-8100, has 33 campsites ($21–25) set high on a hilltop overlooking the harbor. Open mid-May through October, the campground has showers and washrooms and is adjacent to the local information center.

## FOOD AND ENTERTAINMENT
### Food
The **Old Fish Factory** restaurant, 68 Bluenose Dr., tel. 902/634-3333, is above the Fisheries Museum. Specialties include creamy seafood chowder, fish baked on a cedar plank, and a seasonal Seafood Feature, as well as fishermen's favorites such as Solomon Gundy (pickled herring). Non-seafood dishes with a local twist are also offered, such as maple-glazed chicken for $18.50. All other dinner entrées are similarly priced, while lunches run $7.50–12.

One block back from the harbor, several restaurants line Montague Street. All have decks or floor-to-ceiling windows facing the water. The largest of these is the **Rum Runner Inn,** 64 Montague, tel. 902/634-9200, opposite the Fisheries Museum, with upper and lower outside decks; next door, **Big Red's,** 80 Montague, tel. 902/634-3554, caters to families in its upstairs dining room, which has great views of the *Bluenose II* and other ships. The **Grand Banker Seafood Bar & Grill,** 82 Montague St., tel. 902/634-3300, offers similarly great views from an enclosed dining room and serves a wide-ranging menu of seafood, salads, pastas, and sandwiches. A half dozen good beers and a couple of California wines are available. The food is well prepared and the atmosphere pleasant—it feels a little more relaxed and a little less tourist-driven than some of its neighbors. **Dockside Restaurant,** 84 Montague, tel. 902/634-3005, with upper-level decks, specializes in seafood; most dinners run $14–22.

The **Lunenburg Inn** at 26 Dufferin Street creates Mediterranean adaptations of Nova Scotian cuisine in its dining room; entrées run $15.50–22. It's open June through October, and you can dine on the veranda during summer. Reservations are advised; call 902/634-3963.

The **Bluenose Lodge** delights in sophisticated continental fare mixed with Wiener schnitzel and red cabbage with apples and onions; service is quietly quick. Entrées start at $14. Call 902/634-8851 for reservations.

For groceries, **Scotia Trawler Foodmaster** is located at 250 Montague Street.

### Entertainment and Events

The seaport is usually quiet evenings and Sundays. Locals frequent **The Knot Pub,** 4 Dufferin St., tel. 902/634-3334, a comfortable and lively place where you can get "knotwurst" and kraut with your draft beer. The place is reputed to get pretty wild at times; fortunately, the police are right next door. Open Mon.–Sat. to 12:30 A.M.

Drama, dance, puppet shows, children's theater, and music performances regularly take place at **Starlight Theatre,** 37 Hall St. To reach the main office call 902/634-8716 or fax 902/634-9674. The box office numbers are 902/634-9993 and 888/490-1119.

Major annual events include mid-July's two-day **Crafts Festival** and early August's **Lunenburg Folk Harbour Festival,** which attracts a

roster of traditional, roots, and contemporary folk musicians over four days. Tickets are available for the entire festival (about $50) or for single days or evenings; call 902/634-3180.

## OTHER PRACTICALITIES
### Shopping
The **farmers' market,** at the foot of Lincoln Street, lures crowds for fresh produce, smoked meats, and crafts at the former railroad depot grounds; it's open July through October, Thurs. 8 A.M.–noon. Wares are high quality and priced accordingly.

**Montague Gallery,** at Montague and King Streets, tel. 902/634-4333, stocks exquisite sweaters and apparel as well as local arts and crafts. **Houston North Gallery,** 110 Montague St., tel. 902/634-8869, specializes in folk art, Inuit crafts, and imported sculpture.

Nautical gifts are available at the **Yacht Shop,** 280 Montague St., tel. 902/634-4331, which is also a full-service marine-supply center, and at the nonprofit **Bluenose II Company Store,** 121 Bluenose Dr., tel. 902/634-1963 or 800/763-1963, which sells all manner of *Bluenose* clothing, gifts, and art to support preservation of the vessel.

### Information
The **Lunenburg Tourist Office,** tel. 902/634-8100, just east of town on Blockhouse Hill, can make lodging reservations. The office also stocks locally written, informative literature about the port's historic architecture. *Understanding Lunenburg's Architecture* describes the design elements, and *An Inventory of Historic Buildings* provides details on almost every seaport building, organized street by street. The office is open mid-May to mid-October, daily 9 A.M.–6 P.M. (July–August to 9 P.M.). For information in the off-season, call the town offices, tel. 902/634-4410.

**Atlantic Electronics,** 144 Montague St., tel. 902/634-4004, and **Yacht Shop and Marina,** 280 Montague St., tel. 902/634-4331, sell nautical charts.

Genealogical records are kept on the third floor of town hall on Townsend Street; open Wed.–Thurs. 2–9 P.M.

## Services

**Fishermen's Memorial Hospital** is located at 14 High Street (between Dufferin and Green), tel. 902/634-8801. For **police,** call 902/634-4312; for the **RCMP,** call 902/634-8674.

The port has several banks, including the **Bank of Montréal,** at King and Pelham Streets, tel. 902/634-8875. It's open Mon.–Wed. 9:30 A.M.–4 P.M., Thurs.–Fri. 9:30 A.M.–5:30 P.M.

**Canada Post** at King and Lincoln Streets is open Mon.–Fri. 8:30 A.M.–5 P.M. **Bluenose Mini Mart,** 31–35 Lincoln St., has a retail postal outlet. It's open Mon.–Sat. 7 A.M.–midnight, Sun. from 8 A.M.

The **Soap Bubble Cleanette,** 39 Lincoln St., tel. 902/634-4601, is the local launderette. It's open Mon.–Sat. 8 A.M.–8 P.M., Sun. from 10 A.M.

# South Shore

The South Shore is the deeply scored Atlantic coastline that extends from Lunenburg to Yarmouth. It's a three-hour drive between these two towns, but if you have the time, take the coastal detours wherever possible. Follow signs marking the Lighthouse Route to hit all the scenic spots.

Highlights include Sandy Point, near Shelburne, where ground garnet mixed with the sand gives the beach a crimson hue. At Sand Hill Beach Provincial Park near Barrington, the usually chilly Atlantic warms between sandbars at low tide. Take Highway 3 from Barrington to Shag Harbour, where Chapel Hill Museum crests a seaside hill. The museum's belfry tower overlooks the Atlantic and granite-bound coast. Visit at sunset when the sky's pink, rose, and golden hues play across the silvery blue Atlantic.

Naturally, the sea plays a vital role in the South Shore's economy. The industries include fish processing, shipbuilding, ship repair, and fishing (the province's richest lobster grounds lie aside the Pubnico seaports).

*The South Shore is the deeply scored Atlantic coastline that extends from Lunenburg to Yarmouth. It's a three-hour drive between these two towns, but if you have the time, take the coastal detours wherever possible.*

## LUNENBURG TO SHELBURNE

### Ovens Natural Park

Fifteen minutes west of Lunenburg on Highway 232, spectacular sea caves have been scooped out of the coastal cliffs. Early prospectors dis-covered veins of gold embedded in the slate and white quartz cliffs, sparking a small gold rush in 1861. During the following several decades, the cliffs surrendered 15,500 grams of the precious metal. Visitors can try panning for a bit of color themselves. The 81-hectare (200-acre) Ovens Natural Park has a 1.5-km trail (open year-round) leading down to the "ovens"—sea caves—which you also can visit on boat tours ($15). Overnight options include camping ($20–23 per site) and self-contained cottages ($75); call 902/766-4621, www.ovenspark.com. Amenities include a pool, campers' store, and a restaurant. The park is open May 15 to October 15; the day-use fee is $5 adults, $3 seniors and children.

### Bridgewater

The **Wile Carding Mill Museum,** 242 Victoria Rd. (Hwy. 325), tel. 902/543-8233, was a once wool-processing mill. The wool was carded for spinning and weaving or made into batts for quilts. The original machinery is still in operation, powered by an overshot waterwheel, and now demonstrates old carding methods. The museum is open June through September, Mon.–Sat. 9:30 A.M.–5:30 P.M., Sun. 1–5:30 P.M. Admission is $2.

### Rissers Beach Provincial Park

Just one of many parks in Bridgewater and Shelburne, this one boasts a beach of finely ground

NOVA SCOTIA

quartz sand and an area of pristine salt marsh laced with boardwalks.

## Liverpool

The hub of Queens County, Liverpool deals in paper products, foundries, and machine shops, but is worth a stop for the following sights. Housed in the 1901 Town Hall, a National Historic Site in itself, the **Sherman Hines Museum of Photography,** 219 Main St., tel. 902/354-2667, displays the work of prominent Nova Scotian photographers, including the museum's namesake. The building also holds the re-creation of a Victorian-era photography studio, a gallery of changing exhibits, a research library, and a gift shop. In the foyer is an impressive mounted tuna—at 400 kilograms, the largest of its species ever caught on rod and reel. The museum is open May–December, Mon.–Sat. 10 A.M.–5 P.M.

**Perkins House Museum,** 105 Main St., tel. 902/354-4058, is a historic example of a New England planter's adaptation to Nova Scotia. The Connecticut-style white house, built in 1766, is furnished with antiques and is open June to mid-October, Mon.–Sat. 9:30 A.M.–5:30 P.M., Sunday 1–5:30 P.M. Admission is free.

Liverpool was the birthplace of country music legend Hank Snow. The railway station at 148 Bristol Street, tel. 902/354-4675, has been converted to the **Hank Snow Country Music Centre,** with displays following his career; open May through October.

## Kejimkujik National Park Seaside Adjunct

Around 25 km southwest of Liverpool (turn off Highway 103 at Port Joli) is one of the last and largest undisturbed areas of Maritimes coastline. This section of the park, not as popular with visitors as the main, inland park, offers unspoiled beaches and offshore isles. The park is accessible on foot; a two-km walking trail begins at the parking lot on St. Catherine's Road and leads to the St. Catherine's River beach. Some sections of this beach close from late April to late July to protect piping plover nesting sites. Another access trail into the park starts near Willis Lake at South-west Port Mouton; the five-km trail ends at undeveloped Black Point Beach. The Seaside Adjunct has no visitor facilities, and camping is not permitted.

For more information, call the park's inland administration office, tel. 902/682-2772.

# SHELBURNE

Like Lunenburg, Shelburne (pop. 2,000) sits at the innermost end of a long harbor formed between two peninsulas. Teardrop-shaped McNutt Island lies across the harbor entrance; the lighthouse on the island was built in 1788. Getting into Shelburne is quick—it's just minutes from Highway 103 exit 26 to the town, which sits on the harbor's eastern side.

The seaport was established in 1783 when Loyalists fleeing the newly independent American colonies settled here by the thousands (the word

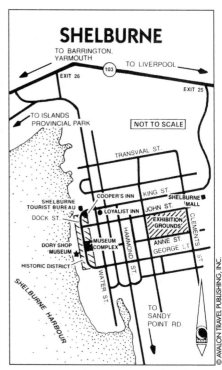

SHELBURNE

TO BARRINGTON, YARMOUTH
TO LIVERPOOL
103
EXIT 26
EXIT 25

TO ISLANDS PROVINCIAL PARK

NOT TO SCALE

TRANSVAAL ST.

COOPER'S INN
KING ST.
SHELBURNE MALL
SHELBURNE TOURIST BUREAU
LOYALIST INN
JOHN ST.
DOCK ST.
EXHIBITION GROUNDS
CLEMENTS
HAMMOND ST.
ANNE ST.
DORY SHOP MUSEUM
MUSEUM COMPLEX
GEORGE ST.
HISTORIC DISTRICT
WATER ST.
SHELBURNE HARBOUR
TO SANDY POINT RD.

Loyalist still appears in the names of numerous local establishments). Rations and free land ran out within a few years, and most would-be settlers moved on to other places. Those who remained started the industries—shipbuilding, fish processing, and fishing—that keep the seaport humming today.

The town is short on lodgings, shorter on restaurants, and long on crowds of tourists who arrive on sightseeing buses. If you intend to stay awhile, advance reservations for lodgings and dining are wise. The historic district lies along Dock Street and is backed by Water Street, the main drag.

## Sights

**Shelburne Historic District** on Dock Street is a hive of historic sites and shops. The **Shelburne County Museum,** 8 Maiden Lane, tel. 902/875-3219, is the hub, with exhibits on Loyalist heritage and shipbuilding history and a 250-year-old fire engine believed to be the oldest in Canada. The museum is open year-round, daily 9:30 A.M.–5:30 P.M. in summer, the rest of the year Tues.–Sat. 2–5 P.M. Admission is $2.

Nova Scotians say the dory was reinvented in Shelburne. The **Dory Shop Museum** on Dock Street, tel. 902/875-3219, the last of seven once-thriving boat factories in town, turned out thousands of handcrafted wooden fishing dories between 1880 and 1970. The shop now houses interpretive displays and gives demonstrations on the dying art. It's open June through September, daily 9:30 A.M.–5:30 P.M. Admission is free on Sunday morning, $2 for the rest of the week.

The **Ross-Thomson House and Store Museum,** 9 Charlotte Lane, tel. 902/875-3141, was built in 1785 as a Loyalist store. The last example of its kind today in Nova Scotia, it depicts the period setting with sample wares and an old-fashioned garden. Scenes for *The Scarlet Letter* were filmed here. It's open June to mid-October, daily 9:30 A.M.–5:30 P.M. Admission $2 adults.

Package admission to the County Museum, the Dory Shop Museum, and the Ross Thomson House and Store Museum costs $4 for adults.

## Accommodations and Camping

The **Loyalist Inn,** 160 Water St., tel. 902/875-2343, a stone's throw from the historic district, has rooms (from $54), two-bedroom housekeeping units (from $75), and a dining room. Open year-round. **Cooper's Inn,** 36 Dock St., tel. 902/875-4656 or 800/688-2011, is a two-story colonial beauty overlooking the harbor and next to the tourist bureau and museum. Built in 1783 by a merchant and restored and opened in 1988, the lodging has six rooms all with private baths ($85–95), one suite ($145), and an outstanding dining room. Rates include a cooked breakfast; open April through October.

Out on Highway 103 at exit 25, the **Ox Bow Motel,** tel. 902/875-3000 or 800/391-7721, combines 40 basic rooms ($60–96) with a dining room, outside pool, and hiking trails.

Rustic and pretty **Islands Provincial Park,** off Highway 3 five km west of Shelburne, tel. 902/875-4304, faces the town across the upper harbor. It offers 64 unserviced sites ($14) with table shelters and grills, pit toilets, running water, and a spacious, modern shower room. Sunbathers can lie on the beach; boaters will find launching areas. The park is open mid-May to early September.

## Food and Drink

With an established reputation for fine dining is the **Charlotte Lane Café,** 13 Charlotte Lane, tel. 902/875-3314. Its Swiss owner-chef, Roland Glauser, specializes in pastas and seafood. Open May–December, Tues.–Sun. 11:30 A.M.–8 P.M.

The dining room at the **Loyalist Inn** on Water Street (reservations are wise, call 902/875-2343) is usually jammed with bus-tour diners. A table is easiest to get before noon, during mid-afternoon, or after 8 P.M. The specialty is seafood ($9–15) prepared any way you like it.

**Tai Woo Family Restaurant,** 165 Water St. (at King St.), serves Chinese cuisine Tues.–Thurs. 11 A.M.–9 P.M., Friday 11 A.M.–10 P.M., Saturday noon–10 P.M., Sunday noon–8 P.M. (closed Mon.).

**Grovestine's Grocery** at 137 Water Street is an old-fashioned grocery with an ample deli for picnic fixings. It's open Mon.–Sat. 8 A.M.–5:30 P.M. The **Shelburne Mall** on King Street has the su-

NOVA SCOTIA

permarkets. Crowds gravitate nightly to **Bruce's Wharf Pub & Grill,** 1 Dock St., where a glass wall overlooks the harbor. Bruce's offers fish and chips and a pool table; it's open Mon.–Sat. to 11:30 P.M.

### Events

Shelburne makes much of **Canada Day** celebrations (July 1) with fireworks, a parade, street vendors, and entertainment. Mid-July's three-day **Founders' Day** festival features yacht races, a crafts sale, music, and food. The **Shelburne County Exhibition** brings country-fair components to the port's exhibition grounds for four days in mid-August.

### Information and Services

**Shelburne Tourist Bureau** on Dock Street, tel. 902/875-4547, stocks literature and self-guided tour maps. It's open June to October, daily 10 A.M.–6 P.M. (9 A.M.–8 P.M. in peak summer season).

**Shelburne Roseway Hospital** is on Lake Road, tel. 902/875-3011. The **RCMP** can be reached by calling 902/875-2490. **Murphy's Convenience,** on King Street just up the hill from Water Street, is one of several launderettes in town; it's open daily 7 A.M.–11 P.M.

## SHELBURNE TO YARMOUTH

### Barrington

Highway 103 takes a mainly inland route between Shelburne and Yarmouth. One place where it does come in contact with the ocean is near Barrington, just off the main highway along Highway 3, where coastal views are exquisite. In Barrington itself, the **Old Meeting House Museum,** 2408 Hwy. 3, tel. 902/637-2185, is a variation on planter life. Built by 50 Cape Cod families in 1765, the New England–style church is Canada's oldest nonconformist house of worship. It's open June–September, Mon.–Sat. 9:30 A.M.–5:30 P.M., Sunday 1–5:30 P.M. Admission is free.

The **Barrington Woolen Mill Museum,** 2368 Hwy. 3, tel. 902/637-2185, presents wool-spinning demonstrations and offers exhibits detailing

wool processing within the old-time water-powered mill; same hours as the meetinghouse. Admission is free.

### Cape Sable Island

Continuing along south on Highway 3, Cape Sable Island is well worth the detour. Connected to the mainland by a causeway, the island forms the southernmost point in Nova Scotia. Feared by early sailors because of its jagged shores, the island was settled by brick-making Acadians during the 17th century. The island also served as a summer base for fishermen from New England, and fishing prevails today as the community's main industry, with tourism a close second.

The island's four main beaches offer surfing, clam digging, swimming, fishing, and bird-watching. At **Hawk Beach,** on the eastern side (turn at Lower Clark's Harbour at Hawk Road and go left), you can see the **Cape Lighthouse** on a small nearby sandbar. The original tower, built in 1861, was Canada's first eight-sided structure; the present lighthouse, a protected heritage building, was constructed in 1923. At low tide on Hawk Beach you can also see the remains of a 1,500-year-old forest.

The **Causeway Beach** (turn right at the Corbett Heights subdivision) is a prime sunbathing and fishing (for mackerel) spot. **Stoney Island Beach,** as the name implies, is not as popular with sunbathers as it is with seals, which like to sun themselves on the rocks. **South Side Beach** (turn on Daniel's Head Road in South Side), too, is popular as a seal-watching and beach-combing locale.

For history buffs, the island's **Archelaus Smith Museum,** on Highway 330 at Centreville, tel. 902/745-3361, features fishing and shipbuilding displays. Open mid-June to late September, Mon.–Sat. 9:30 A.M.–5:30 P.M., Sun. 1:30–5:30 P.M.; free admission.

Services and accommodations are limited. **Penney Estate Bed & Breakfast,** 4 Penney Beach Rd., North East Point, off Rte. 3, tel. 902/745-1516, has a private beach and three rooms with shared bath for $55 single, $60 double, including full breakfast; open year-round.

# Yarmouth and La Côte Acadienne

The South Shore ends at Yarmouth, where the Atlantic meets the Bay of Fundy. Locals say the Vikings came ashore a thousand years ago and inscribed the boulder that now sits at the Yarmouth County Museum's front door. Yarmouth's ragged coastline impressed early explorer Samuel de Champlain, who named the seaport's outermost peninsula Cap Forchu ("Forked Cape").

Like the Vikings, Champlain arrived and departed, as do thousands of visitors who arrive on the ferries and quickly disperse on routes to distant provincial destinations. Their loss is the gain of the tourist who stays. Cyclists like to bike the Yarmouth area's backcountry coastal roads. At Chebogue Point south of the seaport, pink, purple, and white lupines bloom in June, and in summertime white-winged willets roam the marshes.

Another bike route goes to Yarmouth Bar across the harbor. The route begins north of the business district with a turn to the left, where a whisper-thin road lead is to the lighthouse at Cape Forchu's tip. Locals use the road to watch the ferries come and go through the harbor.

## YARMOUTH

Yarmouth (pop. 8,000) was the center of a shipbuilding empire during Canada's Great Age of Sail, when it ranked as the world's fourth-largest port of registry. Still the region's largest seaport, the town is a prosperous and orderly place supported by shipping—primarily lumber products, Irish moss, and Christmas trees—and fishing. Yarmouth's herring fleet is a major contributor to the local economy. The fleet sails at night and anchors with all its lights blazing farther up the Fundy coast, creating a sight known as "herring city." Tourism also helps the port thrive; two ferry lines bring visitors to town in numbers sufficient to establish Yarmouth as the busiest ferry landing in the province.

### Getting Oriented

The town fronts the eastern side of Yarmouth Harbour. Ferries dock at the foot of Forest Street,

where it meets Water Street at the harbor. Main Street parallels Water Street and sits astride a hilly ridge with the port's shops, businesses, and banks. Argyle, Forest, and Parade Streets and Starrs Road spread inland from there. Highway 3 enters Yarmouth on Starrs Road; Highway 103, the other major access route, zips into town on a parallel road and ends at Hardscratch Road, which in turn finishes on Starrs Road.

### Sights

If **historic architecture** interests you, take a leisurely walk along Main Street, where the com-

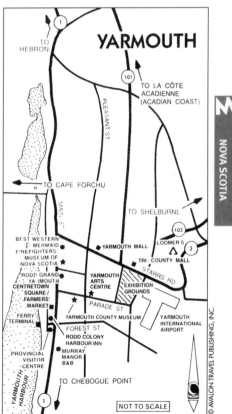

mercial buildings are styled in late 19th-century Classic Revival, Queen Anne Revival, Georgian, and Italianate. The best of Yarmouth was built with Great Age of Sail profits. At the tourist information center on Forest Street, pick up the *Walking Tour of Yarmouth* brochure, which details some two dozen points of architectural and historical interest on a self-guiding four-km walk.

The **Firefighters' Museum of Nova Scotia,** 451 Main St., tel. 902/742-5525, is Atlantic Canada's only museum dedicated solely to firefighting equipment. Among the extensive vintage collection is an 1819 Hopwood & Tilley hand pump and other sparkling equipment. It's open year-round; during the summer season (June–September), hours are Mon.–Sat. 9 A.M.–5 P.M., with longer hours in July and August, 9 A.M.–9 P.M. and Sun. 10 A.M.–5 P.M. Hours in the off-season (October–May) are Mon.–Fri. 9 A.M.–4 P.M., Saturday 1–4 P.M. Admission $3 per person or $5 for families.

The **Yarmouth County Museum,** 22 Collins St., tel. 902/742-5539, showcases Canada's largest ship portrait collection and exhibits a trove of seafaring lore, musical instruments, ship models, furniture, and more. The research library and archives store extensive records and genealogical materials. Also part of the museum complex, the adjacent **Pelton-Fuller House** (open in summer only) was once the summer residence of Fuller Brush Company magnate Al Fuller and his wife. It houses turn-of-the-century furniture and Fuller Brush Company memorabilia. The complex is open year-round. Its summer hours (June to mid-October) are Mon.–Sat. 9 A.M.–5 P.M., Sun. 2–5 P.M.; the rest of the year it's open Tues.–Sun. 2–5 P.M. Admission to both the museum and Pelton-Fuller House is adults $4, children $1, families $8. It costs $2.50 to visit just the museum, and a separate admission is charged for the archives.

## Accommodations and Camping

One block from the ferry terminal, the Gothic-style **Murray Manor B&B,** 225 Main St., tel. 902/742-9625, is a heritage property built circa 1820. It offers three nonsmoking rooms with shared bath ($65 single, $75 double with full breakfast), as well as a beautiful garden and green-

house secluded behind a low stone wall. Open year-round.

The **Comfort Inn,** 96 Starrs Rd., tel. 902/742-1119 or 800/228-5150, is a basic dependable lodging with 80 rooms ($85–140).

The **Rodd Colony Harbour Inn,** 6 Forest St. (overlooking the harbor), tel. 902/742-9194 or 800/565-7633, www.rodd-hotels.ca, occupies the perfect setting for ferry watching. The inn has 65 pleasant rooms with wide windows ($82–122), a restaurant, and a lounge; the highest room rate gets you a harbor view. Part of the same chain, the **Rodd Grand Yarmouth,** 417 Main St., tel. 902/742-2446 or 800/565-7633, www.rodd-hotels.ca, offers 138 rooms ($99–180) in high-rise quarters just north of the business area. Facilities include a dining room, popular lounge, indoor pool, and whirlpool. The **Best Western Mermaid,** 545 Main St., tel. 902/742-7821 or 800/772-2774, www.bestwestern.com, has 45 spacious units ($99–139) and an outdoor heated pool.

Closest camping to Yarmouth is at **Loomer's Campers' Haven,** five km east of Yarmouth off Highway 3 in Arcadia, tel. 902/742-4848. The lakeside campground offers over 200 sites ($16–27), as well as canoe rentals, a pool, camp store, Laundromat, and recreation hall with fireplace. Open May 15 to October 15.

## Food

Yarmouth's waterfront **Rudder's Seafood Restaurant & Brew Pub,** 96 Water St., tel. 902/742-7311, pours a few quaffable micros and offers lots of local seafood in a casual atmosphere.

**Harris' Quick 'n' Tasty** restaurant on Highway 1, three km north of central Yarmouth, tel. 902/742-3467, is a locally owned landmark. For quick and tasty clam, scallop, lobster, and chicken platters ($7–18) and such desserts as "mile-high" lemon or date meringue pie, this is the place. Opposite the Quick 'n' Tasty, try **Fisherman's Shanty Restaurant,** tel. 902/749-7788, which specializes in seafood dishes such as lobster served with steamed mussels and all-you-can-eat seafood chowder.

**Kelley's,** 577 Main St., tel. 902/742-9191, opens daily through summer at 7 A.M. for the best breakfast in town. The lunch and dinner menu features seafood dishes accompanied by local produce. (Check out the 200-year-old "captain's table" in the private dining room. It's built of solid oak and measures six meters in length). In the vicinity, **Five Corners,** 626 Main St., tel. 902/742-6061, is another place popular with Yarmouthers for breakfast, lunch, and dinner. Specialties include beef and homemade chowder and desserts.

The ivy-draped **Manor Inn** on Highway 1 about 10 km north of Yarmouth at Hebron, tel. 902/742-2487, basks in gardens surrounding a pond. Sparkling linens and fresh flowers grace the dining room, where you can order lobster, scallops, salmon, and prime rib ($15.50 and up); it's open May to October.

Up Jenkins Street, **Yarmouth Natural Foods,** tel. 902/742-2336, stocks trail mixes, bulk food, and health foods; it's open Mon.–Sat . For stocking up on regular groceries, the main supermarkets are at the malls on Starrs Road.

## Entertainment and Events

**Yarmouth Cinemas** is at the Kmart Plaza, tel. 902/742-7489. The town's lively nighttime pub scene is concentrated along Main Street. If live entertainment is in town, it's at the **Clipper Ship Beverage Room** on Main Street, Thurs.–Sat. nights. A quieter scene reigns at **Haley's** at the Rodd Grand Yarmouth, which has a piano bar.

The **Yarmouth Arts Regional Centre** (known locally as Th' YARC), 76 Parade St., tel. 902/742-8150, puts on dramas and musicals April–September.

**Yarmouth Lobster Sports,** the first weekend in July, revolves around typical small-town sporting events, but the highlight is a lobster boil. The **Western Nova Scotia Exhibition** spans a week with country fair exhibits and entertainment in early August. Summer finishes with the five-day **Yarmouth Cup Ocean Races** the first weekend of September.

## Recreation

The welter of lakes and rivers inland from Yarmouth and the maze of inlets to the southeast make the county prime canoeing territory.

Pick up the *Canoeing* brochure at the tourist information office, which gives detailed descriptions and directions for 14 paddle trips for boaters of all abilities.

Likewise, the low-lying area makes for wonderful cycling. One easy, rewarding route is the 23-km-round-trip spin out to **Yarmouth Lighthouse** on Cape Forchu. Follow Main Street north and turn left at Vancouver Street. Just past the hospital complex, turn left on Grove Road. The Faith Memorial Baptist Church marks the site where the famous Yarmouth Runic Stone, believed to have been inscribed by Leif Eriksson's men, was found. Next you come to the lighthouse, perched on a stone promontory. Beyond the parking lot, a trail leads down to Leif Ericson Picnic Park, overlooking the rocky coast. Several other trips are outlined in the *Cycling* brochure, available from the tourist office.

## Shopping

From July through fall, a **farmers' market** takes place down on the waterfront by the Rudder's brewpub, Sat. 9 A.M.–3 P.M. It's the place to go for fresh baked goods, marinated or smoked fish, and local crafts. The lively market also features live entertainment.

**R. H. Davis and Company,** 361 Main St., tel. 902/742-3557, sells locally made crafts along with topographical maps and nautical charts. **Gifts Aplenty,** 296 Main St., tel. 902/742-0058, has more of the same, as well as local literature.

## Information and Services

Greeting visitors as they arrive by ferry is the **Provincial Visitor Centre,** 228 Main at Forest St., tel. 902/742-6639, where you'll find literature and information on just about everything imaginable in the city and province. It's open May to mid-October, daily 9 A.M.–5 P.M. (July and August, 8 A.M.–9 P.M.).

The **public library** across from Frost Park alongside Main Street is open Mon.–Fri. 9 A.M.–9 P.M., Sat. to 5 P.M. Local newspapers include Tuesday editions of the *Vanguard* and the Acadians' *Le Courrier* in French.

**Yarmouth Regional Hospital** is at 50 Vancouver Street, tel. 902/742-3541. For the **RCMP,**

call 902/742-8777. In emergencies, dial 911. The port has seven banks downtown and at the malls, and there's also a currency-exchange counter (exchange rates are better at the banks) at the visitor center. **Canada Post** is at 15 Willow Street.

## Transportation

**Air Nova,** tel. 902/742-2458, or 888/247-2262, a connector airline for Air Canada, flies into Yarmouth twice daily on the Halifax-Yarmouth-Boston route. The airport is eight km east of town on Forest Road.

Ferries operate from two points in Maine to Yarmouth, docking right downtown in Yarmouth Harbour. North America's fastest ferry, *The Cat,* tel. 902/742-6800 or 888/249-7245, www.catferry.com, makes the 167-km (100-mile) crossing between Bar Harbor and Yarmouth in around 2.5 hours. Fares: adults US$55, seniors US$50, children US$25, vehicles under 6.6 feet US$95, vehicles under 9.9 feet US$120, bicycles US$30. *The Cat* runs twice daily in each direction through summer and once daily in May and October. The *Scotia Prince,* tel. 207/775-5616 or 800/341-7540, www.scotiaprince.com, is a much slower option, taking 11 hours to negotiate the route between Portland and Yarmouth. The summertime, one-way fare is adults US$86, children US$43, vehicles US$105.

**DRL Coach Lines,** tel. 902/450-1987, run from Yarmouth to Halifax via the south-shore Lighthouse Route. **Acadian Lines,** 65 Starrs Rd., tel. 902/742-0440, offers daily departures to Halifax via the north-shore Evangeline Trail.

**Budget,** tel. 902/742-9500, has desks at the airport and ferry terminal, while **Avis,** tel. 902/742-3323, has a desk at the ferry terminal. For shorter trips, call **Yarmouth Town Taxi,** tel. 902/742-7801.

## LA CÔTE ACADIENNE

North of Yarmouth begins La Côte Acadienne (Acadian Coast), a 50-km coastal stretch populated by descendants of the French who resettled here after the Acadian expulsion of 1755. Between Rivière-aux-Saumon (Salmon River) in the south and Weymouth in the north, the place-names,

the soaring Catholic churches, and the proud Acadian flags (a French tricolor with a single yellow star) announce that you're in the largest Francophone enclave in Nova Scotia. The French spoken by the people here retains vestiges of the 17th-century tongue spoken by the original Acadians, spiced with Mi'kmaq and English words. (You'll also hear this region called the District of Clare, a decidedly non-French name given it in 1767 by Nova Scotia's governor Michael Franklin for the area's resemblance to that Irish county.)

The Ice Age left its mark on this rocky seacoast, where 10,000 years ago the ice mass from New Brunswick and the Nova Scotian ice cap met. At the beach at Salmon River, two levels of glacial till show that the Fundy was 15 meters higher during the Ice Age. At Comeauville, be-

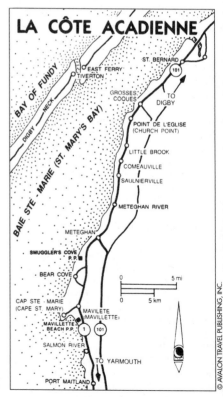

tween Saulnierville and Grosses Coques, the road to the golf club runs atop an Ice-Age moraine.

That made the land a challenge for farmers; draft horses are not powerful enough to pull a plow through the boulder-strewn terrain, and you'll see oxen doing the brute-force job. But the early Acadians persevered here and their hard work and thrifty ways paid off. Today the villages are thriving centers of shipbuilding, fishing, and mink ranching.

The villages appear one after another up the sheltered coast of Baie Sainte-Marie (St. Mary's Bay), which is separated from the Bay of Fundy by the Digby Neck peninsula. The settlements are small, their austere frame houses speckling the flat coastal plain in colors of white, yellow, blue, or green. The Highway 101 expressway from Yarmouth skirts the region on the inland side, while two-lane Highway 1 clings to the coast. The latter route, connecting 14 seaports and inland villages that blend from one to the next, has been called the "longest main street in the world."

## Mavillette Area

For a look at the dynamic Fundy, check out **Mavillette Beach Provincial Park** at Cap Sainte-Marie. The sign for Cape View Restaurant signals the turn from Highway 1; the road peels down to the sea and runs alongside high dunes. Boardwalks cross the dunes to the mile-long beach, where sandbars trap water into warm pools at low tide. On sunny days, beachcombers walk the expanse and hunt for unusual seashells. When fog accompanies the incoming tide, thick mist envelops these trekkers, and shrouds the sun like cotton around a light bulb. Though this is one of the finest beaches in all Nova Scotia, crowds are nonexistent.

Along the beach access road you'll find **Cape View Motel and Cottages,** tel. 902/645-2258. The motel's 10 basic rooms ($80) and five cottages (from $110) overlook sand dunes; open mid-May to October. Across the street is a seafood restaurant specializing in dishes with an Acadian twist.

From Mavillette Beach, you can hike or drive 16-km north to **Smuggler's Cove Provincial Park.** Walkways here lead to great bluff-top views of the coast and down steep tree-lined steps to the rocky shoreline. The coastal cliffs in this area are notched with caves, which were used by Prohibition-era rumrunners. Some of the caves can be explored at low tide. The park also holds numerous picnic tables, making it an ideal lunch stop.

## Meteghan

Settled in 1785, the seaport of Meteghan (from the Mi'kmaq word for blue rocks), 15 km north of Mavillette, is the district's commercial hub, although the population still numbers under 1,000. **La Vieille Maison** (Old House Museum) on Highway 1, tel. 902/645-2389, is in the Robicheau family's former homestead. The museum features 18th-century furnishings and exhibits explaining the area's history, with help from bilingual guides in traditional Acadian costume. Admission is by donation. The museum is open July and August, daily 9 A.M.–7 P.M., June and September, daily 10 A.M.–6 P.M.

For a place to overnight, the tidy **Bluefin Motel,** overlooking the water from 7765 Highway 1, tel. 902/645-2251 or 888/446-3466, charges $55 single, $60 double, including a light breakfast in the motel dining room. Rooms in the historic **Anchor Inn B&B,** 8755 Rte. 1 (two km north of Meteghan), tel. 902/645-3390, which dates to the 1820s, share bathrooms, but for $35 single, $40 double, including a cooked breakfast that is of little consequence.

A seafood cornucopia is brought in daily by the seaport's scallop draggers, herring seiners, and lobster boats. **Blue Rock Restaurant** on Highway 1 near the museum, tel. 902/645-3453, is a good place for seafood dining.

**Meteghan Visitor Centre** is within the walls of La Vieille Maison, along Highway 1, tel. 902/645-2389. It's open the same hours as the museum—July–August , daily 9 A.M.–7 P.M., June and September, daily 10 A.M.–6 P.M.

## North from Meteghan

The village of **Meteghan River,** north of Meteghan, is Nova Scotia's largest wooden-ship-building center. One of the nicest inns along this stretch of coast is **L'Auberge au Havre du Capitain,** 9118 Hwy. 1, tel. 902/769-2001, which offers rooms with private baths ($60–75) and one suite with a whirlpool tub ($110 double). The inn's licensed dining room is locally praised.

Also in Meteghan River, lobster lovers should stop in at **Wright's Lobster** (look for signs along the highway), tel. 902/645-3919, where you can buy one or more of the live lobsters kept in flow-through crates at the large warehouse. It's open Mon.–Fri. 9 A.M.–5 P.M.

The village of **Comeauville,** a bit farther north, is known to golfers for the **Clare Golf and Country Club** off Highway 1, tel. 902/769-2124. It's an 18-hole, par-71 course; handcart and club rentals are available.

## Pointe de l'église (Church Point)

Built between 1903 and 1905, the enormous **église de Sainte-Marie** (St. Mary's Church), the largest and tallest wooden church in North America, dominates this village of 490 inhabitants. The building is laid out in the shape of a cross, and its soaring 56-meter steeple has been ballasted with 40 tons of rock to withstand the winter wind. Inside, **Le Musée Sainte-Marie,** tel. 902/769-2808, exhibits religious artifacts and historical documents and photos. The church is open June to mid-October, daily 9 A.M.–5 P.M. Admission is $2.

The **Université Sainte-Anne,** founded in 1891, is Nova Scotia's only French-language university. The university's **Restaurant Le Casse-Croûte** welcomes visitors and serves a notable selection of Acadian dishes. At the university's Théâtre Marc Lescarbot, the play *Évangéline,* based on the Longfellow poem of love surviving the Acadian deportation, is presented in vernacular Acadian French. But it's not just for French speakers. The highly visual performance includes singing and dancing (and an English translation). Performances are given once a week in June and September and twice a week in July and August (Tues. and Sat. at 8 P.M.); admission is $15 adults, $12 seniors, $8 students. Call 902/769-2114 for reservations.

Accommodations are available nearby at **Le Manoir Samson,** 1768 Hwy. 1, tel. 902/769-2526 or 888/769-8605. The natty road motel offers 13 rooms ($65–78 including continental breakfast). It's open year-round. Campers can head to the full-service **Belle Baie Park,** tel. 902/769-3160, www.bellebaiepark.com, an oceanfront campground offering 150 sites for $15–20, along with a pool, sandy beach, showers, Laundromat, propane station, trailer parts, minigolf, horseshoes, and everything else your little heart desires. It's open mid-May to September.

In town, **Marée Haute,** tel. 902/769-2005, serves heaping portions of Acadian fare to a local crowd.

## Grosses Coques

This small village immediately north of Pointe de l'église takes its name from the huge bar clams harvested here on the tidal flats, an important food source for early settlers.

# Digby and Vicinity

## DIGBY

The busy port of Digby (pop. 2,400) anchors the Annapolis Valley's western end 105 km north of Yarmouth and 235 km west of Halifax. As terminus for the ferry from Saint John, New Brunswick, and home port for the world's largest scallop fleet, the modest town serves as the area's commercial hub. Digby derived its name from Admiral Robert Digby, who sailed up the Fundy in 1793 and settled the place with 1,500 Loyalists from New England.

Lying outside the area's main roads, Digby is easily bypassed. High-speed Highway 101 lies south of Digby and routes sightseers up the St. Mary's Bay coastline into Annapolis Valley. More scenic Highway 1, the pastoral route through the valley, starts beyond Digby to the west. Even the site of Digby's ferry terminal diverts traffic around town, and if you enter the province from New Brunswick, street signs will direct you from Shore Road to Highway 101 via Victoria Street and Highway 303.

### Sights

To get a feeling for the town, head for the waterfront. The scallop fleet ties up off Fishermen's Wharf off Water Street; be there at sunset when the pastel-painted draggers lie at anchor in a semicircle, backlit by the intense setting sun. For a double treat, try the view from a table at the Fundy Restaurant overlooking the Annapolis Basin and a platter of deep-fried or broiled scallops.

Digby's place in history is on display at the harbor-front **Admiral Digby Museum,** housed in a Georgian-era residence at 95 Montague Row, tel. 902/245-6322, with exhibits of old photographs, interesting maps, and maritime artifacts. It's open late June through August, daily 9 A.M.–5 P.M.

### Accommodations

**Summer's Country Inn** at 16 Warwick Street, tel. 902/245-2250, has 10 rooms (from $69 with a full breakfast) and a two-bedroom suite with a kitchen and living room ($109) within a historic building two blocks from the waterfront. All rooms have private baths. Open May through October. The **Coastal Inn Kingfisher,** at the highway end of Warwick Street, tel. 902/245-4747 or 800/401-1155, www.coastalinns.com, has 36 standard rooms ($79 single, $87 double), a family-style restaurant, and a launderette. Open year-round.

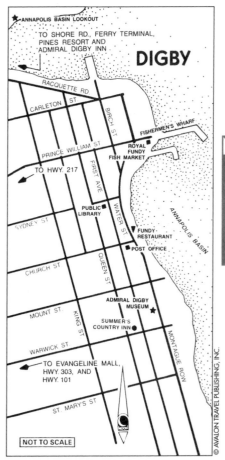

NOVA SCOTIA

NOT TO SCALE

© AVALON TRAVEL PUBLISHING, INC.

The **Admiral Digby Inn,** on Shore Road between the Pines Resort and the ferry terminal, tel. 902/245-2531 or 800/465-6262, www.digbyns.com, has better than average motel accommodations with 44 rooms (from $89) and two cottages ($130), a restaurant, and launderette; it's open mid-May through mid-October.

Appealing to luxury-loving guests, the baronial **Pines Resort** 103 Shore Rd., tel. 902/245-2511 or 800/667-4637, www.signatureresorts.com, peers down over the port from the prow of a hill on the town's outskirts. Its niceties include afternoon tea. Open mid-May to mid-October, the French Norman manor of stucco and stone was built in 1903 and served as a Canadian Pacific Railway hotel until the province bought it in 1965. The accommodations ($145–315) include over 80 rooms in the manor and numerous cottages shaded by spruce, fir, and pine. The hotel offers a dining room of provincial renown, an 18-hole golf course, outdoor pool, fitness center, tennis courts, and hiking trails.

## Food

The **Fundy Restaurant** at 34 Water Street, tel. 902/245-4950, overlooks the Annapolis Basin with dining in the main restaurant, in a solarium, or on balconies. Digby scallops are the specialty, prepared any way you'd like them or in combination with other seafood; reservations are advised.

The **Annapolis Room** of the Pines Resort, 103 Shore Rd., tel. 902/245-2511, has been held in high regard for decades—try the glazed beef tenderloin, chicken basted in white wine, or Digby scallops sautéed in a butter blend of light spices. Also on Shore Road, the **Admiralty Room,** at the Admiral Digby Inn, tel. 902/245-2531, is open for breakfast and dinner daily, May through October, and offers nice views and a gift shop.

For picnic ingredients, check out the **Royal Fundy Fish Market** at Fishermen's Wharf. It offers a tempting showcase of seafood chowder, fresh mussels and salmon, cooked lobster, and smoked cod, haddock, mackerel, and Digby chicks (smoked herring).

## Entertainment and Events

Montague Row to Water Street is the place for people-watching, especially at sunset. **Club 98 Lounge** at 28 Water Street in the Fundy Restaurant has a band (cover charge) or disc jockey, Fri.–Sat. The lounge at the **Pines Resort,** 103 Shore Rd., tel. 902/245-2511, is known for tamer pursuits, low lighting, a comfortable ambience, and finely tuned mixed drinks; it's open Mon.–Sat.

The port's famed scallops attract appropriate fanfare during **Digby Scallops Days** with a parade, scallop-shucking competitions, street vendors, the crowning of the Scallop Queen and Princesses, music, fireworks, and crafts sales over the second week of August.

## Golf

The 18-hole, par-71 **Digby Golf Club** overlooks Digby from a hilltop. Cart and club rentals are available. For tee-off time and reservations call 902/245-4104. The Stanley Thompson– designed course at the **Pines Resort,** north of town, tel. 902/245-2511, has green fees of $35–55, but many golfers play as part of the resort's accommodation packages.

## Services and Information

Three banks in town have similar hours; the **Bank of Nova Scotia** at 61 Water Street is open Mon.–Thurs. 10 A.M.–3 P.M., Fri. to 5 P.M. The nearby **Canada Post** at Water and Church Streets is open Mon.–Fri. 8:30 A.M.–5:15 P.M.; **Marshall's Variety Store** at 101 Water Street is the postal retail outlet; it's open Mon.–Sat. 7 A.M.–midnight, Sunday from 9 A.M.

The **public library** at First and Sydney Streets is open Tues.–Fri. 3–5 P.M., Saturday 10 A.M.–1 P.M. **Digby General Hospital** is at 67 Warwick Street, tel. 902/245-2501; for the **RCMP** call 902/ 245-2579.

The **Digby Visitor Information Centre,** 110 Montague Row, tel. 902/245-5714, is open May to October. The provincial **tourist information center** on Shore Road near the northern outskirts of Digby, tel. 902/245-2201, is open mid-May to mid-October, daily 9 A.M.–5 P.M., from mid-June to 9 P.M.

## Transportation

**Bay Ferries,** tel. 902/245-2116 or 888/249-7245, www.nfl-bay.com, sails the *Princess of Acadia* between Saint John and Digby, Nova Scotia up to three times daily. The 2.5-hour crossing costs adults $35, seniors $30, children $15, vehicles $70 (passenger fares are discounted 40 percent outside of summer).

The **Acadian Lines** bus pulls into Irving gas station at Highways 303 North and 101 on its Fundy loop circuit. Traveling anywhere in Digby by taxi costs about $6, while a cab to the ferry terminal is about $8 from the harbor or $10 from the bus stop. **Basin Taxi,** tel. 902/245-4408, has a stand on Water Street.

## The Digby Neck and Islands

The Digby Neck is a long, spindly peninsula reaching like an antenna for almost 80 km back down the Bay of Fundy from Digby. Highway 217 runs down its center, through the villages of Centreville, Sandy Cove, and Mink Cove, to East Ferry, where a car ferry ($3 per vehicle round-trip) crosses to Long Island. A second ferry (also $3) connects Long Island to Brier Island, the end of the road. Brier Island, Nova Scotia's westernmost extremity, is known for great whale-watching and bird-watching, as well as swimming, fishing, and rockhounding. Ask about it all at the **visitor information center** in Westport, the main community on Brier Island.

Whale-watching excursions are available from numerous companies in the area. Companies generally offer half-day excursions between mid-June and early October, with regular sightings of finback, right, humpback, and minke whales, as well as Atlantic white-sided dolphins and porpoises. Among the many cruise operators in the area are **Brier Island Whale and Seabird Cruises,** operating out of Westport, tel.

902/839-2995 or 800/656-3660; **Mariner Cruises,** Westport, tel. 902/839-2346 or 800/239-2189; **Slocum's,** Westport, tel. 902/839-2110 or 800/214-4655; and **Whale of a Time Sea Adventures,** Little River, tel. 902/834-2867.

For island overnighters, the **Westport Inn,** tel. 902/839-2675, offers comfortable rooms and a delicious breakfast in a 100-year-old home for $45 single, $55 double. Open May through October. **Brier Island Lodge,** tel. 902/839-2300 or 800/662-8355, www.brierisland.com, sits on a bluff overlooking the sea. It has 40 rooms ($70–109), a lounge, and a licensed dining room open for breakfast and dinner. Open April through December.

# KEJIMKUJIK NATIONAL PARK

Deep in the interior of southwestern Nova Scotia, Kejimkujik (pronounced kedgi-muh-KOO-jick, or Keji or Kedge for short) National Park lies off Highway 8, about midway between Liverpool and Annapolis Royal. Encompassing 381 square km of drumlins (rounded glacial hills) and island-dotted lakes—legacies of the last ice age—and hardwood and conifer forests, the park and the adjacent Tobeatic Game Sanctuary are an important refuge for native wildlife and town-weary Nova Scotians.

Wildlife enthusiasts visit the park for bird-watching (including barred owls, pileated woodpeckers, scarlet tanagers, great crested flycatchers, and loons and other waterfowl) and may also spot black bears, white-tailed deer, bobcats, porcupines, and beavers. The many lakes and connecting rivers attract canoeists and swimmers in warm weather, as well as anglers (particularly for perch and brook trout). Hikers can choose from a network of trails, some leading to backcountry campgrounds; some of the campgrounds are also accessible by canoe. In

blue whale

BOB RACE

NOVA SCOTIA

winter, cross-country skiers take over the hiking trails.

Kejimkujik is open year-round; be wary of ticks during May–June and poison ivy throughout the summer. The single-day park entry fee, charged between mid-May and mid-October, is $3.25 adults, $2.50 seniors, $1.75 children, $7.50 families. A four-day pass is also available for three times the single-day rate. For more information call the park office, tel. 902/682-2772, or check website www.parkscanada.ca /kejimkujik.

### Recreation

The **Beech Grove Trail** on a two-km loop starts at the visitor center and wends along the Mersey River, where it climbs a drumlin hilltop swathed in an almost pure beech grove. The **Farmlands Trail** is another drumlin variation, and the 45-minute hike makes its way up a drumlin to an abandoned farm on the hilltop.

The **McGinty Lake Trail** is the ultimate drumlin trek; the two-hour hike starts on the road inland from the lake. Rewards are quick. The first drumlin appears in less than a kilometer, the second crops up before the lake, and the third hill, with an old farm on its crest, lies halfway through the five-km hike.

You can rent canoes, rowboats, and bicycles (all $5 per hour, $24 per day) at Jakes Landing on the northeast side of large Kejimkujik Lake; the adjacent stretch of the Mersey River is placid, suitable for beginning paddlers.

### Camping and Other Acommodations

**Jeremy's Bay Campground,** tel. 902/682-2772 or 800/414-6765 (Parks Canada reservations), on the north side of Kejimkujik Lake, has 360 unserviced sites for tents and trailers ($14), with washrooms and showers, fire pits and firewood ($3.50), a playground, picnic areas, and an interpretive program. Another 46 wilderness sites ($16.25) are scattered in the woodlands with toilets, tables, grills, and firewood; reserve by calling 902/682-2772. The visitor information and administration center, at the park entrance, has free literature and sells a topographical map and seven-day fishing licenses valid within the park.

Hostelling International's **Raven Haven Hostel** is in South Milford, about 20 km north of the park toward Annapolis Royal, tel. 902/532-7320, www.hihostels.ca. Members pay $14, nonmembers $16. Family rooms are available, and you can go swimming or canoeing at adjacent Sandy Bottom Lake. Check-in is any time after 1 P.M.

# The Annapolis Valley

The Annapolis Valley is a haze of white when its apple orchards bloom in late May to early June. Towns from Digby to Windsor celebrate with the **Annapolis Valley Apple Blossom Festival.**

The valley supports more than magnificent apple orchards, however; if you look closely you'll also see hectares of strawberries, plums, peaches, pears, and cherries, as well as crops of hay, grains, and tobacco. Strawberries are ready to harvest during July, and Annapolis Royal sets a day aside for its **Strawberry Tea.** At Port Williams, the Anglican parish of Cornwallis marks each harvest, as it has for a century, with the **Strawberry Supper.** The rich New England planters who settled here in the 18th century built resplendent hous-

es, and many of these have been converted to cozy country inns.

The Annapolis Valley has a legion of fans, among them the early Mi'kmaq Indians, who first settled this region. According to Mi'kmaq legend, Glooscap, a deity taking the form of a giant man, roamed the areas of the upper Fundy. He made his home atop the basalt cliffs of Cape Blomidon—the lofty hook-shaped peninsula that finishes in sea stacks at Cape Split—and buried jewels on the Fundy beaches. (Today's tides still claw at the coastline to reveal agate, amethyst, and zeolite from Hall's Harbour to Cape Split's tip.)

Legend also has it that Glooscap chose the area for its magnificent views. For a sweeping overview of the Annapolis Basin, check out **Old St. Edward's Loyalist Church Museum,** on a hilltop at Clementsport near Digby. Farther up the valley, Bridgetown's **Valleyview Provincial Park** sits high on North Mountain and overlooks the valley's western end. At Wolfville, a drive up Highland Avenue on **Wolfville Ridge** opens up another angle of the western valley, and the town's Gaspereau Avenue climbs a similarly steep hill with more views.

# ANNAPOLIS ROYAL

In 1605, Samuel de Champlain and the survivors of the bitter winter in New Brunswick moved across the Bay of Fundy and established the fortified Port Royal Habitation about five km downriver from what is now Annapolis Royal. The first lasting settlement north of Florida, the outpost also boasted other historic firsts: Canada's first play, *Le Théâtre de Neptune,* was written and produced here by the young Parisian lawyer Marc Lescarbot; the continent's first social club, l'Ordre de Bon Temps ("the Order of Good Cheer") was founded here in 1606; and the New World's first grain mill was built here to grind meal from the first cereal crops. Eight years after its founding, the settlement came to an abrupt end as New Englanders attacked and destroyed the habitation. It has since been reconstructed (see below).

In the 1630s, the French governor Charles de Menou d'Aulnay built a new Port Royal on the south shore of the Annapolis Basin; it included the original earthworks at what is now Fort Anne. The British captured the fort in 1710, renaming it Fort Anne and rechristening the town as Annapolis Royal in honor of their queen. It would serve as Nova Scotia's first capital until 1749, when it was succeeded by the new town of Halifax.

The **Tidal Power Plant** on Highway 1 is the world's only power-generating station to produce electricity from the tides. Its operation is explained inside; it's open May to mid-October, daily 9 A.M.–5 P.M., July–August to 8 P.M. The **tourist office** in the same building, tel. 902/532-5769, stocks area and provincial sightseeing literature; it's open the same hours.

## Fort Anne National Historic Site

This 18th-century fort and grounds, Canada's first national historic site, is on St. George Street, tel. 902/532-2397, and overlooks the confluence of the Annapolis and Allain Rivers. The early French fort was designed with a star-shaped layout, and it's impressively banked with sweeping verdant lawns and deep moats. The British added the 1797 officers' garrison, which houses the fort's museum with historical exhibits. It's open mid-May to mid-October, daily 9 A.M.–6 P.M.; the rest of the year by appointment. Admission is $2.75 adults, $2.25 seniors, $1.35 children, $7 families. The surrounding park grounds are always open.

## Annapolis Royal Historic Gardens

The Historic Gardens, off Upper St. George Street, tel. 902/532-7018, comprise four hectares of theme gardens, demonstrating gardening techniques of the early Acadians as well as the most modern methods, plus two hectares of reclaimed marshland and a waterfowl refuge. It's open mid-May to mid-October, daily 8 A.M. to dusk. Admission is $3.50 adults, $3 seniors and students, $9.75 families.

## Port Royal National Historic Site

The original French settlement of 1605 has been reconstructed at what is believed to be the original site, on the north side of the Annapolis River. Built from Samuel de Champlain's plan, using 17th-century construction techniques, the rustic buildings—governor's house, priest's dwelling, bakery, guardroom, and others, furnished with period reproductions—form a rectangle around a courtyard within the palisaded compound. The knowledgeable staff dresses in period costume.

The site is about 10 km west of Annapolis Royal, off Highway 1A. It's open mid-May to mid-October, daily 9 A.M.–6 P.M.; tel. 902/532-2898. Admission is $2.75 adults, $2.25 seniors, $1.35 children, $7 families.

## Upper Clements

The **Upper Clements Family Vacation Park** off Highway 1 six km southwest of Annapolis Royal, tel. 902/532-7557 or 888/248-4567, is

NOVA SCOTIA

Atlantic Canada's largest theme park. Its style is thoroughly Nova Scotian, featuring a train ride on a historic replica, and a mini-golf course designed as a map of the province. The park also has a roller coaster, flume ride, carousel, pedal boats, live entertainment, dinner theater Fri.–Sat. evenings, a crafts area with demonstrations and a shop, and dining rooms. Entrance admission is $3; passes for rides and shows are additional (an all-day rides pass is available for $12). The park is open June to October, daily 11 A.M.–7 P.M.; open weekends only mid-May to mid-June.

In the vicinity, **Upper Clements Wildlife Park,** tel. 902/532-5924, features indigenous wildlife of the province along with Sable Island horses and the Queen's Royal Red Deer in a natural forested setting. Three trails wind through the park, which is open mid-May to mid-October, daily 10 A.M.–8 P.M. Admission is $3 per person.

### Accommodations and Food

Annapolis Royal boasts a brace of lodgings in vintage homes. Set on two hectares, **Queen Anne Inn,** 494 Upper Saint George St., tel. 902/532-7850, www.queenanneinn.ca, is a restored 1865 Victorian mansion offering 10 rooms with period furnishings (from $55, including full breakfast). Across the road, the **Hillsdale House Inn,** 519 Upper Saint George St., tel. 902/532-2345, www.hillsdalehouse.ns.ca, set on a six-hectare estate, has 10 antiques-furnished bedrooms ($70–110 with full breakfast), a lounge, and a patio.

**Turret Bed and Breakfast,** 372 St. George St., tel. 902/532-5770, is a registered historic property with four guest rooms ($60–80, including full breakfast), one with private bath. Open year-round (although by reservation only in the off-season). The **King George Inn,** 548 Upper St. George St., tel. 902/532-5286, is a Victorian sea captain's home, built circa 1868 and furnished with period antiques. It offers four luxurious guest rooms (from $99) and a two-room family suite ($199). Amenities include a library, pianos, free use of bicycles, and complimentary evening tea and coffee. Open May to October.

East of town across the river, the spacious full-service **Dunromin Campsite and Cabins,** tel. 902/532-2808, has around 150 open and wooded spaces by the riverside, most of them serviced, from $17; camping cabins run $45–55. Amenities include a pool, showers, a Laundromat, a playground, a game room, rental boats, and more. Dunromin is open mid-April through October.

**Kent's,** north of downtown on the causeway, tel. 902/532-5105, has a pleasant outdoor patio offering water views and a menu stacked with seafood. Head to the **Crooked Floor,** 8 Victoria St., tel. 902/532-7602, for fresh and healthy food in an informal setting. Locals gather for afternoon beer and pub grub on the outdoor patio or for nightcaps in the cozy interior of English-style **Ye Olde Towne Pub,** 9–11 Church St., tel. 902/532-2244 (reputed to be the smallest bar in Nova Scotia).

## WOLFVILLE

The Annapolis Valley's genteel town of Wolfville (pop. 3,475) began with the name Mud Creek, an ignoble tribute from the founding New England planters who wrestled with the Fundy coastal area once farmed by early Acadians. Now the town sits in the lushest part of the Annapolis

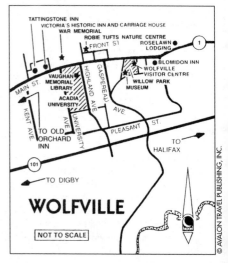

Valley, and you won't want to miss it. Highway 1 runs through town as Main Street, where large houses with bay windows and ample porches sit comfortably beneath stately trees. Acadia University's ivy-covered buildings and manicured lawns lie along Main and University.

The town, just six blocks deep, has an uncomplicated layout alongside Highway 1 and Highway 101. It's a two-hour drive west to Digby; Halifax is almost three hours away to the southeast.

## Sights

**Randall House Historical Museum,** 171 Main St., tel. 902/542-9775, is a historic home (built 1815) with period furnishings and local artifacts from the 1760s to the 20th century. It's open mid-June to mid-September, Mon.–Sat. 10 A.M.–5 P.M., Sun. 2–5 P.M. Admission by donation.

The **Acadia University Art Gallery** in the Beveridge Arts Centre at Highland Avenue and Main Street, tel. 902/585-1373, has a fine-arts collection of local and regional works, highlighted by Alex Colville's oils and serigraphs. It's open year-round, daily 1–4 P.M. Admission is free.

## Accommodations

A registered historic property (1893), **Victoria's Historic Inn and Carriage House,** 416 Main St., tel. 902/542-5744 or 800/556-5744, combines a large Victorian house with an adjacent carriage house and a licensed dining room. Rates start at $98 single, $108 double, including a cooked breakfast. Open year-round. **Roselawn Lodging,** 32 Main St., tel. 902/542-3420, is a modest motel with 28 rooms and another 12 in adjacent cottages; open year-round. Facilities include an outdoor pool, launderette, picnic tables, and a tennis court. Rates range $80–120.

The **Old Orchard Inn,** near Highway 101's exit 11 and visible from the highway, tel. 902/542-5751 or 800/561-8090, includes a motel of 105 rooms ($100–150), 29 cabins ($65–85), tennis courts, an indoor pool, saunas, hiking/ski trails, ski rentals, a popular dining room (for breakfast, lunch, and dinner), and a lounge.

The **Tattingstone Inn** at 434 Main Street, tel. 902/542-7696 or 800/565-7696, www.tattingstone.ns.ca, is casually formal with 10 nonsmoking rooms (from $98 single, $104 double) within the historic main house, as well as a separate carriage house ($98–118 single, $108–125 double) and cottage ($175). Some rooms have whirlpool tubs. The inn also offers a music room, popular licensed dining room, steam room, heated outdoor pool, and tennis court. It's open year-round and rates include breakfast.

The **Blomidon Inn,** 127 Main St., tel. 902/542-2291 or 800/565-2291, www.blomidon.ns.ca, is an imposing three-story sea captain's mansion dating to 1882 and surrounded by expansive grounds. It fronts the town's main drag, with rates starting at $139 per person, including all meals. It's open year-round except Christmas.

## Food

The dining rooms at the local inns are good bets for meals. Expect to pay $15–25 for a main. The **Old Orchard Inn** on Highway 101, tel. 902/542-5751, draws diners to its large restaurant with sea views and good food. Specialties are chateaubriand and cherries jubilee. Reservations required. At **Tattingstone Inn,** 434 Main St., tel. 902/542-7696, innkeeper Betsy Harwood creates feasts (pheasant and wild rice spiced with rosemary, raspberry-glazed chicken, and other gourmet fare); specialties change daily. Reservations are required. The specialties at **Blomidon Inn,** 127 Main St., tel. 902/542-2291, include regional seafood delicacies such as Digby scallops and Atlantic salmon. It's open daily for lunch and dinner.

**Chez la Vigne** at 117 Front Street, tel. 902/542-5077, boasts award-winning owner/chef Alex Clavel. His menu is French-inspired and includes pheasant, rabbit, guinea hen, and seafood dishes ($13–29.50). Terrace dining outside during warm weather augments the pleasant dining room. Reservations are required.

## Events

From July to early September, the **Atlantic Theatre Festival,** 356 Main St., tel. 800/337-6661 or 902/542-4242, stages professional productions of classic drama. Tickets range $12–37.

NOVA SCOTIA

## Information

The **Wolfville Visitor Centre** ensconced at Willow Park on Main Street, tel. 902/542-7000, is open May to mid-October, daily 9 A.M.–5 P.M. The university's **Vaughan Memorial Library** is open Mon.–Thurs. 8 A.M.–10 P.M., Fri. to 4:30 P.M., Sat. 10 A.M.–2 P.M.

The **Blomidon Naturalist Society** is an environmental group. Its interest in local chimney swifts led to the establishment of the **Robie Tufts Nature Centre** at the corner of Front and Elm Streets, where the birds nest in the chimney and cavort at sunset. Society members meet at the university once a month. The town hall has updates; call 902/542-5767.

## Services

**Eastern Kings Memorial Hospital** is at 23 Earnscliffe Avenue, tel. 902/542-2266. Call the **police** at 902/542-3817 or the **RCMP** at 902/679-5555.

The **Bank of Montréal** at 282 Main Street is open Mon.–Thurs. 10 A.M.–4 P.M., Fri. to 5:30 P.M. **Canada Post** is open Mon.–Fri. 8:30 A.M.–5 P.M.

**Wile's** at 210 Main Street has coin-operated laundry machines; it's open daily 8 A.M.–10 P.M.

# VICINITY OF WOLFVILLE

## Starr's Point

**Prescott House,** 1633 Starr's Point Rd. (Hwy. 358), tel. 902/542-3984, harks back to the valley's orchard beginnings, when horticulturist Charles Ramage Prescott imported species to add to the provincial store of fruit trees. His profits built this Georgian-styled homestead. The restored mansion, constructed circa 1812, displays period furnishings and sits amid beautiful gardens. It's open late June to mid-October, Mon.–Sat. 9:30 A.M.–5:30 P.M., Sun. 1–5:30 P.M., with special events celebrating the fall harvest. Admission: adults $3, seniors $2, children $1.

## Grand Pré

**Grand Pré National Historic Site** on Highway 1, tel. 902/542-3631, is all that remains of Acadia's largest settlement, begun in 1680 and put to a premature demise by the 1755 deportation.

Nova Scotia's oldest remaining blockhouse, protected within Fort Edward National Historic Site

That event and the setting of Grand-Pré (Great Meadow) were the inspiration for Longfellow's poem "Evangeline," whose fictional heroine—the faithful Acadian girl separated from her lover by the deportation—is also commemorated with a bronze statue here. The site is open year-round. Saint-Charles Church, built by Acadian descendants in 1922, houses an exhibit on the events of the Acadian diaspora. It's open May-October, daily 9 A.M.–6 P.M.; guided tours are available. Admission to the site is $2.50 adults, $2 seniors, $1.10 children, $7 families.

**Grand Pré Vineyards** on Highway 1 (take exit 10 from Highway 101), tel. 902/542-1753, grows wine grapes on 60 hectares of former Acadian farmland. In the main building you'll find a restaurant, wine shop, and crafts corner. The winery is open year-round, Mon.–Sat. 9 A.M.–6 P.M., Sun. 11 A.M.–5 P.M., with tours offered daily at 11 A.M. and 3 P.M.

## Falmouth

Continuing south toward Halifax, 12-hectare **Sainte Famille Wines,** on the corner of Dyke Road and Dudley Park Lane, tel. 902/798-8311 or 800/565-0993, is another vineyard on former Acadian farmland. The winery's premium red and white wines are sold in the retail shop; open year-round, Mon.–Sat. 9 A.M.–5 P.M., Sun. noon–5 P.M. Tours are offered in summer at 11 A.M. and 2 P.M.

## Windsor

At nearby Windsor, **Fort Edward National Historic Site,** tel. 902/542-3631, preserves the last 18th-century blockhouse in Nova Scotia. Fort Edward was one of the main assembly points for the deportation of the Acadians from the province in 1755. The site is open year-round; the building is open mid-June to late September, daily 10 A.M.–6 P.M. Admission is free.

**Haliburton House,** 414 Clifton Ave., tel. 902/798-5619, was owned by 19th-century author, humorist, and historian Judge Thomas Chandler Haliburton, author of the Sam Slick stories. Among the sayings that originated in Haliburton's writings are "It's raining cats and dogs," "barking up the wrong tree," "facts are stranger than fiction," and "quick as a wink." The Victorian mansion on 10 hectares is open June to mid-October, Mon.–Sat. 9:30 A.M.–5:30 P.M., Sun. 1–5:30 P.M.

The **Shand House,** on Ferry Hill at 389 Avon Street, tel. 902/798-8213, is another vintage beauty and marks the wealthy Shand family's prominence in Windsor. When it was built in the early 1890s, the Queen Anne–style mansion was one of the first residences in the area fitted with electric lights and indoor plumbing. It's open June to mid-October, 9:30 A.M.–5:30 P.M., Sun. 1–5:30 P.M.

## Mount Uniacke

Further south, **Uniacke Estate Museum Park,** 758 Main Rd., tel. 902/866-0032 or 902/866-2560, is a splendid Colonial-style estate on 930 hectares (2,300 acres), built in 1815 by Nova Scotia's attorney general Richard John Uniacke. Uniacke chose this site because the surrounding countryside reminded him of his native Ireland. The home's interior features original furnishings, including four-poster beds and family portraits. The estate offers seven hiking trails and hosts woodworking demonstrations and old-time events such as the provincial Historical Equestrian Society riding exhibits. It's open June to mid-October, Mon.–Sat. 9:30 A.M.–5:30 P.M., Sun. 11 A.M.–5:30 P.M. Admission is adults $2, children $1, families $5.

NOVA SCOTIA

# Eastern Nova Scotia

Nova Scotia's Scottish heritage originated with the first Highland immigrants who trickled into the area: to Pictou County in the 1770s, New Glasgow in the 1780s, and the Arisaig area in the next decade. Loyalists arrived on Nova Scotia's eastern shore in the 1780s, followed by Irish immigrants at Antigonish in 1784.

It was during the early 1800s, however, that the region's decidedly Scottish complexion was firmly established. England and France were engaged in the Napoleonic War, and the French had blocked British ports. England desperately needed food, and began the Highland Clearances—poor tenant farmers in Scotland were turned off their land, their homes were burned, and the farmlands were converted to sheep and cattle pastures. The Clearances continued for almost two decades. Thousands of Scots died of starvation and disease, while thousands more took the Crown up on its offer of free land in Nova Scotia. They left their beloved Highlands forever and re-created their old home in a new land. Intense emotional ties remain to this day, and the Scots' heritage is kept alive with festivals commemorating their history and culture.

dockside fishing gear

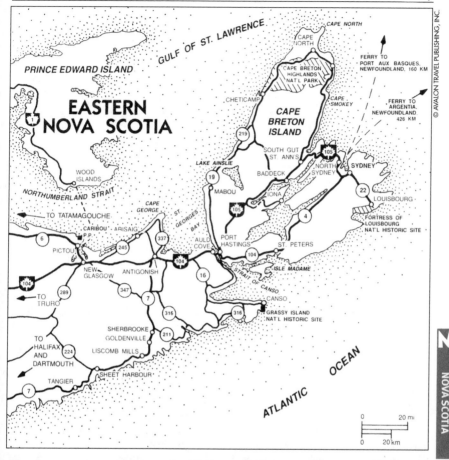

## The Strait Shore

The TransCanada promises little besides uninterrupted speed on its route across the northeastern mainland. The best vistas, beaches, camping, and other attractions lie off the expressway, along the strait's coastal roads between Tatamagouche and Cape Breton. Shallow pools of seawater among sandbars turn warm in the sun, making for comfortable wading and swimming at Rushton's Beach Provincial Park, Tatamagouche Bay, and Melmerby Beach Provincial Park, east of Pictou.

### PICTOU AND VICINITY

Pictou, located on a fine harbor at the confluence of three rivers, was founded by New Englanders in 1767. Six years later, when 33 families and 25 unmarried men arrived from the Scottish Highlands aboard the *Hector,* Pictou (PIC-toe) became the "birthplace of New Scotland." Scots platted the town in 1787. Pictou began at Water and Front streets, and the harbor front is still the town's focus.

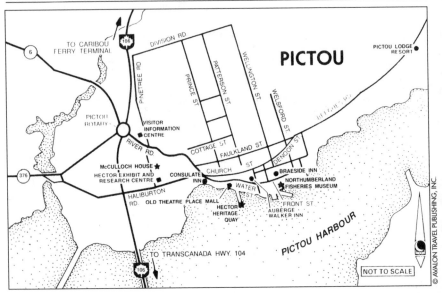

The flamboyant Presbyterian minister and doctor Thomas McCulloch, en route to ministerial duties on Prince Edward Island, arrived here with his family by accident in 1803 when a storm blew his ship into Pictou Harbour. Local immigrants asked him to stay, and McCulloch agreed. In addition to providing medical care to the immigrants, McCulloch tried to reform the province's backward educational system. His efforts helped distance academia from the strictures of the church, and in 1817 he founded the Pictou Academy. He would later become the first president of Dalhousie College in Halifax.

The minister-cum-educator's residence, Sherbrooke Cottage (now McCulloch House), built in 1806 in distinct Scottish vernacular style, is one of many historic stone houses and buildings designed to reflect local lineage. Small Pictou also has numerous fancier styles; you'll see examples of stone Gothic and Second Empire designs along Water, Front, and Church Streets.

Pictou's emergence as a provincial destination is relatively recent. Nothing much happened between the Scots' arrival and the 20th century, and the town dozed through the centuries. The provincial highway system developed and skirted the town. The TransCanada Highway came along and created a fast west-to-east expressway south of Pictou, with Highway 106 as the route's spur up to the ferry at Caribou. The somnolence ended with a waterfront redevelopment and the construction of a full-size *Hector* replica that attracts hordes of visitors to its harbor-front mooring.

## The Town Today

Nearly everything in Pictou happens at waterfront, the stretch from Water and Front streets along Pictou Harbour to the ferry terminal at Caribou on the strait. Besides scenery, the varied shore roads boast a ghost. Try the drive along the strait on a misty autumn evening. Locals have seen the image of a burning ship with billowing sails skimming the strait. Nova Scotians aren't the only ones who have seen the ship. Prince Edward Islanders have seen the same sight from the shore directly across the strait.

The centuries have been kind to the town, and Pictou (pop. 4,000) has evaded tacky commercialism. Its industries include the local paper mill, lobster fishing, shipbuilding, and tire production at the Michelin tire plant. The town had a problem with malodorous emissions from the pulp mill across the harbor, but the mill initiated a $5 million program with a new steam stripper for processing paper in 1989. While sea winds occasionally bring what remains of the odor across the harbor to Pictou, the smell has been reduced by some 65 percent, and efforts are ongoing to eliminate the rest.

## Sights

**Hector Heritage Quay,** 33 Caladh Ave., tel. 902/485-6057, is home to a three-floor interpretation center detailing the Scottish immigrants' arrival and early years. An outside elevated walkway overlooks the harbor. Take time to look over the *Hector.* The three-masted, black-and-off-white replica is a splendid vessel, wide-hulled and round-ended. From the shape of the ship, though, you'll easily see that the voyage from Scotland was not so splendid. The ship's hull is unusually wide, and indeed the *Hector,* owned by the Dutch and chartered by the Scots for the voyage, was built as a freighter and modified only slightly to carry human cargo. Remarkably, the 200-plus immigrants from the Highlands survived, and Nova Scotia owes its Scottish heritage to those seaworthy voyagers. The quay is open daily, mid-May through June, Mon.–Fri. 9 A.M.–5 P.M., July–August 9 A.M.–8 P.M., September and October 9 A.M.–5 P.M. Tours of the quay operate July and August.

East along the waterfront, the **Northumberland Fisheries Museum,** on Front Street within the historic CN railroad station, has a modest fisheries exhibit, including a vintage lobster boat, an aquarium holding local marine species, a mock fisherman's bunkhouse, period photos, and other memorabilia. It's open June–September. Admission is adults $3, children $2. For more information, call 902/485-4972.

**McCulloch House,** 100 Old Haliburton Rd., tel. 902/485-1150, overlooking the harbor, holds period antiques and a small library. The print of a Labrador falcon downstairs was a gift to Mc-

Culloch from artist-naturalist John James Audubon. (McCulloch had his own bird collection, and it is now part of Dalhousie University's exhibits in Halifax.) The museum is open June to mid-October, Wed.–Sat. 9:30 A.M.–4:30 P.M. Admission is $1.

**Hector Exhibit and Research Centre** at 86 Old Haliburton Road near McCulloch House, tel. 902/485-4563, showcases fine arts as part of the national arts exhibit circuit. The site is also one of the province's best genealogical libraries. It's open mid-May to mid-October, Wed.–Sat. 9:30 A.M.–5:30 P.M., Sun. 1–5:30 P.M. Admission to the exhibits is $1; admission to the genealogical library is $5 first visit, $2 subsequent visits.

## Accommodations

Opposite the harbor, the **Consulate Inn,** 157 Water St., tel. 902/485-4554 or 800/424-8263, www.consulateinn.com, dates to 1810. It's a historic building styled in Scottish and Georgian vernacular that was once the American consulate. The restored inn has five guest rooms (from $69, with a light breakfast) and a dining room. It's open year-round. The restored 1865 **Auberge Walker Inn,** 34 Coleraine St., tel. 902/485-1433 or 800/370-5553, has 11 guest rooms ($75–149 with a light breakfast), some with harbor views, and a fully licensed dining room.

**Braeside Inn,** 126 Front St., tel. 902/485-5046 or 800/613-7701, sits back from the harbor on a hillside. It has been restored with oriental touches downstairs and period furnishings upstairs. It has 20 rooms, some with shared baths ($65–85), a dining room, and summer oil-painting classes. It's open year-round and advertises a casual dress code.

**Pictou Lodge Resort,** on Braeshore Road five km east of town, tel. 902/485-4322 or 888/662-7484, www.maritimeinns.com, was built in 1926 on a 67-hectare (165-acre) oceanfront estate overlooking Northumberland Strait. The roomy lodge has been restored with rustic comforts and features

*Besides scenery, the varied shore roads boast a ghost. Try the drive along the strait on a misty autumn evening. Locals have seen the image of a burning ship with billowing sails skimming the strait.*

**NOVA SCOTIA**

a long outside porch, dining in the high-ceilinged rotunda, and a nearby pond with canoes. The 59 guest units include six three-bedroom chalets, 21 suites of various sizes and configurations, and 20 standard motel rooms. All units have private baths, and many have deluxe amenities such as fireplace, kitchen, and living room. Rates range $99–225 per unit. The resort is open May through October.

## Food

For waterfront ambience, head to the **Salt Water Cafe,** next to Hector Heritage Quay at 67 Caladh Avenue, tel. 902/485-2558. Sit inside or out on the screened deck while enjoying the house specialty—seafood, moderately priced. Open for lunch and dinner daily from 11 A.M. Also boasting a waterfront location is **Relics,** 50 Caladh Ave., tel. 902/485-5577, a typical Maritimes pub featuring lots of well-priced seafood and steak in a casual atmosphere.

Several local lodgings offer excellent public dining rooms. The **Vines Restaurant** in the Consulate Inn, 157 Water St., tel. 902/485-4554, has intimate dining June–September. The specialty is seafood, with some beef and chicken dishes. Closed Monday. The dining room at the **Pictou Lodge Resort,** five km east of downtown, backs up on the coastline. You'll enjoy strait views from an intimate setting, with tables centered around a massive stone fireplace. The menu features entrées such as ginger-fried chicken, sauced poached salmon, and smoked trout, with prices ranging $14–25. Reservations are required; call 902/485-4322. **Braeside Inn,** 126 Front St., tel. 902/485-5046, ranks as Pictou's top restaurant and features three-course meals with an emphasis on mixed seafood dishes. Special dishes include Catch 57 (with haddock, lobster, scallops, and shrimp) and Mariner (with halibut and salmon fillets stuffed with scallops and lobster). Meals are served in the formal inside dining room, in the informal greenhouse overlooking the harbor, or on the outdoor deck.

Light fare is the gist of **Stone House Cafe and Pizzeria,** 11 Water St., tel. 902/485-6885. **Smith's Restaurant,** 16 Church St., tel. 902/485-4524, is strong on thick chowders and ample seafood platters.

Sobeys on Haliburton Road near Highway 106 has a deli counter and bakery in its supermarket; open Mon.–Tues., Sat. 9 A.M.–6 P.M., Wed.–Fri. to 9 P.M. There's an **IGA** grocery on Front Street.

## Entertainment and Events

Drinks at the **Braeside Inn,** 126 Front St., tel. 902/485-5046, are served in a stylish lounge off the main lobby and on the deck outside in summer. The **Oceanview Lounge** in the Pictou Lodge Resort on Braeshore Road, tel. 902/485-4322, features varied weekend entertainment and occasional Sunday jazz sessions. Friendly downtown drinking holes include **Relics,** 50 Caladh Ave., tel. 902/485-5577, and the **Old Stone Pub,** both serving up local beers on tap and hearty, well-priced food.

The local performing arts scene is based at **deCoste Entertainment Centre** on Water Street, tel. 902/485-8848, with thrice-weekly drama, concerts, and dance. Look for the *ceilidhs* Tuesday through Thursday nights in July and August.

The four-day **Pictou Lobster Festival** attracts 75,000 revelers with parades, entertainment, and food vendors. It's usually held the second weekend of July. The **Hector Festival** celebrates the 1773 arrival of Pictou's Scottish ancestors through five mid-August days. Most of the action takes place along the waterfront, including concerts, pipe bands, highland dancing, and a re-enactment of the historic landing.

## Shopping

Water Street holds the bulk of the shopping opportunities downtown, including **Water Street Studio,** 110 Water St., tel. 902/485-8398, a crafts outlet with natural-fiber apparel and wares. The **Grohmann Knives** line of cutlery and hunting knives is sold throughout Atlantic Canada. The plant's retail outlet, 116 Water St., tel. 902/485-4224, is open Mon.–Fri. 9 A.M.–3 P.M.; 20-minute plant tours are scheduled May–September at 9 A.M., 11 A.M., and 1 P.M.

## Information and Services

The provincial **Visitor Information Centre** at the Pictou Rotary (where Highway 106 meets

Highway 6), tel. 902/485-6213, is primarily in place for those arriving in Nova Scotia via the ferry from Prince Edward Island, but is also a good source of local information. It's open mid-May to mid-October, daily 8 A.M.–9 P.M. A seasonal information booth operates on Hector Heritage Quay.

**Sutherland–Harris Hospital** is at 1059 Haliburton Road, tel. 902/485-4324. For the **RCMP** call 902/485-4333.

Locals do their banking in style at architecturally resplendent places; the **Bank of Nova Scotia** is in a Second Empire,–style building at the corner of Front and Colerain Streets, tel. 902/485-4378. It's open Mon.–Wed. 9 A.M.–3 P.M., Thurs.–Fri. to 5 P.M. **Canada Post,** 49 Front St., is open Mon.–Fri. 8:30 A.M.–5 P.M.

## Transportation

It's a 10-minute drive from downtown Pictou to Caribou, the departure point for ferries to Prince Edward Island. Vessels operate up to nine times daily in each direction through the May to mid-December sailing season. (Peak summertime waiting lines can be horrendous; try to get to the ferry after 9 A.M. and before 3:30 P.M.). The 75-minute trip over to Prince Edward Island is free, with a fare of $49 per regular-sized vehicle (RVs and trailers $61–74) inclusive of passengers collected only on the return journey. For details call **Northumberland Ferries Ltd.** (NFL), tel. 902/566-3838 or 800/565-0201, website www.nfl-bay.com.

Pictou has several taxi companies, among them **Central Cabs,** tel. 902/755-6074, and **Hillside Taxi,** tel. 902/752-3074. Call **Carefree Cruises,** tel. 902/485-6205, for ocean-fishing charters, sightseeing cruises, or ferry service to Pictou Island. **Jigs and Reels,** tel. 902/396-8855, also offers sightseeing tours out on the water, as well as harbor taxi service between Pictou and New Glasgow.

## Cape George Scenic Drive

The route to fossil hunting at Arisaig and Cape George's ruggedly beautiful eastern coastline lies along Highways 245 and 337 between New Glasgow and Antigonish. Highway 245 passes Merigomish and Lismore and starts to rise as it approaches coastal **Arisaig Provincial Park,** which has picnic tables and a boardwalk over the dunes to the waterfront. As you walk the beach here, you'll see tiny fossils embedded in mudstone—the ancient remnants of the Arisaig coastline's origin as a shallow, warm sea with a silty bottom. A lane beyond the park turns off the highway and leads to Arisaig Point, where the coastline is wrapped in dark green and orange-red rock, a vestige of the area's volcanic past.

The highway rises steadily and peaks at an elevation of 190 meters at **Cape George.** The setting is a bicyclist's favorite scene and a just reward after the steep coastal climb. The panorama from the lighthouse at the cape's tip takes in the manicured farmlands of the Pictou-Antigonish highlands behind you as well as the misty vision of Prince Edward Island across the strait.

Along Cape George's eastern side, the road becomes Hwy. 337 as it peels down from the peak alongside St. Georges Bay. The scenic 53-km route to Antigonish, dubbed a miniature Cabot Trail for its rugged coastal beauty, passes through the tiny communities of Cape George, Lakevale, Crystal Cliffs, Antigonish Harbour, and finally into Antigonish. Just below Cape George, the turn-of-the-century lighthouse at Ballantynes Cove is perched 300 meters above St. Georges Bay.

## ANTIGONISH

First impressions of Antigonish (pop. 4,700) from the west are not promising. Main Street is a thicket of fast-food restaurants and service stations—but the town is not without its charms. Antigonish (from a Mi'kmaq name meaning "place where the branches are torn off by bears gathering beechnuts") is the center of the county. It offers shopping malls, parks, accommodations, and St. Frances Xavier University.

In mid-July, the **Antigonish Highland Games**—the longest-running in North America, celebrated since 1861—kick off with Scottish music, dancing, and sports. Throughout July and August, the **Festival Antigonish,** Nova Scotia's largest and most successful professional summer theater program, features a variety of drama, musicals, comedies, cutting edge improv, and children's entertainment at the university campus. Tickets run $15 for adults, with discounts for children, students, and seniors. Call 800/563-7529.

## Accommodations and Food

**Maritime Inn Antigonish,** 158 Main St., tel. 902/863-4001 or 888/662-7484, www .maritimeinns.com, is open year-round. It has 32 units and a dining room, lounge, and café. Rates range $65–125. **Antigonish Victorian Inn,** 149 Main St., tel. 902/863-1103 or 800/706-5558, is a splendid B&B occupying a William Critchlow Harris–designed Queen Anne mansion. Each of the nine rooms has a private bath and TV. Rates of $69–129 include full homemade breakfast. Closed between Christmas and mid-February.

Antigonish offers a surprising number of good dining options. **Sunshine on Main,** 332 Main St., tel. 902/863-5851, has a homey atmosphere and a good menu of inexpensive, healthy fare. On the same block, **Gabrieau's,** 350 Main St., tel. 902/863-1925, features a diverse menu of seafood, steak, chicken, and vegetarian dishes, all well-presented and reasonably priced (dinner mains $12–17.50).

## Antigonish to Cape Breton Island

From Antigonish, it's a little over 50 km on Highway 104 to the causeway linking the mainland to Cape Breton Island. Along the way, roads such as Highway 4 lead north to **St. George's Bay,** for some of the province's best saltwater sportfishing. The base for much of the fishing action is **Auld Cove,** where the sea meets the Strait of Canso. Late autumn brings bluefin tuna schools close to shore, and a mammoth 679-kilogram bluefin caught here set the world record in 1979.

The bay area, settled by Acadians in the 17th century, also has some fine beaches. Near the village of Pomquet, off exit 35 from the Trans-Canada Highway, is **Pomquet Beach Park,** with supervised swimming and a picnic area. A few kilometers east is another good sandy beach at **Bayfield Provincial Park.**

# The Eastern Shore

The eastern shore, the fretted, rocky Atlantic coastline stretching east from Dartmouth to the Canso Causeway, is as rugged as the Northumberland Strait shore is tame. Two-lane coastal highways 207, 7, 211, and 316 have been designated as Marine Drive, a twisting, 400-km-long scenic route through tiny fishing ports reminiscent of seafaring life decades ago, and rock-bound coves where the forest grows right down to the sea. It's the only major, entirely paved through route to Cape Breton south of the TransCanada, but it's not the highway for those in a hurry. The road unfurls itself at a leisurely pace and it's worth slowing down and taking two or three days to travel its length.

## DARTMOUTH TO SHERBROOKE

Highway 107 is the most direct route east from Dartmouth, but the more scenic Highway 207, which detours along the coast, is worth taking for the section. It loops southward from Dartmouth's eastern suburbs to **Lawrencetown Beach,** Atlantic Canada's premier surfing spot. The surf is best in winter, but surfers can be seen in the water year-round (the beach's southern headland provides a good vantage point). Swimming is safest at the north end of the beach at **Lawrencetown Beach Provincial Park.** The highway swings north from the park, connecting with busy Highway 107. From there, it's 10 km to Musquodoboit Harbour.

## Musquodoboit Harbour and Vicinity

With just 900 people, Musquodoboit Harbour is nevertheless the largest community between Dartmouth and Sherbrooke. The only real attraction in town is **Musquodoboit Harbour Railway Museum,** on Highway 7, tel. 902/889-2689, housed in a 1918 railway station and three

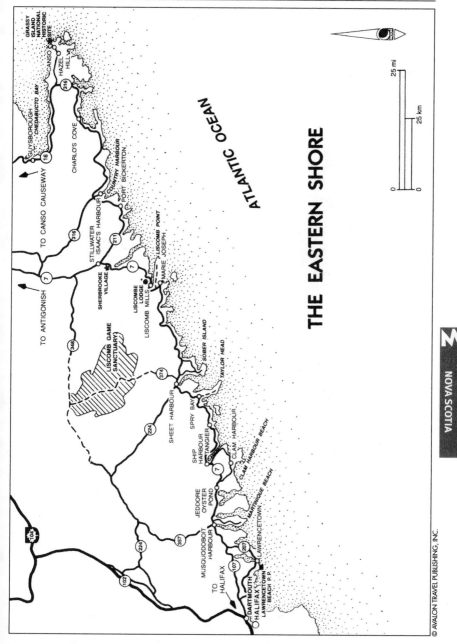

THE EASTERN SHORE

ATLANTIC OCEAN

NOVA SCOTIA

© AVALON TRAVEL PUBLISHING, INC.

Lawrencetown Beach is Atlantic Canada's premier surfing spot.

vintage rail cars. It's open in summer only and admission is free. The **tourist information center** is in the same building.

Five km south of Musquodoboit Harbour on Petpeswick Road, **Martinique Beach Provincial Park** protects the southern end of Nova Scotia's longest beach.

Accommodations in the area include **Salmon River House Country Inn,** 9931 Hwy. 7 (at Salmon River Bridge, just east of Musquodoboit Harbour), tel. 902/889-3353 or 800/565-3353, www.salmonriverhouse.com, occupying historic premises built circa 1855. The inn's six rooms, each with a private bath, rent for $68–124 a night. Two rooms feature whirlpool tubs. The inn is open April–November, as is its licensed dining room.

## Jeddore Oyster Pond to Liscomb Mills

The **Fisherman's Life Museum,** 58 Navy Pool Loop, in the village of Jeddore Oyster Pond just off Highway, tel. 902/889-2053, re-creates the life of an inshore fisherman in the early 1900s in a rustic homestead; it's open June to mid-October, Mon.–Sat. 9:30 A.M.–5:30 P.M., Sun. 1–5:30 P.M. Admission free.

**Clam Harbour** has an excellent white-sand beach—part of the Eastern Shore Seaside Park system. The beach has a lifeguard, changing rooms, picnic areas, and in mid-August a sand-sculpting contest.

Marine Drive skirts the granite-bound coastline at **Ship Harbour,** a tiny mussel-fishing burg. Thousands of white buoys on the bay indicate the location of the "collectors," specially designed nets on which the mollusks develop. Suspended just under the water's surface, the mussels grow faster than normal, and are sweet and free of grit and sand.

Back on Marine Drive, a few other fishing towns line the highway: Murphy Cove, Pleasant Harbour, and **Tangier,** site of Atlantic Canada's first gold mine, where gold was discovered in 1858. Mining still goes on here, but these days Tangier is best known for the smokehouse of **J. Willy Krauch and Sons,** tel. 902/772-2188. The smokehouse's retail shop stocks delicious smoked salmon, mackerel, and eels; it's open year-round, Mon.–Fri. 8 A.M.–6 P.M., Sat.–Sun. 10 A.M.–6 P.M. Tangier is also the place to get outfitted for sea kayaking and canoeing. Call **Coastal Adventures,** tel. 902/772-2774, for lessons, equipment, and information on tripping around the coastline. The company has been in business over 20 years, offering rentals, guided day trips, extended tours, and a paddlers' retreat B&B with a hot tub.

One-half km east of Spry Bay, **Taylor Head Provincial Park** has a beautiful peninsula-tip location. The park has picnic sections, dunes crossed with boardwalks, and a white sandy beach. For hikers, each parking lot marks trails that probe the coastal woodland, where cormorants nest in windswept spruce, maple, and tamarack.

From Highway 7 at Sheet Harbour, Highway 374 heads north to the **Liscomb Game Sanctuary,** a vast wilderness area set aside for native wildlife and for hiking, camping, canoeing, fishing, bird-watching, and snowmobiling.

## Liscomb Mills and Vicinity

More than 10 small-craft harbors line the coast between Sober Island and Liscomb Mills. The most accessible is Marie Joseph, on the south side of the highway. Another setting for nesting rare species, such as Leach's storm petrel and the black guillemot, is Liscomb Point, a remote peninsula that projects into the ocean an hour beyond Spry Bay.

In Liscomb Mills, the elegant **Liscombe Lodge** on Highway 7, tel. 902/779-2307 or 877/375-6343, www.signatureresorts.com, bills itself a "nature lover's resort" and boasts an idyllic setting along the Liscomb River. Amenities include a pool, sauna, hot tubs, a fitness center, hiking trails, tennis courts, a marina with boat, canoe, and fishing-equipment rentals, and a comfortable dining room overlooking the river. Open mid-May to late October, the resort offers a variety of accommodations, all with private baths; choose from among lodge rooms with balconies and river views ($129 single, $139 double), outlying chalets with fireplaces (from $130), and spacious four-bedroom cottages ($180). Meal plans are available.

## SHERBROOKE AND VICINITY

Highway 7 leaves the coast at Liscomb, turning north to Sherbrooke. Popular among salmon anglers, Sherbrooke is a town of just under 400

people on the St. Mary's River. Most of the town has been restored to its 1800s splendor, and **Sherbrooke Village** on Highway 7, tel. 902/522-2400 or 888/743-7845, fills a sightseeing day with a museum including 25 refurbished buildings that date from the gold-mining years (1860-80). Attractions include an ambrotype photography studio for souvenir pictures on glass, craftspeople demonstrating 19th-century skills, several dining rooms, and a water-powered sawmill. The Courthouse Concert Series, over six Saturday nights in mid-summer, brings the past alive through music and dance. The village is open June to mid-October, daily 9:30 A.M.–5:30 P.M. Admission is $7.25 adults, $6 seniors, $3.75 children, $21 families.

### Accommodations and Food

For overnight stays, Sherbrooke offers several choices. **St. Mary's River Lodge,** adjacent to Sherbrooke Village, tel. 902/522-2177, is open year-round. It has five rooms ($68 single, $78 double) and two nearby housekeeping cottages from $75. Its licensed dining room specializes in Swiss cuisine. Within walking distance of the historic village, **Sherbrooke Village Inn and Cabins,** tel. 902/522-2235, is open April through November. It offers various accommodations, including 14 rooms in the main lodge for $67 single, $77 double, and chalets from $87.

Campers head to the **Riverside Campground** on Sonora Road (off Highway 7), tel. 902/522-2913. It's open May 15 through October, and offers showers, a Laundromat, fire pits and firewood, a restaurant, and a small grocery store; $12–16 per site.

### Continuing East toward Canso

Through Sherbrooke, Highway 7 cuts inland across Guysborough County to Antigonish, while Highway 211 (Marine Drive) threads eastward through Stillwater Lake, Jordanville, Indian Harbour Lake, Port Hillford, Port Bickerton, and Isaac's Harbour. The Country Harbour Ferry, seven km northeast from Port Bickerton, is the provincial ferry that runs on the hour from the eastern side of Country Harbour and on the

NOVA SCOTIA

half-hour from the western side. From the other side of the ferry, Highway 316 continues along the coast, joining Highway 16 after 70 km.

# CANSO

At the Highway 316/16 junction, turn right and you'll come to Canso, Canada's oldest fishing village (established in 1605), after 16 km. Canso (from a Mi'kmaq word meaning "opposite the lofty cliffs") sits at the opening to the Chedabucto Bay. The town of 1,000 people is minimally equipped for travelers, with banks, a hospital, a museum, a grocery, a few accommodations, and a couple of places to eat.

## Canso Museum: Whitman House

This museum of county history, 1297 Union St., tel. 902/366-2170, in a handsome three-story house, has displays illustrating the history of Guysborough County and Canso, with period furniture, folk art, and early photos. You can get a panoramic view of the town from the widow's walk on the roof. It's open June through September, daily 9 A.M.–6 P.M. Admission is free.

## Grassy Island National Historic Site

A thriving fishing community in the 18th century, this small island lies one km off the eastern tip of the mainland. The visitor center, tel. 902/366-3136, abuts Canso wharf and details the island's history from Louisbourg times to later seafaring years. Free boat service (on demand) from the visitor center's wharf takes sightseers to the island, where self-guided hiking trails lace the historic reserve. It's open June to mid-September, daily 10 A.M.–6 P.M. Admission: adults $2.50, seniors $2, children $1.25.

## Practicalities

**Seabreeze Cottages,** 230 Fox Island Rd., by the sea in the village of Fox Island (eight km from Canso), tel. 902/366-2352 or 877/366-2352, has four cottages ($59–79) and campsites ($12–15) and offers boat and canoe rentals, swimming, hiking, and fishing. Open May–November.

For something to eat, head for the **Oceanmist Restaurant** on Main Street, tel. 902/366-2338, for good seafood chowder.

Canso Museum, 1297 Union St., tel. 902/366-2170, operates as a **tourist information center;** open June–September, daily 9 A.M.–6 P.M.

# Cape Breton Island

"I have travelled around the globe," wrote Alexander Graham Bell, perhaps Cape Breton Island's most renowned transplant. "I have seen the Canadian and American Rockies, the Andes and the Alps, and the Highlands of Scotland; but for simple beauty, Cape Breton outrivals them all."

Because of its topographical diversity, think of Cape Breton as two separate islands, which it very nearly is. The smaller, eastern part consists of lowlands and rolling hills, with deeply indented Sydney Harbour on its northern coast. The western island is Cape Breton's tourist mecca. Green, steeply pitched highlands begin at the sea in the south and sweep north, cut by salmon-filled rivers. As the elevation increases, the Acadian and boreal forests give way to a taiga tableland of windswept, stunted trees. The western and eastern parts are linked together by a slender isthmus less than a kilometer wide at St. Peters.

In the far northern part of the island, magnificent Cape Breton Highlands National Park stretches from coast to coast, as wild and remote as the Highlands of Scotland. The windswept Cabot Trail, a world-famous, 294-km scenic highway, clings to the park's edges. Nova Scotia's highest point, 532-meter North Barren Mountain, soars within the park near Ingonish.

The Northumberland Strait opens into the Gulf of St. Lawrence on the western coast, while the Atlantic washes the opposite shore. The 1,098-square-km Bras d'Or Lakes forms the island's heart. The saltwater "Arm of Gold," though barely

Black Brook Cove, Cape Breton Highlands National Park

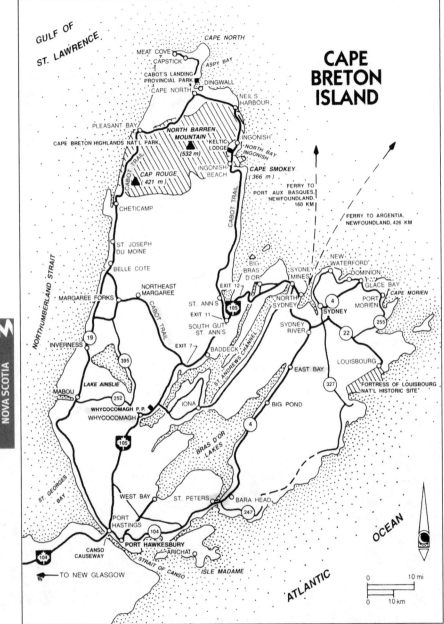

CAPE BRETON ISLAND

influenced by tidal cycles, is an inland arm of the Atlantic consisting of a sapphire blue main lake with numerous peripheral channels, straits, and bays. The two island sections wrap around its edges, connected by bridges, causeways, and ferries.

# The South

## Heading Up Island

Mainland Nova Scotia's roads and highways converge at 1,385-meter-long Canso Causeway, across which all land traffic arrives to reach Cape Breton Island. In addition to linking the island to the mainland, the Canso Causeway—opened in 1955 and created by dumping millions of tons of rock into the strait—blocks ice from getting into the Strait of Canso.

Highways 104 and 105 (the TransCanada) and Highway 19 fan out across the island from here. Highway 19 follows the west coast up to Mabou and Inverness, then links up with the Cabot Trail in the Margaree Valley. The TransCanada Highway lies straight ahead, leading through the center of the island to Baddeck and on to North Sydney. The endless stream of buses packed with tourists makes a beeline along this route, connecting with the Cabot Trail at Baddeck. Highway 4 branches off to the right (or take the more direct Highway 104 for the first 28 km), passing the turn-off to Isle Madame, then following Bras d'Or Lakes, en route to Sydney. Highway 104 is the quickest route to Sydney.

## Port Hastings/Port Hawkesbury

There's little in the Port Hastings/Port Hawkesbury area to linger over, but should you need to stay overnight, there's **Keddy's Inn,** at the junction of Highways 104, 105, and 19, tel. 902/625-0460 or 800/561-7666, www.keddys.ca. It's open year-round, with 70 units and a licensed dining room. Rates are $50–80. Also in Port Hastings, the Auberge Wandlyn **MacPuffin Motel,** a half mile from the causeway down Highway 4 toward Port Hawkesbury, is open April through December; amenities include air-conditioning, full baths, continental breakfast, and an indoor pool. Rates are $79–129; off-season discounts are available. For reservations call 902/625-0621 or 800/867-2212, www.macpuffin.com,

The well-stocked **Visitor Information Centre** is on the right as the TransCanada Highway crosses to the island, tel. 902/625-4201. It's open June–September, daily 9 A.M.–5 P.M. Behind the center, views extend back across to the mainland, and information boards describe the processes involved in constructing the causeway.

## HIGHWAY 4 TO SYDNEY

It's an easy two-hour drive (148 km) from the Canso Causeway to Sydney, via Highway 4 along the southeastern shore of Bras d'Or Lakes. The highway steers away from the lake until passing St. Peters, but if you are planning on overnighting in the area, lakeside **Dundee Resort,** tel. 902/345-2649 or 800/565-1774, www.dundeeresort.com, 12 km from Highway 4, is worth the detour. Set 223 hectares overlooking Bras d'Or Lakes, the resort features motel-style rooms ($75), cottages (from $110), a hot tub, an 18-hole golf course, lighted tennis courts, and a marina with boat rentals. Open May through October.

## Isle Madame

Take Highway 104 for 30 km east from Port Hastings, then Highway 320 south over Lennox Passage Bridge to reach this 43-square-km island. The island takes its name from one of the honorary titles of the queen of France. Founded by French fishermen in the early 1700s, this was one of the first parts of the province to be settled, and it's one of the oldest fishing ports in North America. Isle Madame has four main communities—Arichat, West Arichat, Petit Grat, and D'Escousse.

The wooded island is a popular weekend getaway, with two provincial parks (Lennox Pas-

Arichat Church, Isle Madame

sage to the north and Pondville Beach on the east side) and plenty of picnicking, swimming, and vista spots. In Arichat on the waterfront, **LeNoir Forge Museum,** tel. 902/226-9364, is a restored, working, 18th-century forge open to visitors June–August, daily 10 A.M.–6 P.M.; admission is free.

**L'Auberge Acadienne Inn** on High Road in Arichat, tel. 902/226-2200 or 877/787-2200, www.acadienne.com, is designed as a 19th-century Acadian-style inn, with eight rooms (one with a hot tub) in the main building and nine motel units (from $60 single, $65 double). The licensed dining room serves Acadian dishes, and the inn has bicycles for rent. Another option is **D'Escousse B&B,** tel. 902/226-2936, set on a private beach in D'Escousse, with four rooms with a shared bath for $42 single, $52 double, including full breakfast. It's open mid-May to mid-October.

## St. Peters and Vicinity

This small town lies 48 km east of Port Hawkesbury overlooking the St. Peters Canal, one of two access points for boats entering Bras d'Or Lakes.

The name of Nicolas Denys, the prolific French explorer, merchant, scholar, and author, crops up throughout Atlantic Canada's early history. Denys established one of France's first trading posts at St. Peters, the hamlet alongside the narrow isthmus that links Cape Breton's western and eastern parts. Although Denys is buried in northern New Brunswick, Atlantic Canada's sole museum dedicated to him is the **Nicholas Denys Museum,** 46 Denys St., tel. 902/535-2379, a French-style building reminiscent of the 1650 trading post established here, overlooking St. Peters Canal on Highway 4. It's open June–September, daily 9 A.M.–5 P.M. Admission is 50 cents for adults and 25 cents for kids.

Photography buffs should check out the **MacAskill House Museum,** also in town on Highway 4, tel. 902/535-2531. MacAskill's memorable black-and-white photography depicts the province's seafaring traditions. The museum exhibits a collection of his original photographs; it's open July–August, daily 10 A.M.–6 P.M., September, daily 9:30 A.M.–5:30 P.M. Admission is by donation.

The **MacDonald Hotel,** 9383 Pepperell St.,

just off Highway 4, tel. 902/535-2997, is an old-fashioned hotel with small but cozy rooms, most with shared baths (from $40, with continental breakfast). Rooms over the bar can be noisy until midnight or so. Meals in the dining room—homemade biscuits, seafood, steak, and soup and salad selections—are delicious, and the service is friendly. The hotel is open April–December. Overlooking Bras d'Or Lakes, 1.5 km east of St. Peters, **Joyce's Motel and Cottages,** tel. 902/535-2404, offers accommodations for $50–80. Attractions include a laundry, boating, fishing, and an outdoor swimming pool. It's open mid-May to October.

**Battery Provincial Park,** off Highway 4 one km east of St. Peters, tel. 902/535-3094, has hiking trails and ocean views. Rates are $10 and up for the 52 open, wooded, unserviced campsites. Open mid-June to early September.

### Big Pond

From St. Peters, the run to Sydney takes a little over an hour, with Highway 4 paralleling Bras d'Or Lakes for much of the way. A good halfway-point lunch stop is **Rita's,** in a converted schoolhouse at Big Pond, tel. 902/828-2667, open through summer daily 9 A.M.–7 P.M. Owned by singer Rita MacNeil, who grew up in Big Pond and continues to promote Cape Breton Island around the world, the cafés serves up her own blend of tea, sandwiches, and salads in a country setting. An adjacent room is devoted to her long career.

## HIGHWAY 19 TO THE CABOT TRAIL

### Mabou

A 40-minute drive north up Highway 19 from the Canso Causeway, the town of Mabou (pop. 400) is the center of Gaelic education in Nova Scotia (the language is taught in the local school) and the location of Our Lady of Seven Sorrows Pioneers Shrine. The Mabou Gaelic and Historical Society Museum, or **An Drochaid** (The Bridge), tel. 902/945-2311, focuses on crafts, local music and poetry, genealogical research, and Gaelic culture; open daily 8:30 A.M.–4:30

P.M. In nearby West Mabou and other locales, Saturday-night square dances are held in summer, but the big shindig in these parts is the **Mabou Ceilidh,** a celebration of music and dance, held the closest weekend to Canada Day (July 1). The Mabou Mines area, near the coast, has some excellent hiking trails into a roadless section of the Mabou Highlands.

**The Glenora Inn and Distillery,** nine km north of Mabou on Highway 19, tel. 902/258-2662 or 800/839-0491, www.glenoradistillery.com, is North America's only single-malt whiskey distillery. Better still, it's also a country inn with nine rooms ($109–115), six chalets ($140–200), a dining room (featuring traditional Cape cuisine), and a pub. It's open June 15 through October. Tours are conducted in summer, daily 9 A.M.–5 P.M.

### Inverness

Known for coal mining, this Scottish settlement (pop. 2,000) is the largest town on the west coast. Visitors come for the excellent swimming beaches, windsurfing, and a few shops. The **Inverness Miners Museum,** 62 Lower Railway St., tel. 902/258-2097, gives a slide and film show on local mining history, which dates to 1865. The museum is open June–September, Mon.–Sat. 9 A.M.–7 P.M. Admission is adults $1, children 50 cents.

Free ceilidhs, announced by pipers out front, take place every Thursday evening in the main street fire hall. Nearby, at **Broad Cove,** the annual Broad Cove Scottish Concert offers Highland dancing and music the last Sunday in July at the St. Margaret's Parish Grounds. Admission is $8, and seating is on the grass—bring a picnic blanket or lawn chairs.

**Inverness Beach Village** on Highway 19, tel. 902/258-2653, is open mid-May to mid-October with ocean swimming, horseback riding, tennis, a restaurant with water views, and 41 cottages ($60–110). Camping is also available, with 25 two-way hookup sites and 13 unserviced sites at rates of $15–18. Set on three hectares, **Inverness Lodge Hotel and Motel,** 15787 Central Ave. (Hwy. 19), tel. 902/258-2193, www.invernesslodge.com, is also open May through October. It offers rooms ranging $65–95, a dining room, decks, a patio, and lots of outdoor activities. Ten km north of Inverness on Highway 19 is **MacLeod's Beach Campsite** in Dunvegan, tel. 902/258-2433, www.macleods.com. The campground is open June 15 to October 15, offering 50 sites with full hookups, 25 with two-way hookups, and 69 unserviced sites. Rates range $18–23. Amenities include washrooms, showers, fire pits, a store, a Laundromat, a games room, volleyball, basketball, horseshoes, and more.

## HIGHWAY 105 TO BADDECK

From the Canso Causeway, it's 170 km to Sydney via Baddeck and Highway 105 (TransCanada Highway).

### Whycocomagh

Heading north toward Baddeck on Highway 105 (TransCanada Highway), you'll pass through the town of Whycocomagh, named for a Mi'kmaq word meaning "head of waters." Beyond town is **Whycocomagh Provincial Park,** tel.

902/756-2448. Open mid-June to early September, the park has 61 unserviced sites, a boat launch, and hiking trails. Sites cost $14.

### Iona

Nine km northeast of Whycocomagh, Highway 223 crosses Little Narrows to Iona, then follows the shoreline of St. Andrews Channel all the way to Sydney. It's the least traveled of the many up-island highways, but no less interesting than the other options. The route is posted as Bras d'Or Lakes Drive.

Set on 16 hectares overlooking the narrow body of water between Bras d'Or Lakes and St. Andrews Channel, Iona's **Highland Village,** Hwy. 223, tel. 902/725-2272, features 10 historic buildings as well as many examples of working farm equipment. Admission is adults $5, seniors $4, children $2, families $10. The village is open mid-July to September, 9 A.M.–6 P.M., July–August 9 A.M.–8 P.M.

In a converted convent, **Hector's Arm B&B,** 2504 St. Columbia Rd., Iona, tel. 902/622-1229,

Alexander Graham Bell National Historic Site

is a homey accommodation overlooking the water. Three of the four guest rooms share a bathroom ($70), while a fourth offers an en-suite bathroom ($90).

# BADDECK

Baddeck (from *abadak,* or "place near an island," as the Mi'kmaq called it, referring to Kidston Island just offshore) lies on the misty, wooded shore of St. Patrick's Channel, a long inlet of Bras d'Or Lakes. Halfway between the Canso Causeway and Sydney, Baddeck also marks the traditional beginning and ending point for the Cabot Trail.

Once a major shipbuilding center, Baddeck claims as its most famous resident not a sailor but an inventor—Alexander Graham Bell. The landscape, language, and people all reminded the Scotsman of his native land. He built a grand summer home, Beinn Bhreagh (not open to the public), across the inlet from Baddeck and during the next 37 years carried on countless experiments—with kites, aircraft, hydrofoils, communication devices, genetics, medicine, and more—there and on the lake. In 1904, Bell's *Silver Dart* sped over Bras d'Or Lakes for the first airplane flight in the British Empire.

## Sights

At the east end of Baddeck is the **Alexander Graham Bell National Historic Site,** tel. 902/295-2069, a tremendously satisfying museum with displays on Bell's life, family, and seemingly inexhaustible curiosity about science. The multimedia exhibits include working models of Bell's first telephones, a full-size reproduction of his speed-record-setting HD-4 hydrofoil, kite-building workshops in July and August, a children's science program, and evening programs. The museum is open daily year-round, 9 A.M.–5 P.M. (July–August 8:30 A.M.–7:30 P.M.). Admission is $4.25 adults, $3.25 seniors, $2.25 children, $10 families.

A free ferry runs from Government Wharf out to **Kidston Island,** which has nature trails for exploring and a supervised beach.

## Events

Several events keep Baddeck (pop. 1,100) busy through the summer. The multifaceted **Centre Bras d'Or Festival of the Arts,** running from mid-July to the third week in August, celebrates Maritime, Gaelic, and international culture through dance, music, theater, art, workshops, and children's activities at various venues. Call the festival box office at 902/295-3044 or 800/565-0980 for schedules and ticket information. In August, a favorite tradition is the **Baddeck Regatta,** held since 1904.

## Accommodations

Built in 1860, **Telegraph House & Motel,** in central Baddeck on Chebucto Street, tel. 902/295-1100, has 43 rooms and motel units (from $58) and a dining room. Amenities include a library, sitting room, and great views. Open year-round.

Antiques-furnished **Duffus House Inn,** 108 Water St., tel. 902/295-2172, is open June to mid-October. The seven rooms ($95–165, including continental breakfast) have private baths and water views. Amenities include English gardens and a private dock on Bras d'Or Lakes.

**Silver Dart Lodge** on Shore Road, tel. 902/295-2340 or 888/662-7484, www .maritimeinns.com, sits on a 40-hectare hillside overlooking the lake. It offers Scottish entertainment, a licensed dining room, a heated pool, lake cruises, boat rentals, a beach, and hiking trails. It offers 84 units, including standard lodge rooms ($97–115) and chalets ($110–135). On the lodge grounds, **MacNeil House,** tel. 902/295-2340 or 888/662-7484, www.maritimeinns.com, is a renovated 19th-century country inn with six one- or two-bedroom luxury suites ($165–275; from $115 off-season), each with a whirlpool tub, fireplace, and full kitchen. Guests enjoy use of all Silver Dart Lodge facilities. Both accommodations are open May through October.

**Baddeck Cabot Trail KOA,** on Highway 105 eight km west of Baddeck, tel. 902/295-2288 or 800/562-7452, has lake fishing and camping, canoe rentals, a swimming pool, children's activities, and tours. It has over 170 sites ($19–25), including many with full hookups. The riverside campground is open May 15 to October 15 and also offers camping cabins. **Bras d'Or Lakes Campground,** five km west of Baddeck on Highway 105, tel. 902/295-2329, is open May 15 through September, with 89 unserviced and two-way-hookup sites ($16 and up). Located on Bras d'Or Lakes, it has showers, washrooms, a Laundromat, a pool, and a recreation area. **Silver Spruce Vacation Park,** tel. 902/295-2417 or 800/507-2228, has all the necessary amenities—showers, laundry, pool, fishing, restaurant, and tours. It offers 30 sites with full hookups, 45 with two-way hookups, and 10 unserviced sites; rates range $16–23. It's open mid-June to mid-October.

## Food

The popular and acclaimed **Bell Buoy Restaurant,** on Main Street next to the old library, tel. 902/295-2581, serves seafood, steak, and poultry dishes for lunch and dinner daily, May through October.

For breakfast (7–11 A.M.), sandwiches, pizzas, and light meals, the **Yellow Cello** on Chebucto Street, tel. 902/295-2303, is centrally located and well priced, with an indoor dining room and veranda in front. The calzones are delicious, the beer selection is good, and the people-watching can't be beat. It's open daily. Expect a wait in peak summer season.

# Cabot Trail

Nearly every coastal and inland backcountry road on the western half of the island leads eventually to the Cabot Trail, the scenic highway rimming the unforgettable landscape of northwestern Cape Breton. The 294-km route of steep ascents, descents, and hold-your-breath switchbacks has no official beginning or end, nor, unlike every other highway in the province, is it numbered. From the south, enter the route from Highway 395 near Whycocomagh or from exit 7 of the TransCanada Highway, eight km west of Baddeck. The latter option is most scenic, passing through the Margaree River Valley.

## Margaree River Valley

Eight km west of Baddeck, the Cabot Trail winds northwest through the hills and into the valley of the Margaree River, a renowned salmon-fishing stream and the namesake of seven small communities. Mid-June to mid-July and September to mid-October are the best months for fishing, and many guides are available locally. Near northeastern Margaree, **Margaree Salmon Museum,** 60 East Big Intervale Rd., tel. 902/248-2848, displays the history of fishing on the river. It's open mid-June to mid-October, 9 A.M.–5 P.M. Admission is $1 adults, 25 cents for kids.

**Normaway Inn,** near the village of Margaree Valley, tel. 902/248-2987 or 800/565-9463, www.normaway.com, is an elegantly rustic 1920s resort nestled on 100 hectares in the hills. The main lodge has nine rooms, and the grounds hold 19 one- and two-bedroom cabins. Activities include nightly films or traditional entertainment, tennis, walking trails, bicycling, weekly barn dances, and fiddling contests. Rates range from $89–249, depending on meals; discounts apply to stays of two or more nights. The dining room (open for breakfast and lunch) serves dishes of Atlantic salmon, lamb, scallops, and fresh fruits and vegetables. The Normaway is about 30 km along the Cabot Trail from Highway 105, then three km along Egypt Road.

On Lake O'Law in northeastern Margaree, **The Lakes Campsite,** tel. 902/248-2360 or 888/722-2112, is open mid-May to mid-October, with a licensed restaurant, play area, and store stocked with camping and fishing supplies. It offers sites with or without hookups for $15 and up. Recreational opportunities include boating, fishing, canoeing, mini-golf, and go-carting. **Margaree Lodge and Motel,** tel. 902/248-2193 or 877/242-2193, www.margareelodge.com, is at the junction of Highway 19 and the Cabot Trail. It's open June 15 to October 15, with a licensed lounge, dining room, and pool. The 40 units with private baths run $65–89. In Margaree Harbour, the **Duck Cove Inn,** tel. 902/235-2658 or 800/565-9993, www.duckcoveinn.com, offers 24 motel rooms with private baths from $65 single, $70 double, including continental breakfast. Amenities include a licensed dining room, canoeing, and great area fishing. Open June through October; discounts available before June 30 and after October 12.

## CHÉTICAMP

Chéticamp is an Acadian fishing village (pop. 1,000) and tourism center offering accommodations, restaurants, a museum, craft shops, beaches, and golfing. Deep-sea fishing and whale-watching charter boats leave from the central Government Wharf, and the entrance to Cape Breton Highlands National Park is five km north of town.

The village was settled by Acadians expelled from the Nova Scotia mainland in the 18th century; today, the weeklong **Festival de l'Escaouette,** held the weekend closest to August 1, celebrates aspects of Acadian culture, with a parade, arts and crafts, and music. The first stones for **St. Pierre Catholic Church** were laid in 1893, but it took almost 20 years to finish. Its tower pierces the sky at a height of over 50 meters and can be seen from far up and down the coast. The **Acadian Museum,** 744 Main St., on the highway near the south end of Chéticamp, tel. 902/224-2170, displays artifacts from early settler days, with an emphasis on the sheepherding past, including weaving, spinning, and rug-hooking demonstrations. Open mid-May to mid-June, 9 A.M.–6 P.M., mid-June through September 9 A.M.–9 P.M., October, 9 A.M.–6 P.M. Admission is by donation.

### Arts and Crafts

One of the major cottage industries of this area is the production of hooked rugs, a craft developed by Acadians centuries ago. In the late 1930s, a group of Chéticamp women formed a rug-hooking cooperative that still thrives. The Co-op Artisanale de Chéticamp gives demonstrations and displays its wares at the Acadian Museum. You can also see beautiful hooked rugs and tapestries at **Les Trois Pignons,** 15584 Main St., tel. 902/224-2612 or 902/224-2642, a striking red-roofed building at the northern end of Chéti-

camp (the building also houses the visitor information center). Admission is $3.50 adults, $3.25 seniors and children 12–18, under 12 free.

A number of galleries and shops hereabouts also sell locally produced folk arts—brightly colored, whimsical carvings and paintings of fish, seabirds, fishermen, boats, or whatever strikes the artist's fancy. One km north of the visitor center, the **Sunset Art Gallery,** tel. 902/224-2119, features the colorfully painted woodcarvings of Bill Roach.

### Cruises and Charters

At Government Wharf, **Whale Cruisers,** tel. 902/224-3376, operates two vessels, the *Whale Cruiser* and the *Bonnie Maureen III,* which take guests out on three-hour whale-watching trips three times daily July to mid-September and less frequently in May, June, and late September. Fare is adults $28, children $12. **Acadian Whale Cruise,** La Chaloupe Wharf, tel. 902/224-1088 or 877/232-2522, operates the *Cabot Trail II* on whale-watching cruises three times daily from mid-May through mid-September. The fare is adults $28, children $12.

### Accommodations and Camping

On Main Street, **Fraser's Motel and Cottage,** tel. 902/224-2411, is central and a good value, with five simple but comfortable motel units ($55–65) and one housekeeping cottage ($60) right by the main wharf. It's open mid-May to mid-October. Across the road, **Laurie's Motor Inn,** tel. 902/224-2400 or 800/959-4253, www.lauries.com, offers a three-building complex with 55 motel rooms and suites ($85–175), a licensed dining room and lounge, a playground, and guest laundry facilities. The motel rents bicycles and offers three-hour sightseeing cruises aboard its own two vessels. It's open April through October. On the edge of town and beside the golf course, **Cabot Trail Sea & Golf Chalets,** tel. 902/224-1777 or 877/244-1777, is a complex of modern self-contained units, each with a bathroom, kitchen, deck, and barbecue. Rates range $89–149 for up to four people.

**Germaine's Bed & Breakfast,** tel. 902/224-3459, has sea views and beach access in Point

NOVA SCOTIA

## CAPE BRETON HIGHLANDS NATIONAL PARK CAMPGROUNDS

The following campgrounds are listed in a clockwise direction from the park entrance north of Chéticamp. For reservations, contact Parks Canada, tel. 902/224-2306 or 888/773-8888, www.parkscanada.ca.

**Chéticamp Campground,** five km north of Chéticamp; open mid-May to early October; wheelchair access, fishing, hiking, playground, visitor center; 162 sites; tent sites $15–17, serviced sites $17–21, overflow $15.

**Corney Brook Campground,** eight km north of park entrance; open mid-May to early Oct.; oceanfront camping, unsupervised beach; 20 sites, no reservations; $17.

**Big Intervale Campground,** 15 km east of Pleasant Bay; riverside camping, hiking; open mid-May to early Oct.; 10 sites, no reservations; $15.

**MacIntosh Brook Campground,** five km east of Pleasant Bay; open mid-May to mid-Oct.; wilderness setting, hiking; 10 sites, no reservations; $15.

**Broad Cove Campground,** Ingonish; open mid-May to early Oct.; swimming, hiking, interpretive program; 173 sites; tent sites $15–17, serviced sites $17–21, overflow $15.

**Igonish Campground,** Ingonish Beach; open July to early Sept.; wheelchair accessible, walk to beach, hiking; 90 sites; $15–17.

Cross, eight km south of Chéticamp. Rates are $50 single, $60 double, with full breakfast. Open May through October. Also in the Point Cross area, **Chéticamp Outfitters Inn,** tel. 902/224-2776, offers great views, bicycle rentals, and sporting guide service. Two of the six rooms have private baths. Rates of $55 single, $85 double include full breakfast. Open April–December.

**Plage St Pierre Campground,** tel. 902/224-2112, www.plagestpierre.com, is on Île de Chéticamp (Chéticamp Island), connected by a causeway to the southern end of the village. It has a good sandy beach, open, wooded, serviced and unserviced sites (from $18), showers, mini-golf, and volleyball courts. Open May to mid-September. Farther afield, **Chéticamp Campground,** tel. 902/224-2306, is a few kilometers north of Chéticamp at the southern entrance to Cape Breton Highlands National Park. It's open year-round, with sites ranging $15–21.

### Food

At the north end of town, **Hometown Kitchen,** 15559 Main St., tel. 902/224-3888, is right on the water, but doesn't really take advantage of the location. The food is good, though, with generous portions and inexpensive prices. Expect lots of seafood.

Dine at the **Restaurant Acadien,** 774 Main St., tel. 902/224-3207, for authentic Acadian food: *fricot,* meat pies, fresh fish, blood pudding, and butterscotch pie. Entrées range $10–20. It's open May to October, daily 7 A.M.–10 P.M. **Evangeline,** 15150 Main St., in Chéticamp on the Cabot Trail, tel. 902/224-2044, is a family restaurant specializing in homemade soups and meat pies. Open daily 6:30 A.M.–midnight year-round.

### Information

**Chéticamp Visitor Information Centre,** on the north side of town at 15584 Main Street, tel. 902/224-2642, has information on tours, accommodations, and campgrounds. For national park information, continue into the park to the large visitor center.

## CAPE BRETON HIGHLANDS NATIONAL PARK

Outside Chéticamp, the Cabot Trail begins to climb and enters Cape Breton Highlands National Park five km northeast of town. The park is open year-round, though most facilities operate (and an entry fee is charged) from mid-May to late October. The single-day entry fees are $3.50 adults, $2.50 seniors, $1.50 children (under 6 free), $8 families. A four-day pass costs three times the single-day amount.

## The Land

Heath bogs, a dry rocky plateau, and a high taiga 400 meters above sea level mark the interior of the 950-square-km park. Rugged cliffs characterize the seacoast on the west side, where the mountains kneel into the Gulf of St. Lawrence, and gentler but still wildly beautiful shores define the eastern side.

Typical Acadian forest, a combination of hardwoods and conifers, carpets much of the region. Wild orchids bloom under the shade of thick spruce, balsam fir, and paper birch. The **Grand Anse River** gorge near MacKenzie Mountain is the Acadian forest's showpiece. Its terrain—with sugar maples, yellow birches, and rare alpine-arctic plants—has been designated an international biological preserve. The park is also a wildlife sanctuary for white-tailed deer, black bear, beaver, lynx, mink, red fox, snowshoe hare, and more than 200 bird species, including eagles and red-tailed hawks.

## Hiking

The park offers 26 established hiking trails, ranging from simple strolls shorter than half a kilometer to challenging treks leading to campgrounds more than 20 km away. Many of the trails are level; a few climb up to awesome viewpoints. Some hug the rocky shoreline; others explore river valleys. No matter what your abilities may be, you'll be able to enjoy the park at your own speed.

On the light side, the self-guiding **Le Buttereau** trail leads 1.9 km to wildflowers and good bird-watching opportunities. The **Bog** hike, only 0.6 km and wheelchair accessible, takes you to view the unusual insectivorous pitcher plants, as well as orchids, frogs, and even moose.

For the more hearty, the seven-km **Skyline** loop climbs a headland, from which the lucky can spot pilot whales; along the way, look for bald eagles, deer, and bear. Serious backpackers can take the **Fishing Cove** trail (16 km round-trip), a rugged journey to a campground and beach.

For details on hiking in the park, look for the book *Walking in the Highlands.* Topo maps are available at the park information centers near Chéticamp and at Ingonish Beach.

## Winter Fun

When the snow falls, the park attracts cross-country skiers. To use the groomed trails at Black Brook, Mary Ann Falls, Warren Lake, and Highland Links, you pay $5 per person or $10 per family for a trail pass. These trails are set with both classic and skating tracks. For an extra $2 per person or $4 per family, you get access to an additional 17-km trail system at Cape North and a 12-km system at the end of South Ridge Road. Winter camping is available in your tent at $10 a night, or in one of three shelters for $15–30 a night. For more information, call the Ingonish Warden Office at 902/285-2542. For snow and trail conditions call 902/285-2549.

## Park Information Centre

Turn right as soon as you cross into the park for the excellent Park Information Centre, tel. 902/224-2306. It features natural history exhibits, weather reports, an activities schedule, and helpful staff. Part of the complex is **Le Amis du Plein Ar,** tel. 902/224-3814, a surprisingly large bookstore, with over 1,000 titles in stock.

## North to Pleasant Bay

Within a few kilometers of the west entrance, the highway swoops up again, framed by the boiling gulf surf and **Cap Rouge,** the 421-meter-high inland headland.

At Pleasant Bay, 38 km north along the coast from the park entrance, the **Whale Interpretive Centre,** tel. 902/224-1411, is a good place to learn about the 16 species of whales present in local waters. Admission is adults $4.50, seniors and children $3.50. The center is open May–September 9 A.M.–6 P.M. Below the interpretive center and at the nearby harbor are many whale-watching operators, including **Wesley's Whale Watching,** tel. 902/224-1313 or 866/273-2593. Local guides boast a high success rate when it comes to spotting whales, simply due to the high numbers in local waters.

## Continuing Around the Cape

From Pleasant Bay, the park's northwestern corner, the highway turns inland and wraps upward to 455-meter-high **French Mountain.** From this point, a level stretch barrels across a narrow ridge overlooking deeply scooped valleys. The road climbs up again, this time to **MacKenzie Mountain,** at 372 meters, then switchbacks down a 10–12 percent grade. Another ascent, to **North Mountain,** formed more than a billion years ago, peaks at 445 meters on a three-km summit. The lookout opens up views of a deep gorge and the North Aspy River.

## Cape North and Vicinity

The northernmost point on the Cabot Trail is Cape North. The 19-km road that connects Cape North and Capstick on St. Lawrence Bay rises and dips, affording dizzying ocean views and mountain scenery. En route, **Cabot's Landing Provincial Park,** the supposed landing site of English explorer John Cabot, offers a sandy beach on Aspy Bay (good for clam digging) and a picnic area, and marks the starting point for hikes up 442-meter-high Sugar Loaf Mountain. Whale-watching tours on the northernmost tip of the cape can be arranged at the town of Bay St. Lawrence, four km north.

If boat tours, swimming, whale-watching, and mountain climbing sound appealing, the privately operated **Meat Cove Campground** in Meat Cove, tel. 902/383-2379, is the place to experience the island's raw, northernmost extremity. The campground, overlooking the ocean at road's end, has 25 unserviced campsites ($15 and up).

Set on 25 hectares of oceanfront property, **Markland Coastal Resort,** tel. 902/383-2246 or 800/872-6084, www.marklandresort.com, is in Dingwall, five km off the Cabot Trail. Amenities include gourmet dining, a pool, a playground, and a private beach. Rates are $90–225. Markland is open May to late October.

## Ingonish and Vicinity

From Cape North, the highway heads east to Neil's Harbour and then south past Black Brook Cove's white-sand beach. Clusters of seaports along North Bay are the first signs of civilization. Ingonish (pop. 500) was settled by the Portuguese in the early 1500s, then later by the French, who called it Port d'Orleans. They abandoned the once-vibrant seaport after the destruction of Louisbourg. Today Ingonish is a resort town in operation throughout the year and the eastern entry point for the national park.

Accommodation options include **Sea Breeze Cottages and Motel,** tel. 902/285-2879 or 888/743-4443, eight km north of the national park entrance. It's open year-round. Rates for the cabins, motel units, and cottages range $55–120. **Ingonish Chalets,** tel. 902/285-2008 or 888/505-0552, has access to the beach and hiking trails. Seven two-bedroom log housekeeping chalets go for $129, while five motel suites cost $84. Open year-round.

The Cabot Trail has its devoted fans, and so does the **Keltic Lodge,** tel. 902/285-2880 or 877/375-6343, www.signatureresorts.com, on Middle Head Peninsula. The access lane from the Cabot Trail meanders through thick stands of white birches and finishes at the lodge. The long, low, wood-sided lodge—painted bright white and topped with a bright red roof—is as picturesque as a lord's manor in the Highlands of Scotland. The main lodge has 32 rustic rooms off a comfortable lobby, furnished with overstuffed chairs and sofas arranged before a massive stone fireplace. Another 40 rooms are in the adjacent, newer White Birch Inn. In addition, nine cottages with suite-style layouts (nice for families) are scattered across the grounds. Most guests stay as part of a package, costing from $150 per person per night, inclusive of meals. The lodge is open June through October during tourist season and January through March for cross-country skiers.

Of the lodge's two dining rooms, the formal **Purple Thistle Dining Room** (tie and jacket required) has one of Nova Scotia's finest reputations, especially in seafood. Meals are five courses (about $40) rather than à la carte, with an emphasis on lobster in varied creations and other seafood. If you're tooling along Cabot Trail and hope to stop here for dinner, reservations are very wise. Open late May to mid-October. The informal **Atlantic Restaurant** has lighter fare

© ANDREW HEMPSTEAD

**The first rays of sunlight hit Lakies Head, south of Black Brook Cove.**

and lighter prices. It's open mid-May to mid-October.

The lodge also offers numerous recreational opportunities, including the **Highland Links** golf course, tel. 902/285-2600 or 800/441-1118. Designed by Stanley Thompson and dating to the 1930s, Highland Links is generally regarded as one of the world's top 100 golf courses. Its 6,592-yard layout plays to a par of 72 and a challenging slope rating of 141. Regular green fees are $77; twilight rates $58. Well-marked hiking trails meander through the adjacent national park woodlands and ribbon the coastal peninsula. An outdoor pool (a bit chilly) and tennis courts are also available.

South of Ingonish Beach, the Cabot Trail descends hairpin turns. Stop at 366-meter-high Cape Smokey for a picnic or hiking along the cliff top, which has wonderful views. The steep and twisting road finishes in a coastal glide with views of the offshore Bird Islands. Lying off the northwest side of the Cape at the mouth of St. Ann's Bay, these two islands are the nesting site of a multitude of seabird species; boat tours are available out of Big Bras d'Or.

## ST. ANN'S AND VICINITY

During the 1850s, some 900 of St. Ann's residents, dissatisfied with Cape Breton, sailed away to Australia and eventually settled in New Zealand, where their descendants today make up a good part of the Scottish population. Despite this loss of nearly half its population, St. Ann's is today the center of Cape Breton's Gaelic culture.

The only institution of its kind in North America, the **Gaelic College of Celtic Arts and Crafts,** tel. 902/295-3411, holds classes in Highland dancing, fiddling, piping, Gaelic language, weaving, and other subjects. The summer session attracts Gaelophiles from around the world. For four days in mid-August, students and other participants show off these skills at the Gaelic Mod, a grand Scottish cultural celebration held at the college. The **Great Hall of the Clans Museum,** on the college campus, examines the course of Scottish culture and history, including the migrations that brought Highlanders to Cape Breton. Activities include weaving and instrument-making demonstrations, as well as music and dance performances (July and August, Mon.–Fri.). The museum is open mid-June to mid-October, daily 8:30 A.M.–5 P.M. To reach the museum and affiliated crafts shop, call 902/295-3441.

NOVA SCOTIA

# The East

## SYDNEY AND VICINITY

Nova Scotia's second-largest city and Cape Breton's largest, Sydney (population 24,000) dominates the lowlands of the eastern island. The populated area rims the eastern side of Sydney Harbour. The TransCanada Highway—which turns into Highway 125 at North Sydney—provides road access to the city. The highway curves south of the harbor and arrives in town with exits 6, 7, 8, and 9 leading to the main roads.

Sydney Harbour's configuration is similar to Halifax Harbour's, and just as historic Halifax is concentrated on its own peninsula, so is Sydney's first-settled area. The tourist's Sydney, with the island's greatest concentration of hotels and motels, lies along the Esplanade at waterfront, from the peninsula to the promenade's continuation as Kings Road. The shopping district on Charlotte Street is a block inland. Wentworth Park spreads inland off Kings Road and features walking trails and a lake salted with swans.

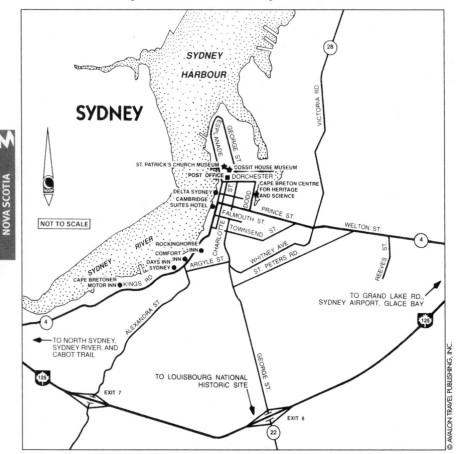

NOVA SCOTIA

© AVALON TRAVEL PUBLISHING, INC.

St. Patrick's Church dates to 1828.

## History

In 1785, Loyalists from New York, and later Scottish Highlanders, settled what was then known as Spanish Bay and renamed it Sydney in honor of England's colonial secretary, Lord Sydney. For the next 35 years, the seaport was the capital of the colony of Cape Breton, until it was united with mainland Nova Scotia in 1820.

Sydney became known as Nova Scotia's Steel City in 1901. Boston entrepreneur Henry Melville Whitney established Dominion Coal and quickly enlarged the operation to include steel production. The Sydney area boomed, and the city ranked as Canada's third-largest steel producer through World War II. Hard times arrived, though, as oil began to displace coal as the industrial fuel of choice. Diminished demand and a half-century of strikes closed the Dominion Mines in 1967. The federal government countered by forming the Cape Breton Development Corporation (DEVCO), a Crown corporation with three operating mines, and the province created Sydney Steel Corporation (SYSCO).

## Sights

**St. Patrick's Church Museum,** 87 Esplanade, tel. 902/562-8237, in Cape Breton's oldest Roman Catholic sanctuary, a Pioneer Gothic–style church built in 1828, showcases the city's history. It's open June–August, Mon.–Sat. 9:30 A.M.–5:30 P.M., Sunday 1–5:30 P.M.; admission is by donation.

**Cossit House Museum,** 75 Charlotte St., tel. 902/539-7973, is almost as old as Sydney itself. The 1787 manse, home to the Reverend Ranna Cossit, Sydney's first Anglican minister, has been restored to its original condition, and costumed guides give tours. It's open June to mid-October, Mon.–Sat. 9:30 A.M.–5:30 P.M., Sun. 1–5:30 P.M. Admission is by donation.

The **Cape Breton Centre for Heritage and Science,** 225 George St., tel. 902/539-1572, offers displays on the social and natural history of eastern Cape Breton, art exhibits, and films. It's open June–September, Mon.–Sat. 9:30 A.M.–5:30 P.M., Sunday 1–5:30 P.M.; the rest of the year Tues.–Fri. 10 A.M.–4 P.M., Sat. 1–4 P.M. Admission is free.

## Accommodations

Right downtown, **Delta Sydney,** 300 Esplanade,

NOVA SCOTIA

tel. 902/562-7500 or 800/268-1133, www .deltahotels.com, is a well-designed, comfortable high-rise with over 150 rooms (from $109), a licensed dining room, indoor pool, whirlpool, sauna, exercise room, and gift shop. Also centrally located is **Cambridge Suites Hotel,** 380 Esplanade, tel. 902/562-6500 or 800/565-9466, www .centennialhotels.com, another nice high-rise, with 150 self-contained units and a licensed restaurant. On the roof level are a pool, sauna, exercise room, and sundeck. Studios cost $109, one-bedroom suites $119, and two-bedroom suites $129.

The following accommodations are south of downtown, along the main access into downtown. The **Rockinghorse Inn,** 259 Kings Rd., tel. 902/539-2696 or 888/664-1010, www .rockinghorse-inn.com, is a registered heritage property furnished with antiques. Open year-round, it offers a full breakfast, a sunroom, and a library. Rates are $70–110 single, $80–120 double. **Cape Bretoner Motor Inn,** 560 Kings Rd., tel. 902/539-8101 or 888/793-9555, is set back from the busy road with 71 rooms ($75–95), a dining room, lounge, and indoor pool. **Comfort Inn,** 368 Kings Rd., tel. 902/562-0200 or 800/228-5150, www.choicehotels.ca, overlooks the waterfront two km south of downtown with 62 rooms (from $77 single, $82 double, with morning coffee and newspaper). **Days Inn Sydney,** 480 Kings Rd., tel. 902/539-6750 or 877/834-0333, www.daysinnsydney.com, completes Sydney's high-rise hotel contingent with 167 rooms and junior suites ($109–129 single, $119–139 double) overlooking the harbor. It also offers a restaurant, lounge, indoor pool, whirlpool, sauna, and exercise equipment.

## Food

**Joe's Warehouse,** 424 Charlotte St., tel. 902/539-6686, began as a converted Canadian Tires warehouse. It's spacious enough to accommodate crowds, who come for the specialty prime rib and New York strip steak; weekend reservations are wise. Open daily year-round, for dinner nightly and for lunch Mon.–Sat.

**Jasper's Family Restaurant** at George and Dorchester streets, tel. 902/539-7109, is one of three local Jaspers restaurants. It's a trusty, reliable place with summer lobster in the shell, seafood, and steak; open daily 24 hours.

The major hotels all have dining rooms tending toward steak and seafood. Reservations recommended.

## Entertainment and Events

The **Vogue Theatre,** 392 Charlotte St., tel. 902/564-8221, presents movies nightly, as does **Empire Theatres,** an octoplex at 325 Prince Street, tel. 902/539-9049. **Centre 200,** 481 George St., tel. 902/595-2130, brings in concerts and large shows; check the billboard for current events. You can watch big-screen sports television at **Steel City Sports Bar,** 252 Townsend St., tel. 902/562-4501.

**Smooth Herman's,** tel. 902/539-0408, downstairs at Joe's Warehouse at 424 Charlotte Street, has been around for years and lures a chummy bar crowd with nightly dancing, Mon.–Sat. to 3 A.M. The major hotels all have lounges catering to older, tamer crowds and tourists.

The **Festival on the Bay** puts on live theater and cabaret, late June–August, while the eight-day **Action Week** has town-fair trappings during early August.

## Information and Services

The local **information center** is a five-minute drive from the Sydney harbor at 220 Keltic Drive, Sydney River, tel. 902/539-9876. It's open year-round, Mon.–Fri. 9 A.M.–5 P.M., July–August 8:30 A.M.–7:30 P.M. **McConnell Memorial Library,** 50 Falmouth St., tel. 902/562-3161, is open Tues.–Fri. 10 A.M.–9 P.M., Sat. to 5:30 P.M. The daily *Cape Breton Post* newspaper circulates in Sydney and throughout Cape Breton.

**Cape Breton Regional Hospital** is at 1482 George Street, tel. 902/567-8000. For the **RCMP** call 564-7171, or 911 in emergencies.

Sydney has numerous banks downtown and in shopping malls. **Canada Trust,** 257 Charlotte St., tel. 902/539-3640, is open Mon.–Fri. 8 A.M.–8 P.M., Sat. 9 A.M.–5 P.M. **Bank of Nova Scotia** has a branch at 258 Charlotte Street. **Canada Post,** 75 Dodd St., tel. 902/564-7400, is open Mon.–Fri. 8 A.M.–5 P.M.

**Vogue Cleaners,** 470 Prince St., tel. 902/539-1250, has a launderette; it's open Mon.–Fri. 8 A.M.–10 P.M., Sat. to 9 P.M., Sun. to 5 P.M.

## Transportation

Sydney Airport is served by **Air Nova/Air Canada,** tel. 902/539-7501 or 888/247-2262, with flights from Halifax. **Air St. Pierre,** tel. 902/562-3140, flies twice weekly to and from St-Pierre, in St-Pierre and Miquelon. The airport is 14 km northeast of town; a taxi ride costs about $10 per person.

**Avis** and **Budget** have car-rental counters at the airport and offices in town.

**Briand's Taxi,** tel. 902/564-6151, is one of numerous Sydney taxi outfits; rides in town are metered and start at around $2. **Transit Cape Breton,** tel. 902/539-8124, provides public bus service in Sydney and area towns, Mon.–Sat. 7 A.M.–11 P.M. **Acadian Lines,** 99 Terminal Rd., tel. 902/564-5533, is open daily 6:30 A.M.–1 A.M. and has luggage-storage lockers; buses run regularly from Sydney to Baddeck and Chéticamp.

## North Sydney

North Sydney, 25 km from Sydney, is the terminus for Marine Atlantic ferries to Port aux Basques (year-round) and Argentia (mid-June to October only) in Newfoundland. The former takes 5–7 hours, depending on the season, with up to 16 crossings per week year-round (adults $22, seniors $20, children $11, vehicles from $67). The latter, to Argentia, takes around 14 hours, with two crossings per week (adults $60, seniors $55, children $30, vehicles from $135). Marine Atlantic contacts are tel. 902/794-5254 or 800/341-7981, www.marine-atlantic.ca.

The **Best Western North Star Inn,** 39 Forrest St., tel. 902/794-8581 or 800/561-8585, www.bestwestern.com, is next to the ferry terminal. It's open year-round, with a licensed dining room, a lounge, and a whirlpool. Rates are $96–110 for rooms; $200–275 for suites.

## Glace Bay

Glace Bay, 21 km northeast of Sydney, is the former heart of Cape Breton's once-flourishing coal-mining industry. As early as the 1720s, the French exploited the area's extensive bituminous deposits, digging coal to serve the new capital of Louisbourg and initiating North America's first commercial coal-mining enterprise. Much of the reserves lie below the Atlantic, and the submarine seams have been worked as far as 15 km offshore. The industry supported a population of 28,000 in the 1960s, but Glace Bay has since shrunk to 19,500, which still makes it Cape Breton's fourth-largest community.

Today, the **Miners' Museum** is the main attraction for visitors. Retired miners guide you on an underground tour of a real mine, the Ocean Deeps Colliery, to show the rough working conditions under which workers manually extracted coal. The adjacent Miners' Village recreates a miner's modest home, circa 1850–1900, and company store of the same period. A new attraction is a simulated, multimedia trip into the workings of a modern mine, using laser-disc projection and other special effects. On Tuesday evenings, the Men of the Deeps, a local singing group comprised of miners, gives concerts at the museum. The Miners' Museum, tel. 902/849-4522, is at 42 Birkley Street, at Quarry Point, 1.6 km from central Glace Bay via South Street. It's open year-round: June to early September, daily 10 A.M.–6 P.M. (till 7 P.M. on Tuesday); the rest of the year weekdays 9 A.M.–4 P.M. Admission is adults $4.50, children $2.50.

Glace Bay's other claim to fame is that the "Wizard of Wireless," Guglielmo Marconi, sent the first west-to-east trans-Atlantic wireless message from here on December 15, 1902. The **Marconi National Historic Site,** on Timmerman Street at Table Head, tel. 902/295-2069, explains Marconi's experiments and achievements and features a model of the original wireless radio station. It's open June to mid-September, daily 10 A.M.–6 P.M. Admission is free.

# FORTRESS OF LOUISBOURG

After their defeat by the British at Port Royal in 1713, the French regrouped on Île Royale (Cape Breton Island), which they were allowed to keep under the terms of the Treaty of Utrecht. By 1720, their new capital, Louisbourg, was underway. It was planned not only as a fortified military center but also as their embodiment of a new Paris—France's governmental, commercial, and cultural center in the New World—situated on an uncomplicated small harbor fronting the Atlantic.

The dream might have worked. Louisbourg, with its transplanted French culture and social hierarchy, fed by trade from France, survived untouched by British reprisals for more than 20 years. Life in the French outpost went along placidly for the 2,000 transplanted French inhabitants, whose numbers swelled to 5,000 when ships from abroad were in port. But they lived with a sense of anxiety and expected England's invasion at any time.

In 1745, England struck for the first time, with horrendous force. The British Royal Navy blockaded the harbor. A massive volunteer militia led by a merchant from Maine pounded the seaport for seven weeks. Louisbourg fell, and the French were deported.

England controlled Louisbourg until 1748, when a treaty returned the fortress to France. Under French control, Louisbourg thrived again, but briefly. Led by James Wolfe, English forces attacked the port again in 1758 and Louisbourg fell for the final time.

"Louisbourg must be most effectively, and most entirely, demolished," Prime Minister William Pitt advised in London in 1760. Across the Atlantic, the British forces complied, blowing up every building, bastion, and wall. France's dream of a new Paris lay in ruins, never to rise again as a threat to the British. Some of the stones were used as ship ballast; some were used in buildings such as Government House in Halifax. Sydney's Anglican Church of St. George incorporated Louisbourg stone in its construction in 1785, as did Sydney's Roman Catholic Church of St. Patrick's in 1828.

## The Fortress Grounds

For 200 years, the site was just weeds and piles of rubble. In the 1930s, private individuals established a small museum as a way to help preserve Louisbourg's legacy, but it wasn't until the 1960s, with federal government investment, that massive restoration efforts were undertaken. Today, at **Fortress of Louisbourg National Historic Site,**

Parks Canada has reconstructed 50 of the original 80 buildings, right down to the last window, nail, and shingle, based on historical records. Two of the seven original bastions are in place. The site represents Canada's largest—and most magnificent, many people say—national historic park. The bulk of Louisbourg's $25 million reconstruction took place between 1961 and 1984, and the 10-hectare site is now nearly complete.

Louisbourg reveals itself slowly. The seaport covers 10 hectares, and you can spend the better part of a day exploring. From the visitor center, it's a brief bus ride across fields and marsh to the back of the fortress. You walk from there. The reconstructed fortress and town open a window on New France; they are designed to reflect Louisbourg on a spring day in 1744, the year preceding England's first attack, when the seaport hummed with activity. The houses, fortifications, ramparts, and other structures—as authentically 18th-century French as anything you will find in France—were conceived as a statement of grandeur and power in the New World. Louisbourg's polarized social structure mirrored that of homeland France. The fancy houses lining cobbled lanes belonged to the elite, who ate sumptuous meals on fine china and drank the finest French wines. The simpler houses are the rustic cottages of the working class.

Well-informed guides and animators—portraying soldiers, merchants, workers, and craftspeople—are on hand to answer questions and demonstrate military exercises, blacksmithing, lace making, and other skills. L'Epée Royale and the Hotel de la Marine serve meals with an 18th-century flair, and hungry visitors can buy pastries at the Destouches House, and hearty, freshly baked soldiers' bread at the brick-oven bakery.

The 25 August **Feast of St. Louis** at Louisbourg attracts more than the usual number of sightseers. Celebrations finish with fireworks at 9 P.M.

## Practicalities

Be prepared for walking, and bring a sweater or jacket in case of breezy or wet weather. Louisbourg's reconstructed buildings stretch from the bus stop to the harbor. Remaining ruins lying beyond the re-creation are marked by trails. You can wander on your own or join a tour: usually 10 A.M. and 2 P.M. for English tours and 1 P.M. for the French-language tour.

The Fortress of Louisbourg on Highway 22, tel. 902/733-2280, is open, fully staffed, and operates shuttle bus service in July and August, daily 9 A.M.–6 P.M. In May, June, September, and October, it's open daily 9:30 A.M.–5 P.M. Admission June–September is $11 adults, $8.25 seniors, $5.50 youths, $27.50 families. Admission in May and October is by guided tour only (departs daily 10 A.M. and 2 P.M.); $4.50 adults, $3.50 seniors, $2.25 youths, $11.25 families.

## Nearby Accommodations

Several accommodations are nearby. **Camilla Peck Tourist Home B&B,** 5353 Hwy. 22, tel. 902/733-2649, is a working 100-acre farm on a hilltop eight km from Louisbourg. Three rooms, one with private bath, rent for $40 single, $50 double, including full country breakfast. Open June through mid-October. **Fortress Inn Louisbourg,** 7464 Main St. in Louisbourg, tel. 902/733-2844 or 888/367-5353, www.louisburg.ns.ca, is wheelchair accessible. It's open year-round and has rooms ranging $54–79, a restaurant, and lounge. Overlooking the fort and harbor, **Stacey House B&B,** 7438 Main St., tel. 902/733-2317 or 888/924-2242, is open June through October. It offers four rooms, two with private baths, for $45 (double), including full breakfast.

**Louisbourg RV Park,** tel. 902/733-3631, is a campground on the harbor, open June through September. It offers tenting ($10 per night) and fully serviced sites ($15).

# Prince Edward Island

# Introduction

Canada's smallest province, Prince Edward Island is only about as big as the state of Delaware, or twice the size of Luxembourg. Its shape could be likened to a tattered butterfly, its wings outstretched and poised for flight at the sheltered southern edge of the Gulf of St. Lawrence.

Prince Edward Island, or PEI, is beautifully manicured and predominantly rural. The fields of nodding wheat and neatly combed rows of potato plants that yield the island's agricultural mainstays spread across thousands of acres, interrupted by spanking-white farmhouses and tracts of woodland.

The last ice age is responsible for the ragged shape of the island, which in places seems only tenuously sutured together by slender isthmuses. The retreating ice sheets shoved several chunks of land together to form one landmass. The component parts are still clearly discernible: the island's central part is flanked, for example, with wing-shaped additions on both sides. The configuration is most noticeable at Summerside, which sits on a mere slip of a six-km-wide isthmus connecting the western and central sections. Nowadays, counties mark the province's three parts: Kings County on the east, Queens County in the center, and Prince County on the island's western side.

Just 225 km from end to end (275 km by road), PEI may seem small enough to skim in a long day. But everything is spread out and the roads are narrow, undulating, and sometimes unpaved, forcing you to slow down and move at the island's more leisurely pace.

Over the years, PEI has acquired numerous nicknames. The province is known as the "Birthplace of Canada," a distinction earned in 1864 when representatives of England's colonies in eastern Canada convened for informal meetings in Charlottetown. Those meetings resulted in

Green Gables House, of *Anne of Green Gables* fame, is the island's most popular tourist attraction.

© ANDREW HEMPSTEAD

the creation of the Confederation of Canada three years later. *Fathers of Confederation,* the nationally esteemed painting that marked the event, was painted by island artist Robert Harris.

In literary circles, Prince Edward Island is known as the pastoral Avonlea of island author Lucy Maud Montgomery's *Anne of Green Gables.* This juvenile novel and its sequels, set in the Cavendish area on PEI's gulf seacoast, draws many thousands of visitors from around the world to the area each year—visitors who read the books as children and fell in love with the stories and their setting.

As for the rest of the Atlantic Canadians, they've dubbed PEI "Spud Island," a tribute of sorts to Canada's major producer of table and seed potatoes. Islanders themselves see their fertile province—about half of which is given over to farmland—as the "Garden of the Gulf" or the "Million-Acre Farm."

All of which hardly hints at what it is that attracts nearly three-quarters of a million visitors a year to PEI. The province is a tranquil and harmonious reminder of what the world was like decades ago. Its long, empty roads for biking, quiet woods and trails for hiking, scores of excellent beaches, and several splendid golf courses invite you to enjoy the outdoors. Island cuisine takes full advantage of local produce and the rich surrounding seas. Add summertime dinner theaters and plays, friendly people, shops with quality crafts, and a gentle, lovely landscape, and you'll understand what brings visitors back again and again.

## THE LAND

At its highest, Prince Edward Island rises to a mere 152 meters, at Springton in northern Queens County. Its topography of predominately low, rolling countryside is a result—like the shape of the island—of the ice ages, when the islands were the highest level points on the rim of a plain that extended onto New Brunswick and Nova Scotia. As the ice sheet melted and retreated, it scooped out part of the plain and created the arc-shaped hollow that became Northumberland

Strait. Then it gouged its fingers into the island edges and created fringing coastlines of bays, river estuaries, offshore islets, and dangling peninsulas.

The soil is another ice-age legacy—made up of benevolently light and loamy glacial debris, it's responsible for the province's notable success with agriculture. The soil's color is often a surprise to visitors. Its cinnamon-red hue is yet another ancient heritage, caused by iron-oxide compounds—rust—churned up by the ice sheets. (And the rust will stain clothing, so think twice before sitting on damp soil or red-tinged sand.) The burnished red hue also colors coastal headlands and sandstone cliffs.

## Seacoasts and Ports

The northern coast, along the Gulf of St. Lawrence, is the tourist's PEI. Lucy Maud Montgomery described the foaming perfection to a friend in Scotland in 1906: "Some of our dips were taken in heavy surf. It was the cream of bathing to stand there and let a wave break up around one's neck in a glorious smother of white foam."

The gulf coast forms an almost even, curved line, and the sea sweeps in on a long roll through shallow waters, churning up silt along the way. The waves carry the silt to the shore, so much so that silt deposits clog harbors and river mouths, which must be dredged continually to keep the ports navigable. The north-coast bays are protected by long sand spits and barrier islands.

The gulf coast's most famous stretch lies in Prince Edward Island National Park in northern Queens County. Red cliffs up to 30 meters high peer over the surf, and the sea washes up on pink- and white-sand beaches. Ribbons of wooden boardwalks, bike paths, hiking routes, and roads thread across the slender 40-km-long park.

Along this same stretch of coast, three bays—Tracadie (TRAK-a-dee), Rustico, and New London—are popular with tourists. To the west, Malpeque Bay nearly splits Prince County and gives PEI's Malpeque oysters their name. Mollusk aquaculture began here decades ago. Today, oysters are farmed throughout the bay, helping make PEI Canada's number-one oyster-producing province.

PEI's Northumberland Strait coastline is distinctly different. Its jagged headlands are spliced with the majority of the island's 60 harbors. Charlottetown is situated on its own harbor at the confluence of the wide Hillsborough, North, and West Rivers. It's the province's best-known port and a cruise ship port of call. Summerside, an hour northwest of Charlottetown, ranks as PEI's major produce-shipping port and is protected behind a peninsula. Other major ports include Georgetown—an hour east of Charlottetown and one of the province's oldest deepwater ports—and Souris, the fishing and ferry seaport, 45 minutes beyond Georgetown toward the island's eastern tip.

## CLIMATE

PEI basks in a typical maritime climate with one major exception: its growing season of 110–160 days is Atlantic Canada's longest. Moderated by open seas, frost-free days can extend from late April through mid-October.

Spring is short, lasting from May until mid-June. Summer is pleasant and warm and spans late June through early September. Summer temperatures peak July–August, with highs ranging 18–23° C; an unusually warm day can reach 35° C, while, at the other extreme, some summer days can be cool at just 5° C. Most islanders rarely take the blankets off beds, even during summer.

The island is sun-washed and gleaming during summer. Showers come and go. When clouds move in and unite as a singular dull white sky, expect one to three days of showers. Annual precipitation amounts to 106 centimeters, half of that falling from May to October.

Autumn spans mid-September through October, and brings with it Atlantic Canada's brightest and most dramatic fall foliage. Colors peak from early to mid-October, finishing with a flourish as pre-winter breezes strengthen to full-blown winds that bring the leaves down late in the month.

The island gets more than its share of year-round breezes and winds. Summer breezes can be pleasantly warm, but the pace can occasionally pick up to outright gales, especially during late autumn.

The climate's fast-changing moods can make for dramatic photography. Storms create intensely contrasting sea and land colors; winds churn up the sea floor for waters as red as the soil, and puffy white clouds hurry across a lapis-blue sky. Summer showers enrich the farmlands with glistening freshness.

The island lures very few winter tourists. Winter temperatures can dip from -21 to 6° C after Christmas, and average -7° to 3° C.

## FLORA AND FAUNA

In 1534, the explorer Jacques Cartier described the island as "wonderfully fair, filled with goodly meadows and trees." Cartier's goodly trees were typical Acadian forest, similar to the Great Lakes and St. Lawrence woodlands. Forest variety was plentiful and included spruce, birches, pines, elm, and the regal northern red oak, the provincial tree.

But centuries of downing trees for shipbuilding and clearing land for farms altered the landscape, leaving the island with the least amount of original wilderness of any Canadian province. In the 1950s, the provincial government began to reforest the island. The effort was led by J. Frank Gaudet, the first provincial forester, whose name now graces numerous provincial reforestation projects. For a close-up look at new projects underway, check out the provincial J. Frank Gaudet Tree Nursery, Upton Road at West Royalty, near Charlottetown, tel. 902/368-4700. It's open June–August, Tues.–Fri. 10 A.M.–noon.

The province's six "demonstration woodlots," an outgrowth of the nursery, represent the provincial nursery's work in action. "Woodlots" as an image hardly describes the landscape to the uninitiated; rather, visualize plantations of mixed trees that welcome visitors with hiking trails beneath the leafy canopies.

Late spring and summer's warm temperatures urge columbines, bachelor buttons, pansies, lilacs, wild roses, and pink clover into blossom. The delicate lady's slipper is the provincial flower, most abundant in the shady woods in the Valleyfield area in Kings County. In summer, roadsides are splashed with the color of abundant wildflowers—the white umbels of Queen Anne's lace, yellow daisies, lupine, and the showy spikes of purple loosestrife, a pretty but aggressive and unwelcome pest.

Ruffled grouse, gray partridge, red fox, raccoon, and woodcock are spread throughout the province. Foxes are particularly important. The world's first successful captive breeding of silver foxes occurred in Prince County in the late 1800s.

Hundreds of varieties of birds inhabit PEI and some 303 species migrate through in spring and fall. The noisy blue jay, at home throughout the island, is the official provincial bird. The showiest species is the enormous, stately great blue heron, which summers on the island from May to early August. The rare piping plover may be seen (but not disturbed) on national park beaches. Arctic terns nest along Murray Harbour coastlines.

# HISTORY

## The First Visitors

The island's first visitors were the Mi'kmaq Indians, a branch of the eastern Algonquins. The island was their Abegweit ("land cradled on the waves"), and they summered on the island for centuries. A Mi'kmaq legend relates that Glooscap, a god who roamed the earth as a giant man, fashioned the island out of clay in the shape of a crescent, set its trees and flowers in place, and transported it on his shoulders to its place at the gulf's edge.

Jacques Cartier bumped into the island on his first New World voyage, claimed it for France, and sailed

off to explore the rest of the gulf and the St. Lawrence River. European settlers and subsequent turbulence followed. Queen Anne's War between England and France concluded with the Treaty of Utrecht, which awarded the island to the French. Port la Joye, established in 1719 where Charlottetown Harbour meets Hillsborough Bay, was the island's first settlement. It was the fortified military hub for farms across the island that contributed foodstuffs to the Fortress of Louisbourg on Cape Breton.

## Settlement

In 1755, England deported the Acadians from Acadia (Prince Edward Island, Nova Scotia, and New Brunswick) and swept the area again for Acadians in 1758, after capturing Louisbourg. Port la Joye was renamed Fort Amherst, and the English Crown dispatched surveyor Samuel Holland to survey, parcel out, and name various places and sites on the newly acquired island.

One would think the most logical way to divide the island into counties would be along its own natural divisions. But for reasons known only to himself, Holland chose to ignore PEI's natural configuration. He drew county lines on perplexing slants and added some of the central island to the western county (Prince) and did a cut-and-paste job in the east as well.

Holland laid out Charlotte Town as the capital in 1763. The rest of the island was divided into 67 parcels and sold to absentee landlords at a lottery in England. On the island, tenant farmers worked the land and paid quitrents on leases controlled in England.

Prince Edward Island paid its own way as a self-sustaining outpost of the empire. The island became a separate colony independent of Nova Scotia in 1769, and quitrents paid for the maintenance of the colonial government.

Many Acadians managed to elude the net of deportation, and

Jacques Cartier

the province's contemporary Acadians are the descendants of those resourceful original settlers. Other immigrants followed, and Loyalists fleeing the American Revolution added an Anglo presence in the 1780s. Scotch and Irish emigrants, displaced by land clearances, poverty, and religious persecution in the British Isles, began to arrive in the early 1800s.

## Boom Decades

The thickly wooded island began to change. A road network was laid out by 1850. And by 1860, some 176 sawmills were transforming forests into lumber, greasing the island's economy and providing the raw materials for a thriving shipbuilding industry. The first census in 1798 had counted 4,371 islanders; by 1891, the number had grown to 109,000, close to the current population. Land ownership was a hotly contested, ongoing issue, and by the 1850s many islanders acquired title to their own land. By the time PEI joined the Confederation of Canada, half of the parcels were owned free and clear by the island's residents.

Confederation was another issue. In 1867, the island ducked the first opportunity to unite with the other eastern Canadian colonies but joined in 1873, lured by the promise of federal railroad financing. Two years later, the Land Purchase Act settled the issue of land ownership, and the remaining landowners' parcels were sold to the farmers holding the leases on them.

## The Twentieth Century

PEI flourished during the Great Age of Sail. Charlottetown, as the center of government and commerce, was enriched with splendid stone churches and public buildings. In the early 20th century, silver fox–breeding profits brought riches to western PEI. The lowly lobster, once used as fertilizer, caught the fancy of seafood gourmets and became the leading fisheries product by 1897.

In 1905, Ottawa turned down the provincial request for a tunnel to the mainland. But scheduled ferry service with the mainland started in 1916.

The island's good luck soured as World War I wound down. An epidemic nearly destroyed Malpeque Bay's fledgling oyster industry in 1917. The Great Depression took hold in the 1930s, and the population plummeted to 88,000 as islanders left for work elsewhere in Canada and the United States.

The provincial economy withered, and it was decades before it recovered. Scheduled icebreaker ferry service improved year-round transportation to the mainland in 1947. The confederation centennial in 1964 prompted the federal government to mark the event by establishing the

## ISLAND DEVELOPMENT ISSUES

For land developers, Prince Edward Island is a delectable plum that's ripe for picking. The land lies mainly in farmlands and pleasant woodlands, and developers for years have eyed the province as a gold mine for luxury summer homes, hotels, and resorts. Environmentally conscious islanders have opposed absentee-landlord development and formed watchdog groups, such as **Friends of the Island,** and other environmental committees to keep an eye on development schemes.

Land-use conflicts have pitted farmers, fishermen, and environmentalists against powerful local business and tourism interests, as well as the federal government. The provincial govern-

ment has walked the middle ground between the camps.

After more than a century of debate and three years of construction, Confederation Bridge was completed in spring of 1997. The bridge spans the narrowest part of Northumberland Strait, providing a "fixed link" between the island and the New Brunswick mainland. PEI commercial interests long favored the 13-km bridge, contending that it would move produce to market more efficiently than the ferry system. Tourism interests wanted more tourists. The federal government wanted to improve PEI's overall economy and agreed that the bridge was a key component in realizing this goal.

**Government House, Charlottetown**

Confederation Centre of the Arts in Charlottetown, and the new complex became PEI's proud showplace for theater, art exhibits, and other presentations.

The province today maintains the tranquility associated with a rural countryside. The ravaged woodlands began to be restored by the provincial Forestry Act in 1949. Tourism developed in the 1960s as backcountry roads were paved, and the province added a second ferry service to the mainland. Higher education became more cohesive when Prince of Wales College and St. Dunstan's University were absorbed into the University of Prince Edward Island in the late 1960s.

## GOVERNMENT AND ECONOMY

The province has a parliamentary government with a 32-seat provincial assembly for 16 electoral districts. PEI contributes four parliament members and four senators to the federal government.

Diminutive PEI supplies one third of Canada's supply of potatoes. Half of the crop is grown in Prince County, and the remainder is produced by farms scattered across the province. Local farmers travel abroad to 32 nations to advise their foreign counterparts on varieties and farming methods. The province also ranks first in Canadian oyster production, harvesting 10 million oysters annually and exporting most of them.

The island's beauty may be partially attributed to its agriculture, which accounts for 9.5 percent of the province's gross domestic product (GDP). The sector yields $120 million a year and employs 4,000 islanders on 2,200 farms, each of which averages 140 hectares. Grains, fruits, beef, pigs, sheep, and dairy products are other components of agricultural production.

Fishing is another strong income producer, reeling in $51.9 million annually. Some 2,400 fishermen on 800 vessels ply the sea for lobsters and cod, in addition to oysters. Island blue mussel cultivation is the province's newest aquaculture project—a highly successful venture that has produced mussels freer of salt and sand than their wild counterparts.

Farming and fishing remain crucial, but the economy is slowly changing. Tourist numbers have been growing steadily for the last three decades, but have risen exponentially since the Confederation Bridge opened in 1997. The 1.2 million visitors the island hosted in 2001 injected around $300 million into the local economy.

The province's GDP is about $2.5 billion. Inflation is just under 4 percent, lower than the national average. Unemployment measures

PRINCE EDWARD ISLAND

10–15 percent, due to the seasonal nature of fishing and farming.

## THE PEOPLE

Some 138,000 islanders are dispersed among almost 500 hamlets, villages, towns, and one city, Charlottetown, the provincial capital. Prince Edward Islanders are a special breed of Canadians, no matter their ethnic origin. An easygoing way of life places high on their list of priorities; people here tend to be relaxed, pleasant, and helpful, and are resistant to being hurried or hustled. They're courteous and they expect similar courtesies from their guests—aggressive mannerisms and loudness will get you nowhere.

The island has a youthful population: 40 percent of islanders are under 25 years old. Sixty percent of the people live in the countryside, while most of the others are concentrated in the urban centers of Charlottetown and Summerside.

With 22.8 people per square km, PEI has the highest population density of all the provinces. It's also said to be Canada's most ethnically homogeneous province. Anglos make up 80 percent of the population (a third are Irish and the remainder are Scottish). Acadians represent 16 percent of the population, of whom five percent speak French. The Mi'kmaqs form 4 percent of the population. PEI still lures immigrants, mainly from Ontario, Nova Scotia, and New Brunswick.

Islanders value their ethnic identities. Lineage details are abundant, carefully documented, and available at carefully maintained archives throughout the island, including the **Charlottetown Public Archives,** Coles Building (beside Province House), Richmond St., tel. 902/368-4290.

### Local Idioms

Stay tuned to the expressions islanders use to describe the island. For example, everyone who is not from the island they say is "from away." Prince County has numerous grandiose "fox houses" that were built with silver-fox fortunes decades ago, and if you hear an islander explain that a town has been "foxified," it means that it has a number of such lavish houses. On the roads,

signs warn of "bad bumps," and sometime advise drivers to "squeeze" left or right.

A route on foot through an interesting sightseeing place is called a "walk-about." A "run" is an entrance into a bay through flaking sand dunes. And a "feed" is the most lavish of dinners, usually a bountiful summertime lobster supper at one of the island's community supper halls.

### Religion

Religious affiliations are important to islanders, who are overwhelmingly Christian. More than half are Roman Catholic, and the remainder belong to the Protestant sects, mainly Presbyterian and Anglican.

### Crime

Islanders pride themselves on an almost crime-free environment. Part of the reason is the obvious fact that this is an island; what bank robber wants to wait around for the ferry to make his getaway? A crime of passion may happen every so often, but the most you can expect is minor theft. To eliminate temptation, lock your car, keep your luggage in the trunk, and take cameras and other valuables with you.

## ARTS, CRAFTS, AND SHOPPING

Local artists capture the island in masterful watercolors, acrylics, oils, and sculpture. Local crafts include finely made quilts, knits and woolens, stained glass, jewelry, pewter, pottery, and handsome furniture. The Anne doll is the most popular souvenir, and it's produced in innumerable variations for as little as $20 to as much as $800.

An exquisite handmade quilt costs $400–800—seldom a bargain. But well-crafted quilts are sturdily constructed and will last a lifetime with good care. Sweaters ($75–300) are especially high quality. One of the best sources is **Great Northern Knitters,** tel. 800/565-9665, which operates a factory outlet at West Royalty Industrial Park in Charlottetown, tel. 902/566-5850. It's open year-round, weekdays 10 A.M.–5 P.M. The company owes its origin to the provincial Comprehensive Development Plan. Great

Northern Knitters sells its line of warm, bulky sweaters in two Charlottetown shops and has another store in Nova Scotia, where the crew of the *Bluenose II* adopted one of the styles for their official racing sweater.

Much of the creativity here springs from **Holland College,** the provincial applied-arts school. If you're interested in latest crafts trends, check out the college's gallery in Charlottetown.

The **P.E.I. Crafts Council** is another driving force. It counts about 100 provincial craftspeople among its esteemed ranks. **Island Crafts Shop,** 156 Richmond St. in Charlottetown, tel. 902/892-5152, functions as the council members' outlet; if you're interested in locating council crafts producers, ask for a membership list with shop or studio addresses and phone numbers.

## Shopping Hours

In tourist areas, shops generally open daily between 8 and 10 A.M. and close between 8 and 10 P.M. Stores catering to islanders are normally open Mon.–Sat. from about 9 A.M. to 5 P.M.; most stores stay open until 8 or 9 P.M. on Friday nights. From late May to early September, provincial liquor stores at 16 locations are open Mon.–Fri. 10 A.M.–10 P.M.; most close Saturday at 6 P.M., while Charlottetown Mall and Oak Tree Place outlets are open until 10 P.M.

# ENTERTAINMENT AND EVENTS

## Charlottetown Festival

The province enthusiastically promotes this event, and it's worth it; an island visit without seeing *Anne of Green Gables* is like bread without butter. The Anne musical is just one of a number of theatrical, cabaret, and musical productions staged concurrently mid-June to early September in the capital's sumptuous **Confederation Centre of the Arts** and smaller nearby theaters.

## Other Events

Scores of local and regional events fill the province's festival calendar; the provincial *Visitors Guide* lists each and every event across the island, in chronological order. Some of the best are listed here.

Most major events take place in the capital, Charlottetown. Early in the year these include the **Spring Wine Festival** on the last weekend of May and the **Biggest Backyard Barbeque** along the waterfront in mid-June. In late June Summerside hosts the **Highland Gathering.** Also in late June is the **Montague Homecoming Festival,** a typical small-town get-together with a parade, Celtic music, and fun events such as log-rolling.

On July 1, **Canada Day** culminates on the Charlottetown waterfront with the **Festival of Lights.** Mid-July brings the **Strawberry Festival** at Orwell Corner (a provincial historic site that marks the early settlement), the **PEI Bluegrass & Old-Time Music Festival** in rural Rollo, and Summerside's **Lobster Carnival,** which attracts hungry lobster fans to its week of festivities. Mid-August's **PEI Provincial Exhibition,** Atlantic Canada's largest agricultural exposition, includes a sentimental tribute to islanders who have left the island and returned for the week.

# RECREATION

Lucy Maud Montgomery's sudsy, soft, and pervading image of the province as the politely genteel Avonlea is a bit deceiving. It's not all croquet and tea parties: the island abounds in opportunities for exciting sports and other outdoor activities.

Various packages are described under "Island Value Vacations" in the *Visitors Guide.* Sports like golf, fishing, biking, and camping can be booked before arrival and are often linked with accommodations with good value for the dollar. Other packages focus on dining, sightseeing, theater, or photography.

## Bicycling

The narrow roads that slice through the rolling countryside are sublime avenues for biking. The biking terrain is classified by the province as rolling, hilly, or level, though it's all pretty gentle. The highest peaks present no more than a four-degree incline. The greatest impediment is the wind, which can blow steadily at times. Apart from some stretches along the TransCanada Highway and some primary highways, road shoulders are narrow or nonexistent. Traffic is normally light, but bicycle helmets are recommended.

You'll find rentals in all resort towns as well as in the capital at **MacQueen's Travel & Bike Shop,** 430 Queen St., tel. 902/368-2453. Mac-Queens has one of the island's most complete selections and charges around $25 a day for standard and mountain bikes.

## Hiking

While there's nothing resembling remote wilderness on the island, the rolling countryside nevertheless lends itself to relaxed hiking on a variety of trails. Many short trails lie within the provincial park system; the national park has 11 marked trails. The province has been busy converting abandoned rail lines into hiking and bicycling trails that will eventually extend for 270 km across the island—from Tignish in the west to Elmira in the east—as the **Confederation Trail.**

## Golf

Golf isn't a sport here, it's a religion. And no wonder—the whole island looks like one big golf course. Many farms have been converted to courses in recent years, and currently visitors have the choice of 28 different links. Golf season starts in late May when the ground dries out and finishes in mid-October. Green fees range from $20 up to $80 for a round on a world-class course such as the Links at Crowbush Cove near Charlottetown. Details about all courses can be found on the website www.golfpei.com.

Island born and raised Lorie Kane is a perennial local heroine on the LPGA circuit. She actively promotes the island as a golfing destination and hosts an annual skins game that brings the world's best women golfers to PEI.

## Hunting and Inland Fishing

Hunters "from away" will need a $75 nonresident license and a provincial Firearm Safety Certificate, and bird hunters must buy a Canada Migratory Game Bird permit; for details, contact the **Department of Fisheries, Aquaculture, and the Environment,** Fish and Wildlife Branch, tel. 902/368-4683, or write to them at P.O. Box 2000, Charlottetown, PE C1A 7N8.

Open season on gray partridge, ruffled grouse, and migratory birds is early October to mid-December. **North Shore Outfitters,** tel. 902/963-3449 or 902/569-3423, charges around $600 and up per person for a guided, three-day bird hunt with lodgings and meals.

Brook trout, found in virtually all streams, rivers, and ponds, are the most popular quarry of inland anglers; less common are rainbows, found mainly in the Dunk, Cardigan, and Sturgeon Rivers and in Glenfinnan and O'Keefe Lakes. Trout fishing requires a license; contact the Fish and Wildlife Branch in Charlottetown at the above address.

## Sea Sports

**Deep-sea fishing** is popular here, with the primary game fish being the giant bluefin tuna, feisty enough to battle for 10 hours. Its season runs midsummer through October. Fishing charter companies are located mainly along the gulf seaports, with sizable concentrations at the Rustico ports and North Lake Harbour. Three-hour trips cost about $25 per person, with gear provided. Expect to pay about $350 for an eight-hour trip with four anglers. Charters are geared for groups of four to six anglers and depart between 8 and 10 A.M. No license is required. For details, contact the **Fish and Wildlife** branch office listed under Hunting and Inland Fishing, above.

**Outside Expeditions,** tel. 902/963-3366 or 800/207-3899, www.getoutside.com, outfits half-day to five-day kayaking trips, including instruction and equipment. Prices start at $45 for

rainbow trout

BOB RACE

PRINCE EDWARD ISLAND

a half-day trip. **Paddle PEI,** tel. 902/569-1352, offers guided kayak, canoe, and mountain-bike tours with an emphasis on the natural environment. Most of the tours are at Brudenell River Provincial Park.

**Windsurfing** is best in northern Queens County on the gulf, where the winds are steadiest. **Beachcombing and sunbathing** are alternatives to getting out in the water. Beaches on the island are comprised of either white or red sand. If your beach of the day has red sand, bring a chair or old blanket—the iron-oxide stains garments. Along southeastern Kings County's Montague Harbour and Murray Harbour coastlines, you'll see seals by the dozens; they like the warm waters of Northumberland Strait.

## ACCOMMODATIONS AND FOOD

PEI offers more lodgings per square kilometer than any other Canadian province. You'll have a choice from among 2,000 bed-and-breakfasts, country inns, vacation farms, lodges, tourist homes, hotels, motels, resorts, houses, and apartments, not to mention campgrounds. The abundance can be baffling, but the *Visitors Guide* describes nearly all of them, arranged by sightseeing regions and type. Some lodgings are listed with a one- to five-star rating, but as the grading system is strictly voluntary, an absence of a rating carries little weight. If you have questions about where to stay, call **PEI Tourism** (the provincial information service) at tel. 902/368-5540 or 888/734-7529. This same office operates a Vacancy Information Search hotline at 888/268-6667, or click through the accommodations section on the website www.gov.pe.ca.

**Rates** range from extraordinarily inexpensive to inordinately pricey. Overall, lodging costs are among Atlantic Canada's lowest. Generally, costs are highest in Charlottetown and Queen County's North Shore, both longtime tourist meccas. Best buys are in the hinterlands at either end of the province. Regardless, rates are fair, with good value for the dollar; count on clean and tidy rooms, and courteous and helpful hospitality.

Rates given in this chapter are in Canadian dollars, and do not include taxes.

### Food and Drink

Island fare is *good.* Seafood lovers will be particularly enthralled. Where else in the world would McDonald's offer lobster burgers?

Summertime offers a feast of shellfish—Atlantic Canada's most abundant variety. If you're interested in Malpeque oysters on their own turf, the sweet mollusks are prepared island-wide in season. And the popularity of lobster as an entrée has spawned a half dozen community halls known especially for boiled lobster and fixings.

Local produce and dairy products are delicious. Chefs make the most of island-grown succulent berries, locally produced maple syrup, and thick, sweet honey.

Restaurants run the gamut from purposely rustic or plain places furnished in early Formica, to haute-decor dining rooms with artfully created interior ambience. Plain or fancy, count on consistently good cooking—you can't go wrong. Charlottetown and Queens County's North Shore offer the most abundant dining choices. Options are sparse however on backcountry roads; it's wise to plan to arrive in towns at mealtimes when you're exploring the hinterlands. Acadian fare—found in abundance in southern Prince County's Mont-Carmel area—is excellent and reasonably priced.

If you're interested in bending an elbow with the locals, check out Canadian Legion halls and neighborhood taverns, where beer drinking is serious business. As for mixed drinks, a finely tuned martini is hard to find; basic scotch and water is a wiser choice. Restaurant wine lists are nothing to rave about, but a few places, such as the Inn at Bay Fortune's dining room at Bay Fortune, and the Delta Prince Edward's Lord Selkirk Room in Charlottetown, have worthy offerings.

## INFORMATION AND SERVICES
### Visitor Information

Your first point of contact should be **Tourism PEI,** P.O. Box 940, Charlottetown, PE C1A

**PRINCE EDWARD ISLAND**

7M5, tel. 902/368-5540 or 888/734-7529, www.gov.pe.ca. Request a copy of the excellent, detailed 202-page *Visitors Guide,* which will be sent by post—along with an island map—to any address in the world.

The government operates **Visitor Information Centres** in 10 locations across the island, including in the gateway communities of Wood Islands and Borden and along the Charlottetown waterfront. The latter two are open year-round; the others May or June to September or early October. Most towns without an official information center hold a **Welcome Center.** Generally attached to a gift shop or museum, these centers are good sources of localized information.

## Publications

The daily *Guardian* ("Covers Prince Edward Island Like the Dew") is published in Charlottetown and circulates in Queens and Kings Counties. The *Journal-Pioneer,* another daily, covers Prince County. The *Graphic* ("The Lively One") is a local newsweekly, while *La Voix Acadienne* is the Acadian newsweekly. A handy free tabloid, published monthly, is the *Buzz,* which lists entertainment and events, mainly in and around Charlottetown.

Though a bit cluttered with ads, a helpful 100-plus-page booklet available free at tourist information centers is *This Week on PEI,* which lists events, ferry schedules, accommodations, and the like, and gives a bit of background on places.

## Health and Safety

No special inoculations or other health precautions are required to enter the province. Canadians are covered by national health care. For non-Canadians, a day's basic hospital costs (exclusive of doctor fees and treatment) are high. Charlottetown's Queen Elizabeth Hospital is the largest medical center; smaller hospitals are located in Summerside, Alberton, O'Leary, Tyne Valley, Montague, and Souris.

Dentists can be found in Charlottetown, Summerside, Tignish, O'Leary, Wellington, Kensington, Hunter River, Crapaud, Cornwall, Parkdale, Southport, Morell, Montague, and Souris.

The **Royal Canadian Mounted Police** headquarters is at 153 Maypoint Road, Charlottetown, tel. 902/368-9300. It's open daily, 24 hours.

## Communications

The main **Canada Post** office is at 135 Kent Street, Charlottetown. Numerous retail post offices are scattered across the province; hours vary—some open at 7 A.M. and close at midnight.

PEI's area code is **902,** the same as Nova Scotia's. **Island Tel,** tel. 800/565-4737, www.islandtel.pe.ca, is the main telecommunication provider.

# GETTING THERE

Most visitors to Prince Edward Island arrive by road, traveling either across the **Confederation Bridge** or on the ferry from Caribou, Nova Scotia (see By Sea, below). The bridge opened on May 31, 1997, linking Cape Jourimain (New Brunswick) to Borden-Carlton. The drive over this impressive 12.9-km span takes around 10 minutes (views are blocked by concrete barriers erected as a windbreak). Crossing to the island by either bridge or ferry is free. The crossing fee is collected upon leaving the island. The bridge toll is $37.25 per vehicle including passengers; more for RVs and trailers. Payment (credit card, debit card, or cash) is collected on the island side of the bridge. (The ferry fare is higher than the bridge toll, so smart travelers catch the ferry over to the island and use the bridge to cross back to the mainland). Call 902/437-7300 or 888/437-6565, and, yes, even the bridge has its own website: www.confederationbridge.com.

## By Air

Most air service to the island is direct, but not nonstop, which means that the plane sets down someplace else before it arrives at the Charlottetown airport. International flights are routed through Halifax, Montréal, or Toronto. **Air Canada/Air Nova,** tel. 888/247-2262, www.aircanada.ca, connects Charlottetown with Toronto via Ottawa, and with Montréal, Boston, and Newark via Halifax. **Prince Edward Air,** tel. 902/566-4488 or 800/565-5359, www.peair.com, is a local charter operator with scheduled flights between Halifax, Moncton, Charlottetown, and Summerside.

## By Sea

Scheduled ferries depart regularly from Caribou, Nova Scotia, landing at Wood Islands, a scenic 62-km drive from Charlottetown. The service is operated by **Northumberland Ferries Ltd.** (NFL), tel. 902/566-3838 or 800/565-0201, www.nfl-bay.com. The 75-minute crossing operates May to mid-December, with up to nine crossings in each direction daily during peak summer season. The large ferries offer plenty of vantage points to soak up the ocean views, as well as a cafeteria, an ice cream booth, and a staffed information booth. The fare, collected only when you leave the island, is $49 per vehicle,

no matter how many people you cram into it. Walk-on passengers over age 12 pay $11. Bicycles cost $20, motorcycles $25, and motor homes, campers, and cars with trailers charged by length, $61–74. Allow plenty of time going either direction; during the tourist season, the waiting lines for cars can be horrendously long—up to two or three hours. Tune in to local radio stations, such as 720 AM, which give regular status reports on crossing conditions and estimated waiting times. Schedules are posted at ferry terminals and roadside tourist centers.

**CTMA Ferry,** tel. 418/986-3278 or 888/986-3278, operates the M.V. *Madeleine* car/passenger ferry between Souris and Cap-aux-Meules on Québec's Îles-de-la-Madeleine (Magdalen Islands). The 134-km crossing takes five hours. The ferry runs between April and January, with up to 10 sailings weekly in each direction (including daily at 8 A.M. from Cap-aux-Meules and daily at 2 P.M. from Souris). Peak one-way fares are adults $37, seniors $30, children $18.50, vehicles from $70.

## GETTING AROUND
### The Road System

The island is webbed with highways and roads of all types. High-speed highways are numbered with single digits and include the TransCanada (Highway 1), which runs along the strait and connects the Confederation Bridge with the ferry terminal at Wood Islands; Highway 2 in Queens and Prince Counties; and Highways 3 and 4 in Kings County, which slice through PEI's interior.

Primary and secondary highways are numbered with double and triple digits, respectively. Think of them as paved, two-lane rural routes, especially useful as driving entrées into the island's scenic countryside. At the bottom of the provincial road classification are paved, unpaved, and unnumbered local roads—the narrow driving lanes that angle across farmland fields and wander into remote places. They're gorgeous roads, most memorable when the surfaces are red clay. But they can be unexpectedly dangerous with steep, drop-off shoulders and surfaces that during rainstorms can become slippery as grease.

© ANDREW HEMPSTEAD

PEI is linked to the mainland by bridge, but the ferry makes for a more enjoyable introduction to the island.

Seat belts are mandatory, as are safety restraints for child passengers; violations cost $60. Drinking while driving and "impaired driving" bring severe penalties.

## Scenic Roads

Three established scenic drives grace Prince Edward Island: the 190-km **Blue Heron Drive** in Queens County, the 375-km **Kings Byway Drive** in Kings County, and the 288-km **Lady Slipper Drive** in Prince County.

Note that the circuits are named "drives." That's no exaggeration. PEI may be Canada's smallest province, but to circumnavigate the island's perimeter on the scenic routes takes more than 14 hours. The routes are well marked with symbols: a drawing of the island's blue heron for Blue Heron Drive; a crown of royal purple as the symbol for Kings Byway Drive; and the provincial orchidlike flower depicted in red for Lady Slipper Drive.

And if you think the foregoing coastal routes are feasts for the eye, try the provincial **heritage roads**—stretches of pastoral roads untouched

*Note that the circuits are named "drives." That's no exaggeration. PEI may be Canada's smallest province, but to circumnavigate the island's perimeter on the scenic routes takes more than 14 hours.*

by commercialism or 20th-century changes. Marked with the silhouette of two trees on a maroon field, the roads run mainly across the island's interior. If you're a photographer or painter, bring appropriate gear. The old-time byways run through rolling countryside speckled with weathered barns and verdant farms.

## Car Rentals, Taxis, and Tours

Major car-rental agencies have offices in Charlottetown and counters at the airport: **Avis,** tel. 902/892-3706; **Buget,** tel. 902/566-5525; **Hertz,** tel. 902/966-5566; **National,** tel. 902/368-2228; and **Rent-a-wreck,** tel. 902/566-9955.

You'll find taxi service in all major towns.

**Abegweit Tours,** tel. 902/894-9966, conducts guided tours of Charlottetown ($10.50 adults, $1 children), the North Shore ($60/$28), South Shore ($60/$28), and other destinations in red double-decker London buses that depart from Confederation Centre and the Rodd Charlottetown.

# Queens County

Queens County is the definitive PEI, as you imagined the province would be. The region is temptingly photogenic, a meld of small seaports with brightly colored craft at anchor, and farmland settings with limpid ponds and weathered barns.

Rural roads are snugly narrow and punctuated every so often with smaller-than-small villages. Red-clay lanes depart the main paved roads and wrap up and across the undulating countryside like burnished red ribbons laced on verdant velvet. Barns crest the hilltops like lofty crowns, and boats with billowing sails skip across the bays that reach inland from the gulf coastline.

Visualize Queens County in two parts. The North Shore lies along the Gulf of St. Lawrence and

has enjoyed decades of tourist renown. Here the sea is always at your shoulder, and the land is dotted with tiny villages. The South Shore rims Northumberland Strait's jagged seacoast, which holds seaports like Victoria and historic sites such as Orwell Village, the re-created settlement of PEI's early Scottish and Irish immigrants. This coast may be on the beaten tourist path someday. But for now, it's the lesser-known side of Queens County and only lightly explored by visitors. Queens County as a whole is divided in half by Highway 2, the expressway that slices across the island's midsection from Charlottetown to Summerside.

Province House, Charlottetown

# Charlottetown and Vicinity

As Atlantic Canada's smallest capital, Charlottetown (pop. 32,000)—the island's governmental, economical, cultural, and shopping center—makes no pretense of being a big city. Rather, this attractive town is walkable, comfortable, and friendly. Its major attractions include a beautiful harbor-side location, handsome public and residential architecture, sophisticated art and cultural happenings, and plentiful lodgings and appealing restaurants.

The city also makes a good sightseeing base. From centrally located Charlottetown to most any place on the island and back again is a feasible day's distance; for example, it's a quick 40 minutes by car northwest to Cavendish, and a mere two-hour drive to the island's most distant points, at the northeastern or northwestern tip.

## HISTORY

After the fall of Louisbourg in the mid-1700s, the French abandoned their Prince Edward Island holdings at Port la Joye. The English renamed it Fort Amherst and fortified the site, then moved the settlement to the more defensible inner peninsula tip within Hillsborough Bay. By 1758, they had established Charlotte Town, named for the consort of King George III. The town's grid was laid out in 1764 and was named the island's capital the next year. During the American Revolution, American privateers sacked the capital, then added insult to injury when they stole the island's government seal and kidnapped the colonial governor.

Charlottetown has always been the island's main market town; the land now occupied by Province House and Confederation Centre was once the colony's thriving marketplace. As in most early island towns, the majority of buildings were constructed of wood rather than stone, and many were subsequently leveled by fire. The stone buildings, however, survived. One of these is the small, brick building at 104 Water Street—one of the capital's oldest buildings and

now site of the Strawberry Patch restaurant and crafts shop.

## Where Canada Began

In the fall of 1864, the colonial capital hosted the Charlottetown Conference, which led to establishment of the Dominion of Canada. The delegates who became Canada's founding Fathers of Confederation agreed that the city was the ideal, neutral site for the conference. Islanders were neither for nor against the idea of a dominion. But just in case the fledgling idea of forming a union did come to something, the islanders appointed several delegates to represent them.

The other delegates arrived by sea in groups from New Brunswick, Nova Scotia, and Upper and Lower Canada, now Québec and Ontario. Their respective ships docked at the harbor, and one by one, the delegates walked the short blocks up Great George Street to the Colonial Building, as Province House was known then. The meeting led to the signing of the British North America Act in London in 1867 and the beginnings of modern Canada on July 1 of that year. The initial four provinces were Nova Scotia, New Brunswick, Québec, and Ontario. Prince Edward Island originally passed on membership and didn't join the Confederation until 1873.

## Growth

Charlottetown's development paralleled the growth in profits from the Great Age of Sail. The building of St. Peter's Anglican Church at Rochford Square transformed a bog into one of the capital's finest areas in 1869. Beaconsfield, a tribute of Second Empire and Victorian gingerbread style at Kent and West streets, was designed by architect William Critchlow Harris for wealthy shipbuilder and merchant James Peake in 1877. The Kirk of St. James was architect James Stirling's tribute to early Gothic Revival. The brick Charlottetown City Hall, at Queen and Kent streets, was a local adaptation of Romanesque Revival.

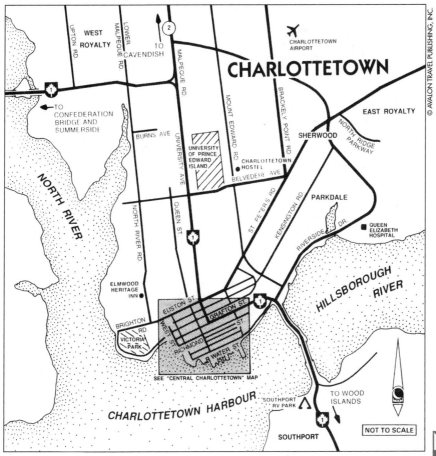

© AVALON TRAVEL PUBLISHING, INC.

PRINCE EDWARD ISLAND

## GETTING ORIENTED

The city, small as it is, may be baffling for a new visitor due to the way historic and newer streets converge. The town began with a handful of harbor-front blocks. The centuries have contributed a confusing jumble of other roads that feed into the historic area from all sorts of angles.

From either direction, the **TransCanada Highway** will take you right into the heart of town. From the west, it crosses the North River, turns south at the University of Prince Edward Island campus and becomes University Avenue, then hits Grafton and turns east to head out of town across the Hillsborough River. Upon entering downtown, head for the waterfront (take the Water Street exit from the west) and the **Visitor Information Centre.** Visitors to the city enjoy one hour of free parking at the center (take the stub into the center to be stamped)—enough time to collect a pile of brochures and take a quick stroll along the harbor.

Extending from the harbor to Euston Street, the commercial area is pleasantly compact, attractive, and easily covered on foot. **Old Charlottetown** (or Old Charlotte Town, depending on who's describing the area) has been restored with rejuvenated buildings and brick walkways, lit at night with gas lamps. **Peake's Wharf,** where the Fathers of Confederation arrived on the island, is now a tourist hub of sorts with restaurants and shops, and there's plentiful vacant land for more development.

The most-sought-after residential areas, with large, stately houses (some designed by noted architect William Critchlow Harris), rim Victoria Park and North River Road. Working-class neighborhoods fan out farther north beyond Grafton Street and are marked with small, pastel-painted houses set close to the streets.

## Tours

The **Confederation Players,** tel. 800/955-1864, are a group of keen local historians who dress in period costume to conduct walking tours of downtown Charlottetown from Founders Hall through summer. The regular one-hour tour departs daily at 10 A.M., 11 A.M., noon, 1 P.M., 3 P.M., and 4 P.M.; the one-hour Waterfront Story Telling tour departs at 1 P.M.; and the 90-minute Merchants and Mansions tour leaves at 7 P.M. Tours cost a reasonable $3.50 per person.

**Abegweit Tours,** tel. 902/894-9966, operates the red double-decker bus that lopes through Charlottetown on sightseeing tours ($10.50 for a 50-minute tour). The bus stops at Confederation Centre on Queen and Grafton Streets, and runs mid-June through September, daily 10:30 A.M.–6:15 P.M. At the harbor, **Peake's Wharf Boat Tours,** 1 Great George St., tel. 902/566-4458, offers a 70-minute sightseeing cruise (1 P.M.; $15) and a 2.5-hour seal-watching cruise (2:30 P.M.; $21). Children age 12 and under pay half price. The tours run June to early September.

## SIGHTS

The following sightseeing starts on the harbor at the information center and takes in about two dozen blocks.

## Founders Hall

Years of restoration saw a historic railway building transformed into Founders Hall, which opened in 2001 and quickly became Charlottetown's number-one attraction. Located on the harbor beside the information center, this state-of-the-art facility combines the latest technology, dynamic audiovisuals, holo-visuals, and interactive displays to create a very different museum experience. You'll enter the Time Tunnel and travel back to 1864, when the Fathers of Confederation first met to discuss the union of Canada. You'll proceed through history, from the formation of each province and territory to modern times. Admission is adults $7.50, seniors $6, children $4. Summer hours are 9 A.M.–8 P.M., shorter the rest of the year. For more information call 800/955-1864 or go to the www.foundershall.com.

## Province House National Historic Site

The nation of Canada began at Province House, four blocks up Great George Street from the harbor. Now protected as a National Historic Site, the buff sandstone Neoclassical edifice at the high point of downtown was erected in 1847 to house the island's colonial legislature. It quickly became the center of public life on the island. It was the site of lavish balls and state functions, including the historic 1864 conference on federal union. The provincial legislature still convenes here; meetings are in session between mid-February and early May for 5 to 17 weeks, depending on how much provincial government haggling is underway.

In the late 1970s, Parks Canada undertook restoration of the age-begrimed building, a five-year task completed in 1983. Layers of paint came off the front columns. The double-hung windows throughout were refitted with glass panes from an old greenhouse in New Brunswick. About 10 percent of the original furnishings remained in the building before restoration and were retained. Most of the rest were replaced by period antiques obtained in the other provinces and northeastern United States. A flowered rug was woven for Confederation Chamber, where the Fathers of Confederation convened. Every nook and corner was refurbished and polished until the interior gleamed. Today, Province House, tel. 902/566-7626, is one of Atlantic Canada's most significant public buildings. The building is open to the public in June, daily 9

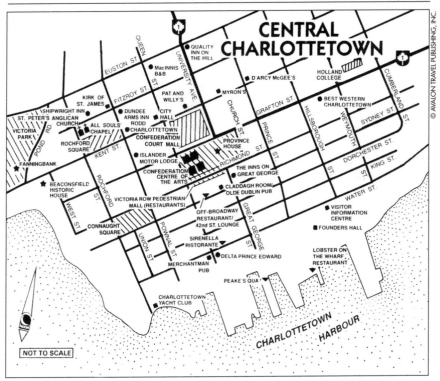

© AVALON TRAVEL PUBLISHING, INC.

# CENTRAL CHARLOTTETOWN

NOT TO SCALE

---

A.M.–5 P.M., July–September daily 8:30 A.M.–5 P.M., the rest of the year Mon.–Fri. 9 A.M.–5 P.M. Admission is free.

## Confederation Centre of the Arts

Confederation Centre of the Arts, 145 Richmond St., tel. 902/628-1864, is the other half of the imposing complex shared by Province House. The promenades, edged with places to sit, are great places for people-watching, and kids like to skateboard on the walkways.

The center opened in 1964 to mark the centennial of the Charlottetown Conference, as the confederation meeting became known in Canadian history. It's a great hulk of a place, compatible with its historic neighbor in its design and coloring.

The center houses an art gallery, a museum, the provincial library, and four theaters. The emphasis at the museum and gallery is on the province—expect to see some of island artist Robert Harris's paintings, and one or two of Lucy Maud Montgomery's original manuscripts—but national arts exhibits also come through regularly. Regular gallery lectures explore the varied Canadian schools of art. The art gallery and museum, tel. 902/628-6142, are open June–September, daily 10 A.M.–7 P.M.; shorter hours October–May. Combined admission is $4. A gift shop stocks wares by the cream of PEI's artisans, and an informal courtyard restaurant serves sandwiches, salads, quiches, and desserts.

Summertime's **Charlottetown Festival** lures locals and tourists to the center's theaters for dramatic and musical productions—most notably the popular *Anne of Green Gables*. Reservations can be made by phone, tel. 902/566-1267 or 800/565-0278. In summer, free lunchtime performances are staged Monday through Saturday

in the amphitheater between the art gallery and
adjacent library.

## City Hall

The redbrick city hall, at the corner of Kent and
Queen Streets, was built in 1888. Free summertime walking tours of the historic streets depart
from here, July–August, weekdays 10 A.M.–5
P.M. Inside is a municipal **visitor information
office,** tel. 902/566-5548.

## All Souls' Chapel

A few blocks west of city hall, this remarkable
chapel next to **St. Peter's Anglican Church** on
Rochford Street, tel. 902/628-1376, was a joint
Harris family creation. The architect William
Harris styled it in island sandstone with a dark
walnut interior. His brother Robert painted the
murals and deftly mixed family members and

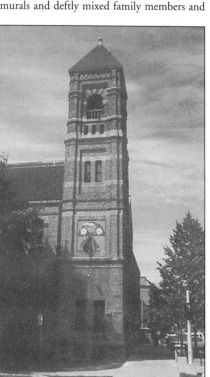

City Hall

friends among the religious figures. The chapel is
open daily 8 A.M.–6 P.M.

## Beaconsfield Historic House

This bright yellow 25-room mansion, 2 Kent St.
(at West St.), tel. 902/368-6600, was built in
1877 from a William Critchlow Harris design.
The building has survived more than a century of
varied use as a family home, a shelter for "friend-
less women," a YWCA, and a nurses' residence. It
was rescued in 1973 by the PEI Museum and
Heritage Foundation, which turned it into foundation headquarters and a heritage museum.

A good bookstore is on the first level, and genealogical archives are kept across the hall and
also upstairs. Outside, you can sit on the wide
front porch overlooking the harbor across the
long lawn—it's a great place to have tea and
scones. Beaconsfield is open year-round; daily
10 A.M.–5 P.M. in summer, Wed.–Thurs. noon–5
P.M. the rest of the year. Admission is $3.50, free
for age 12 and under.

## Victoria Park

Victoria Park, adjacent to Beaconsfield House,
reigns as one of Charlottetown's prettiest settings, with 16 wooded and grassy hectares overlooking the bay at Battery Point. The greenery
spreads out across the peninsula tip; to get there
follow Kent Street as it turns into Park Road-
way. The park's rolling terrain is the result of
moraines, heaps of gravelly deposits left behind by
ice-age glaciers.

Joggers like the park's winding paths, and birders find abundant yellow warblers, purple finch-
es, and downy woodpeckers nesting in the
maples, firs, oaks, pines, and birches. The white
palatial mansion overlooking the water is Fan-
ningbank (Government House), the lieutenant
governor's private residence—nice to look at,
but it's closed to the public.

## Outskirts

**Farmers' Market** is an island institution. The
indoor market holds about 40 vendors selling
everything from flowers and crafts to baked
goods, produce, and fish. It's located in a long,
spacious building on Belvedere Avenue across

Beaconsfield Historic House

from the university campus; open year-round, Sat. 9 A.M.–2 P.M. and Wed. 10 A.M.–5 P.M. in July and August.

**Holland College** is a tidy teaching center at Weymouth and Grafton Streets, tel. 902/566-9500. Arts and crafts are on exhibit in the gallery. It's open year-round, weekdays 8:30 A.M.–10 P.M., Sat.–Sun. 10 A.M.–6 P.M.; shorter summer hours.

## ACCOMMODATIONS

You'll find every kind of lodging, from plain budget places to sumptuous, expensive rooms in Charlottetown's 100-plus lodgings. Unless noted otherwise, prices given below are for a double room; sales tax is not included in these prices.

### Budget and Camping

Hostelling International's **Charlottetown Hostel,** 153 Mt. Edward Rd. (near Belvedere Ave.), tel. 902/894-9696, www.hihostels.ca, has 52 beds, showers, and a place for cooking in spartan quarters. It's open June through Labour Day; $15.50 for HI members, $18.50 for non-

members. Check-in is 7–10 A.M. and 4 P.M.–midnight.

The only campground within city limits is a convenient five-minute drive east across the Hillsborough River at five-hectare **Southport RV Park,** 20 Stratford Rd., tel. 902/569-2287. The park, open mid-May to mid-October, has tent and full-hookup spaces, a Laundromat, a kitchen shelter, and a waterside location looking across the harbor to Charlottetown; $21.50 per site. A year-round motel and housekeeping cottages ($75–93) are also offered here.

### Inns and B&Bs

The least expensive of Charlottetown's many historic accommodations is **MacInnis Bed and Breakfast,** 80 Euston St., tel. 902/892-6725, a homey, centrally located choice with three basic rooms that share bathrooms ($60 single, $70 double) and one room with an en-suite bath ($100). It's open year-round.

The elegant 1860s **Shipwright Inn,** 51 Fitzroy St., tel. 902/368-1905 or 888/306-9966, www.shipwrightinn.com, was originally the home of shipbuilder James Douse. The inn has eight rooms and suites, all with private baths and furnished in a nautical theme; from $135 with breakfast.

A few steps from Province House on a designated national historic street, **Inns on Great George,** 58 Great George St., tel. 902/892-0606 or 800/361-1118, www.innsongreatgeorge.com, is a complex of three townhouses bookended by two hotels, all five tastefully restored in a Georgian-era theme,. Offerings include bed-and-breakfast accommodations in the hotels (from $115) to deluxe suites in the townhouses ($150–180). A nice experience, and right in the heart of Charlottetown.

The **Dundee Arms Inn,** conveniently located between downtown and Victoria Park at 200 Pownal Street, tel. 902/892-2496 or 877/638-6333, www.dundeearms.com, is a restored turn-of-the-century mansion awash with antiques. It offers eight gorgeously appointed, nonsmoking guest rooms ($140–180 with a light breakfast) as well as an adjacent motel with 10 units ($125).

**Elmwood Heritage Inn,** 121 North River Rd., tel. 902/368-3310 or 877/933-3310, www.elmwoodinn.pe.ca, is an 1889 country inn with three suites ($125–185 with a light breakfast) furnished with antiques. Finding the inn can be a challenge—it's hidden at the end of a tree-lined driveway (look for the red fire hydrant opposite the entrance).

## Motels and Hotels

Least expensive of the downtown hotels is the old two-story **Islander Motor Lodge,** 148 Pownal St., tel. 902/892-1217 or 800/268-6261, www.islandermotorlodge.com, which charges $96–115 in high season and has an on-site restaurant.

**Quality Inn on the Hill,** 150 Euston St., tel. 902/894-8572 or 800/466-4734, www.innonthehill.com, is a basic motel with 62 rooms ($116–127 double, $137–174 suite) and a locally esteemed dining room, just three blocks from Province House.

**Best Western Charlottetown,** 238 Grafton St., tel. 902/892-2461, www.bestwesternatlantic.com, is also a three-block jaunt from Province House. It has 143 rooms ($139–154; $154–199

Rodd Charlottetown, a grand city lodging

© ANDREW HEMPSTEAD

for a suite) fronting both sides of the street, connected beneath the road by a tunnel. Facilities include a restaurant, indoor pool, sauna, hot tub, and launderette.

The **Rodd Charlottetown,** 75 Kent St. (at Pownal St.), tel. 902/894-7371 or 800/565-7633, www.rodd-hotels.ca, is a grand redbrick 1931 Georgian gem with magnificent woodwork and furnishings made by island craftspeople. It offers 115 rooms and suites and a restaurant, whirlpool, indoor pool, and sauna. Summer rates start at $182, but check the Rodd website for packages and off-season rooms for around $100.

The boxy expensive high-rise the **Delta Prince Edward,** 18 Queen St., tel. 902/566-2222 or 800/268-1133, www.deltahotels.com, overlooks Charlottetown's waterfront with over 200 spacious rooms and suites. It offers saunas, hot tubs, a spa, restaurants, and a shopping arcade. Rack rates start at around $190 in summer, but many packages are offered, including some with local golf courses.

Charlottetown's least expensive motels are on the outskirts of the city. One concentration is at the junction of Highway 1 and 2 at West Royalty. Near here you'll find **Queen's Arms Inn,** 20 Lower Malpeque Rd., West Royalty, tel. 902/368-1110 or 800/539-1241, with spacious landscaped grounds, an outdoor pool, and a restaurant. Rates are $78–108.

At the intersection itself, **Rodd Confederation Inn,** tel. 902/892-2481 or 800/565-7633, www.rodd-hotels.ca, features 62 rooms and housekeeping units ($85–145), a restaurant, an outdoor pool, and some nonsmoking rooms.

**Holiday Inn Express,** also on the Trans-Canada Highway near the intersection of Highways 1 and 2, tel. 902/892-1201 or 800/465-4329, www.holiday-inn.com, has 137 rooms ($112–142) and suites (from $155, some with an in-room hot tubs), an outdoor heated pool, and a sundeck.

## FOOD

Some of the island's best dining is found in Charlottetown. Reservations are a wise precaution, especially during tourist season.

### Victoria Row

For a selection of cozy restaurant-cafés, most with a street-side patio, stroll along Richmond Street between Queen and Great George. Known as Victoria Row, this block of vintage buildings is usually buzzing with diners and shoppers ducking in and out of the adjacent crafts shops. In the evenings, musicians set up and entertain. Restaurants here include **Meeko's Mediterranean Cafe & Grill,** 146 Richmond St., tel. 902/892-9800, where you'll find appetizers such as hummus and spanakopita, entrées ($8–13) including chicken, pastas, and more Greek dishes, and, best of all, a singing chef; **Fishbones,** 136 Richmond St., tel. 902/628-6569, offering specialty seafood dishes in the $16–24 range and occasional live jazz; **Brennan's,** 132 Richmond St., tel. 902/892-2222, which serves up pizzas, pastas, salads, steaks, and specialties ($6–18) for diners and nightly live music for drinker-dancers; and **Cafe Diem,**

128 Richmond St., tel. 902/892-0494, whose café mochas are delicious.

### Down the Hill

Walking down toward the waterfront from Victoria Row, you'll pass a couple of other blocks harboring culinary finds.

The **Off Broadway Restaurant,** 125 Sydney St., tel. 902/566-4620, is a local favorite for lunch and dinner with poached seafood, lobster crepes, shrimp Provençal, and luscious desserts. And its upstairs **42nd St. Lounge** is by far the best place in town for a quiet drink and conversation; ask one of the affable bartenders for a Cognac, kick back in one of the overstuffed chairs, and listen to soft jazz on the sound system. Highly recommended.

The **Claddagh Room,** 131 Sydney St., tel. 902/892-9661, is authentically Irish, starting with owner Liam Dolan from County Galway. Seafood is the specialty ($17–25); for lunch the Claddagh offers an all-you-can-eat mussel-and-chowder special for $8.95. Open weekdays for lunch and dinner, weekends dinner only. Reservations are advised. Upstairs, the **Olde Dublin Pub,** tel. 902/892-6992, serves an array of pub-style seafood, including a great seafood chowder ($8).

Farther down the hill, **Sirenella Ristorante,** 83 Water St., tel. 902/628-2271, is the place for upscale Italian fare—from a choice of *antipasto* to the Linguine allo Scoglio (shellfish linguine) to the extensive list of Italian wines. Prices are reasonable (entrées range $16–24), and the atmosphere and food are outstanding. For less upscale Italian fare, head next door to **Piazza Joe's,** a casual bistro at 189 Kent Street, tel. 902/894-4291.

The **Merchantman Pub,** 23 Queen St. (at Water St.), tel. 902/892-9150, has a nice atmosphere, a wide-ranging menu that includes some Thai and Cajun dishes, and a good beer selection. But the place seems overpriced, probably due to its location across the street from the upscale Delta Prince Edward.

### On the Waterfront

Keep heading downhill and you'll end up on the waterfront, where you'll find a few more noteworthy eateries. **Peake's Quay,** 1 Great George St., tel. 902/368-1330, boasts a harbor-side location, with informal indoor and outdoor dining and an enviable seafood selection ($11–22); try the scallops sauced with honey butter. Peake's Quay is also arguably the hottest nightspot in town, drawing locals, landlubber tourists, and yachties (who tie up at the adjacent marina) alike to see and be seen while listening or dancing to top touring bands.

More staid is **Lobster on the Wharf** at the foot of Prince Street, tel. 902/368-2888, which combines a harbor view and open-air deck with delectable fresh and well-presented food. Lobster and beef entrées start at $20, while all other dishes (including delicious pan-fried halibut) cost under $20.

## Dining Rooms

Many of the city's hotels have noteworthy dining rooms. The Dundee Arms Inn, away from the tourist crush at 200 Pownal Street, tel. 902/892-2496, is a restored three-story manor offering rooms (see above) and the choice of dining in a pub, out on a large deck, or in the more formal **Griffon Room,** which combines a well-appointed historic setting with elegantly conceived fine cuisine emphasizing red meats and seafood. It's open for breakfast, lunch, and dinner.

The **Inn Restaurant** at the Quality Inn on the Hill, 150 Euston St. (at University Ave.), tel. 902/894-8572, whets the appetite with a creative menu of steamed island blue mussels, Malpeque oysters, some of the best beef in town, and rich chocolate desserts.

The **Selkirk,** in the lobby of the Delta Prince Edward at 18 Queen Street, tel. 902/894-1208, is open throughout the day and features fine dining at dinner. Entrées are unsurpassed in creativity and fine preparation—try chicken breast stuffed with duck sausage and awash in rich wine sauce.

The **Carvery,** in the Rodd Charlottetown, 75 Kent St., tel. 902/894-7371, is known for its steak and prime rib, as well as a lavish seafood buffet; summer nightly 5–9 P.M. Diners chose one main and enjoy a lavish all-you-can-eat spread for a reasonable $26.95.

One more dining room worthy of mention is not associated with a hotel but with a school. The **Lucy Maud Dining Room,** the dining room of the Culinary Institute of Canada, 4 Sydney St., tel. 902/894-6868, is open year-round, its student chefs preparing lunch Tues.–Fri. and dinner Tues.–Sat. Look for four- to six-course formal dinners (around $28), as well as occasional theme menus. Reservations are required.

## Around Town

Popular **Pat and Willy's Cantina,** 119 Kent St., tel. 902/628-1333, specializes in Mexican food but also offers Italian and Canadian fare. Dinners run $8–17.

Named for a father of confederation, **D'Arcy McGee's,** 185 Kent St. (at Prince St.), tel. 902/894-3627, serves steak and seafood in a casual atmosphere; open for lunch and dinner.

At the Confederation Centre of the Arts, the **Courtyard Restaurant,** tel. 902/628-6107, provides a culinary respite within the sunny dining room; entrées ($8–11) are geared to light fare—try crepes stuffed with crab and asparagus. For a variety of seafood and grill combinations, try the family-oriented **Town and Country,** 219 Queen St., tel. 902/892-2282.

The **Lone Star Café & Saloon,** in University Plaza, 449 University Ave., tel. 894-STAR, is the local microbrewery. It complements its decent if not earthshaking homebrews with pretty good Southwest-style fare—fajitas, mesquite-grilled steaks, and the like.

## Local Treats and Light Bites

Ice-cream fanciers whoop it up at **Cow's** on Queen Street (across from Confederation Centre), tel. 902/892-6969, and at Peakes Wharf, tel. 902/566-4886, where a dozen different flavors are scooped each day. The shop also stocks Cow's T-shirts, the ones you'll see coming and going everywhere on the island. Health-food addicts go to the **Root Cellar,** 34 Queen St., tel. 902/892-6227, for power drinks and sandwiches on whole-wheat bread.

**Beanz Espresso Bar,** 38 University Ave., tel. 902/892-8797, is the place for a cup of gourmet coffee or steeped tea with muffins, cinnamon rolls, and other delectables. Breakfasts are hearty and well priced, with an inexpensive special of eggs, toast, sausage, and hash browns. Open Mon.–Sat.

## Groceries

**Sobey's Food Warehouse,** 679 University Ave., tel. 902/566-3218, is as large and well stocked as the name implies and has a deli with picnic ingredients. Another major and centrally located market is **Island Food Centre,** on Queen Street opposite the Confederation Centre of the Arts, tel. 902/894-8557.

## ENTERTAINMENT AND EVENTS

### Movies

**Charlottetown Mall Cinemas** screens current films nightly and for weekend matinees; for show times call 902/892-0943. The **City Cinema,** 64 King St., tel. 902/368-3669, will appeal more to the art-house crowd. It presents two different films nightly—mostly a good selection of European and independent films.

### Theater

The **Confederation Centre of the Arts,** 145 Richmond St., tel. 902/628-1864, is the performing-arts capital of the province and the site of the **Charlottetown Festival,** which runs from mid-June to early September. The festival is best known for the *Anne of Green Gables* musical; tickets cost $16–36. Also on the bill are repertory productions in the center's main theater and cabaret-style productions at the **MacKenzie Theatre,** the festival's second stage at University Avenue and Grafton Street. For tickets to either theater, call 902/566-1267, or 800/565-0278 within the Maritimes (May–September only).

### Music and Nightlife

Charlottetown once rolled up the sidewalks at night, but in recent years a rousing nightlife and pub scene has emerged, centered on drinking and dancing. Last call for drinks is at 1:30 A.M.; the doors lock at 2 A.M.

Several nightspots are attached to restaurants already mentioned above. **Peake's Quay,** 1 Great George St., tel. 902/368-1330, is one of the most popular dance venues in town; the **Olde Dublin Pub,** 131 Sydney St., tel. 902/892-6992, offers Irish folk music nightly in summer; **D'Arcy McGee's,** 185 Kent St., tel. 902/894-3627, offers a variety of live rock, blues, and other entertainment; and **Fishbones,** 136 Richmond St., tel. 902/628-6569, presents occasional live jazz at its prime Victoria Row location.

A venerable mainstay of the club scene is cavernous **Myron's,** 151 Kent St., tel. 902/892-4375, which might offer anything from country to hard rock for the dancing masses. As closetlike as Myron's is cavernous, **Baba's Lounge,** upstairs above Cedar's Eatery, 81 University, tel. 902/892-7377, is a "hipoisie" hangout extraordinaire. "Intimate" is an understatement here; bodies writhe to the rhythm on a dance floor about the size of a postage stamp. Wear your most outrageous costume and, if you're over 25, be prepared to feel old.

On the entertainment spectrum's more sedate side, you'll find dim lights, comfortable surroundings, and a piano bar at the **Quality Inn on the Hill,** 150 Euston St., tel. 902/894-8572. Another good choice is **Provinces Lounge** at street level in the Rodd Charlottetown, 75 Kent St., tel. 902/894-7371. The plushest place for a relaxing nightcap is the **42nd Street Lounge,** part of the Off Broadway Cafe, 125 Sydney St., tel. 902/566-4620.

> *Charlottetown once rolled up the sidewalks at night, but in recent years a rousing nightlife and pub scene has emerged, centered on drinking and dancing.*

### Events

Should you find yourself in town in the off-off-season, you might enjoy the hockey tournament and other winter sporting activities of the **Charlottetown Winter Carnival,** held in early February; tel. 902/892-5708.

The June to mid-October **Charlottetown Fes-**

PRINCE EDWARD ISLAND

tival presents musical theater and cabaret at the Confederation Centre and the nearby MacKenzie Theatre. Two musicals are presented, including one centering on *Anne of Green Gables*. For ticket information, call 902/566-1267 or 800/565-0278.

The summer season opens in Confederation Park the middle weekend of June with the **Biggest Backyard Barbeque. Canada Day** is celebrated on the waterfront with a food fare, island music, and the **Festival of Lights,** fireworks display. Call 902/629-1784. During mid-July's **Charlottetown Race Week,** yacht races take place from the Charlottetown Yacht Club on Pownal Street, tel. 902/892-4455. Mid August's **PEI Provincial Exhibition,** Atlantic Canada's largest agricultural exposition, incorporates **Old Home Week,** a sentimental tribute to islanders who are now home "from away." The city unofficially shuts down for the harness racing, horse and livestock shows, and week-ending **Gold Cup Parade** through the streets of Charlottetown—said to be Atlantic Canada's biggest and best-attended parade. For exhibition information call 902/892-6623. Summer ends with the **International Shellfish Festival,** tel. 902/892-4455, which centers on a large tent set up beside Peake's Wharf the middle weekend of September. Festivities include an oyster-shucking contest, a Chowder Challenge, "touch tanks," cooking classes, and cruises.

## RECREATION
### Outdoor Adventures
**MacQueen's Travel & Bike Shop,** 430 Queen St., tel. 902/368-2453, provides complete bike and accessory rental and repairs and can also arrange cycle-touring packages. **Smooth Cycle,** 172 Prince St., tel. 902/566-5530, also offers rentals and repairs. Both charge $16 for four hours or $24 for a full day.

Dive shops in Charlottetown include **Black Dolphin Diving & Water Sports,** 106 Hillsboro St., tel. 902/894-3483; and **Diver's Quarters,** 4 Watts Ave., tel. 902/894-7080. You can rent canoes and kayaks at **Sporting Intentions,** 570 N. River Rd., West Royalty, tel. 902/892-

4713. **Island Rods and Flies** at 18 Birch Hill Drive in nearby Sherwood, tel. 902/566-4157, stocks fly-fishing equipment and materials. It also offers fishing guide service.

## SHOPPING
### Arts and Crafts
If you're an avid shopper with a penchant for crafts, head for the **Island Crafts Shop** at 156 Richmond Street, tel. 902/892-5152. It's the PEI Crafts Council's retail outlet. A thorough browse among quilts, glassware, sculpture, clothing, knitted apparel, and jewelry ad infinitum will provide you an insight into what's available in the city and province. Craftspeople demonstrate their trades at the shop from time to time. The wares here tend to be one-of-a-kind. If you don't see exactly what you want, you could go directly to the maker; the membership list is available at the shop.

**Two Sisters,** 150 Richmond St., tel. 902/892-7711 (Confederation Court Mall, tel. 902/368-1428, and the Charlottetown Mall, tel. 902/628-6740), is a Crafts Council member and stocks a luscious variety of island crafts. **Great Northern Knitters** has a retail outlet at 77 Water Street, tel. 902/566-5302. Knitted of oiled wool (oil makes the wool softer and warmer), the sweaters are mass produced, but each knitter works on the same sweater from start to finish—an arrangement that allows custom sizing as well as run-of-the-line production. The stores are open Mon.–Sat. 10 A.M.–5:30 P.M., and until 9 P.M. on Thurs. and Fri .

At **Artworks,** 525 N. River Rd., tel. 902/368-3494, you'll find a worthy collection of fine art by PEI artists. It's open year-round, Mon.–Sat. 9 A.M.–5 P.M.

### Sundries
The **Confederation Court Mall,** 134 Kent St., holds some 90 shops and 10 restaurants, taking up a city block in the heart of downtown. The **Charlottetown Mall,** 670 University Ave., is just north of town, where the TransCanada hits University. The latter is home to the island's

largest department store, **Zellers,** tel. 902/892-8571, which stocks camping gear and also has a well-stocked deli and bakery; open Mon.–Sat. 9 A.M.–5 P.M., Fri. to 9 P.M.

For all your camera and film needs head to **PEI Photo Lab,** 55 Queen St., tel. 902/892-5107.

# INFORMATION AND SERVICES
## Visitor Information
Charlottetown's main **Visitor Information Centre,** beside the harbor at 173 Water Street, tel. 902/368-4444, answers questions and stocks a good supply of literature about the province and Charlottetown. It's open in summer, daily 8 A.M.–10 P.M.; spring and fall, daily 9 A.M.–6 P.M.; winter, weekdays only 9 A.M.–6 P.M. Inside city hall, at the corner of Kent and Queen Streets, is a smaller seasonal information booth.

## Library and Bookstores
The **public library,** tel. 902/368-4642, is part of the Confederation Centre (access from Richmond St.), open Tues.–Thurs. 10 A.M.–9 P.M., Fri.–Sat. 10 A.M.–5 P.M., Sun. 1–5 P.M. September–May weekday hours are shorter.

**Island Information Service** at 11 Kent Street near Beaconsfield House, tel. 902/368-4000, is the best source for information on the island's environment, population, and economy; open weekdays 8 A.M.–4 P.M. in summer, 8:30 A.M.–5 P.M. the rest of the year. For island literature and especially architecture and history coverage, check out the bookshop at **Beaconsfield House.** Gift boutiques and crafts shops also stock some island-related books.

**The Bookman,** 177 Queen St., tel. 902/892-8872, carries new, used, and rare books. **Book Emporium,** 169 Queen St., tel. 902/628-2001, is a general bookstore with a good PEI section.

Bookshops in the malls stock current books. **Coles** at Charlottetown Mall, tel. 902/628-8252, and **Bookmark** at Confederation Court Mall, tel. 902/566-4888, have the widest selections. If you like browsing for used books, head for the shops along University Avenue near the campus.

# Health and Safety
**Queen Elizabeth Hospital** is on Riverside Drive, tel. 902/894-2200. For **police** call 902/566-7112.
## Post and Internet
**Canada Post** at 135 Kent Street, tel. 902/628-4400, is open Mon.–Fri. 8 A.M.–5:15 P.M. The philatelic bureau is open daily 9 A.M.–4 P.M. For public Internet access, head to the library in the Confederation Centre, Richmond St., tel. 902/368-4642. Across from the library, **Cafe Diem,** 128 Richmond, tel. 902/892-0494, has a row of computers with high-speed Internet access; $2 for 15 minutes.

## Laundries
Coin laundries are plentiful; they're generally open daily 8 A.M.–11 P.M. Among them, **Better Than Home Laundromat,** 73 St. Peters Rd., tel. 902/628-1994; and **Mid Town Laundromat,** 238 University Ave., tel. 902/628-2329, advertise drop-off service.

# TRANSPORTATION
**Charlottetown Airport** lies eight km from Charlottetown in the northern suburbs, on Brackley Point Road at Sherwood. **Air Canada,** tel. 902/892-1007, offers nonstop flights from Toronto and up to seven flights a day to Halifax. Though open daily 24 hours, it's a small airport sans banks, lockers, or a duty-free shop. For sightseeing and other information, use the free phone line to the tourist office. Between flights, the terminal is almost vacant, with no one at the car rental counters. Taxis wait outside during flight arrivals and charge about $12 for two for the 15-minute drive to town. Avis, Budget, and Hertz rent vehicles at the airport.

## Getting Around
Use **Charlottetown Transit,** tel. 902/566-5664, to get anywhere in Greater Charlottetown for $1.50; buses run weekdays only. Another option is with **Abegweit Tours,** tel. 902/894-9966, which charges $9 for city tours aboard an old English double-decker bus.

Charlottetown taxis are plentiful; you'll pay $3.50–5 to get almost anywhere downtown. Taxis cruise the streets or wait at major downtown hotels. Taxi companies include **City Cab,** tel. 902/892-6567; **Co-op,** tel. 902/628-8200; and **Yellow Cab,** tel. 902/566-6666.

Local rental-car agencies include **Avis,** tel. 902/892-3706; **Budget,** tel. 902/566-5525; **Hertz,** tel. 902/966-5566; **National,** tel. 902/368-2228; and **Rent-a-Wreck,** tel. 902/566-9955. **Smooth Cycle Bicycle Rentals,** 172 Prince St., tel. 902/566-5530, rents bikes from $7 per hour and $28 per 24 hours.

# The South Shore

While the North Shore of Queen's County is the island's premier destination, the South Shore is closer to Charlottetown and possessed of its own charms. Provincially operated information centers are located in Borden-Carleton (in the Gateway Village), tel. 902/437-8570, and at the Wood Islands ferry terminal, tel. 902/962-7411, which is open for ferry arrivals.

## CORNWALL AND VICINITY

A sense of city quickly fades as the TransCanada/Highway 1 peels out of Charlottetown and continues south and then southwest along Northumberland Strait. This is farming country, richly productive in grains, potatoes, and orchard fruits. The TransCanada Highway makes a direct route to the Confederation Bridge at Borden-Carleton, but numerous side roads invite exploring off the main highway.

Cornwall, about 10 minutes west of Charlottetown, is one of the main service centers on the South Shore, with a concentration of restaurants, accommodations, and shopping.

### Accommodations and Food

**Obanlea Century Farm Tourist Home,** 40 York Point Rd. (Hwy. 248), near North River (ask for directions), tel. 902/566-3067, is surrounded by a pastoral landscape devoted to potato farming and cattle grazing; the farmhouse has three basic guest rooms ($50 includes a light breakfast).

**Chez-Nous** on Ferry Road (Highway 248), tel. 902/566-2779 or 800/566-2779, www.cheznous.pe.ca, offers four rooms with cable TV/VCRs and private baths; two have in-room whirlpool tubs. It's open June–September; rates of

$75–135 include breakfast. **Pye's Village Guest Home,** on the main highway through town, tel. 902/566-2026, offers one room with a double bed and en-suite bath and another, much larger suite; from $45.

Dating to 1862, **Strathgartney Homestead Inn,** on the TransCanada Highway at the hamlet of Strathgartney (midpoint between Charlottetown and Borden), tel. 902/675-4711, www.strathgartney.com, is an architectural heritage clone of Cavendish's pretty Green Gables House farmhouse. The historic inn has eight antiques-furnished guest rooms ranging $60–90 including a light breakfast. Dinner is also available. The inn is open year-round.

**Holiday Haven Campground,** tel. 902/566-2421, on Highway 248 two km east of Cornwall, spreads across 25 beautiful hectares along the West River. Rates are $18–20. Amenities include a Laundromat, fireplaces, showers, toilets, and a kitchen shelter; open June through October. Camping is also available at **Strathgartney**

BOB RACE

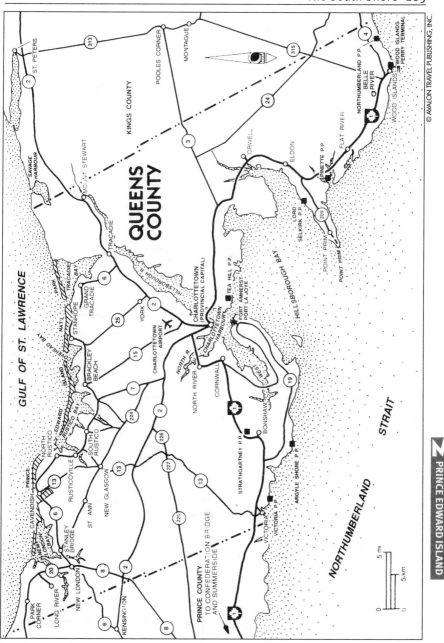

**Provincial Park,** tel. 902/675-7476, on the Trans-Canada at the village of Churchill, about 20 km southwest of Charlottetown. The park's 132 acres encompass inland woodlands spliced by (and providing delightful views of) the Strathgartney River (with fishing). Facilities include unserviced campsites ($17) and two-way hookup sites ($19), hiking trails, hot showers, a launderette, kitchen shelters, and nearby campers' store; open mid-June to early September.

Dinnertime lures crowds to **Bonnie Brae Restaurant** on Highway 1 near Cornwall, tel. 902/566-2241. Open year-round, 11 A.M.–9 P.M. daily, the restaurant is an islander favorite for Canadian, Swiss, and continental fare, as well as the mid-June to mid-September nightly lobster buffet ($27).

## Where PEI Began
**Fort Amherst/Port-la-Joye National Historic Site,** 35 minutes from Charlottetown on Hillsborough Bay, provides sublime views of the capital from its site on a peninsula tip. The island's first permanent European settlement began here in 1720 when three French ships sailed into Port la Joye (today's Charlottetown Harbour) carrying some 300 settlers. Most of them moved to the North Shore and established fishing villages, but the rest remained here at the military outpost.

Within just four years, adverse conditions had driven out most of the French. The British burned Port la Joye in 1745 and took control of the island. The French later returned to rebuild their capital, but were compelled to surrender Port la Joye to a superior British force in 1758. The British renamed the post Fort Amherst. After the British established the new capital at Charlottetown, Fort Amherst fell quickly into disrepair.

Nothing much remains of the fortifications today. A visitor center presents historical exhibits and displays explaining the history of the site; it's open mid-June to Labour Day, 9 A.M.–5 P.M. The grounds, which have picnic tables, are open May–November. The site is on Blockhouse Point Road, off Highway 19 near Rocky Point; tel. 902/566-7626.

# VICTORIA

Victoria (pop. 200), about 30 minutes from Charlottetown, marks Queens County's southwestern corner. The town owed its start to shipbuilding, and by 1870, Victoria ranked as one of the island's busiest ports. As the demand for wooden ships faded, the seaport turned to cattle shipping—herds of cattle were driven down the coastal slopes to water's edge, where they were hoisted on slings to waiting ships.

Today Victoria shows just a shadow of its former luster. The seaport slipped off the commercial circuit decades ago, and the settlement shrank to a handful of waterfront blocks. Happily, island craftspeople discovered the serene setting. It's still a quiet place where the fishing fleet puts out to sea early in the morning as the mist rises off the strait. But now the peaceful seaport also holds a modest arts colony, with outlets along the main street.

Two km east of the wharf area is **Victoria Provincial Park,** really nothing more than a waterfront picnic area but a good place to kick back with a packed lunch nevertheless.

## Entertainment
If an evening at the theater sounds good, try the **Victoria Playhouse** on Howard Street, the repertory theater that showcases historically themed comedy and drama (adults $14, children under 12 $7), as well as concerts of jazz and folk music. It's open late June to early September, Tues.–Sun. For reservations and dinner/theater packages, call 902/658-2025 or 800/925-2025.

## Accommodations and Food
Next to the Victoria Playhouse on Howard Street, **Victoria Village Inn,** tel. 902/658-2483, is an 1870s heritage inn, awash with lustrous antiques in its four nonsmoking guest rooms. Rates range $65–85. **Dunrovin Lodge Cottages and Farm,** tel. 902/658-2375, is 1.2 km off the TransCanada Highway, overlooking Victoria and the sea. Features include farm animals and children's activities for younger guests; babysitting is available. Two lodge rooms and seven housekeeping cottages are available. Open mid-June to mid-Sep-

PRINCE EDWARD ISLAND

Confederation Bridge

tember; rates are $60–85. Victoria's most up-market accommodation is the **Orient Hotel,** Main St., tel. 902/658-2503 or 800/565-6743. It features a few smallish guest rooms (from $80) as well as larger suites ($129–139). Rates include breakfast, and tea and coffee throughout the day. The Orient is open June to October.

The best option for a meal is the **Actors' Retreat Café** in the Victoria Village Inn, tel. 902/658-2483. Expect a healthful approach to cooking—no deep-fat frying or processed food and an emphasis on whole grains and fresh ingredients. Two or three entrées are offered daily ($15–23). At the end of the town's main wharf is **Seawinds,** tel. 902/658-2200, open daily for lunch and dinner but most popular for the Wednesday night lobster buffet and Sunday brunch.

## BORDEN-CARLETON

Borden-Carleton, 56 km west of Charlottetown, is the main gateway to Prince Edward Island. Since the opening of the Confederation Bridge in 1997, many tourist facilities have been developed, including a profusion of restaurants in the Gateway Village. Also in the village is a gateway

**Visitor Information Centre,** tel. 902/437-8570, open year-round, daily 9 A.M.–6 P.M., with extended hours in spring and fall (until 8 P.M.) and summer (until 10 P.M.)

Back in the late 1700s, iceboats carrying mail and passengers crossed the strait when the island was icebound from December to early spring. The voyages were filled with hair-raising tales of survival, and the iceboats—rigged with fragile sails and runners—were often trapped in the strait's ice. Male passengers were sometimes put into harnesses to haul the boats over the uneven ice ridges.

By 1900, though, the province had turned to icebreaker boats that nosed through the winter ice. In 1916 the first car ferry sailed from Borden near Summerside, and the last made its crossing in the spring of 1997, when the bridge opened.

### Accommodations
**Dutchess Gateway Bed and Breakfast,** 264 Carleton St., tel. 902/855-2765, is close to the bridge, with dining nearby. Rates for the basic rooms run $30–40. Open year-round.

West of town, south of Central Bedeque (Prince County) on Highway 171, **Pine-Lawn B&B,** tel. 902/887-2270 or 800/419-2270, charges $50 for a single, $60 for a double and is open year-round. In the same vicinity, **Mid Isle Motel,** tel. 902/887-2525 or 877/877-2525, 13 km west of Borden, offers 10 basic rooms for $60; a small adjacent cafÑ is open for breakfast.

## Confederation Bridge

If you've arrived in Borden-Carlton via the Confederation Bridge, you'll have enjoyed a free ride. If you're leaving the island, it's time to pay. The toll is $37.25 per vehicle, including passengers; from $42 for RVs and trailers. Payment by credit card, debit card, or cash is collected on the island side of the bridge.

# EAST OF CHARLOTTETOWN

The TransCanada/Highway 1 departs Charlottetown and finishes at the Wood Islands ferry terminal. Turnoffs lead to several interesting places. Highway 2 runs northeast through Tracadie and continues all the way to Souris.

## Orwell

About a 25-minute drive east of Charlottetown, a marked road off the TransCanada leads to **Orwell Corner Historic Village,** a restored mid-19th-century farm village founded by early Scottish and Irish settlers. Buildings include the farmhouse, general store, dressmaker's shop, blacksmith's shop, church, and barns. The village is open mid-May to mid-October. During the prime summer season, from late June to early September, it's open daily 9 A.M.–5 P.M. In early and late season, it's open Mon.–Fri. 10 A.M.–3 P.M. Admission charged. For more information on tours, crafts demonstrations, and events call 902/651-8510.

Wednesday evenings from early June to late September, there's a *ceilidh,* featuring traditional music and song, with refreshments available; adults $5, children under 12 free. On the second Sunday of August, **Kilts and Cabers** celebrations, tel. 902/651-8510, provides the chance to sample haggis and enjoy pipers, fiddlers, dancers, and traditional games such as caber tossing.

## Lord Selkirk Provincial Park

Tucked on the eastern shore of Orwell Bay, an inlet off the larger Hillsborough Bay, is beachfront Lord Selkirk Provincial Park, tel. 902/659-7221. The park, named for the Scottish leader of one of the early immigrant groups, is right off the TransCanada, a stone's throw west of Eldon. Though the beach here isn't good for swimming, it's great for walking, beachcombing, and clam digging. The park's unserviced campsites ($17) and hookup sites ($20) are accompanied by an extra-charge pool, nine-hole golf course, and mini-golf, as well as a launderette, kitchen shelters, fireplaces, and a nearby campers' store.

A naturalist program runs throughout summer, and the first weekend of August, the park is the site of the annual **Highland Games,** which include piping, dancing competitions, Scottish athletic competitions, and lobster suppers. The park is open late June to early September.

## Point Prim Lighthouse

Point Prim Lighthouse is at the end of Highway 209, which peels off the TransCanada and runs 10 km down the long, slender peninsula jutting into Hillsborough Bay. The unusual, 20-meter-tall tower, built in 1845, was designed by Isaac Smith, architect of Province House. It's Prince Edward Island's oldest lighthouse and Canada's only round, brick lighthouse tower. The view overlooking the strait from the octagonal lantern house at the top is gorgeous. It's open daily July–August; tel. 902/659-2412. Admission free.

The **Chowder House** at Point Prim, tel. 902/659-2023, serves fresh local clams and mussels, chowder, sandwiches, and homemade breads and pastries. It's open daily, mid-June to mid-September.

## Wood Islands and Vicinity

Highway 1 (the TransCanada) officially leaves Prince Edward Island at Wood Islands, terminus for the **Northumberland Ferries,** tel. 902/566-3838 or 800/565-0201, service to Caribou, Nova Scotia. Up to nine crossings daily are made in each direction through the May to mid-December operating season. Travel to the island is free, with the ferry back to the mainland costing $49 per vehicle (includes driver and passengers). Other fares include: walk-on passengers $11, bicycles $20, motorcycles $25, RVs or trailers $61–74. The crossing takes 75 minutes, but expect to wait in line at least that long during peak sailings.

A road runs along the eastern side of the ferry terminal access road to the **Visitor Information Centre,** tel. 902/962-7411, open daily mid-May to mid-June 8 A.M.–6 P.M., mid-June to early September 8 A.M.–10 P.M., early September to late October 8 A.M.–6 P.M.

**Meadow Lodge Motel,** tel. 902/962-2022 or 800/461-2022, on the TransCanada two km west of the terminal, is a convenient accommodation if you're leaving the island early or arriving late. Rooms run $60–77, and it's open in summer only.

A five-minute drive east from the ferry terminal, **Northumberland Provincial Park** on Highway 4, tel. 902/962-7418, fronts the ocean, near enough to the terminal to see the ferries coming and going to Caribou. The park offers rental bikes, hayrides, a nature trail, a stream for fishing, an ocean beach with clam digging, and miniature golf. Facilities include 60 sites ($17–20), many with hookups, plus a launderette, kitchen shelters, a nearby campers' store, and hot showers. It's open late June to early September.

## Continuing East into Kings County

From Wood Islands, Highway 4 continues into Kings County, making a sharp left inland to Murray River. Highway 18 sticks to the coast, wrapping around Murray Head before leading into the town of Murray Harbour and then into **Murray River.**

# The North Shore

Queens County's North Shore is a long swatch of PEI's loveliest landscapes, with much of the actual coastline protected by Prince Edward Island National Park. Visitors in the know and the discerning carriage trade have retreated here for decades. Outside of popular Cavendish, the rest of the North Shore is low-key and quiet.

## Utopian Avonlea

The author Lucy Maud Montgomery penned northern Queens County's Cavendish into literary stardom. Montgomery as a young writer portrayed the village, and indeed the whole area, as an idyllic "neverland" called Avonlea, imbued with innocence and harmony.

As you drive the rambling red-clay lanes, and walk the quiet woods, meadows, and gulf shore, you'll have to agree the lady did not overstate her case. The North Shore's most pastoral and historic places are preserved as part of **Prince Edward Island National Park.** And if you're in pursuit of the bucolic dream that Montgomery created, don't limit yourself to Cavendish. Queens County—especially the Gulf of St. Lawrence

coastline—is virtually untouched by tacky, 20th-century commercialism.

Florid writing style notwithstanding, Montgomery created perfection on earth within the pages of her books, and through the decades more affection for a place has centered on Cavendish than perhaps anyplace else in North America. Montgomery's Anne, the winsome, impressionable, and spunky heroine of *Anne of Green Gables,* has been loved by generation after generation of young readers around the world. And those children, as adults, are among the island's most numerous visitors.

## Getting There

The most direct route between Charlottetown and Cavendish is to take Highway 2 west from the capital for 25 km, then head north from Hunter River on Highway 13. This drive takes less than one hour to reach the coast. A more leisurely alternative, and the one followed below, begins by taking Highway northeast from Charlottetown, then Highway 6 north to Grand Tracadie.

PRINCE EDWARD ISLAND

# THE EASTERN END

## Grand Tracadie

Grand Tracadie is easily reached in around 40 minutes from Charlottetown. It is the eastern gateway to Prince Edward Island National Park, but is best known for a historic inn, which lies within the park, two km from the town center. Elegant, green-roofed **Dalvay by the Sea,** tel. 902/672-2048, www.dalvaybythesea.com, appeals to guests who like an old-money ambience. The rustic mansion was built in 1895 by millionaire American oil industrialist Alexander MacDonald, who used the lodging as a summer retreat. Today the hotel, its antiques, and its spacious grounds are painstakingly maintained by the national park staff. Its 26 rooms rent for $175–325, breakfast and dinner included. Four cottages on the grounds ($360) are most popular with honeymooners. The hotel's dining room is locally renowned. Entrées ($17–34) feature formal Canadian cuisine prepared with a French flair. The emphasis is on the freshest produce, best seafood (try the poached salmon), and finest beef cuts; reservations are required. Other facilities at the hotel include a well-stocked gift shop, a nearby beach, a tennis court, bike rentals, a lake with canoes, and nature trails. Open mid-June to early October.

## Stanhope

From Grand Tracadie, there are two options for westbound travelers: one along the coast within the national park (see below), the other through Stanhope. Golfers like **Stanhope Golf and Country Club** for its relaxing 5,800-yard layout overlooking Covehead Bay. The course is open May through October; green fees are $40 weekdays, $42 weekends. Clubs can be rented.

In Stanhope itself, **Campbell's Tourist Home and Housekeeping Unit,** tel. 902/672-2421, offers year-round B&B units for $50, including a light breakfast, and one housekeeping apartment for $100. Another option is **Stanhope by the Sea,** tel. 902/672-2047 or 877/672-2047, on Bay Shore Road (Highway 25), which overlooks Covehead Bay and the national park. The inn offers 60 lodge rooms ($120), 22 motel units

($140), and eight suites ($180–200). Rates include a buffet-style breakfast and a discount on dinner. Resort facilities include tennis, croquet, a pool, bike and canoe rentals, and an adjacent golf course. Open June to October 15.

## Brackley Beach

With its proximity to the national park, excellent beaches, golf, deep-sea fishing, and other attractions, Brackley Beach is a popular place. Accommodations are plentiful.

**Blue Waters Tourist Home & Executive Cottages** on Highway 15, tel. 902/672-2720 or 800/616-9436, is a large country home on spacious grounds overlooking Brackley Bay, with five guest rooms for $58 (summer only). **Shaw's Hotel,** on an unmarked lane off Highway 15, tel. 902/672-2022, overlooks the bay from a 30-hectare peninsula at the edge of Prince Edward Island National Park. This was the Shaw family's homestead in the 1860s and it's still in the family. The property has 16 antiques-furnished guest rooms in the main house, as well as 25 adjacent historic cottages and 15 newer upscale waterfront chalets. Rates start at $120, or you can pay $110–150 per person including breakfast and dinner. The cottages are available year-round (from $85 in winter); the inn is open June to October. The ambience is informal and friendly—a nice place for meeting islanders and other visitors. The dining room at Shaw's Hotel is consistently good; start with a chowder appetizer and stick to the chef's daily choices, prepared from whatever seafood is in season ($22–28). Two nights a week (on a rotating basis), the hotel hosts **Rustico Shindigs,** concerts of local Maritime music; admission $3.50. The **Lobster Trap Lounge,** tel. 902/672-2769, is another dining option, a pub-style restaurant set off by itself. The mood is informal, as is the menu, with seafood platters, hamburgers, and fries.

In the vicinity, the **Dunes Studio Gallery and Cafe** on Highway 15, tel. 902/672-2586, is an architecturally distinctive building with lots of exposed wood. It's worth browsing for porcelains crafted by owner Peter Jansons; the shop is also an outlet for island craftspeople with a line of stoneware, framed photography, gold jewelry, pottery, watercolors, oils, and sculptures. The café is open May through October, daily 9 A.M.–10 P.M.

Camping is available nearby at the 30-acre **Vacationland Travel Park,** east of Highway 15 overlooking Brackley Bay, tel. 902/672-2317 or 800/529-0066, www.vacationland.pe.ca. Facilities include a dump station, store, canteen, Laundromat, heated pool, hot showers, mini-golf, and other recreational activities. The park is open May 15 to September 15. Rates are $21–25 for up to two adults and four kids under 16.

### Oyster Bed Bridge

This small village three km southwest of Brackley Beach is worth a stop for **Café St. Jean,** tel. 902/963-3133, which hosts shindigs of traditional island music on Tuesday and Friday evenings. The menu combines French and Cajun fare ($14–25) in an informal atmosphere. It's open June–September, 11:30 A.M.–9:30 P.M.

**Cheeselady's Gouda** in Winsloe North, tel. 902/368-1506, is owned by Dutch immigrants who make a variety of Gouda cheeses just like in the Netherlands. Visitors are welcome to watch the production process. It's open year-round, Mon.–Sat. 10 A.M.–6 P.M. To get there take Highway 223 east from Oyster Bed Bridge. The road soon bends southeast to Winsloe North.

## PRINCE EDWARD ISLAND NATIONAL PARK

Prince Edward Island National Park's sandy beaches, dunes, sandstone cliffs, marshes, and forestlands represent Prince Edward Island as it once was, unspoiled by the crush of 20th-century development.

The park protects a slender, 40-km-long coastal slice of natural perfection, extending almost the full length of Queens County, as well as a six-square-km spit of land further east in St. Peters Bay (see below). The park extends inland at Cavendish to include Green Gales House and Green Gables Golf Course (both detailed below). The main body of the park is bookended by two large bays. At the eastern end, Tracadie Bay spreads out like an oversize pond with shimmering waters.

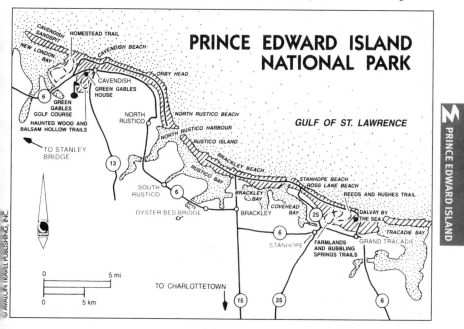

Forty km to the west, New London Bay forms almost a mirror image of the eastern end. In between, long barrier islands define Rustico and Covehead Bays, and sand dunes webbed with marram grass, rushes, fragrant bayberry, and wild roses front the coastline.

Sunrise and sunset here are cast in glowing colors. All along the gulf at sunrise, the beaches have a sense of primeval peacefulness, their sands textured like herringbone by the overnight sea breezes.

Getting around is easy. Highway 6 lies on the park's inland side, connecting numerous park entrances, and the Gulf Shore Parkway runs along the coast nearly the park's entire length. You can drive through the park year-round. Cyclists will appreciate the smooth, wide shoulders and light traffic along the Gulf Shore Parkway, which runs most of the length of the park.

From early June to early September, the entrance fee for a one-day pass is adults $3.50, seniors $2.50, and children $1.75, to a maximum of $8 per vehicle.

## Environmental Factors

The national park was established in 1937 to protect the fragile dunes along the Gulf of St. Lawrence, as well as cultural features such as the Green Gables House. Parks Canada walks a fine line, balancing environmental concerns with the responsibilities of hosting half a million park visitors a year. Boardwalks route visitors through dunes to the beaches and preserve the fragile landscape.

Bird-watchers will be amply rewarded with sightings of some of the more than 100 species known to frequent the park. Brackley Marsh, Orby Head, and the Rustico Island Causeway are good places to start. The park preserves nesting habitat for some 25 pairs of endangered piping plovers—small, shy shorebirds that arrive in early April to breed in flat sandy areas near the high-tide line. Some beaches may be closed in spring and summer when the plovers are nesting; it's vital to the birds' survival that visitors stay clear of these areas.

piping plover

## Recreation

If you'd like to learn more about the park's ecology, join one of the **nature walks** led by Parks Canada rangers. The treks lead through white spruce stunted by winter storms and winds, to freshwater ponds, and into the habitats of such native animal species as red fox, northern phalarope, Swainson's thrush, and junco.

The unbroken stretches of sandy beaches—some white, others tinted pink by iron oxide—are among the best in the province. Half a dozen public beaches lie between Blooming Head and Orby Head, many backed by steep, red-sandstone cliffs. On warm summer days, droves of sunbathers laze on the shore and swim in the usually gentle surf. Stanhope, Ross Lane, Brackley, North Rustico, Cavendish, and Cavendish Campground beaches all have lifeguards on duty, and a variety of visitor facilities.

Established **hiking trails** range from the half-km, wheelchair-accessible Reeds and Rushes Trail, beginning at the Dalvay Administration Building near Grand Tracadie, to the eight-km Homestead Trail beginning near the entrance to Cavendish Campground. The latter wends inland alongside freshwater ponds and through woods and marshes and is open to both hikers and bikers. Be wary of potentially hazardous cliff edges, and of the poison ivy and ticks that lurk in the ground cover.

## Campgrounds

The park's three campgrounds are distinctly different from one another. **Stanhope Campground,** east of Brackley Beach, is closest to the seacoast and has 90 unserviced sites ($17–19), 16 sites with two-way hookups ($20), and 14 sites with full hookups ($21). Open mid-June to early October. **Cavendish Campground,** closest to Cavendish and center of the park's naturalist programs, is most popular and has 230 unserviced sites ($17–19) and 78 full hookup sites ($21). It's open late May to early October. More remote **Robinsons Island**

BOB RACE

© ANDREW HEMPSTEAD

The national park protects long stretches of undeveloped oceanfront.

**Campground** occupies a 35-acre spread on Rustico Island, the lengthy sandbar that lies across Rustico Bay's mouth. The campground's 148 unserviced sites ($15–17) are four km inland from the sea in a wilderness setting that appeals to naturalists. Open late June to late August. Campground facilities include campers' stores (in the campgrounds or nearby), kitchen shelters, launderettes, flush toilets, and hot showers (except at Robinsons Island). For reservations call 902/672-6350 or 800/414-6765.

### Information

The main **Park Information Centre** is in the provincially operated Visitor Information Centre, 50 meters north of the Highway 6 and Highway 13 intersection in Cavendish, tel. 902/963-2391. It's open June–September, daily 9 A.M.–5 P.M., with extended hours of 9 A.M.–9 P.M. in July and August. As well as general park information, displays depict the park's natural history, and a small shop sells park-related literature and souvenirs. To the east, the **Brackley Visitor Information Centre,** at the intersection of Highways 6 and 15 in Brackley Beach, tel. 902/672-7474, supplies park information. Write

the island's park office at Parks Canada, 2 Palmer Lane, Charlottetown, PE C1A 5V6; tel. 902/672-6350; www.parkscanada.gc.ca/pei.

## AROUND RUSTICO BAY

A decade after the French began Port la Joye near Charlottetown, French settlers cut through the inland forest and settled Rustico Bay's coastline. England's Acadian Deportation in 1755 emptied the villages, but not for long. The Acadians returned, and the five revived Rusticos—Rusticoville, South Rustico, Anglo Rustico, North Rustico (pop. 600, the area's center), and North Rustico Harbour—still thrive and encircle Rustico Bay's western shore. Expect a composite of French Acadian and Anglo cultures on the gulf coast.

### South Rustico

For a look at old-time Acadian culture, check out the imposing two-story **Farmers' Bank Museum** on Church Road, tel. 902/963-2304. Built in 1864 as Canada's first chartered people's bank, the building served as the early Acadian banking connection, then as a library. Exhibits at this national historic site include heritage displays plus

PRINCE EDWARD ISLAND

artifacts from the life of the Reverend Georges-Antoine Belcourt, the founder. The museum is open late June to early September, Mon.–Sat. 9:30 A.M.–5 P.M., Sun. from 1 P.M. A small admission fee is charged.

The 1870 **Barachois Inn,** overlooking Rustico Bay from Highway 243, tel. 902/963-2194, www.barachoisinn.com, offers four guest rooms ($140–185, including full breakfast) brimming with antiques and paintings. All rooms have private baths, and two of them are suites with soaker tubs. The inn is open May through October.

**Rustico Resort Golf & Country Club,** at the intersection of Highways 6 and 242, tel. 902/963-2909, www.rusticoresort.com, boasts golf greens known far beyond Atlantic Canada and described as user-friendly by *Golf Digest.* The 18-hole, par-73 course rents carts and clubs and offers lessons from a pro. It's open May through October; green fees run $35, but guests at the resort play free (up to two adults per unit).

The resort's motel units run $115 nightly; suites $135 nightly; and self-contained cottages from $900 weekly. Other amenities include grass tennis courts, a heated pool, and a dining room with a lounge.

**Cymbria Tent and Trailer Park,** on Highway 242 off Highway 6, tel. 902/963-2458, occupies a quiet, 12-hectare location close to the beach; sites cost $18 unserviced, $20–22 with hookups. Facilities include a store, rec room, playground, dump station, and hot showers. Open mid-May to Labour Day.

## North Rustico

Half a dozen charter fishing operators tie up at North Rustico and North Rustico Harbour. The average rate is about $15 per person for a three-hour outing or $150 for a full day's charter, for cod, mackerel, flounder, and tuna. Most charters operate July to mid-September or mid-October. The crew will outfit you in raingear if

# LUCY MAUD MONTGOMERY

Lucy Maud Montgomery, known and beloved around the world as the creator of *Anne of Green Gables,* was born at New London, Prince Edward Island, in 1874, a decade after the Charlottetown Conference. When Lucy was only two, her mother died and her father moved to western Canada. Maud, as she preferred to be called, was left in the care of her maternal grandparents, who brought her to Cavendish.

Cavendish, in northern Queens County, was idyllic in those days, and Montgomery wrote fondly about the ornate Victorian sweetness of the setting of her early years. As a young woman, she studied first at the island's Prince of Wales College, later at Dalhousie University in Halifax. She then returned to the island as a teacher at Bideford, Lower Bedeque, Belmont, and Lot 15. In 1898, her grandfather's death brought her back to Cavendish to help her grandmother.

The idea for *Anne of Green Gables* dated to the second Cavendish stay, and the book was published in 1908. In 1911, Montgomery married the Rev. Ewen MacDonald at her Campbell relatives' Silver Bush homestead overlooking the Lake of Shining Waters. (The Campbell descendants still live in the pretty farmhouse and have turned their home into a museum.) The couple moved to Ontario, where Montgomery spent the rest of her life, returning to PEI only for short visits. Though she left, Maud never forgot Prince Edward Island. Those brief revisitations with her beloved island must have been painful; after one trip, she wistfully recalled in her journal:

*This evening I spent in Lover's Lane. How beautiful it was—green and alluring and beckoning! I had been tired and discouraged and sick at heart before I went to it—and it rested me and cheered me and stole away the heartsickness, giving peace and newness of life.*

Montgomery died in 1942, and lay in state at the Green Gables House in the new national park before burial in the Cavendish Cemetery. As an author, she left 20 juvenile books and a myr-

needed, provide tackle and bait, and clean and fillet your catch. **Beauty and the Beast,** tel. 902/963-3130, caters to casual anglers with three scheduled trips daily.

**Andy's Surfside Inn,** off Gulf Shore Parkway just 100 meters from the beach, tel. 902/963-2405, offers a sundeck, bikes, and a barbecue. The inn's eight rooms rent for $40–55, including continental breakfast. **St. Lawrence Motel,** tel. 902/963-2053 or 800/387-2053, is on Gulf Shore Road in the national park between Cavendish and North Rustico. Set on eight hectares, this 16-room property overlooks the gulf a short walk from the water. It offers kitchen-equipped suites, a recreation room, horseshoe pits, barbecues, croquet, and other recreational facilities. The St. Lawrence is open late May to late September. Rates are $85–135. **Saint Nicholas Motel,** tel. 902/963-2898, is on Highway 6 on the outskirts of North Rustico. The 18 units have refrigerators, and dining is available

nearby. Open mid-May through mid-October; rates are $70–85.

**Fisherman's Wharf Lobster Suppers,** at North Rustico's busiest intersection, tel. 902/963-2669, is a cavernous 500-seat restaurant that attracts the tour bus crowd from Cavendish. Choose from three different sized lobsters ($26–32), pay your money, and join the fray. The cost includes one full lobster and unlimited trips to the buffet counter, including chowder, mussels, hot entrées, salad, dessert, and hot drinks. The restaurant is open mid-May to mid-October, daily noon–9 P.M.

## CAVENDISH

Thanks to Lucy Maud Montgomery and a certain fictional character named Anne, Cavendish is the county's (and the island's) main attraction. Unfortunately, those who come here expecting to find a bucolic little oasis of tranquility

---

iad of other writings. Her works have been published worldwide, translated into 16 languages. In Japan, Montgomery's writings are required reading in the school system—which accounts for the island's many Japanese visitors.

Montgomery also inadvertently created an island phenomenon, giving PEI the persistent image as the utopian Avonlea, the name she had given the Cavendish area during her long years in publishing. Her heroine Anne is recreated in Charlottetown's annual summertime musical, and seems to be everywhere in PEI tourist advertising. The once rural Cavendish area has become a maze of theme parks, fast-food outlets, and souvenir shops in parts, and the village has repositioned itself as an official resort municipality to try to grapple with fame. Remarkably, obtrusive commercialism has made no inroads be-

yond the Cavendish area on Queens County's North Shore.

Montgomery wrote for children, and she viewed Cavendish and Prince Edward Island with all the clarity and innocence that a child possesses. Her books are as timeless today as they were decades ago. Some critics have described Montgomery's writings as mawkish. Contemporary scholars, however, have taken a new look at the author's works and have begun to discern a far more complex style. The academic community may debate her literary prowess, but no matter—the honest essence of Montgomery's writings have inspired decades of zealous pilgrims to pay their respects to her native Cavendish. To islanders, she is Lucy Maud, their literary genius, on a first-name basis.

will be sorely disappointed. Fame has transformed this small town and its environs into a tourist theme park, replete with tacky commercial trappings such as garish roadside signs, amusement parks, and shopping malls. On weekends and holidays in summer, hordes of visitors converge here, and traffic backs up for miles along the highway. To dedicated readers of Montgomery's sentimental books, the village's lure is emotional. For others—those who don't know Anne of Green Gables from Anne Frank—it might best be avoided. Still, if you end up here and are looking for something to do, you'll have a multitude of choices—including heading into adjacent Prince Edward Island National park (see above), golfing at the Green Gables Golf Course, or browsing through a multitude of crafts shops

## History

Immigrants fleeing Scotland's poverty and religious persecution arrived at New London and Stanhope in the mid-1700s. By the 1790s, other Scots settled Cavendish—L. M. Montgomery's ancestors among them. The town was named for Field Marshall Lord Frederick Cavendish, patron landowner who acquired title in the 1760s.

## Green Gables House

Located on the west side of the Highway 6 and Highway 13 intersection, Green Gables House, tel. 902/963-3370, reigns as the idyllic hub of a Montgomery sightseeing circuit. The restored 19th-century farmhouse, once home of Montgomery's elderly cousins and the setting also for her most famous book, *Anne of Green Gables*, is furnished simply and stolidly, just as it was described in the novel. A fire in 1997 badly damaged portions of the house, but repairs commenced immediately and within a couple of weeks the landmark was back in perfect condition. Among other memorabilia in the pretty vintage setting are artifacts such as the author's archaic typewriter, on which she composed so many well-loved passages. Period-style gardens, farm buildings, and an interpretive center and gift shop complete the complex. Also on the

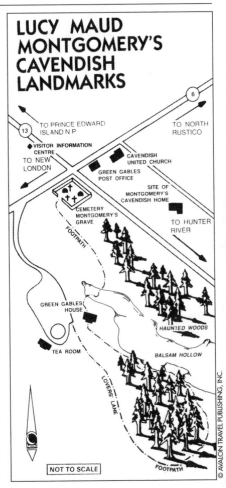

LUCY MAUD MONTGOMERY'S CAVENDISH LANDMARKS

grounds, the Balsam Hollow and Haunted Woods trails feature some of Montgomery's favorite woodland haunts, including Lover's Lane. Green Gables is open May through October, daily 9 A.M.–5 P.M. (until 8 P.M. from late June to late August); plan to visit early in the day to miss the crowds. Admission is $7 adults, $5.50 seniors, $3 youths, $16 families.

## Other Montgomery Sights

**Site of Lucy Maud Montgomery's Cavendish Home,** Highway 6 near the United Church, tel.

902/963-2231, is the location of Montgomery's grandparents' homestead (now gone), where Lucy lived from 1876 to 1911 and wrote *Anne of Green Gables*. "I wrote it in the evenings after my regular day's work was done," she recalled, "wrote most of it at the window of the little gable room that had been mine for many years." The site includes the house's stone cellar, set amid woods and gardens, now a bookstore with works by and about Montgomery. It's open June through September, daily 10 A.M.–5 P.M. (9 A.M.–7 P.M. in July and August). Admission is adults $5, children $1.

Montgomery is buried at the nearby United Church cemetery.

## Accommodations

**Kindred Spirits Country Inn and Cottages** on Highway 6, tel. 902/963-2434, www .kindredspirits.pe.ca, lies beside Green Gables House and the surrounding golf course. It offers 25 B&B rooms (from $135 high season) and 12 outlying housekeeping cottages ($175–205, for one to four guests). All units have private baths; some have whirlpool tubs. Rates include a light breakfast. Open mid-May to mid-October.

**Silverwood Motel,** west along Highway 6, tel. 902/963-2439 or 800/565-4753, www .silverwoodmotel.com, features 27 rooms ($100) and 23 self-contained suites (from $150). The motel is open mid-May to mid-October.

**Our Lady of the Way Tourist Lodge,** tel. 902/963-2024 or 888/963-5239, is on Highway 13, 1.5 km south of Cavendish Beach. It offers 10 units, a sundeck, and a picnic area. Licensed dining is nearby. Leashed pets are allowed. Rates are $65–80.

**Cavendish Motel,** tel. 902/963-2244 or 800/565-2243, www.cavendishmotel.pe.ca, is at the intersection of Highways 6 and 13. The motel offers 35 standard rooms and 10 housekeeping units. Amenities include TVs, barbecues, a heated pool, a dining room, and a playground. Rates are $85–165 s or d. Open June through September.

**Cavendish Beach Cottages,** on Gulf Shore Road within Prince Edward Island National Park, tel. 902/963-2025, www.cavendishbeachcot-tages.com, boasts 13 simply furnished yet mod-ern cottages, each with a deck offering ocean views ($125–175). The cottages, set back 200 meters from the beach, are just a few steps from the park's jogging and hiking trails. They're open mid-May to mid-October.

## Campgrounds

What **Cavendish Campground** lacks in facilities it makes up for in location, close to the ocean within Prince Edward Island National Park and just a few km from downtown Cavendish, tel. 902/672-6350 or 800/414-6765. Unserviced sites run $17–19 (depending on the view), serviced sites $21, including the use of kitchen shelters and showers. Two other national park campgrounds lie to the east.

**Marco Polo Land,** on Highway 13 two km from Cavendish Beach, tel. 902/963-2352 or 800/665-2352, is the island's definitive commercial campground, replete with resort trappings. Facilities at the 40-hectare park include 497 sites ($24–31), tennis courts, mini-golf, two heated pools, a licensed dining room, a campers' store, a Laundromat, and hot showers; open June to mid-October.

The 120-hectare, 415-site **Cavendish Sunset Campground** is on Highway 6 opposite Cavendish Boardwalk and the entrance to the national park, tel. 902/963-2440 or 800/715-2440. Leashed pets are allowed, and amenities include bike and movie rentals, a Laundromat, mini-golf, tennis, a store, hot showers, and kitchen shelters. Dining is within walking distance. The campground is open mid-June to Labour Day. Rates are $23–26.

## Food

On the eastern side of the Highway 6 and Highway 13 intersection, the **Friendly Fisherman,** tel. 902/963-2234, offers inexpensive breakfasts from 8 A.M., then seafood and steak choices the rest of the day. **Fiddles & Vittles** on Highway 6, tel. 902/963-3003, has pleased islanders for decades with bountiful seafood platters ($14–21). The particularly kid-friendly restaurant is open June to early September, daily 11:30 A.M.–9 P.M. Numerous fast-food places clog the area's arteries—you won't go hungry here.

For do-it-yourself meals, take your choice of markets along major highways; shops at **Cavendish Beach Shopping Plaza** answer most needs. **Cavendish Boardwalk** mall is another source and also boasts **Cow's** ice-cream shop, tel. 902/963-2692.

## Recreation and Entertainment

You'll see **Sandspit** amusement park right on Highway 6, tel. 902/963-2626. The huge park, a magnet for kids on vacation, features a roller coaster (The Cyclone—billed as the largest in the Maritimes), a carousel, and other rides, rides, rides. It's free to get in, but each ride costs a small amount. All-day ride packages are available. In the vicinity, you'll find a number of enthralling attractions, including **Black Magic,** indoor black-light mini-golf; the **Fantazmagoric Museum,** promising "strange and unusual subjects presented in thought-provoking exhibits and displays"; and yet more mini-golf (outdoors).

**Rainbow Valley,** a quarter mile from Green Gables on Highway 6, tel. 902/963-2221, is where islanders take their kids for tame entertainment ($12 adults, $10 seniors, $9 children, preschoolers free). The 16-hectare park offers water slides, rides, and picnic places. It's open early June to early September, Mon.–Sat. 9 A.M.–8 P.M., Sunday 11 A.M.–8 P.M.

And what tourist mecca would be complete without a **Ripley's Believe It or Not! Museum,** in Cranberry Village on Highway 6, tel. 902/963-2242 ($8 adults, $6.50 seniors, $5 kids 6–15), or a wax museum—in this case the **Royal Atlantic Wax Museum,** at the junction of Highways 6 and 13, tel. 902/963-2350 (around $7 adults, $5.50 ages 13–17, $3.50 ages 5–12, $18 families).

For more pastoral pursuits, **Cavendish Sunset Campground,** on Highway 6 next to Cavendish Boardwalk, tel. 902/963-2440 or 800/715-2440, rents standard and mountain bikes from $16 per day; open mid-June to early September, daily 8 A.M.–10 P.M. For a round of golf at **Green Gables Golf Course,** expect to pay around $40. It's open May through October; reservations are advised during July and August, call 902/963-2488.

## Information and Services

The provincial **Visitor Information Centre** at the intersection of Highways 13 and 6, tel. 902/963-7830, is open June to mid-October, daily 9 A.M.–6 P.M., with extended hours in mid-summer (till 9 P.M. mid- to late June, till 10 P.M. July to mid-August). It holds local and provincial information, as well as national park displays and details.

# VICINITY OF CAVENDISH

A web of hamlets encircles Cavendish. The rural scenery is lovely, and exploring the beaches and back roads should help you sharpen your appetite for a night at one of PEI's famed lobster-supper community halls, which are scattered hereabouts.

## Stanley Bridge

For seaworthy sightseeing, check out **Stanley Bridge Marine Aquarium,** on Highway 6 west of Cavendish, tel. 902/886-3355. The privately operated aquarium has native fish species in viewing tanks and exhibits on natural history and oyster cultivation; seals are kept outside in penned pools. The complex is open mid-June to mid-September, daily 9 A.M.–8 P.M. Admission is charged. Part of the complex is an oyster bar with a deck built over the water.

In the vicinity, shoppers like the **Stanley Bridge Studios** on Highway 6, tel. 902/886-2800 or 902/621-0314, where shelves and floor space overflow with woolen sweaters, quilts, apparel, stoneware, porcelain, jewelry, and Anne dolls. It's open mid-May to mid-October, daily 10 A.M.–5 P.M. (9:30 A.M. until dusk in July and August). **Old Stanley Schoolhouse** at the intersection of Highways 6 and 224, five km from Cavendish, tel. 902/886-2033, handles island-made quilts, weaving, pottery, pewter, folk art, and sweaters. It's open daily May to mid-October.

Overlooking the river west of downtown, **Stanley Bridge Country Resort** on Highway 6, tel. 902/886-2882 or 800/361-2882, is a large complex comprising motel-style rooms ($85–170), self-contained cottages ($135–220), a café and restaurant, and an outdoor heated pool scattered around spacious grounds dotted with Adirondack chairs and picnic tables.

## St. Ann

The **Dyed in the Wool** shop on Highway 224 between New Glasgow and Stanley Bridge, tel. 902/621-0699, is Jill Allman's creation and melds crafts with wares woven from her own sheep's wool. The shop is open early June to early October, daily 10 A.M. to 5 P.M.

**Blue Jay Cottages,** off Highway 224 on New London Road, tel. 902/621-0709 or 800/663-0709, offers eight fully equipped one- to three-bedroom housekeeping cottages at $120 for up to six people. Amenities include a heated pool, playground, and Laundromat.

## New London

The **Lucy Maud Montgomery Birthplace,** at the junction of Highways 6 and 20, tel. 902/886-2099, lies 10 minutes from Cavendish at what was once Clifton. The author was born in the unassuming house in 1874. Among the exhibits are her wedding dress, scrapbooks, and other personal items. The site is open daily mid-May to Thanksgiving. Hours are 9 A.M.–7 P.M. in July and August and 9 A.M.–5 P.M. the rest of the season. Admission is $2 adults, 50 cents children 6–12, under six free.

If you're on the prowl for a place to eat close by, check out the **New London Seafood Restaurant** on Highway 20, tel. 902/886-3000; the waterside dining room serves basic, hearty seafood ($7–25) June through September.

Questions on the area's highlights may be directed to **New London Tourist Information Centre,** in the community complex east of Stanley Bridge, tel. 902/886-2315 or 888/886-2315. It's open June–September, daily 9 A.M.–8 P.M. and on Saturday from late March to June.

## Continuing North Toward Park Corner

From New London, Highway 6 cuts southwest across the island to Kensington, and Highway

20 heads north around New London Bay to Park Corner. If you're looking for somewhere to eat, consider the short detour off the highway to the hamlet of **Long River** and the **Kitchen Witch Tea Room,** tel. 902/886-2294, occupying a two-room schoolhouse dating to 1832. As the name implies, you can have your future read in your tealeaves if you like. The cozy restaurant is known for chowders, sandwiches, salads, and extraordinarily rich desserts. It's open mid-June to September for breakfast, lunch, and dinner.

At **French River,** eight km northwest of New London on Highway 20, **Wild Goose Lodge,** tel. 902/886-2177 or 800/463-4053, www.wildgooselodge.com, is a gem of a contemporary-style lodge, gorgeously designed with six housekeeping suites ($105–125 for up to four people) that converge on a central lounge area; outside, there's a viewing deck that overlooks the countryside (and flocks of geese during autumn). The lodge is open mid-May to mid-September.

## Park Corner

**Anne of Green Gables Museum at Silver Bush,** on Highway 20, tel. 902/436-7329 or 902/886-2884, another Montgomery landmark and the ancestral home of the author's Campbell relatives, spreads out in a farmhouse setting in the pastoral rolling countryside. Montgomery described the house as "the big beautiful home that was the wonder castle of my dreams," and here she was married in 1911. The museum's exhibits include Montgomery's personal correspondence and first editions of her works. It's open June through October, daily 9 A.M.–6 P.M.; July–August until dark. Admission is $2.50 for adults, 75 cents for children under 16. The Lake of Shining Waters, described in *Anne of Green Lakes,* lies across the road.

The adjacent **Shining Waters Tea Room,** tel. 902/886-2003, serves island-style light fare, and the crafts shop sells Montgomery souvenirs as well as wind chimes, quilts, and other crafts.

# Prince County

Along the southern portion of Prince County—the province's slender western part—the land is level, and the pastoral farmlands flow in gentle, serene sweeps to the strait coastline. Thick woodlands span the county's midsection, and you'll see fields of potatoes that blossom in July and green carpets of wheat nodding in the summer breezes. The northern tip is a remote and barren plain with a windswept coast, where farmers known as "mossers" use stout draft horses to reap Irish moss (a seaweed) from the surf.

Summerside, the province's second-largest town, boasts an ample supply of lodgings, restaurants, and nightlife. Just west of there is the province's largest Acadian area, the **Région évangéline.**

Count on high-quality crafts and wares at town boutiques and outlying shops throughout the region; the region's craftspeople are renowned for quilts, knitted apparel, Acadian shirts, and blankets.

The **climate** here is not so much moody as it is variable—be prepared to dress like an onion, ready to peel as you go from one area to another.

## GETTING AROUND

**Highway 2,** PEI's main expressway, enters Prince County at the town of Kensington, glides past the seaport of Summerside on a narrow isthmus, and leads inland for 100 km to finish at the village of Tignish, near the island's northwestern tip.

This route is dubbed the Lady Slipper Scenic Drive, one of the provincial scenic sightseeing routes; it's signposted with a red symbol of the orchidlike flower. But the scenic route designation is somewhat misleading. The county's most idyllic scenery—and some of PEI's most spectacular sea views—lie well off this beaten path, at the sea's edges along Northumberland Strait and the Gulf of St. Lawrence.

Nonetheless, Highway 2 is useful as an access road through the region. Narrow roads amble along the coastline close to the sea. These byways—**Highways 11, 12, and 14**—are incorporated as part of Lady Slipper Scenic Drive, and though the route numbers change, the symbol

Summerside Harbour

© ANDREW HEMPSTEAD

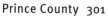

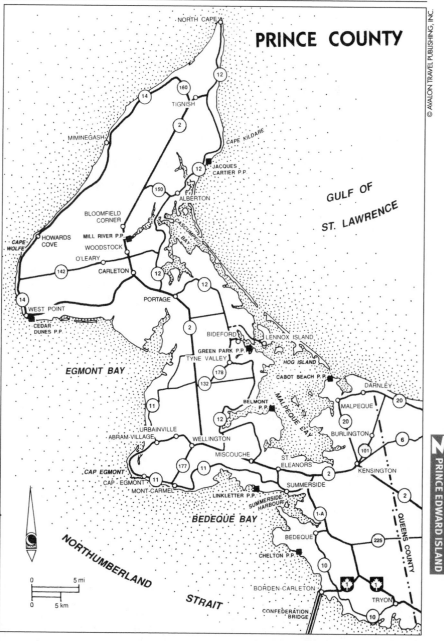

PRINCE COUNTY

GULF OF
ST. LAWRENCE

NORTH CAPE

TIGNISH

MIMINEGASH

CAPE KILDARE

JACQUES
CARTIER P.P.

ALBERTON

BLOOMFIELD
CORNER

CAPE
WOLFE

HOWARDS
COVE

MILL RIVER P.P.

WOODSTOCK

O'LEARY

CARLETON

PORTAGE

WEST POINT

CEDAR
DUNES P.P.

EGMONT BAY

BIDEFORD

LENNOX ISLAND

GREEN PARK P.P.

TYNE VALLEY

HOG ISLAND

CABOT BEACH P.P.

DARNLEY

BELMONT
P.P.

MALPEQUE BAY

MALPEQUE

BURLINGTON

URBAINVILLE

ABRAM-VILLAGE

WELLINGTON

MISCOUCHE

ST
ELEANORS

KENSINGTON

CAP EGMONT

CAP-EGMONT

MONT-CARMEL

LINKLETTER P.P.

SUMMERSIDE

SUMMERSIDE
HARBOUR

BEDEQUE BAY

BEDEQUE

CHELTON P.P.

NORTHUMBERLAND

QUEENS COUNTY

BORDEN-CARLETON

TRYON

CONFEDERATION
BRIDGE

STRAIT

0    5 mi

0    5 km

PRINCE EDWARD ISLAND

© AVALON TRAVEL PUBLISHING, INC.

will guide you to awesome coastal vistas. About 50 meandering side roads also turn off Highway 2 and connect with other secondary paved and clay roads. You may become temporarily lost on the roads, but not for long—the blue sea invariably looms around the next bend.

# Eastern Prince Country

## KENSINGTON AND VICINITY

Kensington lies at the intersection of five highways—including the trans-island Highway 2— 48 km west of Charlottetown, 38 km north of the Confederation Bridge, and 38 km southwest of Cavendish. It's a small place, but worth visiting nonetheless.

Make your first stop **Kensington Railyards,** where you'll find the **Welcome Centre,** tel. 902/836-3031 or 877/836-3031, and a **farmers' market,** a good place to come for fresh produce, baked goods, snacks, and crafts; it's open July–September, Sat. 10 A.M.–2 P.M. On the main highway through town, **Kensington Towers and Water Gardens,** tel. 902/836-3667 or 902/836-3336, is worth a look for Tudor castles large and small, and kid-friendly water attractions. Admission is $5 adults, $2 children 6–12.

**Green Valley Cottages and Bed & Breakfast,** tel. 902/836-5667 or 888/283-1927, www.malpeque.ca, is about five km north of town on Highway 102, surrounded by birch-studded farmland. Seven cottages rent for $100–150 (up to six guests allowed in each); a room in the main house runs $60 double, with light breakfast. The inn is open mid-May through October. The renovated turn-of-the-last-century **Victoria Inn,** 32 Victoria St. E, tel. 902/836-3010 or 800/439-6769, offers two B&B rooms ($75 single, $80 double, including breakfast) and four housekeeping units ($80 each). All rooms have private baths. The inn is open June to September 15.

### Woodleigh Replicas & Gardens

Take Highway 101 north for 10 km from Kensington to Highway 234 to reach this attraction, a sort of Lilliputian Disneyland for Anglophiles. It was the creation of E. W. Johnstone, a retired World War I colonel who made it his life's obsession to re-create on Prince Edward Island some 30 British buildings with historical or literary significance—buildings that had impressed him during his service in Britain. His magnificently crafted, minutely detailed, scaled-down reproductions of British Isles landmarks include Dunvegan Castle, the Tower of London, St. Paul's Cathedral, Robbie Burns's cottage, Shakespeare's birthplace, and other sites, displayed over 18 hectares of lovingly landscaped grounds. Johnstone was in his eighties and still at work on his chef d'oeuvre at the time of his death in 1984. Woodleigh is open June to mid-October, daily 9 A.M.–5 P.M. (until 7 P.M. in July and August). Admission is adults $8.50, seniors $8, children $4.50, preschoolers free. For details call 902/836-3401.

## SUMMERSIDE

Summerside (pop. 14,000) is PEI's major shipping port. It's got all the bustle, yet none of the seaminess usually associated with seaports. Here you'll find stately old homes with wide lawns, and quiet streets edged with verdant canopies. The town provides a plentiful mix of lodgings, dining places, and nightspots—a rare combination on PEI outside of Charlottetown.

### History

Summerside began in 1800 as Green's Shore, named after the tract's owner. By 1840, the settlement had an inn, the new name of Summerside, and a shipbuilding yard at the harbour. Its role as an important port began with rail service in the 1870s; potatoes from O'Leary were among the first exports. During World War II, a military installation was built on the outskirts of town and became a major contributor to the local economy. To everyone's chagrin, the base closed in the late 1980s. A growing tourism industry is helping to fill the gap left by the closure.

PRINCE EDWARD ISLAND

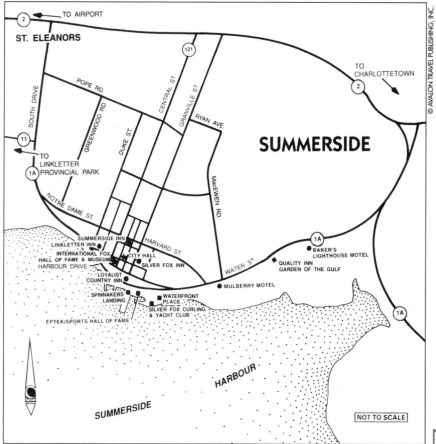

NOT TO SCALE

## Sights

The tourist's Summerside lies along Water Street, Harbour Drive, and the first few blocks back from the harbour. This downtown area holds the port's most exemplary historic buildings, such as the Gothic-styled **City Hall,** 45 Summer St. (at Fitzroy St.). Like Charlottetown, Summerside has revitalized parts of its harbour, notably at Spinnakers' Landing, a complex of tourist shops and wharves begun several years ago when the military base was phased out.

Taking its name from the Mi'kmaq Indian word for hotspot, the **Eptek National Exhibition Centre,** in front of Spinnakers' Landing at

130 Harbour Drive, tel. 902/888-8373, has a spacious main gallery hosting touring national fine arts and historical exhibits. The adjacent **PEI Sports Hall of Fame and Museum** catalogues the achievements of the island's best athletes. Both are open June through October, Mon.–Sat. 9 A.M.–5:30 P.M. Admission is charged.

Fox farming began on the island in 1894 and soon grew into big business, accounting for nearly one-fifth of the provincial economy within a couple of decades. In 1911, Frank Tuplin, one of the first to commercialize the industry, traded a breeding pair of silver foxes for a luxurious new home; by 1920, when the fashion for fur was in its heyday, a pair of prime silver foxes could fetch $35,000. The **International Fox Hall of Fame and Museum,** 286 Fitzroy St., tel. 902/436-2400, explains the region's heady fox boom and the methods of raising and pelting the animals. It's open June–September, Mon.–Sat. 8 A.M.–4 P.M.; admission by donation.

## Accommodations and Camping

Summerside's least expensive motel is **Baker's Lighthouse Motel,** two km east of downtown at 802 Water Street, tel. 902/436-2992, charging $46 single, $52 double for each of its seven guest rooms. In the same vicinity, but within walking distance of the waterfront, is the **Mulberry Motel,** 6 Water St. E., tel. 902/436-2520 or 800/274-3825. Each of the rooms is spacious and has basic cooking facilities. On the downside, the televisions are very small, but for $60 single, $65 double, that's of little consequence.

**Quality Inn Garden of the Gulf,** 618 Water St. E., tel. 902/436-2295 or 800/265-5551, has 92 rooms and suites ($109–179), a restaurant and coffee shop, indoor and outdoor pools, and a nine-hole, par-three golf course.

**Travellers Inn & Convention Centre,** on Highway 2 at St. Eleanors on Summerside's northern outskirts, tel. 902/436-9100 or 800/268-7829, has better-than-average motel trappings with 24 rooms and 16 housekeeping units ($85–155), an indoor heated pool, a hot tub, and a pleasant atmosphere. The motel's restaurant serves basic beef and seafood dishes ($13–24.50).

The 108-room **Linkletter Inn,** 311 Market St., tel. 902/436-2157 or 800/565-7829, is centrally located and offers large rooms (some with kitchenettes), a restaurant, a lounge, and amenities for the physically challenged. Summer rates are $120–170, but rooms go for well under $100 through the cooler months.

The **Loyalist Country Inn** faces Spinnakers' Landing from 195 Harbour Drive, tel. 902/436-

*Fox farming began on the island in 1894 and soon grew into big business, accounting for nearly one-fifth of the provincial economy within a couple of decades.*

3333 or 800/361-2668. It features 95 spacious, sunny rooms ($121–197), a cocktail lounge, a tennis court, an outside patio, and the Prince William Dining Room. Forty-eight of the rooms have whirlpool tubs.

Summerside has two recommended bed-and-breakfasts. In a stately 100-year-old mansion, **Summerside Inn,** three blocks from the harbor at 98 Summer Street, tel. 902/436-1417 or 877/477-1417, features six guest rooms with en-suite bathrooms, as well as comfortable lounge and living areas. Rates of $70–85 include a cooked breakfast. **Silver Fox Inn,** 61 Granville St., tel. 902/436-1664 or 800/565-4033, www.silverfoxinn.net, reigns locally as one of the seaport's "fox houses," built with a silver fox fortune and designed by architect William Critchlow Harris. The comfortable inn has six rooms furnished with antiques ($85–125, including breakfast).

Summerside's closest campground is in **Linkletter Provincial Park,** eight km west of town on Highway 11, tel. 902/888-8366. This 30-hectare park on Bedeque Bay has 84 serviced and unserviced sites ($17–23), hot showers, and a Laundromat, dump station, kitchen shelter, and nearby store. It's open mid-June to mid-September.

## Food

**Little Mermaid,** on the waterfront at 240 Harbour Drive, tel. 902/436-8722, proudly declares that it's operated by a fishing family. Seafood is the specialty. Prices on lobster, Malpeque oysters, and fish are reasonable, though most everything is fried. It's open for lunch and dinner April through October.

**Brothers Two Restaurant** at the Quality Inn Garden of the Gulf, 618 Water St. E, tel. 902/436-9654, is a local favorite for entrées ($11–23) such as hip of beef and sautéed scallops in white wine sauce. The restaurant has been a social hub for decades. The **Prince William Dining Room,** in the Loyalist Country Inn, 195 Harbour Dr., tel. 902/436-3333, offers specials like lobster crepes and poached salmon drenched with lobster sauce (mains from $15); reservations are required.

**Minh-Wang Family Restaurant,** 601 Water St. E., tel. 902/436-3838, sets an all-you-can-eat buffet. Chinese is also the specialty at **King Wok,** 239 Water St., tel. 902/436-6333. The Silver Fox Curling and Yacht Club's **Beacon Lounge,** 110 Water St., tel. 902/436-2153, serves lunch 11:30 A.M.–2 P.M. and has good sea views.

## Entertainment

Summerside has a fairly lively night scene. **Shaker's,** 250 Water St., tel. 902/436-9828, revels in rock 'n' roll and country music. For a tamer evening drink, check out the **Green Lantern Pub** at Gentleman Jim's, 480 Granville St., tel. 902/888-2647, or the Loyalist Country Inn's **Crown and Anchor Tavern** at 195 Harbour Drive, tel. 902/436-3333.

The **College of Piping,** 619 Water St. E., tel. 902/436-5377, affiliated with Scotland's College of Piping in Glasgow, presents a Highland summer concert series featuring pipers, step dancers, fiddlers, and singers in its Ceilidh Cafe. The program, called "Come to the Ceilidh," takes place June–August, Mon.–Thurs. at 7:30 P.M. Admission is adults $12, seniors $11, children $7. The college also offers short-term summer classes (about $25 hour) in Highland dancing, piping, and drumming. For details, go to the website www.collegeofpiping.com.

**Feast Dinner Theatre,** produced by a local thespian troupe, offers musical comedy spoofs hilarious enough to lure an audience from Charlottetown. The dinner theater shows ($30) are held at the Brothers Two Restaurant, 618 Water St. E., late June to early September, Mon.–Sat. at 6:30 P.M. Dinner choices include salmon, chicken, or roast beef with fixings; reservations are required, call 902/436-7674.

The **Harbourfront Jubilee Theatre,** tel. 902/888-2500, presents professional theater focusing on Maritimes history and culture. Performances are scheduled year-round, including July–August, Tues.–Sat. at 8 P.M.

In summer, **Spinnakers' Landing** at the waterfront puts on music and dance at its outdoor stage Fri.–Sun. at 6 P.M.; call 902/436-6692 for details.

## Events

Hosted by Summerside since the 1950s, the **Lobster Carnival,** lasting two weeks in July, attracts islanders from across the province for lobster suppers, livestock exhibitions, harness racing, and entertainment including a parade and a midway. Celebrations are centered on the Recreation Centre, 511 Notre Dame St., tel. 902/436-4925.

## Recreation

**Summerside Golf and Country Club,** off Highway 11 a few kilometers west at Linkletter, tel. 902/436-2505, is among PEI's finest championship terrains, with 18 holes across 6,300 yards overlooking the strait. Facilities include a clubhouse, a pro shop, and a lounge overlooking the 18th green; call for reservations and tee-off times. Open May through October.

**Summerside Raceway,** 477 Notre Dame St., tel. 902/436-7221, is a scaled-down version of Charlottetown Driving Park's harness-racing facilities. The races are just as intense but fewer in number. It's open May–November, with a race once a week over most of the season and nightly during the July Lobster Carnival. Admission is $1.

## Services and Information

**Prince County Hospital** is at 259 Beattie Avenue, tel. 902/432-2500. For the **RCMP,** call 902/436-9300.

The **Visitor Information Centre,** on Highway 1A at Wilmot between Summerside and North Bedeque, tel. 902/888-8364, www.city.summerside.pe.ca, answers questions and stocks free sightseeing literature on Summerside and the province. It's open early June to early October, 9 A.M.–4:30 P.M. (to 9 P.M. July to early September).

The **Rotary Regional Library,** 192 Water St., near Spinnakers' Landing, tel. 902/436-7323, is open weekdays 10 A.M.–5 P.M. The best local bookstore is **Coles,** in the County Fair Mall on Granville Street, tel. 902/888-2925. The county's news is covered by the daily *Journal-Pioneer* and the weekly *La Voix Acadienne.*

PRINCE EDWARD ISLAND

## Transportation

**Prince Edward Air,** tel. 800/565-5359, flies between Summerside and Halifax. Summerside's airport, Slemon Park, is about 10 km north of town on Highway 2. **Courtesy Cab,** 15 Spring Street, tel. 902/436-4232, is one of several taxi outfits; expect to pay about $10 one way for a ride to or from the airport. **Silver Fox Curling and Yacht Club** has marina space for visiting boats. Call 902/436-2153.

# Around Malpeque Bay

Sheltered from the open gulf by the long, narrow sandbar of Hog Island, the shallow waters of broad Malpeque Bay are tranquil and unpolluted. The bay's long, fretted coastline is deserted, nearly bereft of development apart from three small provincial parks. Conditions are perfect for the large oyster fishery that thrives here. Ten million Malpeque oysters—Canada's largest source of the shellfish—are harvested each year. The purity of the bay water in part accounts for the excellent flavor of the oysters, which has made them famed worldwide as a gustatory treat. You'll find them served in a variety of ways at restaurants in the region.

## Cabot Beach Provincial Park

This 140-hectare park, 30 km north of Summerside on Highway 105, is the most worthwhile attraction along the east side of Malpeque Bay. It occupies a gorgeous setting on a peninsula tip just inside the bay, including a coastline of sandy beaches broken by rocky headlands. At the park's day-use area is **Fanning School,** a schoolhouse built in 1794 and unique (for the time) for having two stories. Finally closed in 1969, it's now open to the public mid-June to mid-September, daily 10 A.M.–dusk. Facilities at the park campground include over 150 sites (unserviced sites $17, hookups $20–23), a supervised ocean beach, a launderette, hot showers, kitchen shelters, and a nearby campers' store. The park is open late June to early September. For more information call 902/836-8945.

**Cabot's Reach Restaurant,** on Highway 105 nearby, tel. 902/836-5597, is an unassuming roadside eatery that gets ongoing rave reviews for Malpeque oyster chowders and platters ($8–15.50); open June–September.

# TYNE VALLEY

Quiet and bucolic, the crossroads hamlet of Tyne Valley (pop. 200), at the intersection of backcountry Highways 12, 178, and 167, lies on the west side of Malpeque Bay two hours from Charlottetown, 45 minutes from Summerside, and uncountable kilometers from the rest of the modern world.

In the 1800s, Tyne Valley began as a Green Park suburb. Two generations of the Yeo family dominated the island's economy with their shipbuilding yards on Malpeque Bay, and the empire begun by James Yeo—the feisty, entrepreneurial English merchant who arrived in the 1830s—spawned the next generation's landed gentry.

The empire's riches are gone, but the lovely landscape remains, like a slice of Lucy Maud Montgomery's utopian Avonlea, transplanted from Cavendish to this corner of Prince County. To get there, follow Highway 12 around Malpeque Bay or from Highway 2, turn east on Highway 132 or 133. The paved and red-clay roads ripple across the farmlands like velvet ribbons on plump quilts.

The quiet village stirs to life on the first weekend of August with the **Tyne Valley Oyster Festival,** a three-day tribute to Malpeque oysters. Daytime oyster-farming exhibits and evening oyster and lobster dinners are accompanied by talent shows, oyster-shucking demonstrations, fiddling and step-dancing contests, a parade, and a dance.

## Shopping

Tyne Valley is also known for handmade sweaters, and you'll find none better than Lesley Dubey's original Shoreline designs sold at **Tyne Valley**

**Studio** on Highway 12, tel. 902/831-2950 (open July–August, daily 9:30 A.M.–5 P.M.

## Accommodations

**Doctor's Inn** on Highway 167 in Tyne Valley, tel. 902/831-3057, belonged to the village doctor during the late 1800s, and the inn's luster still sparkles, polished by innkeepers Jean and Paul Offer. The Offers are also organic produce farmers, and during the mid-May to September growing season, they conduct garden tours Tues.–Fri. at 1 P.M. Let them know you're coming 24 hours in advance.

The inn has a formal front entrance, but everyone arrives at the side kitchen door and enters the busy kitchen fray, as the Offers process, can, and preserve the backyard's produce. Beyond the door to the dining room, the inn's interior gleams with antiques. Dinner is served on request ($35 with wine) in the elegant, spacious dining room. Upstairs are two guest rooms ($60 double, with breakfast).

# VICINITY OF TYNE VALLEY

## Green Park Provincial Park

Take Highway 12 northeast from Tyne Valley and continue north through the hamlet of Port Hill to reach this beautiful park, protecting a peninsula that juts into Malpeque Bay. From the end of the road (at the Shipbuilding Museum; see below), a three-km hiking trail brings you as deep into the bay as you can go without getting your feet wet. (Wear sneakers anyway, and bring insect repellent; mosquitoes flourish in the marsh pools.) The trail starts among white birches, short and stunted due to the bay's winter winds and salt. Beyond there, the path wends through hardwood groves, brightened with ground cover of pink wild roses, bayberries, and goldenrod. Eventually, the trail gives way to marshes at the peninsula's tip. The small inland ponds at the bay's edge are all that remain of a local effort to start oyster aquaculture decades ago. Marsh hay and wild grasses bend with the sea winds. Minnows streak in tidal pools, and razor clams exude streams of continuous bubbles from their invisible burrows beneath the soggy sand.

A 58-site **campground** fronts the bay beneath tree canopies on a sheltered coastal notch. It offers a launderette, kitchen shelters, hot showers, Frisbee golf, a river beach, and nature programs. Sites range $17–23, and the campground is open late June to early September; for details, call 902/831-2370.

## Green Park Shipbuilding Museum and Yeo House

This heritage attraction lies on the edge of the provincial park, tel. 902/831-7947. The Yeo House sits back on a sweep of verdant lawn. It's a gorgeous estate, fronted by a fence that rims the curving road. Inside, rooms are furnished with period antiques. Up four flights of stairs, the cupola—from which James Yeo would survey his shipyard—overlooks the grounds and sparkling Malpeque Bay. Behind the house, the museum has exhibits explaining the history and methods of wooden shipbuilding, Prince Edward Island's main industry in the 19th century. The shipyard features a partially finished vessel cradled on a frame, plus historic shipbuilding equipment. Open early June to early September, daily 9 A.M.–5 P.M.; admission $4.

## Bideford

You'll find the modest **Ellerslie Shellfish Museum** at the end of a red-clay road off Highway 166, about 10 minutes from Tyne Valley, tel. 902/831-2934. Everything you could ever want to know about oysters and mussels is explained. A small aquarium contains mollusks, lobsters, snails, and inshore fish; outside, experimental farming methods are underway in the bay. Admission is adults $2, children $1. The museum is open late June to early September, Sun.–Fri. 10 A.M.–4 P.M.

## Lennox Island

A causeway off Highway 163 brings you to this small island, home to 220 people of Mi'kmaq ancestry, intent on cultivating oysters, spearing eels, trapping, and hunting, while pursuing recognition of the 18th-century treaties with England that entitled them to their land. The province's Mi'kmaqs are said to have been the first native

Canadians converted to Christianity. Their history is kept alive at the **Mi'kmaq Cultural Centre,** tel. 902/831-2702, open in summer Mon.–Sat. 10 A.M.–7 P.M., Sunday noon–6 P.M. and through Wednesday night concerts. The

1895 **St. Anne's Roman Catholic Church,** a sacred tribute to their patron saint, grips the island's coastline and faces the sea. A crafts shop just north of the church markets Mi'kmag baskets, silver jewelry, pottery, and other wares.

# Région Évangéline

The bilingual inhabitants of the Région évangéline, the province's largest Acadian area, date their ancestry to France's earliest settlement efforts. The region offers French-flavored culture at more than a dozen villages spread west of Summerside between Highway 2 and the strait seacoast. Miscouche, the commercial center, is a 10-minute drive west of Summerside on Highway 2; 30 minutes from the seaport along the coastal Highway 11 is Mont-Carmel, the region's seaside social and tourist hub.

## MISCOUCHE

As you approach from the east, the high double spires of St. John the Baptist Church announce from miles away that you've left Protestant, Anglo Prince Edward Island behind and are arriving in Catholic territory.

The village of 700 inhabitants at the intersection of Highways 2 and 12 began with French farmers from Port la Joye in the 1720s, augmented with Acadians who fled England's Acadian Deportation in 1755. The settlement commands a major historical niche among Atlantic Canada's Acadian communities and was the site of the 1884 Acadian Convention, which adopted the French tricolor flag with the single gold star symbolizing Mary.

The **Musée Acadien** (Acadian Museum) at

the east side of town on Highway 2, tel. 902/432-2880, is geared as a genealogical resource center and also has exhibits of early photographs, papers, and artifacts, and a book corner (mainly in French) with volumes about Acadian history and culture since 1720. Admission is $2.75; children under 6 admitted free. The museum is open year-round. Hours are daily 9:30 A.M.–7 P.M. in July and August; daily 9:30 A.M.–5 P.M. in late June and early September; Mon.–Fri. 9:30 A.M.–5 P.M. and Sun. 1–4 P.M. the rest of the year.

## MONT-CARMEL

Two km south of Miscouche, the backcountry Highway 12 meets the coastal Highway 11 (Lady Slipper Drive), which lopes south and west across Acadian farmlands to this hamlet, best known for Le Village, a complex of lodgings with a restaurant. Mont-Carmel, 16 km from Miscouche, makes a handy sightseeing base for touring the Région évangéline.

the Acadian flag

### Sights

Facing the sea, **Le Village de l'Acadie** (Pioneer Acadian Village) on Highway 11, tel. 902/854-2227 or 800/567-3228, is a re-creation of a 1920s Acadian settlement with a school, church, blacksmith shop, store, and houses. The complex also includes Le Village Resort accommo-

a typical Acadian residence

dations, étoile de Mer restaurant, and La Cuisine à Mémé dinner theater. It's open early June to late September, daily 9 A.M.–7 P.M.

**Our Lady of Mont-Carmel Acadian Church** on Highway 11 reflects the cathedral style of France's Poitou region, where the French settlers originated. The cathedral is open Sunday during Mass. For permission to enter at other times, ask at the **Musée Religieux** (Religious Museum) across the road, tel. 902/854-2260; open July–August, daily 1–5 P.M.

### Accommodations and Food
Within the Acadian Village complex, **Le Village Resort,** tel. 902/854-2227 or 800/567-3228, offers good value with 56 modern rooms (18 with kitchenettes) ranging $74–105, plus two housekeeping cottages for $112. Open early June to late September.

Le Village's **étoile de Mer** restaurant, tel. 902/854-2227, gets rave reviews for Acadian dishes (lunch $6.50–12, dinner mains $11–23), especially the *rapûre*—luscious potato pie brimming with chicken chunks; open early June to late September. **La Cuisine à Mémé,** the com-

plex's **dinner theater** with a comedy in French and English, includes a buffet and dessert ($32). It's offered July–August , Tues.–Sat. at 6:30 P.M.; reservations are required.

### Shopping
**Artisanat du Village** (Village Craft Shop), tel. 902/854-3208, is an area outlet of locally created crafts. It features quilts, hooked mats, and apparel; open mid-June to mid-September, daily 9 A.M.–7 P.M.

## OTHER ACADIAN SETTLEMENTS
### Cap-Egmont
Other Prince Edward Island oddities are the **Bottle Houses,** on Highway 11 overlooking the strait, tel. 902/854-2987. They are the work of Edouard Arsenault, who in the 1970s mortared together 25,000 glass bottles of all colors, shapes, and sizes to form three astonishing buildings—a chapel with altar and pews, a tavern, and a six-gabled house. The structures qualified for inclusion in *Ripley's Believe It or Not.* The admission of

© JAYME LYNES

Cap-Egmont's striking six-gabled "bottle house," constructed in the 1970s by Edouard Arsenault

$3.25 adults, $1 children 6–16 allows you to roam the buildings and gardens. The site is open early June to late September, daily 10 A.M.–6 P.M. with extended hours in July and August of 9 A.M.8 P.M.

## Abram-Village

From Cap-Egmont, the scenic coastal Highway 11 wends north for 10 km and turns inland to this hamlet known for crafts. **Le Centre d'Artisanat d'Abram Village** (Abram's Village Handcraft Co-op), at the intersection of Highways 11 and 124, tel. 902/854-2096, is the area's definitive crafts source. Here you'll find weavings, rugs, Acadian shirts, pottery, and dolls. It's open mid-June to mid-September, Mon.–Sat. 9 A.M.–6 P.M., Sunday 1–5 P.M.

Acadian festivals are centered here, too. During September's first weekend, look for **L'Exposition Agricole et Festival Acadien de la Région évangéline** (Evangeline Region Agricultural Exposition and Acadian Festival), which includes dances, concerts, competitions, lobster suppers, and a fishing-boat parade.

# Western Prince Country

PRINCE EDWARD ISLAND

Beyond Summerside and the Région évangéline, Highway 2 cuts into the interior out of sight of the seas. Nonetheless, most backcountry roads off the main route eventually finish at the water. To the west, the Northumberland Strait is the pussycat of summer seas, and the warm surf laps peacefully along the southern and western coastlines. The Gulf of St. Lawrence, however, is more temperamental, with a welter of rolling waves breaking onto the north shore.

For sightseeing information, stop at the provincial **Visitor Information Centre** in Portage, tel. 902/859-8795. It's open July–August, daily 9 A.M.–7 P.M., and in June and September 9 A.M.–4:30 P.M.

## MILL RIVER PROVINCIAL PARK

As you exit Highway 2 at Woodstock, you enter a wooded realm on a ribbon of a road into Mill River Provincial Park, tel. 902/859-8786. The park meshes lush landscapes with contemporary-style resort trappings and full recreation facilities, including the championship-quality Mill River Provincial Golf Course.

## Accommodations and Camping

The park's riverfront **campground** has 72 sites: 18 unserviced ($17), 18 with two-way hookups ($20), and 36 with full hookups ($23). Amenities include kitchen shelters, hot showers, a launderette, nature programs, and plentiful recreation opportunities. The 32-hectare park is open mid-June to late September. For more information call Parks Division West at tel. 902/859-8790.

The three-story **Rodd Mill River,** tel. 902/859-3555 or 800/565-7633, www.rodd-hotels.ca, is a sleek, wood-sided hotel with 90 spacious rooms (from $140 in summer) and suites (from $185) and an indoor heated pool overlooking the woodlands. It's open May through October, and February and March for cross-country skiers.

The resort's **Hernwood Dining Room,** tel. 902/859-3555, boasts regionally renowned dining that draws an appreciative clientele from Summerside; expect a reasonably priced menu (from $14.50) featuring seafood specialties with a dish-of-the-day emphasis on salmon, halibut, or lobster (usually around $20); reservations are required during summer.

### Recreation

Campers, resort guests, and day visitors all have access to the park's sports facilities. The eight tennis courts (lit for night games) beside the hotel are free (but hotel guests play first). At the campground, there's a marina with equipment for river exploring; canoes and boats rent for $5 an hour and $18 a day. Sailboards cost $10 per hour, $32 per half-day, and $52 per day.

The 18-hole, par-72 **Mill River Provincial Park Golf Course,** tel. 902/859-8873 or 800/377-8339, is generally regarded as one of Canada's top 50 courses and has hosted many national events through the years. The course spans 6,747 yards and is open May through October. During July and August, you'd be wise to make reservations 48 hours in advance. Greens fees range $45–50.

- The **Rodd Mill River Aquaplex and Racquet Club,** a one-of-a-kind recreational facility in the province, houses a pool, water slide, whirlpool, sauna, two squash courts, an exercise room with Nautilus equipment, a sundeck, and changing rooms with lockers; open Mon.–Fri. 7 A.M.–10 P.M., Sat. from 8 A.M., Sun. 8 A.M.–9 P.M. A day-use pass costs $10 per person or $22 for a family; for details call 902/859-3555.

## O'LEARY

On Prince Edward Island, O'Leary is synonymous with potatoes. Legend has it that the hamlet took its name from an Irish farmer who settled here in the 1830s. By 1872, rail service connected the hamlet with the rest of the island, and

with that link in place, O'Leary was on its way to becoming Canada's largest potato producer.

O'Leary straddles backcountry Highway 142, a five-minute drive from Highway 2 and 50 minutes from Summerside. You might expect mountains of potatoes. Rather, O'Leary (pop. 900) is a tidy place, nestled in the midst of surprisingly attractive fields of low-growing potato plants. If you're in the area during the autumn harvest, you'll see the fields lit by tractor headlights, as the farmers work late at night to harvest the valuable crop before frost.

### Prince Edward Island Potato Museum

The museum, 22 Parkview Dr. (at Centennial Park, off Main St.), tel. 902/859-2039, is a must stop for true spud fanatics. Interpretive exhibits combine local history with potato lore and agricultural methods. The museum is open mid-May to mid-October, Mon.–Sat. 9 A.M.–5 P.M., Sun. 1–5 P.M. Admission is $5 per person or $12 per family.

### Food

Expect plenty of potato recipe variations hereabouts. Potato burgers and potato "candy bars" are sold as snacks at the museum, and the **Railway Cafe** on Main Street at O'Leary's former rail depot gets rave reviews for its fluffy potato pancakes.

## THE STRAIT COAST

Highway 14 (Lady Slipper Drive) exits the main highway at Carleton, doglegs west across the verdant farmlands, and heads to West Point at the island's western tip. From there, the scenic coastal route hugs the strait shore and brings some of the island's most magnificent sea views.

Potato fields peter out at the strait coastline, which is definitely off the beaten tourist route. The coast's long stretches of beach are interspersed with craggy red cliffs.

### West Point

**Cedar Dunes Provincial Park,** on Highway 14 south of O'Leary, tel. 902/859-8790, fronts the strait at a windy beach backed by sand dunes.

DAVID KIEFER

**West Point Lighthouse**

The small campground, tel. 902/859-8785, includes 20 unserviced campsites ($17) and another 39 two-way hookup sites ($20), a supervised beach, an activities program, a nature trail, kitchen shelters, a nearby campers' store, and hot showers. It's open late June to early September.

Within the park is one-of-a-kind **West Point Lighthouse,** tel. 902/859-3605, a functioning Coast Guard lighthouse (in operation since 1875) that also serves as an inn. The access road runs through the park. Inside the lighthouse and the adjacent house are nine rooms ($80–125), two of which have a whirlpool tub. Also here are a museum ($2 adults, free to overnight guests) replete with historic artifacts; a gift shop; and a dining room serving basic seafood and beef ($6–16) and overlooking the sea through wide windows. The **West Point Lighthouse Festival** in mid-July brings together a concert, children's activities, fishing-boat races, and a dance.

### North of West Point

Beyond West Point, the scenic road cleaves to the coastline and heads north, first to **Cape Wolfe,** where British General James Wolfe is said to have stepped ashore on the way to battle the French in 1759; and then to **Howards Cove,** fronted with precipitous cliffs of burnished red.

Storm winds whip the sea on this side of the island into a frenzy, churning sea-floor plants into a webbed fabric that floats to the surface and washes to shore. This seaweed, known as **Irish moss,** is used commercially as a stabilizer in ice cream and other foods. It is harvested from the sea by boat, and also from along the shore—after a storm you may see workers raking the surf's edge from Miminegash around North Cape to Cape Kildare, reaping the Irish moss and hauling it away with the help of draft horses.

In **Miminegash,** you can learn about all there is to know about Irish moss farming at the **Irish Moss Interpretive Centre,** housed in a vessel off Highway 152, tel. 902/882-4313. The center and a gift shop are open from early June to late September, daily 10 A.M.–7 P.M. Admission is $1. The Seaweed Pie Café serves light meals such as chowder and its namesake Mon.–Sat. 11 A.M.–7 P.M., Sun. noon–8 P.M.

## ALBERTON AND VICINITY

The seaport of Alberton (pop. l,200) is the northern area's largest town. Named for Albert, the Prince of Wales, the town began in 1820 with 40 families who worked at the shipyards in nearby Northport. Deep-sea fishing aficionados will readily find charter boats here.

The **Alberton Museum** on Church Street, tel. 902/853-4048, ensconced within the old courthouse (a national historic site), exhibits the town's history with antiques, clothing, and farm tools and chronicles the region's fox-farming past. It's open June–September, Mon.–Sat. 10 A.M.–5:30 P.M., Sun. 1–5 P.M.; adults $3, students and seniors $2, families $7.

### Accommodations and Food

**Travellers Inn Motel** on Highway 12, tel. 902/853-2215 or 800/561-7829, has 14 basic rooms and eight housekeeping units (from $90) and a dining room and lounge on premises.

For a snack or a meal, the **Revilo Restaurant,** 519 Main St., tel. 902/853-2323, serves worthy seafood chowder and burgers concocted of scallops.

## Jacques Cartier Provincial Park

It's only a short hop from Alberton back to Highway 2, then 16 km north to Tignish, but a worthwhile detour is to continue north on Highway 12 along the gulf shore to this eight-hectare provincial park, tel. 902/853-8632, occupying the site where explorer Cartier is believed to have stepped ashore in 1534. The eight-hectare campground rims the gulf. It offers a supervised ocean beach, 23 unserviced campsites ($17), 30 sites with two-way hookups ($20), hot showers, a launderette, varied programs, and Frisbee golf. It's open late June to early September.

## TIGNISH AND VICINITY

Stories of legendary riches and the fur that created a haute-couture sensation almost a century ago embellish the lore of the remote northern peninsula. The world's first successful silver fox breeding began in the Tignish area in 1887. Charles Dalton—later knighted by the queen—was the innovator, and he joined with Robert Oulton from New Brunswick to breed the foxes. The pelts sold for thousands of dollars in fashion salons worldwide.

From 1890 to 1912, the Dalton and Oulton partnership kept a keen eye on the venture and the number of silver fox breeding pairs. As luck would have it, generosity was their downfall: their empire fell apart when one of the partners gave a pair of the breeding foxes to a relative. The cat—the fox, that is—was out of the bag. That single pair begat innumerable descendants that were sold worldwide, and breeding became an international business.

The area earned itself another major entry in national history when local fishermen organized Canada's first fishermen's union; the cooperative still processes and markets the bulk of the island's tuna. During summer, expect to see the "mossers"—Irish-moss harvesters clad in high rubber boots—in town.

Tignish (pop. 850) is simply laid out with Church Street/Highway 2 as the main street. The town is 20 minutes from Alberton, a half hour from O'Leary, and 80 minutes from Summerside.

## Sights

Make your first stop the **Tignish Cultural Centre** on Maple Street, tel. 902/882-1999, which tells the natural and human history of the area, holds the usual array of tourism brochures, and offers public Internet access. It's open late May to early September, daily 8 A.M.–4 P.M. Nearby, the **St. Simon and St. Jude Church,** tel. 902/882-2049, is the town's stellar attraction, notable for its frescoes of the apostles and its mighty pipe organ. The organ, built by Louis Mitchell of Montréal, features 1,118 pipes from six inches to 16 feet in length. It was installed in 1882, and until the 1950s the organ was pumped by hand. The church is open daily, 8 A.M.–7 P.M.

## Accommodations

**Chaisson Homestead,** 156 Chaisson Rd., tel. 902/882-2566, is on a potato farm and offers one B&B room ($50) and three housekeeping cottages ($50–80 for one to four people). Features include a beach, restaurant, and nearby fishing area. Open year-round. **Murphy's Tourist Home and Cottages,** 325 Church St. (Hwy. 153), tel. 902/882-2667, has three guest rooms ($40 single, $50 double including a light breakfast) and five one- and two-bedroom housekeeping cottages ($55–65). It's open May 15 to October 15. **Island's End Motel,** on Doyle Road off Highway 12 at Sea Cow Pond, six km north of Tignish, tel. 902/882-3554, overlooks the Gulf of St. Lawrence and has a nearby beach. Open May through October. Rates are $60–70.

## North Cape

Some 20 minutes directly north of Tignish on Highway 12, the **Atlantic Wind Test Site** juts up from the windy plain with a federal project complex that tests and evaluates wind turbines. The visitor center, tel. 902/882-2746, presents an audiovisual show; open July to late August, daily 10 A.M.–8 P.M. Admission is charged.

Dining is very fine at **Wind and Reef** on Highway 12 preceding the wind site, tel. 902/882-3535; the low profile roadside restaurant is among the island's best seafood places, overlooking the windy coastal setting; open June to mid-October.

# Kings County

Kings County, at Prince Edward Island's eastern end, is cultivated in farms of corn, berries, grains, potatoes, and tobacco, and is rimmed on the north by forests and tracts of provincial woodlot plantations. The long northern coast is nearly straight and uninterrupted, except at large St. Peter's Bay and smaller Savage and North Lake harbors. The northern area is remote, lightly populated and developed, and, inland, thickly wooded. As any islander will tell you, the county's northern portion is "far out," i.e., far out of sight and out of mind from mainstream PEI and a world away from the tourist circuit.

The more heavily touristed eastern shore, by contrast, is tattered with little offshore islands and dozens of deeply indented bays and river estuaries. The region's southern climate is warm, humid, and almost tropical; islanders refer to this part of Kings County as PEI's "banana belt," and even such crops as tobacco thrive here.

## Sightseeing Highlights

Kings County is quiet compared to Queens County. It has none of the hype of Cavendish, and its activities and sights are more limited. But the pastoral countryside is beautiful. If you're looking for sightseeing and recreation combined with naturalist attractions—coastal windswept peninsula beaches, sand dunes, and inland, an improbable herd of provincial bison—you'll find that and more in Kings County.

The region appeals to eclectic interests. Hikers like the provincial woodlot plantations with self-guided trails. Sightseers go for seal-watching cruises at seaports along the Northumberland Strait coastline. Anglers intent on catching trophy bluefin tuna head for the county's northeastern tip, where the strait meets the Gulf of St. Lawrence in a turbulent clash of seas. Golfers tee off at the 36-hole Brudenell River Resort near Montague or combine the game with scenery at Sea Cove Golf Course alongside Murray Harbour, where seals on offshore rocky islands share the day.

Gorgeous pastoral interior (especially in the southern area)

King's County lighthouse

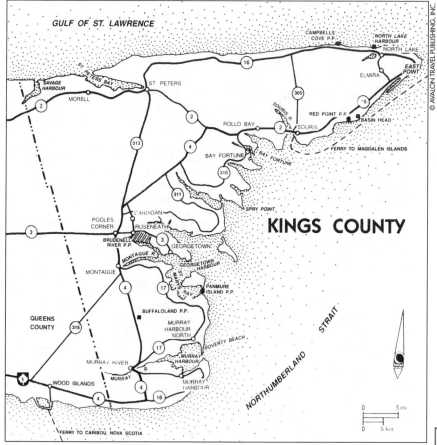

notwithstanding, the sightseers' circuit lies along the county's sea-rimmed perimeter. This chapter divides the county into northern and southern halves, with Cardigan at roughly the midpoint.

## HISTORY

### Early Settlements

Unaware of the benevolent climate in the region's southern area, early French settlers from Port la Joye made their way up the Hillsborough River to the Souris area's inhospitable wilderness by 1724. Conditions were wretched. Plagues of field mice ravaged the fields and Souris village through the 1750s. Though the infestations eventually petered out, a reputation for rodents followed the seaport through the centuries, and gave the village its name; *souris* is French for mouse.

Another early French settlement was centered at Trois Rivières, between what is now Montague and Georgetown. The French merchant John-Pierre de Roma saw the potential for an Acadian village with bridges, wharves, and houses. De Roma was able to realize his ambitious scheme, but a party of New England raiders leveled the place in 1745.

## Growing Economy

Souris welcomed the Scots in 1772 and Irish immigrants in the early 1800s. The town soon emerged as an island shipbuilding center and retained the role until the Great Age of Sail ended in the late 19th century. Simultaneously, canning as a method of preserving food developed as a seaport specialty, and for decades islanders stuffed lobster ad infinitum into cans for international export.

The seaport always held a prominent role in island life. Indeed, it was the port's reputation as an economic kingpin, as well as the Souris area's seacoast carved with attractive bays, that lured playwright Elmer Harris and his arts colony to Bay Fortune in the 1880s, and American actor Charles Flockton and a similar enclave to nearby Abell's Cove.

The naming of Georgetown was surveyor Samuel Holland's tribute to George III of England. The port boasted one of the island's most perfectly created deep-water harbors. Its early economy was built with British money, however, and when England's economy had a short-lived collapse, Georgetown lost its economic edge and never regained it. Georgetown slid into the shadows, replaced by Montague first as a shipbuilding and shipping center and then as the area's principal market town.

## HIGHWAYS AND BYWAYS

From Charlottetown, getting into the county is efficiently quick. The provincial road system lies across the region's interior like a fork with the tines splayed out to the different parts.

The TransCanada/Highway 1 leaves the capital heading east and connects with fast-moving Highway 3, the main access route into the county's interior, at Cherry Valley. From there, Highway 3 lopes across the countryside to Pooles Corner, the highway circuit hub, and on to Georgetown on the strait. Alternatively, stay on Highway 1 around the south coast to Wood Islands, where the coastal road becomes Highway 4, then Highway 18 to Murray Harbour, then Highway 17 to Montague, the southern area's main market town.

Highway 4's north-south route zips from Murray River to Souris, 81 km from the capital. Souris is also the departure point for the ferry to Québec's Îles-de-la-Madeleine. Narrower Highway 313 splays northwest off Highway 4 above Pooles Corner and routes traffic to St. Peters near the gulf coast. Highway 2 is the county's major access road to the north coast; it runs from Charlottetown to Souris, and intersects Highway 4 at St. Peters.

It's helpful to study a highway map before getting off the main roads onto the county's rambling network of paved and unpaved roads. The pace is slow on the scenic backcountry roads that link the county's more than 100 out-of-the-way hamlets.

# Southern Kings County

## AROUND MURRAY HARBOUR

Beyond Wood Islands, the 350-km-long Kings Byway Drive (signposted with the symbol of a purple crown) winds up the coast on its way north, changing route numbers innumerable times. The narrow seacoast road is scenic, with farmlands laid out on the intensely red earth on one side, and the sea and sapphire-blue sky on the other. On a clear day, you can see Nova Scotia's northern coast across the strait.

You'll pass through remote hamlets like Little Sands and White Sands, marked more by road signs than clusters of houses. At Murray Harbour's entrance, the road cuts across the tip of a peninsula studded with three lighthouses. The 35-km-long harbor-front road on Highways 18 and 17 rims the harbor's perimeter.

Enormous numbers of seals live in this well-sheltered harbor, and they love to loll about on offshore islands. You can see some of them from the beach at Beach Point's Lighthouse, situated closest to the harbor entrance.

The Murray family settled the area, and has namesakes everywhere: the Murray River flows into Murray Harbour, whose entrance is marked by Murray Head; seal colonies cluster on the harbor's Murray Islands; and the three seaport villages are Murray Harbour, Murray River, and Murray Harbour North.

### Town of Murray Harbour

**Alpha and Omega Resort** on Highway 18 east of the seaport, tel. 902/962-2888, operates seal-watching cruises ($18; campers get a 10 percent discount) and has a campground beside Fox River with 30 unserviced and 12 serviced sites ($14–18), river fishing, rowboats, a beach, pool, mini-golf, and showers. Alpha and Omega also offers five housekeeping cottages ($70) and seven motel rooms ($45). It's open mid-June through September.

Set on a five-hectare property, **Fox River Cottages** on Machon Point Road off Highway 18, tel. 902/962-2881, offers three two-bedroom housekeeping cottages ($100–116) with screened porches overlooking the Fox River. Amenities include a canoe, rowboat, and laundry. It's open May through October. Also in the area, **Harbour Motel** on Mill Road, tel. 902/962-3660, has seven housekeeping units ($60 each) within walking distance of town. Open year-round.

### Town of Murray River

The oval-shaped harbor is centered on the town of Murray River, southeastern Kings County's shopping hub. Seal-watching excursions are popular in these parts. If you like woodland walking, stretch your legs at **Murray River Pines,** a provincial woodlot near town. The site off Highway 4 is remote. Look for an abandoned mill, the former provincial Northumberland Mill and Museum, now closed; the woodlot is set inland behind the site. A 30-minute hike on the red-clay road leads to dense groves of red and white pines, abutted by stands of balsam, red maple, and red spruce. The largest pines date to the 1870s, when England's Royal Navy cut down most of the forest for masts. Somehow these trees survived, and they have become havens for birds of all kinds, including blue herons, kingfishers, swallows, blue jays, and chickadees.

**Captain Scotty's Deep-Sea Fishing** at the Highway 4 wharf, tel. 902/962-2494 or 902/962-3846, takes anglers and sightseers on all-weather vessels through the Murray Islands, with trips from $20 per person. The four-day **Northumberland Provincial Fisheries Festival** during late July features country-fair hoopla with lobster suppers, a parade, races, a dance, and the opportunity to watch fish filleting and scallop shucking by local experts.

The **Old General Store** on Main Street, tel. 902/962-2459, ranks as one of the island's best crafts sources and stocks folk art, linens, and domestic wares. It's open mid-June to mid-September. From July 1 to Labour Day, hours are Mon.–Sat. 9:30 A.M.–5:30 P.M., Sun. noon–5 P.M. In early and late season, it's open Mon.–Sat. 10 A.M.–4 P.M.

PRINCE EDWARD ISLAND

## Murray River to Montague Via Highway 17

From Murray River, Highway 4 cuts inland to Montague via Alliston, but a more scenic route is Highway 17, which skirts Northumberland Strait on a more leisurely route to Montague. The first worthwhile stop is **Murray Harbour North** and **Lady Catherine's Bed and Breakfast,** tel. 902/962-3426 or 800/661-3426. Views are fantastic from the veranda of this Victorian farmhouse, and recreation options include a nearby beach, a golf course, seal-watching tours, and bikes. Open year-round. Rooms start at $65, including breakfast. In the area, privately operated **Seal Cove Campground,** tel. 902/962-2745, overlooks offshore seal colonies. It has 22 unserviced and 78 serviced sites ($15–19), a bayside beach, a launderette, and a nine-hole golf course. Open mid-May to October.

Through the village of Murray Harbour North, **Poverty Beach,** at the end of a spur off Highway 17, is a long, narrow sandbar that separates the sea from the harbor. It's quiet, remote, and wrapped in a sense of primeval peacefulness. The peninsula is worth a trek, but think twice about swimming in the surf; powerful sea currents can be dangerous and no lifeguards are around to rescue floundering bathers.

**Panmure Island,** a similar remote and windswept wilderness, lies 15 minutes farther north off Highway 17. Take the Highway 347 spur as it rambles out the flag-shaped peninsula that wags between St. Marys Bay, Georgetown Harbour, and the sea. A supervised beach fronts the strait, and a wisp of a road angles into the interior and emerges at waterfront with views of Georgetown across the harbor. Back on the mainland, **Panmure Island Provincial Park** shares the remote location just north of Gaspereaux on Highway 347, tel. 902/838-0668. A campground here has 22 unserviced sites and 16 two-way hookup sites ($17–19), supervised ocean swimming off a beautiful white-sand beach, a launderette, a campers' canteen, fireplaces, and hot showers; open late June to early September.

## MONTAGUE AND VICINITY

Montague (pop. 1,900), Kings County's largest town, 46 km east of Charlottetown and 28 km north of Wood Islands, has always been known for the Main Street bridge over the Montague River. In fact, the town began as Montague Bridge in 1825, when the bridge was made of logs, and the area had just four farms. Shipbuilding brought riches to the town, and many a schooner and other sailing craft was launched here on the broad river.

The town is uncomplicated, pretty, clean, and friendly. Everything important lies along Main St., which slices through town and proceeds up, over, and down the bridge. Montague secured its place as Kings County's main market center in the 1850s, and since the 1960s, the town has benefited from the county's expanding dairy and tobacco production.

> *Montague (pop. 1,900), Kings County's largest town, has always been known for the Main Street bridge over the Montague River. In fact, the town began as Montague Bridge in 1825, when the bridge was made of logs, and the area had just four farms.*

The **Garden of the Gulf Museum,** 2 Main St. S, tel. 902/838-2467, is housed in an old post office overlooking Montague River at the bridge. The building is an impressive hulk of red brick with a steeply pitched roof, showing its French architectural influence. The collection includes exhibits on local history, including tidbits on de Roma's pioneer French settlement. The museum is open mid-June to September 30, Mon.–Sat. 10 A.M.–5 P.M. Admission is $3.

### Accommodations and Food

The deliberately rustic riverside **Lobster Shanty Motel,** 102 Main St. S. (at the town outskirts), tel. 902/838-2463 or 800/418-9430, has 10 motel rooms ($55) and suites (from $77). The motel's river-view restaurant reigns as one of the island's best dining rooms and serves fried or broiled seafood, thick steaks, and roast beef. Open year-round.

On the northern outskirts of Montague at Pooles Corner, the **Whim Inn,** at the intersection of Highways 3 and 4, tel. 902/838-3838 or 800/563-9446, is a basic motel in an area where large-scale lodgings are scarce. Facilities include 24 rooms ($70; suites $120), 12 housekeeping units ($80–100), a dining room, and a lounge. Open year-round.

## Boat Tours

**Cruise Manada Seal-Watching Boat Tours,** tel. 902/838-3444, leave from the town's marina on Highway 4 or from the Brudenell River resort wharf on Highway 3. Both two-hour cruises sail two to three times daily. An onboard narrator provides information on local history and wildlife such as harbor seals, great blue herons, gulls, and ospreys. The Montague-based tours operate mid-May to October 1, while the Brudenell tours run July–August only; tickets for either are adults $20, seniors $16, children 4–14 $10. The outfit also handles river transport for the dinner theater at Georgetown.

## Information and Services

The provincial **Visitor Information Centre,** north of Montague at Pooles Corner, tel. 902/838-0670, answers travel questions and stocks island information. It's open in June, daily 9 A.M.–5 P.M.; July and August, daily 9 A.M.–7 P.M.; September 9 A.M.–4:30 P.M.

**Kings County Memorial Hospital** is at 409 McIntyre Avenue, tel. 902/838-0777. You'll find the **RCMP** at 38 Wood Island Hill Road, tel. 902/838-2352.

**CIBC bank,** tel. 902/838-2134, is one of several town banks. It's open Mon.–Thurs. 9:30 A.M.–4:30 P.M., Fri. to 5 P.M. **Montague Taxi** is at 138 Sackville Street, tel. 902/838-3000.

## Buffaloland Provincial Park

Six km south of Montague at the intersection of Highways 4 and 317, the 40-hectare Buffaloland Provincial Park, tel. 902/652-8950, may

seem deserted at first glance. If you look closely, though, you'll spot bison and white-tailed deer roaming the woodlands.

The bison herd here began with 14 bison imported from Alberta in 1970, as part of a federal experiment to help preserve the almost-extinct species. There's still no population explosion, but the herd numbers 24 buffalo now. Between 3 and 5 P.M. the bison herd emerges to feed near the Highway 4 fence. The day-use park is open daily year-round. Admission is free.

# BRUDENELL RIVER PROVINCIAL PARK AND RESORT

This 30-hectare park-cum-resort occupies a gorgeous pastoral setting on the peninsula that juts out into Cardigan Bay between the Brudenell and Cardigan Rivers. You enter the park from Highway 3 about 10 minutes beyond Pooles Corner, and the road winds through manicured grounds to the resort's main house and nearby chalets.

## The Park

Facilities at the provincial park, tel. 902/652-8966, include 94 unserviced campsites ($17) and 16 two-way hookup sites ($20–25), hot showers, kitchen shelters, a launderette, interpretive programs, a riverfront beach, and a multitude of recreational opportunities. The campground is open mid-June through September; reservations are accepted beginning April 1.

Golfers here enjoy the 36-hole **Brudenell River Resort,** tel. 902/652-8965 or 800/377-8336, which comprises the "Brudenell 18" and the newer Dundarave course, which plays to a challenging 7,300 yards from the back tees. The courses rank among Atlantic Canada's superior golf greens and have been the site of various national and CPGA tournaments. Greens fees are $50 and $60 respectively. Open May through October.

Other park sports include canoeing ($22 a day), windsurfing ($32 for a partial day), horseback riding ($16 per hour), tennis, and boat tours. All sports in the park are open to campers, resort guests, and day visitors alike.

## The Resort

**Rodd Brudenell River** (part of the Rodd Hotels & Resorts group), the park's resort component, tel. 902/652-2332 or 800/565-7633, www.rodd -hotels.ca, has 100 rooms of varying configuration ($110–199) in the main lodge, 50 basic "country cabins" (from $85), 16 two-bedroom cottages ($140–300), and an indoor heated pool. It's open May–December. The ambience is friendly and relaxed—a nice place to meet islanders and other visitors.

The resort's licensed **Gordon Dining Room** is casually upscale and specializes in seafood entrées ($18–24); try the poached salmon awash in lemon sauce and, for dessert, shortbread squares topped with lemon meringue or the homemade parfait.

The region's night scene, quiet though it is, is also centered at the resort. The **Nineteenth Hole** lounge is a golfers' domain by day, but at night it comes alive to the sounds of recorded oldies and some rock; open nightly to midnight.

## VICINITY OF BRUDENELL RIVER PARK

### Georgetown

At the end of Highway 3, beyond the park, Georgetown was once a major shipbuilding center. It is now best known for the **Georgetown Theatre Festival—King's Playhouse** in the village's center. The local repertory company stages dramas and comedies mid-July to mid-September; for current plays and details on dinner theater packages, call 902/652-2053.

### Cardigan

At this hamlet five km north of the provincial park, the **lobster suppers** are well worth partaking in. You'll find them at the Olde Store, tel. 902/583-2020; open late June to late September. The supper price is $25.95 adults, $14.95 children.

At the former railroad depot, **Cardigan Craft Shop**, tel. 902/583-2930, is a reliable source of high-quality crafts including handmade textiles, stained glass, and warm sweaters. It's open June to November, Mon.–Sat. 10 A.M.–5:30 P.M., Sun. noon–5 P.M. The tearoom is open Mon.–Sat. 10 A.M.–4 P.M., Sun. noon–4 P.M.

# Northern Kings County

From Cardigan Bay northeast to Souris, the Kings County coastline is deeply notched with a series of bays. The Kings Byway Scenic Drive is extremely circuitous hereabouts, taking long, lazy loops out along the intervening peninsulas. Along the route you'll find scattered backcountry hamlets, rivers, secluded coves, and empty beaches. If you're in a hurry, Highway 4 and then 2 will take you directly from Pooles Corner to Souris in just half an hour or so.

## BAY FORTUNE AND VICINITY

Around 60 km north of Cardigan along the Kings Byway, Fortune River flows into Bay Fortune, whose name originated long before the fortunes of Broadway fueled the local retreats of producer David Belasco and playwright Elmer

Harris. Upriver six km is the hamlet of Dingwells Mills, where *Johnny Belinda,* one of Harris's most successful Broadway plays and later a movie, was set.

## Inn at Bay Fortune

In the late 1800s, Harris bought a chunk of land fronting the bay and set a sprawling summer house on a rise that peeled back from the sea. An entourage of thespians traveled with Harris, and for them the playwright designed the 19th-century version of a motel. The L-shaped addition, fronted with a porch, ended at the lighthouse-style tower, once Harris's study, and linked the "motel" with the main house. Actors Colleen Dewhurst and George C. Scott later took over the place, and it has since been transformed into a highly esteemed country inn, the

Inn at Bay Fortune on Highway 310, tel. 902/687-3745, www.innatbayfortune.com. David Wilmer, the present innkeeper, bought the property from Dewhurst and extensively restored the interiors of the main house, tower, and adjacent wing rooms. The refurbished inn opened in the late 1980s and is among the island's most celebrated lodgings. The 18 impeccably furnished suites with fireplaces run $140–280 with full breakfast. The tower suite overlooking the sea is the prized place for an overnight, and the tower's top floor serves as a lounge with sea views.

A strong sense of conviviality pervades the inn's dining room, downstairs in the main house. Meals are served on the front enclosed porch during summer or inside with tables arranged before the fireplace when the weather is cooler. The creative menu features entrées emphasizing poultry (try the roasted duck covered with a sauce of peach and raspberry vinegar preserves) and red meats, accompanied by an unusually full choice of wines. In 1993, *Where to Eat in Canada* proclaimed the cuisine "without question the best on the Island." The inn is open late May to mid-October.

### Continuing North Toward Souris

Beyond the Bay Fortune hamlet, the Kings Byway Scenic Drive parallels the Fortune River and crosses a bridge to riverside Fortune Bridge, once the site of Broadway producer David Belasco's summer home. At this point, the coastal circuit meets Highway 2, which cuts westward to St. Peters and heads in a northeasterly direction the Souris.

At **Rollo Bay,** eight km from Fortune Bridge, the **Rollo Bay Inn,** tel. 902/687-3550 or 877/687-3550, fronts the highway. The inn combines a re-created Georgian setting with 20 rooms, housekeeping units, and suites ($83–98 with breakfast) on spacious grounds with a licensed restaurant serving basic island cuisine. No pets.

Fiddlers from all over North America converge here for the **Rollo Bay Fiddle Festival** in mid-July. Events include open-air concerts and old-time dances. For details, call 902/687-2584.

# SOURIS

Any islander will tell you that Souris is "far out," the end of the line on the beaten tourist track. The seaport (pop. 1,200), notched on the strait seacoast 80 km east of Charlottetown and 44 km north of Montague, garners unqualified raves for its setting. The port overlooks the sea from sloping headlands, bounded in part by grasslands that sweep down to the water and in other parts by steeply pitched red cliffs. On the port's southern boundary, the Souris River rushes toward the sea with a gush of red-colored water and pours into the blue strait, like a palette of blended watercolor pigments.

Souris is an active offshore-fishing port, a rarity on the island nowadays when mammoth trawlers flying international flags have almost depleted the once-abundant offshore fisheries' stock. And the seaport boasts more than its share of seafaring legends. On a misty night, you may see an apparition of a ship returning to port. Some folks swear the ship is the *Lydia*, built in a local shipyard and subsequently lost at sea on its first voyage in 1876. The valiant, drowned crew aboard the brigantine, the local legend claims, still attempt to return to home port.

Consider Souris as a sightseeing base. Souris to Grand Tracadie is a mere two-hour drive, and Cavendish lies another half hour beyond there. The port's "far out" location translates as good value for the dollar in lodgings and dining. The restaurants are plainly furnished and specialize in seafood platters, ranked by islanders among the province's best and freshest.

### Recreation

Nearby Basin Head is a popular destination for local cruise operators. Daytime sailings feature coastal bird-watching, and sunset cruises are timed to take in the colorful twilight. Cruises (usually around $30 per person) depart the Souris town wharf regularly, with all-day **lobster-fishing** expeditions offered in summer ($100 per person, with all gear supplied). Call the Visitor Information Centre, tel. 902/687-7030, for a list of operators.

The highlight of the event calendar is the **Souris Regatta** in mid-July, which features a

PRINCE EDWARD ISLAND

## ÎLES DE LA MADELEINE

Souris is the departure point for ferries to Québec's Îles de la Madeleine (Magdalen Islands), in the Gulf of St. Lawrence, 105 km from the northern tip of Prince Edward Island and 215 km from the closest point of Québec in. This remote archipelago comprises 12 islands, six of which are linked by low, rolling sand dunes, and totals 200 square km. The islands are renowned as a remote wilderness destination, featuring great beaches and abundant birdlife. Villages dot the islands, and each has basic tourist services.

**CTMA Ferry,** tel. 418/986-3278 or 888/986-3278 (call 902/687-2181 from Souris) operates the MV *Madeleine* car/passenger ferry between Souris and Cap-aux-Meules on Québec's (Mag-

dalen Islands). The 134-km crossing takes five hours. Amenities onboard the modern vessel include a dining room, cafeteria, cocktail lounges, a movie theater, and a children's play area. The year-round schedule includes up to 10 sailings weekly in each direction during the peak summer months. Most runs leave Souris at 2 P.M. and leave Cap-aux-Meules for the return at 8 A.M. One-way passenger fares are adult $37, senior $30, child $18.50, vehicle from $70.

For information on the Magdalens, contact the local **tourism office,** 128 Chemin Debarcadere, tel. 418/986-2245. This office also maintains the excellent website, www.ilesdelamadeleine.com, with detailed island information and links to accommodations.

---

sailing regatta, tub races, a midway, wood-carving demonstrations, and an arm-wrestling competition.

### Accommodations and Food

**Lighthouse and Beach Motel,** across the Souris River at Souris West, tel. 902/687-2339 or 800/689-2339, fronts the sea with 15 rooms and two housekeeping units ($55–84), as well as the whirlpool-equipped Keeper's Suite (in the lighthouse; $700 per week) and a white, sandy beach; open mid-June to mid-September.

**Hilltop Motel,** off Main Street near the ferry terminal in Souris, tel. 902/687-3315 or 800/445-5734, fills the bill as a better-than-average motel with 12 rooms and 10 housekeeping units ($72–80) and a restaurant; open year-round.

**Church Street Tourist Home,** 8 Church St. (opposite the Ultramar gas station), tel. 902/687-3065 or 800/242-8361, offers three B&B rooms with a shared bath. A kitchen and a phone are available. Open April through January; the nightly rate is $35 single, $40 double.

Dining choices are limited, but the fare is worth savoring. The **Blue Fin Restaurant** at 10 Federal Avenue, tel. 902/687-3271, has earned decades of plaudits for its lavish, deep-fried

seafood platters ($9–21). On Highway 2 across the river in Souris West, the licensed **Platter House Seafood Restaurant,** tel. 902/687-2764, matches basic beef and seafood dishes with prime views of the sea and harbor through large windows; open May through October.

## THE EASTERN CORNER

If you like photogenic landscapes, windy seacoasts washed with tossing surf, and weathered seaports, consider northeastern Kings County for a revealing glimpse of this seafaring island as it once was. Beyond Souris, the strait seacoast stretches 25 km to windswept East Point, PEI's east tip. Between the two points lie the "walking" sand dunes and superb beach at Basin Head, as well as a pristine ecological spread and Red Point Provincial Park. On the equally remote gulf coast in this region, you'll find few tourists, a dozen tiny seaports, and a handful of lonesome lighthouses that stand as sentinels along the 75-km-long coastline, strewn with centuries of shipwrecks.

### Townshend Woodlot

Townshend Woodlot is a 106-hectare spread that closely resembles the island's original Acadian forest. In 1970, the International Biological Program designated the setting as one of PEI's finest examples of old-growth hardwood groves. To get there, take Highway 16 north from Souris and turn inland at Highway 305 to the hamlet of Souris Line Road. The woodlot plantation lies off the road, is fairly well hidden, and obscurely marked—you may want to ask for directions in Souris. Acquired by the province in 1978, the woodlot lacks a clear hiking route, but it's easily walkable on a level grade of sandy loam. The groves meld beech trees—a species that once dominated half the island's forests—with yellow birch, red maple, and sugar maple, whose dark brown trunks stretch up as high as 32 meters. Eastern chipmunks nest in underground tunnels here. And dwarf ginseng—rare on the island—and nodding trillium thrive.

## Basin Head and Vicinity

Formed by the winds, most sand dunes grow and creep along, albeit at a snail's pace. Basin Head's dunes are known as "walking" dunes for their windblown mobility. The high silica content of the sand here causes it to squeak audibly when crunched underfoot. Islanders poetically describe the phenomenon as "singing sands." The beaches at both Basin Head and adjacent Red Point Provincial Park are composed of singing sands. At Basin Head, the dunes are high and environmentally fragile; visitors should stay off the dunes and tread instead along the beach near the water's edge.

Behind the Basin Head dunes, **Basin Head Fisheries Museum,** off Highway 16, tel.

**Basin Head Fisheries Museum**

902/357-7233, sits high on the headland overlooking an inlet. Here you'll find boats, nets, and a museum with expertly conceived exhibits detailing the historic inshore fishing industry and local coastal ecology. The museum is open mid-June to late September. Hours are daily 10 A.M.–7 P.M. in July and August; Sun.–Fri. 10 A.M.–3 P.M. in June and September. Admission is $4. Behind the museum, a boardwalk leads across the dunes to the ocean.

**Red Point Provincial Park,** 13 km east of Souris off Highway 16, tel. 902/357-2463, has supervised ocean swimming with a campground of 32 unserviced and 58 serviced campsites ($17–23), kitchen shelters, fireplaces, and hot showers. It's open late June to early September.

Beyond Basin Head, the landscape is pure drama. White, puffy clouds hurry across a Wedgwood-blue sky. At the northeastern tip, the strait and gulf meet in a lathered flush of cresting seas, sometimes colored blue and often tinged with red from oxide-colored silt.

Along the gulf, a score of lighthouses jut up from the coastline, silent witnesses to ships wrecked by the tumult of sea and wind. At the gulf's most easterly point stands the octagonal tower of **East Point Lighthouse,** off Highway 16, tel. 902/357-2106, which is open to visitors. Admission is $2.50 adults, $2 seniors, $1 children. Guided tours are available mid-June to August 30.

## Elmira

**Elmira Railway Museum,** inland on Highway 16A, tel. 902/357-7234, was once the terminus of rail service to the area. The former depot serves as the unspoken testament to the island railroad's halcyon years with the province's only exhibits and documentation on rail service. It's open mid-June to early September, daily 9 A.M.–5 P.M.; admission $1.50. Outside, you can hike into the interior along the abandoned railroad track.

## North Lake and Vicinity

North Lake harbor is one of four departure points for deep-sea fishing; anglers try for trophy catches of bluefin tuna. Expect to pay $20–30 per person for a three- to four-hour trip or about

$400 for an eight-hour charter with four fishermen aboard. Trips depart daily during the July to mid-September season from North Lake, Naufrage, Launching, and Red Head harbors. **North Lake Tuna Charters** at North Lake harbor, with five tuna charter boats, is among the best; for details, call 902/357-2055.

**Bluefin Motel** on Highway 16 at North Lake harbor's coast, tel. 902/357-2053, caters to fishermen with 10 basic rooms ($48) and a beach with clam digging; open June 30 to September 30.

**Campbells Cove Provincial Park,** on Highway 16 five km west of Elmira, tel. 902/357-3080, fronts the gulf with a beach, hot showers, kitchen shelters, and 48 serviced and unserviced sites ($17–20); open late June to early September.

# THE GULF SHORE

## St. Peters and Vicinity

If you're in the area in late July or early August, check out the port's five-day **Blueberry Festival,** an islander favorite with concerts, entertainment, blueberry dishes, lobster and beef barbecue, and a pancake brunch. It's held at **St. Peters Park** on Highway 2.

The park also has a campground with a choice of 24 unserviced sites and 44 full-hookup sites ($15–19); tel. 902/961-2786. The town operates the campground, which has a launderette, kitchen shelters, free firewood, two pools, minigolf, and hot showers; open mid-June through September.

Take Highway 313 west from St. Peters along the north side of St. Peters Bay to reach the Greenwich Peninsula, part of **Prince Edward Island National Park** (see Queens County, earlier in this chapter). The six-square-km park encompasses a fragile dune system and wetlands, with a 4.5-km trail leading over the dunes. At the end of the road is **Greenwich Interpretation Centre,** tel. 902/963-2391, open July–August 9 A.M.–8 P.M. and June, September, and October, 9 A.M.–5 P.M. Admission is adults $6, seniors $4.50, children $3.

## Morell

Berries are the focus at Morell, 40 minutes from Charlottetown. The St. Peters Bay seaport makes much of the harvest at mid-July's six-day **Strawberry Festival,** with a parade, concerts, dances, barbecues, strawberry desserts, and other community events.

A relatively new, highly acclaimed, 18-hole, par-73 golf course, the **Links at Crowbush Cove,** tel. 902/961-3100 or 800/377-8337 (reservations), lies five km north of Morell off Highway 2. A true links course in the Scottish tradition, Crowbush challenges players with nine water holes and eight holes surrounded by dunes. It's open daily May through October. Green fees are $50–55. **Kelly's Bed and Breakfast** on Highway 2, tel. 902/961-2389, is conveniently close to the beach and the course. Its five rooms go for $45–65 double; open June through October.

The **Morell Canadian Legion** on Queen Elizabeth Drive, tel. 902/961-2110, puts on lobster and salmon suppers; open June to early September, nightly 4:30–9 P.M.

# Newfoundland and Labrador

# Introduction

The province of Newfoundland and Labrador, situated at North America's northeastern edge, is composed of two parts: the 110,681-square-km island of Newfoundland (pronounced "Noof 'n-LAND"), the world's 16th-largest island; and Labrador, which lies across the narrow Strait of Belle Isle from the island and forms the 295,039-square-km eastern flank of Canada's mainland.

The combined area is three times the size of New Brunswick, Nova Scotia, and Prince Edward Island put together, and more than twice the size of America's New England region. Cape Spear, the windy, boulder-bound promontory near the provincial capital of St. John's, is North America's most easterly point and lies closer to Ireland than to central Canada.

The province's nearest neighbor is mainland Québec, which lies on Labrador's southern and western borders. The islands of St-Pierre and Miquelon, France's last vestiges of colonialism in North America, lie 25 km off Newfoundland island's southern coast. Nova Scotia and the rest of Atlantic Canada lie southwest across Cabot Strait, the 125-km-wide channel between the Atlantic Ocean and the Gulf of St. Lawrence.

Access to the province is not difficult. Labrador's western area is connected to Québec with air, rail, and road links. Labrador's eastern area and the island of Newfoundland are linked by air to Halifax, Nova Scotia, Atlantic Canada's gateway. Newfoundland's capital of St. John's is also an international gateway, served by Air Canada's nonstop flights from London. By sea, two ferry routes connect Newfoundland island with North Sydney, Nova Scotia. One leaves from Channel-Port aux Basques at the southwestern tip, the other from Argentia on the Avalon Peninsula.

The province is a veritable ethnic stew, home to a number of different cultures. You'll hear an accent not unlike an Irish brogue across the Avalon Peninsula and in outports all along the island's

Newfoundland's rugged coast offers many hidden delights, such as this west coast beach.

ragged coastlines. The King's English savored in St. John's is a reminder of the province's historic link with the mother country, severed only as recently as 1949. An ancient French dialect is spoken on the Port au Port Peninsula in southwestern Newfoundland. And in the communities on the north coast's Fogo Island, remnants of Elizabethan dialect mark the islanders' speech.

In Labrador, the ethnic mix includes Innu and Inuit communities, year-round and summertime Newfoundlanders; and French Canadians from Québec.

## SIGHTSEEING HIGHLIGHTS
### The Great Outdoors

Seabirds by the thousands—Atlantic Canada's largest concentrations—nest on the Avalon Peninsula coastlines. Whales cruise offshore, lured by spawning, smeltlike capelin. Moose and caribou graze peacefully alongside the roads, particularly at dawn and dusk. Icebergs float south from the arctic in summer and bob off the island's seacoasts, occasionally drifting into harbors and inlets.

In Labrador, when the sun goes down, look up. The aurora borealis—the magnificent northern light show caused by charged particles in the upper atmosphere—provides a stellar attraction, illuminating the sky up to 243 nights a year. The northern lights appear to float lazily in the pale moonlight, and it's said they'll dance to your tune if you whistle.

Labrador's rare labradorite, or firestone, is a type of feldspar with iridescent peacock blue, green, gold, purple, or pink streaks. Found also in Finland and Madagascar, it's the best known and showiest of the province's 20 precious and semiprecious gems.

In summertime, wild berries of many varieties ripen in the province. Bakeapples, similar to Scandinavia's cloudberries, go into tasty desserts and preserves. Others include wild partridgeberries, squashberries, marshberries, blueberries, blackberries, plum boys, bunchberries, dewberries, crackerberries, crowberries, strawberries, and black currants.

Apart from all that, many consider the fishing and hunting in Newfoundland and Labrador to be Atlantic Canada's best. Hikers will find both marked and roughly cut wilderness trails, and enthusiasts of water sports can avail themselves of a number of activities, including canoeing, ocean kayaking, and scuba diving. In the winter, crosscountry skiing and snowmobiling are as much a mode of transportation as they are the recreation of choice, while several ski resorts provide the thrill of speeding down snowy slopes. As in other regions of vast wilderness, eco-tourism adventure tours are becoming an increasingly popular way to experience the natural rugged beauty of Newfoundland and Labrador.

### History and Tradition

The province's history is well documented provincewide in a trove of museums and attractions. St. John's traces its history to the 1500s, as do Trinity, the heritage village on Trinity Bay, and Red Bay, where Basques established a series of whaling stations that constituted North America's largest industrial enterprise of the period. South of St. John's, Ferryland began as Lord Baltimore's first New World settlement for English Roman Catholics. Its inland location, away from the often-present coastal fog, made Gander a prime candidate for a military air base during World War II, and the town now keeps its heritage on display with a collection of notable aircraft.

Evidence of the province's original inhabitants can be seen at the several burial mounds and settlement sites that have been excavated in recent years. Interpretive centers housing artifacts of Maritime Archaic, Dorset Eskimo, and Beothuk communities include sites at Port au Choix, Boyd's Cove, Burnside, Cape Ray, and L'Anse Amour, in Labrador.

The tip of the Northern Peninsula claims North America's first known Viking settlement—at L'Anse aux Meadows, where a re-creation of the thousand-year-old encampment lies adjacent to the grassy mounds of the original site. Nearby St. Anthony owes its fame to Sir Wilfred Grenfell, the medical missionary who initiated medical care in the remote areas and encouraged the making of crafts that are still produced and sold across the province.

Expect an astonishing variety of sweaters, jew-

© LISA COSTANTINO

**a reconstruction of North America's first known Viking settlement—at L'Anse aux Meadows**

elry embellished with labradorite and other gems, hooked mats, pottery, dolls, weavings, apparel created in the finest fabrics, and carvings of moose or caribou antlers, whalebone, soapstone, and ivory.

The summertime festivals go on and on. Folk festivals are particularly notable, showcasing traditional music from new and established talents from the province, Canada, and abroad. Folk music fills the local pubs, too, especially in St. John's, which has a rousing night scene. In July, both Trinity's Summer in the Bight festival and the Stephenville Theater Festival (on the west coast) take to the boards—and their fame has spread far beyond the province. In Forteau, a coastal village in Labrador, the annual Bakeapple Folk Festival in August is an unqualified must-see.

## THE LAND
### "The Galápagos of Geology"

"What the Galápagos are to biology, Gros Morne is to geology," declared Britain's Prince Edward when he formally opened Gros Morne National Park in 1973. UNESCO concurred, and one of the world's rarest windows on the ancient

world's formation was designated a world heritage site in 1987.

Plate tectonics theory holds that the earth's crust is broken into many huge plates that float on the molten rock beneath them. The movement of the plates dictates the creation, position, and shape of the continents. According to this theory, long before Newfoundland was an island, it was a landlocked part of a great supercontinent formed during Precambrian times; the oldest rocks in both Newfoundland and Labrador are 3.8 billion years old. When the supercontinent broke apart, the land plates drifted and a rift formed. Water filled the rift during the Cambrian period, creating the Iapetus Ocean.

After another 50 million years, give or take, the land plates, which had previously moved apart, reversed direction and moved toward each other. As the land plates closed together, the continents converged with a profound smack. The plates were pushed together and up like a squeezed accordion. Pangaea, the second supercontinent, was the result, and Newfoundland, not yet an island, perched high and dry near the center. At that point, Newfoundland's only distinctive characteristic was a mountain rib (the budding Ap-

# THE BERGS OF SUMMER: ICEBERGS ON PARADE

The spectacular icebergs that float past New-foundland and Labrador every summer originate from southwestern Greenland's ice cap, where great chunks of ice calve off the coast and cascade into the bone-chilling Davis Strait. The young bergs eventually drift out to the Labrador Sea, where powerful currents route them south along the watery route known as Iceberg Alley.

The parade usually starts in March, peaks in June and July, and in rare cases continues into November. Iceberg-watching was spectacular in 1991. No one dares to predict the next exemplary year; icebergs have their own agenda.

Though no one actually counts icebergs, an educated guess has 10,000–30,000 of them migrating down from the north annually. Of those, about 1,400-2,000 make it all the way to the Gulf Stream's warm waters, where they finally melt away after a two- to four-year, 3,200-km journey.

No two bergs are exactly the same. Some appear distinctly white. Others may be turquoise, green, or blue. Sizes vary, too. A "growler" is the smallest, about the size of a dory, and weighs about 1,000 tons. A "bergy bit" weighs more, about 10,000 tons. A typical "small" iceberg looms 5–15 meters above water level and weighs about 100,000 tons. A "large" ice mass will be 51–75 meters high and weigh 100–300 million tons. Generally, you'll see the largest bergs—looking like magnificent castles embellished with towers and turrets—farther north; the ice mountains diminish in size as they float south and eventually melt. No matter what the size, what you see is just a fraction of the whole—some 90 percent of the iceberg's mass is hidden beneath the water.

Occasionally, a wandering berg may be trapped at land's edge or wedged within coves and slender bays. Should you be tempted to go in for a closer look, approach with caution. As it melts and its equilibrium readjusts, an iceberg may roll over. And melting bergs also often fracture, throwing ice chips and knife-sharp splinters in all directions.

### Iceberg-watching

Iceberg-watching opportunities start along Labrador's coastline. Your best berg bet hereabouts is the view from one of the coastal ferries running along the coast of Labrador.

Farther south on the coastline, sea currents diverge, and the parade separates. One route takes some of the smaller ice masses through the shallow, fast-flowing Strait of Belle Isle and into the Gulf of St. Lawrence. Based in Cartwright, **Experience Labrador,** tel. 709/653-2244 or 877/938-7444, www.experiencelabrador.com, offers a variety of tours that combine kayaking and iceberg-watching.

Another flock of bergs bypasses the strait and drifts toward Newfoundland's northern coast, where some loll aimlessly about the offshore islands. Concentrations are thickest at the seaport of **Twillingate** on Twillingate Island. The Long Point Lighthouse at the island's most northern point makes a good viewpoint.

**Twillingate Island Boat Tours** at the Iceberg House, Hwy. 340, tel. 709/884-2317 or 800/611-2374, offers both iceberg-watching (best July–Aug.) and whalewatching tours with photo opportunities, from May to early September. **Fogo Island,** east of Twillingate, is another of the province's prime iceberg-watching locations.

Continuing south, the icebergs glide along the eastern coast of Newfoundland, propelled by the Labrador Current. Some wander close to shore and ditch among Terra Nova National Park's fjord-like bays. At the park's Newman Sound, **Ocean Watch Tours,** tel. 709/533-6024, operates federally approved ocean-exploration and research programs, and offers three-hour boat tours from mid-May to late October. Activities on the natural-history tours include sea-floor dredging, plankton trawling, and coastline exploring combined with iceberg- and whalewatching.

**St. John's** counts iceberg-watching as a city attraction. Two of the best views are from the lofty Signal Hill promontory by the seaport's harbor entrance, and Cape Spear at the harbor's southeastern tip.

Throughout the province, expect to pay $25–35 per person for a guided, two- to three-hour iceberg-watching boat tour.

palachian Mountains), formed from the earth's earlier faulting and upheavals. Later, the plates moved again, and Pangaea split apart. The Eurasian/African plate drifted east and southeast and settled in its present position as the continents of Europe, Asia, and Africa. The mountains of Great Britain and Scandinavia were formed from the mountain rib's northern end— the rib had severed at midpoint and half had traveled with the Eurasian/African plate.

The world as we know it began to settle into place. The Appalachian Mountains rimmed North America's eastern edge from Alabama in the southern United States to Nova Scotia's Cape Breton Highlands. Northeast of Nova Scotia, the mountain chain's low-lying peaks dipped beneath the Cabot Strait and reemerged on Newfoundland's western coast as the Long Range Mountains. Strewn among the mountains were a colossal geological heritage: remnants from the world's first supercontinent and parts of the Iapetus Ocean's sea floor. East of the mountains, the island's central plateau portion was made up of a great rectangular swatch of the crumpled, ancient seabed, 200–250 km in width and length.

A geological oddity was responsible for the island's southeastern portion; though most of the Eurasian/African landmass had wandered east and southeast, a chunk of the plate remained. It comprises the island's southeastern corner and the Avalon Peninsula.

Between then and now, the eons added a few more topographical touches. The retreating ice sheet uncovered the Labrador Trough, scooped out the Strait of Belle Isle, cut fjords into the coastlines, and pocked the interiors to create myriad ponds and lakes, and the short Gander, Humber, and Exploits Rivers. Subsequent erosion shaved the peaks of the Long Range Mountains.

## The Contemporary Island

Newfoundland island rises from the sea as a massive, brooding countenance of rock. Numerous peninsulas radiate from its lofty central plateau into the sea to the northeast, ending in precipitous cliffs, massive headlands, and sandy or cobble beaches. Deepwater fjords, small coves, and great bays serrate the coastline. A 10-km-wide

isthmus threads the main part of the island to the smaller Avalon Peninsula at Newfoundland's southeastern corner. The hilly interiors of both the main island and the peninsula are cloaked in dense woodlands and open barrens laced with bogs, swamps, and muskegs. Scoured and shaped by ice, the island's rocky terrain is said to hold 11,000 ponds.

The Atlantic Ocean embraces the northern, eastern, and southern coastlines, while the Gulf of St. Lawrence lies on the west. The narrow Strait of Belle Isle separates the island from Labrador to the north. The Grand Banks, once some of the world's richest fishing grounds, lie southeast, offshore at the continental shelf's edge.

Much of the island is exposed bedrock, mantled with a thin soil layer. The bedrock, consisting of sedimentary, volcanic, and granitic components, is littered in places with oddly placed boulders called erratics. Carried, then dropped, by retreating glaciers, the erratics are vestiges of the Ice Age. The Long Range Mountains, rimmed with a narrow coastal plain, dominate the western coastline. Agricultural regions and meadows are rare, but where they occur they are exceptionally lush. The island reaches its peak at 815-meter-high Lewis Hill, on the western coast near Corner Brook, the island's second-largest city.

## Labrador

The province's mainland is known as the "The Big Land," a fitting handle for the triangle-shaped region that's three times as big as the island. The name Labrador comes from the Portuguese *terra del lavrador,* land of the farmer—a name bestowed upon it most likely by an early Portuguese fisherman or explorer traveling west from his home in the Azores.

Along the 7,886-km coastline of granite boulders, jagged fjords, coves, and harbors, a string of islands clutches at the Labrador Sea's chilly edge. Farther south, sandy beaches mix with headlands on the strait seacoast. The province's highest peak is 1,729-meter-high Mt. Caubvick, which overlooks the northern coast in the dark, ragged Torngat Mountains.

The interior's diverse terrain can be roughly divided into three regions. Across the triangle's broad southern plateau lie luxuriously thick woodlands ribboned with bogs. The midsection holds Labrador's slice of civilization, and is rimmed in part with the 160-km-long wall of the Mealy Mountains. The Labrador Trough—a region of swift rivers, waterfalls, rich iron-ore deposits, and a mammoth hydroelectric plant—anchors the western midsection. The twisting, west-to-east TransLabrador Highway—in part a roughly cut forest-access road and, nearer to Labrador City, a gravel highway—connects western Labrador to the head of the 200-km-long Hamilton Inlet/Lake Melville fjord.

North of the midsection, Labrador's triangular tip narrows and ends in remote wilderness. The subarctic taiga, studded with a stunted coniferous forest, melds at timberline to the arctic tundra, which makes up the northernmost reaches of the province. Here lichens, sedges, and dwarf shrubs cross barren valleys, and steeply walled basins cut into angular mountains. From the northern shore, the Hudson Strait and the Arctic's Baffin Island are north, and Greenland lies northeast.

## Parks and Protected Areas

Virtually all of Newfoundland and Labrador is protected land, and the plethora of parks preserve the best of the best. The province's two national parks showcase the best of Newfoundland's splendid landscape. **Terra Nova National Park** is a scenic beauty with 400 square km of boreal forests, ponds, bogs, and hills embraced by a fjord-streaked coastline on the island's Eastport Peninsula. **Gros Morne National Park,** northwest of Deer Lake, melds geological history with nine spectacular scenic areas across 1,805 square km. For national park information, check the Parks Canada website, www.parkscanada.gc.ca.

The province also counts 95 provincial parks, the majority of them on the island. Most provincial parks offer such amenities as picnic tables and supervised beaches. Some parks have campgrounds, playgrounds, marked hiking trails, and scenic views; a few have visitor centers with interpretive programs. Notable provincial parks include **J. T. Cheeseman Provincial Park** near Port aux Basques, where pearly everlast-

ing, violet bog aster, and yellow clintonia grow on the coastal barrens, and **Black Bank Provincial Park** near Stephenville and **Northern Bay Sands Provincial Park** on northern Conception Bay above Carbonear, both renowned for their beaches. Provincial parks open between late May and late June, generally closing on the first weekend of September. For details on the provincial parks, contact the **Parks and Natural Areas Division,** Department of Tourism, Culture, and Recreation, tel. 709/729-2424, www.gov.nf.ca/parks&reserves. The provincial highway map lists the provincial parks and provides some details.

Six wilderness and ecological reserves feature seabirds by the thousands and extraordinary views, but for the most part no visitor facilities. **Cape St. Mary's Ecological Reserve** is the exception, with its summertime interpretive program.

## CLIMATE

On a typical summer day, the weather's mood can swing from sultry to chilly. Brilliant sunshine one moment can turn into dark clouds the next, often bringing rain ranging from light sprinkles to drenching downpours. The island's eastern and southern seacoasts are frequently foggy due to the offshore melding of the warm Gulf Stream and the cold Labrador Current. Be prepared to dress like an onion—ready to peel—and keep a lightweight raincoat, umbrella, or hooded slicker handy.

### Newfoundland Island

Overall, the island has a cool, moist maritime climate. Annual rainfall averages 105 cm. Summer high temperatures average 16° C, but hot spells (up to 24° C) are common, and the swimming season starts by late June. Summer's overnight lows range 9-129–12° C. The island's interior and low-lying coastal areas are the warmest and sunniest areas in summer.

Frost begins in early October on the southern coast, earlier farther north. Winter brings overnight lows down to -8° C and snowfall averaging 300 cm a year.

Expect year-round blustery winds along the Marine Drive and nearby Cape Spear on the eastern coast and peninsulas, and warmer and generally better weather on the west coast. The Northern Peninsula, especially at the tip, can have snow patches and chilly winds into July. Finally, conditions are almost always severe at upper altitudes in the Long Range Mountains; the peaks are snow-covered year-round, and winds can blow to gale force.

## Labrador

Labrador summers are short, generally cool, and usually brilliantly sunny except for periodic showers. The average summertime high temperature here is 18° C, but temperatures vary widely from one part of Labrador to another. In the western area, summer highs range 11–33° C. To the north, the subarctic region has cool and dry summers averaging 11° C during the day, though in the far north near Nain, pack ice and snow showers are common during July. Summer's fair weather notwithstanding, the temperature can drop rapidly after mid-August; bring gloves, rain gear, insulated underwear, lined rubber boots, and warm sweaters.

Frost starts during late August. Winter temperatures dip down to the -20s across Labrador and have plunged off the scale with a brutally cold -51° C in the western area.

Annual precipitation is 800 mm in the north and central regions, half of which falls as snow between October and May. As much as 1,000 mm fall in southern Labrador. During the winter months, an average 481 cm of snow falls across the central plateau.

**puffin**

### Weather Information

**Environment Canada** provides 24-hour weather forecasts and marine conditions for St. John's, tel. 709/772-5534, and the west coast (from Corner Brook), tel. 709/637-4570. Environment Canada's website, www.weatheroffice.com, is another good source of weather information.

## FLORA AND FAUNA

The forests of Newfoundland island are comprised mainly of black spruce and balsam fir, with occasional stands of larch, pin cherry, pine, paper birch, aspen, red maple, mountain maple, and alder. If you're hiking in alpine or coastal areas, you'll likely encounter the formidable "tuckamore," a canopy-shaped, wind-weathered thicket of stunted, hopelessly entwined fir and spruce. Walk around the thicket, not through it—the dense web mercilessly tears skin and clothing.

In Labrador, the southern forests are cloaked with 12- to 27-meter-high spruce, tamarack, juniper, and birch. Thirty-meter-high white spruce dominates the central area, while black spruce, a mere meter high, speckles the timberline area.

Wildflowers blossom profusely in summer; for an impressive sampler, check out Terra Nova National Park, home to 350 plant species. Across the island's marshes and bogs, expect to see white water lilies, rare orchid species, yellow lady's slipper, purple iris and goodwithy, and insectivorous plants such as the pitcher plant (the provincial flower). Daisies, blue harebells, yellow goldenrod, pink wild roses, and deep pink fireweed thrive in the woodlands. Bright yellow marsh marigolds are native to the western coast's Port au Port Peninsula. Yellow beach groundsel, island gentian, pink sea rocket, and the braidlike hooded ladies' tresses are among the hardy vegetation that grows along the rugged shoreline of the Northern Peninsula.

Northern Labrador's tundra brightens with yellow poppies, heather buttercups, miniature purple rhododendrons, violets, and deep blue gentian, mixed among the white cotton grass. Bushy yellow moss campion thrives on the barrens' gravel surface, while farther south, daisylike arnica and purple saxifrage grow in rock niches.

No poison ivy, poison oak, or ragweed grows

BOB RACE

anywhere in the province. Mushrooms are everywhere, however; the chanterelles are culinary prizes, but the amanitas are deadly poisonous. Be safe and leave identification to the experts.

## Birds

The province is alive with birds; the island counts 343 species, while Labrador has 90. Songbirds such as robins and black-capped chickadees are found in the island's interior. The sooty shearwater can be seen near Gander, and red-throated loons and snowy and great horned owls inhabit the woodlands. The island's raptors include ospreys, gyrfalcons, and eastern North America's largest bald eagle population. Willow ptarmigan habitats include the Burin Peninsula; the rock ptarmigan is native to the Long Range Mountains. Labrador is home to ruffled and spruce grouse, ptarmigans, boreal owls, woodpeckers, ravens, gyrfalcons, jays, chickadees, and nuthatches.

In summer, an estimated 35 million seabirds arrive and gather in 20 major colonies. These coastal colonies harbor 95 percent of North America's Atlantic puffins (the province's official bird), as well as countless common murres—Newfoundlanders call them "turres"—and gannets. Three of North America's six major gannet colonies can be found on Newfoundland's coastal cliffs.

If you're an avid birder, the ecological reserves will leave you breathless. The **Witless Bay Ecological Reserve,** offshore south of St. John's, harbors North America's largest breeding colonies of Atlantic puffins and black-legged kittiwakes (known locally as "tickle aces"). The reserve is also the summer home of murres, Leach's storm petrels, gannets, black guillemots, and herring gulls. The **Cape St. Mary's Ecological Reserve,** North America's third-largest gannetry, is cloaked with 5,400 nesting pairs of gannets, and augmented with common and thick-billed murres, kittiwakes, black guillemots, great black-headed and herring gulls, and razorbills.

The **Funk Island Ecological Reserve** lies 50 km offshore from Musgrave Harbour and is North America's largest murre colony and second-largest gannetry. Off Labrador's coast, the **Gannet Islands Ecological Reserve** is equally remote and lies alongside the Marine Atlantic ferry route to Labrador; from the ferry you can catch awesome displays of 50,000 common murres, 35,000 puffins, and thousands of other seabirds. North America's largest razorbill population, estimated at 24,000, nests at this site off the coast of Cartwright.

Seabird-watching is best late May to mid-July, though seabirds cluster on the coastal cliffs through August and sometimes into mid-September.

## Whales

Some 17 whale species can be seen off Newfoundland island's coastlines, and 10 species cruise Labrador's seacoast. The humpback, minke, fin, right, pothead, pilot, blue, sperm, and sei are most common; the beluga and narwhal are also occasionally seen. June and July are the prime whale-watching months. Most species, however, roam local waters longer, and the minke and pothead whale-watching season extends from May to October.

For the best whale shows, check out the island's Atlantic coastlines, from Fogo Island to St. Mary's Bay. Pods of humpbacks frequent Bonavista and Trinity bays, especially off Trinity and Terra Nova National Park. Sperm and pothead whales are especially fond of the giant squid in Conception Bay near St. John's. An array of humpback, minke, and fin whales, bobbing amid tour boats, usually adds excitement to the seabird show at the Witless Bay Ecological Reserve.

On the western coast, fin, minke, humpback, and pilot whales are sighted offshore at Gros Morne National Park.

## An "Impoverished" Animal Region

With only 14 species of indigenous mammals, the island is considered an impoverished animal region. On the other hand, some of these 14 species have proliferated in amazing numbers. Moose number 150,000; Newfoundland's unique subspecies of black bear number 6,000 to 10,000. Caribou are even more numerous: 12

# THE NEWFOUNDLAND DOG AND LABRADOR RETRIEVER

The large, long-haired Newfoundland dog is believed to have originated with the early Portuguese, who brought mountain sheepdogs across the Atlantic with them. Considered one of North America's finest show dogs, the Newfoundland is better known locally as a working dog. Its swimming prowess in rescuing shipwrecked fishermen and sailors from stormy seas has inspired local legends.

Contrary to the name, the Labrador retriever originated on the island of Newfoundland as a descendant of the Newfoundland dog. The retriever was known as the "lesser Newfoundland," "St. John's dog," or "St. John's water dog," until its debut in London at the English Kennel Club in 1903.

herds roam the island and are most plentiful in the Avalon Wilderness Reserve and across the Northern Peninsula. Four caribou herds inhabit Labrador, the most famous of which is the George River herd. Its 450,000 caribou migrate eastward from Québec in late spring to calve in the Torngat Mountains. This calving ground is currently under consideration for a national park. Among the island's native animals are the hare, lynx, beaver, otter, muskrat, marten, mink, and fox. Labrador's northern tundra coastline is home to populations of red wolves, wolverines, porcupines, squirrels, weasels, and polar bears. No skunks, snakes, or porcupines inhabit the area.

## HISTORY

### Early Inhabitants

The province's earliest human history dates back some 8,000 to 10,000 years, when Maritime Archaic people followed the retreating Laurentide glacier into southern Labrador. By 7500 B.C., they were hunting seals and whales in the Labrador Straits; by 5000 B.C., they'd reached northern Labrador. At L'Anse-Amour, a Maritime Archaic burial mound, discovered in 1973, dates from about 7500 B.C. From here, these people migrated farther south, to Newfoundland, and occupied much of the island's coastline by 4000 B.C. Another burial site at Port au Choix on the island dates to 4,300 years ago. After this culture disappeared from the region, about 3,000 years ago, other aboriginal cultures—known only to archaeologists as "Intermediate" and "Recent"—

settled the Labrador Straits. The present-day Innu may be descended from these mysterious peoples.

Paleo-Eskimo groups began to arrive between 4,000 and 7,000 years ago. Among the various peoples that migrated south from the high Arctic, the Dorset culture is probably the most interesting to anthropologists. The Dorsets roamed as far south as Newfoundland's Port au Choix on the Point Riche Peninsula 1,500 to 2,200 years ago, but they vanished from the island between A.D. 1000 and 1200 and from Labrador about 600 years later.

A third Arctic group, the Thule (TOO-lee), migrated south about A.D. 1400. Their descendants are the Inuit who today make up a large percentage of Labrador's population.

The Beothuks (Bay-AW-thuk), who adorned themselves with red ochre and lived on the island as early as A.D. 200, were part of the Algonquin-speaking group and probably descended from a Labrador group that came over from Québec. Beothuk encampments have been found throughout central Newfoundland. The arrival of European settlers proved fatal to the Beothuk, however, and they were extinct by 1829.

### Earliest Explorers

As early as the fifth century, Brendan the Navigator, an Irish monk, sailed across the Atlantic in search of the "wonderful island of the saints." Some say he found it on Newfoundland; the *Navigatio Sancti Brendani Abbatis,* penned in the ninth century, described an island of steep cliffs, rocky inlets, fog, icebergs, and seabirds—all hallmarks of the island. Intriguingly, a stone found near L'Anse aux Meadows bears a inscription believed to use an ogham style of writing, a Celtic alphabet used by the Irish monks of the 5th and 6th centuries.

The Norsemen, or Vikings, from Greenland and Iceland sailed along Labrador's coast and up Hamilton Inlet. About A.D. 1000, they established a foothold at L'Anse aux Meadows, possibly as a base camp for collecting timber. The site was North America's earliest European settlement, and has been designated a national historic park and a UNESCO world heritage site.

By the 1500s, European fishermen were familiar with the island and Labrador coastlines. Basques from Spain fished for cod off the Grand Banks—drying and salting the fish on the island's seacoasts—and hunted whales in the Strait of Belle Isle. From 1540 to 1610, five whaling stations employing 1,900 men served the area. The *San Juan,* one of the Basque whaling ships, sank at Red Bay; archaeological work dates the ship to 1565, and experts say the sunken ship, perfectly preserved by the cold sea, is North America's best-preserved shipwreck.

England's claim to the area dates to Giovanni Caboto (better known as John Cabot), the Venetian explorer-for-hire who sighted the "New Founde Lande" on a 1497 voyage. He had apparently learned about the island from Basque fishermen. Where Cabot actually stepped ashore is anyone's guess. Some scholars now believe it was somewhere in Labrador. The folks in St. John's say it was on their shores; others in the province believe it was at Bonavista, which is where the 500th anniversary celebration of the landing took place in 1997.

### French and English Claims

France's claim of sovereignty dates to the early 16th-century fishing fleets that dropped anchor from the Burin Peninsula to Channel-Port aux Basques. French explorer Jacques Cartier followed, skirting the coastlines of the island and Labrador on voyages between 1534 and 1542, and claiming for France all the land he saw. On the island, France claimed and defended the French Shore, from Cape Bonavista's tip to Cape

Ray near Port aux Basques. The 1763 Treaty of Paris awarded fishing rights off the island to the French, but prohibited the western coast's permanent settlement. In 1783, the Treaty of Versailles limited France's fishing rights to solely the western coast.

Great Britain, for its part, was eager to establish trading centers in the New World. In 1558, private mercantile interests from England's West Country settled **Trinity,** the pretty historic village on Trinity Bay. Trinity predates St. Augustine, Florida, which was settled by the Spaniards in 1564. The settlement emerged as a major trading and fishing center several decades later, and was also the site of England's first overseas court of justice, a vice-admiralty court established in 1615.

The fishing admirals evolved a system of raw justice. In lieu of a governor, the admirals of the season's first fishing ships ruled St. John's and each major bay. The nations jockeyed for dominance, but England eventually controlled the system. As a U.S. diplomat described the situation in the late 1700s, "Newfoundland has been considered, in all former times, as a great ship moored near the Grand Banks during the fishing season for the convenience of English fishermen."

### Settlements: Legal and Illegal

The Crown granted Lord Baltimore the Avalon Peninsula for Roman Catholic settlement in 1621. But after he arrived at Ferryland in 1627 and endured a harsh winter, Baltimore petitioned for another grant and a decade later moved the Catholics south to Maryland. With Baltimore out of the picture, Sir David Kirke, the British merchant and adventurer, received a grant for the island in 1637. Kirke, who had fled political upheaval in England, set himself up in Baltimore's baronial quarters at Ferryland, where he remained until his death in 1655.

Less pretentious outports such as Pouch (pronounced "pooch") Cove began as illegal refuges for sailors and fishermen who had jumped ship and married local women. For them, any dent on the rocky shore would do, and the rockier the better. Settlements were discouraged by British and French ships patrolling the coast-

# NEWFOUNDLAND'S COD INDUSTRY: A CHRONOLOGY

Newfoundland's rich cod-fishing heritage began with waters so thick with fish they could, it was said, be harvested by the bucketful. This wealth of resources engendered long-running battles between nations for fishing rights, and the battles continue to this day. The seemingly endless supply of cod resulted inevitably in overharvesting on a massive scale. Now, despite moratoriums placed on the fisheries through the 1990s, fish numbers remain low. Recent aquaculture endeavors are proving moderately successful, as are various diversification programs, and there is hope that the industry will rebound.

**1550s** Basque and Portuguese fleets begin fishing the Strait of Belle Isle and the Grand Banks.

**1600s** French and English fleets begin fishing the Grand Banks and the waters of the Avalon Peninsula.

**1713** The Treaty of Utrecht grants Newfoundland Island to the British, though France retains some fishing rights along the south coast.

**1750s** Newfoundland fishing is dominated by fisheries from England's West Country

**1763** The Treaty of Paris cedes French possessions in Canada to the English, including Labrador.

**1832** England's wars with France and the U.S. end, causing a boom in Newfoundland settlement. Fisheries, including those based on the Labrador coast, continue to expand and prosper.

**1850s** Newfoundland battles England for jurisdiction over its own resources.

**1890s** Ninety percent of Newfoundland's workforce is involved in the fishing industry.

**1904** Britain and France sign agreements ceding control of the West Coast and the Northern Peninsula to Newfoundland.

**1908** The powerful Fishermen's Protective Union is established by William Coaker. (The union's power will diminish by 1932.)

**1911** The Hague Tribunal awards control over its bays to Newfoundland.

lines. Any sign of life, such as fireplace smoke issuing from a chimney, spelled eviction, but a dangerous shore dissuaded royal navy ships from landing.

## Early St. John's

St. John's evolved independently as a supply and fisheries center. Its mixed population of Spaniards, Portuguese, and French was hardly Anglo; consequently, the island's first officially chartered English colony was Cupers (now Cupids) Cove, on Conception Bay, founded in 1610.

Still, St. John's was hard to ignore, and by 1675 a string of British forts guarded the harbor. England's most formidable foe was the French, entrenched since 1662 at Plaisance on Placentia Bay. After ongoing assaults, Plaisance slipped from French control with the Treaty of

Utrecht in 1713. The British renamed the place Placentia and took over the fortified town.

## England's New Colony

In 1711, a naval governor was appointed to strengthen England's control of the fishing-admiral system. Part-time government, administered by a summertime governor, followed in the late 1720s. Sporadic settlements took hold as immigrants, who had settled on the Avalon Peninsula, moved westward. Twillingate, begun by Breton fishermen about 1700, had 159 inhabitants by 1739. Bell Island, in Conception Bay, was settled by English and Irish immigrants in the 1750s.

The persistent French attacked St. John's from the Fortress of Louisbourg on Cape Breton, but the British finished off Louisbourg in 1758. A French contingent subsequently sailed across the

**1949** Newfoundland joins the Canadian Confederation. As a result, it cedes exclusive fishing rights to its waters.

**1960s** Overharvesting by foreign trawler fleets results in depletion of cod stocks.

**1971** The Newfoundland Fishermen, Food and Allied Workers' Union is established and becomes the first provincial fishers' union to wield effective power.

**1977** A 200-mile economic limit is placed on Newfoundland waters.

**1986** Aquaculture industries begin experimental cod-farming and find limited success.

**1990** Severe decline in northern cod stocks reaches lowest levels on record.

**1992** A two-year moratorium on commercial cod fishing is enacted.

**1994** Yearly cod catch has declined by 90 percent in five years. The moratorium of 1992 is extended. Provincewide, scores of fisheries and processing plants are closed. The Atlantic Groundfish Strate-

gy is put into action, providing economic assistance and job training for displaced fishery workers.

**1996** Foreign fishing trawlers continue to overharvest fish stocks straddling the 200-mile limit on the Grand Banks. The jurisdictional boundary around the French-owned St-Pierre and Miquelon Islands remains in dispute.

**1997** Cod farms continue to supply juvenile cod to fishery waters, an enterprise that will continue to be necessary even if wild cod stocks return to healthy numbers.

**1999** Cod fisheries reopen and the fishing sector experiences its best year ever, employing 15,000 Newfoundlanders and adding over $500 million to the economy.

**2000** Cod stocks waver, but a diversification programs see high returns of shellfish, such as shrimp and crab.

**2001** As cod numbers return to normal in some areas, factors outside Newfoundland's control affect the industry, such as poor market conditions, which forced the July closure of the shrimp fishery.

Atlantic from Brest, and was defeated at the Battle of Signal Hill in 1762. That battle ended the Seven Years' War. The 1763 Treaty of Paris awarded the island and a mainland strip to England, while France acquired **St-Pierre and Miquelon,** small islands off Newfoundland's southern shore.

Navigator and explorer Capt. James Cook was dispatched in 1762 to survey England's new colonial acquisition. Cook's explorations probed Labrador's seacoast, and the Burin Peninsula and Corner Brook areas on the island. He also ventured inland—up the island's Humber River as far as Deer Lake. On the western coast, Anglo immigration soon followed to the Bay of Islands, Humber Arm coastline, and St. George's.

French Acadians from Nova Scotia, who had fled France's defeat at Louisbourg, settled on the Port au Port Peninsula in 1758. France wanted

fishing rights on the island's western coast, and the Treaty of Versailles granted the request in 1783. England bitterly contested this claim through the late 1800s. In fact, when plans were made for the new railroad's terminus, England chose the more neutrally located Port aux Basques, rather than St. George's in the Acadian area, which the French claimed was within their jurisdiction. The sun was setting, however, on Atlantic Canada's French presence, and, in 1904, France relinquished the island's territorial fishing claims in a swap with England for Morocco.

## The Beothuks' Demise

Across the island's central area, the arrival of Europeans foretold grave consequences for the Beothuks, who had migrated from Labrador in A.D. 200 and spread across the Baie Verte Peninsula to Burnside, Twillingate, and the shores of the Exploits River and Red Indian Lake.

In 1769, a law prohibiting murder of the indigenous people was enacted, but the edict came too late. The Beothuks were almost extinct, and in 1819 a small group was ambushed by settlers near Red Indian Lake. In the ensuing struggle, a 23-year-old woman named Demasduit was captured, and her husband and newborn infant were killed. The government attempted to return her to her people when she contracted tuberculosis, but she was too ill, and she died in Botwood. In 1823, her kinswoman, Shanawdithit, was also taken by force. Shanawdithit told a moving tale of the history and demise of her people, punctuating it with drawings, maps, and a sampling of Beothuk vocabulary before she died in 1829, the last of her race.

### Labrador Develops

Settlements spread to Labrador. The lure was trade, and by 1870, five hundred schooners plied the coast. English law was administered first by a circuit court of justice, then with Labrador's first permanent court of justice at Rigolet, established in 1826. Trading posts started at North West River, Cartwright, and L'Anse au Clair, and English immigrants and Newfoundland *livyers* (permanent coastal residents) followed.

Remote Labrador also lured the missionaries. German Moravians set up outposts at Nain, Hopedale, and other coastal sites in the 1700s. The area's famed medical missionary, Dr. Wilfred Grenfell of England, established a mission hospital at Battle Harbour in 1893—the first of many remote medical centers and nursing stations. Grenfell also encouraged Inuit crafts and trade and opened the first cooperative at Red Bay.

### Fuller Government Evolves

Meanwhile, full-fledged dominion status came to the island. The former part-time governor was replaced by a full-time governor in 1811. The issue of land ownership was resolved, and settlers were allowed to own land by 1813. Newfoundland was granted self-government, and the first assembly was held in St. John's in 1855. Splendid official buildings went up: the Commissariat

House, for Fort William's assistant commissary general; and the Government House—an expensive residential replica of the Admiralty House at Plymouth, England—for the governor.

Immigration fleshed out the island. A second wave of Acadians from Nova Scotia immigrated to the Port au Port Peninsula in the 1840s. Mass Irish immigration spread across the Avalon Peninsula's Southern Shore, and by 1850 half of Newfoundland's inhabitants were Irish. Aside from the western coast's French ports, the island was decidedly pro-British, and when the question of Confederation arose in 1869, Newfoundlanders held a general election and voted resoundingly against it.

### Communications and Industry

By 1844, steamer service linked St. John's with Halifax, and island-wide rail service started in the 1880s. The first transatlantic telegraph cable to Europe was laid from **Heart's Content** on Trinity Bay in 1866; Guglielmo Marconi received the first transatlantic wireless message from Signal Hill at St. John's in 1901.

Copper was first mined at Tilt Cove in 1864, and the discovery of iron ore on Bell Island led to over 70 years of prosperity, from 1893 to 1966. During that period, the Wabana Mines produced 30 percent of the iron ore smelted in Canada. Pulp and paper industries developed in the early 1900s at Grand Falls and Corner Brook. In Labrador, Garland Lethbridge of Paradise River developed a flash-freeze food-preservation method. Lethbridge shared the secret with Clarence Birdseye, an American who spent a year at Sandwich Bay in 1916. Birdseye subsequently sold the concept to General Foods for $22 million—without a cent to Lethbridge.

### The Bad-luck Years

Bad luck struck Newfoundland in the early 1900s. In Labrador, the Spanish flu arrived aboard a supply ship, and a third of the region's 1,200 Inuits perished. During World War I, cod and fur prices slumped, and the island's railroad went bankrupt. The Great Depression aggravated conditions, and in St. John's, a mob tried to lynch the prime minister. By 1933, Newfoundland was insolvent. England paid the debts (based on the personal credit of Sir Robert Bond, the St. John's millionaire who later became Newfoundland's prime minister), stripped Newfoundland of its dominion status, and returned it to the status of a crown colony, suspending the assembly and appointing a six-member commission to govern the island and Labrador.

The island, nevertheless, fared better during the Great Depression than the rest of Atlantic Canada. Zinc, lead, copper, silver, and gold were discovered at Buchans. The economy was aided coincidentally with the unprecedented economic boom that accompanied World War II. The location of Newfoundland and Labrador at North America's eastern edge was an enviable asset. Canadian, British, and U.S. military bases were built in rapid succession from Gander to Goose Bay.

Nazi submarines plied the island's waters. In St. John's, Signal Hill was fortified against invasion, as was nearby Cape Spear. The Germans chose Bell Island in Conception Bay for an incursion attempt. They sank ships laden with iron ore and burned the piers. No place on the island or mainland was safe: a submarine sank the *Caribou*, a Nova Scotia ferry, off Port aux Basques; and in northern Labrador, the Germans actually landed and set up a weather station, probably the Nazis' only foothold in North America.

## Confederation and Its Consequences

Wartime tolls notwithstanding, the economy had never been better. Buoyed by improved conditions, Newfoundlanders questioned the existing Crown commission-government arrangement. Confederation was rejected by the voters in 1946 and 1948. But when it appeared on the ballot again in 1949, a slender majority voted for union with Canada, and Newfoundland became the nation's 10th province.

A rite of passage can have pitfalls. Joey Smallwood, a schoolteacher and journalist from St. John's, carried the Liberal banner for confederation and assumed government reign during the early confederation years. Smallwood saw a profitable, efficient industrial society as the province's hope, and he advised Newfoundlanders to "Burn your boats." Under that strategy, the island's innu-

merable outports, many without municipal governments or services, were victims of the times.

A resettlement scheme began—still painfully remembered—under which many small outports were forcefully abandoned, with the inhabitants relocated to new or larger communities with services. Critics lambasted the displacement as a horrendous blow to the island's social texture. Other islanders saw a glimmer of hope and said that feudalism, the system that had prevailed since the fishing-admiral system, had finally ended.

## The New Newfoundland

From this, a new Newfoundland emerged. Municipal government and town planning, both new concepts, began in the 1950s. Memorial University in St. John's, founded in 1925 as a college, was granted university status in 1949. Access to Labrador improved, as rail service and a road linked Labrador City with the province of Québec.

The provincial economy is now in flux. The seal industry, censured by animal activists, has been limited to the 30,000 seals legally culled by First Nations people each spring. In 1977, the federal government sought to curb depletion of the Grand Banks fisheries by establishing a 320 km offshore fishing zone. That was admirable defensive thinking on the part of the Canadian government, but parts of the Grand Banks lie outside the designated zone, and these areas still draw mammoth foreign trawlers that contribute to the depletion of the once-rich fisheries.

The codfish landings remained sparse, and in 1992, the Canadian government took drastic steps. Ottawa banned commercial salmon fishing in Newfoundland for five years and commercial cod fishing in the province's northeastern waters for two years. The moratorium put 19,000 fishers and fish processors out of work for the first time in 500 years. The two-year codfishing ban expired in 1994, and fishery employees prepared to go back to work. But, to everyone's horror, the codfish populations off Newfoundland had not only recovered during the ban but had actually diminished further—to almost nothing. The fishing ban was extended, and the future of this industry now looks exceedingly bleak.

# NEWFOUNDLAND'S ROLE IN AVIATION HISTORY

As the continent's closest gateway to Europe, Newfoundland played a significant role in the development of air travel across the Atlantic. Capt. John Alcock and Lt. A. W. Brown made the first successful transatlantic flight in 1919, taking off from St. John's in a twin-engine biplane and landing tail-up in an Irish peat bog 16 hours later. Charles Lindbergh, the pioneer American pilot, flew over St. John's on a 33.5-hour nonstop New York–Paris solo flight in 1927, and in 1933 he touched down at Nain, Labrador, on another transatlantic flight. American aviator Amelia Earhart chose Trepassey on the southern Avalon Peninsula as the departure point for her 1928 transatlantic flight to Wales. On that flight, Earhart flew as a passenger. Her next flight, however, in 1932, won Earhart honors as the first woman to solo across the Atlantic. She left from Harbour Grace, near St. John's.

**Wartime Aviation**

By 1939, England was locked in mortal combat with Nazi Germany and needed aircraft and supplies. The British Air Ministry selected Gander (now nicknamed Crossroads of the World) as a landing and refueling base on the transatlantic supply route. Goose Bay Air Base, in Labrador, opened shortly thereafter; by 1940, the joint Cana-

dian and U.S. airbase had a staff of 5,000 military and 3,000 civilian personnel.

At the war's height, American-built aircraft destined for England touched down in Newfoundland and Labrador. About 500,000 U.S. pilots and crew members passed through major installations, such as Ft. Pepperell, the military headquarters at St. John's, and bases at Goose Bay, Gander, Torbay, Argentia, and Stephenville.

**Postwar Developments**

Most military operations ceased in the 1960s, and U.S. Air Force involvement was taken over by the Canadian Ministry of Transport. The U.S. still has a small military presence at the Argentia, Gander, and Goose Bay bases. The former Goose Bay Air Base kept its military functions and has evolved as the Canadian Forces Air Base Goose Bay. It added a NATO Tactical Fighters Weapons Training Centre in the early 1990s, while the emergence of Happy Valley–Goose Bay as central Labrador's air gateway prompted the development of the commercial Goose Bay Airport. The former Gander base made the transition to a commercial airport. It offered polar flights to Europe and served as the gateway for political refugees from Cuba and the Eastern European nations, who touched down briefly before flying to other parts of Canada.

Provincial economic expectations are now tied to offshore petroleum and natural gas fields at the edge of the Grand Banks, with over $3 billion spent on exploration alone through the 1990s. The Hibernia oilfield—said to be the world's largest offshore oil reserve—has been producing over 150,000 barrels of oil a day since 1999. Along with the nearby Hebron/Ben Nevis and White Rose fields, which began producing in late 2001, total yield for the region is currently around 500,000 barrels per day.

## GOVERNMENT AND ECONOMY

The province's government is modeled on the British parliamentary system. The lieutenant-

governor, appointed by the prime minister to a four-year term, heads the executive council and the legislative House of Assembly. The House of Assembly's 52 members are elected from the provincial districts. On the national level, the province sends seven members of parliament and six senators to Ottawa.

The Liberal Party has been in power since 1989, with most opposition coming from the Progressive Conservatives, who held power through most of the 1970s and 1980s.

On the local level, the province has about 1,500 settlements, of which three—St. John's, Corner Brook, and Mount Pearl (a St. John's suburb)—are cities, 168 are towns, and 140 are communities. The remaining settlements are organized around local churches rather than municipal governments; in these hamlets, provincial taxes and services are lacking.

## Economy

The gross provincial product was more than $9.5 billion in 2001. Mining (at $1.1 billion) was the top revenue earner. Most mining revenues come from offshore oilfields and western Labrador, where about 80 percent of Canada's iron ore is extracted. Other commercially mined minerals include copper, lead, zinc, gold and silver, chromium, limestone, gypsum, aluminum silicate, and asbestos. Labrador also holds Canada's sole commercial deposit of pyrophyllite, which is used in the production of ceramics. The mining industry directly employs around 2,500 people. Manufacturing ($1 billion), construction ($900 million), and government ($600 million) are also important revenue earners. Electric power and water utilities bring in some $500 million.

Fishing is still an integral part of the Newfoundland economy.

Fisheries, a chronic boom or bust industry, contributed $511 million to the provincial economy in 1999. This was a record, and the figure has decreased slightly in the ensuing years. With diminished cod stocks, larger fishing boats have moved further offshore, filling their holds with crab, shrimp, lobster, capelin, and lumpfish. The industry employs around 14,000 Newfoundlanders, half involved in harvesting and the half in processing.

Tourism is also important. Around 400,000 nonresident visitors injected $287 million into the provincial economy in 1999. Logging earned $75 million, while its offshoot, pulp and paper factories, earned $120 million. Agriculture earns around $33 million annually—the bulk of it in hay, root crops, vegetables, berries, and mink farming.

## PEOPLE

The province (pop. 530,000) is lightly settled, with a density of fewer than two people per square km. Cities, towns, and communities hold about 60 percent of the population; the remaining residents inhabit outports and remote areas.

On the island, many settlements lie along the coastline. About 40 percent of the population is found in St. John's and on the Avalon Peninsula. Labrador's 31,100 residents are concentrated east to west across the central plateau, while the seacoast is sparsely settled.

### Early Ancestors

Most residents of the island trace their ancestry to England and Ireland. The Irish are well represented—you'll find plenty of O'Rourkes, Murphys, and Mooneys at settlements from St. John's to Placentia Bay. Merchants from Scotland also settled in St. John's, and were joined by Nova Scotian Scots who migrated from Cape Breton to the western coast. English descendants are spread throughout the province and trace their roots to the West Country—Devon, Dorset, Somerset, Hampshire—and the Channel Islands. The population of St. John's is a mix of English and Irish.

© ANDREW HEMPSTEAD

Among the ethnic groups here are the southwestern coast's small French population; the Mi'kmaq community of Conne River; and an American population that originated with a small number of military personnel who stayed on after being stationed here in World War II.

In Labrador, most of the inhabitants are "from away," meaning from other parts of Canada. Mixed among these are the Newfoundlanders who made their homes in Labrador long ago; some Newfoundlanders who summer there at the family fishing stations; and the indigenous Innu and Inuit peoples, who live primarily at Davis Inlet, Sheshatsheits, the Lobstick Lake area, and along the northern coastline.

## Religion

The island's Irish and French are Roman Catholics, while the English belong to the Anglican or United churches. Protestant evangelical denominations have strong followings and include the Salvation Army, Pentecostal, and Seventh-day Adventists. Labrador has a similar distribution, as well as Moravian, Church of the Nazarene, Plymouth Brethren, Baptist, and Methodist denominations. There's also a small Jewish population in St. John's.

## Language

English—rich with clipped British accents and softly brushed Irish lilts—is the province's dominant language, spoken by more than 98 percent of the population. French is spoken on the southwestern coast, where Newfoundlanders are mainly bilingual (a mere 1.4 percent of the population speaks only French). Other languages occasionally heard among the population include Innu, Inuit, Chinese, German, and Spanish.

The English spoken in Newfoundland is a dialect unique to the province. It's so distinctive, it prompted Memorial University scholars to compile the province's own *Dictionary of Newfoundland English,* the definitive reference to the local language since 1982.

Every immigrant group to come along has contributed to Newfoundland English. For example, *droke,* a Celtic word, translates as a steepsided valley cut with a stream. The Inuit

contributed *komatik* (sled), among others. A number of local words deal with dining. If you're invited to "have a scoff" or "boil up," be prepared to pull up a chair and share a meal; if it's a "mug up," you'll have tea or a snack.

Many words relate to fishing. A "tilt" translates as an open fishing shelter; a "hangashore" or "angishore" describes a man too lazy to fish; a "tickle" is a small narrow that's dangerous to navigate; and "stages and flakes" are fish-drying racks set up on stilts. You'll hear a misty day described as "mauzy." The 400,000-plus visitors who arrive in the province each year are known as "mainlanders," who have "come from away"—"CFAs" for short.

## Conduct and Customs

Historically at odds with the inhospitable land, treacherous seas, and capricious weather, Newfoundlanders have emerged from the centuries as passionate, resourceful survivors. Their long link with England has imbued them with a preference for formal courtesies (a Newfoundlander expects to finish a sentence without interruption). You'll find the people here, like other Atlantic Canadians, friendly, hospitable, patient, and sincere.

None of which precludes the passion with which they live. They're quick to joke and quicker to laugh. Further, Newfoundlanders are habitual iconoclasts, who lambaste issues from religion to social conventions. They enjoy satire, and their political brickbats saturate the local newspapers. They're intuitively creative, and their music, crafts, and fine arts are among Canada's best.

In a sense, Newfoundland has never quite fit the Canadian mold. Its culture has always been more entwined with the traditions of England and Ireland than the rest of Canada. This has occasionally led to tensions between citizens of the province and Canadians elsewhere in the country. In the 1940s, when Newfoundland was considering confederation with Canada, some ethnocentric Canadians used the word "Newfie" as a slur, belittling their culturally distinct Newfoundland cousins. To this day, the word amuses no one here.

## Genealogy Resources

The best source for genealogical tracing is the **Provincial Archives of Newfoundland and Labrador** in the Colonial Buildings on Military Road in St. John's, tel. 709/729-3065 (open Mon.–Fri. 9 A.M.–4:15 P.M.; also 6:30 P.M.–9:45 P.M. Wed.). Its free *Genealogical Package* describes the archives' holdings and how they can help trace family roots, and provides a list of private genealogists. Access the archives through the Distance Research Division; details are at www.gov.nf.ca/panl.

Memorial University's **Centre for Newfoundland Studies,** tel. 709/737-7475, has directories of names and addresses dating to the 1800s, plus the nominal censuses for 1921, 1935, and 1945. The center is part of the university's Queen Elizabeth II Library on Elizabeth Avenue; open Mon.–Thurs. 8:30 A.M.–10.45 P.M.

In Labrador, **Them Days,** 3 Courtemanche St., Happy Valley–Goose Bay, tel. 709/896-8531, www.hvgb.net/~themdays, publishes a quarterly magazine of the same name, with features about the region's history and people. The company is also a source for historic diaries, letters, and other records. If you want to do a roots search, you'll need to know your family's name, regional relatives' names, and where family members lived. Be aware that Them Days is a publishing company, not a genealogical society. But Labrador's early years are important to the staff members, and they'll help you as best they can. A subscription to the magazine costs $20 in Canada, $25 in the United States.

## Crime

With no history of violent crime or multiracial upheavals, the province is among North America's safest places. It's so free of violent crime that the provincial police do not carry guns. Petty theft is more common; lock vehicle doors and keep valuables out of sight.

Don't ask for trouble, however, especially if you are a woman traveling alone. St. John's, as an international port, has a lively bar scene that, depending on the number of ships in port, can be rife with sailors. In the hinterlands, service stations are sparse, and the back roads are lightly traveled; bring a spare tire and make sure your vehicle is in good working condition.

## CRAFTS

Newfoundland's exciting crafts scene owes its genesis to the province's demanding setting. Winters here are long and harsh, many areas are remote, and money is short during the fisheries' slack periods. Crafts, which can be produced in the home at any time of year, were taken advantage of early on to contribute a margin of comfort to the subsistence economy. The Nonia Handicrafts shop in St. John's, for example, is an outlet for the Newfoundland Outport Nursing and Industrial Association, an organization begun in 1924 to raise money for medical care in the remote outports.

Handmade crafts became an industry with clout in the 1970s, when the provincial government eyed them as a potential revenue earner. The **Craft Council of Newfoundland and Labrador** is charged with developing the crafts industry, as well as running the Devon House gallery and retail shop in St. John's and hosting crafts shows four times a year. Contact the council at 709/753-2749, www.craftcouncil.nf.ca.

Privately owned crafts shops flourish across the province. Every area has a crafts specialty. Tourist chalets on the TransCanada Highway are stuffed with bulky, warm fishermen's sweaters; knitted mittens and hats whose linings are "thrummed" with fleece; embroidered parkas trimmed with fox fur; and landscapes depicted on hooked mats and hangings. Gander is known for hand-woven woolens; St. Alban's and the Conne River Indian Reserve feature carvings in bone, wood, rock, and moose or caribou antlers. The crafts shops of Labrador's northern Inuit settlements are centers for soapstone sculpture, caribou-leather moccasins, labradorite jewelry, and woven-grass baskets. Another irresistible buy is **Terra Footwear;** the deftly crafted suede hiking boots are manufactured in Harbour Grace and exported worldwide.

### Typical Prices

When shopping around, expect superbly crafted wares at reasonable prices. A wool sweater, for example, will cost from $85 to $200, depending on the design's complexity; when it's washed, you'll smell the aroma of fresh lamb's wool. Yard goods are hand woven. Linen costs about $30 a meter, wool $50 a meter. The exquisitely crafted Grenfell-style coats have a hefty price tag, though, and you'll pay about $375 for a full-length coat or around $315 for a three-quarter-length model. Raw, gem-quality labradorite is $50 or more a pound.

## EVENTS AND ENTERTAINMENT

### Folk Festivals

Provincial folk festivals originated as family reunions decades ago and have grown to country-fair proportions—tempting enough to lure distant relatives from afar and visitors from all over the province. The festivals are consistently good summer entertainment. Local lodgings can be hard to get at festival time, so it's wise to make reservations early.

The **Festival of Folk Song and Dance** at Burin kicks off the season with authentic island songs, music, dance, and dance workshops in early July. The **Iron Skull Folk Festival** at Belleoram and the **Exploits Valley Salmon Festival** at Grand Falls–Windsor follow with more of the same in mid-July. The **Fish, Fun, and Folk Festival** at Twillingate, the **Southern Shore Shamrock Folk Festival** at Ferryland, and the **Conception Bay Folk Festival** at Carbonear round out the month.

The festival season ends by mid-August. The **Newfoundland and Labrador Folk Festival,** held in early August in St. John's, ranks as the province's grandest folk hoopla and draws large crowds with its mix of folk ingredients and country-fair trappings. The **Heritage Folk Festival** at Terra Nova National Park features old-time Newfoundland music and recitations over three days in mid-August.

### Other Festivals and Outdoor Entertainment

If you're interested in French-inspired airs and dance, head to the Port au Port Peninsula and check out **Une Journée dans l'Passé** in late July at La Grand Terre.

The smaller festivals are equally entertaining. In late June, for example, the western coastal town of Cow Head puts on a daily lobster spread

at its **Lobster Festival.** In late July, North West River's **Beach Festival** combines Labradorian food with the sounds of local musicians. In August, the **Triton Caplin Cod Festival** celebrates the return of two important ocean resources at Triton on the northeast coast. And bountiful feeds take place during the **Bakeapple Folk Festival,** held in the Labrador Strait community of Forteau in mid-August.

Count on summertime street entertainment, too. **Buskers,** many of whom are Memorial University music students, perform at the drop of a hat in St. John's and other island towns. More events are described in the travel chapters below, but for a complete list of the sports events, country and town fairs, food festivals, regattas, and more folk festivals, see the provincial *Tourist Guide.*

### Kissing the Cod

Newfoundlanders dote on the codfish, and visitors are invited to pledge piscatorial loyalty to King Cod in hilarious induction ceremonies regularly conducted on tour boats and in restaurants. To be "screeched-in" in proper style, a visitor dons fishing garb, downs several quick shots of Screech rum, kisses a cod, joins in singing a local ditty, poses for a photograph, and receives an official certificate. It's strictly tourist nonsense, but visitors love it.

### Provincial Holidays

Newfoundland celebrates all of the national holidays, plus St. Patrick's Day, March 17; St. George's Day, April 24; Discovery Day, June 24; Dominion (Memorial) Day, July 1; and Orangemen's Day, July 12. The holidays are observed on the nearest Monday in order to provide a long weekend. St. John's also unofficially shuts down on St. John's Regatta Day, the first Wednesday in August, weather permitting.

## RECREATION

Newfoundland, with its thousands of square kilometers of parks and untouched wilderness, offers the perfect backdrop for the ultimate in outdoor recreation. The province boasts every option in Atlantic Canada's sports repertoire.

Consider the choices: scuba diving and kayaking in the Gulf of St. Lawrence or the Atlantic; golfing at the capital's Pippy Park, the Twin Rivers links at Terra Nova National Park's edge, or in Corner Brook; inland and coastal biking and hiking; big-game hunting; and angling for trophy-size fish.

On the island, canoeists explore whitewater and placid water alike on the Upper Humber, Main, and Gander Rivers. The Avalon Peninsula attracts scuba divers, anglers, canoeists, hikers, and backpackers. The western coast caters to kayakers, the mountains to horseback riders, bikers, and climbers. Labrador attracts die-hard anglers and hunters to backwoods sports camps, while naturalists take air tours along the seacoast in search of polar bears and caribou.

## Adventure-Travel Experts

Whether you're an experienced adventure enthusiast, or a novice who wants to learn the ropes, numerous licensed adventure-travel companies and sports outfitters are available to help make the route smoother.

**Wildland Tours,** tel. 709/722-3123, www .wildlands.com, operates naturalist trips led by academically trained guides and specializes in packages across the Avalon Peninsula, with a stop in historic St. John's. The eight-day Newfoundland Adventure, offered mid-May to August, includes wildlife sightings at Witless Bay, Cape St. Mary's, and Avalon Wilderness Reserve. The price is $2,000 per person for double occupancy, all-inclusive except for suppers.

**Gros Morne Adventures,** tel. 709/458-2722 or 800/685-4624, www.grosmorneadventures.com, leads geology and natural history tours through the park of the same name between June and September and backcountry ski tours come winter and spring. Kayaking is another specialty; a day with instructions and lunch costs around $100 per person, a two-hour paddle at sunset costs $35. Weeklong kayaking excursions run $1,300.

## Fishing

The province's reputation for first-class fishing attracts anglers from across Canada, the United States, and Europe. Inland waterways are choked with trout: speckled, rainbow, lake, brook, and brown. Atlantic salmon, some up to 18 kg, migrate on 200 rivers. In Labrador, a landlocked salmon (known locally as *ouananiche,* pronounced "WIN-a-nich") set the record at 10.29 kg in 1982. Lake trout and northern pike can tip the scales at up to 18 kg, and brook trout are trophy size. Wilderness fishing camps are abundant, and typically charge $250 per person and up per day, all-inclusive with a guide.

Fishing seasons vary. Labrador's arctic char season spans mid-June to mid-September and peaks during August. In the Gros Morne area, brook trout are most plentiful June to mid-September, while the Atlantic salmon season spans mid-June to early September. Among the best salmon rivers are the island's Humber and Lomond Rivers, along with Labrador's Eagle and Pinware Rivers. You'll need a provincial fishing license ($53 for salmon, $8 for trout); in most cases, you'll also need an outfitter or a Newfoundlander relative with you as a guide. At the national parks, salmon fishing is restricted to fly-fishing on scheduled rivers; the required federal salmon permit costs $13 (a trout permit costs $4), and whatever you hook and keep has to be reported for statistical purposes.

The provincial waters are strictly monitored. For details, get in touch with the provincial tourist office for a copy of the federal Department of Fisheries and Oceans' free *Angler's Guide,* containing nonresident guide requirements, river statistics, and bag limits.

## Hunting

Nonresident hunting is strictly regulated. Even if you have traveled and hunted in Newfoundland before, request a copy of the Firearms Act—it was rewritten in 2001. Call 506/624-5380 or 800/731-4000, for a copy. You'll also need an RCMP gun permit (available at retail stores or from an outfitter), and if you plan to light a fire to keep warm, you'll need a fire permit, available from the provincial Department of Forestry.

Big-game licenses are available only through licensed outfitters. Requirements and prices vary. On the island, for example, one male caribou can be taken per license ($405 for a Canadian hunter, $605 for non-nationals). Bears and moose are two other popular big-game species. A small-game license for grouse, ptarmigan, and hare costs $25; a waterfowl permit costs $12. Hunters favor the Long Range Mountains in fall for moose and black bear, northern Labrador in spring for caribou.

The provincial tourist office has free copies of the *Newfoundland and Labrador Hunting and Fishing Guide,* which details regulations and lists outfitters. Another contact is the **Fish & Wildlife Division,** tel. 709/729-2815, or click through the government website, www.gov.nf.ca.

## ACCOMMODATIONS AND CAMPING

St. John's boasts the province's finest accommodations, with dozens of hotels, stunning historic inns and bed-and-breakfasts, functional motels, and smaller guesthouses and hospitality homes (variations on B&Bs). Outside the capital, motels lie along the TransCanada Highway at the major towns. Off the beaten track, accommodations are smaller and fewer, although new B&Bs are opening all around the province.

All the major motel and hotel groups are represented: Best Western, Holiday Inn, Fairmont, and Delta. The locally owned Atlantic Inns of Newfoundland has lodgings at Corner Brook, Grand Falls–Windsor, and Gander.

### Standards, Rates, and Reservations

Lodgings are licensed for minimum standards; the newer motels and hotels are equipped for wheelchair access. The star-grading system is operated to Canada Select guidelines, and all accommodations listed in the various government tourism guides have received a minimum of one star (clean, comfortable). The grading is strictly voluntary, so an absent listing has no real weight. The provincial *Travel Guide* lists the approved lodgings by sightseeing regions.

Rates (posted in each room) are set by the property owner; if the price you're charged differs from the posted rate, discuss it with the lodging manager or contact **Hospitality Newfoundland and Labrador,** tel. 709/722-2000 or 800/563-

0700, www.hnl.nf.net. The HST (harmonized sales tax) is applied to all lodgings except campgrounds and hospitality homes with fewer than four rooms. The city of St. Johns also applies a 3 percent accommodations tax within city limits.

For reservations, phone the property directly or use the listed websites to make online bookings; in July and August, reservations are a good idea throughout the province. The **Department of Tourism, Culture, and Recreation,** tel. 709/729-2830 or 800/563-6353, www.gov.nf .ca/tourism, operates a reservations system for accommodations, tours, and car rentals. Hotels and motels accept major credit cards, but many bed-and-breakfasts don't; check the *Travel Guide* or call ahead to confirm payment details.

### Campgrounds

Campers will find some 2,500 campsites spread among the province's parks. Most sites are unserviced ($9) and include a table, fire pit with free wood, drinking water, cleared space or wooden platform for a tent, and pit toilets; partially serviced sites ($11) have showers. Most commercial campgrounds have full facilities. For a full list, see the provincial *Travel Guide,* available through the **Department of Tourism, Culture, and Recreation,** tel. 709/729-2830 or 800/563-6353, www.gov.nf.ca/tourism. Reservations can also be made through the above contacts.

Campgrounds in Newfoundland's two national parks offer modern facilities and limited hookups. Sites range $12–18 and can be reserved through the Department of Tourism, Culture, and Recreation, tel. 709/729-2830 or 800/563-6353, www.gov.nf.ca/tourism.

## FOOD

Some visitors prefer basic, unadorned dining fare, and will find it in the standard steak, chops, seafood, and salads available at most restaurants across the province. Newfoundlanders, on the other hand, prefer their own culinary creations based on historical recipes and the ingredients available locally. If you're a culinary adventurer, you've arrived in the right province.

Many dishes originated from the province's

## A FEW FAVORITE LOCAL FOODS

**blood pudding**—parboiled, fatty sausage fried for a main meal

**crubeens**—pigs' feet pickled in a brine

**figgy duff**—boiled or baked dried-fruit dessert pudding

**fish 'n' brewis**—salted cod, potatoes, and hard biscuits cooked as a hash

**jiggs dinner**—boiled salted meat, cabbage, and vegetables in broth

**pork scrunchions**—diced pork fat used in fish 'n' brewis and other dishes

**screech pie**—rum-flavored chocolate pie baked in gingerbread crust

**seal flipper pie**—nutritious, dark, gamy meat parboiled, baked in crust

**soused herring**—herring pickled in a brine and bottled

**thimbles**—shortbread embellished with coconut and jam

**yum yums**—sweet shortbread cookies

or roasted caribou, moose, partridge, duck, and rabbit on upscale restaurant menus. Moose meat is also available as fast-food mooseburgers served at some summer festivals and occasionally at hinterlands restaurants.

Available veggies consist of root vegetables such as parsnips, turnips, and carrots, plus local (thanks to hydroponic nurseries) and imported tomatoes, lettuce, and green vegetables. Nutritious reconstituted dried peas are used liberally in soups. At certain times of the year, fresh vegetables get more difficult to find the farther you get from St. John's.

With a fledgling tourism industry, Labrador has far fewer culinary dining opportunities. Deep-fried fish, fried or broiled steaks, and grilled hamburgers are the usual fare. Roast game and broiled Atlantic salmon and char are the real treats, and in Labrador City, French Canadian dishes such as *poutine* (French fries and cheese curds doused with gravy) are frequently on the menu. Credit cards are accepted for lodging and dining in the major towns; outlying settlements prefer cash.

### Area Specialties

Some of the province's best meals are served at motel dining rooms along the TransCanada and other highways. Look for mooseburgers at Conception Bay and Northern Peninsula restaurants. Shrimp are Port au Choix's specialty, and the area's succulent scallops come from Port au Port Peninsula outports. Consider yourself lucky to sample the western coast's rhubarb—cooked in pies, served as a sauce, and bottled as a relish or jam. It's said to be Atlantic Canada's finest rhubarb variety. The province's many berry varieties ripen August–September; in season, they're good buys from roadside vendors.

### Drink

Be on the lookout for iceberg cubes in your cocktails. In summer, icebergs float south from the Arctic, and a few ditch in coves and bays on the island's northern and eastern coastlines. Stranded at land's end, the bergs explode and splinter in pieces, and entrepreneurial iceberg vendors sell the remains to local restaurants. You'll know the real thing when you see it; iceberg pieces sizzle as they melt.

ties with England and Ireland. Locals may enjoy full English breakfasts in the morning; tea biscuits (sweet cakes) with an afternoon snack; dumplings served with supper's stew; or hardtack, a dough mixture that when cooked with flaked, salted fish is known as "fish and brewis." For a special dessert, there's trifle, concocted of a cake layer, fresh summer berries, homemade vanilla custard, and a thorough dousing of sweet sherry, all topped with whipped cream.

Seafood is always on the menu, and if the menu says "fish," here that translates as cod. All other fish species on the menu will be specifically named. Local cooks use every part of the ubiquitous cod. Fillets (pronounce the "t" here) are broiled or dipped in batter or breaded and deep-fried. Cod tongues and cheeks are unusual taste sensations—the fish nuggets, encased in fish gelatin, are poached in a fish stock or fried, then served with lemon and tartar sauce.

Flounder, mackerel, shrimp, capelin, lobster, herring, and blue mussels frequently appear on menus. Wild game is abundant, and you'll find luscious pâtés and gourmet variations of smoked

Rum ("dark and dirty," as locals describe it) is imported from Barbados; Screech, London Dock, and Old Sam brands are bottled in St. John's and sold locally. Gold Ribbon Deluxe and Kingsway rye whiskeys are bottled locally and sold everywhere. Newfoundlanders are avid beer drinkers and favor Labatts, potent Black Horse, Guinness Stout, and Dominion. No grapes are grown locally, but wine imports are plentiful from Chile, Australia, Europe, and the United States. Restaurants tend to charge hefty prices for wine, but don't count on bringing your own bottle—that's considered improper here.

Liquor outlets are owned by the province or privately operated as agency stores. Hours are Mon.–Sat. 9:30 A.M.–5:30 P.M.; some outlets stay open until 10 P.M. on Friday and Saturday nights. In bars, pubs, and taverns, alcohol is served Mon.–Sat. 9 A.M.–2 A.M., Sun. noon–midnight.

### Dining Details

There's always a motel or hotel dining room open, but independent restaurants may close on Monday and sometimes Sunday. Service can be slow. If you've run out of patience and want to prod the server, a polite inquiry gets more response than a rude request. A tip is usually *not* included on the bill, and 10–15 percent is customary. Most restaurants accept Visa (the favored plastic money) and other major credit cards.

## INFORMATION AND SERVICES

### Visitor Information

The **Department of Tourism, Culture, and Recreation,** P.O. Box 8730, St. John's, NF A1B 4K2, tel. 709/729-2830 or 800/563-6353, www.gov.nf.ca/tourism., publishes the free *Travel Guide.* This useful booklet details auto tours, attractions and activities, accommodations, campgrounds, events, and crafts stores—arranged by region on the island and in Labrador. The department also produces a free highway map that includes provincial park listings, local ferry phone numbers, and other travel information.

Provincial **visitor information centers** are open late May to early October. Locations at provincial gateways include **North Sydney,** Nova Scotia (at the Marine Atlantic Ferry Terminal), tel. 902/794-7433, **Port aux Basques,** tel. 709/695-2262, and **Argentia,** tel. 709/227-5272. Others are located at **Whitbourne,** tel. 709/759-2170, **Clarenville,** tel. 709/466-3100, **Notre Dame Junction,** tel. 709/535-8547, and **Deer Lake,** tel. 709/635-2202.

Many municipalities operate their own tourist centers. The centers are open year-round at St. John's, Corner Brook, Gander, Grand Falls–Windsor, Springdale, and Happy Valley–Goose Bay, while operations at Mount Pearl, Baie Verte, Eastport, Glovertown, Goobies, Harbour Grace, Hawke's Bay, St. Antony, L'Anse au Clair, Labrador City, Marystown, Newville (near Twillingate), Port au Port East, Southern Bay, Stephenville, and Witless Bay are seasonal.

### Communications and Time

The area code for Newfoundland and Labrador is **709.**

**Canada Post** has province-wide branch offices, open Mon.–Fri. 9 A.M.–5 P.M. The main office is in St. John's at 354 Water Street. Retail outlets augment the Canada Post and are open longer hours.

Time zones vary within the province. Newfoundland island and Labrador Straits communities are on **Newfoundland standard time,** a half hour ahead of the other Atlantic Canada provinces. The rest of Labrador sets the clock on **Atlantic standard time. Daylight saving time** starts the last Sunday in April and continues until the first Sunday in October.

### Publications

On the island, the *Evening Telegram* publishes provincial news daily from St. John's. Regional newspapers are published in Gander, Stephenville, Port aux Basques, Corner Brook, St. Anthony, and Grand Falls–Windsor. In Labrador, the weekly *Aurora* covers western Labrador news from Labrador City; the *Labradorian* and *Examiner* handle weekly central and coastal news at Happy Valley–Goose Bay. Another dozen weekly and quarterly newspapers are published in the outlying areas.

**Breakwater Books** in St. John's ranks among

the province's most esteemed sources for provincial books. *Newfoundland Lifestyle* is a glossy quarterly magazine published in St. John's with cultural coverage and insights into the province's lifestyle. *Newfoundland and Labrador Business Journal,* based in St. John's, covers provincial business developments monthly. *Them Days* magazine, a quarterly publication, covers Labrador's heritage and historical events from its base in Happy Valley–Goose Bay.

## GETTING THERE
### By Air
**Air Canada,** tel. 709/726-7880 or 888/247-2262, www.aircanada.ca, flies nonstop from Halifax and Toronto to St. John's, while **Air Nova,** Air Canada's affiliated carrier, flies from Halifax, to St. John's, Gander, Deer Lake, Stephenville, and Goose Bay (Labrador). Air Nova also flies between Montreal and St. Johns. Flights originating farther afield are routed through Halifax. The only direct international flights are with Air Canada between London (England) and St. Johns.

### By Land
The Iron Ore Company of Canada operates the **Québec, North Shore, and Labrador Railway,** with thrice-weekly service from Québec's Sept-Îles (accessible by air from Québec City with Air Nova) on the northern St. Lawrence River to western Labrador's towns. The railroad's main job is hauling iron ore, but a separate passenger service operates as well, and passengers ride along in comfort in a dome-topped passenger car equipped with lunch/snack facilities. For details and reservations, call 709/944-8205.

For road travelers, Highway 389 from Baie-Comeau (Québec) leads 581 km to Labrador City/Wabush, continuing eastward a further 520 km through the heart of Labrador to Happy Valley–Goose Bay.

### By Sea
**Marine Atlantic** operates two ferry routes (reservations required) from North Sydney, Nova Scotia. One docks at Port aux Basques at the island's southwestern tip; the five- to seven-hour sailing operates year-round, with up to 16 crossings per week. One-way fares and rates: adults $22, seniors $20, children $11, vehicles from $67; reclining chairs $8 (only offered on some sailings), bunk beds $14, cabins $37–125. The other route, to Argentia (131 km south of St. John's), takes about 14 hours and operates mid-June to mid-October twice a week. One-way prices: adults $60, seniors $55, children $30, vehicles from $135; reclining chairs $16, bunk beds $22, cabins $125. The latter crossing is occasionally rough, so bring along motion-sickness medication. For ferry reservations and information, contact Marine Atlantic at tel. 902/794-5254 (North Sydney), tel. 709/695-4266 (Port aux Basques), tel. 709/227-2431 (Argentia), tel. 800/341-7981 (toll-free), or the website www.marine-atlantic.ca.

## GETTING AROUND
### By Air
The provincial carrier, **Provincial Airlines,** tel. 709/576-1666 or 800/563-2800, www.provair .com, connects St. John's, St. Anthony, Deer Lake, and Goose Bay, as well as Québec's Blanc Sablon (the air gateway to Labrador's Strait of Belle Isle settlements) and France's St-Pierre and Miquelon islands.

**Air Labrador,** the region's airline, flies from Goose Bay to remote settlements on the northern and southern coastline, plus St. Johns. Contact the airline at tel. 709/753-5593 or 800/563-3042, www.airlabrador.com.

**Air Canada/Air Nova,** tel. 888/247-2262, www.aircanada.ca, also links many communities within the province, including St. Johns to Corner Brook, Gander, Goose Bay, and Wabush.

### By Land
One is never quite sure if the province's lack of consistent roads and sightseeing markers is a humorous intrigue to confuse visitors or a get-to-know-the-Newfoundlanders promotion sponsored by the tourist office. Regardless, you'll need logistical help getting around and sightseeing. Use a map to plot a day's itinerary before starting out, and be prepared to ask for direc-

NEWFOUNDLAND & LABRADOR

# CAUTION: MOOSE ON THE LOOSE

Some Newfoundlanders won't drive between dusk and dawn on the island. The reason? Moose on the loose.

About 400 moose-and-car collisions occur annually, causing some $600,000 in damage. A moose collision is no mere fender-bender. These animals are big and heavy, and hitting one at speed will make a real mess of your car (it doesn't do the unfortunate moose much good, either). Consequences can be fatal to both parties. Vehicular collisions with the animals are rising, simply because there are both more vehicles and more moose on the island each year. Vehicle numbers are increasing by 30 percent every five years, and the dozen moose imported from Nova Scotia and New Brunswick in the late 1800s have now multiplied to about 150,000.

Seventy percent of the year's collisions occur between May and October. Accidents occur mainly from 11 P.M.–4 A.M.

© ANDREW HEMPSTEAD

(but that's no guarantee collisions won't happen at any hour). If you must drive after dark, use the high beams, scan the sides of the road, and proceed with caution.

Not to say that a moose makes a beeline for your speeding car. Moose, accompanied by swarms of biting insects, inhabit the remote interior. When the swarms thicken during the warm, moist summer, a severely bitten animal may stampede anywhere for relief. Some moose stray onto the TransCanada, perhaps attracted to the bright headlights, or enticed by roadside puddles, which provide drinking water and salt.

The province is aware of the situation and posts signs marked with the figure of a moose along the most dangerous stretches. Some 31 high-risk stretches lie along the TransCanada, especially from Terra Nova National Park to Gander and from Deer Lake to Corner Brook.

tions along the way; Newfoundlanders are very helpful. If you arrive on the island with your own vehicle, you'll find service centers are often widely spaced. Make sure your vehicle is operating perfectly, and carry a spare tire, preferably new, with good tread.

On the island, the TransCanada Highway wraps around the island's perimeter in a 905-km-long horseshoe. **DRL Coachlines,** tel. 709/738-8088, a long-haul bus system, follows the route and stops in towns and settlements; terminals are in St. John's, Gander, Grand Falls–Windsor, Corner Brook, and Port Aux Basques. Numerous private bus companies link major towns with outlying areas. St. John's has limited public transit service. There's no public transportation in Labrador.

The major car rental firms are plentiful at the airports and main towns. Companies represented in St. John's include locally owned **Cabot,** tel. 709/738-5502, as well as **Avis,** tel. 709/722-6620; **Budget,** tel. 709/747-1234; **Discount,** tel. 709/722-6699; **Enterprise,** tel. 709/739-6570; **Hertz,** tel. 709/722-4333; **National,** tel. 709/722-4307; **Rent-a-Wreck,** tel. 709/753-2277; and **Thrifty,** tel. 709/722-6000.

**Islander RV,** based in St. Johns, tel. 709/738-7368 or 888/848-2267, www.islanderrv.com, is Newfoundland's only RV rental outlet.

In Labrador, the Happy Valley–Goose Bay area, western Labrador towns, and strait settlements have road networks. Highway 500, the 520-km TransLabrador Highway, opened fully in 1992 and links Happy Valley–Goose Bay with Churchill Falls, Wabush, and Labrador City. In southern Labrador, Highway 510 links coastal communities to Blanc Sablon (Québec), the arrival point for ferries from Newfoundland. This highway is currently in the throes of a massive extension project. In 2001 a new stretch of highway opened, linking Red Bay to Mary's Harbour. It is planned to reach Cartwright in 2004 and will eventually link up with the existing TransLabrador Highway.

## By Sea

The province operates a number of ferry routes connecting Newfoundland Island with the Labrador mainland. A couple of these routes haul freight up to remote outports along the northern Labrador coast, making them spectacular off-the-beaten-track sailings perfect for adventure travelers. Along the way you'll see an incredible array of whales, seals, seabirds, passing icebergs, and, if it's early or late in the season, some pack ice.

The **M/V *Sir Robert Bond*** car ferry runs from Lewisporte on the island's central northern coast to Goose Bay. Some sailings go direct (38 hours each way), others stop in Cartwright. One-way fare for the entire run is adults $97, seniors $87.25, children $48.50, vehicles $160. From Lewisporte to Cartwright, the fare is $97 vehicles, $60 adults. From Goose Bay to Cartwright it's $65 vehicles, $40 adults. Two to three sailings on each route are offered in June, three to four in July and August, and one in September.

Across the Strait of Belle Isle, ferry service runs from St. Barbe on the Northern Peninsula to Blanc Sablon, Québec, from early May to late December, once or twice daily. One-way fares for the 90-minute crossing are adult $9, seniors $7.50, children $4.75, vehicles $18.50. A dozen other shorter-haul provincial ferry routes connect Newfoundland island to the offshore islands and remote coastal spans.

If that's not enough adventure for you, book passage on the **M/V *Northern Ranger*** passenger ferry, which leaves St. Anthony at the tip of Newfoundland's Northern Peninsula and steams all the way north to Nain and back—a 12-day trip. Along the way, it makes brief stops at 48 ports of call along Labrador's rugged coastline. The ferry has always been the sea link between Newfoundland and the Labrador coast for fisheries workers and supplies, but there's always room for adventure travelers and sightseers interested in the southern coast's tiny outports and the northern coast's Inuit settlements. The *Northern Ranger* offers basic services, comfortable cabins (three classes, all at extra charge—from 11 cents per nautical mile) with views, regional cuisine, and the opportunity to rub elbows and sea legs, as it were, with the locals. Fares are calculated at 25 cents per nautical mile for adults, 22.5 cents for seniors, and 12.5 cents for children. The distance from St. Anthony to Nain is 1,038 nautical miles, yielding a maximum base adult fare of $233.55 each way.

For more information or to make reservations on any of the provincial ferries, call 800/563-6353 or check the website www.gov.nf.ca/ferryservices.

# Newfoundland

## INTRODUCTION

Visualize the island of Newfoundland as not one island but two, similarly shaped but different in size—a mammoth main island and a smaller one, the Avalon Peninsula, threaded to the larger by a slender isthmus. The interiors of both sections rise in barren, lofty plateaus, while capes dotted with seaports angle out to the northeast and southwest.

### Sightseeing Highlights

At 111,390 square km in area, Newfoundland is the world's 16th-largest island. If you're short on time, consider concentrating your itinerary on the smaller Avalon Peninsula, which offers more manageable sightseeing.

If you have two or three weeks, however, invest some time exploring the main island. Bluish-green waters shimmer in limestone-cupped lakes at **Blue Ponds Provincial Park** near Corner Brook. Majestic icebergs wander into fjords and coves on the eastern and northern coastlines. And all along the seacoasts, photogenic lighthouses perch atop precipitous cliffs overlooking the surf.

The ancient world heaved and formed richly diverse landscapes at **Gros Morne National Park.** A millennium ago, the Vikings arrived and established a coastal camp (North America's first European settlement), now re-created at **L'Anse aux Meadows National Historic Site.** Before the Spaniards settled St. Augustine, Florida, the British created a mercantile center at **Trinity;** today it's a provincial heritage village, with brightly painted, saltbox-style houses lining its narrow lanes.

The appeal of raw wilderness aside, the main island caters to numerous other interests. Golfers like the 18-hole links at **Terra Nova National Park** and **Corner Brook.** Sightseers line up for boat tours led by knowledgeable skippers or academically trained

Lobster Head Cove Lighthouse

© ANDREW HEMPSTEAD

guides, whose vessels nose among whales, seals, and icebergs. If you're interested in a quick trip to France, Fortune on the Burin Peninsula lies a two-hour boat ride from **St-Pierre**, the capital of France's archipelago province of St-Pierre and Miquelon.

## Navigating Newfoundland

Think of the **TransCanada Highway** as a long Main Street. The horseshoe-shaped route edges the interior and connects the Avalon Peninsula with Channel-Port aux Basques—a 14-hour nonstop drive. Well-marked side roads split off the main highway and whisk drivers onto the peninsulas. Aside from the Burin Peninsula's efficient Highway 210 and the Northern Peninsula's relatively uncomplicated Highway 430, the other side roads to the peninsulas and coastlines meander interminably.

Don't underestimate the peninsulas' sizes. On the Burin Peninsula, for example, it's a three-hour drive on Highway 210 from Goobies to Grand Bank near the tip. On the Bonavista Peninsula, count on an hour's drive from Clarenville to Trinity, and another hour to Cape Bonavista. The Eastport Peninsula is more manageable; above Port Blandford, pull off the TransCanada to the lane designated for park visitors and meander into Terra Nova on the short network of landscaped, shady roads.

# St. John's and Vicinity

St. John's, the provincial capital, is a colorful and comfortable city. Situated on the steep inland side of St. John's Harbour, the city's rooftops form a tapestry: some are gracefully drawn with swooping mansard curves, some are pancake-flat or starkly pitched, while others are pyramidal with clay pots placed atop the central chimneys. Against this otherwise picture-perfect tapestry, the tangle of electrical wires strung up and down the hillside is a visual offense.

Contrasts of color are everywhere. House windows are framed in deep turquoise, red, bright yellow, or pale pink and are covered with starched white-lace curtains. Window boxes are stuffed to overflowing with red geraniums and purple and pink petunias. Along the streets, cement walls brace the hillside, and any blank surface serves as an excuse for a pastel-painted mural. The storefronts on Water Street, as individual as their owners, stand out in Wedgwood blue, lime green, purple, and rose. At streetside, public telephone booths are painted the bright red of old-time fire hydrants.

As the Newfoundlanders say, St. John's offers the best for visitors—another way of saying that Newfoundland is short on cities and long on coastal outports. But without question, St. John's thrives with places for dining, nightlife, sight-seeing, and lodging—more than anywhere else across the island and Labrador. Simply put, the Newfoundlanders have carved a contemporary, livable, and intriguing niche in one of North America's most ancient ports. Come to St. John's for some of Atlantic Canada's most abundant, high-quality shopping; unusual dining in lush surroundings; interesting maritime history displayed in fine museums; rousing nightlife and music; and an emerging, eclectic fine-arts scene.

## HISTORY

St. John's officially dates to 1497, when Newfoundlanders say the explorer John Cabot sailed into the harbor and claimed the area for England. Portugal's Gaspar Côrte-Real arrived about 1500 and named the harbor (or a tributary river) the Rio de San Johem, which appeared on a 1519 Portuguese map. Although undocumented, European fishermen probably knew about the port in Cabot's time—perhaps before. By the early 1540s, St. John's Harbour was a major port on Old World maps, and the French explorer Jacques Cartier anchored there for ship repairs.

### The British Presence

The British—who arrived, conquered, and remained for centuries—have had the greatest impact here. By 1528, the port had its first residence, and the main lanes were the Lower Path (Water Street) and Upper Path (Duckworth Street). In 1583, Sir Humphrey Gilbert arrived with four ships, disembarked on a harbor beach, and reiterated England's claim to the area. Harbourside Park, between Water and Duckworth Streets, marks the landfall, known also as the King's or Gilbert's Beach.

Fishing thrived, but settlement was slow. Early on, the defenseless port was ready game for incursions by other European imperialists, and in 1665 the Dutch plundered the town. Nevertheless, by 1675, St. John's had a population of 185, as well as 155 cattle and 48 boats anchored at 23 piers. The English protected the harbor with Forts William, George, Castle, and Battery. They blocked the harbor's narrows with chains and nets, and used lofty Signal Hill as a lookout to monitor both friendly and hostile ships.

By 1696, the French emerged as England's persistent adversary. Based at Plaisance (Placentia), the French launched destructive attacks on St. John's in 1696, 1705, and 1709. Simultaneously, England developed Halifax, Nova Scotia, as a naval hub, and by 1762, dispatched a fleet that vanquished the French at the Battle of Signal Hill, North America's final land battle of the Seven Years' War.

## The Early Port

St. John's was a seamy port through most of its early years. In a town bereft of permanent settlement and social constraints, 80 taverns and innumerable brothels flourished on Water Street, with a few stores on Duckworth Street and Buckleys Lane (George Street). The port's inhabitants were a motley mix of Spaniards, Portuguese, French, and British; as the latter gained dominance, Anglo immigration was encouraged.

Almost 4,000 settlers from England and Ireland arrived in the early 1800s, followed by another 10,000 in 1815. The new immigrants had fled the poverty of the British Isles, but they found the St. John's cupboard equally bare. They rioted en masse, and uncontrollable fires worsened conditions.

St. John's history has been punctuated with great fires. Those early conflagrations were fueled by various sources. Fish caught on the Grand Banks were often brought to port and laid out to dry on streetside fish flakes (wooden racks). During the great fires from 1816 to 1819, sparks ignited the flakes' dry timbers and tree boughs, sending fires racing across the hillside. In 1846, the scene repeated itself, when sparks ignited barrels of seal and codfish oil.

## Troubles and Triumphs

St. John's, like Halifax, was a British garrison town. With no foreseeable enemy, England withdrew the troops in 1870. The Royal Newfoundland Constabulary, modeled after England's occupying police force in Ireland, made its headquarters at Fort Townshend in 1871.

In 1892, another huge fire destroyed the city from Water Street to the East End, leveling 1,572 houses and 150 stores and leaving 1,900 families homeless. St. John's rebuilt *again*. The stores, commercial buildings, and merchant mansions were re-created in Gothic Revival and Second Empire styles. The Anglican Cathedral of St. John the Baptist, on the site of the first 1720 church, was rebuilt within the Gothic stone walls.

The fire coincided with rail transportation's emergence, and St. John's was designated as the island's rail headquarters in 1892. The main Water Street rail station was styled with a flourish of Victorian gingerbread. In 1907, the fledgling Newfoundland Museum found a permanent home in the twin-towered brick building on Duckworth Street.

## Inheritances and Additions

St. John's was beautiful at the turn of the century. From the British military occupation, the city inherited grandiose buildings. The Georgian-style Commissariat House on King's Bridge Road was built in 1821; the stately, pillared Colonial Building on Military Road now houses the provincial archives. St. Thomas's Anglican Church, built first in 1699 as Fort William's garrison church, was torched by the French, then rebuilt in 1836. Prosperous citizens donated choice land for Bannerman and Bowring Parks. Trolley cars tooled along the downtown streets and served as public transit until 1948. Atop Signal Hill, the city added Cabot Tower in 1897 as a tribute to both the 400th anniversary of Cabot's discovery and Queen Victoria's Diamond Jubilee.

## World War II and After

St. John's thrived during World War II. Fort Pepperell served as the operations headquarters for military bases across the island and Labrador. As defenses against the German submarines that stalked the harbor entrance and local waters, Signal Hill and Cape Spear were fortified with antiaircraft batteries, and nets were stretched across the Narrows' 174-meter-wide entrance. After the war, the U.S. Northeast Command, followed by NATO's 64th Air Division, occupied Fort Pepperell until the base was deactivated in 1960.

Newfoundland joined the Confederation in 1949. An infusion of federal funding and 4,000 civil service posts buoyed the city's economy. In the 1960s, the city lost its commercial and residential cores as people and business fled to the suburbs, with their new malls, industrial parks, and housing. In 1966 downtown merchants and private parties galvanized interest in an almost abandoned downtown with the Downtown Development Corporation, and in 1985 the federal government initiated the Main Street Program, Canada's first urban-rejuvenation project.

## The Contemporary City

St. John's today is a handsomely historic and stylishly new city with a metropolitan-area population of around 200,000. The town grew up from the harbor, which is still the city's most colorful part—a promenade aside a long string of ships at anchor. Harbour Drive is lined with modern office buildings and the Murray Premises—a group of warehouses built in 1846 and now a national historic site holding a mall and museum complex. Water and Duckworth Streets offer a colorful array of storefronts, while the lively night scene continues until early morning at the bars, pubs, and clubs on pedestrian-friendly George Street. The city hall, built at a cost of $3.5 million, opened in 1970 on New Gower Street.

Overlooking the city is C. A. Pippy Park, the

1,343-hectare gift of the town's famous millionaire merchant, and the Memorial University of Newfoundland. Nearby are the Arts and Culture Centre and the Aquarena, the recreational mecca added to the city during the Canada Summer Olympic Games in 1977.

# SIGHTS
## Getting Oriented

The city's Old World street layout defies modern logic. The streets follow footpaths laid out by European fishermen and sailors centuries ago, when towns were not planned but simply evolved for everyone's convenience. Water Street (one of North America's oldest streets) and the other main streets rise parallel to the waterfront, and are intersected by roads meandering across the hillside. Historic stone staircases climb grades too steep for paved roads.

The following sights are listed starting at city hall near the harbor and proceeding horizontally, wherever possible, across the hillside. Although locals lope up and down the hillside like agile mountain goats, beware of the steep inclines. Centuries ago, one pitched lane was known as Burst Heart Hill.

Be prepared to trek across the downtown area and drive everywhere else. Nobody covers St. John's in one day.

## Near the Waterfront

The spacious wharf anchors half a dozen city blocks and provides a panorama of international ships and sightseeing boats. Depending on your orientation, the TransCanada Highway either starts in Newfoundland and ends in British Columbia, or vice versa. Outside **St. John's City Hall,** a large sign marked Kilometer 0 (on New Gower Street's northern side) initiates the national highway. Inside the building, displays of provincial fine arts adorn the lobbies; open Mon.–Fri. 9 A.M.–4:30 P.M., tel. 709/576-8106.

Inside the splendidly restored and gleaming Apothecary Hall, the **James J. O'Mara Pharmacy Museum,** 488 Water St., tel. 709/753-5877, recalls a pharmacy of 1895. It's open mid-June to mid-September, daily 10 A.M.–5

NEWFOUNDLAND & LABRADOR

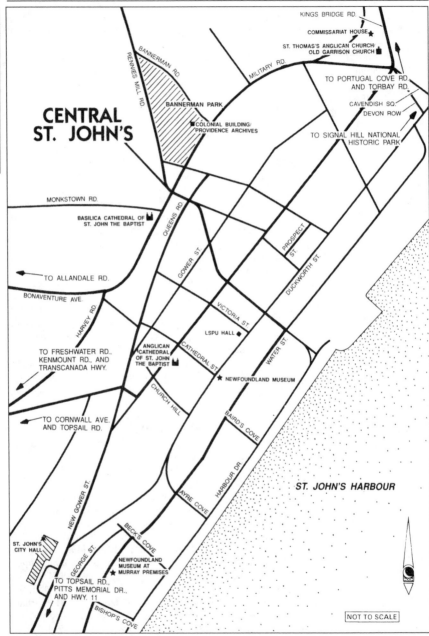

# CENTRAL ST. JOHN'S

KINGS BRIDGE RD.

COMMISSARIAT HOUSE

ST. THOMAS'S ANGLICAN CHURCH/
OLD GARRISON CHURCH

MILITARY RD.

BANNERMAN RD.

RENNIES MILL RD.

BANNERMAN PARK

COLONIAL BUILDING/
PROVIDENCE ARCHIVES

TO PORTUGAL COVE RD.
AND TORBAY RD.

CAVENDISH SQ.
DEVON ROW

TO SIGNAL HILL NATIONAL
HISTORIC PARK

MONKSTOWN RD.

BASILICA CATHEDRAL OF
ST. JOHN THE BAPTIST

QUEENS RD.

PROSPECT ST.

DUCKWORTH ST.

TO ALLANDALE RD.

BONAVENTURE AVE.

GOWER ST.

HARVEY RD.

VICTORIA ST.

LSPU HALL

WATER ST.

TO FRESHWATER RD.,
KENMOUNT RD., AND
TRANSCANADA HWY.

ANGLICAN
CATHEDRAL
OF ST. JOHN
THE BAPTIST

CATHEDRAL ST.

NEWFOUNDLAND MUSEUM

TO CORNWALL AVE.
AND TOPSAIL RD.

CHURCH HILL

BAIRD'S COVE

HARBOUR DR.

ST. JOHN'S HARBOUR

NEW GOWER ST.

AYRE COVE

ST. JOHN'S
CITY HALL

GEORGE ST.

BECK'S COVE

NEWFOUNDLAND
MUSEUM AT
MURRAY PREMISES

TO TOPSAIL RD.,
PITTS MEMORIAL DR.,
AND HWY. 11

BISHOP'S COVE

NOT TO SCALE

© AVALON TRAVEL PUBLISHING, INC.

P.M.; by appointment year-round. Admission is free.

At the **Newfoundland Museum,** 285 Duckworth St. (opposite Cathedral St.), tel. 709/729-2329, the exhibits showcase Newfoundland's 9,000-year history with an emphasis on natural wonders, aboriginal inhabitants, early European discoveries and settlements, and the towns and outposts of the 1800s. The museum is open daily 9 A.M.–4:45 P.M. (closed Monday outside summer). Admission is adults $3, seniors $2.50, children free.

The **Anglican Cathedral of St. John the Baptist,** 22 Church Hill (at Gower St.), tel. 709/726-5677, is a national historic site revered by locals (and said to be haunted by a resident ghost). English architect Sir George Gilbert Scott designed the impressive Gothic Revival edifice in Newfoundland bluestone. The cornerstone was laid in 1847, and the Great Fire of 1892 almost gutted the structure. Reconstruction within the walls started the next year. Of special interest are the carved furnishings and sculpted arches and a gold communion service presented by King William IV. The sanctuary and small museum are open for tours daily mid-June through September, 10:30 A.M.–4:30 P.M.; by appointment the rest of the year.

## Signal Hill National Historic Site

In the 1700s, this hill, once known as the Lookout, served as part of a British signaling system; news of friendly or hostile ships was flagged from Cape Spear to Signal Hill, where the message was conveyed to Fort William in town. In 1762, the Battle of Signal Hill marked the Seven Years' War's final North American land battle, with England victorious and France the loser.

The hilltop is pocked with historical remnants. England's Imperial Powder Magazine stored gunpowder during the Napoleonic Wars, and the Queen's Battery—an authentic outport tucked beneath the cliff—guarded the harbor Narrows from 1833. Public hangings were held at Gibbet Hill, the slope overlooking Deadman's Pond. The pond served as the port's reserve water supply in the event of a siege. Guglielmo Marconi

received the first transatlantic wireless message atop the hill, and exhibits within the Cabot Tower detail his work.

To get to the park, follow Duckworth Street across town until it turns into Signal Hill Road. The tower and nearby visitor center (containing more historical displays) are open daily year-round, 8:30 A.M.–4:30 P.M. (till 8 P.M. mid-June to early September). Admission is $2.50 adults, $2 seniors, $1.50 children 6–16, $6 families. A two-site pass is available in conjunction with Cape Spear National Historic Site (see below); the pass costs $4 adults, $3 seniors, $2 children, $9 families. Call 709/772-5367 for more details.

For hiking, the **North Head Trail** peels off the hill and follows along the cliffs to Fort Chain Rock. The Cuckold's Cove Trail wends across Signal Hill's leeward side to Quidi Vidi Village.

## Returning to Town

**St. Thomas's Anglican Church,** at King's Bridge and Military Roads, is known as the Old Garrison Church. The city's oldest surviving church building houses a cast-iron Hanoverian coat of arms over the door, attesting to the royal lineage. Sanctuary tours are available July through August, Mon.–Sat. 2:30–4:30 P.M. and Sun. 10:30 A.M., by appointment the rest of the year. For more information, call 709/576-6632.

Now a national and provincial historic site, the three-story **Commissariat House** on King's Bridge Road, tel. 709/729-6370, began in 1818 as a residence and office for Fort William's assistant commissary general. Over the years, it was used as the St. Thomas's Church rectory, a nursing home, and a hospital. The interior, furnished with antiques, has been restored to the style of the 1830s. The house is open mid-June to mid-October, daily 10:30 A.M.–5:30 P.M. Admission is $2.50.

**Government House** on Military Road, one of few structures that escaped damage in the Great Fire of 1892, now houses the province's lieutenant governor. The impressive 1831 building was constructed of red sandstone quarried from Signal Hill and features a moat, ceiling frescoes, and floral gardens. The grounds are open daily, year-round between dawn and dusk.

NEWFOUNDLAND & LABRADOR

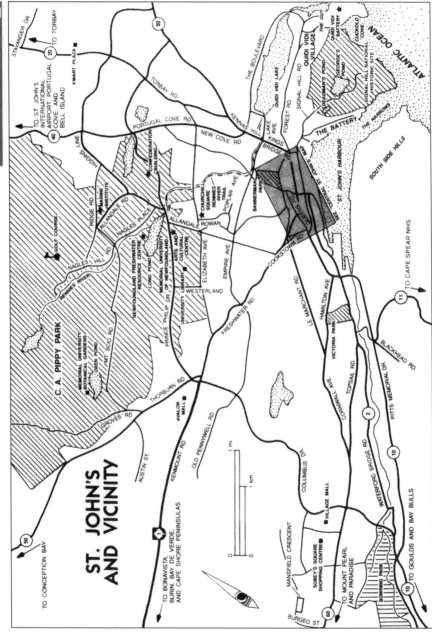

ST. JOHN'S AND VICINITY

© AVALON TRAVEL PUBLISHING, INC.

The **Colonial Building,** located at Military and Bannerman Roads, was the meeting place for Newfoundland and Labrador's House of Assembly from 1850 until 1959. The handsome white building of imported Irish limestone now houses the **Provincial Archives,** tel. 709/729-3065. It's open year-round, Mon.–Fri. 9 A.M.–4:15 P.M. and Wed. 6:30–9:45 P.M. Admission is free.

The early Roman Catholics aimed to make an impact on the St. John's skyline and did so in the mid-1800s with the **Basilica Cathedral of St. John the Baptist,** 200 Military Rd., tel. 709/754-2170. The Romanesque cathedral, built of stone and shaped like a Latin cross with twin 43-meter-high towers, is now a national historic site. Guided tours point out the ornate ceilings embellished with gold leaf, numerous statues, and other features. The church is open year-round, Mon.–Sat. 10 A.M.–5 P.M. Admission is free.

## Quidi Vidi Area

The Atlantic's watery inroads permeate the St. John's area. Aside from the city's famed harbor, another sizable pocket of the sea—**Quidi Vidi Lake**—lies nearby. Its azure-blue waters meet a boulder-bound coastline, all within the bustling city limits.

Quidi Vidi Lake ("kiddie viddie" is the local pronunciation) is best known as the site of the Royal St. John's Regatta, held on the first Wednesday in August, weather permitting. The lake's choppy water also lures windsurfers. Locals enjoy strolls along the grassy banks. Picturesque **Quidi Vidi Village** shows off colorful fishing boats anchored at the wharves and weathered houses strung along winding lanes.

To get there, start from the intersection of Military and King's Bridge Roads, then follow King's Bridge a block up the hill. Make a right onto Forest Road, which turns into Quidi Vidi Village Road.

The **Quidi Vidi Battery** on Cuckold's Cove Road, tel. 709/729-2977, sits high on a hill off Quidi Vidi Village Road, overlooking the lake and village. The site owes its origin to the French,

who built the battery in their effort to capture St. John's in 1762. France lost, and the British took the battery and rebuilt it in 1780. The site has been restored to the War of 1812 glory years, when England fortified the battery in anticipation of a U.S. attack that never materialized. The battery is now staffed by guides dressed in period uniforms of the Royal Artillery. It's open June through August, 10 A.M.–5:30 P.M. daily. Admission is $2.50.

## Cape Spear National Historic Site

Cape Spear's eminently photogenic lighthouse crowns a windy, 75-meter-high promontory above the Atlantic Ocean. Built in 1836, the lighthouse ranks as the province's oldest extant beacon and was used until 1955, when the original lighting apparatus was moved to a more efficient building nearby. The keeper's living quarters have been restored. The visitor center displays antiques and maritime artifacts.

Outside the lighthouse, the precipitous slopes hold the rusting remains of World War II gun batteries. Hiking trails fan out from the peak. The 10-km trail to Maddox Cove starts here and winds south along the coast, through gullies, bakeapple bogs, and berry patches. If you're lucky, you'll see a family of shy foxes in the high grasses.

The cape, North America's most easterly point, lies six km southeast of St. John's Harbour as the crow flies and 11 km around Highway 11's coastal curve. To get there, follow Water Street to the exit for Pitts Memorial Parkway and turn

BOB RACE

**The Cape Spear Lighthouse overlooks North America's easternmost point.**

left to Highway 11 (Blackhead Road). Children from the nearby residential area often use the road as a sidewalk, so be sure to drive carefully and follow the posted speed limits.

The grounds are open 24 hours year-round. The lighthouse and visitor center are open mid-May to mid-October, daily 10 A.M.–6 P.M. Admission is $2.50 for adults, $2 for seniors, $1.50 for children 6–16, $6 for families. A two-site pass is also available in conjunction with Signal Hill National Historic Site (see above); the pass costs $4 adults, $3 seniors, $2 children, $9 families. For more information call 709/772-5367.

## City Parks

The mood is Old English at **Victoria Park.** The spread offers paths and formal gardens beneath shade trees, and is situated a half-dozen blocks from the harbor's western end. Take Water Street west to find the park's entrance.

**Bowring Park,** arguably the city's prettiest park, has hosted significant guests for many tree-planting ceremonies, including a visit from Queen Elizabeth for the Cabot celebrations in 1997. Crocus and hyacinth beds make a colorful impact during spring, swans glide across the tranquil ponds in summer, and the setting is transformed into a canvas of dappled oranges and reds during autumn. Statues are everywhere, the most famous being of Peter Pan. It's a replica of the original in England's Kensington Gardens, and serves as a memorial to Sir Edgar Bowring's godchild, who died in an offshore shipwreck.

To get there, stay on Water Street until the road splits into Waterford Bridge and Topsail Roads; continue on Waterford Bridge Road for three km to the park's entrance.

## C. A. Pippy Park

Civilization ends and wilderness begins at this preserve, which covers 1,343 hectares of woodlands, grasslands, and rolling hills on the steep hilltop plateau overlooking St. John's. The park also features a botanical garden and a "fluvarium"—an exhibit that allows a close look at a stream's underwater inhabitants.

Developed along the rim of the hill, the park fronts Confederation Parkway/Prince Philip Drive and encompasses Memorial University's campus and the government Confederation Building complex. Barrens, marshes, woodlands, ponds, and streams make for a splendid landscape. Moose, muskrat, mink, snowshoe hare, meadow vole, and common shrew roam the hilly terrain, which is studded with balsam fir, spruce, and juniper. The green-winged teal, black and pintail duck, sora rail, American bittern, gyrfalcon, and pie-billed grebe are among the birds lured to Long Pond, the oval lake near the park's edge. Long Pond marks the start of the seven-km Rennies River Trail across the city's hillside to Quidi Vidi Lake.

Recreational facilities are spread across the park's developed edge. Off Ridge Road, just above the hollow, there's an 18-hole golf course with spectacular views. The **Newfoundland Freshwater Resource Centre,** tel. 709/754-3474, is nearby. Park in the lot near the road and walk down the hillside to the handsome wooden building wrapped with an open porch. You'll enter on the second floor, a spacious room with ecological exhibits depicting Atlantic salmon and other fish species, marsh birds, and carnivorous plants. If you ask, you can see a natural-history audiovisual show. The center's pièce de résistance occupies the first floor. Nine windows pierce the walls and provide spectators a below-water-level look at the brook and brown trout, arctic char, and salmon in Nagle's Hill Brook. It's an innovative variation on the traditional aquarium. The center is open year-round; summer hours daily 9 A.M.–5 P.M. (fish feeding at 4 P.M.). Admission is adults $2.75, senior s$2.25, children $1.50.

At Oxen Pond, the 38-hectare **Memorial University Botanical Garden,** 306 Mount Scio Rd., tel. 709/737-8590, is the province's only botanical garden. Garden environments include heather beds, a cottage garden, a rock garden, and a wildflower garden. Hiking trails wind through a boreal forest and a fen, both resplendent with native flowers, shrubs, and trees. The gardens feature a medley of soft colors. Blue forget-me-not, white turtlehead and rhododendron, and pink Joe-pye-weed bloom among spirea, northern wild raisin, dogwood, and high-bush cranberry. White birch, chokecherry, trembling aspen, ash, willow, and maple surround the botanical medley.

To get to the gardens, follow Allandale Road until it ends at Mt. Scio Road. The gardens are open May–November, daily 10 A.M.–5 P.M. Garden tours are available by advance reservation, and bird-watching walks are conducted the second Sunday of each month during the season, weather permitting. Admission to the gardens is $2 adults, $1 children and seniors, free for preschoolers.

## Academia

The nonsectarian provincial **Memorial University of Newfoundland,** spread out on 30 hectares in St. John's, trains physicians, nurses, and teachers, and also grants liberal arts degrees in English literature, economics, languages, and other majors. Other fields include the sciences with anthropology, engineering, biochemistry, and marine research—the latter offered at the Ocean Sciences Centre on the Logy Bay campus. The center is open to the public and offers interpretive tours, aquariums, touch tanks, and diving displays. Admission is $4.50 adults, $3.50 children. Hours vary by season; call 709/737-3706 for details.

The university also functions as the keeper of provincial history and culture. Separate departments specializing in history include the **Centre for Newfoundland Studies** and the **Labrador Institute of Northern Studies.** In addition, 40 off-campus colleges are located across the province.

Other provincial colleges in St. John's include the **Fisheries and Marine Institute,** specializing in ocean studies, the **Cabot Institute,** emphasizing applied arts and technology, and the **College of the North Atlantic,** offering a wide range of courses from its 18 campuses across the province.

### Sightseeing Tours
**McCarthy's Party Tours** has been on the sightseeing-tour scene for decades. From June to August, the company offers daily 2.5-hour guided tours to Signal Hill, the cathedrals, and other major sites. For reservations, pickup anywhere

in the city, and details, call 709/781-2244 or 888/660-6060.

**British Island Tours,** tel. 709/738-8687, operate distinctive red double-decker buses along a loop through the city, with 14 stops; adults $20, seniors $18, children $10.

**City & Outport Adventures,** tel. 709/754-8687, combines city and coastal sightseeing year-round in three- or four-day packages. They also offer daily 2.5-hour tours (under $30) pickup service from anywhere in St. John's.

Several informal walking tours of St. John's start from locations near the waterfront, including **Terry's Tours,** tel. 709/726-0262, and **St. John's Historic Walking Tours,** 709/738-3781. Tours run one and a half to two hours and range in price $10–20.

**Universal Helicopters,** tel. 709/576-4611, whisks passengers aloft for aerial sightseeing from St. John's International Airport. Flights are offered year-round, but the weather is most cooperative April to October. Rates run around $450 for a half hour (up to six passengers).

**Wildland Tours,** tel. 709/722-3123, is a St. Johns–based tour company that leads eight-day trips through the capital and across the Avalon Peninsula.

## ACCOMMODATIONS

St. John's boasts the province's most varied and impressive lodgings. The high-rise harbor-front properties are stunning and offer the city's best facilities. . . and highest prices. Costs are considerably less at the city's plentiful motels, historic inns, B&Bs, and heritage homes. Contact the hotels and motels in advance to inquire about any discounted weekend or unpublished rates. At the smaller inns and bed and breakfasts, ask about parking facilities; a few depend on metered street parking (free on weekends and Mon.–Fri. after 5 P.M.).

### Inns and B&Bs
**Prescott Inn Bed and Breakfast,** 19 Military Rd., tel. 709/753-7733 or 888/263-3768, www.prescottinn.nf.ca, has 18 rooms, most with fireplaces and views, for $60–105 including a full breakfast. The splendidly restored setting

won the townhouse a Heritage House award. There's a spacious bathroom on each floor (one with a whirlpool) and a library with art and books about the province. The inn has a great location (with free, streetside parking) near historic St. Thomas's Anglican Church. Open year-round.

**Roses Bed and Breakfast,** 9 Military Rd., tel. 709/726-3336 or 877/767-3722, is a restored Victorian-style heritage home within walking distance of downtown. The house is also located near several scenic trails and many St. John's historic sites. Four large rooms with private baths and fireplaces run $60–85 and include a full breakfast in a dining room that overlooks the harbor.

**Compton House,** 26 Waterford Bridge Rd., tel. 709/739-5789, once served as the mansion of C. A. Pippy, the merchant who donated St. John's local hilltop to the city for a park. The house has been grandly restored. Each of the five standard guest rooms has a private bath, and two have a whirlpool and fireplace or a full kitchen. Suites available. Parking is free, and the house is just a 15-minute walk to downtown. Rates range anywhere from $69 to $199 per room, including full breakfast.

In a central downtown location, **Bonne Esperance House,** 20 Gower St., tel. 709/726-3835 or 888/726-3835, built by a fishing captain in the 19th century, features antique furnishings, a collection of local arts and crafts, and a sundeck. The 12 rooms all have private baths; some have fireplaces. Rates are $75–120 with full gourmet breakfast.

A restored Queen Anne–style townhouse, the **Balmoral Inn,** 38 Queen's Rd., tel. 709/754-5721 or 877/428-1055, www.balmoralhouse.com, offers three large guest rooms, each with a fireplace, private bath, antique furnishings, local art, and an expansive view of the harbor. The rate of $75–145 includes a full breakfast and free off-street parking.

**Waterford Manor,** 185 Waterford Bridge Rd., tel. 709/754-4139, www.waterfordmanor.nf.ca, is a beautiful Queen Anne–style mansion near Bowring Park and furnished with antiques of the late 19th century. The three guest rooms have private baths and sitting areas, while the three suites feature whirlpool baths and fireplaces. Rates range $80–120 and include full breakfast.

**Winterholme Heritage Inn,** 79 Rennies Mill Rd., tel. 709/739-7979 or 800/599-7829, www.winterholme.nf.ca, offers seven rooms and four apartments ranging $99–179 including breakfast. The century-old Queen Anne–style inn is a National Historic Site. It includes a hot tub.

## Motels and Hotels

**Quality Hotel Harbourfront,** 2 Hill O'Chips, tel. 709/754-7788 or 800/228-5151, www.choicehotels.ca, offers similar trappings with superb waterfront views. It has 162 rooms ($140 with complimentary coffee and newspaper), a popular restaurant overlooking the harbor, and a prime downtown location (next to the Fairmont Newfoundland).

**Holiday Inn St. John's,** 180 Portugal Cove Rd., tel. 709/722-0506 or 800/933-0506, www.holidayinnstjohns.com, is near Pippy Park, Memorial University, and the Confederation Building complex. It's a five-minute drive from downtown. The popular hotel has 250 rooms and suites; summer rates are $165. Amenities include dining rooms and a lounge, a shopping arcade with a launderette, a hairdresser and barber, a heated pool, and a driving range. Parking is free.

**Fairmont Newfoundland,** at Cavendish Square near the intersection of King's Bridge and Military Roads, tel. 709/726-4980 or 800/441-1414, www.fairmont.com, has an auspicious location, on the former site of Fort William. The first Hotel Newfoundland, one of Canadian Pacific's deluxe properties, opened in 1925. After many years' service, it was demolished to make room for this handsome hotel. Opened in 1982, the hillside property has over 300 guest rooms, restaurants and a bar, a fitness center (with indoor pool, table tennis, squash courts, sauna, and whirlpool), a shopping arcade with a hairdresser, and free parking. In summer, standard rooms cost $189, with rooms on the Entrée Gold floor costing $249.

**Delta St. John's,** 120 New Gower St., tel. 709/739-6404 or 800/268-1133, website www.deltahotels.com, is a stunning, avant-garde high-rise that offers 276 rooms and suites starting at $185 (check the Delta website for packages); restaurants and a pub; fitness facilities including an indoor heated pool, exercise equipment, a whirlpool, sauna, and squash courts; a shopping arcade; and free covered parking.

The **Battery Hotel and Suites,** 100 Signal Hill Rd., tel. 709/576-0040 or 800/563-8181, www.batteryhotel.com, is the most easterly hotel in North America. Located on historic Signal Hill, the Battery has 126 rooms and suites (from $99 single, $109 double), a restaurant, a bar, a sports bar, an indoor swimming pool, laundry services, a hair salon, and free parking. Nonsmoking rooms are available and pets are allowed.

The **Airport Plaza Hotel,** 106 Airport Rd., tel. 709/753-3500 or 800/563-2489, www.cityhotels.ca, is conveniently located across from St. John's International Airport and features 100 rooms and suites ($72–95), a restaurant and lounge, airport transfers, and free continental breakfast. **Hotel St. John's,** 102 Kenmount Rd., tel. 709/722-9330 or 800/563-2489, www.cityhotels.ca, near the Avalon Mall, has 84 comfortable rooms ($76–114), a restaurant, a lounge with weekend entertainment, and an airport shuttle.

**Best Western Travellers Inn,** a smart two-story property at 199 Kenmount Road (also near Avalon Mall), tel. 709/722-5540 or 800/261-5540, www.bestwestern.com, is a full-service hotel with has 88 rooms, a restaurant, a nightclub, and a lounge. Parking is free. Rack rates start at $149, but rooms under $100 are usually available through the Best Western Bestrates program (check the website).

## Campground

**Pippy Park Trailer Park,** northwest of downtown on Nagle's Place, tel. 709/737-3669, www.pippypark.com, offers basic city camping, with 184 sites, access to hiking trails, a general store, and a playground. Tent sites cost $14 per night, serviced sites range $18–20. The park is open May through September on a first-come, first-served basis.

# FOOD

## Dinner

**East Side Mario's,** 180 Portugal Cove Rd. (in the Holiday Inn), tel. 709/722-6900, specializes in Italian cuisine and also offers chicken, ribs, and steaks. Dinner entrées range $13–22. The restaurant is open daily for breakfast, lunch, and dinner.

**Woodstock Colonial Restaurant,** tel. 709/722-6933, boasts a trove of exotic game selections—rabbit or seal-flipper pie; stuffed, roasted partridge—as well as seafood or steak ($15–24). Reservations are required for the game dishes. The restaurant is a 25-minute drive on Topsail Road/Highway 60 from St. John's to the town of Paradise; the brown building fronts the road.

**Cellar Restaurant,** tel. 709/579-8900, has cozy downstairs quarters on Baird's Cove, the short lane between Water Street and Harbour Drive, across from the former courthouse. This is the place for Newfoundland nouvelle continental ($15.50–26.50) and such dishes as spicy pan-roasted chicken breast and tiger shrimp or mixed seafood in creamy saffron risotto. Reservations are recommended.

The Delta St. John's **Portos Garden Grill,** 120 New Gower Rd., tel. 709/570-1660, serves up fine Mediterranean-style cuisine in a harbor setting. Known for its elegant dinners (entrées $25 and under), it's also popular for lunches ($12.50 and under) and a sumptuous Sunday brunch ($22.95). Thursday and Friday nights, Portos features prime rib and roasted chicken at its Horn and Feather Buffet ($22.95).

**Cabot Club,** Cavendish Square, tel. 709/726-4980 (reservations required), the Fairmont Newfoundland's signature dining room, combines a superb view of the harbor's narrows with an elegant menu ($19–27) featuring prime chateaubriand, steak Diane, or pepper steak prepared tableside; classic seafood dishes; and the five-course table d'hôte. The **Outport,** the hotel's daytime dining room, lures locals with huge buffets served Mon.–Fri. at noon ($15); at Sun. at brunch ($18.50); and Thurs. 5:30–8 P.M. (the keenly popular Newfoundland spread, $20).

**Classic Café,** 364 Duckworth St., tel. 709/579-4444, fills quickly each night with diners seeking delicious lobster dinners, seafood chowder, seal flipper pie, and other traditional Newfoundland fare at moderate prices in a cozy atmosphere. One of St. John's few 24-hour restaurants, the Classic is a popular place for cheesecake and coffee after the pubs close.

Encircled by gardens, the **Stonehouse Restaurant,** 8 Kenna's Hill, between Torbay and New Cove Roads, tel. 709/753-2425, offers classic continental dining in an 1834 heritage building near Memorial Stadium. Traditional Newfoundland dishes are served along with local fish and wild game ($20–30). Reservations are advised.

**Stella's Natural Foods,** 106 Water St., tel. 709/753-9625, serves gourmet vegetarian cuisine along with selected meat and seafood dishes. Stella's offers an eclectic menu that includes Thai vegetable stir fry, Indian curry, and Sicilian fettuccine, plus such non-veggie dishes as curried scallops and raspberry chicken. Stella's is also very popular with the lunch crowd; be prepared for a wait.

Fine Indian cuisine can be found at **India Gate,** 286 Duckworth St., tel. 709/753-6006. The extensive menu includes Tandoori dishes; prawns, lamb, beef, and chicken cooked in the masala, korma, and vindaloo styles; and a wide array of vegetarian entrées. Prices are inexpensive to moderate, portions are generous, and the atmosphere is quiet and relaxed.

**Bruno's Ristorante D'Italia,** 248 Water St., tel. 709/579-7662, prepares fresh Italian dishes in a romantic setting. Entrées include red snapper, halibut, pasta dishes, bruschetta, and more. Reservations suggested.

## Light Meals

**Cavendish Café,** 73 Duckworth St., tel. 709/579-8024, is popular with locals for it home-baked breads and pastries, healthy sandwiches made to order, and country-style hot meals. Open daily. **Auntie Crae's,** 72 Water St., tel. 709/754-0661, cooks home-style fare and packages it to go. Its deli, bakery, and dining area are open daily 8 A.M.–9 P.M.

**Ches's Snacks,** 9 Freshwater Rd., tel. 709/722-4083, is one of St. John's numerous fish and chips places and ranks among the best. Tender, deep-fried fillets and crisp french fries (from $6.50) are served in an atmosphere of Formica and bright lights. Other Ches's shops are at 655 Topsail Road and 29–33 Commonwealth Avenue.

Downtown, everyone meets at **Living Rooms Café** at Murray Premises, tel. 709/753-7666, for such delectables as French onion soup, stuffed crepes, salads, and desserts such as cheesecake or French truffle pie. It's open 11:30 A.M.–5 P.M. **Pasta Plus Cafe** at Churchill Square, tel. 709/739-5818, features a bistro menu with homemade pastas, quesadillas, curries, pizzas, and a gourmet-to-go counter.

**Nautical Nellies,** 201 Water St., tel. 709/738-1120, has stouter fare such as Cornish beef pasty, fried cod or cod tongues, and steak and kidney pie. The **Ship Inn,** 265 Duckworth St. (Solomon's Lane), tel. 709/753-3870, features good pub grub including Cornish pasties, savory pies, chowders, and salads. At night, the Ship turns into one of St. John's most vibrant pubs.

The convenient fast-food place is **Ports of Food,** a food court at the Atlantic Place mall on Water Street. If afternoon tea sounds appetizing, take your place at the table with scones, crumpets, and small sandwiches at the **Court Garden,** Fairmont Newfoundland, Cavendish Square, tel. 709/726-4980, Mon.–Sat. afternoon.

Several coffeehouses offer lattes, Americanos, mochas, and rich desserts in casual spaces frequented by St. John's young and hip. **Hava Java Coffee House,** 216 Water St., tel. 709/753-5282, and of course **Starbucks,** 70 Kenmount Rd., tel. 709/726-0420, are two such purveyors of caffeinated bliss.

## Stores and Supermarkets

You'll find plenty of places to pick up do-it-yourself picnic ingredients. For some of the freshest produce, stop at **Lar's Fruit Mart,** 79 New Gower St., tel. 709/753-9270. **Stockwood's Bakery and Delicatessen,** 316 Freshwater Rd., tel. 709/726-2083, stocks fresh sandwiches, cold plates, salads, cakes, and baking supplies and is open 24 hours a day. **William's Fine Foods and**

**Deli,** 516 Topsail Rd., tel. 709/364-2820, is a good choice for pastas, salads, sandwiches, soups, and desserts.

For fancier deli, bakery, and takeout food, **Manna European Bakery & Deli** fills the bill at 342 Freshwater Road, tel. 709/739-6992. It's open Mon.–Sat. 9 A.M.–9 P.M., Sun. 10 A.M.–9 P.M. **Michel's Bakery,** 799 Water St., tel. 709/579-0670, is another source for French breads and croissants, pâtés, homemade soups, and hot dishes. Michel's is open Mon.–Fri. 9 A.M.–7 P.M., Sat.–Sun. 10 A.M.–6 P.M.

Head to the **Seafoods Shop,** 7 Rowan St., Churchill Square, tel. 709/753-1153, for fresh and packaged seafood such as cod, shrimp, halibut, mussels, and scallops. For a tantalizing overview of Newfoundland cuisine, the centuries-old **Bidgood Supermarket,** tel. 709/368-3125, stocks every taste sensation known to the province, including seal, caribou, salted fish, salmon, and cod tongues and cheeks. It's open Mon.–Sat. 9 A.M.–6 P.M. Not much is prepackaged here, but the produce (especially western coast strawberries), berry preserves, shellfish, smoked or pickled fish, and sweet tea biscuits make delicious picnic additions. Bidgood's is in the town of Goulds, a 10-minute drive south of St. John's on Highway 10.

**Sobey's,** one of the province's largest supermarket chains, has branches at the Avalon Mall, another mall on Torbay Road, and the Sobey's Square Shopping Centre at 760 Topsail Road.

# ENTERTAINMENT AND EVENTS
## Cinemas
The Empire Theatres chain, tel. 709/726-9555, operates **Avalon Mall Cinemas** at Avalon Mall on Kenmount Road and **Empire Cinemas,** at 760 Topsail Road. The two multiplex theaters offer nightly shows and weekend matinees.

## The Night Scene
It's said St. John's has more pubs, taverns, and bars per capita than anyplace else in Atlantic Canada. The city's international port status is partly the reason. Even better, these watering holes serve double duty as venues for music of various styles, including traditional Newfoundland, folk, Irish, country, rock, and jazz.

The nightlife originated on George Street—once a derelict back street—and spread from there to other downtown-area bars and clubs. The weekend starts late Friday evening, picks up again on Saturday afternoon and lasts until 2 A.M. (and at some places keeps up through Sunday).

Among George Street's abundance of pubs and eating establishments, **Trapper John's Museum and Pub,** 2 George St., tel. 709/579-9630, ranks as a city entertainment mainstay, hosting notable provincial folk groups and bands. The patrons will gladly initiate visitors to Newfoundland with a screech-in ceremony for free. The **Yellow Dory,** at 6 George St., tel. 709/579-2101, features Newfoundland country and folk music until 2 A.M. **Greensleeves Pub and Lounge,** 14 George St., tel. 709/579-1070, doubles as a weekend hub for traditional, rock, and Irish concerts and jam sessions; on weeknights, the satellite-dish TV is tuned to sports events. The **Fat Cat,** 5 George St., tel. 709/722-6409, presents the blues seven night a week, with concerts, open mike, blues rock, and women's jam sessions scheduled on different nights.

The **Ship Inn,** 265 Duckworth St., tel. 709/753-3870, has been a venue for local and provincial recording acts for years and continues to draw Newfoundland's hottest up-and-coming bands. The **Blarney Stone** on George Street, tel. 709/754-1798, hosts the Folk Art Council's popular folk night every Wednesday night (cover charge). Touring acts headline the show, while local and visiting musicians sign up to perform between sets in a convivial atmosphere where performers chat and drink with the audience when they're not on stage.

Near the harbor, **Erin's Pub,** 186 Water St., tel. 709/722-1916, has Irish and local artists six nights a week, 9:30 P.M.–2 A.M. (cover charge Fri.–Sat.). **Nautical Nellies,** 201 Water St., tel. 709/738-1120, offers more of the same on Saturday nights.

**Sundance,** 33A New Gower St., tel. 709/753-7822, features top-40 music during the week; Sat.–Sun. it showcases local bands on its huge patio deck. **Cornerstone Video Dance Bar,** 16

Queen St., tel. 709/754-1410, is one of the town's few dance clubs (you'll pay a cover charge). It features dancing to videos Thurs.–Sat.

If you're seeking nightlife without music, try the English-style **Duke of Duckworth,** 325 Duckworth St., tel. 709/739-6344, where you'll find pool, darts, and imported draft beers. **Calio's,** 193 Water St., tel. 709/739-6100, is a comfortable lounge with both pool tables and private nooks for intimate conversation.

The hotel lounges share the weekend scene. Folk and Irish groups play at the **Narrows** lounge in the Fairmont Newfoundland on Fridays 5–8 P.M. At the **Blue Puttee Lounge** in the Delta St. John's, jazz serves as a mellow backdrop to billiards and scotch; open daily noon to midnight.

## Performing Arts

The **Resource Centre for the Arts,** LSPU Hall, 3 Victoria St., tel. 709/753-4531, stages productions by the resident RCA Theatre Company and also hosts professional touring groups throughout the year. Ticket prices vary depending on the event.

The **Arts and Culture Centre,** near Memorial University at Allandale Road and Prince Philip Drive, tel. 709/729-3900, presents a wide range of theater, music, and dance on its Main Stage, with artists and troupes from across Canada. In early July, the St. John's Players, the center's resident company, hosts the annual **International Drama Festival.** Experimental theater, comedy, poetry readings, and children's entertainment are performed in the center's Basement Theatre. The center is also home to the **Newfoundland Symphony Orchestra,** tel. 709/753-6492.

**Concerts Under the Dome** is a year-long series of classical, chamber, and sacred music performed in the acoustically perfect environment of the Cochrane Street United Church. Call 709/722-3023 for information.

**Pigeon Inlet Productions** is a leader in the promotion of traditional music and dance in St. John's. Its regular events include the **Culture Club,** a showcase of local singers, poets, and musicians every Saturday night at the Ship Inn, and **Dance Up,** which takes place every Wednesday at Rocky's Place in Trinity. Come early for informal dance lessons. For local event details, call 709/754-7324.

**Mile One Stadium,** on King's Bridge Road at Lake Avenue near Quidi Vidi Lake, is the venue for most big concerts and theatrical productions that come to town. For upcoming events, ticket prices, and details, call the info line at 709/576-7688 or the box office at 709/576-7657.

## Festivals and Events

Most of the action through the first few months of the year centers on **Mile One Stadium** on Kings Bridge Road, tel. 709/576-7657, where the St. Johns Maple Leafs hockey franchise competes one level below the NHL. The last weekend of April, **Outdoor Newfoundland and Labrador** prepares locals for the warmer months with displays of new-season equipment and destinations around the province and beyond. Children will enjoy the **Teddy Bears' Picnic** on the Arts and Culture Centre lawn in late June, tel. 709/729-0128.

For theater lovers, the **Shakespeare by the Sea Festival** presents outdoor productions of the Bard's best by the acclaimed Loyal Shakespearean Company. Performances run July and August at Cape Spear National Historic Site; call 709/576-0980 for details. The fledgling St. John's **Fringe Festival** takes place in odd-numbered years, presenting innovative and experimental drama for five days in mid-June at various venues downtown. For show information, call 709/722-5581.

Another summer-long event, **Pirates at the Pier,** features pirates relating tales of locally buried treasure. The action takes place Sat.–Sun. at 2 P.M. The venue is Harbourfront Park, tel. 709/685-3444.

The city shines as a music-festival venue. The biggest and best is early July's nine-day **Festival 500,** held in odd-numbered years. Highlights include the noontime medley of harbor ship horns; citywide theater, workshops, and dance; and Newfoundland, folk, electronic, jazz, New Age, and African concerts. In late July/early August, Prince Edward Plaza on George Street is the outdoor setting for the five-night **George Street Festival,** which offers a variety of performances by top entertainers.

The **Signal Hill Tattoo** is a tribute to the landmark Battle of Signal Hill that ended the war between the English and French in North America. The military event is staged dramatically with military drills by foot soldiers, artillery detachments, fife and drum bands, and more. It all takes place early July to mid-August on Wednesday, Thursday, Saturday, and Sunday at 3 and 7 P.M. For details, call 709/772-5367.

In early August, the province's best performers take to the boards at the **Newfoundland and Labrador Folk Festival** in Bannerman Park. The festival also presents folk dancers, storytellers, crafts shows, and festivities. It's one of the largest festivals in the province. For more information, call 709/576-8508.

The **Royal St. John's Regatta,** another city tradition, ranks as North America's oldest ongoing sporting event. It began in 1826 with fishermen at the helm; nowadays, the regatta combines experienced crews with sleek racing shells and 50,000 cheering spectators. It's held at Quidi Vidi Lake on the first Wednesday in August, tel. 709/576-8921. The country comes to the city for the **Annual Farm Field Day,** held at the Atlantic Cool Climate Crop Research Centre, tel. 709/772-0461, the second Saturday of August. As well as displays of current research center projects, you'll enjoy a petting zoo, tractor rides, and food sampling.

Later in the year, the four-day Halloween Mardi Gras brings partying to George Street. And there's no place better to celebrate New Year's Eve than at the **North America's First New Year's Festival,** held along Harbour Drive on the waterfront. Fireworks usher in the New Year here at North America's easternmost edge.

# RECREATION
## Water Sports
Situated on Atlantic Canada's oldest ship routes, the St. John's area is incredibly rich in shipwrecks. What's more, the waters here are as clear as the Caribbean—20- to 30-meter visibility is common—and reasonably warm from summer to autumn, though a wetsuit is advisable. **Sub Aqua Diving,** tel. 709/364-3483, leads dives year-round in the waters along the Avalon Peninsula. Sub Aqua also offers rentals and sails from its Topsail Road location. **Rockwood Adventures,** 50 Pippy Place, tel. 709/738-6353, is another local dive operator.

If you're interested in kayaking through local waters, contact **Whitecap Adventures,** tel. 709/726-9287.

The **Aquarena** at Westerland Road and Prince Philip Drive, tel. 709/737-3799, has adult swims and a variety of water slides. Indoor pools are also located at **H. G. R. Mews Community Centre** on Munday Park Road and the **Wedgewood Park Recreation Centre** at 47 Gleneyre Street. **Municipal pools** at Bowring, Victoria, and Bannerman Parks are open July and August.

## Golf
**Pippy Park,** tel. 709/753-7110, features 9- and 18-hole golf courses ($15 and $30 respectively) on Nagle's Hill near the botanical gardens. Playing to 6,532 yards and a par of 71, the 18-hole Admiral's Green course has hosted numerous national events. The **Clovelly Golf Club,** east of downtown, tel. 709/722-7170, comprises two 18-hole courses, including the 7,080-yard Black Duck course, one of Atlantic Canada's best. Green fees range $32–45, with power carts and rentals available. **The Wilds at Salmonier River,** tel. 709/229-9453, is a challenging par-72 course carved into the boreal forest. Green fees are $43. A good contact for golfers heading to Newfoundland is the website www.golfnewfoundland.ca, with links to all of the above courses.

## Other Sports
**Lakeview Downs,** a 15-minute drive from St. John's in Goulds, has weekly live and simulcast harness racing. The live racing season begins in June and runs through August. Post time is 2 P.M. Call 709/747-7223 for details.

For hockey or ice skating, head to **Mile One Stadium** on King's Bridge Road, tel. 709/576-7657.

## SHOPPING

### Crafts

Crafts shops downtown offer every conceivable craft available, and new developments continually increase the variety. One of the best places to start is **Devon House,** at 59 Duckworth St. near the Hotel Newfoundland, which is the Newfoundland and Labrador Crafts Development Association's gallery and retail crafts shop. It offers an excellent sampling of traditional and contemporary wares. Open in summer Mon.–Wed. 10 A.M.–5 P.M., Thurs.–Fri. 10 A.M.–9 P.M., Sat. 10 A.M.–5 P.M., and Sun. 1–5 P.M.; the rest of the year Mon.–Sat. 10 A.M.–5 P.M. and Sun. 1–5 P.M.; tel. 709/753-2749.

For designer pieces, check out retail sales outlets in the artists' workroom/studios. **Woof Design,** 181 Water St., tel. 709/722-7555, sells mohair, woolen, and angora apparel, plus whalebone carvings and other crafts. The workroom and a retail outlet are open year-round Mon.–Sat. 10 A.M.–5 P.M.; in summer Sun. 12:30–4:30 P.M.

Other shops operate as cottage-industry outlets. **Nonia Handicrafts,** 286 Water St., tel. 709/753-8062, is among the best crafts shops, carrying hand-woven apparel, weavings, parkas, jewelry, hooked mats, domestic wares, and handmade toys. The **Cod Jigger,** 245 Duckworth St., tel. 709/726-7422, a similar cooperative, is another good source for parkas, hooked mats, bone and talc carvings, quilts, knits, mittens and hats, crocheted items, and jewelry.

Some shops showcase the newest designs and first-quality wares of selected producers. **Newfoundland Weavery,** 177 Water St., tel. 709/753-0496, handles Bogside Weaving clothing, Placentia West Mat Makers' hooked mats, and other weavings, whalebone carvings, and jewelry from across the province.

For crafts, antiques, and collectibles, visit **Mallard Cottage** in Quidi Vidi Village, tel. 709/576-2266. This 18th-century cottage houses glassware, china, crockery, pewter, stained glass, prints, and old books. Open June through October, daily 10 A.M.–6 P.M.; the rest of the year it's closed Tuesday, but the other hours are roughly the same, weather permitting.

Other shops sell a variety of wares: Grenfell parkas from St. Anthony, books about Newfoundland, local Purity-brand candies, tinned biscuits or seafood, bottles of savory spice, pottery and porcelain, handmade copper and tin kettles, model ships, soapstone and stone carvings, fur pelts and rugs, apparel, folk art, and handwoven silk, wool, cotton, and linen. Expect to find most of these goods at **Melendy's Kuffer Korner,** 336 Water St., tel. 709/753-8021, and the **Downhomer Shoppe & Gallery,** 303 Water St., tel. 709/722-2970.

### Art Galleries

For an overview of Newfoundland's outstanding traditional and avant-garde fine arts, spend several hours at the **Art Gallery of Newfoundland and Labrador,** in the brown-brick Arts and Culture Centre at Prince Philip Drive and Allandale Road, tel. 709/737-8209. The AGNL holds the city's most extensive exhibits; open Tues.–Sun. noon–5 P.M. and Fri. 7–10 P.M.

The **Resource Centre for the Arts,** LSPU Hall, 3 Victoria St., tel. 709/753-4531, is another notable gallery with regularly changing exhibits and periodic shows of Newfoundland and Canadian artists. The **Eastern Edge Art Gallery,** 73 Harbour Dr., Baird's Cove, tel. 709/739-1882, is an artist-run gallery dedicated to the promotion of provincial and Canadian arts. Open Tues.–Fri. noon–5 P.M., Sat.–Sun. 1–5 P.M.

Top-notch private galleries are plentiful. **Christina Parker Gallery,** 7 Plank Rd., tel. 709/753-0580 (ask for directions), showcases Newfoundland's avant-garde spectrum; open Mon.–Fri. 10 A.M.–6:30 P.M., Sat. 11 A.M.–5 P.M. For traditional art, check out the **Emma Butler Gallery,** 111 George St., tel. 709/739-7111, **James Baird Gallery,** 221 Duckworth St., tel. 709/726-9193 or 800/563-9100, and **Pollyanna Art and Antique Gallery,** 206 Duckworth St., tel. 709/726-0936. All showcase local paintings, sculpture, and photography.

### Stores and Malls

Among half a dozen suburban shopping malls, the largest are **Avalon Mall,** with a 150-plus shops on Kenmount Road near Confederation Parkway; **Village Mall,** with 80 stores at Columbus Drive and Topsail Road; and **Sobey's Square Shopping Centre,** with more than 30 stores and services at 760 Topsail Road. In general, mall hours are Mon.–Sat. 10 A.M.–10 P.M. The better clothing shops are found at the Village Mall and at **Churchill Square,** a small complex on Elizabeth Avenue near the Arts and Culture Centre.

# INFORMATION AND SERVICES
## Visitor Information
The **City of St. John's Economic Development and Tourism Division,** at City Hall on New Gower Street, tel. 709/576-8106, www.city .st-johns.nf.ca, answers questions and stocks free literature. The office is open year-round, Mon.–Fri. 9 A.M.–4:30 P.M. It has branch locations at the airport (also open year-round) and at the **Railcar Chalet,** on the harbor (open June–August). Available literature includes various city maps and the following booklets: *A Step Back in Time,* describing self-guided walks through the city's five historic areas; *Walking Tour of Old St. John's,* which sums up most of the foregoing with written descriptions and a map; and the *St. John's Visitor Guide,* with details on lodgings, dining and shopping places, and sightseeing highlights.

You'll find other free, privately published tourist literature at stores, hotels and motels, and restaurants. Among the most informative are *What's Happening,* with monthly updates and sightseeing coverage, and the *Newfoundland & Labrador Vacation Guide,* a softcover tourist guide crammed with details on sightseeing.

## Bookshops and Libraries
Books about St. John's and the province are plentiful. **Wordplay,** 221 Duckworth St., tel. 709/726-9193, has the widest selection of new titles, as well as used books and public Internet access. It's open Mon.–Sat. 10 A.M.–6 P.M., Sun. noon–5 P.M. Two other esteemed sources are **Dicks and Company,** 385 Empire Ave., tel. 709/579-5111, and the **Newfoundland Book-** **store,** 100 Water St., tel. 709/722-5830. **Chapters–Indigo** is at 70 Kenmount Road, tel. 709/726-0375. For secondhand and rare editions, check out **Afterwords Bookstore,** 245 Duckworth St., tel. 709/753-4690.

The city's largest library is Memorial University of Newfoundland's **Queen Elizabeth II Library,** tel. 709/737-7425. Open Mon.–Thurs. 8:30 A.M.–11:30 P.M., Friday 8:30 A.M.–5:45 P.M., Saturday 10 A.M.–5:45 P.M., Sun. 1:30–9:30 P.M. (Mon.–Fri. 8:30 A.M.–4:15 P.M. when school is not in session). To get there, turn into the campus at Westerland Road off Prince Philip Drive and head for the massive building with windows tiered like steps.

Smaller public libraries include the **Michael Donovan Library,** 655 Topsail Rd., tel. 709/737-2621, and **Marjorie Mews Library,** 18 Highland Dr., tel. 709/737-3020. Call 709/737-2348 for the location and hours of all city-run libraries.

## Health and Safety
Local hospitals under the jurisdiction of the Health Care Corporation of St. Johns include the **General Hospital,** 300 Prince Philip Dr., tel. 709/737-6300; **Janeway Child Health Centre** at Janeway Place, tel. 709/778-4222, and **St. Clare's Mercy Hospital,** 154 LeMarchant Rd., tel. 709/777-5000.

The **Royal Newfoundland Constabulary,** tel. 709/729-8333 or 911 for emergency assistance, handles local police matters; the **Royal Canadian Mounted Police** phone number is 709/772-5400. St. John's **Marine Rescue Centre** can be reached at 709/772-5151.

## Banks and Postal Outlets
Several major banks are located in metro St. John's. **Royal Bank,** tel. 709/576-4222, has 10 locations in the city and suburbs. Most are open Mon.–Fri. 9:30 A.M.–5 P.M., while the office at 45 Commonwealth Avenue in Mt. Pearl stays open Thurs.–Fri. to 8 P.M. and offers Saturday hours of 10 A.M.–3 P.M. You'll be charged a service fee on each traveler's check transaction, but nothing extra to exchange U.S. or U.K. currencies.

The city has three main **Canada Post** offices. For buying stamps and mailing letters, the best bet is the office at 354 Water Street, tel. 709/758-1003, open Mon.–Fri. 8 A.M.–5 P.M.; the philatelic window is open weekdays, 8 A.M.–noon and 1–4 P.M. Retail postal outlets have longer hours.

## GETTING THERE
### By Air
Frequent nonstop and direct flights serve St. John's from provincial, regional, national, and international gateways.

For flight information or reservations, call **Air Canada/Air Nova** at 709/726-7880 or 888/247-2262. For onward travel, contact **Provincial Airlines,** tel. 709/576-1666 or 800/563-2800, or **Air Labrador,** tel. 709/753-5593 or 800/563-3042.

**St. John's International Airport,** off Portugal Cove Road, is a 15-minute drive from downtown. Taxis all charge a flat rate to any of the major downtown hotels; $14 for the first person, $2 per each additional person. The airport is open 24 hours daily and has a duty-free shop. Avis, Budget, Hertz, National, and Thrifty have counters here. The city's **Tourist Information Kiosk** at the airport, tel. 709/772-0011, is open daily until the arrival of the last flight.

### By Sea
From mid-June through mid-October, **Marine Atlantic** offers ferry service between North Sydney, Nova Scotia, and Argentia, 131 km south of St. John's. Sailings are three times a week in July and August and twice weekly in late June and early September.

Rates for the 14-hour sailing one-way are adults $60, seniors $55, children $30, vehicles from $135, reclining chairs $16, bunk beds $22, cabins $125. For details, contact Marine Atlantic in North Sydney at 902/794-5254, in Argentia at 709/227-2431, or toll-free at 800/341-7981; www.marine-atlantic.ca. Reservations are required on all crossings, and you should arrive an hour before departure.

If you're arriving on your own yacht, you can tie up at **Royal Newfoundland Yacht Club** on Greenslades Road in Long Pond on Conception Bay, tel. 709/834-5151. The club offers guest slips, a dining room and bar, laundry, and showers. To arrange for customs clearance before arrival, call the **Canadian Customs** office at 709/772-5544.

## GETTING AROUND
### Driving and Buses
Locals complain that downtown parking space is scarce. Not so, the city says, countering that there are 1,500 parking slots at the Municipal Parking Garage on Water Street, other downtown garages, and on the streets. Some 800 street spaces are metered for loonies (the $1 coin) and quarters; when the time is up, the cops are quick to ticket expired meters.

Expect the demand to outpace supply, however. It's just as easy to park uptown on an unmetered street and walk or take a bus downtown. St. John's Transportation Commission's **MetroBus** operates public transit ($1.50 adults, $1 children, in exact change); for a recorded schedule, call 709/722-9400.

**DRL Coachlines,** tel. 709/738-8088, operates long-haul bus service along the TransCanada Highway's length, with daily service from St. Johns airport. The ride to the ferry terminal at Port-aux-Basques costs $104 one-way. Other long-distance buses leaving from St. Johns include **Venture,** tel. 709/722-4249, to and around the Bonavista Peninsula; **Fleetline,** tel. 709/722-2608, to Carbonear; and **Newhook's,** tel. 709/726-4876, to Placentia.

### Taxis, Bikes, and Rental Cars
Taxis cruise downtown and also wait at the hotels and motels. **Gullivers Cabs,** tel. 709/722-0003, is among the largest outfits. **Bugden's,** tel. 709/726-4400, and **Citywide,** tel. 709/722-0003, have stands all over the city. **Jiffy Cabs,** tel. 709/722-2222, and **Co-op Cabs,** tel. 709/726-6666, also offer personalized tours of the city and environs at $25–30 an hour.

Bike rental places are scarce. **Earle Industries,** 51 Old Pennywell Rd., tel. 709/576-1951, rents mountain bikes and all the equipment you'll need for a day ($25–35) or a week ($119). It also operates **Avalon Bicycle Tours** and provides information about Avalon Peninsula trips. To get to the store, follow Empire Avenue until it turns into Old Pennywell Road, then look for the buff-colored brick Bay Bulls Trading Company building.

All major rental car companies are represented in St. Johns, but check local restrictions, such as bans on traveling in certain parts of the island.

Contact **Avis,** tel. 709/722-6620; **Budget,** tel. 709/747-1234; **Cabot,** tel. 709/738-5502; **Discount,** tel. 709/722-6699; **Enterprise,** tel. 709/739-6570; **Hertz,** tel. 709/722-4333; **National,** tel. 709/722-4307; **Rent-a-Wreck,** tel. 709/753-2277; and **Thrifty,** tel. 709/722-6000. **Islander RV,** based in St. Johns, tel. 709/738-7368 or 888/848-2267, rents a variety of campers and RVs.

# Avalon Peninsula

If sightseeing time is short and you must bypass the rest of Newfoundland, consider the Avalon Peninsula as a manageable stand-in. Life on the Avalon has a long history. The Basques and French fished the Southern Shore and Cape Shore seacoasts as early as the 1500s. The peninsula's name is attributed to Sir George Calvert (Lord Baltimore), who was evidently a passionate fan of the Arthurian legends. To him, the peninsula was akin to King Arthur's heavenly paradise, a haven for the beleaguered Roman Catholics from England. Or so he thought. Once settled at Ferryland in the early 1600s, Calvert's colony endured diminishing supplies and harsh winters. His wife and son and a number of other colonists headed south to Maryland, and Calvert followed, leaving the plantation and the name of Avalon. Farther south on the peninsula, the *Mayflower* stopped at Renews during the Pilgrims' transatlantic sailing from England to Massachusetts.

## Remnants from the Past

Early French and British military incursions also molded the area. The HMS *Sapphire* sank during a 1696 naval battle and lies off Bay Bulls. The same year, the French burned Carbonear, and they returned to torch the settlement again in 1705. The English settlers retreated to Carbonear Island, now a national historic site, for England's only early successful defense against the French in Newfoundland.

During World War II, German submarines saturated the offshore waters; sensitive harbors such as Bay Bulls were strung with nets to prohibit entry. At Bell Island's Lance Cove, German submarines sank four ships at their berths and badly damaged the pier.

The Avalon is still making history. In the 1960s, Parks Canada archaeologists initiated a project that stabilized the French and British fortification ruins at Castle Hill National Historic Site near Placentia. And another dig at Mistaken Point yielded one of Canada's most spectacular marine fossil finds in the 1980s.

## Getting Around

You will be wise to tackle one peninsula at a time. For the Bay de Verde Peninsula, take the TransCanada/Highway 1 out of St. John's and turn north at Highway 70 to Carbonear, a two-hour drive from the city. From Carbonear, Victoria is a quick 10 minutes, and Heart's Content on Trinity Bay is another 15 minutes on Highway 74. Highway 70 follows the coastline of Conception Bay to the tip of the peninsula; Highway 80 returns south on the Trinity Bay side.

The Southern Shore is quicker to navigate, along faster-moving Highway 10, which follows the eastern side of the peninsula. Ferryland lies an hour from St. John's, and Mistaken Point Reserve is another two hours south. To reach Salmonier Nature Park, simply take the TransCanada Highway, turn off on Highway 90, and you're there in an hour. The Cape Shore deserves a full day. The Cape Shore Loop, as it's known, peels off the TransCanada and rims the peninsula along Highways 100 and 92. It's paved alongside Placentia Bay, but the remainder of the route is gravel.

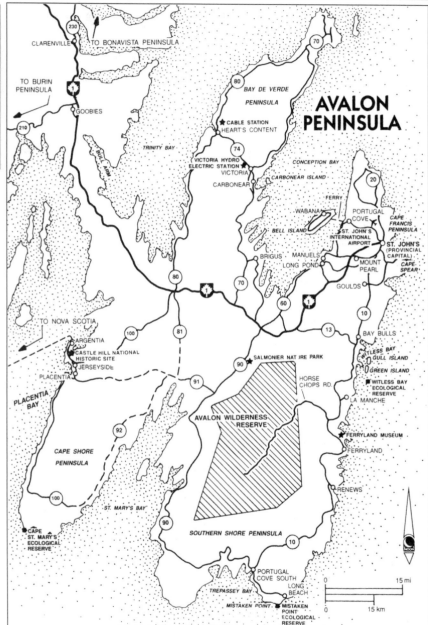

CLARENVILLE   TO BONAVISTA PENINSULA

TO BURIN
PENINSULA

GOOBIES

BAY DE VERDE

PENINSULA

AVALON
PENINSULA

CABLE STATION
HEART'S CONTENT

TRINITY BAY

VICTORIA HYDRO
ELECTRIC STATION
VICTORIA

CARBONEAR

CONCEPTION BAY

CARBONEAR ISLAND

FERRY

WABANA   PORTUGAL
COVE

CAPE
FRANCIS
PENINSULA

BELL ISLAND

ST. JOHN'S
INTERNATIONAL
AIRPORT

ST. JOHN'S
(PROVINCIAL
CAPITAL)

BRIGUS   MANUELS
LONG POND

MOUNT
PEARL

CAPE
SPEAR

GOULDS

TO NOVA SCOTIA

ARGENTIA

CASTLE HILL NATIONAL
HISTORIC SITE

JERSEYSIDE

PLACENTIA

PLACENTIA
BAY

SALMONIER NATURE PARK

HORSE
CHOPS RD.

BAY BULLS

WITLESS BAY
GULL ISLAND

GREEN ISLAND

WITLESS BAY
ECOLOGICAL
RESERVE

LA MANCHE

AVALON WILDERNESS
RESERVE

FERRYLAND MUSEUM

FERRYLAND

CAPE SHORE

PENINSULA

ST. MARY'S BAY

RENEWS

CAPE
ST. MARY'S
ECOLOGICAL
RESERVE

SOUTHERN SHORE PENINSULA

PORTUGAL
COVE SOUTH

LONG
BEACH

TREPASSEY BAY

MISTAKEN POINT   MISTAKEN
POINT
ECOLOGICAL
RESERVE

0                 15 mi

0         15 km

© AVALON TRAVEL PUBLISHING, INC.

# NORTHERN AVALON

## Bell Island

The Newfoundlanders boast an incredible flair for artistic expression, an ability displayed by the **Bell Island murals.** Large-scale scenes painted on the sides of buildings depict the community's life and people during the Wabana Mines' ore-mining decades. John Littlejohn, a Bell Island native and now an Ontario-based wildlife artist, heads the ambitious, ongoing project. You'll find the half-dozen murals in different locations across the tiny island's northeastern corner, mainly in and near **Wabana,** the largest settlement. One assumes the murals were painted from historical photographs, yet there's a sense of real life to each painting—from a car's black luster to the animated figures and even the clear gleam of a miner's eyes. The murals are easy to locate; for directions, call 709/488-2602.

To get to Bell Island, follow Highway 40 out of St. John's to Portugal Cove's ferry terminal. The ferry, tel. 709/895-6931, operates daily year-round, 7:15 A.M.–11:10 P.M. from Portugal Cove, 6:45 A.M.–10:30 P.M. from Wabana. Crossings are fewer on weekends.

## Brigus

Picturesque Brigus's most famous native son, Captain Robert Bartlett, was an Arctic explorer who accompanied Commodore Robert E. Peary on his 1908 North Pole expedition. Bartlett's house is now the **Hawthorne Cottage National Historic Site.** Built in 1830, the cottage is a rare intact example of the *cottage ornè* style. Hawthorne Cottage is open mid-May to October, daily 10 A.M.–6 P.M.; admission is $2.50 adults, $1.75 seniors, $1.25 children, $5.50 families. For more information call 709/528-4004.

## Cupids

Plantation owner John Guy established Cuper's Cove in 1610, making what is now called Cupids the oldest British settlement in Canada. At the **Cupids Cove Archaeological Site,** an ongoing dig continues to unearth the remains of Guy's plantation. Visitors are welcome to view the dig

in progress during summer. Artifacts can be seen at the **Cupids Museum** on Seaforest Drive, tel. 709/596-1906. The museum is open mid-June to September, daily 10 A.M.–6 P.M.

## Harbour Grace

Once the second-largest town in Newfoundland, Harbour Grace suffered a series of setbacks when seven fires besieged the town over the span of a century. Many of its oldest buildings survived and now make up the **Harbour Grace Heritage District.**

Named Havre de Grace by the French in the early 16th century, the town boasts both pirates and pilots in its heritage. The **Conception Bay Museum** on Water Street, tel. 709/596-1309, is open daily June through September and by appointment the rest of the year; free admission. The building it occupies sits on the former site of the lair of Peter Easton, a notorious pirate of the early 1600s. Three centuries later, in 1932, Harbour Grace gained notoriety when Amelia Earhart took off from the local airfield to become the first woman to fly solo across the Atlantic. Harbour Grace airfield is now a national historic site.

## Victoria

The **Victoria Hydro Electric Station,** tel. 709/596-9000, a provincial heritage site, was the site of one of Newfoundland's earliest hydroelectric plants (1904). The United Towns Electrical Company once owned the plant. Restored as a museum, the site showcases the original turbines and generators as well as other exhibits on early electrical technology. One turbine is still in operation. The museum is open July and August daily 10 A.M.–6 P.M.; admission is free.

## Grates Cove

The peninsula's northernmost village, Grates Cove retains the look and feel of Ireland perhaps more than any other Irish-settled community, thanks to the hundreds of rock walls erected as livestock and farm enclosure by the original set0ed a national historic site. Off the eastern end of the peninsula's tip, the **Baccalieu Island Ecological Reserve** shelters 11 species of seabirds, including Leach's storm petrels, black-legged kittiwakes, gannets, fulmars, and puffins. Boat tours offer a closer view of the seabird colonies.

## Heart's Content

The first successful transatlantic telegraph cables came ashore here and received the first message in 1866. The original cables, which extended from Valentia Island on the west coast of Ireland, are still visible at shoreline. The restored Cable Station, formerly a cable-relay station and now a provincial heritage site, displays some of the original equipment, plus the town's heritage artifacts. **Heart's Content Cable Station Provincial Historic Site,** one km northeast of Heart's Content on Highway 74, is open mid-June to late October, daily 10:30 A.M.–5:30 P.M.; by appointment the rest of the year. Admission is $2.50. For more information call 709/583-2163.

## Dildo

The history of the 19th-century codfish hatchery on Dildo Island—the first commercial hatchery in Canada—is depicted at the **Dildo Interpretation Centre** on Highway 80, tel. 709/582-2687. Dorset Eskimo harpoon tips estimated to be 1,700 years old, other artifacts from Dildo Island, and Maritime Archaic artifacts from nearby Anderson's Cove are also housed at the center; ask for information on the ongoing digs. The center is open May through October. The **South Dildo Whaling and Sealing Museum,** a few km to the south on Highway 80, tel. 709/582-3083, has exhibits and artifacts from the area's whaling past. Also on display are artifacts from an excavation at nearby Russell's Point, where the site of a Beothuk camp was discovered in the 1990s. The museum is open late June to August; admission is $2 for adults, free for kids.

## SOUTH OF ST. JOHN'S

### Witless Bay Ecological Reserve

Newfoundland's seabird spectacle spreads across three offshore islands near Witless Bay, 31 km south of St. John's. Overwhelming displays of more than a million pairs of Atlantic puffins, Leach's storm petrels, murres, black-legged kittiwakes, herring gulls, Atlantic razorbills, black guillemots, and black-backed and herring gulls are the attraction here. The season spans May–August and peaks from mid-June to mid-July.

To get there, take Highway 10 to Bay Bulls and turn off on the unmarked road to the wharf. For a close view from a boat, make trip arrangements beforehand. Sightseeing boats depart from Bay Bulls to roam among the sanctuary islands, where you may also see icebergs and humpback or minke whales in addition to the countless seabirds. **O'Brien's Whale and Puffin Tours,** tel. 709/753-4850 or 877/639-4253, runs daily 2.5-hour trips from May to mid-October. The cost is $40 per person, including pickups at any St. John's lodging.

## Avalon Wilderness Reserve

The Avalon Wilderness Reserve is a 1,070-square-km reserve, home to woodland caribou by the thousands. It lies within the Avalon Peninsula's remote interior, southwest of St. John's. The reserve lacks visitor facilities, and you'll need a permit to enter the grounds. The free permits, valid for 90 days, are available from the provincial **Parks and Natural Areas Division,** tel. 709/729-2429, www.gov.nf.ca/parks&reserves. To get to the reserve, follow coastal Highway 10 south from St. John's, look for the first inland turn after La Manche Provincial Park (20 km south of Witless Bay), and follow Horse Chops Road, a winding backcountry lane, into the reserve. Several rudimentary hunting lanes also enter the reserve from the west on Highway 90.

You can also obtain a permit from the office at **La Manche Provincial Park,** a wildlife-rich area in its own right, where you can canoe the La Manche River, paint or photograph the colorful marsh wildflowers, bird-watch, and hike via a suspension bridge to the abandoned fishing village of La Manche.

## Ferryland

This east coast port is one the province's earliest fishing villages, and the site of the colony founded by Sir George Calvert in 1621. Although Calvert abandoned the colony in 1629 and relocated to what would become Maryland, others remained. In 1637, London merchant David Kirke took control and developed a successful plantation and fishery. After Kirke's death, his wife, Sara, ran the plantation for another 25 years.

The settlement is the site of an ongoing archaeological dig. A well, smithy, stables, vegetable garden, cobblestone street, and what is believed to be Calvert's mansion have all been uncovered thus far. The colony's history is depicted in exhibits at the on-site **Colony of Avalon Interpretation Centre,** where hundreds of artifacts fill drawers and glass display cases. Guided tours of the excavations and the archaeology lab are offered. The center, tel. 709/432-3200, is open mid-May to mid-October, daily 9 A.M.–7 P.M.; admission $4.

Artifacts and other exhibits on the area's history can also be seen at the **Historic Ferryland Museum,** tel. 709/432-2155. It's inside the courthouse, near the church on the main street; open mid-June to early September, Mon.–Sat. 10 A.M.–noon and 1–5 P.M., Sun. 1–5 P.M.

If you have time, drive or hike out to the old lighthouse, about a 20-minute walk from the edge of the dig. Here is where renowned artist Gerry Squires lived for 12 years, creating stunning paintings inspired by the lonely beauty of Ferryland Head. Now empty, the lighthouse is said to be haunted.

The two-day **Southern Shore Shamrock Folk Festival,** held in Ferryland in late July, ranks among the province's most exuberant festivals of traditional Newfoundland music, dance, crafts, and food. For more information, call 709/432-2052.

## Mistaken Point Ecological Reserve

Now being considered for designation as a UNESCO world heritage site, the Mistaken Point Ecological Reserve lies alongside a remote coastline at the southern shore's tip. To explore the area, turn off Highway 10 at Portugal Cove South and follow the unmarked gravel road 16 km to Long Beach, where the reserve's gently rolling headland stretches to the sea. Bring a warm jacket to fend off the strong winds, and be ready for thick fogbanks from June to mid-July.

Hikers enjoy the trails that meander across the reserve, and photographers relish the offshore boulders and turbulent surf. The rocks at the ecological reserve, acclaimed as one of Canada's most important fossil sites, contain impressions of 20 different species of multicelled marine creatures that lived 620 million years ago.

Look, but don't touch. Fossil poachers are severely prosecuted. For details and a copy of *Mistaken Point Ecological Reserve,* which describes the site and fossils, contact the provincial Parks and Natural Areas Division, tel. 709/729-2429, www.gov.nf.ca/parks&reserves.

## Salmonier Nature Park

The facility, on Highway 90 halfway between the TransCanada Highway and St. Catherines, tel. 709/229-7189, is well worth searching out. A two-km boardwalk and wood-chip trail runs through a sample forest and across bogs, which back up to the Avalon Wilderness Reserve. Moose, caribou, lynx, bald eagles, snowy owls, beavers, and other indigenous species are exhibited in natural-habitat enclosures. Facilities include a visitor center and shaded picnic tables. The park is open June–August, daily 10 A.M.–6 P.M., September, daily 10 A.M.–4 P.M. Admission is free.

# THE CAPE SHORE
## Placentia

France chose the magnificent coastal forest area overlooking Placentia Bay for its early island capital, Plaisance, and colonists and soldiers settled here in 1662. The early military fortification crowned a high hill overlooking the port at what is now Jerseyside. The French launched assaults on St. John's from Le Gaillardin, the first small fort of 1692, and then from Fort Royal, the massive stone fortress built the following year.

England gained possession of the settlement in 1713 under the terms of the Treaty of Utrecht and renamed it Placentia. The hill on which the fortress stands became known as Castle Hill. Ruins of Fort Royal include a blockhouse, barracks, and guardrooms. Exhibits at the visitor center of **Castle Hill National Historic Site,** tel. 709/227-2401, document French and English history at Placentia. Guided tours are offered in summer. Picnic tables are available and trails run along the peak's fortifications and the bay's stone beach. The park is open daily, 8:30 A.M.–8 P.M. in summer, 8:30 A.M.–4 P.M. the rest of the year. Admission is $2.50 for adults, $1 for children.

The 19-room **Harold Hotel,** on Main Street in Placentia, tel. 709/227-2107 or 877/227-2107, is just five km from the Argentia ferry terminal (see below) and therefore makes a handy overnight stop. Rates start at $55. The hotel is open year-round, with a restaurant and lounge on the premises.

### Argentia

Argentia, five km north of Placentia, is the arrival point for ferries from Sydney, Nova Scotia. Formerly a U.S. naval base, the bay is now dominated by the ferry terminal, but trails lead to lookouts, abandoned bunkers, and good vantage points for watching local birds.

**Marine Atlantic** ferries arrive in the bay two times weekly during a mid-June to mid-October sailing season. One-way fares and rates for the 14-hour sailing include adults $60, seniors $55,

children $30, vehicles from $135, reclining chairs $16, bunk beds $22, cabins $125. For reservations and information, contact Marine Atlantic, tel. 709/227-2431 or 800/341-7981, www .marine-atlantic.ca.

### Cape St. Mary's Ecological Reserve

This spectacular seabird reserve lies at the Cape Shore's southern tip, 16 km down a gravel road off Highway 100. A 40-minute walk leads across the steeply banked headland to a seastack jammed with some 60,000 seabirds. The rocky pyramid seems to come alive with fluttering, soaring birds, whose noisy calls drift out to sea on the breezes. Expect to see northern gannets in one of North America's largest colonies—12,000 birds), common and thick-billed murres, and black-legged kittiwakes, along with some razorbills, black guillemots, great black-backed gulls, and herring gulls.

The sanctuary's interpretive center, at the gravel road's end, tel. 709/337-2473, stocks informative literature and sponsors guided walks. It's open May to October, 10 A.M.–7 P.M. The well-marked seastack trail also starts from here. Stay on the trail and don't wander; the headland is edged by precipitous, 100-meter-high cliffs—a fall would be fatal.

## Eastern Newfoundland

### BURIN PENINSULA

The 200-km-long Burin Peninsula angles like a kicking boot off Newfoundland's southeastern coastline. The peninsula's interior is a primeval, barren moonscape—if the moon held water, that is—for every hollow and depression in these barrens is filled with bogs, marshes, and ponds. But the coastline rims the edge of the Grand Banks, historically one of the most fertile fishing regions in North America. Along the shore are scattered fishing villages and several burgeoning towns. Marystown, one of the fastest-growing towns in the province, is supported by one of the largest fish processing plants in eastern Canada, and its shipyard supplies vessels to the booming North

Atlantic oil industry. St. Lawrence is the exception to the region; as Canada's only producer of fluorspar, it has relied on mining as much as marine-related industries. For the most part, however, fishing has been the mainstay of the peninsula's communities since the 1500s.

### Boat Harbour

A cottage industry here produces hand-hooked scenic mats made of reused fabric scraps. The mats and other homemade wares are sold at reasonable prices at the **Placentia West Craft Shop,** on Highway 210 about one km south of the Boat Harbour intersection, tel. 709/443-2312. The shop is open in summer, daily 8:30 A.M.–6 P.M.

## Burin

Near the "heel" of the boot-shaped peninsula, Burin, settled in the early 1700s, lies in the lee of offshore islands. The islands generally protect the town from the open Atlantic, though they weren't enough to stop a destructive tidal wave in 1929. The islands also were a refuge for pirates, who could escape their pursuers among the dangerous channels. During his mapping expeditions of the Newfoundland coast in the 1760s, Captain James Cook used Burin as a seasonal headquarters. A high hill above the town, where watch was kept for smugglers and illegal fishing, still bears his name—Cook's Lookout.

In early July, the **Festival of Folk Song and Dance** kicks off three days of Irish-inspired song and dance, children's games, seafood meals, and crafts shows and sales. The festival ranks among Newfoundland's most popular heritage events. Call 709/891-1546 for more information.

## Grand Bank

Grand Bank, on the "toe" of the Burin boot, is the best known of the peninsula's towns. Settled in the 1650s by the French and taken over by the British in the early 1700s, Grand Bank (pop. 2,500) has always been associated with the rich fishing grounds of the same name, the Grand Banks to the south and west of Newfoundland. The coastal waters still provide the town's livelihood.

The Grand Bank Town Council, tel. 709/832-1600, has outlined a Heritage Walk, which visits the province's largest number of Queen Anne–style homes outside of St. John's. The heritage district's architectural treasures include the 1905 **Masonic Lodge,** the 1917 **Thorndyke House** (with its Masonic symbolism integrated into the interior design), and the **George C. Harris House,** 16 Water St., tel. 709/832-1574, a 1908 Queen Anne housing the town's museum of local history. The Harris House is open daily and admission is free. Complementing the Heritage Walk is the Nature Trail, leading to a lookout and salmon spawning beds, and the Marine Trail, which closely follows the shoreline of Fortune Bay.

You can't miss the **Southern Newfoundland Seamen's Museum,** 54 Marine Dr., tel. 709/832-

1484. Styled as an angular white sailing ship, the museum has exhibits on the Grand Banks fisheries and maritime history, with photographs, ship models, and other artifacts. It's open July–August, daily 9 A.M.–4:45 P.M.; the rest of the year, Mon.–Fri. 9 A.M.–5 P.M., Sat.–Sun. 2–5 P.M. Admission is free.

## Fortune

The growing port town of Fortune, 10 minutes southwest of Grand Bank, is the terminus for the St-Pierre Ferry Service (see below). In Fortune, the **Fair Isle Motel** on Main Street, tel. 709/832-1010, is two km from the ferry terminal and operates year-round. The 13 rooms run $59 single, $64 double, or you can stay in the adjacent cottage for $89. A restaurant is also on the premises.

# ST-PIERRE AND MIQUELON

Centuries of fierce British and French battles ended in the mid-1700s with Britain's dominance firmly stamped across eastern Canada—*except* on St-Pierre and Miquelon, a trio of islands 25 km south of the Newfoundland mainland. In 1713, the Treaty of Utrecht awarded the islands to England. But France regained possession in the Treaty of Paris in 1763, and the islands have remained strongly French ever since.

During the Prohibition era in the United States, St-Pierre served as a distribution center for bootleg alcohol that was stockpiled in warehouses by Canadian, American, and European rumrunners. An 80-boat fleet delivered cargoes of illicit liquor up and down the Eastern Seaboard from 1920 to 1933.

While French and Newfoundland inhabitants have coexisted peacefully and intermarried for centuries, the nations are periodically at political odds. In 1992, St-Pierre's confrontations with Canada made the headlines when scallop fishermen from Newfoundland were met by a French gunboat off the island. The fishermen had entered St-Pierre's 24-nautical-mile fishing zone, and the French vessel confronted and escorted the boats back to their home port. A political up-

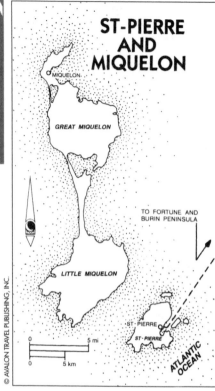

ST-PIERRE
AND
MIQUELON

MIQUELON

GREAT MIQUELON

TO FORTUNE AND
BURIN PENINSULA

LITTLE MIQUELON

ST-PIERRE
ST-PIERRE

ATLANTIC OCEAN

0          5 mi
0     5 km

© AVALON TRAVEL PUBLISHING, INC.

Miquelon, joined by a sand-dune isthmus, lie to the west and north.

The capital, St-Pierre, on the island of the same name, is the most popular destination. It dates to the early 1600s, when French fishermen, mainly from Brittany, worked offshore. The port's mood and appearance are pervasively French, with bistros, cafés, bars, brasseries, wrought-iron balconies, and an abundance of Gallic pride. St-Pierre borders a sheltered harbor filled with colorful fishing boats and backed by narrow lanes that radiate uphill from the harbor. The cemetery, two blocks inland from rue du 11 Novembre, has an interesting arrangement of aboveground graves, similar to those in New Orleans. The **St-Pierre Museum,** at 15 rue Docteur Dunan, open by chance, documents the islands' history.

One of the islands' greatest attractions, of course, is the low duty rates on French wines and other goods. Visitors may bring back $200 worth of duty-free purchases after a 48-hour visit. You'll find shops with French wines, perfumes, and jewelry.

## Practicalities

Most visitors arrive as part of a package, including ferry transportation from Fortune. For details, contact **St. Pierre Tours,** 116 Duckworth St., St. John's, tel. 709/832-2006 or 800/563-2006. Starting from $160 per person per night (from $60 for extra nights), packages include bus shuttle from St. John's, the Fortune-to-St-Pierre ferry, and lodgings. Also contact this company for general ferry information and a schedule; the trip takes 70 minutes and costs $75. Plan to arrive a half-hour before departure and park in the lot near the Canadian customs building. To clear customs, Canadians and Americans need a passport, a driver's license, or a Social Security card; visitors from European Community nations and Japan are required to have a passport. Travelers from everywhere else need a passport and a French visa.

**Air St. Pierre,** tel. 902/873-3566, flies to the island year-round from Halifax, Nova Scotia. Flights are also available from St. John's and from Sydney, Nova Scotia.

roar ensued. Newfoundland contended that reciprocal fishing rights existed offshore, and that Newfoundland's fishing rights were ensured by existing Canadian-French agreements. High-level negotiations eventually smoothed out the problem.

## France's Far-Flung Archipelago Province

The province consists of three islands, with a combined land area of about 242 square kilometers. Tiny St-Pierre (pop. 5,500) anchors the southeastern corner. The topography of this triangular island includes hills, bogs, and ponds in the north, lowlands in the south. The larger islands of Little Miquelon (pop. 600), sometimes called Langlade, and uninhabited Great

On the island, **Tour Explorateau** offers 90-minute minibus tours of St-Pierre ($6). Tours depart the l'Hôtel Robert's parking lot near the harbor, daily from July to early September. You'll need a local contact for other sightseeing and also for trips to the Miquelons; the best source is **l'Agence Régionale du Tourisme,** which can provide literature and a list of lodgings, restaurants, and other services. The office is on place du General de Gaulle, tel. 800/565-5118. The website: www.st-pierre -et-miquelon is another good source of general island travel information.

Among the dozen small hotels, pensions, and bed-and-breakfasts, the largest lodging is the 54-room **l'Hôtel Robert,** tel. 508/41-24-19, on rue du 11 Novembre near the harbor, which hosted the American gangster Al Capone in the 1920s.

## THE SOUTH COAST

Here on the most isolated of Newfoundland island's populated regions, many of the communities are accessible only by local ferry. For information on traveling between Rose Blanche (near Port aux Basques), Burgeo, and Hermitage, call 709/551-1446.

Despite its remoteness, the region maintains a steady economy. The Bay d'Espoir area is

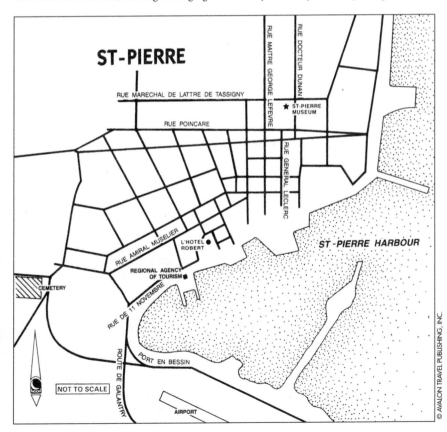

dominated by a hydroelectric plant that provides electricity for half the province. The largest salmon hatchery in Newfoundland operates near the hydro plant. Lumber and a strong crafts tradition fuels the Mi'kmaq community of Conne River. Fine woolens and other knitwear have put English Harbour West on the map.

For a true Newfoundland experience, hike or canoe into the remote **Bay Du Nord Wilderness Reserve,** or attend one of the local summer festivals, such as Belleoram's popular **Iron Skull Folk Festival,** in mid-July, when renowned provincial musicians travel to this scenic coastal village for three days of the best of traditional Newfoundland music. For details, call 709/881-6181.

## Harbour Breton

Harbour Breton, with its picturesque landlocked harbor, sits at the terminus of Highway 360. Established in the 17th century as a French fishing camp, Harbour Breton grew into a year-round town when the prominent Newman family arrived from England and began a long history of commercial enterprise. In summer, at the 1907 **Sunny Cottage Heritage Centre,** tel. 709/885-2425, costumed interpreters relate the history of the Newman company, the area's resettlement, and the town's colorful past. The mid-July **Tradition by the Sea** festival features music, a garden party, dory races, and a dramatic telling of the true story of ill-fated love between an English countess and a Newman & Company clerk—a romance that shocked the town in the 1800s. The town office, tel. 709/885-2354, can supply details.

## Burgeo

Lonely Highway 480, which branches off the TransCanada Highway near Stephenville, passes through 150 km of woodlands, barrens, and caribou country before coming to its end at Burgeo, a fishing community since the end of the 18th century. The remote village is also linked to the outside world by government ferry—from Rose Blanche to the west and Hermitage to the east. Call 709/551-1446 for a schedule.

Burgeo's population of 1,500 continues to depend on the sea. Visitors, too, rely on Burgeo's fish-filled waters—the many rivers and lakes in

this area yield some of the best trout and salmon fishing in the province. Burgeo offers other outdoor activities as well—the many small islands along the rugged coastline provide excellent kayaking and diving opportunities, while nearby **Sandbanks Provincial Park** has rare sand dunes, wide sandy beaches, good bird-watching, and a seven-km nature trail that winds through a variety of ecosystems.

Overnights in Burgeo are limited to camping in Sandbanks Provincial Park ($12) or a stay at **Burgeo Haven B&B,** a two-story waterfront home at 111 Reach Road, tel. 709/8865-2544 or 888/603-0273 ($45–55 single, $55–65 double, including breakfast).

# BONAVISTA PENINSULA

The Bonavista Peninsula rises off the eastern coastline as a broad, bent finger covered with verdant woods, farmlands, and rolling hills. Paved Highway 230 runs along the peninsula's length, from the TransCanada to the town of Bonavista at the tip; Highway 235 returns to Highway 1 along the peninsula's west side.

## Clarenville

Founded in 1890, Clarenville serves as the gateway to Terra Nova National Park and the Bonavista Peninsula. Though relatively new compared to other Newfoundland towns, Clarenville has its share of history. It was the starting point for an 1827 expedition to find the last of the Beothuks. In 1933, the town was paid a visit by Italian general Italo Balbo's flying boat squadron. And in 1957, Clarenville's modern tradition produced Newfoundland's first woman mayor.

As the TransCanada Highway's area service center, Clarenville offers a variety of lodgings and places to eat. The **Clarenville Inn,** tel. 709/466-7911 or 877/466-7911, fronts the road with 64 rooms (from $77 single, $93 double), a steakhouse, a lounge and patio bar, and an outdoor heated pool. The **St. Jude Hotel,** tel. 709/466-1717 or 800/563-7800, www.stjudehotel.nf.ca, also lies on the TransCanada. It has 64 rooms (from $85; nonsmoking rooms available), a restaurant, and a fireside lounge. The **Restland Motel,**

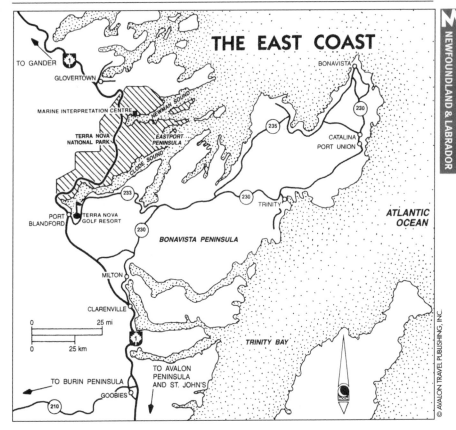

off Memorial Drive, tel. 709/466-7636, is centrally located and offers 33 rooms, suites, and housekeeping units ($65–85), an outdoor pool, and a picnic/play area. The **Pasta Plus Café,** in the motel's lobby, features inexpensive pastas, pizzas, curries, and traditional entrées.

## Trinity

Just three years after John Cabot bumped into Newfoundland, Portugal commissioned mariners Gaspar and Miguel Côrte-Real to search for a passage to China. That mission failed, but Gaspar accidentally sailed into Trinity Bay on Trinity Sunday in 1501. In 1558, merchants from England's West Country founded a settlement on the same site, making Trinity even older than St. Augus-

tine, Florida. Pirates and the French navy frequently attacked this British fishing and mercantile center in the early 18th century. In defense, the settlers constructed fortifications along the coast, some remains of which can still be seen.

The attractive village (pop. 500) has changed little since the late 1800s. White picket fences, small gardens, and historic sites are everywhere. The best photo vantage point of Trinity is from the Highway 239 coastal spur, the narrow road also known as Courthouse Road. The road peels across the headlands, turns a quick corner, and suddenly overlooks the seaport. Ease into the turn so you can savor the view. To get your photograph, park your car in the village and walk back up the road.

© LISA COSTANTINO

Trinity

A cluster of historic sites sits atop a hillside along Highway 239. The **Trinity Interpretation Centre,** in a handsomely restored building, has historical exhibits about the village. It's open from late June to early September, daily 10 A.M.–5:30 P.M., tel. 709/464-2042. The **Lester-Garland Premises** is a restored 19th-century mercantile, while the Georgian-style brick **Lester Garland House,** tel. 709/464-3706, has been restored to its 1820s appearance and now houses a museum. The **Green Family Forge,** in a restored 1895 building on Church Road, is a blacksmith museum displaying more than 1,500 tools, products and other artifacts of the blacksmith trade. Also on Church Road is an 1880 saltbox-style house that now serves as the **Trinity Historical Society Museum and Archives,** tel. 709/464-2244, displaying more than 2,000 fishing, mercantile, medical, and fire-fighting artifacts. All of these historical properties/museums are open mid-June to mid-September and charge $2 adults, $3 families.

For Trinity's other sites, drive into the village, park anywhere, and walk. Expect to wander; locals place more value on oral tradition than street signs. Emma Hiscock and her two daughters lived in the restored mustard-and-green **Hiscock House,** a block inland from the government wharf, tel. 709/464-2042. They operated a forge, retail store, and telegraph office in the saltbox-style house in the 1800s. Costumed guides give free tours of this provincial historic site. It's open June–November, daily 10 A.M.–5:30 P.M.; by appointment the rest of the year.

The **Village Inn,** Taverner's Path, tel. 709/464-3269, offers six guest rooms (from $59), all with private baths, in a heritage house with a long open porch, as well as a separate guesthouse that rents as a single unit ($160). Innkeeper/co-owner Christine Beamish lures gourmets from St. John's with sautéed cod tongues or capelin appetizers, and entrées such as fried cod, halibut, scallops, and poached salmon. Lodging and meal reservations are advised.

The other half of the inn's talented duo is Dr. Peter C. Beamish, who is also the director of Ceta-Research, an outfit devoted to communication research with whales, dolphins, porpoises, and many other species. **Ocean Contact,** the company's seafaring component, takes sightseers along while conducting research out in the bay; guests actually take part in the research. The excursions ($45 for four-hour trips; longer packages available) depart daily mid-June to mid-September, weather permitting. For details or reservations, call 709/464-3269, www .oceancontact.com.

The summer solstice kicks off Rising Tide Theatre's **Summer in the Bight** festival, presenting original musical and dramatic productions written and performed by some of Newfoundland's best. The festival runs July through Labour Day, Tues.–Sun., in a re-created fishing shed on the harbor front. For information, call Rising Tide Theatre at 709/464-3847 or 888/464-3377.

## Port Union

The only town in Canada to have been established by a labor union, Port Union was the home of Sir William Coaker, leader of the Fishermen's Union Trading Company. His legacy lives on: one of the largest fish-processing plants and the largest trawler fleet in the province are both based here. Coaker's grand presence is still evident in his gravesite memorial, a sar-

cophagus topped by a statue overlooking the town. At **The Bungalow,** tel. 709/469-2728, artifacts of Coaker's life and times fill the influential labor man's 1917 home. Open mid-June through early September, Wed.–Sun. 9:30 A.M.–5:30 P.M.; the guided tour costs $4 for adults, $2 for children.

## Bonavista

Fifty kilometers from Trinity up Highway 230, Bonavista (pop. 5,000) began in the 1600s as a French fishing port. It was later taken over and fortified by the British. Many believe that the barren shoreline at **Cape Bonavista,** six km north of town, was the first landfall Giovanni Caboto (better known as John Cabot) spied in North America, on June 24, 1497. In 1997 the 500th anniversary of Cabot's discovery was celebrated all around the province, and nowhere more grandly than at Bonavista. The normally quiet town came alive with more than 25,000 visitors to witness the arrival of the *Matthew,* a

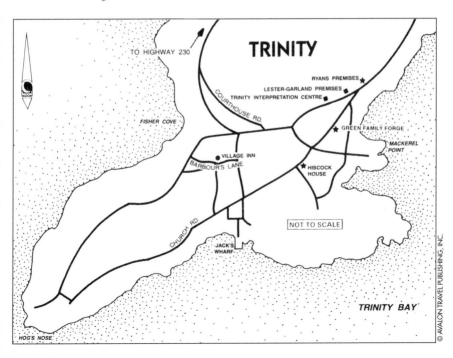

replica of Cabot's ship that left Bristol, England, on May 2, 1997, tracing the probable route of Cabot's expedition. A visit from Queen Elizabeth and other dignitaries, musical performances, theatrical reenactments, an air show, and other events created what was billed as the most spectacular celebration in Newfoundland's history.

With or without the celebrations, Bonavista has its share of historic sites worth seeing. The 1871 **Mockbeggar Plantation** on Mockbeggar Road, tel. 709/468-7300, has been a residence, carpenter's shop, and fish store. The house's last resident was F. Gordon Bradley, the province's first senator and a member of the federal cabinet in the 1950s. Bradley donated the property to the village. Open daily 10 A.M.–5:30 P.M. June–November; admission is $2.50.

At the intersection of Ryan's Hill and Old Catalina Road lies the **Ryan Premises,** tel. 709/468-1600, where merchant James Ryan established his salt-fish enterprise in the mid-1800s. The waterfront site's collection of white clapboard buildings includes the manager's residence, the fish store, and the retail shop, all filled with exhibits and artifacts of the era. In the salt shed, local crafters demonstrate such skills as furniture making; their goods can be purchased in the retail shop. Also here is the **Bonavista Museum,** tel. 709/468-2909, which houses genealogical records and exhibits on the area's history. The site and museum are open June 15 through October 15, daily 10 A.M.–6 P.M. Admission is $2.50 adults, $2 seniors, $1.50 children 6–16, $6 families.

The photogenic 1843 **Cape Bonavista Lighthouse** on Highway 230, tel. 709/468-7444, crowns a steep and rocky headland. The keeper's quarters inside the red-and-white-striped tower have been restored to the 1870 period. A climb up steep steps leads to the original catoptric light with Argand oil burners and reflectors. A more efficient but far less attractive metal tower, outfitted with an electric light, replaced the beacon in 1962. From early June to early October, the lighthouse is open daily 10:30 A.M.–5:30 P.M.; by appointment the rest of the year.

# TERRA NOVA NATIONAL PARK

Above Port Blandford, the TransCanada Highway runs along Terra Nova National Park's western edge. Moose, black bear, beaver, rare pine martens, lynx, and bald eagles inhabit the hilly, inland boreal forest and wetlands of the 404-square-km preserve. Ocean currents push icebergs up to the rugged shoreline in summer, and from mid-May to mid-August, whales roam the deep-water fjords. Water temperatures vary: the sea can be as warm as 20° C in the sheltered bays from late summer to early autumn, but temperatures never rise above a chilly –2° C in the fjord's depths.

Terra Nova National Park is open year-round. Admission to the park during the summer is adults $3.25, seniors $2.50, children $1.75; admission is free from mid-October to mid-May. Pets are allowed but must be leashed.

## Marine Interpretation Centre

Make your first stop the Marine Interpretation Centre, which overlooks Newman Sound at the Saltons Day Use Area, just off the TransCanada Highway, tel. 709/533-2801. The center features aquariums, touch tanks, live feed from an underwater camera, exhibits on the various marine habitats within the park, interactive computer displays, and films, plus a restaurant and gift shop. It's open mid-May to late June, 10 A.M.–5 P.M., late June to early September 9 A.M.–8 P.M., and early September to early October 10 A.M.–5 P.M. The center's gift shop sells topographical maps of the park and stocks books about the province's flora, fauna, and attractions.

## Park Recreation

More than a dozen trails thread through the park, providing some 60 km of hiking. Most are uncomplicated loop routes that meander easily for an hour's walk beneath tree canopies. The longest trek, the five-hour round-trip **Outport Trail,** connects the Newman Sound Campground with the fjord's southern coast. If icebergs or whales are offshore, you'll see them from the lookout tower on the sound.

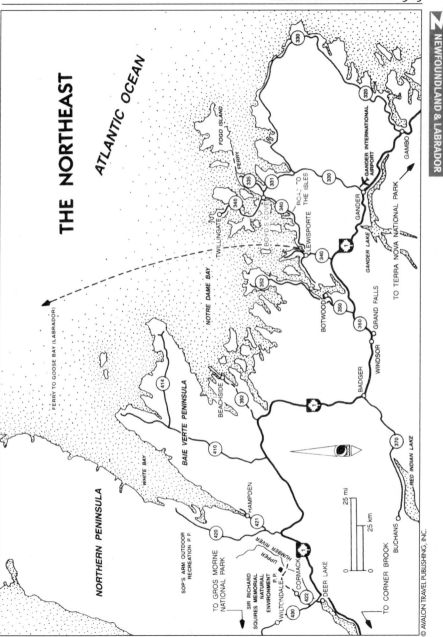

NEWFOUNDLAND & LABRADOR

THE NORTHEAST

ATLANTIC OCEAN

NORTHERN PENINSULA

WHITE BAY

BAIE VERTE PENINSULA

NOTRE DAME BAY

FOGO ISLAND

FERRY

TWILLINGATE

BOYD'S COVE

ROAD TO THE ISLES

LEWISPORTE

GANDER INTERNATIONAL AIRPORT

GANDER

GAMBO

TO TERRA NOVA NATIONAL PARK

GANDER LAKE

BOTWOOD

GRAND FALLS

WINDSOR

BADGER

RED INDIAN LAKE

BEACHSIDE

HAMPDEN

HUMBER RIVER

UPPER P.P.

SIR RICHARD SQUIRES MEMORIAL NATURAL ENVIRONMENT P.P.

SOP'S ARM OUTDOOR RECREATION P.P.

TO GROS MORNE NATIONAL PARK

CORMACK

WILTONDALE

DEER LAKE

TO CORNER BROOK

BUCHANS

FERRY TO GOOSE BAY (LABRADOR)

330

320

330

335

331

340

340

340

352

350

360

370

392

414

410

420

421

422

430

25 mi

25 km

0

0

© AVALON TRAVEL PUBLISHING, INC.

Fishing is good in the park's many lakes and streams; game fish include brook trout and arctic char. A national park fishing permit is required for inland fishing ($4.50 daily; $6.50 for seven days) but not for saltwater angling for mackerel, cod, and other species.

**Terra Nova Golf Resort,** tel. 709/543-2525, lies at the park's southern entrance, where 27 holes overlook Clode Sound. The resort's 18-hole Twin Rivers course is one of Canada's top 50 courses, while Eagle River is an easier nine-hole layout. Green fees are $68 and $22 respectively.

For informative boat trips, check out **Ocean Watch Tours,** tel. 709/533-6024, located at Saltons Wharf near the Marine Interpretation Centre. The three-hour morning trip (9 A.M. departure) noses among the fjord fingers looking for icebergs and whales, while the two afternoon trips (departing at 1 and 4 P.M.) are geared to sightseeing. The shorter sunset tour (7 P.M.) explores an abandoned outport. Tour season runs mid-May through October.

**Sandy Pond Rentals,** tel. 709/677-2221, rents canoes, kayaks, and paddle boats for visitors interested in taking their own boat trips. The Southwest Arm and Sandy Pond/Dunphy's Pond are two of the most popular paddling routes.

## Accommodations and Camping

**Terra Nova Golf Resort,** tel. 709/543-2525, www.terranovagolf.com, is a family-oriented lodge in a huge, blue wooden building on the golf course. The lodge offers comfortable accommodations with 82 rooms (from $95), a dining room and pub, exercise facilities, an outdoor heated pool, and walking trails overlooking Clode Sound.

Further north, **Clode Sound Motel,** located within the park off Highway 1 in Charlottetown, tel. 709/664-3146, has 19 rooms, a swimming pool, a playground, and a highly regarded restaurant/bakery that serves wonderful desserts created with apples from the motel's 90-year-old orchard. Rates run $65–80. The motel and restaurant are open May through October.

Wooded **Newman Sound Campground** has 387 full- and semi-serviced campsites ($14–18), as well as kitchen shelters and heated washrooms

with hot showers. It's open year-round and staffed from late May to early September, when you'll find interpretive programs presented in the **Activity Centre.** At the campground's **Service Centre,** you'll enjoy a restaurant, campers' store, rental store, and launderette. Reservations are accepted at tel. 709/533-3187. **Malady Head,** the park's more rustic campground, features a kitchen/activity area and playground equipment. The campground, located off Highway 310 along the Southwest Arm, has 99 semi-serviced sites ($12).

# GANDER TO TWILLINGATE

From the high central plateau, rolling hills descend gradually to the sea, where the northern coast is fringed with offshore islands. The Trans-Canada Highway cuts across the interior in a rambling inland path, sometimes angling north to touch a deeply carved bay or reaching into the interior to amble amid the plateau's seemingly endless stretches of tree-blanketed hills.

It's a six-hour drive across the island from Glovertown near Terra Nova National Park to Deer Lake, the gateway to western coast sightseeing highlights such as Gros Morne National Park. You can drive it in one day, but take more time if you can and wander north to explore the fishing communities strewn across the small peninsulas and islands that line the edge of Notre Dame Bay and Hamilton Sound.

## Gander

The town of Gander, 60 km west of Glovertown, was founded only in 1951, when the military decided to convert Gander Airport to civilian operations. Adjoining the TransCanada Highway, Gander proudly displays its memorials to aviation history. Gleaming, full-size models of World War II Hudson, Voodoo, and Canso water bombers, a Beech 18 aircraft, and a reconstructed De Havilland Tiger Moth greet visitors to the **North Atlantic Aviation Museum** on Highway 1, tel. 709/256-2923. Inside, exhibits on Gander's strategic role in World War II and the development of transatlantic aviation include early equipment, uniforms, photographs, and a reconstructed DC-3 cockpit. The museum

TWILLINGATE AREA

ATLANTIC OCEAN

LONG POINT
LONG POINT LIGHTHOUSE

NORTH TWILLINGATE ISLAND

NOTRE DAME
BAY

MAIN ST
MAIN ST.

TWILLINGATE
HARBOUR

BACK HARBOUR
TWILLINGATE
MUSEUM
& CRAFTS

ICEBERG SHOP

TOULINGUET
ST.

340

TO TRANSCANADA HIGHWAY

SOUTH
TWILLINGATE
ISLAND

NOT TO SCALE

© AVALON TRAVEL PUBLISHING, INC.

road turns off the highway and peels down to the lake. A group of statues, of an American soldier and two children, backed by Canadian, U.S., and Newfoundland flags, overlooks the lake. The park spreads across the remote, rocky hillside, and flower bouquets lie here and there.

Gander is a convenient stop for travelers crossing Newfoundland's interior and it provides a wide choice of accommodations. The spacious **Hotel Gander,** tel. 709/256-3931 or 800/563-2988, www.hotelgander.com, fronts the Trans-Canada Highway and offers 148 rooms and suites ($65–99), a dining room, a lounge with entertainment, an indoor pool, and an exercise room. The modern **Comfort Inn,** on the TransCanada Highway, tel. 709/256-3535 or 888/256-3535, www.comfortinn.com, has 66 large rooms (from $66, $70 with a kitchenette, including a breakfast buffet), a family restaurant, and a picnic area.

## Boyd's Cove

From Gander, Highway 330 heads north to Gander Bay, where Highway 331 curves farther northwest and lopes onto the northern archipelago as Highway 340, better known as the Road to the Isles.

Boyd's Cove, at the intersection of Highways 331 and 340, is a small village with a large attraction: the **Boyd's Cove Beothuk Interpretation Centre.** Designed to mimic the shapes of Beothuk dwellings, the center lies at the end of a two-km gravel road. The detour is worth it, though, for the artifacts, dioramas, films, and exquisitely expressive paintings depicting the history of the Beothuk people. Take the 20-minute walk down to the site of the 17th-century Beothuk encampment, excavated in the early 1980s. Eleven house pits, clearly defined by earthen walls, were discovered here, along with countless artifacts such as beads, stone tools, and iron. The center, tel. 709/656-3114, is open daily 10 A.M.–5:30 P.M. during summer. Admission is $2.50.

## Twillingate

A series of causeways connects roads across the islands. One of the prettiest drives in the province, the narrow highway passes farmland (where you might catch a glimpse of the rare Newfoundland

is open year-round, daily 9 A.M.–9 P.M. mid-May to Labour Day (Mon.–Fri. 9 A.M.–5 P.M. the rest of the year). Admission is $3 adults, $2 seniors and children. At **Gander International Airport,** a massive mural inside the international lounge depicts more aviation history.

The **Silent Witness Memorial,** four km east of town off the TransCanada Highway, marks the site of an aviation disaster. On a cold December day in 1985, the airport was a scheduled refueling stop for a DC-8 flight from the Middle East. The flight carried the U.S. 101st Airborne Division, better known as the Screaming Eagles, who were returning home from a United Nations peacekeeping mission in the Sinai. The plane, with 248 soldiers and an eight-member crew, crashed shortly after takeoff between the highway and Gander Lake. The memorial park marks the crash site. As you drive through Gander on the TransCanada Highway, look for the sign on the highway's southern side. An access

**shipwreck near Musgrave Harbour, north of Boyd's Cove**

Dorset Eskimo artifacts. One room is devoted to the career of Dr. John Olds, Twillingate's famous expatriate surgeon who came from the United States to pioneer medicine in remote Newfoundland. The intriguing medical artifacts include a collection of early 20th-century pharmaceuticals and glass eyes. There are also details about local opera star Georgina Stirling, who took the stage name of Marie Toulinguet. She performed in Paris and Milan in the late 19th century, but her voice gave out prematurely, cutting short her concert career. She retired to Newfoundland to live out her days here in her hometown. Stirling now lies buried in St. Peter's Cemetery. The museum is open mid-May to early October, daily 9 A.M.–9 P.M.; admission is $1 for adults, 50 cents for kids.

Icebergs, which wander offshore and sometimes ditch at land's end in Notre Dame Bay, are one of Twillingate's main claims to fame. If you're interested in getting up close, take one of the three daily cruises offered by **Twillingate Island Boat Tours.** Their office, in the Iceberg Shop on the eastern harbor front at 50 Main Street, tel. 709/884-2242, is open May through October. You may also see an offshore iceberg from Back Harbour, the semicircular bay a short walk behind the museum. Otherwise, head for Long Point, the high, rocky promontory that juts into the Atlantic Ocean aside Notre Dame Bay. Take Main Street north and follow the narrow road to **Long Point Lighthouse,** the local iceberg vantage point. Bring rubber-soled shoes for scrambling across the boulders, and don't forget your camera—the beacon backed by the sea and sky makes a beautiful picture, particularly at sunset.

Visitors to Twillingate often find themselves captivated by the town's charm, and because of this, numerous accommodations can be found. **Harbour Lights Inn,** 189 Main Street, tel. 709/884-2763, is a restored early-19th-century home overlooking the harbor. The nine-room inn features nonsmoking rooms with private baths; two suites have whirlpool baths. Rates range $60–85, including a cooked breakfast. If you prefer more privacy, consider **Cabins by the Sea,** 11 Hugh Lane, tel. 709/884-2158, www.cabinsbythesea.com, comprising small

pony); gentle, island-filled bays; and tiny outports to finish at South and North Twillingate islands. The archipelago's most northwesterly point, the islands are washed by the Atlantic and shouldered by Notre Dame Bay. The road crosses the southern island and eases into the tiny port at Twillingate Harbour.

Cross the causeway to Twillingate (pop. 3,500) on the northwestern island. Main Street runs alongside the scenic harbor before it zips north and climbs to Long Point. If you're interested in local lore, stop at the **Twillingate Museum and Crafts,** on the western island, tel. 709/884-2825. The gleaming, white-painted wooden building sits back from the road behind the 1839 St. Peter's Anglican Church and is bordered by a white picket fence—altogether as proper as a former Anglican manse should be. The museum's extensive exhibits include historic fishing gear and tools, antique dolls, and several rare

self-contained cabins for a reasonable $70 per night. Four km from town, in the village of Little Harbour, the **Beach Rock Bed & Breakfast,** tel. 709/884-2292, overlooks the protected waters of Notre Dame Bay. Open year-round, it offers four guest rooms, a light breakfast, and dinners by reservation. Rates are $40 single, $45 double.

The popular weeklong **Twillingate Fish, Fun, and Folk Festival,** in late July or early August, is another reason to visit. It features seafood, boat tours, music and dance, crafts, and fireworks at Twillingate and nearby outports. For details, call 709/884-2678.

## GRAND FALLS–WINDSOR

Grand Falls-Windsor lies almost exactly halfway along the Newfoundland leg of the TransCanada Highway; St. Johns is 428 km to the east, and Port aux Basques is 476 km to the west. The two towns, as separate entities, predate the TransCanada Highway by decades. In an efficient political move, the towns joined into a single municipality in

1991. Keep in mind that Windsor lies north of the TransCanada Highway and Grand Falls south. Each town has its own shopping area, and the shops lining the highway make up a third.

## Sights

Grand Falls offers the most sightseeing. Turn south off the highway to the **Mary March Regional Museum,** 22 St. Catherine St., tel. 709/292-4522, where exhibits about the area's Beothuk people, natural history, geology, and regional industry fill the modern center. The museum is named for Demasduit, a Beothuk woman kidnapped in 1819. Her captors, who renamed her Mary March, were attempting to return her to her people when she died of tuberculosis. Open mid-May to mid-September, daily 9 A.M.–4:45 P.M., admission to the museum is adults $2.50, seniors and children $2. In the woodlands behind the museum is **Beothuk Park,** tel. 709/489-3559, a re-created Beothuk village, featuring a sweat lodge and summer and winter dwellings. Open mid-June to early September, daily 10 A.M.–6 P.M. Admission to the village is adults $3, children $2.

The town is aptly named for its Grand Falls, a thunderous, whitewater gush from the Exploits River as it speeds alongside the town. To see the falls, take Scott Avenue off the TransCanada Highway or drive through town, turn west at the pulp and paper mill, and head north on a narrow, gravel lane. The river's famous for its Atlantic salmon. You can get a close look at them at the **Grand Falls Fishway–Salmonid Interpretation Centre,** the wooden A-frame building next to the river, tel. 709/489-7350. The Environment Resources Management Association, a private conservation group, operates the center. The main floor's exhibits explain the salmon's life cycle and habitat, while on the observation

level you can watch the migratory salmon through the viewing windows. The center is open mid-June through mid-September, daily 8 A.M. to dusk. Admission is $3 adults, $2 children.

During mid-July, the six-day **Exploits Valley Salmon Festival** takes over the whole area. Up to 10,000 spectators come for the province's only horse show, music (Irish, rhythm and blues, funk, and rock), a Newfie night, fishing derby, a crafts fair, and traditional Newfoundland food with an emphasis on salmon dinners. Call 877/585-9762 for details.

## Accommodations

**Mount Peyton Hotel** 214 Lincoln Rd., tel. 709/489-2251 or 800/563-4894, www .mountpeyton.com, has an array of accommodations, including 102 hotel rooms, 32 motel rooms, and 16 housekeeping units ranging $76–116. The motel's dining room is locally known for fresh salmon, trout, crab, and lobster; locally grown vegetables; and, for dessert, berries in all forms.

In the residential outskirts of Windsor, **Carriage House Inn,** 181 Grenfell Heights, tel. 709/489-7185 or 800/563-7133, is a nicely appointed private home that rents four spic-and-span guest rooms from $69 single, $79 double, with full breakfast. Outside you'll find a pool, sundeck, and stables. It's open year-round.

**Hotel Robin Hood,** 78 Lincoln Rd., tel. 709/489-5324, fax 709/489-6191, is Grand Falls–Windsor's newest new hotel. Small and charming, it's set off from the road and run by a couple from Nottingham, England. The 14 rooms ($70–80), all air-conditioned and with private baths, are comfortable and spacious. Friar Tuck's Restaurant serves up British-style meals and is locally known for its fish and chips.

# Western Newfoundland

The TransCanada Highway's route across the central island finishes at **Deer Lake,** the western coast gateway. Be prepared to make a directional decision here. At Deer Lake, Highway 430, also known as the Viking Trail, heads northwest to stunning scenery and archaeological treasures on the remote Northern Peninsula, while the TransCanada Highway turns southwest to Corner Brook, Newfoundland's second-largest city, and Port aux Basques, terminus for the Nova Scotia ferry.

Western Newfoundland may seem remote, but the area is surprisingly developed. Along the northwestern coast, Gros Morne National Park works nicely as a sightseeing base. Park campgrounds and community lodgings are plentiful. To the south, Corner Brook, the western coast business hub, offers city comforts.

## GROS MORNE NATIONAL PARK

UNESCO world heritage sites are scattered across the world. Egypt boasts the pyramids at Giza. France is known for Chartres Cathedral. Australia has the Great Barrier Reef. And Newfoundland boasts Gros Morne National Park, a spectacular geological slice of the ancient world.

The Gros Morne Park fronts the Gulf of St. Lawrence on a coastal plain rimmed with 72 km of coast edging sandy and cobblestone beaches, seastacks, caves, forests, peat bogs, and breathtaking saltwater and freshwater fjords. The flattened Long Range Mountains, part of the ancient Appalachian Mountains, rise as an alpine plateau cloaked with black and white spruce, balsam fir, white birch, and stunted tuckamore thickets. Bare patches of peridotite, toxic to most plants, speckle the peaks, and at the highest elevations the vegetation gives way to lichen, moss, and dwarf willow and birch on the arctic tundra.

Innumerable moose, arctic hares, foxes, weasels, lynx, and a few bears roam the park. Two large herds of woodland caribou inhabit the mountains and migrate to the coastal plain during winter. Bald eagles, ospreys, common and arctic terns, great black-backed gulls, and songbirds nest along the coast, while rock ptarmigans inhabit the mountain peaks. You might see willow ptarmigans on the lower slopes or, especially during the June to early July capelin run, a few pilot, minke, or humpback whales offshore.

### The User-Friendly Park

The park is remarkably user-friendly. Although the preserve spans 1,805 square km, it's not so large that sightseeing is unmanageable. And while the majority of the park is mountainous wilderness, a narrow coastal plain contains rare, ancient landscapes, one of Gros Morne's most significant attractions.

Some 120 km of roads thread through this outdoor geological museum. The park highway divides at Wiltondale. From this point, Highway 431 leads west through the Tablelands to the village of Trout River (50 km from Wiltondale), and Highway 430 leads northwest to the main park information center (34 km) and Rocky Harbour Township (39 km) and north along the coast to Western Brook Pond and Cow Head (87 km). Park entry costs adults $5, seniors $4, children $2.50 per day.

More than 100 km of marked and unmarked hiking trails lead novice to expert trekkers into the park's nooks and crannies. Several privately operated boat tours probe the fjords, and if you're adventurous, private outfitters can make sea kayaking arrangements. A provincial fishing license (available at any sports store) opens up angling for brook trout and arctic char on the fast-flowing streams and rivers. If you'd like to know more about Gros Morne's natural history and geology, scheduled interpretive programs and evening campfires run from late June to early September.

### Climate

The park enjoys a pleasant, cool climate, averaging 10 days of precipitation each month during summer. At Rocky Harbour, a typical summer

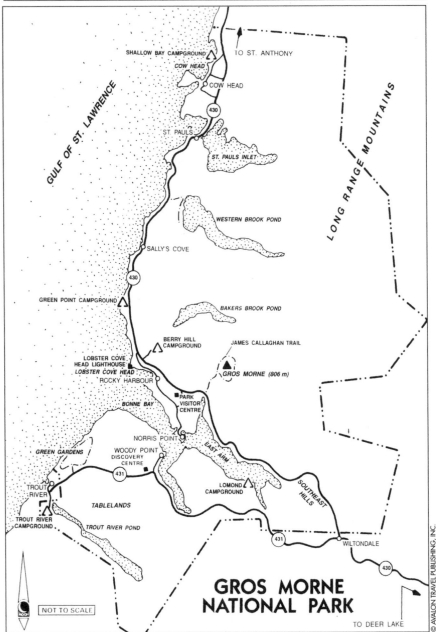

GULF OF ST. LAWRENCE

LONG RANGE MOUNTAINS

SHALLOW BAY CAMPGROUND

*COW HEAD*

TO ST. ANTHONY

COW HEAD

430

ST. PAULS

*ST. PAULS INLET*

*WESTERN BROOK POND*

SALLY'S COVE

430

GREEN POINT CAMPGROUND

*BAKERS BROOK POND*

BERRY HILL CAMPGROUND

JAMES CALLAGHAN TRAIL

LOBSTER COVE HEAD LIGHTHOUSE

*LOBSTER COVE HEAD*

ROCKY HARBOUR

*GROS MORNE (806 m)*

PARK VISITOR CENTRE

*BONNE BAY*

NORRIS POINT

*GREEN GARDENS*

WOODY POINT DISCOVERY CENTRE

EAST ARM

LOMOND CAMPGROUND

SOUTHEAST HILLS

TROUT RIVER

431

TABLELANDS

TROUT RIVER CAMPGROUND

*TROUT RIVER POND*

431

WILTONDALE

430

## GROS MORNE NATIONAL PARK

NOT TO SCALE

TO DEER LAKE

day is breezy with southwesterly winds. The temperature averages 15° C—cooler and windier at higher elevations. For weather information, contact the **Newfoundland Weather Centre,** tel. 709/256-6600.

## Discovery Centre

If you've entered the park on Highway 431, make your first stop the Discovery Centre, on the hill above Woody Point, tel. 709/458-2417. This modern park facility showcases everything the park is renowned for. The main display area holds an impressive 3-D map of the park, geological samples and descriptions, a human history display, and a theater. Also in the building is a gift shop selling park literature and a café specializing in regional cuisine. Outside, a short trail leads through a garden planted with species native to the park. The center is open June through October, daily 9 A.M.–4:30 P.M., with extended hours in July and August.

From the Discovery Centre, Highway 431 climbs to the Tablelands, described below.

## Touching Base with the Ancient World

The **Tablelands,** the park's most prized geological tract, lies along Highway 431, halfway between Wiltondale and Trout River. It's an odd sight, more resembling Hudson Bay's bleached, brown barrens than verdant Newfoundland. The 12-by-7-km chunk once lay beneath the ancient Iapetus Ocean. Violent internal upheavals eventually thrust the unearthly landscape to the surface. The parched yellow and tan cliffs and boulders that resulted are formed of peridotite, an igneous rock found in the earth's mantle.

In contrast, the **Green Gardens** originated as lava from erupting volcanoes in the Iapetus Ocean. Look for a marked trailhead on Highway 431, just it descends from the Tablelands. A 16-km (five-hour) round-trip hiking trail starts out across Tablelands's crusty terrain and emerges on a high headland cloaked in rich green grasses overlooking the gulf. Below the headland, seastacks and caves rise from the beach floor beside

the lunarlike landscape of Gros Morne's Tablelands

© ANDREW HEMPSTEAD

cliffs pocked with pillow lava, the solidified remnants of molten rock from 100 km beneath the ancient seafloor.

## North along Highway 430

The park's northern section is typical of the island's rocky seacoast and verdant hills and mountains, a distinct contrast to the southern area. To get there, retrace Highway 431 to Wiltondale and turn northwest on Highway 430, passing the main park information center and the service town of Rocky Harbour. Unusual groups of faulted and folded rock layers lie along this coastline. An example is **Lobster Cove Head,** a kilometer west of the village of Rocky Harbour. Its layers formed as the North America plate slid beneath the eastern Eurasia/Africa plate 450–500 million years ago.

Check out the Lobster Cove Head lighthouse. The site is one of several places in the park offering guided walks, evening campfire programs, and weekend crafts demonstrations. Inside the lighthouse, exhibits depict local lore, geological facets, and ancient natural history. It's open June to late September, daily 9 A.M.–6 P.M.

More dramatically formed coastal rock lies farther north. **Green Point,** 10 minutes beyond Lobster Cove, presents a tilted, textured surface of ribbon limestone and shale embedded with fossils from the Cambrian and Ordovician periods. **Cow Head,** 40 minutes farther north, features a similar angled formation with limestone breccia (jumbled limestone chunks and fossils) spread across a small peninsula. The areas are richly textured. At Cow Head, the breccia looks like light-colored rock pillows scattered across a dark rock surface, while Green Point's surface is a rich green and textured like crushed velvet. The rock layers at both places originated during deepwater avalanches as the Iapetus Ocean formed 460–550 million years ago.

## James Callaghan Trail

**Gros Morne Mountain,** part of the Long Range Mountains but set off by itself, dominates the central section of the park and provides a challenging hike to its summit. You'll see the mountain's flattened peak as Highway 430 threads westward from Wiltondale through the park's interior, curves along the Southeast Hills, and dips down to sea level alongside the east arm of Bonne Bay.

The 16-km round-trip James Callaghan Trail to the 806-meter summit begins from a trail-

## THE FJORDS OF GROS MORNE

Like Scandinavia, Gros Morne National Park is famous for fjords, fringed sea arms carved by the last ice sheet and shouldered by forests and cliffs. And like their Scandinavian counterparts, both the **Bonne Bay** and **St. Paul's Inlet** fjords open directly to the sea. The park's other fjords, however, are actually landlocked fjord lakes and are known as "ponds." These ponds—**Trout River, Ten Mile, Bakers Brook,** and **Western Brook**—were carved by the ice sheets just like the other fjords. But in each case, when the enormous ice sheet melted out, the coastline—which had been compressed by the sheer weight of the glacier—rebounded like a sponge, rising above sea level and cutting the fjord off from the sea.

**Boat Tours**

Daily boat tours explore some of the fjords from late May or June to October, weather permitting. Tours generally last two to two-and-a-half hours and cost $25–35 per person. **Bontours,** tel. 709/458-2730 or 800/563-9887, offers a cruise on spectacular Western Brook Pond. This fjord is in the north of the park, and is reached by an easy three-km hiking trail. During July and August, three tours depart daily, at 10 A.M. and 1 and 4 P.M.; in June and September, one daily tour departs, at 1 P.M. Book by calling the above numbers, or through the Bontours reservations desk at the Ocean View Motel in Rocky Harbour.

In the park's southern reaches, **Tableland Boat Tour,** tel. 709/451-2101, cruises 15-km-long Trout River Pond, passing between the Tablelands and the Gregory Plateau's towering cliffs. Cruises leave three times daily in July and August. **Seal Island Tours,** tel. 709/243-2278, provides tours of St. Paul's Inlet and the coastline beyond on a similar schedule.

© LISA COSTANTINO

**Western Brook Pond**

head on Highway 430, some 30 km northwest of Wiltondale. Plan for a full day and wear sturdy high hiking boots. It's wise to bring raingear, a topographical map and compass, a first aid kit, and extra food, clothing, and drinking water.

The trail starts with about an hour's walk toward the mountain across a gently rising spruce and fir woodland, threaded with a dirt path and boardwalks. Tightly packed boulders mark the beginning of the actual ascent, which takes 2–2.5 hours (it may seem longer, as you negotiate the boulder trail). Unexpectedly, the trail empties at a corner of the flattened peak. The air is clear and exhilarating, but surprisingly chilly. Far below, climbers scramble fitfully up the rocky ascent. To the west rise the Long Range Mountains. Looking south, you'll see a sapphire fjord, laid like an angled ribbon across the green woodlands. Exploring the peak takes minutes. The surface is mainly bare shale, limestone, and quartzite rock sprinkled with wild grass tufts. The sun feels deliciously warm, though the wind whistles across the stark terrain. Savor the peak's views.

A few hikers backtrack and return on the boulder trail, but most climbers follow the cairns across the peak and go down Gros Morne's back side. Be careful, though—rain sometimes washes out the trail, which is steeper than the ascent described above.

## Park Campgrounds

Almost 300 campsites at five campgrounds lie within Gros Morne National Park. No electrical hookups are available, but all sites except Green point have hot showers, flush toilets, fire pits (firewood costs $3 per bundle), at least one kitchen shelter, and a playground.

Two campgrounds are staffed from mid-June to early September and offer evening campfire programs. Near Rocky Harbour, the **Berry Hill** site, open June through October, has 146 sites ($15.25), while further north along Highway 430, **Shallow Bay Campground** offers 50 ocean-front sites.

Small (40 sites) **Trout River Campground,** situated near the Tablelands, Green Gardens, and the Trout River boat tour dock, boasts the park's most exotic setting; $15.25 per night. It's open

mid-June to early September. The only campground open year-round, seaside **Green Point Campground,** near a cobble beach, has 31 campsites ($11) with fireplaces and kitchen shelters. The **Lomond Campground** edges Bonne Bay's east arm. Open mid-June to early September, Lomond offers 25 sites ($15.25), a range of facilities, and proximity to fishing streams.

## Rocky Harbour

Those not camping will find a variety of accommodations in Rocky Harbour, the park's major service area.

**Parsons Harbour View Cabins,** tel. 709/458-2544 or 877/458-2544, charges $55–60 for rooms or housekeeping units in the main house or adjacent motel. It's open May through October. The sunny, small dining room is known for fried halibut and salmon and flaky pies and tarts. The **Ocean View Motel,** tel. 709/458-2730 or 800/563-9887, www.oceanviewmotel.com, enjoys a prime location across from the water in the heart of Rocky Harbour. Rooms in the older wing are high quality and spacious ($65 single, $75 double), while those in the newer wing offer a patio or balcony with ocean views ($85 single, $95 double). The motel also has a downstairs bar and an upstairs restaurant. It's open year-round. Continue around the southern side of Rocky Harbour to reach **Gros Morne Cabins,** tel. 709/458-2020, also open year-round. This lodging comprises 22 one- and two-bedroom log chalets ($75–125) right on the harbor. For bed-and-breakfast accommodations, **Evergreen B&B,** Evergreen Lane, tel. 709/458-2692 or 800/905-3494, has four bedrooms ($40 single, $45 double, with full breakfast) and a large patio with barbecue facilities. It's open year-round.

**Fisherman's Landing** restaurant, opposite the Ocean View Motel, tel. 709/458-2060, is a good dining choice. It offers delectable fish dishes, such as a heaping platter of fried or broiled salmon, cod, or lobster (from $15), and a reputation for some of the best fried capelin, cod burgers, and bakeapple pies in the park.

## Cow Head

In Cow Head, 48 km north of Rocky Harbour,

**Shallow Bay Motel and Cabins,** tel. 709/243-2471 or 800/563-1946, www.shallowbaymotel.com, lies close to long stretches of sandy beach, hiking trails, and Arches Provincial Park. The 35 rooms and 17 housekeeping cabins run $80–90; a dining room serves home-style cooking. **J & J Hospitality Home,** tel. 709/243-2521, features four comfortable rooms ($45–50), full breakfast, and a library of Newfoundland books.

On the last weekend of June, the small town hosts the big **Cow Head Lobster Festival,** where residents and visitors from up and down the Northern Peninsula come for lobster dinners, entertainment, traditional music and dancing, and fireworks. For more information, call 709/243-2471.

### Woody Point

In Woody Point, on Highway 431 overlooking Bonne Bay's southern coastline, you'll find a row of waterfront shops and eateries, while one block back from the harbor is **Victorian Manor B&B,** tel. 709/453-2485. This imposing 1920s heritage home offers three guest rooms (from $55).

### Information

The **Park Visitor Centre,** on Highway 430 near Rocky Harbour, tel. 709/458-2066, stocks literature, sells books about the park and Newfoundland, presents slide shows, and has changing exhibits on the park's geology, landscapes, and history. The center is open daily 9 A.M.–4:30 P.M., and from mid-June to early September until 10 P.M. Along Highway 431, the **Discovery Centre** in Woody Point, tel. 709/458-2417, is another source of park information. A good source of pre-trip information is www.parkscanada.gc.ca/grosmorne.

## THE NORTHERN PENINSULA

North of Gros Morne National Park, the Northern Peninsula sweeps northeast across mountainous, flat-topped barrens and ends in tundra strewn with glacial boulders. Highway 430 runs alongside the gulf on the coastal plain and extends the peninsula's full length, finishing at St. Anthony. For meals and lodgings, stop anywhere;

one place is as good as the next. Make sure your car is in good operating condition and watch the gas gauge: service stations are located at widely spaced settlements.

As you drive the lonely stretch of Highway 430 between Cow Head and Eddies Cove, where the road turns inland, you'll notice, depending on the time of year, either small black patches of dirt or tiny flourishing vegetable gardens lining the road. These roadside gardens belong to the people of the nearby villages; because of the region's nutrient-poor soil, people plant their gardens wherever they find a patch of fertile ground.

### Port au Choix

The Maritime Archaic people and the later Dorset and Groswater Eskimos migrated from Labrador, roamed the Northern Peninsula, and then settled on this remote cape. In the 1960s, archaeological digs revealed Dorset dwellings in Phillip's Garden and an incredible wealth of Maritime Archaic cultural artifacts buried with almost 100 bodies at three nearby burial grounds. At the **Port au Choix National Historic Site,** tel. 709/861-3522, the three cultures are represented by artifacts, exhibits, and a reconstruction of a Dorset Eskimo dwelling at the newly expanded Visitor Reception Centre. It's open June to early September, daily 9 A.M.–8 P.M., 9 A.M.–5 P.M. until mid-October. Admission is $2.75 adults, $2.25 seniors, $1.50 children 6–16. Outdoors, a trail leads to the Phillip's Gardens site. Visitors are welcome to visit the dig underway at Garganelle Cove, where archaeologists hope to uncover evidence of Maritime Archaic dwellings.

As the town of Port au Choix continues to unfold its rich archaeological heritage, it also continues to expand its visitor services. One of these is **French Shore Inn & Cottages,** tel. 709/861-3824 or 888/801-3824, with six motel rooms ($54 single, $59 double, including a light breakfast) and six self-contained cottages (from $65). The **Anchor Café,** on Main Street near the national historic site, tel. 709/861-3665, serves fine fresh seafood, Italian, and vegetarian dishes.

### St. Barbe

From St. Barbe, 80 km north of the turn-off to

Port au Choix, the **MV *Apollo*** ferry makes two daily round-trip crossings to Blanc Sablon, Québec, early May to early January. The 90-minute crossing costs adults $9, seniors $7.50, children $4.75, vehicles $18.50 and up. Vehicle reservations are accepted from mid-June to late October. For reservations, call 866/535-2567, or check the schedule at www.gov.nf.ca/ferryservices.

## St. Anthony

Dr. Wilfred Grenfell, a medical missionary from England, traveled to the Labrador Straits in 1892. Struck by the lack of medical services, he soon established a hospital at Battle Harbour. In 1900 Grenfell chose St. Anthony, 443 km north of Deer Lake, as the site of his medical mission headquarters and supervised the construction of a new hospital. The largest town on the Northern Peninsula, St. Anthony (pop. 3,000) still serves as the International Grenfell Association headquarters. Grenfell dedicated his life to building and raising funds for area hospitals, stores, schools, and orphanages. He also helped foster financial independence for remote outports through profitable organizations such as **Grenfell Handicrafts,** tel. 709/454-3576, which still produces hand-embroidered cassocks, parkas, and jackets at its workroom/retail shop in the **Grenfell Interpretation Centre** (by Curtis Memorial Hospital on the village's western side), tel. 709/454-4010. This is the source for the fox-trimmed parkas, hooked rugs, and crafts sold islandwide. It's open mid-May to mid-October, daily 9 A.M.–8 P.M., weekdays 9 A.M.–6 P.M. in the off-season. The Interpretation Centre also holds two floors of panels and videos detailing Grenfell history; the $4 adult admission fee (discounts for children and families) includes admission to the Grenfell House Museum.

Grenfell was knighted for his efforts, once in 1907 and again in 1927. He and his wife, Anne Elizabeth, are buried on Tea House Hill. Exhibits at the stately **Grenfell House Museum,** on the other side of the hospital about a block from the Interpretation Centre, tel. 709/454-2281, teach about Dr. Grenfell's work. The green house is open 9 A.M.–6 P.M. in mid-May and early June, 9 A.M.–8 P.M. through September, by appointment the rest of the year.

Near the waterfront, the **Dock House Museum** exhibits artifacts from the days when Grenfell's mission hospital ships plied the waters of the Strait of Belle Isle. Open June–September; admission is free. A tribute to the life and works of Dr. Grenfell lives in the **Jordi Bonet Murals,** impressive ceramic panels adorning the walls of the Curtis Memorial Hospital foyer.

St. Anthony traces its origins back to its days as a seasonal settlement for Basque and French fishing fleets in the early 16th century. Today it's the region's main service center, offering visitors a wide range of accommodations and dining options. **Haven Inn,** on Goose Cover Road, tel. 709/454-9100 or 877/428-3646, has 29 rooms ($70–110), including two suites with hot tubs and fireplaces, a restaurant serving home-style cooking, and a lounge.

The **Lightkeeper's Café,** tel. 709/454-4900, serves seafood specialties, chicken, burgers, pasta, and vegetarian dishes in the old Fishing Point Light Station lightkeeper's residence. The views from the windows and from nearby Fishing Point Park offer excellent opportunities to see whales and drifting icebergs. The restaurant often features live music and is smoke-free.

## L'Anse aux Meadows

The island has no grapes, so this impressive Norse settlement couldn't have been the Norse "Vinland." It's believed the fossilized grapes found here originated farther south, perhaps in New Brunswick. Nonetheless, the current **L'Anse aux**

BOB RACE

reconstructed remains of the Viking village at L'Anse aux Meadows

**Meadows National Historic Site** was once a full-fledged Norse village serving as a sailing base for explorations throughout the area about A.D. 1000.

Long before archaeologists arrived, Newfoundlanders were aware of the odd-shaped, sod-covered ridges across the coastal plain. Newfoundland historian W. A. Munn speculated about the contents and origin decades ago. George Decker, a local fisherman, led Norwegian scholar-explorer Helge Ingstad and his wife, archaeologist Anne Stine Ingstad, to the area in the 1960s. The subsequent digs uncovered eight complexes of rudimentary houses, workshops with fireplaces, and a trove of artifacts, which verified the Norse presence. National recognition and site protection followed in 1968. More digs by Parks Canada archaeologists led to the site's designation as a national historic park in 1977. UNESCO named the settlement a world heritage site the following year.

A gravel path and boardwalk across the grassy plain lead to re-created buildings overlooking Epaves Bay. Here costumed interpreters reenact the roles and work of the Norse captain, his wife, and four crewmembers. Nearby, all that remains of the original settlement are depressions in the grass-covered field. You can see the artifacts, site models, and an audiovisual presentation at the Visitor Reception Centre on Highway 436, a half-hour's drive north of St. Anthony. The center is open mid-June to early September, daily 9 A.M.–8 P.M., then 9 A.M.–5 P.M. until mid-October. Admission is $5 adults, $4.25 seniors, $2.75 youths, $10 families. For more information, call 709/623-2608.

# CORNER BROOK

Called the hub of the province, Corner Brook is the western coast's commercial, educational, service, and governmental center. The area ranks as Newfoundland's second-largest city, combining the city of Corner Brook (pop. 24,000) with outlying settlements on the Humber Arm (another 20,000).

Fifty km inland from the Gulf of St. Lawrence, Corner Brook lies picturesquely cupped in a 20-square-km valley bowl, rimmed by the deepwater Humber Arm—one of three fjords that branch off the Bay of Islands. Farther inland beyond Corner Brook, the Humber Arm narrows to meet the Humber River, one of the province's finest fishing rivers.

The auspicious peaks of the Long Range Mountains rise around the city. To the southwest lie the 815-meter **Lewis Hills,** the island's highest mountains. At 472 meters, **Marble Mountain,** 10 minutes northeast, ranks as one of eastern Canada's finest ski mountains. And the barren orange-brown **Blow Me Down Mountains** are 35 minutes northwest on the gulf, commanding a stunning view of the Bay of Islands.

## History

The area was known to early French fishermen and explorers, but it was England's Captain James Cook who surveyed the bay and fjords in 1767 and named the Bay of Islands, River Hamberg (Humber), and Cook's Brook. Between 1771 and 1840, English Loyalist settlers founded Birchy Cove (Curling), Gillams, and Summerside. The area remained lightly settled through 1911, when a census counted 382 inhabitants.

Corner Brook, as a place-name, dates to 1864, when Gay Silver from Halifax started a sawmill operation on what is now the Corner Brook Stream. Meanwhile, the area became part of the new railroad's network in 1890, and Humbermouth served as the line's regional maintenance center. Curling on the Humber Arm emerged as the transportation link between the railroad and ships at the docks.

Silver sold his sawmill and land to Christopher Fisher in 1881. Fisher resold the vast tract to the Newfoundland Power and Paper Company, a British company that then built a pulp and paper mill on the site in 1923. Andrew Cobb, a Halifax architect, designed the Tudor-style Glynmill Inn as construction crew quarters, and the Townsite, the management families' residential area. The handsomely styled company town is now a heritage conservation district. Corner Brook East and Corner Brook West developed haphazardly through the years for the workers' families.

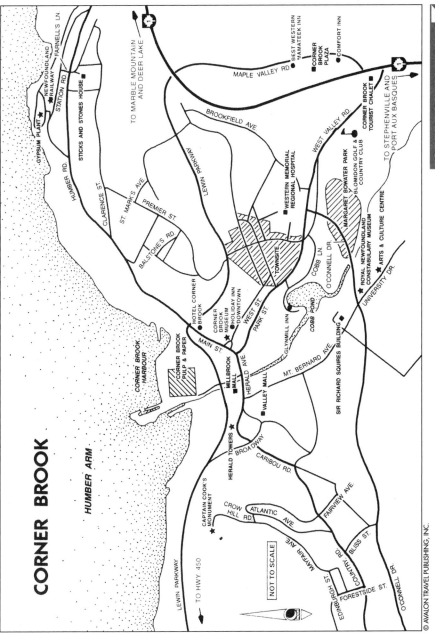

© AVALON TRAVEL PUBLISHING, INC.

In less than 10 years, the area's population jumped from 6,000 to 10,000. The British company sold the mill to International Power and Paper Company in 1928, who in turn sold the mill to the Bowater Company. Townsite, Curling, Corner Brook East, and Corner Brook West joined as the municipality of Corner Brook in 1956. Today, the city remains dependant on its pulp and paper operation, but is also a major provincial port and center for fish processing, as well as cement and gypsum production.

## Getting Oriented

Corner Brook lacks a central hub, so an uninitiated visitor may tend to wander. Locals say getting around is a breeze, but you may encounter some confusion at the TransCanada Highway, where the highway cuts a half-circle swath. Four roads peel off the highway in quick succession and lead into the city. The easiest access is West Valley Road. It leads directly into town past the historic Townsite—the prettiest residential area—and finishes at downtown West Street.

## Sights

Grab a city map from the information center and head straight for **Captain Cook's Monument** to get a feeling for the layout of the city. On the road to the monument, the traveler is rewarded with glorious views as far as the Bay of Islands. Follow O'Connell Drive across town, turn right (north) on Bliss Street, make another right on Country Road, turn left onto Atlantic Avenue with another left to Mayfair Street, and right to Crow Hill Road. The monument itself commemorates Cook's Bay of Islands explorations with a plaque and sample chart.

In the wide bowl containing downtown, West Valley Road roughly divides the city in half. Near the bottom end of this thoroughfare and overlooking Remembrance Square is **Corner Brook Museum,** 2 West St., tel. 709/634-2518, housed in a historic building that has served as a post office, courthouse, and customs house through the years. Displays center around the various local industries and their impact on the city's growth. The museum is open in summer, daily

10 A.M.–8 P.M., the rest of the year, Mon.–Fri. noon–5 P.M.

On land donated by the Bowater operation and named for the chairman's wife, the delightful grassy and wooded **Margaret Bowater Park** is pierced by a fast-flowing river and waterfall. Locals enjoy the walking trails, river swimming, supervised outdoor pool, and picnics on the pitched hillside beside O'Connell Drive off West Valley Road. At the **Royal Newfoundland Constabulary Museum,** tel. 709/634-4222, artifacts, uniforms, and photographs depict the Royal Newfoundland Constabulary's history in Corner Brook. It's open year-round, daily 9 A.M.–5 P.M. To get there, follow O'Connell Drive to University Drive and turn south; the brown-brick building on University Drive sits back from the corner.

Railroad buffs should head for the waterfront and an old-time narrow-gauge railroad assemblage with a gleaming locomotive and box, baggage, day, dining, and sleeping cars. Once part of the **Newfoundland Railway,** the train has been beautifully restored by the Railway Society of Newfoundland. The locomotive and cars lie on an old track beside the gypsum plant at the waterfront. To get there, take Humber Road to steep Farnell's Lane, turn left, then make another left on Station Road. Open June 15 through September 15. For a tour, call 709/634-6089.

## Accommodations

Budget-priced **Hotel Corner Brook,** on Main Street near Lewin Parkway, tel. 709/634-8211 or 800/738-8211, has 45 plainly furnished rooms ($55–70) and a restaurant and lounge in a downtown setting.

The **Best Western Mamateek Inn,** on Maple Valley Road, tel. 709/639-8901 or 800/563-8600, www.mamateekinn.com, is arguably the city's most attractive contemporary lodging and is conveniently located beside the TransCanada Highway. A *mamateek* is a Beothuk winter wigwam, and though this motel bears no resemblance, it's cozy with an accommodating, friendly staff. Fifty-five rooms ($69 single, $79 double) fan out from the stylish lobby, and the dining room has splendid views of the city nestled in the valley. Also just off the highway through town, the **Comfort Inn,** 41 Maple Valley Rd., tel. 709/639-1980 or 800/228-5150, www .comfortinn.com, offers 81 no-frills but comfortable rooms ($79–95) and a restaurant.

The lovely **Glynmill Inn** on quiet Cobb Lane, tel. 709/634-5181 or 800/563-4400, www .glynmillinn.ca, lies near the historic Townsite residential area. It's a charming inn banked with gardens of red geraniums. Rambling ivy, with leaves as large as maple leaves, covers the half-timber, Tudor-style exterior. The wide front steps lead to an open porch, and the English-style foyer is comfortably furnished with wing chairs and sofas. Between the reception desk and dining room there's a privately operated art gallery. The original inn of the 1920s had far fewer rooms, but a new wing brought the room count to 81 ($75–165). All the rooms are comfortably furnished, but the older ones feature old-time spaciousness and antique marble in the bathroom. The main-level restaurant has end windows overlooking the gardens, and room enough for the many tour groups that frequent

Glynmill Inn

the inn. However, the best restaurant is downstairs, appropriately named the Wine Cellar. It does full justice to tender, juicy beef from western Canada.

The **Holiday Inn Downtown,** 48 West St., tel. 709/634-5381 or 800/399-5381, www .holidayinncornerbrook.com, has a splendid location. With 103 rooms ($115 single, $120 double), the hotel boasts the city's best facilities: a restaurant and lounge, outdoor and indoor heated pools, spa facilities, a fitness room, barber and beauty shops, a launderette, and free underground parking.

Corner Brook offers a choice of bed-and-breakfast accommodations as well. The **Townsite Inn,** 15 East Valley Rd., tel. 709/634-7379, www.townsiteinn.com, is a renovated 1920s-era home within walking distance of Margaret Bowater Park. Four rooms with private baths, one featuring a whirlpool, start at $55. **Bell's Inn B&B,** 2 Fords Rd., tel. 709/634-5736 or 888/634-1150, offers eight nonsmoking rooms, each with private bath, in an attractive clapboard house with a large garden and play area. Rates range $56–96 and include full breakfast. Some rooms have whirlpool tubs.

Those planning on enjoying the Humber Valley's abundant recreational opportunities may wish to lodge closer to nature. Opposite Marble Mountain alpine resort, 12 km northeast of Corner Brook, **Marble Mountain Inn & Cabins,** tel. 709/634-2237, www.explorekayaking .com, offers 10 modern rooms in the main lodge and 18 cedar cabins and efficiency units tucked away in the trees. Many cabins have fireplaces, and all have kitchens. Amenities include a heated pool, a playground, canoe and kayak rentals, and a dock on the Humber River. Lodge rooms range $70–80, and cabins start at $79.

## Food

You'll find an adequate mix of fish, red meat, and provincial culinary specialties in Corner Brook, but locals favor beef—the rarer and thicker the better. Reservations are wise at all restaurants, especially during the mid-June to mid-September tourist season.

Don't miss Glynmill Inn's **Wine Cellar,** Cobb Lane, tel. 709/634-5181, a cozy setting in high demand (reservations are required). The restaurant boasts a fine wine list and serves some of the city's best unadorned beef. Entrées ($22–31) include grilled juicy filet mignon ($29) served in 12-ounce cuts. Upstairs, the **Carriage Room** specializes in Newfoundland fare ($12.50–20.50) with fried, poached, or broiled salmon, cod, halibut, and lobster.

**Thirteen West,** at 13 West St., tel. 709/634-1300, serves an outstanding array of entrées that reaches far beyond the typical Newfoundland dinner menu. This is the place to come for pasta ($11–17), including lemon pepper linguini with scallops, pasta primavera in a basil cream sauce, and curried salmon fettuccine. Filet mignon ($22.50), rack of lamb ($25.50), and stuffed breast of chicken ($15) also populate the menu. Reservations are recommended.

The Holiday Inn's **Newfoundland Meat and Beverage Company Restaurant,** 48 West St., tel. 709/634-5381, does a succulent Steak Napoleon (tender sirloin awash in a mushroom wine sauce, $16) and its barbecued chicken and ribs dish ($14) is temptingly browned, crispy, and spicy. Overall, the entrées range $12–19.50. The buffet lunch (Mon.–Fri. noon–2 P.M., $9) includes soup, salad, hot dishes, and dessert. Sunday brunch ($12) is similarly bountiful. The **Beothuk Dining Room** at the Best Western Mamateek Inn on Maple Valley Road, tel. 709/639-8901, offers tempting three-course table d'hôte meals for $16–24. For dessert, the berry and cream pies are light and flaky, and the cheesecakes with berry toppings are creamy and smooth.

For do-it-yourself meals and picnic fare, check out **Sobey's,** one of the town's largest supermarkets, at Valley Mall on Mt. Bernard Avenue. **More F or Less Food,** 9 Herald Ave. near Canadian Tire, tel. 709/634-1452, sells natural foods in bulk as well as Newfoundland specialties, such as Mt. Scio savory spice and Purity candy. **Back to Basics,** in the Corner Brook Plaza, tel. 709/634-2580, also stocks bulk natural foods and vitamins.

## Entertainment and Events

The **Majestic Theatre** on Church Street shows two films nightly. Call 709/634-6816 for the latest films. Inside the Millbrook Mall, each of the two theaters at **Millbrook Cinema,** tel. 709/634-6064, has two shows nightly. For a run-down on other performances in town, contact the **Arts and Culture Centre,** on University Drive next to the Newfoundland Constabulary, tel. 709/637-2582. The 400-seat performing arts hall hosts performances by Theatre Newfoundland Labrador touring symphonies and also features a visual arts gallery exhibiting local as well as touring exhibits.

Changing exhibits of contemporary Canadian artists can be viewed at the **Sir Wilfred Grenfell College Art Gallery** on University Drive, tel. 709/637-6209.

Another venue for events is the **Regional Civic Centre,** tel. 709/634-1999, which features two ice arenas, a fitness center, a restaurant, convention facilities, and a 4,800-seat concert hall.

## Summer Recreation

**Blomidon Golf and Country Club,** off West Valley Road beside the TransCanada Highway, tel. 709/634-5550, has a rolling 18-hole, par-70 course, a restaurant, and scenic city views. It's open from June to mid-October. The greens fee is $35; cart and club rentals are available.

At the **Arts and Culture Centre,** the heated indoor pool ($3 admission) is open daily. For details, call 709/637-2546. Sir Wilfred Grenfell College also has an indoor pool available to the public; call 709/637-6258. **Margaret Bowater Park** has an outdoor, supervised pool; open July to late August, daily noon–6 P.M.

There are plenty of hiking opportunities in the mountains surrounding the area. For a convenient, in-city hike, walk the **Corner Brook Stream Trail,** which cuts through the heart of the city along the Corner Brook Stream and visits Glynmill Inn Pond and Glynmill Inn Pond Marsh and continues upstream to Three Mile Dam. To the northeast of the city, the hike to **Steady Brook Falls** attracts summer visitors. Follow the signs to Marble Mountain and park in the back parking lot. A marked 15-minute trail to the left (rocky in parts) leads up the mountain, with views of the waterfalls. From there, a 3.5-km (one-way) unmarked trail continues and brings you nearer to the peak. The views of the Humber Valley and Bay of Islands are splendid.

## Marble Mountain

Right beside the TransCanada Highway, 12 km northeast of downtown Corner Brook, Marble Mountain is Atlantic Canada's largest and best-known alpine resort. Open December–April, it offers 27 runs (the longest is 3.6 km) and lifts including a high-speed quad. The mountain averages almost five meters of snow annually, with snow-making facilities for the lean times. Snowboarders enjoy a small terrain park and a half-pipe. The base area is dominated by a magnificent four-story, 6,400-square-meter day lodge, home to a ski and snowboard school, rental shop, café, restaurant, and bar. Lift tickets cost adults $30, seniors $25, children $15. For information, contact the resort at tel. 709/637-7600, www.skimarble.com.

## Shopping

Stores with a variety of wares line West Street and Broadway, the city's historic shopping district. General hours are Mon.–Sat. 9:30 A.M.–5 P.M., and Thurs.–Fri. until 9 P.M. Many shops have relocated to shopping centers such as the **Millbrook Mall** on Main Street; **Valley Mall,** a large shopping center at 1 Mt. Bernard Avenue; and **Corner Brook Plaza,** situated behind McDonald's on the TransCanada Highway. Sundays from 11 A.M. to 4 P.M., the Valley Mall is home to the west coast's largest flea market.

For traditional, local crafts, head to **Sora Fine Gifts and Crafts,** 54 Maple Valley Rd., tel. 709/634-8859, selling hand knits, quilts, jewelry, pottery, and pewter, or to **Newfoundland Emporium** 7 Broadway, tel. 709/634-9376, which stocks, among other things, whalebone and soapstone carvings, sealskin products, and parkas from Labrador, and also has a well-stocked book corner with provincial tomes. The **Corner Brook Tourist Chalet** on the TransCanada Highway features the **Nortique Fashions and Specialty Gift Shop,** tel. 709/634-8344, carrying handmade sweaters ($65–165), locally made

wares, music, and souvenirs. It's open Mon.–Fri. 8:30 A.M.–10 P.M. in summer and until 4:30 P.M. the rest of the year.

For local art, the **Ewing Gallery,** located in the Glynmill Inn's foyer, tel. 709/634-4577, showcases painting and original prints by western coast and provincial artists. It's open daily 11 A.M.–4 P.M. and 7–9 P.M. The **Franklyn Gallery,** 90 West St., tel. 709/639-7100, is another source for Canadian paintings, prints, and three-dimensional works.

**Alteen's Jewellers,** 74 Broadway, tel. 709/639-9286, features labradorite jewelry.

## Information

The **Corner Brook Tourist Chalet,** on the Trans-Canada Highway opposite the Comfort Inn, tel. 709/639-9792, stocks city and area literature and maps. The chalet is open Mon.–Fri. 8:30 A.M.–4:30 P.M. and from June to early September until 10 P.M. The **Corner Brook Chamber of Commerce,** tel. 709/634-5831, shares the same building and hours.

The **city library** in the Sir Richard Squires Building, the city's 10-floor high-rise on Mt. Bernard Avenue, tel. 709/634-0013, is open Tues.–Thurs. 10 A.M.–8:45 P.M., Fri. to 5:45 P.M.

Bookstores are sparse. **Coles Book Store,** tel. 709/634-4125, has a shop at the Valley Mall on Mt. Bernard Avenue. The **Family Bookstore** in the Corner Brook Plaza, tel. 709/639-9813, stocks Newfoundland books and tapes.

The daily *Western Star* newspaper covers the western coast.

## Services

The **Western Memorial Regional Hospital,** tel. 709/637-5000, is at 1 Brookfield Avenue. Other important emergency numbers include the **Royal Newfoundland Constabulary,** tel. 709/637-4100, and the **RCMP,** tel. 709/637-4433.

All major **banks,** such as the CIBC, Royal Bank, and Banks of Montréal and Nova Scotia, have branch offices in the city. **Bank of Nova Scotia** has offices at the Corner Brook Plaza on the TransCanada and in town on Broadway. It is open Mon.–Wed. 10 A.M.–3 P.M., Thurs.–Fri. to

5:30 P.M. There's no fee to change U.S. or U.K. currency or traveler's checks to Canadian dollars.

Canada Post is on Main Street near Park Street, tel. 709/637-8807. Hours are Mon.–Fri. 8 A.M.–5 P.M. (philatelic window: 8:30–11:30 A.M. and 1–5:15 P.M.). Canada Post retail outlets are at the Shoppers Drug Mart, 93 West St. and Millbrook Mall, and Allen's Foodland, 13 Killick Place.

Launderettes are scarce. The New-Lee Done Laundromat has coin-operated laundry facilities at 15 Fairview Avenue, open daily 10 A.M.–10 P.M.

### Transportation

Deer Lake Airport is the western coast's air hub and has service from across the province and from Halifax and Montréal. Located 45 minutes northeast of Corner Brook, the small airport has Avis, Budget, Thrifty, and National car rentals. Air Nova, Air Canada's affiliated carrier, flies in from Halifax and other provincial gateways. For details, call Air Canada at 888/247-2262.

The city has half a dozen cab companies whose cabs wait at lodgings, cruise business streets, and take calls. City Cabs, 4 Caribou Rd., tel. 709/634-6565, is among the largest outfits.

DRL Coachlines, tel. 709/738-8088, operates frequent bus service along the Trans-Canada Highway, with daily stops in Corner Brook (at Pike's Irving Station), Deer Lake, and Port aux Basques. Departures from St. John's at 8 A.M. arrive in Deer Lake at 5:15 P.M. For west coast bus travel, check out the Viking Express, tel. 709/634-4710. Buses depart from the Millbrook Mall and go north to Rocky Harbour ($11 one-way) and St. Anthony ($41 one-way) on Monday, Wednesday, and Friday and return to Corner Brook on Sunday, Tuesday, and Thursday.

## HIGHWAY 450 WEST FROM CORNER BROOK

This winding highway follows the south shore of Humber Arm for 50 km, ending beyond the fishing village of Lark Harbour at a picturesque protected cove.

### Blow Me Down Provincial Park

About an hour's drive northwest of the city, past a dozen or so Humber Arm fishing settlements, is Blow Me Down Provincial Park on the Bay of Islands' southwestern corner, tel. 709/681-2430. Incidentally, the park isn't extraordinarily windy, as the name might imply. Legend holds that a sea captain saw the mountain centuries ago and exclaimed, "Well, blow me down." The name stuck. Views of the bay, spread across 355 square km and speckled with islands, are worth the trip. You'll see the bay's fjord arms and the Lewis Hills, as well as bald eagles and ospreys gliding on the updrafts, and perhaps caribou and moose roaming the preserve's terrain. The remote park has 28 campsites ($11), pit toilets, a comfort station, a lookout tower, and hiking trails.

© ANDREW HEMPSTEAD

Highway 450 ends at aptly named Little Port.

# CORNER BROOK TO PORT AUX BASQUES

## Blue Ponds Park

A half hour on the TransCanada Highway southwest from Corner Brook, the park has two limestone lakes with crystalline, blue-green waters, hiking trails through the woodlands, and 61 unserviced campsites ($10); tel. 709/639-7740.

## Stephenville

With a population of more than 8,000, Stephenville is the business hub for the Bay St. George-Port au Port region. Once home to the U.S. Harmon Air Force Base, the town's airport now rivals Deer Lake Airport as the gateway to the west coast, with daily flights to the mainland and throughout Newfoundland with Air Nova.

Stephenville offers a selection of hotels and restaurants to travelers heading out onto the Port au Port Peninsula, including the **Holiday Inn,** 44 Queen St., tel. 709/643-6666 or 800/465-4329, with 47 rooms ($79–120) and a popular pub and eatery.

**Beavercraft,** 108 Main St., tel. 709/643-4844, is best known for Winterhouses sweaters ($120–175), designed locally and produced by 60 cottage-industry knitters. Top shops in St. John's also sell Winterhouses' knitwear.

The shop is also a source for thrummed mittens ($20–30) and caps. This revived traditional craft combines a knitted woolen facing backed with raw fleece. The shop shelves are stuffed with top-quality wares including Woof Design sweaters, Random Island Weaving cotton placemats, King's Point Pottery platters and bowls, and handmade birch brooms. Open Mon.–Sat. 9 A.M.–5:30 P.M., and Thurs.–Fri. until 9 P.M.

From mid-July to mid-August the **Stephenville Theatre Festival** presents original and Broadway-style productions at the Stephenville Arts and Culture Centre and other venues. Call 709/643-4982 for a schedule of events.

## Barachois Pond Provincial Park

One of the province's most popular preserves, Barachois Pond is popular with hikers for the 3.2-km trail through birch, spruce, and fir trees to Erin Mountain's barren summit. Be on the lookout for a rare Newfoundland pine marten along the way. The view at 305 meters overlooks the Port au Port Peninsula.

There's a commendable summertime interpretive program with guided walks and evening campfires, a lake for swimming and fishing, minigolf, and 150 unserviced campsites ($14), some situated atop the mountain. A $4 per vehicle park entry fee is charged. For more information, call 709/729-2429.

## Port aux Basques

Just over 900 km from its starting point in St. Johns, the TransCanada Highway reaches its western terminus at Port aux Basques, a town of about 5,000 with a deepwater port used by French, Basque, and Portuguese fishing fleets as early as the 1500s. Arriving in town from the north, the main highway continues two km to the ferry terminal, and a side road branches west, past hotels and fast food restaurants to the township proper. Here you'll find a cluster of commercial buildings along the harbor, including the **Gulf Museum,** around the south side of the harbor at 118 Main Street, tel. 709/695-7604. The highlights of this small museum are an astrolabe, a navigation aid dating to the early 1600s, and remnants from the SS *Caribou,* a ferry torpedoed by a German submarine as it crossed the Cabot Strait during World War II. It's open July–August, daily 10 A.M.–8 P.M. Admission is $2. Beyond the museum, turn left at the church and climb through a residential area to a lookout that affords 360-degree views of the town, open ocean, and ferry terminal.

At the turn-off to town are two hotels. **Hotel Port aux Basques** on Grand Bay Road, tel. 709/695-2171, offers 50 rooms ($69–89) and a restaurant and lounge. The nearby **St. Christopher's Hotel** on Caribou Road, tel. 709/695-7034 or 800/563-4779, www.stchrishootel.nf.net, has 52 rooms ($69–99). Its restaurant is well known for fresh and innovative seafood entrées.

If you're camping, your best choice is six km north of town at **J. T. Cheeseman Provincial**

**Park,** tel. 709/695-7222. Over 100 sites ($10) are spread along a picturesque stream. Facilities are limited, but the park is renowned as a nesting ground for the endangered piping plover.

Port aux Basques is the northern terminus of year-round ferry service from North Sydney, Nova Scotia. It's the shorter and least expensive of the two crossings to Newfoundland from North Sydney. One-way fares and rates for the five- to seven-hour sailing are adults $22, seniors $20,

children $11, vehicles from $67, reclining chairs $8 (only on some sailings), bunk beds $14, and cabins $37–125. Make reservations with **Marine Atlantic** at tel. 709/227-2431, 800/341-7981, or www.marine-atlantic.ca.

Housed in a distinctive pyramid-shaped building just north of the turn-off to town is a provincial **Visitor Information Centre,** tel. 709/695-2262, which opens in summer 9 A.M.–8 P.M. and for all ferry arrivals.

# Labrador

## Introduction

### THE LAND AND PEOPLE

Spanning 294,330 square km, two and a half times the size of Newfoundland island, Labrador dominates Atlantic Canada. Known as the Big Land, it covers more than twice the expanse of the Maritime Provinces. The region resembles an irregular wedge pointing toward the North Pole, bordered on the east by 8,000 km of coastline on the Labrador Sea, and on the west and south by the remote outskirts of Québec. Thorfinn Karlsefni, one of several Norse explorers who sailed the coastline around A.D. 1000, is said to have dubbed the region Helluland for the large flat rocks, and Markland for the woodlands. Jacques Cartier described the coastline as a "land of stone and rocks" during a 1534 voyage. The region once was Atlantic Canada's last frontier. But it's no longer isolated, having crossed the threshold from untamed wilderness into the modern world decades ago.

Spruce forests, interspersed with bogs and birch and tamarack stands, dominate the wilderness of southern Labrador. Along the Strait of Belle Isle, the narrow passage between Labrador and Newfoundland island, lie eight tiny ports within striking distance of Newfoundland's Great Northern Peninsula. This area was a Basque whaling center in the 1500s, and modern sightseers have rediscovered the strait and its archaeological treasures at Red Bay and L'Anse-Amour.

Highlights of the more remote southeastern coast include the Wunderstrands—a 56-km beach named by early Norse explorers—and the Gannet Islands Ecological Reserve. Both are located near Cartwright.

The watery complex of Lobstick Lake, Smallwood Reservoir, Michikamau Lake, and the Churchill River and its tributaries marks central Labrador. The Churchill flows out of the western saucer-shaped plateau and rushes eastward, widening into Lake Melville at Happy Valley–Goose Bay.

© ANDREW HEMPSTEAD

A Labrador boy watches an ocean-bound fishing boat.

The river meets the sea at Groswater Bay. Happy Valley–Goose Bay, now Labrador's second-largest town, began with tents and tarpaulins as the Goose Bay airbase civilian settlement. One of North America's prime military installations in World War II, the airbase was once a berry farm at the head of Lake Melville.

In western Labrador, iron-ore mining developed in the late 1950s. The twin cities of Labrador City and Wabush started as mining towns, and together they now serve as the region's economic and transportation center. With a population of 11,300, Labrador City/Wabush is Labrador's largest municipality. The air gateway to Labrador is based at Wabush Airport. Northeast of the twin cities, a massive hydroelectric plant, developed in the late 1960s, spawned another company town—Churchill Falls.

Heading north, the forests diminish in density and size until the tree line is reached. There barren, mountainous tundra continues north into a terrain of caribou moss (lichen), ferns, and stunted birch. The landscape is brightened with summertime's tiny purple rhododendron, poppies, heather, buttercups, and violets.

The northern coast evokes images of another world. It's the Labrador as you may imagine: raw and majestic with the craggy Torngat, Kaumajet, and Kiglapait mountain ranges rising to the north. The region is sparsely populated with Inuit communities, made up of people who came off the ice to live in small, coastal settlements decades ago. Moravian mission sightseeing is a splendid bonus. You'll also find centuries-old German-style buildings at Nain, Makkovik, and at the national historic sites in Hopedale and Hebron.

## LAYING CLAIM TO LABRADOR

For centuries the French Canadians have asserted, "Labrador is part of Québec." And the British and the Newfoundlanders have traditionally countered, "Never!"

Labrador is a choice piece of property, and Québec has been a longtime avid suitor of North America's northeastern edge. Québec's interest in Labrador dates to 1744, decades before the British vanquished the French at the Fortress of Louisbourg in Nova Scotia and on Québec City's Plains of Abraham. At that time, the French cut a deal with the British: Québec got jurisdiction over Labrador, but the island of Newfoundland got fishing rights in Labrador's coastal waters.

The Treaty of Paris of 1763 went one step further, however, and awarded all of Labrador (not defined by a precise border) to Newfoundland. Newfoundland's claim gained more substance in 1825, when the British North America Act set Labrador's southern border with Québec at the 52nd parallel. Little by little, England whittled away Québec's share of Labrador.

### Canadian Confederation

In the 1860s, Canadian nationalism emerged, as Nova Scotia, New Brunswick, Ontario, and Québec banded together to form the Dominion of Canada. Prince Edward Island joined the Confederation a few years later. The dispute over Labrador, formerly between France and England, now involved the new Confederation of Canada.

From England's point of view, its colonial possession included the island of Newfoundland *and* mainland Labrador. Québec did not dispute England's sovereignty over Labrador. It did, however, continue to question the location of the border. Canada, ever aware that Québec was a founding Confederation member, backed the French Canadians' land claims.

By 1898, Québec pushed the Labrador border far eastward to what is now the Happy Valley–Goose Bay area at the head of the Hamilton Inlet. In 1900, Newfoundland acquired 50-year timber rights and licensed a Nova Scotian outfit to build two sawmills and a lumberjacks' camp at Mud Lake just north of Happy Valley–Goose Bay. Six years later, Québec challenged the legality of the sawmill's location and surveyed the area.

### For Sale: Labrador

Labrador's precise border became a tedious issue for

## Climate

Labrador's climate is subject to great extremes. Summers are short, range from cool to sometimes hot, and are brilliantly sunny with periodic showers. Daytime highs in July can rise to 30° C at Happy Valley–Goose Bay. Temperatures drop rapidly after mid-August; by November, daytime highs at Goose Bay fall to 0° C.

Winters are very cold, with temperatures ranging from −10° C to −15° C. Snowfall is heavy, with an average of 481 cm in Churchill Falls and 424 cm in Nain. Snow blankets the ground for six months out of the year in the south and eight months in the far north.

Summertime, then, is the optimal season for traveling in Labrador. From July to August, the mean temperature is 13° C. August brings cooler temperatures. Rainfall averages for the summer season are generally 275 mm in the south and 175 mm in the north. Expect thunderstorms during July, and periodic fog on the coast. Summertime snow showers fall on the northern coast. Black flies and other biting insects are most numerous from July to early September.

Transportation in Labrador is conducted on a weather-permitting basis. Early-season ice packs and late-season storms can delay the ferries. The region's smaller aircraft need daylight and good visibility for flights. An absence of both may ground flights for days. Therefore, it's wise to add a few extra days at both ends of your itinerary and bring extra money, in case your plans are held up.

## The Thinly Settled Region

Labrador (pop. 31,100) is sparsely settled. A

England. Newfoundland put Labrador up for sale. The land was first offered to Canada at $9 million in 1909. Canada ducked. Labrador went on the market again for $110 million in 1932. Again, Canada passed.

By 1927, the Mud Lake sawmill operation was bankrupt, and the border issue was still unresolved. It came before the Privy Council's Judicial Committee in London. In a sweeping decision, the committee set Labrador's western border far west of Mud Lake at the "height of the land," the watershed line separating the Atlantic Ocean from Ungava Bay. It now marks the boundary between Labrador and Québec Province. In the decision, Labrador acquired the wedge-shaped "Labrador Trough," a delta area rich in iron ore deposits and hydroelectric power.

### Québec's Clout Emerges

By the 1970s, Québec became a major player in Labrador's economy. Ironically, Québec bought into Labrador's hydroelectric fortune during the reign of Newfoundland premier Joey Smallwood, who led the move to Confederation in the 1940s and advocated industrialization as an edge against the capricious fisheries. Based on his belief that hydroelectric power would bring in a modest financial return, Smallwood convinced the French Canadians to join in a development project. The potential wealth of the province's latent hydroelectric resources had been explored during the 1960s, and the Labrador Hydro Electric Company at Churchill Falls was formed by 1974.

As oil prices shot up in the mid-1970s, hydroelectric power became the cheaper energy alternative. Québec Province's Hydro-Québec, the project's largest shareholder, now earns $200 million annually, while Newfoundland, another company shareholder, earns $12 million. But the island receives none of the energy. In the late 1970s, Newfoundland considered a tunnel beneath the Strait of Belle Isle to transmit power. Costs, at $30–40 million, were considered prohibitive.

The western border remains to be fully surveyed, and Québec does not consider the issue settled. A fragile status quo exists between the two provinces, but the renaming of Newfoundland to Newfoundland and Labrador in 2001 brought official recognition to Labrador as part of Newfoundland.

small population of Innu inhabit Davis Inlet and Sheshatsheits, while coastal settlements north of the Hamilton Inlet are mostly Inuit communities. The rest of the inhabitants—descendants of European settlers and others from Newfoundland and southern Canada—populate the coastal and inland areas or are scattered in the larger regional towns and settlements.

Almost 70 small outports and settlements span the coastline's sheltered coves and harbors, while Labrador's larger commercial towns—Happy Valley–Goose Bay, Churchill Falls, Wabush, and Labrador City—lie inland across the midsection.

## HISTORY

### Indigenous Peoples

The Maritime Archaic people arrived in Labrador about 9,000 years ago, camping near the large rivers and hunting seals and walrus during the summer. Their domain included the strait coast. An archaeological dig at L'Anse-Amour uncovered a burial site of a 12-year-old child dating from 7500 B.C. The Maritime Archaic people eventually crossed the Strait of Belle Isle into Newfoundland, but they vanished from both Newfoundland and Labrador about 3,000 years ago.

About that time, an aboriginal group known to archaeologists as the Intermediate or Recent people began to populate the Labrador Straits. Little is known about them, but some speculate that they were the ancestors of the present-day Innu.

Other cultures moved into the area, including the Dorset Eskimos. The earliest Inuit presence in the region dates to about 700 years ago, when the Thule people—the ancestors of the Inuit—migrated into Labrador.

### Early Europeans

Basque whalers created the world's largest whaling port at Red Bay in the early 1500s and lived on nearby Saddle Island, where the whaling stations' red roof tiles still litter the beaches. Historians estimate that between 1550 and 1600, these whalers extracted some 500,000 gallons of oil annually from harpooned right and bowhead whales.

England's interest in Labrador began in the 16th century. Stories of the riches of the Orient fueled the search for a Northwest Passage, and the king sent John Davis to discover the route. The mission failed, but the navigator accidentally sailed into Davis Inlet on his second voyage in 1586 and returned to England with reports of seas teeming with cod, and black bears roaming the woodlands.

In 1668, King Charles II chartered the Hudson's Bay Company and charged the merchants with developing Labrador trade. Captain James Cook surveyed the coastline a century later. After the mid-1700s, pioneer merchants built coastal trading posts and an English fishing firm established the strait's largest fishing stations at L'Anse au Loup.

The French staked claim to Labrador in 1702, granting to nobleman Augustin de Courtemanche all the land from the Gulf of St. Lawrence to Hamilton Inlet. Trading posts followed at L'Anse-au-Clair, Forteau, West St. Modeste, and L'Anse-au-Loup on the strait. The merchant Louis Fornel solidified France's coastal control by garnering posts at Cape Charles, Davis Inlet, and Rigolet from 1743 to 1747.

Nonetheless, settlement was slow. Although the Treaty of Paris in 1763 ceded the Labrador coastline to Britain's Newfoundland colony, Newfoundlanders and Anglo immigrants didn't start settling the strait until the 1830s. The imprint of European architecture only reached the northern seacoast when the Moravians, an evangelical Protestant sect from Bohemia, established mission stations with prefabricated wooden buildings at Hopedale, Nain, Hebron, and other sites during the mid-18th and early 19th centuries.

### Into the Twentieth Century

The economy slipped into a depression as codfish and fur prices dropped during World War I. The Moravian mission stores were absorbed by the Hudson's Bay Company, which eventually closed all hinterlands outlets except Rigolet, Cartwright, and North West River. An epidemic of Spanish flu—introduced from a supply ship—decimated a third of the indigenous population on the northern coast. The Inuit who survived resettled at Nain in 1918.

BOB RACE

During World War II, central Labrador thrived. The Canadian forces selected the Goose Bay site and, with assistance from the British Air Ministry and the U.S. Air Force, built a massive airbase and two airstrips there. Before the war ended, 24,000 aircraft set down for refueling during the transatlantic crossing. After the war, the United States used the base for its Northeast Air Command, followed by the Strategic Air Command in the 1950s. Currently operated by the Canadian Armed Forces, Goose Bay Airport serves as central Labrador's commercial air gateway and as a low-level flight-training center for British, Dutch, and German air forces.

During the 1940s and 1950s, tuberculosis was rampant among the Innu. Medical authorities ordered almost one-fifth of the Innu population into sanatoriums far from their northern domain. Never having been away from the North, the Innu suffered a severe sense of disorientation. Eventually, the Innu were moved away from their nomadic life in order to "benefit" from Canada's social welfare system of health care, education, and housing.

### The Western Boom

Industrial western Labrador is booming. Labradorians knew of the area's iron-ore potential in the late 1800s, and massive ore deposits were discovered in 1958. The Iron Ore Company of Canada and Wabush Mines, both near the twin cities of Labrador City and Wabush, together rank as the Canadian steel industry's largest supplier. The two extract 20 million metric tons of iron ore a year. At Churchill Falls, the 5,225-megawatt hydroelectric plant ranks as one of the western hemisphere's largest single-site operations. The northern seacoast has shared western Labrador's industrial prominence since the discovery of uranium at Makkovik in 1973.

## RECREATION

Many visitors to Labrador are anglers and hunters, who rank the sportfishing and trophy-

northern pike

size wildlife hunting here among the world's best. The fishing is said to be Atlantic Canada's finest: it's not uncommon to land an *ouananiche* (landlocked salmon) weighing four kilograms. Brook trout here range 3–4 kg, lake trout to 18 kg, northern pike 9–14 kg, and arctic char 5–7 kg. Wild game includes caribou, moose, black bear, ruffled and spruce grouse, ptarmigan, ducks, and rabbit.

Naturalists and adventure travelers make up a new breed of visitors. Travelers interested in other cultures visit the indigenous peoples' settlements, while sports enthusiasts enjoy wilderness rafting, kayaking, canoeing, rock climbing, hiking, backpacking, and camping.

### Outfitters

Many outfitters catering to sportfishers and hunters are based in Happy Valley–Goose Bay. An outfitter is a requirement for any nonresident fishing beyond 800 meters of a provincial highway, and for all nonresident big-game hunters.

Outfitters are licensed, and their wilderness lodgings are inspected by the province. An all-inclusive week's package has the highest price and usually includes license fees, lodgings, meals, a guide, and fly-in transportation from Goose Bay. One such place is **Rifflin' Hitch Lodge,** a 50-minute flight southeast from Goose Bay, tel. 709/634-2000 or 877/433-5461, www.rifflinhitchlodge.nf.ca. Located on the Eagle River, one of the richest Atlantic salmon rivers in North America, the lodge supplies anglers with some of the world's best fishing and all the comforts of home. Guests enjoy luxuries such as gourmet meals and a hot tub, comfortable private rooms, and fishing from the shore or boats at a ratio of one guide to every two guests. The seven-night all-inclusive package, including transfers from Goose Bay, costs US$4,400.

The *Newfoundland and Labrador Hunting and Fishing Guide,* available from the provincial tourist office, tel. 709/729-2830 or 800/563-6353, www.gov.nf.ca/tourism, lists outfitter packages and provincial regulations.

## Tours

**Labrador Scenic Ltd.,** tel. 709/497-8326, specializes in tours to Labrador's central and northern wilderness areas, with an emphasis on wildlife and Innu and Inuit history and culture. Expect to pay $200–300 a day for all-inclusive arrangements, with travel by boat, air, or snowmobile.

**Atsanik Lodge,** tel. 709/922-2910, offers weeklong boat trips to Hebron and trips for hikers and climbers to the mountains of northern Labrador. **True North Outfitting Co.,** tel. 709/896-4292, leads snowmobile trips into Labrador's interior from its base at Happy Valley–Goose Bay, as well as canoeing, kayaking, and hiking excursions.

For other sports ideas and outfitters, see the provincial tourism guide. Finally, if you plan any kind of independent excursion or camping trip, register your itinerary with the RCMP; Labrador's wilderness is beautiful, but it's easy to become disoriented in the vast spaces.

# TRANSPORTATION

## By Air

**Air Nova,** tel. 888/247-2262, www.aircanada.ca, flies daily between St. Johns and Goose Bay and from St. Johns and Québec City to Wabush. **Provincial Airlines,** tel. 709/576-1666 or 800/563-2800, www.provair.com, connects St. John's with Goose Bay and Blanc Sablon, Québec's gateway to Labrador's Strait of Belle Isle settlements. **Air Labrador,** tel. 709/753-5593 or 800/563-3042, www.airlabrador.com, flies throughout Labrador, including between Goose Bay and remote settlements on the northern and southern coastline.

## By Land

The 520-km TransLabrador Highway (Highway 500) crosses the region from Labrador City, Wabush, and Churchill Falls to Happy Valley–Goose Bay with a western Labrador extension (Highway 501 or the Esker Road) to Esker; for road conditions and weather updates, contact the **Department of Works, Services, and Transportation** at 709/896-7888, www.gov.nf.ca/wsf/roads. The communities of Labrador Straits are linked by Highway 510 from Blanc Sablon, where ferries land from Newfoundland. This highway currently extends as far north as Mary's Harbour, with a planned extension to Cartwright scheduled for completion in 2004.

In western Labrador, the **Québec, North Shore, and Labrador Railway,** tel. 709/944-8205, departs three times a week from Labrador City to Sept-Îles.

## By Sea

The **M/V *Sir Robert Bond*** ferry runs between Lewisporte, Newfoundland, and Goose Bay. The 38-hour trip costs adults $97, seniors $87.25, children $48.50, vehicles $160. From St. Barbe, Newfoundland, another service links the communities of Labrador Straits to the outside world from early May to early January, once or twice daily. One-way fares for the 90-minute crossing are adults $9, seniors $7.50, children $4.75, vehicles $18.50.

The **M/V *Northern Ranger*** is a cargo and passenger ferry that runs between St. Anthony (Newfoundland) and Nain on a continuous 12-day round-trip routing, stopping at 48 remote communities along the way to load and unload goods. Passenger space is limited, and vehicles are not accepted. Fares are calculated on distance traveled rather than destination. St. Anthony to Nain, for example, is 1,038 nautical miles, equal to $233.55 one way. Cabins are available.

For more information or to make reservations on any of the above ferries, call 800/563-6353 or check the website www.gov.nf.ca/ferryservices.

# South and Central Labrador

## HAPPY VALLEY–GOOSE BAY AND VICINITY

Happy Valley–Goose Bay (pop. 7,500) spreads across a sandy peninsula bordered by the Churchill River, Goose Bay, and Terrington Basin at the head of Lake Melville. The city is 210 km inland from the Labrador Sea, and serves as the region's administrative, service, and transportation center. The town garnered this role thanks to both its prominence as a military airbase and the area's accessibility. The town is situated on a fog-free plateau allowing dependable air service, and its location at the head of Hamilton Inlet provides easy access for the Newfoundland coastal ferries.

Before the war, the area had a few small settlements, such as Kenemich, Mulligan, and Otter Creek. Robert Michelin, owner of Uncle Bob's Berry Patch, sold the land for the airbase and later supplied cream, eggs, and salmon to the installation's messes. The town evolved as two distinct areas: Goose Bay, rimming the base; and adjacent Happy Valley, which became the base's residential and commercial sector. In 1961, the two areas joined as Happy Valley–Goose Bay and elected the first town council, which was Labrador's first municipal government.

The distinction between the two areas remains firm, so be prepared to consult a map as you wander around. Goose Bay connects to Happy Valley by the L-shaped Hamilton River Road, the main drag. Loring Drive, the base's access road, feeds off Hamilton River Road and is another orientation point. You're never far from either road.

Shops, restaurants, sightseeing, and lodging are sprinkled liberally on or near the two main streets.

**North West River,** a settlement founded by fur traders, and adjacent **Sheshatsheits,** an Innu community, lie 38 km northeast and are considered the town's suburbs. Illustrious **Mud Lake,** site of the contentious lumber operation in the border dispute between Newfoundland and Québec, lies directly east across the Churchill River; to get there, follow Hamilton River Road east through Happy Valley to the river and ask around for a boat ($5–10) to take you across.

### Town Sights

The white clapboard **Labrador Heritage Museum** at the corner of Hamilton River Road and Halifax Street on the former airbase, tel. 709/497-8858, provides rare insights into Labrador's early years with photographs, manuscripts, books, artifacts, furs, native minerals, and other displays. It's open July–August, Mon.–Fri. 9 A.M.–5 P.M.; admission is $1.

In the **Northern Lights Building** at 170 Hamilton River Road, the **Northern Lights Military Museum,** tel. 709/896-5939, offers exhibits pertaining to military history from World War I to the Vietnam War. Displays include uniforms, medals, documents, weapons, and photographs. Across the hall, the **Trapper's Brook Animal Display** exhibits stuffed native animals and birds—from beavers and bears to bald eagles. Also in the building is the **Labrador Institute,** tel. 709/896-6210, with various craft displays and an archive of maps and photographs. All of the above are open summer Mon.–Sat. 9 A.M.–5:30 P.M.; Tues.–Sat. the rest of the year.

### North West River

This community of 500, 38 km northeast of Goose Bay on Highway 520, was the center of the area until the 1940s. The settlement began as a French trading post in 1743, and the inhabitants are descendants of

caribou

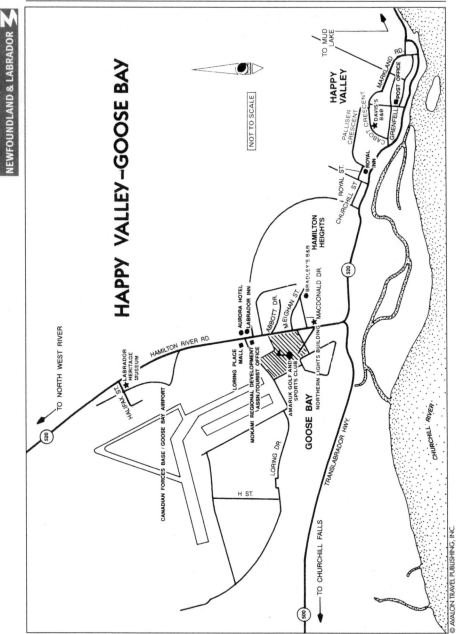

HAPPY VALLEY–GOOSE BAY

NOT TO SCALE

French, British, and Scottish settlers. The highlight of a visit is the **Labrador Interpretation Centre,** tel. 709/497-8566, filled with interesting exhibits that catalogue the natural and human history of "the Big Land." The center is open in summer, Tues.–Sun. 1–4 P.M. The road along the waterfront leads to piers and pleasant views. If you'd like to meet some of the locals, arrive in late afternoon, when the Innu fishers collect the day's catch from nets strung across the waterway.

## Accommodations

Bed-and-breakfasts offer the least-expensive lodgings. **Davis's Bed and Breakfast,** 14 Cabot Crescent in Happy Valley, tel. 709/896-5077, has four guest rooms with private baths ($40–50 single, $50–60 double). Rates include a continental breakfast (a full breakfast costs extra). Facilities include a dining room, laundry, and outside patio. The B&B is open year-round. **Bradley's Bed and Breakfast,** 13 MacKenzie Dr., Hamilton Heights, tel. 709/896-8006, offers three rooms ($40–60 with a cooked breakfast), a picnic area, and laundry facilities.

Happy Valley–Goose Bay has several motels. The **Royal Inn,** 3 Royal Ave., Goose Bay, tel. 709/896-2456 or 888/440-2456, has 18 rooms, a picnic area, a deck with barbecue facilities, and basic to deluxe housekeeping suites. Rates range $63–95 and include continental breakfast; open year-round.

The town's two other motels are situated side by side on Hamilton River Road opposite Loring Drive, the airport's access road. The **Labrador Inn,** 380 Hamilton River Rd., tel. 709/896-3351 or 800/563-2763, www.labradorinn.nf.ca, has 74 basic to deluxe rooms ($75–100), a suite ($150), a restaurant, a lounge, and airport shuttles. The **Aurora Hotel,** 382 Hamilton River Rd., tel. 709/896-3398 or 800/563-3066, www .aurorahotel.com, is smaller, with 40 rooms ($86 single, $98 double), a restaurant, and a lounge.

## Food

Fast-food places line Hamilton River Road, including the ubiquitous and ever-popular **Tim Hortons,** 220 Hamilton River Rd., tel.

709/896-5666. Further down the hill, the **Daybreak Café,** 178 Hamilton River Rd., tel. 709/896-0936, serves up hearty breakfasts and healthy lunches daily.

Hungry locals who love beef head for **Tricia Dee's Steak and Rib Dining Room,** 96 Hamilton River Rd., tel. 709/896-3545, where diners enjoy prime beef from western Canada and barbecued ribs. All manner of steak cuts are also prepared anyway you'd like. For a homemade dessert, try the dark, rich black forest cake ($5) or fruit or cream pies.

The casual **Caribou Restaurant,** in the Aurora Hotel at 382 Hamilton River Road, tel. 709/896-3398, features a menu of typical Canadian dishes, as well as a few local specialties like lunchtime moose and caribou burgers ($7); dinner mains range a reasonable $13–22. The **Naskaupi Dining Room,** next door in the Labrador Inn, 380 Hamilton River Rd., tel. 709/896-3351, is slightly more formal, with linen tablecloths laid out in the evening. The menu features lots of Labrador cuisine and pasta dishes, New York sirloin, T-bone steaks, and pork chops—all in the $14–26 range.

Also in the inn, the **FlightDeck Pub** offers basic pub grub.

The **Terrington Co-op,** ensconced in a brown building on Abbott Drive in Goose Bay's Hamilton Heights, is the town's largest grocery. It has a deli, canned goods, and fresh meat and produce; open Mon., Tues., and Sat. 9 A.M.–6 P.M., Wed.–Fri. until 9 P.M. **Pleasant Grocery,** 132 Hamilton River Rd. in Goose Bay, has longer hours (daily 10 A.M.–11 P.M.).

## Golf

At the **Amaruk Golf and Sports Club,** alongside Hamilton River Road, tel. 709/896-2112, local golfers play the 3,122-yard, nine-hole course as soon as the snow's off the ground, usually mid-May or early June. The greens fee is $20 weekdays, $25 weekends. Club rental costs $6.50. Motorized carts rent for $25. A pull cart rents for $5.

## Entertainment and Events

Head to the **FlightDeck Pub** at the Labrador

Inn, 380 Hamilton River Rd., tel. 709/896-3351, for occasional live entertainment and a wide choice of beers on tap. The interior is filled with aviation memorabilia, worth a look in itself. **Trapper's Cabin Bar and Grill,** on Aspen Road near Hamilton River Road and Loring Drive, tel. 709/896-9522, regularly has live bands and other music Wed.–Sun. You'll pay a cover charge. The **Sand Bar** at Amaruk Golf and Sports Club, tel. 709/896-8839, features local guitarists and other musicians, Sun. 2–5 P.M.

In March the town stages its **Winter Carnival,** with outdoor and indoor activities including snow-sculpting, ice-fishing, tobogganing, dances, and a parade. The last weekend of July, **North West River Beach Festival** is a big weekend bash with food, boat rides, square dances, crafts, and contemporary and traditional provincial and Innu music set on the beach at North West River. The first weekend in August, Happy Valley–Goose Bay hosts the three-day **Labrador Canoe Regatta** on Gosling Lake, with voyageur canoe racing, music, and traditional food. For details and exact dates, call 709/497-8506.

## Services

**Melville Hospital** (also called Grenfell Hospital), is located at Building 550, G Street (near Fifth Avenue). The **RCMP** is at 149 Hamilton River Road, tel. 709/896-3383.

**Bank of Nova Scotia** and **Royal Bank** have branches in town; Royal Bank has an office at 36 Grenfell Street, Happy Valley, and at the airport's Building 381 (the Canex Building) near the terminal. All are open Mon.–Fri. 9 A.M.–5 P.M.

**Canada Post** has branches on Hamilton River Road near the Aurora Hotel, tel. 709/896-2771, and on the base, tel. 709/896-2261. It's open Mon.–Fri. 9 A.M.–5:15 P.M.

**Sheppard's Laundry and Dry Cleaning** at 17 Aspen Road has coin-operated washers and dryers; open Mon.–Fri. 9 A.M.–6 P.M., Sat. 10 A.M.–4 P.M. **March's Laundry and Cleaners,** next to El Greco, is another option.

## Transportation

Air Canada's affiliated airline, **Air Nova,** tel. 800/247-2262, flies to Goose Bay from Hali-

fax, Toronto, and Montreal, with all flights routed through St. Johns. **Air Labrador,** tel. 709/896-6777 or 800/563-3042, serves as a regional carrier, with service to a dozen remote settlements on Labrador's coastline as well as St. Anthony, Deer Lake, and St. John's. **Provincial Airlines,** tel. 709/576-1666 or 800/563-2800, has flights from St. John's and Blanc Sablon. The **Goose Bay Airport** has an easy-in, easy-out terminal open 24 hours a day, with car rentals, a coffee shop/lounge, and a gift shop. Taxis meet incoming flights.

The town is served by the provincially operated vehicular ferry from Lewisporte, Newfoundland, once weekly. The one-way fare is adults $97, seniors $87.25, children $48.50, vehicles $160. For more information or to make reservations on any of the above ferries, call 800/563-6353 or check the website www.gov.nf.ca/ferryservices.

**Budget,** tel. 709/896-2973, and **National,** tel. 709/896-5575, have rental cars in town, but don't allow their vehicles on the TransLabrador Highway. **Deluxe Cabs,** tel. 709/896-2424, charges around $5 per trip anywhere within Goose Bay, and $10 between the airport and Happy Valley.

# LABRADOR WEST
## Churchill Falls

Churchill Falls, located 288 km west of Happy Valley, is a relatively modern town with few attractions. The waters of the Churchill River drop more than 300 meters over a 32-km section—ideal for one of the world's largest hydroelectric generators. In an incredible feat of engineering, the water is diverted underground to the massive generators, which produce 5,428 megawatts of electricity. Organized tours of the facility (around two hours) can be arranged at the town office, tel. 709/925-3335.

**Churchill Falls Inn,** tel. 709/925-3211 or 800/229-3269, is a modern lodging attached to the main town office complex. Rooms cost $82 single, $92 double.

## Labrador City/Wabush

West of Churchill Falls, the twin mining towns of

Labrador City and Wabush—just 23 km from the Québec-Labrador border—process the diggings from North America's largest open-pit iron-ore mine. The towns, five km apart, are surrounded by rolling hills and abundant lakes.

This area also attracts cross-country skiers to the **Menihek Nordic Ski Club** on Smokey Mountain Road, tel. 709/944-5842. The club has twice hosted World Cup events. The facility features more than 30 km of groomed trails, with 3 km lighted for night skiing. It's open mid-November through April.

Labrador City/Wabush's limited accommodations include three hotels. **Two Seasons Inn,** Avalon Drive, tel. 709/944-2661 or 800/670-7667, www.twoseasoninn.nf.ca, offers 37 rooms ($89), airport shuttle service, a restaurant, and all the amenities of a big-city hotel. It's open year-round.

The **Wabush Hotel,** 9 Grenfell Drive, tel. 709/282-3221, also operates year-round. It features a Chinese/Canadian buffet lunch and dinner in its restaurant and a convenience store. The 65 standard rooms go for $84 single, $90 double; suites run from $110. The **Carol Inn,** 215 Drake Ave., tel. 709/944-7736 or 888/799-7736, has 20 rooms ($87 single, $92 double), as well as a dining room, lounge, and playground.

Labrador City has two nearby camping areas. **Duley Lake Family Park,** 10 km west of Labrador City, tel. 709/282-3660, has a 100-site campground ($8 per night), a sandy swimming beach, and boating, fishing, and picnicking. **Grande Hermine Park,** tel. 709/282-5369, is 33 km from the city. It offers 45 semiserviced and 30 unserviced sites from $12 per night. Facilities include a boat launch, a convenience store, and paddle boat rentals.

Each March the twin towns swell with participants and spectators for the **Labrador 120 Sled Dog Race.** While 20 or so sled-dog teams compete in the grueling, 120-mile race, spectators can enjoy a variety of Winterfest activities. For more details, call 709/944-5949. For tamer pursuits, the 18-hole **Tamarack Golf Course,** tel. 709/944-3007, features well-maintained greens and a tight, tree-lined layout. Green fees are $20, with club and cart rentals available.

# LABRADOR STRAITS

The communities of Labrador Straits lie across the Strait of Belle Isle from Newfoundland. They are linked by a 160-km stretch of road that extends between Blanc Sablon (Québec) and Mary's Harbour. The northern limit of this highway, between Red Bay and Mary's Harbour, opened in 2000. Constuction continues, and the highway is scheduled to reach Cartwright in 2004 and eventually join with the TransLabrador Highway.

The **M.V. *Apollo*** ferry from St. Barbe, Newfoundland, to Blanc Sablon, tel. 800/563-6353, www.gov.nf.ca/ferryservices, operates between early May and early January, when shifting sea ice begins moving through the strait. The crossing takes 90 minutes. On board is a café and a craft shop. The one-way fare is adults $9, seniors $7.50, children $4.75, vehicles $18.50, RVs or campers from $40.

## History

In 1973, archaeologists uncovered a Maritime Archaic burial site at L'Anse-Amour, which contains artifacts dating back nearly 8,000 years. The aboriginal caribou hunters who lived here among retreating glaciers left only a few primitive campsites and ancient gravesites. In contrast, the Basque whalers of the 16th century left behind plenty of evidence of their whaling port along the strait, much of which can be seen in Red Bay. L'Anse-au-Loup, Capstan Island, Forteau, and West St. Modeste were once seasonally inhabited by fisherfolk from Newfoundland, England, and the island of Jersey.

## L'Anse-au-Clair

Founded in the early 18th century by French sealers, L'Anse-au-Clair is the closest strait community to the Québec border. Fishing is still the livelihood for the outport's population of about 300, although crafts also contribute to its economy. The **Gateway Visitor Centre,** tel. 709/931-2360, the region's interpretive center, is located in a handsomely restored, early 20th-century Anglican church. Inside are exhibits, photographs, and artifacts representing the area's fishing heritage.

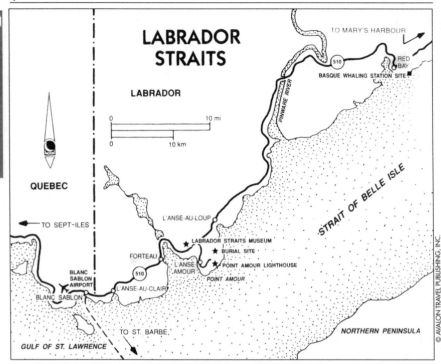

Local crafts can be found at **Moore's Handicrafts,** 8 Country Rd., tel. 709/931-2022, including hand-knit woolens, winter coats, cassocks, and moccasins. The shop is open daily 8:30 A.M.–10 P.M.

The largest accommodation along the Labrador Straits is the **Northern Light Inn,** 58 Main St., tel. 709/931-2332 or 800/563-3188, with 54 rooms ($75 single, $85 double), 10 RV sites with hookups ($15), a gift shop, an indoor pool, a laundry, and a restaurant. Open 7 A.M.–10 P.M., the restaurant is renowned for its traditional Labrador and Basque cuisine, including a great seafood platter and delicious bakeapple jam.

## Forteau

Established as a cod-fishing settlement by islanders from Jersey and Guernsey in the late 1700s, Forteau remains a fishing community,

not only in the cod industry but also as a base for anglers fishing the salmon- and trout-filled Forteau and Pinware Rivers.

Forteau's accommodations include the **Grenfell Louie A. Hall Bed and Breakfast,** tel. 709/931-2916, located at 3 Willow Avenue in the old Forteau Nursing Station built by the International Grenfell Association. Five rooms ($45 single, $55 double) and a dining room are complemented by antiques, artifacts, crafts, and reading materials and videos on the area's history. The **Seaview Restaurant and Cabins,** 33 Main St., tel. 709/931-2840, offers eight cabins ($65) and dining.

The **Labrador Straits Bakeapple Folk Festival,** held over three days in mid-August, is always popular. The gathering includes traditional music, dance, storytelling, crafts, and Labrador foods. Call 709/931-2545 for details.

## L'Anse-Amour and Vicinity

This tiny community was originally named Anse aux Morts ("cove of the dead") for the many shipwrecks that occurred in the treacherous waters offshore. A mistranslation by later English settlers resulted quite charmingly in the name L'Anse Amour ("cove of love").

After leaving L'Anse Amour, turn off the main road past English Point and head toward the peninsula coastline. The Maritime Archaic people were the first known humans in the area. A cairn and national historic plaque mark the **Maritime Archaic Burial Mound National Historic Site,** the New World's earliest known burial site. A 12-year-old native boy was buried here about 6900 B.C. Evidence shows that a ceremonial feast took place at the burial. A trail with interpretive markers rings the site; the artifacts found here are on display at the Newfoundland Museum in St. John's.

Nearby is the **Point Amour Lighthouse Provincial Historic Site,** tel. 709/927-5825. The strait's rich sea has attracted intrepid fishing fleets

Communities along the Labrador Straits cling tenuously to the coastline.

through the centuries: the early Basques sailed galleons into Red Bay, followed by English and French fleets, and eventually Newfoundlanders arrived in schooners to these shores. By 1857, shipwrecks littered the treacherous shoals, and the colonial government erected this 33-meter-high beacon, Atlantic Canada's tallest. Now restored, the lighthouse and lightkeeper's residence (now the interpretive center) features displays and exhibits on the history of those who have plied the strait's waters. The 122-step climb to the top (the final section is a ladder) affords excellent views of the strait and the surrounding land. It's open in summer, daily 10 A.M.–5:30 P.M.

## Red Bay

Back on Highway 510, Red Bay is reached after a further 40 km drive north. Between 1540 and 1610, the bay was the site of five whaling stations operated by an estimated 1,900 Basques. At **Red Bay National Historic Site,** you will likely see Memorial University archaeologists scouring the rocky coastline for artifacts, and Parks Canada divers surfacing in the cold waters. Parks Canada discovered the Spanish galleon *San Juan,* the oldest shipwreck north of the Caribbean, perfectly preserved here in the bone-chilling sea. Smaller whaling boats, called *chalupas,* have subsequently been recovered, and at least two more whaling ships await excavation.

**Red Bay Visitor Centre,** tel. 709/920-2051, displays a multitude of artifacts found at the site, including clothing, tools, glassware, ceramics, and harpoons. An hour-long video explains the *San Juan* discovery and other excavations. During the summer months, visitors can take a boat ride to nearby Saddle Island, where the remains of the 16th-century whalers' living and work areas and their cemetery have been discovered. The center is open from June 15 to October 15, daily 9 A.M.–8 P.M. Admission to the center is adults $5, seniors $4, children $3; the ferry to Saddle Island is $2 round-trip.

## Mary's Harbour

Though isolated until 2000, when Highway 510 was extended, Lodge Bay—once a winter sta-

## THE GRENFELL LEGEND

Labrador's harsh living conditions and lack of medical care attracted Dr. Wilfred Grenfell, the British physician-missionary. Dr. Grenfell worked with the Royal National Mission to Deep Sea Fishermen on the North Sea. A visit in 1892 convinced him that serving the people of remote Labrador and northern Newfoundland was his calling. He established Labrador's first coastal hospital at Battle Harbour the next year, followed by a large mission at St. Anthony. From the mission, he sailed along the coast in mission boats, treating 15,000 patients in 1900 alone. By 1907, he had opened treatment centers at Indian Harbour, Forteau, North West River, and seven other remote settlements. For his efforts, he was knighted.

Dr. Grenfell initiated a policy of free medical treatment, clothing, or food, in exchange for labor or goods. Funded by private contributions and the Newfoundland government, he opened cooperative stores, nursing homes, orphanages, mobile libraries, and lumber mills. He also initiated the Grenfell Handicrafts programs and home gardening projects. In 1912, he formed the International Grenfell Association to consolidate the English, Canadian, and American branches that funded his work. The physician was subsequently knighted a second time, in 1927, and also awarded recognition by the Royal Scottish Geographical Society and other notable organizations.

later with the arrival of seasonal fishers from Newfoundland. A fire in 1930 forced the residents to move to Mary's Harbour, but a number of buildings remained undamaged. Now restored to their 19th-century appearance, they make up the **Battle Harbour National Historic Site,** tel. 709/921-6216, including the oldest Anglican church in Labrador, the original mercantile salt fish premises, an interpretation center, and more.

**Battle Harbour Inn,** tel. 709/921-6216, is a restored two-story house overlooking the water. The five guest rooms cost $86–130 per person including meals. The owners also run boat tours and operate transfers from Mary's Harbour. If you're on the mainland and would like to visit Battle Harbour for the day, contact **Jones Charters** in Mary's Harbour, tel. 709/921-6249.

## CARTWRIGHT

Highway 510 is slated to open as far north as Cartwright in 2004. In the meantime, its only link to the outside world are coastal ferries that arrive once a week from Lewisporte, Newfoundland, and even less frequently from St. Anthony via Red Bay. For details contact the provincial operators at tel. 800/563-6353, www.gov.nf.ca/ferryservices.

### Sights

Named for 18th-century merchant adventurer and coastal resident Captain George Cartwright, **Flagstaff Hill Monument,** overlooking the town and Sandwich Bay, still has the cannons Cartwright installed to guard the harbor two hundred years ago.

**Gannet Islands Ecological Reserve,** farther north off the coast, is a breeding colony for common murres, puffins, black-legged kittiwakes, and the province's largest razorbill population. The local tour operator is **Experience Labrador,** tel. 709/653-2244 or 877/938-7444, with a wide variety of scheduled kayaking tours costing $180–200 per person per day.

North of Cartwright lies the spot where Norse sailors first laid eyes on the coast: the Wunderstrands (now known as the Porcupine Strand), a remarkable 56-km stretch of sandy golden beach.

tion for the fishers of nearby Cape St. Charles—and Mary's Harbour are small commercial centers. In Mary's Harbour, the **Riverview Inn,** tel. 709/921-6948, offers four comfortable rooms ($65–79), a restaurant, and a lounge.

### Battle Harbour

A few kilometers to the east of Mary's Harbour, on a small island, is Battle Harbour, a fishing village since 1759 and one of the oldest European settlements on the Labrador coast. By 1775, Battle Harbour's salt fish industry had made the settlement the economic center of the region, a status that faded and then rebounded a century

## Practicalities

The **Cartwright Hotel,** tel. 709/938-7414, www.cartwrightlabrador.com, holds 10 basic motel rooms ($82 single, $98 double), each with cable TV and a coffeemaker. The hotel also has a restaurant offering everything from southern fried chicken to Atlantic salmon, and a bar that comes alive on Saturday with dancing.

# North Coast

Labrador's cold jagged coast, with its countless inlets, bays, and islands, has harbored fishing settlements for centuries. Today these communities are reached by **Air Labrador,** tel. 709/753-5593 or 800/563-3042, www.airlabrador.com, from Goose Bay, or by a cargo and passenger ferry that takes six days to reach its northern turnaround point, Nain. Riding the ferry, the **M/V Northern Ranger,** is a real adventure. Its southern starting point is St. Anthony (Newfoundland), where it crosses the Strait of Belle Isle, stopping at many communities between Red Bay and Cartwright before heading down Hamilton Inlet to Goose Bay, then commencing its long trek along the north coast to Nain. In total, 48 stops are made, usually just long enough to drop off supplies. All fares are calculated on the distance traveled. The one-way fare for an adult between St. Anthony and Nain—1,038 miles at 25 cents per nautical mile—works out to be $233.55. A single berth in a cabin costs 11.7 to 19.5 cents per mile, while a private cabin costs 50.5 cents per mile. For more information, call 800/563-6353. The website www.gov.nf .ca/ferryservices lists a schedule and prices, with distances included to make calculations easy.

## GOOSE BAY TO NAIN

After stopping at communities along the Labrador Straits, the M/V *Northern Ranger* starts its long haul to Nain, 478 nautical miles north of Goose Bay. As one travels farther north, the coastal settlements thin out. It is in these remote north coast villages—Rigolet, Postville, Makkovik, and Nain—that the original inhabitants, the Inuit, have settled. The tradition of fishing and trapping is alive in **Rigolet,** a community between the Hamilton Inlet and Groswater Bay. Few aspects of this town have changed over the last century, and the lifestyle of northern peoples here remains traditional. Visit the local craft shops for unique grass basketwork, a specialty of the area.

## Makkovik

First settled in the early 1800s by a Norwegian fur trader, the M/V *Ranger* arrives at Makkovik 18 hours after leaving Goose Bay and makes a two-hour stopover before continuing north. In 1896 a Moravian mission was built in town. It was used until the late 1940s. Today this two-story building holds the **White Elephant Museum,** open July–August, daily 1–5 P.M. (or call 709/923-2262 for an appointment). Local shops such as the **Makkovik Craft Centre,** tel. 709/923-2246, sell Inuit crafts, including fur caps, boots and mittens, parkas, moose-hide moccasins, and bone and antler jewelry.

Right on the water, the **Adlavik Inn,** 7 Willow Creek Lane, tel. 709/923-2389, has the only five guest rooms in town, so call ahead if your itinerary includes an overnight stay in Makkovik. Rates are $85 single, $120 double, with meals served in an adjacent dining room.

## Postville

Postville, four hours and 40 nautical miles north of Makkovik, lies at the western end of Kaipokok Bay. This settlement has been visited by indigenous people for fishing and hunting every spring for over 4,000 years. A fur trading post was established here in 1843.

## Hopedale

Around 70 nautical miles north of Postville and 122 miles short of Nain, the M/V *Ranger* makes a 90-minute stop at Hopedale, just enough time to go ashore and visit the 1782 **Hopedale Mission National Historic Site,** containing the oldest wooden frame building east of Québec. Stores, huts, a residence, a storehouse, and a graveyard share the area with the Moravian church. Admission is $5; guided tours are available. For more information, call the local Agvituk Historical Society, tel. 709/933-3777.

Accommodations are provided at **Amaguk Inn,** tel. 709/933-3750, which charges $85 single, $95 double for one of its 12 rooms. Meals are available at the inn for both guests and non-guests.

## NAIN AND THE FAR NORTH

Nain, with a population of just over 1,000, is the northern turnaround point of the M/V *Ranger* and the northernmost municipality on the Labrador coast. Prior to the cod-fishing moratorium, the fishing industry dominated here, but now nickel mining at Voisey's Bay appears to be the economic engine of the future. Life is rugged this far north—electricity is provided by diesel generator; fuel and wood are used for domestic heat; local transportation is by boat in the summer and snowmobile in the winter. The only roads are within the town itself.

Nain is home to the **Labrador Inuit Association,** which is slowly but surely working toward securing a self-governed territory. To be called **Nunatsiavut,** their land claim encompasses the entire northern half of Labrador. For progress call the association at tel. 709/922-2942 or check its website, www.nunatsiavut.com.

The settlement's history is depicted at the **Nain Piulimatsivik** (Inuit for "Nain Museum")

through Inuit and Moravian artifacts, vessels, and other displays. The museum, tel. 709/922-2842, is open July through September. Admission is free, though donations are welcome. The Moravians built a mission church here in 1771, but the structure was subsequently destroyed by fire.

### Practicalities

If you've arrived on the ferry (see above), you'll have just four hours ashore to explore the town before the return journey. The alternative is to take the ferry one way and an **Air Labrador,** tel. 709/753-5593 or 800/563-3042, flight the other.

The only accommodation in town is the **Atsanik Lodge** on Sand Banks Road, tel. 709/922-2910. Each of the 25 rooms has cable TV, a phone, and a private bathroom ($87 single, $98 double). The lodge also has a lounge, restaurant, and laundry. It's also open year-round. Other services include three retail shops, a takeout food joint, and a snowmobile dealership.

### Continuing North

Labrador's northernmost remaining Moravian mission is protected at **Hebron Mission National Historic Site,** on the shores of remote Kangershutsoak Bay, 140 nautical miles north of Nain. Building began on the mission complex, including a church, residence, and store, in 1829. The mission remained in operation until 1959. The best way to get there is with **Torngat Mountain Labrador Tours,** tel. 709/896-4292. Another tour company that operates this far north is **Nature Trek Canada,** tel. 250/653-4265, www.naturetrek.ca.

# Resources

# Suggested Reading

## NEW BRUNSWICK

### History and Culture

Collie, Michael. *New Brunswick.* Toronto: Macmillan, 1974. Much has changed in the more than 20 years since this book was written, but much still rings true. Collie provides a poetic, highly personal, and often moving overview of the province, its history, and the psyche of its people.

De Mont, John. *Citizens Irving: K.C. Irving and His Legacy, The Story of Canada's Wealthiest Family.* Toronto: Doubleday Canada, Ltd., 1991. The Irving family is *very* private, and this unofficial biography is stuffed with well-documented unfavorable and favorable facts, legends, and speculation.

MacDonald, M.A. *Rebels and Loyalists: The Lives and Material Culture of New Brunswick's Early English-Speaking Settlers, 1758-1783.* Fredericton: New Ireland Press, 1990. MacDonald's slice of history is narrow, and his view is interestingly pervasive.

MacNutt, W.S. *New Brunswick: A History, 1784-1867.* Toronto: Macmillan of Canada, 1984. A penetrating overview of New Brunswick history, from the days of the founding Loyalists until Confederation—a time line of major and minor events.

Pincombe, C. Alexander, and Edward W. Larracey. *Resurgo: The History of Moncton.* Fredericton: Centennial Print and Litho Ltd., 1990. Moncton's official biography is short on scandal, long on personal and political tidbits, and altogether interesting from a historical point of view.

Wibur, Richard. *The Rise of French New Brunswick.* Halifax: Formac Publishing, 1989. Splendid academic treatise on early Acadians.

Wright, Esther Clark. *Loyalists of New Brunswick.* Yarmouth, NS: Sentinel Printing, 1985. More insights on the founding Loyalists.

### Natural History

Folster, David. *Great Trees of New Brunswick.* Fredericton: Canadian Forestry Association of New Brunswick, 1987. An asset for every naturalist's bookshelf, the lavishly detailed coverage on provincial trees is a feast of information. Illustrated with color and black-and-white pictures.

Morton, John Edward. *Shorelife between Fundy Tides.* Toronto: University of Toronto Press, 1991. A detailed look at the sessile lifeforms that inhabit the Bay of Fundy's shoreline.

Shaw, M. *Mount Carleton Wilderness: New Brunswick's Unknown North.* Fredericton: Fiddlehead Poetry Books and Goose Lane Editions, 1987. Marvelous descriptive and factual coverage with black-and-white photography of the highest mountain in the Maritimes.

Thurston, Harry. *Tidal Life: A Natural History of the Bay of Fundy.* Halifax: Nimbus Publishing, 1998. The lavishly illustrated contents describe natural habitats formed by the Fundy.

### Recreation

Eiselt, Marianne, and H.A. Eiselt. *A Hiking Guide to New Brunswick.* Fredericton: Goose Lane Editions, 1991. Extensively detailed with abundant maps, the guide describes 107 hikes throughout the province.

Gillis, Stephen, and John Gillis. *No Faster Than A Walk: The Covered Bridges of New Brunswick.* Fredericton: Goose Lane Editions, 1988. An illustrated guide to the province's significant covered bridges.

Thomas, Peter. *Lost Land of Moses: The Age of Discovery on New Brunswick's Salmon Rivers.* Fredericton: Goose Land Editions, 2001. Thomas combines his knowledge of New Brunswick history with his love of angling in this new title.

Tracy, Nicholas. *Cruising Guide to the Bay of Fundy and the Saint John River.* Toronto: Stoddart Publishing, 1999. A useful guide to Fundy and Saint John sailing.

# NOVA SCOTIA

## Culture

Carter, Pauline. *The Great Nova Scotia Cookbook.* Nimbus Publishing: Halifax, 2001. In depth look at local cuisine including many traditional dishes incorporating modern trends in cooking.

Field, Richard Henning. *Spirit of Nova Scotia: Traditional Decorative Folk Art 1780-1930.* Toronto: Dundurn Press, 1985. The Nova Scotians' historic use of textiles, sculpture, paintings, and decorated utilitarian objects is expertly explained by subject and splendidly illustrated with photographs.

Harper, Marjory. *Myth, Migration and the Making of Memory: Scotia and Nova Scotia.* Halifax: John Donald Publishers, 2000. Explores Nova Scotia's Scottish heritage and the importance of the province's links to Scotland through the years.

Lynch, Allan. *Discover Nova Scotia: Museums and Art Galleries.* Halifax: Nimbus Publishing, 1999. The perfect companion for anyone planning to visit the province's many cultural facilities.

Metcalfe, Robin. *Studio Rally.* Halifax: Goose Lane Editions, 2001. A coffee-table book highlighting 52 Nova Scotian artists and their work.

Parsons, Catriona. *Gaidhlig Troimh Chomhradh (Gaelic Through Conversation).* South Gut St. Ann's: Gaelic College of Celtic Arts and Crafts. The college's mission is to keep the language alive, and it does so with this text and accompanying cassette tapes as well as a number of other books and varied literature. For information or to order, contact the Gaelic College of Celtic Arts and Crafts, P.O. Box 9, Baddeck, NS B0E 1B0, tel. (902) 295-3411.

Penney, Allen. *Houses of Nova Scotia: An Illustrated Guide to Architectural Style Recognition.* Halifax: Nova Scotia Museum and Formac Publishing, 1989. Penney, a professor of architecture, sums up provincial architectural styles and explains how to identify styles by dates, similarities, and differences. Available from the Nova Scotia Government Bookstore (see below).

## History

Bruce, Harry. *An Illustrated History of Nova Scotia.* Nimbus Publishing: Halifax, 1998. Primarily aimed for the younger set, this book is highly readable and well worth a look even for adults.

Candow, James E. *Industry and Society in Nova Scotia.* Toronto, Ontario: Fernwood Books, 2001. The history of industry and the way it has shaped the people of Nova Scotia today. One section is devoted to the phenomenal growth and importance of tourism.

Crowell, Clement W. *Novascotiaman.* Halifax: Nova Scotia Museum, 1979. A sea captain's correspondence forms the basis for a retelling of the story of Nova Scotia's Great Age of Sail. Available from the Nova Scotia Government Bookstore (see below).

Ledger, Don. *Swissair Down.* Halifax: Nimbus Publishing, 2000. The story of the September 1998 crash of a Swissair jetliner off the village of Peggy's Cove from a pilot's point of view.

Lyell, Charles. *Travels in North America in the Years 1841-2*. New York: Arno Press, 1978. The author included Nova Scotia in his 19th-century travel observations.

Oickle, Vernon. *Busted: Nova Scotia's War on Drugs*. Halifax: Nimbus Publishing, 1997. Stories of local lawmen and their struggle to curb the trade of illicit drugs along Nova Scotia's remote coastline.

Sanderberg, Anders and Peter Clancy. *Against the Grain: Foresters and Politics in Nova Scotia*. Vancouver: University of British Columbia Press, 2000. A detailed look at the province's forestry practices and the viability of the industry in the new millenium.

## Natural History and Geography

Dawson, Joan. *The Mapmaker's Eye: Nova Scotia Through Early Maps*. Halifax: Nova Scotia Museum, 1988. Nova Scotia evolved over the centuries, as did the art of mapping. This illustrated book is a cartographer's dream. Available from the Nova Scotia Government Bookstore (see below).

Lee, Albert (photographer) and Alexa Thompson. *Destination Nova Scotia*. Halifax: Nimbus Publishing, 2000. Stunning photography and lyrical descriptions of the landscape are combined in this coffee-table book.

Lyell, Charles. *Geological Observations on the U.S., Canada, and Nova Scotia*. New York: Arno Press, 1978. During an early 1840s' visit, Lyell thought enough of Nova Scotia's unusual landscape and geology to give it equal space among the nations in this insightful account.

MacAskill, Wallace R. *MacAskill Seascapes and Sailing Ships*. Halifax: Nimbus Publishing. Cape Breton's famed photographer captures the misty moods of fishermen, schooners, seaports, and seacoasts.

*Natural History of Nova Scotia*. Halifax: Departments of Education and Lands and Forests, two volumes. Everything on land or beneath the nearby seas is comprehensively detailed here with illustrations. Available from the Nova Scotia Government Bookstore (see below).

*Nova Scotia Resource Atlas*. Halifax: Nova Scotia Department of Development, 1986. An exhaustive compilation of facts about the land, resources, and people, augmented with oversize maps and detailed statistics. Available from the Nova Scotia Government Bookstore (see below).

Saunders, Gary. *Discover Nova Scotia: The Ultimate Nature Guide*. Halifax: Nimbus Publishing, 2001. Perfect for a day-pack, this handy guide includes maps, trail descriptions, and the natural wonders of Nova Scotia's parks.

Stephens, Clarence. *Birding in Metro Halifax*. Halifax: Nimbus Publishing, 1996. This 300-page book details the many species of shore and inland birds present in and around the capital.

Towers, Julie and Anne Camozzi. *Discover Nova Scotia: Wildlife Viewing Sites*. Halifax: Nimbus Publishing, 1999. Another of Nimbus's popular "Discover Nova Scotia" titles, this one gives detailed directions to over 100 sites.

## Recreation

Sienko, Walter. *Nova Scotia & the Maritimes by Bike*. Seattle: Mountaineers Books, 1995. Detailed description of 21 routes across the province and beyond, with details of highlights along the way.

*Canoe Routes of Nova Scotia*. Halifax: Canoe Nova Scotia and Camping Association of Nova Scotia, 1983. A description of canoe routes for novice to expert paddlers. Available from the Nova Scotia Government Bookstore (see below).

*Hiking Trails of Nova Scotia.* Halifax: Canadian Hostelling Association, 1990. A guide to the province's better known hiking trails, accompanied by topographical data and maps. Available from the Nova Scotia Government Bookstore (see below).

# PRINCE EDWARD ISLAND

## Culture

Arsenault, Georges. *Les Acadiens de l'Ile, 1720-1980.* Ottawa: Lemeac, Inc., 1980. Insightful look in French at the province's Acadians by an islander who knows the culture and history from the inside.

Bolger, F.W.P. *Spirit of Place: Lucy Maud Montgomery and Prince Edward Island.* Toronto: Oxford University Press, 1982. Among the best of the photography books depicting Montgomery's Island. Augmented with text, Bolger matches selected Montgomery quotes with glossy pictures by Wayne Barrett and Anne MacKay.

Heibron, Alexandra (editor). *Lucy Maud Montgomery Album.* Markham, Ontario: Fitzhenry and Whiteside, 1999. Thoroughly researched, this huge compilation includes everything there is to know about Montgomery, her writing, and her home province. It was released in 1999 to commemorate the 125th anniversary of her birth.

Montgomery, Lucy Maud. *The Alpine Path.* Markham, Ontario: Fitzhenry and Whiteside, Ltd., 1999. Some of Montgomery's most vivid descriptions of the island are found in this recounting of the author's life.

Montgomery, Lucy Maud. *Anne of Green Gables.* New York: Bantam Skylark, 1984. The juvenile story that started Montgomery's popularity as an author is as interesting today as when it was written.

Perlman, Ken. *The Fiddle Music of Prince Edward Island.* Pacific, Missouri: Mel Bay Productions, 1996. Over 400 traditional Celtic and Acadian tunes.

Rootland, Nancy. *Anne's World, Maud's World: The Sacred Sites of L. M. Mongomery.* Halifax: Nimbus Publishing, 1998. This thought-provoking book reflects on how Montgomery's island home was reflected in her writing, with references to many sites that remain today.

Rubio, Mary, and Elizabeth Waterston, ed. *Selected Journals of Lucy Maud Montgomery.* Toronto: Oxford University Press, Vol. I, 1985, Vol. II, 1987. The editors have sifted through Montgomery's vast store of writing and selected some of the most interesting pieces.

## History

Bolger, F.W.P., ed. *Canada's Smallest Province: A History of P.E.I.* Charlottetown: PEI Centennial Commission, 1973. Bolger has selected some of the most interesting historical highlights of the island.

Bumstead, J.M. *Land, Settlement and Politics in 18th Century P.E.I.* McGill/Queen's University Press, 1987. The intellectual treatment will appeal to scholars.

Callbeck, Lorne C. *My Island, My People.* Charlottetown: P.E.I. Heritage Foundation, 1979. As the title implies, the author's roots go way back on the island, and the stories take in many major historical events.

De Jong, Nicholas J., and Marven E. Moore. *Launched from PEI—A Pictorial Review of Sail.* Charlottetown: P.E.I. Heritage Foundation, 1981. The illustrated book covers the province's Great Age of Sail.

Greenhill, Basil, and Ann Giffard. *Westcountrymen in PEI's Isle: A Fragment of the Great Migration.*

Toronto: University of Toronto Press, 1975. Painstakingly researched and well written, the book looks into the island's share of the immigrant outpouring from across the Atlantic.

MacDonald, Edward. *If you're Stronghearted: PEI in the Twentieth Century.* Charlottetown: PEI Museum Heritage Foundation, 2000. This hardcover book tells the story of the people, their culture, and a changing economy through a turbulent 100 years that ended with the construction of a bridge to the outside world.

Smith, H.M. Scott. *Historic Churches of Prince Edward Island.* Erin, ON: Boston Mills Press, 1998. The story of the province's churches and their place in the island's history and architecture.

Tuck, Robert C. *Island Family Harris—Letters of an Immigrant Family in British North America: 1856-1866.* Ragweed Press, 1983. Read Tuck's book on architect Harris first, and if it whets your interest, follow it with Tuck's collection of the Harris family letters.

## Natural History and Geology

Clark, Andrew *Three Centuries and the Island: A Historical Geography of Settlement and Agriculture in PEI.* Toronto: University of Toronto Press, 1959. The island's history is explored in a thorough geographical approach.

*Cummins' Atlas of Prince Edward Island, 1928.* Charlottetown: P.E.I. Historical Foundation, 1990. All the details are here, from maps and lists to history.

Gaudet, J.F. *Forestry Past and Present on PEI.* Charlottetown: PEI Department of Energy and Forestry, 1979. The province put Gaudet at the helm of its forestry department decades ago to assess the condition of the provincial woodlands. His book details what he found

and the historical reasons for the forests' decline over centuries.

*Meacham's Illustrated Historical Atlas of the Province of Prince Edward Island, 1880.* Charlottetown: P.E.I. Historical Foundation, 1989. A helpful guide to tracing family roots.

# NEWFOUNDLAND AND LABRADOR

## General

Andrieux, J.P. *St. Pierre and Miquelon: A Fragment of France in North America.* Ottawa: O.T.C. Press, 1986. One of the most thorough books about France's overseas province, the small volume details sightseeing within a historical context, and is illustrated with historical photography.

Norman, Howard. *The Bird Artist.* NY: Picador, 1995 (paperback). This tale of murder, passion and betrayal is set in the remote village of Witless Bay, Newfoundland. The book was a 1994 National Book Award finalist.

O'Flaherty, Patrick. *Come Near at Your Peril: A Visitor's Guide to the Island of Newfoundland.* St. John's: Breakwater, 1992. Often hilarious and always insightful, the author meanders across the island, explains the sights as no one but a Newfoundlander sees them, and reveals travel's potential tangles and torments.

Oppersdorff, Tony. *Coastal Labrador: A Northern Odyssey.* Halifax, NS: Nimbus Publishing, 1991. A visual feast of Labrador's dramatic scenery.

Proulx, E. Annie. *The Shipping News.* New York: Touchstone, 1994. Pulitzer Prize-winning story of a widowed journalist rebuilding his life on the Newfoundland coast. Reprinted in hardcover in 1999.

## Culture

Guy, Ray. *Ray Guy's Best.* St. John's: Breakwater, 1987. Every word from the local humorist's hilarious, often satirical, pen is worthwhile, and these short pieces—rueful insights on the province from oil expectations to fisheries woes—represent the local writer's finest columns.

Mannion, John J., ed. *Peopling of Newfoundland: Essays in Historical Geography.* St. John's: Memorial University of Newfoundland, 1990. Collected essays exploring the combination of history and geography that influenced the native peoples and settlers through the centuries.

Paddon, Harold G. *Green Woods and Blue Waters: Memories of Labrador.* St. John's: Breakwater. Life in Labrador is probed through Paddon's own settlement experiences and the yarns of fishermen and trappers.

Richardson, Boyce, ed. *Drumbeat: Anger and Renewal in Indian Country.* St. John's: Breakwater, 1992. Essays by prominent Innu leaders relate the often troubled, historic relationships with the federal and provincial governments and suggest solutions to the rising native anger.

Story, G.M., W.J. Kirwin, and J.D.A. Widdowson, eds. *Dictionary of Newfoundland English.* St. John's: Breakwater, 1990. The Newfoundlanders use their own version of the King's English—from "aaron's rod," a roseroot's local name, to "zosweet," a Beothuk word for the ptarmigan. This remarkably researched compilation translates words and adds historical, geographical, and cultural insights.

Zimmerly, David William. *Cain's Land Revisited: Cultural Changes in Central Labrador, 1775-1972.* St. John's: Memorial University of Newfoundland, 1975. Originally written as a doctoral dissertation, the incisive text is a rare look into the modern world's often-harsh effect on Labrador's peoples.

## History

Alia, Valerie. *Names, Numbers and Northern Policy.* Toronto, Ontario: Fernwood Books, 1999. A disturbing look at the facts and figures as they relate to the Inuit of Canada and government policy.

Barkham, Selma. *The Basque Coast of Newfoundland.* St. John's: Great Northern Peninsula Development Corp., 1989. The author, an expert in early Basque history, presents rare, historic maps with a detailed text and takes the reader on a journey from the southwestern island to the Strait of Belle Isle.

Davidson, James. *Great Heart: The History of a Labrador Adventure.* Tokyo, Japan: Kodansha International, 1997. In 1903, an adventure across the Ungava-Labrador Peninsula came to a tragic end with the death of leader Leon Hubbard. This highly readable story was written from original expedition diaries and notes taken by Hubbard's wife who spent years searching for the truth about his death.

Neary, Peter, and Patrick O'Flaherty. *Part of the Main: An Illustrated History of Newfoundland and Labrador.* St. John's: Breakwater, 1983. The province's early years are clearly detailed and embellished with interesting graphics and black-and-white photography.

Roberts, Dr. Harry D. and Michael Nowlan. *Newfoundland Fish Boxes: A Chronicle of The Fishery.* Fredericton: Brunswick Press, 1982. The story of "fish boxes" the name given to Newfoundland's small fishing boats, including their history and that of the industry, along with statistics and illustrations.

Rompkey, Ronald. *Grenfell of Labrador: A Biography.* Toronto: University of Toronto Press, 1991. Sir Wilfred Grenfell, the physician/missionary whose work left an indelible imprint on the province's remote areas, has had several biographers, but none as meticulous and incisive as Rompkey.

Tuck, James A., and Robert Grenier. *Red Bay, Labrador: World Whaling Capital, A.D. 1550-1660.* St. John's: Atlantic Archaeology, 1989. Recent archaeological discoveries form the gist for relating the early Basque whaling industry. Splendid color photography and black-and-white graphics.

## Geology and Natural History

Beamish, Peter. *Dances with Whales.* St. John's: Robinson-Blackmore Printing and Publishing Ltd., 1993. Dr. Beamish, who has researched Trinity Bay's whales for decades, explains the methodology involved in studying the various species' habits, peculiarities, and migrations.

## Recreation

Gard, Peter, and Bridget Neame. *Trails of the Avalon: Hiking in Eastern Newfoundland.* Torbay, Newfoundland: Gallow Cove Publishing, 1989. Many of the Avalon's most interesting trails are detailed with text insights, photography, and directions.

Maryniak, Barbara. *A Hiking Guide to the National Parks and Historic Sites of Newfoundland.* Fredericton: Goose Land Editions, 1996.

Nicol, Keith. *Best Hiking Trails in Western Newfoundland.* Independent Publishers Group, 1987. Another fine hiking guide, this handy paperback includes trails from Port aux Basques to the Northern Peninsula, with maps and handsome color photography.

Walsh, David. *Intriguing Waters of Newfoundland.* St. John's: Jesperson Press, 1980. Details intriguing, shipwreck-littered scuba-diving sites and offers diving advice.

# REGIONWIDE

*Atlantic Canada Road Atlas.* Oshawa, Ontario: Map Art, 2000. The best of many road atlas' to the region. Purchase online at www.mapart.com.

Bedford, David and Danielle Irving. *Tragedy of Progress: Marxism, Modernity and the Aboriginal Question.* Toronto, Ontario: Fernwood Books, 2000. Catalogues the struggle for justice by native Canadians. Although published in Ontario, the book's New Brunswick-based authors provide plenty of local content.

Daigle, Jean, Ed. *Acadians of the Maritimes.* Moncton: Chaire d'Études Acadiennes, Université de Moncton, 1995. The history of the Acadians in Atlantic Canada is a tangled tale of upheaval and survival, cultural clashes and passions. Daigle's collection of Acadian literature is among the best on the bookshelves.

Griffin, Diane. *Atlantic Wild Flowers.* Toronto: Oxford University Press, 1984. A glorious combination of text by Griffin and photography by Wayne Barrett and Anne MacKay—a must for every naturalist who revels in wildflowers.

Hardy, Anne. *Where to Eat in Canada.* Ottawa: Oberon Press, 2001. The author and her compatriot reviewers list the best dining across the nation, much of it in Atlantic Canada.

Medjuck, Sheva. *Jews of Atlantic Canada.* St. John's: Breakwater, 1986. The Jews are among Atlantic Canada's smaller ethnic groups. The author traces their impact on, and roles in, the various communities across the region.

Nightingale, Richard. *Atlantic Salmon Chronicles.* Boulder, Colorado: Sycamore Island Books, 2000. Incorporates aspects of salmon fishing, from its earliest beginnings to modern-day techniques. But at $150, it's for the real enthusiast.

Paul, Daniel N. *We Were Not the Savages.* Toronto, Ontario: Fernwood Books, 2000. A fascinating look at the unhappy relationship between the Mi'kmaq of Atlantic Canada and Europeans.

Sherwood, Roland H. *Maritime Mysteries: Haunting Tales from Atlantic Canada.* Hantsport, NS: Lancelot Press, 1991. No one takes ghosts, burning ships, and natural oddities lightly in Atlantic Canada. These mysteries are deftly handled in a collection of stories that are stranger than fiction.

## Sources
**Nova Scotia Government Bookstore** lists its publications in the *Publications Catalogue.* The Bookstore is at One Government Place, 1700 Granville St., Halifax; or contact it at P.O. Box 637, Halifax, NS B3J 2T3, tel. (800) 526-6575, www.gov.ns.ca/snsmr.

**University College of Cape Breton Press** publishes numerous titles in addition to those listed here. Contact the press at P.O. Box 5300, Sydney, NS B1P 6L2, tel. (902) 539-5300, www.uccb.ns.ca.

Suggested Reading

# Internet Resources

## ACCOMMODATIONS

Auberge Wandlyn Inns:
www.wandlyninns.com
Bed and Breakfast Online:
www.bbcanada.com
Best Western: www.bestwestern.com
Choice Hotels Canada:
www.choicehotels.ca
City Hotels: www.cityhotels.ca
Country Inns and Suites:
www.countryinns.com
Days Inn: www.daysinn.com
Delta Hotels and Resorts:
www.deltahotels.com
Fairmont Hotels and Resorts:
www.fairmont.com
Hilton Worldwide: www.hilton.com
Holiday Inns: www.holiday-inn.com
Hostelling International Canada:
www.hihostels.ca
Howard Johnson: www.hojo.com
International Youth Hostel Federation:
www.iyhf.com
Keddys Hotels and Inns: www.keddys.ca
Maritime Inns and Resorts: www.mar-
itimeinns.com
Radisson: www.radisson.com
Ramada: www.ramada.com
Rodd Hotels and Resorts:
www.rodd-hotels.ca
Signature Resorts: www.signatureresorts.com

## AIRLINES

Air Canada: www.aircanada.ca
Air China: www.airchina.com
Air New Zealand: www.nzair.com
Alaska Airlines: www.alaksaair.com
All Nippon Airways: www.ana.co.jp

American Airlines: www.aa.com
British Airlines: www.britishairlines.com
Continental Airlines: www.continental.com
Eva Air: www.evaair.com.tw
Horizon Air: www.horizonair.com
Japan Airlines: www.jal.co.jp
KLM: www.klm.nl
Korean Air: www.koreanair.com
Lufthansa: www.lufthansa.de
Northwest Airlines: www.nwa.com
Philippine Airlines: www.philippineair.com
Qantas: www.qantas.com.au
Singapore Airlines: www.singaporeair.com
Skywest: www.skywest.com
United Airlines: www.ual.com
WestJet: www.westjet.com

## BUS, FERRY, AND RAIL

Bay Ferries: www.nfl-bay.com
Greyhound: www.greyhound.ca
Marine Atlantic: www.marine-atlantic.ca
Northumberland Ferries: www.nfl-bay.com
*Scotia Prince:* www.scotiaprince.com
*The Cat:* www.catferry.com
VIA Rail: www.viarail.ca

## CAR AND RV RENTAL

Alamo: www.alamo.com
Avis: www.avis.com
Budget: www.budget.com
Cruise America: www.cruiseamerica.com
Discount: www.discountcar.com
Dollar: www.dollar.com
Enterprise: www.enterprise.com
Hertz: www.hertz.com
National: www.nationalcar.com
Rent-a-wreck: www.rentawreck.ca
Thrifty: www.thrifty.com

## TOURISM OFFICES

Canadian Tourism Commission:
www.canadatourism.com

### New Brunswick
Tourism New Brunswick:
www.tourismnbcanada.com

### Newfoundland and Labrador
Department of Tourism, Culture and Recreation: www.gov.nf.ca/tourism

### Nova Scotia
Department of Tourism and Culture:
www.explore.gov.ns.ca

### Prince Edward Island
Tourism PEI: www.gov.pe.ca

## GOVERNMENT

Government of Canada: www.gc.ca
Citizenship and Immigration Canada:
www.cic.gc.ca
Canada Customs and Revenue Agency
(Visitor Rebate Program):
www.ccra-adrc.gc.ca/visitors
Government of New Brunswick:
www.gov.nb.ca
Government of Newfoundland and
Labrador: www.gov.nf.ca
Government of Nova Scotia: www.gov.ns.ca
Government of Prince Edward Island:
www.gov.pe.ca
Parks Canada: www.parkscanada.gc.ca

Internet Resources

# Index

**Index**

## A
Abram-Village: 310
Acadian Coast (New Brunswick): 122–145
Acadian Coast (Nova Scotia): 214–216
Acadian Festival: 142
Acadian Historical Village: 143
Acadian Museum: 245
Acadia University Art Gallery: 223
Acadien Festival: 132
accommodations: 35–40; *see also specific place*
Action Week: 252
Admiral Digby Museum: 217
agriculture: 20
air travel: 42, 43, 44; *see also specific place*
Aitken Bicentennial Exhibition Centre: 104
Aitken, William Maxwell: 59, 125
Alberton: 312–313
Alberton Museum: 312
alcoholic beverages: 40; New Brunswick 64; Newfoundland and Labrador 347–348; Nova Scotia 160–161
Alexander Graham Bell National Historic Site: 243
Alexander Keith's Original Brewery: 180
All Souls' Chapel: 276
Amherst: 167–169
Amherst Point Migratory Bird Sanctuary: 168
amusement parks: Kensington Towers and Water Gardens 302; Magic Mountain Water Park 130; Palais Crystal 135; Rainbow Valley 298; Sandspit 298; Upper Clements Family Vacation Park 221–222
An Drochaid: 241
Anglican Cathedral of St. John the Baptist: 357
animals: 10–12
Annapolis Royal: 221–222
Annapolis Royal Historic Gardens: 221
Annapolis Valley: 220–225
Annapolis Valley Apple Blossom Festival: 220
*Anne of Green Gables*: 294, 296–297, 299
Anne of Green Gables Museum at Silver Bush: 299
Antigonish: 231–232
Antigonish Highland Games: 231
Antique Automobile Museum: 86
Apple Blossom Festival: 156
Aquarena: 367

Aquarium and Marine Centre: 141
aquariums: Aquarium and Marine Centre 141; Huntsman Marine Science Centre and Aquarium 93; Stanley Bridge Marine Aquarium 298
archaeological sites: 373
Archelaus Smith Museum: 210
architecture: Grand Bank 377; Halifax 178; Saint John 104; Yarmouth 211–212
Argentia: 376
Arisaig Provincial Park: 231
art galleries: Acadia University 223; Aitken Bicentennial Exhibition Centre 104; Art Gallery of Nova Scotia 179; Confederation Centre of the Arts 275–276; Eptek National Exhibition Centre 303; Fredericton 72, 77; Galerie d'Art et Musée Acadien 128; Galerie Restigouche 145; Hector Exhibit and Research Centre 229; Mount Saint Vincent University Art Gallery 183; Owens 119; Sir Wilfred Grenfell College Art Gallery 402; St. John's 368
Art Gallery of Nova Scotia: 179
Atlantic Film Festival: 189
Atlantic Fringe Theatre Festival 189
Atlantic National Exhibition: 111
Atlantic Theatre Festival: 223
Atlantic Wind Test Site: 313
Auld Cove: 232
Avalon Peninsula: 371–376

## Arts and Crafts
general discussion: 34
Boat Harbour: 376
Charlottetown: 282
Chéticamp: 245
Crafts Festival: 206
Gaelic College of Celtic Arts and Crafts: 249
Halifax: 190–191
New Brunswick: 62
Newfoundland and Labrador: 343–344
Nova Scotia: 155
Prince Edward Island: 262–263
Saint John: 112
Stanley Bridge: 298
St. John's: 368

Avalon Wilderness Reserve: 374
aviation: 340
Avonlea: 289

**B**
Baccalieu Island Ecological Reserve: 374
Baddeck: 243–244
Baddeck Regatta: 243
Baie des Chaleurs: 142–145
Balmoral Grist Mill Museum: 173
Balmoral Mills: 173
banks: *see specific place*
Barachois Pond Provincial Park: 405
Barbour's General Store: 103
Barrington: 210
Barrington Woolen Mill Museum: 210
Bartibog Bridge: 141
Bartlett, Robert: 373
Bas-Caraquet: 142
Basin Head: 323
Basin Head Fisheries Museum: 323
Bathurst: 144
Battery Provincial Park: 241
Battle Harbour: 420
Battle Harbour National Historic Site: 420
Bay Du Nord Wilderness Reserve: 380
Bayfield Provincial Park: 232
Bay Fortune: 320–321
Beaconsfield Historic House: 276
Bedford Basin: 183
Bedford Institute of Oceanography: 182
beer: 40, 64, 180
Bell, Alexander Graham: 153, 243
Bell Island: 373
Beothuk Park: 390
Beothuk people: 12, 13, 334, 337–338, 387, 390
bicycling: 32–33; Cavendish 298; Charlottetown 282; Edmundston 84; Fredericton 76; Halifax 190; Kouchibouguac National Park 138; New Brunswick 60; Nova Scotia 157; Prince Edward Island 265–266; Yarmouth 213
Bideford: 307
Biggest Backyard Barbeque: 265, 282
Big Pond: 241
birds: 10–11; Newfoundland and Labrador 333; Nova Scotia 151–152
bird-watching: Amherst 168; Baccalieu Island Ecological Reserve 374; Blow Me Down Provincial Park 404; Cape St. Mary's Ecological Reserve 376; Fundy Coast 98, 115; Gan-
net Islands Ecological Reserve 420; Gros Morne National Park 391; Irving Eco-Centre 137; Jourimain Nature Centre 135; Kejimkujik National Park 219; Murray River 317; Neguac and Val-Comeau Parks 141; Nova Scotia 158; Prince Edward Island National Park 292; Sackville 120; Saint John 106; Shepody National Wildlife Area 117–119; Tintamarre Sanctuary 121; Witless Bay 374
Black Cultural Centre for Nova Scotia: 183
Blacks Harbour: 96
Blow Me Down Mountain: 398
Blow Me Down Provincial Park: 404
Blueberry Festival: 324
blueberry picking: 99
*Bluenose* and *Bluenose II*: 154, 203
Blue Ponds Park: 405
Blue Rocks: 204
Boat Harbour: 376
boating: 33; Baddeck Regatta 243; Fundy National Park 116–117; Royal St. John's Regatta 367; Saint John 106; Yarmouth Cup Ocean Races 213
Boiestown: 140–141
Bonar Law Historic Site: 137
Bonavista: 383–384
Bonavista Museum: 384
Bonavista Peninsula: 380–384
booklist: 424–431
bookstores: Charlottetown 283; Fredericton 77; Halifax 191; Moncton 133; Saint John 112–113; St. John's 369
Borden-Carleton: 287–288
Bore Park: 128
botanical gardens: *see* gardens
Bottle Houses: 309–310
Bouctouche: 136–137
Bowring Park: 360
Boyd's Cove: 387
Boyd's Cove Beothuk Interpretation Centre: 387
Brackley Beach: 290–291
breweries: 180
Bridgewater: 207
bridge, world's longest covered: 82
Brigus: 373
Broad Cove: 241
Brudenell River Provincial Park and Resort: 319–320
Buffaloland Provincial Park: 319
Bungalow, The: 383

Index

Burgeo: 380
Burin: 377
Burin Peninsula: 376–377
business hours: 35
Buskers Festival: 110, 189
bus travel: 44; *see also specific place*

**C**
Cabot Beach Provincial Park: 306
Cabot Institute: 361
Cabot, John (Giovanni Caboto): 13–14,
    383–384
Cabot's Landing Provincial Park: 248
Cabot Trail: 244–249
Campbellton: 144–145
camping: 32, 40; Fundy National Park 117; Gros
    Morne National Park 395; Kouchibouguac
    National Park 137–138; New Brunswick 63;
    Newfoundland and Labrador 345; Nova Sco-
    tia 159–160; Prince Edward Island National
    Park 292–293; Saint John 108; Terra Nova
    National Park 386
Campobello Island: 96–97
Canada Day: 210, 282
Canada Select: 37
canoeing/kayaking: Brudenell River 319; Char-
    lottetown 282; Fredericton 76; Halifax 190;
    Kejimkujik National Park 219–220; Kouchi-
    bouguac National Park 138; Labrador Canoe
    Regatta 416; Newfoundland and Labrador
    344; Nova Scotia 157; Prince Edward Island
    266–267; Saint John 111–112; St. Andrews
    93; St. John's 367; Tangier 234–235; Terra
    Nova National Park 386; Yarmouth 213
Canso: 236
Canso Museum: 236
Cape Bonavista: 383–384
Cape Bonavista Lighthouse: 384
Cape Breton Centre for Heritage and Science: 251
Cape Breton Highlands National Park: 246–249
Cape Breton Island: 237–255
Cape George Scenic Drive: 231
Cap-Egmont: 309–310
Cape Lighthouse: 210
Cape North: 248
Cape Sable Island: 210
Cape Shore: 375–376
Cape Spear National Historic Site: 359–360
Cape St. Mary's Ecological Reserve: 376
Cape Tormentine: 135

Cape Wolfe: 312
C. A. Pippy Park: 360–361
Cap-Pelé: 135
Cap Rouge: 247
Captain Cook's Monument: 400
Caraquet: 142–143
Cardigan: 320
Carleton Martello Tower National
    Historic Site: 106
Cartier, Jacques: 261, 313
car travel: 41, 43; *see also specific place*
Cartwright: 420
Castle Hill National Historic Site: 375–376
Cavendish: 295–298
Cedar Dunes Provincial Park: 311–312
*ceilidhs:* Mabou 241; Orwell 288
cemeteries: Fredericton 72; Loyalist Burial
    Ground 105; Old Burying Ground,
    Halifax 179
Centennial Park: 129, 132–133
Central New Brunswick Woodmen's Museum:
    140–141
Centre Bras d'Or Festival of the Arts: 243
CFB Gagetown Museum: 80
Charlotte County Court House: 92
Charlottetown: 272–284
Charlottetown Festival: 265, 281–282
Charlottetown Winter Carnival: 281
Cherry Brook Zoo: 106
Chester: 199–201
Chester Theatre Festival: 200
Chéticamp: 245–246
Chignecto Isthmus: 90
churches: Annapolis Valley 221; Charlottetown
    276; Chéticamp 245; Fredericton 73; Grand
    Pré 225; Halifax 179, 180–182; Lennox Is-
    land 308; Lunenburg 204; Mont-Carmel 309;
    Pointe de l'église 216; Saint John 105; St.
    John's 357, 359; Sydney 251; Tignish 313
Churchill Falls: 416
Church Point: 216
cinema: Atlantic Film Festival 189; Charlotte-
    town 281; Corner Brook 402; Festival interna-
    tional du cinéma francophone en Acadie 132;
    Fredericton 75; Halifax 188; St. John's 365;
    Sydney 252; Yarmouth 213
Clam Harbour: 234
Clarenville: 380–381
climate: 6–8; *see also specific place*
clothing: 49

Coaker, William: 383
Colchester Historical Society Museum: 171
College of Piping: 305
College of the North Atlantic: 361
Colony of Avalon Interpretation Centre: 375
Comeauville: 216
Commissariat House: 357
communications: 48; *see also specific place*
Conception Bay Museum: 373
concerts: *see* music
Confederation Bridge: 43, 268, 288
Confederation Centre of the Arts: 275–276
Confederation Players: 274
Conservation Council of New Brunswick: 78
Constitution Act: 17, 19
Cook, James: 377, 398
Cook's Lookout: 377
Corner Brook: 398–404
Corner Brook Museum: 400
Cornwall: 284–286
Cossit House Museum: 251
Covenhoven: 92
Cow Head: 395
Cow Head rock formation: 394
Crafts Festival: 206
crime: 46
cross-country skiing: *see* skiing
cruises, sightseeing: Charlottetown 274; Chéti-camp 245; Digby 219; Gros Morne National Park 394; Halifax 192–193; Lunenburg 203; Montague 319; Souris 321; Terra Nova National Park 386; Twillingate 388
Crystal Crescent Beach Provincial Park: 190
Cumberland County Museum: 168
Cupids: 373
Cupids Cove Archaeological Site: 373
Cupids Museum: 373
currency: 46–48
customs regulations: 45
cycling: 32–33; Cavendish 298; Charlottetown 282; Edmundston 84; Fredericton 76; Halifax 190; Kouchibouguac National Park 138; New Brunswick 60; Nova Scotia 157; Prince Edward Island 265–266; Yarmouth 213

**D**
Daly Point Wildlife Reserve: 144
Dartmouth Heritage Museum: 182
*Day Adventures* catalog: 60
Deer Island: 96–97

Deer Lake: 391
Denmark: 173
deportation, Acadian: 15–16, 124
Depression: 17
Dieppe: 135
Digby: 217–219
Digby Neck and Islands: 219
Digby Scallops Days: 218
Dildo: 374
Dildo Interpretive Centre: 374
Dingle Tower: 184
Discovery Centre: 393
diving: Charlottetown 282; Halifax 190; Nova Scotia 157; Saint John 111; St. John's 367
Doak Historic Site: 140
Doaktown: 140
Dorchester Peninsula: 120
Dorset people: 12
Dory Shop Museum: 209
drama: *see* theater

**E**
East Point Lighthouse: 323
ecological organizations: 78, 133–134
ecological reserves: Baccalieu Island 374; Cape St. Mary's 376; Gannet Islands 420; Mistaken Point 375; Witless Bay 374; *see also* wilderness areas, parks, and reserves
economy: 19–21; *see also specific place*
Edmundston: 84–86
église de Sainte-Marie: 216
Elderhostel: 39
electrical voltage: 49
Ellerslie Shellfish Museum: 307
Elmira: 323
Elmira Railway Museum: 323
employment in Canada: 46
Enclosure Park: 139–140
entertainment: 32–35; *see also specific place*
environmental conflicts: 262
Eptek National Exhibition Centre: 303
Eskimos: *see* Inuit people
Évangéline: 216
experimental farm: 169
Exploits Valley Salmon Festival: 390
export details: 35

**F**
factory tours: Glenora Inn and Distillery 241; Grohmann Knives 230

Fairbanks Interpretive Centre: 182
Fairmont Algonquin: 94
Falmouth: 225
Fantazmagoric Museum: 298
Farmers' Bank Museum: 293–294
farmers' markets: Amherst 168; Charlottetown 276–277; Kensington 302; Lunenburg 206; Yarmouth 213
Farm Field Day: 367
Fathers of the Confederation: 17
fauna: 10–12
Feast of St. Louis: 254
Ferryland: 374–375
ferry travel: 41, 43–44; *see also specific place*
Festival Acadien: 110–111
Festival Antigonish: 231–232
Festival by the Sea: 110
Festival de l'Escaouette: 156, 245
Festival 500: 366
Festival Francophone: 76
Festival international du cinéma francophone en Acadie: 132
Festival of Folk Song and Dance: 344, 377
Festival of Lights: 265, 282
Festival on the Bay: 252
festivals: 34; Acadian Festival 142; Acadien Festival 132; Action Week 252; Annapolis Valley Apple Blossom Festival 220; Annual Farm Field Day 367; Antigonish Highland Games 156, 231; Apple Blossom Festival: 156; Atlantic Film Festival 189; Atlantic Fringe Theatre Festival 189; Atlantic National Exhibition 111; Baddeck Regatta 243; Biggest Backyard Barbeque 282; Blueberry Festival 324; Buskers Festival 110, 189; Canada Day 210, 265, 282; Centre Bras d'Or Festival of the Arts 243; Charlottetown Festival 265, 281–282; Charlottetown Winter Carnival 281; Chester Theatre Festival 200; Crafts Festival 206; Digby Scallops Days 218; Exploits Valley Salmon Festival 390; Feast of St. Louis: 254; Festival Acadien: 110–111; Festival Antigonish 231–232; Festival by the Sea 110; Festival de l'Escaouette 156, 245; Festival 500 366; Festival Francophone 76; Festival international du cinéma francophone en Acadie 132; Festival of Folk Song and Dance 377; Festival of Lights 265, 282; Festival on the Bay 252; Founders' Day 210; Fringe Festival 366; George Street Festival 366; Harvest Festival 132; Hector Fes-

tival 230; Heritage Folk Festival 344; Highland Games and Scottish Festival, 76; Highland Games, Lord Selkirk Provincial Park, 288; Highland Gathering 265; International Gathering of the Clans 156; International Shellfish Festival 282; Irish Festival 138–139; Iron Skull Folk Festival 380; Journées Acadienne de Grand-Pré 156; Kilts and Cabers 288; Labrador Straits Bakeapple Folk Festival 418; Lamèque International Baroque Music Festival 141; L'Exposition Agricole et Festival Acadien de la Région évangéline 311; Lobster Carnival 305; Loyalist City Heritage Festival 110; Lunenburg Folk Harbour Festival 206; Mabou Ceilidh 241; Miramichi Folksong Festival 139; Montague Homecoming Festival 265; New Brunswick Competitive Festival of Music 110; Newfoundland and Labrador Folk Festival 344, 367; North America's First New Year's Festival 367; North West River Beach Festival 416; Northumberland Provincial Fisheries Festival 317; Nova Scotia International Tattoo 156, 189; Outdoor Newfoundland and Labrador 366; PEI Bluegrass & Old-Time Music Festival 265; PEI Provincial Exhibition 265, 282; Pictou Lobster Festival 230; Race Week 200; Rollo Bay Fiddle Festival 321; Royal St. John's Regatta 367; Saint John YM/YWCA Quilt Fair 110; Shakespeare by the Sea Festival 366; Shediac lobster festival 136; Shelburne County Exhibition 210; Signal Hill Tattoo 367; Snow Jam 189; Southern Shore Shamrock Folk Festival 375; Spring Wine Festival 265; Stan Rogers Folk Festival 156; Stephenville Theatre Festival 405; Strawberry Festival 324; Summer in the Bight 383; Teddy Bears' Picnic 366; Tradition by the Sea 380; Twillingate Fish, Fun, and Folk Festival 389; Tyne Valley Oyster Festival 306; Victoria Park Craft Fair 132; Western Nova Scotia Exhibition 213; West Point Lighthouse Festival 312; Winter Carnival 416; Wooden Boat Festival 201; World Wine Festival 132; Yarmouth Cup Ocean Races 213; Yarmouth Lobster Sports 213
Firefighters' Museum of Nova Scotia: 212
fish: 11–12
Fisheries and Marine Institute: 361
Fisheries Museum of the Atlantic: 204
Fisherman's Life Museum: 234

fishing, commercial: 13, 19–20, 336–337, 339, 341

fishing, recreational: 32; Burgeo 380; Charlotte-town 282; Fundy National Park 117; Ke-jimkujik National Park 219; Labrador 411–412; Miramichi River 139; Murray River 317; New Brunswick 61; Newfoundland and Labrador 344; North Lake 323–324; North Rustico 294–295; Nova Scotia 157–158; Prince Edward Island 266; Saint John 106; Terra Nova National Park 386

fjords: 394

Flagstaff Hill Monument: 420

flora: 8–10; *see also specific place*

food: 40; New Brunswick 63–64; Newfoundland and Labrador 346–347; Nova Scotia 160; Prince Edward Island 267; *see also specific city*

forests: 8

Fort Amherst/Port-la-Joye National Historic Site: 286

Fort Anne National Historic Site: 221

Fort Beauséjour: 120–121

Forteau: 418

Fort Edward National Historic Site: 225

Fort Howe National Historic Site: 106

Fortress of Louisbourg: 253–255

Fortune: 377

Founders' Day: 210

Founders Hall: 274

Fredericton: 67–80

Fredericton Exhibition: 76

Fredericton Lighthouse: 72

French Mountain: 248

French River: 299

Friends of the Island: 262

Fringe Festival: 366

Fuller, Alfred: 153, 212

Fundy Coast: 87–121

Fundy Geological Museum: 170

Fundy National Park: 116–117

**G**

Gaelic College of Celtic Arts and Crafts: 249

Gagetown: 80

Galerie d'Art et Musée Acadien: 128

Galerie Restigouche: 145

Gander: 386–387

Gannet Islands Ecological Reserve: 420

Garden of the Gulf Museum: 318

gardens: Annapolis Royal Historic Gardens 221; Bowring Park 360; Memorial University Botanical Garden 360–361; New Brunswick Botanical Garden 84–86; Prescott House 224; Public Gardens (Halifax) 183; Victoria Park 360; Woodleigh Replicas & Gardens 302

Gateway Visitor Centre: 417

genealogy: 59, 78, 155, 229, 343

geography: 2–6

geology: 4, 149–150, 328–330

George C. Harris House: 377

Georges Island: 182

George Street Festival: 366

Georgetown: 320

Glace Bay: 253

Glenora Inn and Distillery: 241

Gold Cup Parade: 282

gold-panning: 207

Goose Bay: 413–416

## Golf

Amherst: 168

Bathurst: 144

Brudenell River: 319

Cavendish: 298

Comeauville: 216

Corner Brook: 402

Digby: 218

Edmundston: 84

Fredericton: 76

Fundy National Park: 116

Halifax: 190

Happy Valley–Goose Bay: 415

Ingonish: 249

Labrador City/Wabush: 417

Lunenburg: 205

Mactaquac: 81

Mill River: 311

Moncton: 132

Morell: 324

Nova Scotia: 158

Prince Edward Island: 266

Saint John: 112

South Rustico: 294

St. Andrews: 94

Stanhope: 290

St. John's: 360, 367

Summerside: 305

Terra Nova National Park: 386

government: 18–19; *see also specific place*
Government House: 357
Grand Anse River: 247
Grand Bank: 377
Grande-Anse: 143
Grand Falls (Grand-Sault): 82–84
Grand Falls Fishway–Salmonid Interpretation Centre: 390
Grand Falls–Windsor: 389–390
Grand Manan Island: 97–99
Grand Pré: 224–225
Grand Pré National Historic Site: 224–225
Grand Pré Vineyards: 225
Grand Tracadie: 290
Grassy Island National Historic Site: 236
Grates Cove: 373–374
Great Hall of the Clans Museum: 249
Green, The: 69–70
Green Family Forge: 382
Green Gables House: 296
Green Gardens: 393
Green Park Provincial Park: 307
Green Park Shipbuilding Museum and Yeo House: 307
Green Point: 394
Greenwich Peninsula/Interpretation Centre: 324
Grenfell House Museum: 397
Grenfell, Wilfred: 397, 420
Grohmann Knives: 230
Gros Morne Mountain: 394–395
Gros Morne National Park: 391–396
Grosses Coques: 216
Gulf Coast: 141–142
Gulf Museum: 405

**H**
Haliburton House: 225
Halifax: 174–195
Halifax Citadel National Historic Site: 180
Halifax Harbour: 176
Hank Snow Country Music Centre: 208
Happy Valley–Goose Bay: 413–416
Harbour Breton: 380
Harbour Grace: 373
Harmonized Sales Tax (HST): 47–48
harness racing: 305, 367
Harvest Festival: 132
Harvest Jazz and Blues Festival: 76
Harvey: 119
Hawthorne Cottage National Historic Site: 373

health and safety: 46
Heart's Content: 374
Heart's Content Cable Station Provincial Historic Site: 374
Hebron Mission National Historic Site: 422
Hector Exhibit and Research Centre: 229
Hector Festival: 230
Hector Heritage Quay: 229
helicopter tours: 361
Hemlock Ravine Park: 183
Heritage Folk Festival: 344
Highland Games: *see* festivals
Highland Village: 242
hiking: 32; Cape Breton Highlands National Park 247; Corner Brook 402; Fundy National Park 116; Gros Morne National Park 394–395; Kejimkujik National Park 219–220; Kouchibouguac National Park 138; New Brunswick 60; Nova Scotia 157; Prince Edward Island 266; Prince Edward Island National Park 292; Saint John 106; St. John's 357; Sugarloaf Mountain Provincial Park 145; Terra Nova National Park 384
Hiscock House: 382
Historic Ferryland Museum: 375
historic sites: Acadian Historical Village 143; Alexander Graham Bell 243; Anglican Cathedral of St. John the Baptist 357; Battle Harbour 420; Bonavista 384; Cape Spear 359–360; Carleton Martello Tower 106; Castle Hill 375–376; Charlotte County Court House 92; Doak 140; Fort Amherst/Port-la-Joye 286; Fort Anne 221; Fort Edward 225; Fort Howe 106; Fortress of Louisbourg 253–255; Grand Pré 224–225; Grassy Island 236; Halifax Citadel 180; Hawthorne Cottage 373; Heart's Content Cable Station 374; Hebron Mission 422; Hopedale Mission 421–422; L'Anse aux Meadows 397–398; Loyalist House 104; MacDonald Farm 141; Marconi 253; Maritime Archaic Burial Mound 419; Minister's Island 92; Monument-Lefebvre 135; Old Burying Ground 179; Point Amour Lighthouse 419; Port au Choix 396; Port Royal 221; Province House 274–275; Red Bay 419; Saint John City Market 104–105; Sheriff Andrews House 91–92; Signal Hill 357; St. Andrews Blockhouse 91; Trinity 382; York Redoubt 182
history: 12–18; *see also specific place*

hockey: 33, 34; St. John's 366, 367
holidays: 35, 344
Holland College: 265, 277
Hopedale: 421–422
Hopedale Mission National Historic Site: 421–422
Hopewell Cape: 119
horseback riding: Brudenell River 319; Saint John 106
hospitals: *see specific place*
Hostelling International (HI): 39
hotels: 35–40; *see also specific place*
houseboating: New Brunswick 60; Saint John River 81
Howards Cove: 312
hunting: 32; Labrador 411–412; NewBrunswick 61; Newfoundland and Labrador 344–345; Prince Edward Island 266
hydroelectricity: 21, 373, 416

**I**

icebergs: 329
ice-skating: 33; Halifax 190; Saint John 106; Sugarloaf Mountain Provincial Park 145
Île Lamèque: 141
Île Miscou: 142
Îles de la Madeleine: 322
Indians: 22–24
industry: 21
information and services: 45–49; *see also specific place*
Ingonish: 248–249
Inn at Bay Fortune: 320–321
insurance: 46
International Fox Hall of Fame and Museum: 303–304
International Gathering of the Clans: 156
International Shellfish Festival: 282
internet: 48; Nova Scotia 161; St. Andrews 96
internet resources: 432–433
Inuit people: 12, 23–24, 422
Inverness: 241–242
Inverness Miners Museum: 241
Iona: 242–243
Irish Festival: 138–139
Irish moss: 312
Iron Skull Folk Festival: 380
Irving Eco-Centre: 137
Irving, Kenneth Colin: 59
Isle Madame: 239–240

**J**

Jacques Cartier Provincial Park: 313
James Callaghan Trail: 394–395
James J. O'Mara Pharmacy Museum: 355–357
Jeddore Oyster Pond: 234–235
Jewish Historical Museum: 104
Joggins: 169
Joggins Fossil Centre: 169
Jordi Bonet Murals: 397
Jost Vineyards: 170
Jourimain Nature Centre: 135
Journées Acadienne de Grand-Pré: 156
judicial system: 19
J. Willy Krauch and Sons Smokehouse: 234

**K**

kayaking/canoeing: Brudenell River 319; Charlottetown 282; Fredericton 76; Halifax 190; Kejimkujik National Park 219–220; Kouchibouguac National Park 138; Labrador Canoe Regatta 416; Newfoundland and Labrador 344; Nova Scotia 157; Prince Edward Island 266–267; Saint John 111–112; St. Andrews 93; St. John's 367; Tangier 234–235; Terra Nova National Park 386; Yarmouth 213
Kejimkujik National Park: 208, 219–220
Kensington: 302
Kensington Railroads: 302
Kensington Towers and Water Gardens: 302
Kidd, William: 200
Kidston Island: 243
Kilts and Cabers celebration: 288
Kings County: 314–324
Kings Landing Historical Settlement: 81–82
King's Square: 105
kissing the cod: 344
Kouchibouguac National Park: 137–138

**L**

Labrador: 407–422
Labrador Canoe Regatta: 416
Labrador City: 416–417
Labrador Heritage Museum: 413
Labrador Institute: 413
Labrador Inuit Association: 422
Labrador 120 Sled Dog Race: 417
Labrador Retrievers: 334
Labrador Straits: 417–420
Labrador Straits Bakeapple Folk Festival: 418
Lac-Baker: 86

La Côte Acadienne: 214–216
Lakeview Downs: 367
La Manche Provincial Park: 374
Lamèque International Baroque
    Music Festival: 141
land: 2–12; *see also specific place*
language: 26–27
L'Anse-Amour: 419
L'Anse-au-Clair: 417–418
L'Anse aux Meadows: 397–398
L'Anse aux Meadows National Historic Site:
    397–398
La Vieille Maison: 215
Law, Andrew Bonar: 59, 137
lawn bowling: Fundy National Park 117
Lawrence House Museum: 174
Lawrencetown Beach: 232
Le Musée de Kent: 136
Le Musée Sainte-Marie: 216
Lennox Island: 307–308
LeNoir Forge Museum: 240
Leonowens, Anna: 153
Le Pays de la Sagouine: 136
Lester Garland House: 382
Le Village de l'Acadie: 308–309
Lewis Hills: 398
L'Exposition Agricole et Festival Acadien de la
    Région évangéline: 311
libraries: Charlottetown 283; Confederation
    Centre of the Arts 275–276; Corner Brook
    403; Digby 218; Fredericton 77; Halifax 192;
    Moncton 133; Saint John 112–113; St. John's
    369; Summerside 305; Sydney 252;
    Yarmouth 213
Linden: 170

Liscomb Game Sanctuary: 235
Liscomb Mills: 235
Liverpool: 208
Lobster Carnival: 305
Lobster Cove Head Lighthouse: 393
Long Point Lighthouse: 388
Long River: 299
Lord Beaverbrook: 59, 125
Lord Selkirk Provincial Park: 288
Louisbourg: 253–255
Loyalist City Heritage Festival: 110
Loyalist House National Historic Site: 104
Lucy Maud Montgomery birthplace: 299
lumber mills: 20
Lunenburg: 202–207
Lutz Mountain Heritage Museum: 129

**M**
Mabou: 241
Mabou Ceilidh: 241
Mabou Gaelic and Historical
    Society Museum: 241
MacAskill House Museum: 240
MacDonald Farm Historic Site: 141
MacKenzie Mountain: 248
Mactaquac: 80–81
Madawaska: 84–86
Madawaska Historical Museum: 84
Magaguadavic Falls: 96
Magic Mountain Water Park: 130
Magnetic Hill: 129–130
Magnetic Hill Zoo: 129–130
Mahone Bay: 201–202
Maisonnette Beach Park: 143
Maitland: 173–174
Makkovik: 421
Malagash: 170
Maliseet people: 23
Malpeque Bay: 306–308
manufacturing: 21
maps: 48–49
Marble Mountain: 398, 403
Marconi, Guglielmo: 253, 357
Marconi National Historic Site: 253
Margaree River Valley: 244–245
Margaree Salmon Museum: 244
Margaret Bowater Park: 400
Maritime Archaic Burial Mound National
    Historic Site: 419
Maritime Command Museum: 182

## Lighthouses

Cape Bonavista: 384
Cape Lighthouse: 210
Cape Spear: 359–360
East Point: 323
Fredericton: 72
Lobster Cove Head: 393
Long Point: 388
Point Amour: 419
Point Prim: 288
West Point: 312
Yarmouth: 213

Maritime Museum of the Atlantic: 178–179
Martinique Beach Provincial Park: 234
Mary March Regional Museum: 390
Mary's Harbour: 419–420
Mary's Point: 118–119
Mavillette: 215
Mavillette Beach Provincial Park: 215
McCulloch House: 229
McCulloch, Thomas: 228
McNab's Island: 182
medical care: 46
Memorial University Botanical Garden: 360
Memorial University of Newfoundland: 361
Meteghan: 215
Meteghan River: 215–216
Métis: 22–24
metric system: 49
Mi'kmaq Cultural Centre: 308
Mi'kmaq people: 23, 308
Military Compound: 71–72
Mill River Provincial Park: 310–311
Miminegash: 312
Miners' Museum: 253
Mines & Minerals Interpretation Centre: 144
miniature golf: Cavendish 298
mining: 20
Minister's Island Historic Site: 92
Miquelon: 377–379
Miramichi City: 138–139
Miramichi Folksong Festival: 139
Miramichi River: 138–141
Miramichi Salmon Museum: 140
Miscouche: 308
Mispec Beach: 112
Mistaken Point Ecological Reserve: 375
Mockbeggar Plantation: 384
Moncton: 126–135
Moncton Museum: 128
money: 46–48
Montague: 318–319
Montague Homecoming Festival: 265
*Mont Blanc:* 175
Mont-Carmel: 308–309
Montgomery, Lucy Maud: 289, 294–295,
    296–297, 299
Monument-Lefebvre National Historic Site: 135
moose: 350
Morell: 324
motels: 35–40; *see also specific place*
Mount Carleton Provincial Park: 86

Mount Saint Vincent University Art Gallery: 183
Mount Uniacke: 225
mountain biking: *see* cycling
movies: *see* cinema
Mud Lake: 413
murals: 373, 397
Murray, Anne: 170
Murray Harbour: 317
Murray River: 317
Musée Acadien (Miscouche): 308
Musée Acadien de Caraquet: 142
Musée des Papes: 143
Musée Religieux: 309
Museum of Natural History: 180
museums: 34; Acadian Museum 245; Acadia
    University Art Gallery 223; Admiral Digby
    Museum 217; Alberton Museum 312; Anne
    Murray Centre 170; Anne of Green Gables
    Museum at Silver Bush 299; Antique Auto-
    mobile Museum 86; Archelaus Smith Muse-
    um 210; Art Gallery of Nova Scotia 179;
    Balmoral Grist Mill Museum 173; Barbour's
    General Store 103; Barrington Woolen Mill
    Museum 210; Basin Head Fisheries Museum
    323; Beaconsfield Historic House 276; Bonav-
    ista Museum 384; Boyd's Cove Beothuk Inter-
    pretation Centre 387; Bungalow, The 383;
    Canso Museum/Whitman House 236; Cape
    Breton Centre for Heritage and Science 251;
    Central New Brunswick Woodmen's Museum
    140–141; CFB Gagetown Museum 80;
    Colchester Historical Society Museum 171;
    Colony of Avalon Interpretation Centre 375;
    Conception Bay Museum 373; Confederation
    Centre of the Arts 275–276; Corner Brook
    Museum 400; Cossit House 251; Cumberland
    County Museum 168; Cupids Museum 373;
    Dartmouth Heritage Museum 182; Dory
    Shop Museum 209; Ellerslie Shellfish Muse-
    um 307; Elmira Railway Museum 323; Fan-
    tazmagoric Museum 298; Farmers' Bank
    Museum 293–294; Firefighters' Museum of
    Nova Scotia 212; Fisherman's Life Museum
    234; Fort Anne National Historic Site 221;
    Founders Hall 274; Fundy Geological Muse-
    um 170; Galerie d'Art et Musée Acadien 128;
    Galerie Restigouche 145; Garden of the Gulf
    Museum 318; Great Hall of the Clans Muse-
    um 249; Green Park Shipbuilding Museum
    and Yeo House 307; Grenfell House 397; Gulf

M

Index

Museum 405; Hank Snow Country Music Centre 208; Historic Ferryland Museum 375; International Fox Hall of Fame and Museum 303–304; Inverness Miners Museum 241; James J. O'Mara Pharmacy Museum 355–357; Jewish Historical Museum 104; Labrador Heritage Museum 413; La Vieille Maison 215; Lawrence House 174; Le Musée de Kent 136; Le Musée Sainte-Marie 216; LeNoir Forge 240; Lutz Mountain Heritage Museum 129; Mabou Gaelic and Historical Society Museum (An Drochaid) 241; MacAskill House 240; Margaree Salmon Museum 244; Maritime Command Museum 182; Maritime Museum of the Atlantic 178–179; Mary March Regional Museum 390; McCulloch House 229; Miners' Museum 253; Mines & Minerals Interpretation Centre 144; Miramichi Salmon Museum 140; Moncton Museum 128; Mount Saint Vincent University Art Gallery 183; Musée Acadien (Miscouche) 308; Musée Acadien de Caraquet 142; Musée des Papes 143; Musée Religieux 309; Museum of Natural History 180; Musquodoboit Harbour Railway Museum 232–234; Nain Piulimatsivik 422; New Brunswick Agricultural Museum 116; New Brunswick Museum 103; Newfoundland Museum 357; Nicholas Denys Museum 240; North Atlantic Aviation Museum 386–387; Northern Lights Military Museum 413; Northumberland Fisheries Museum 229; Old Meeting House Museum 210; Old St. Edward's Loyalist Church Museum 221; Parrsboro Rock and Mineral Shop Museum 170; PEI Sports Hall of Fame and Museum 303; Perkins House 208; Prince Edward Island Potato Museum 311; Queens County Museum 80; Randall House 223; Ripley's Believe It or Not! 298; Ross Farm Living Museum of Agriculture 200–201; Ross-Thompson House and Store Museum 209; Royal Atlantic Wax Museum 298; Royal Newfoundland Constabulary Museum 400; Settlers Museum 201; Shearwater Aviation Museum 183; Shelburne County Museum 209; Sherbrooke Village 235; Sherman Hines Museum of Photography 208; Sir Wilfred Grenfell College Art Gallery 402; South Dildo Whaling and Sealing Museum 374; Southern Newfoundland Seamen's Museum 377; Springhill Miners' Museum 170; St. Patrick's Church Museum 251; St-Pierre 378; Sutherland Steam Mill Museum 173; Trinity Historical Society Museum and Archives 382; Twillingate 388; Uniacke Estate Museum Park 225; West Point Lighthouse 312; White Elephant Museum 421; Wile Carding Mill Museum 207; Yarmouth County Museum 212
music: Broad Cove Scottish Concert 241; Festival 500 366; Festival of Folk Song and Dance 344; George Street Festival 366; Harvest Jazz and Blues Festival 76; Heritage Folk Festival 344; Highland summer concert series 305; Iron Skull Folk Festival 380; Labrador Straits Bakeapple Folk Festival 418; Lamèque International Baroque Music Festival 141; Lunenburg Folk Harbour Festival 206; Miramichi Folksong Festival 139; New Brunswick Competitive Festival of Music 110; Newfoundland and Labrador Folk Festival 344, 367; PEI Bluegrass & Old-Time Music Festival 265; Outdoor Summer Music Series 76; Rollo Bay Fiddle Festival 321; Saint John concerts 110; Saint John Jazz and Blues Festival 110; Southern Shore Shamrock Folk Festival 375; Stan Rogers Folk Festival 156; St. John's 366; Summer in the Bight 383
Musquodoboit Harbour: 232–234
Musquodoboit Harbour Railway Museum: 232–234

**N**
Nain: 422
Nain Piulimatsivik (Museum): 422
Nappan: 169
Natal Day: 189
national historic sites: *see* historic sites
National Parks: general discussion, 2–4; Cape Breton Highlands, 246–249; Fundy, 116–117; Gros Morne, 391–396; Kejimkujik, 208; Kouchibouguac, 137–138; Prince Edward Island, 291–293; Terra Nova, 384–386
National Wildlife Areas: Shepody 117–119; Tintamarre 121
native people: 22–24
Neguac Park: 141
New Brunswick: 51–145
New Brunswick Agricultural Museum: 116
New Brunswick Competitive Festival of Music: 110
New Brunswick Day: 76

## National Parks
Cape Breton Highlands: 246–249
Fundy: 116–117
Gros Morne: 391–396
Kejimkujik: 208
Kouchibouguac: 137–138
Prince Edward Island: 291–293
Terra Nova: 384–386

New Brunswick Museum: 103
Newfoundland: 352–406
Newfoundland and Labrador Folk Festival:
    344, 367
Newfoundland dogs: 334
Newfoundland Freshwater Resource Centre: 360
Newfoundland Museum: 357
Newfoundland Railway: 400
New London: 299
New Ross: 200–201
newspapers: 48; *Daily Gleaner* 64; *Evening
    Telegram* 348; *Guardian* 268; *Journal-Pioneer*
    268; *Telegraph-Journal* 64; *Times-Globe* 64;
    *Western Star* 403
Nicholas Denys Museum: 240
nightlife: Charlottetown 281; Halifax 188–189;
    Happy Valley–Goose Bay 415–416; Moncton
    132; Saint John 110; St. John's 365–366;
    Summerside 305
North America's First New Year's Festival: 367
North Atlantic Aviation Museum: 386–387
Northern Lights Military Museum: 413
North Lake: 323–324
North Mountain: 248
Northport Beach Provincial Park: 170
North Rustico: 294–295
North Sydney: 253
Northumberland Fisheries Museum: 229
Northumberland Provincial
    Fisheries Festival: 317
Northumberland Provincial Park: 289
North West River: 413–415
North West River Beach Festival: 416
Nova Scotia: 147–255
Nova Scotia Centre for Craft and Design: 179
Nova Scotia International Tattoo: 156, 189
nuclear power: 21; Point Lepreau 99
Nunatsiavut: 422

## O
Odell Park: 73
oil industry: 20
Old Home Week: 282
Old Meeting House Museum: 210
Old Sow tidal whirlpool: 97
Old St. Edward's Loyalist Church Museum: 221
O'Leary: 311
Oromocto: 80
Orwell: 288
Orwell Corner Historic Village: 288
Outdoor Newfoundland and Labrador: 366
Ovens Natural Park: 207
Owens Art Gallery: 119
Oyster Bed Bridge: 291

## PQ
packing: 49
Palais Crystal: 135
Panmure Island: 318
parades: 282
Park Corner: 299
parks: *see* provincial parks; national parks
Parlee Beach Provincial Park: 136
Parliament: 18
Parrsboro: 170
Parrsboro Rock and Mineral Shop Museum: 170
Partridge Island: 106
passports: 45
Peake's Wharf: 274
Peggy's Cove: 198–199
PEI Bluegrass & Old-Time Music Festival: 265
PEI Provincial Exhibition: 265, 282
PEI Sports Hall of Fame and Museum: 303
Pelton-Fuller House: 212
Pennfield Ridge: 99
people: 22–26; *see also specific place*
Perkins House Museum: 208
photography seminars: 61
photography supplies: 49
Pictou: 227–231
Pictou Lobster Festival: 230
Pier 21: 180
pirates: 200
Pirates at the Pier: 366
Placentia: 375–376
plants: 8–10
Point Amour Lighthouse Provincial Historical
    Site: 419
Pointe de l'église: 216

Point Lepreau Nuclear Generating Station: 99
Point Pleasant Park: 183
Point Prim Lighthouse: 288
Pomquet Beach Park: 232
population: 22–26; *see also specific place*
Pork and Beans War: 85
Port au Choix: 396
Port au Choix National Historic Site: 396
Port aux Basques: 405–406
Port Hastings: 239
Port Hawkesbury: 239
Port-la-Joye: 286
Port Royal: 152
Port Royal National Historic Site: 221
Port Union: 383
postal abbreviations: 47
postal service: 48
Postville: 421
Poverty Beach: 317
Prescott House: 224
Prince County: 300–313
Prince Edward Island: 257–324
Prince Edward Island National Park: 291–293
Prince Edward Island Potato Museum: 311
Province House (Halifax): 179
Province House National Historic Site
  (Charlottetown): 274–275
provinces: 4–6; highlights 28–31; population
  information 24–26
provincial parks: Anchorage, The 60; Arisaig
  231; Barachois Pond 405; Battery 241; Bay-
  field 232; Blow Me Down 404; Brudenell
  River 319–320; Buffaloland 319; Cabot
  Beach 306; Cabot's Landing 248; Cedar
  Dunes 311–312; Chaleur 60; Crystal Crescent
  Beach 190; Enclosure 60; Green Park 307;
  Herring Cove 97; Jacques Cartier 313; La
  Manche 374; Lawrencetown Beach 232; Les
  Jardins de La République 84; Lord Selkirk
  288; Mactaquac 80–81; Martinique Beach
  234; Mavillette Beach 215; Mill River
  310–311; Mount Carleton Provincial Park 86;
  Murray Beach 60; Northport Beach 170;
  Northumberland 289; Panmure Island 318;
  Parlee Beach 60, 136; Red Point 323; Rissers
  Beach 207–208; Sandbanks 380; Smuggler's
  Cove 215; Strathgartney 284–286; Sugarloaf
  Mountain 145; Taylor Head 235; Valleyview
  221; Victoria 286; Whycocomagh 242;
  William E. deGarthe Memorial 199

Public Gardens: 183
Queens County: 271–299
Queens County Museum: 80
Quidi Vidi Battery: 359
Quidi Vidi Lake: 359
quilts: 110, 264

**R**
Race Week: 200
Rainbow Valley: 298
Randall House Historical Musem: 223
recipes: 158–159
recreation: 32–35; *see also specific place and type
  of recreation*
Red Bank Indian Band: 140
Red Bay: 419
Red Bay National Historic Site: 419
Red Point Provincial Park: 323
Région évangéline: 308–310
religion: 22; provincial distinctions 24–26;
  *see also specific place*
Remote Islands: 141–142
resources: 423–433
restaurants: *see specific place*
Reversing Falls: 105–106
Rexton: 137
Rigolet: 421
Ripley's Believe It or Not! Museum: 298
Rissers Beach Provincial Park: 207–208
Rockwood Park: 106
Rocky Harbour: 395
Rodd Mill River Aquaplex and Racquet Club: 311
Rollo Bay: 321
Rollo Bay Fiddle Festival: 321
Roosevelt Campobello International Park: 97
Ross Farm Living Museum of Agriculture:
  200–201
Ross-Thompson House and Store Museum: 209
Royal Atlantic Wax Museum: 298
Royal Canadian Mounted Police (RCMP): 46
Royal Newfoundland Constabulary Museum: 400
Royal St. John's Regatta: 367
Rustico Bay: 293–295
Ryan Premises: 384

**S**
Sackville: 119–120
Sackville Waterfowl Park: 120
sailboarding: *see windsurfing*
sailing: Race Week 200

Sainte Famille Wines: 225
Saint-Jacques: 84–86
Saint John: 99–114
Saint John City Market: 104–105
Saint John River Valley: 66–86
Saint John YM/YWCA Quilt Fair: 110
Saint-Joseph-de-Memramcook: 135
Salmonier Nature Park: 375
Sandbanks Provincial Park: 380
Sandspit amusement park: 298
seal-watching: 317, 319
Seaview Park: 183
Settlers Museum: 201
Shakespeare by the Sea Festival: 366
Shand House: 225
Shearwater Aviation Museum: 183
Shediac: 136
Shelburne: 208–210
Shelburne County Exhibition: 210
Shelburne County Museum: 209
Shepody National Wildlife Area: 117–119
Sherbrooke: 235
Sherbrooke Village: 235
Sheriff Andrews House Historic Site: 91–92
Sherman Hines Museum of Photography: 208
Sheshatsheits: 413
Ship Harbour: 234
Shippagan: 141
shopping: 34; *see also specific place*
Shubenacadie River: 173–174
Shubenacadie Wildlife Park & Environmental
    Centre: 173
sightseeing highlights: 28–31; *see also specific place*
Signal Hill National Historic Site: 357
Signal Hill Tattoo: 367
Silent Witness Memorial: 387
Sir Sandford Fleming Park: 183–184
Site of Lucy Maud Montgomery's Cavendish
    Home: 296–297
skiing: general discussion, 33; Cape Breton
    Highlands National Park, 247; Halifax, 189,
    190; Kouchibouguac National Park, 138;
    Labrador City/Wabush, 417; Saint John, 106;
    Sugarloaf Mountain Provincial Park, 145
sled dog races: 417
Slocum, Joshua: 153
Smuggler's Cove Provincial Park: 215
snowboarding: 189
Snow Jam: 189
snowmobiling: 33; Sugarloaf Mountain

Provincial Park 145
Souris: 321–322
Souris Regatta: 321–322
South Dildo Whaling and Sealing Museum: 374
Southern Newfoundland Seamen's Museum: 377
Southern Shore Shamrock Folk Festival: 375
South Rustico: 293–294
spectator sports: 34
Springhill: 170
Springhill Miners' Museum: 170
Spring Wine Festival: 265
St. Andrews: 91–96
St. Andrews Blockhouse National Historic Site: 91
Stanhope: 290
Stanley Bridge: 298–299
Stanley Bridge Marine Aquarium: 298
St. Ann: 299
St. Ann's: 249
Stan Rogers Folk Festival: 156
St. Anthony: 397
Starr's Point: 224
St. Barbe: 396–397
Steady Brook Falls: 402–403
Ste.-Anne-du-Bocage Shrine: 142
Stephenville: 405
Stephenville Theatre Festival: 405
St. George: 96
St. George's Bay: 232
St. John's: 353–371
St. Martins: 115–116
St. Patrick's Church Museum: 251
St. Patrick's Day celebrations: 110
St. Peters (Nova Scotia): 240
St. Peters (Prince Edward Island): 324
St-Pierre: 377–379
St-Pierre Museum: 378
Strait Coast (New Brunswick): 135–138
Strait Coast (Prince Edward Island): 311–312
Strait Shore: 227–232
Strathgartney Provincial Park: 284–286
Strawberry Festival: 265, 324
Strawberry Tea/Dinner: 220
student visas/regulations: 46
Sugarloaf Mountain Provincial Park: 145
suggested reading: 424–431
Summer in the Bight: 383
Summerside: 302–306
Summerside Raceway: 305
Sunbury Shores Arts and Nature Centre: 93
Sunny Cottage Heritage Centre: 380

M
Index

surfing: Lawrencetown Beach 232;
   Nova Scotia 157
Sussex: 116
Sutherland Steam Mill Museum: 173
swimming: 33; Corner Brook 402; Fundy National Park 116; Halifax 190; Kouchibouguac National Park 138; Moncton 132–133; Saint John 112; St. Andrews 93–94; St. John's 367; Sugarloaf Mountain Provincial Park 145
Sydney: 250–253

**T**
Tablelands: 393
Tangier: 234–235
Tantramar Marshes: 120–121
taxes: 47–48
Taylor Head Provincial Park: 235
Teddy Bears' Picnic: 366
telephone area codes: 47
telephone service: 48
temperature: 6–8
tennis: Brudenell River 319; Fundy National Park 117; Sugarloaf Mountain Provincial Park 145
Terra Nova National Park: 384–386
Thomas Williams Heritage House: 128
Tidal Bore Rafting Park: 173
Tidal Power Plant: 221
tidal whirlpools: Old Sow 97
tide-watching: Bay of Fundy 166; Moncton 128; St. Andrews 93; Truro 171
Tignish: 313
Tignish Cultural Cenre: 313
time zones: 47
Tintamarre Sanctuary/National Wildlife Area: 121
*Titanic*: 175
tourism: 21
tourism offices: 45
tours: Charlottetown 274; Halifax 192–193; Labrador 412; Lunenburg 204–205; Saint John 102–103; St. John's 361; St-Pierre 378–379; wilderness 344
Townshend Woodlot: 322–323
Tradition by the Sea: 380
train travel: 41–42; *see also specific place*
transportation: 41–44; *see also specific place*
Trapper's Brook Animal Display: 413
Treaty of Utrecht: 14–15
Trinity: 381–383
Trinity Historical Society Museum and Archives: 382

**Theater**
Atlantic Fringe Theatre Festival: 189
Charlottetown: 281
Chester Theatre Festival: 200
Corner Brook: 402
Fredericton: 75
Halifax: 188
Lunenburg: 206
Moncton: 132
Pictou: 230
Saint John: 110
Stephenville Theatre Festival: 405
St. John's: 366
Summer in the Bight: 383
Summerside: 305
Université Sainte–Anne: 216
Victoria: 286
Wolfville: 223
Yarmouth: 213

Trinity Interpretation Centre: 382
Truro: 170–173
Twillingate: 387–389
Twillingate Fish, Fun, and Folk Festival: 389
Twillingate Museum and Crafts: 388
Tyne Valley: 306–307
Tyne Valley Oyster Festival: 306

**UV**
UNESCO world heritage sites: Gros Morne National Park 391–396; L'Anse aux Meadows 397–398
Uniacke Estate Museum Park: 225
Université de Moncton: 130
Université Sainte-Anne: 216
Upper Clements: 221–222
Upper Clements Family Vacation Park: 221–222
Upper Clements Wildlife Park: 222
Val-Comeau Park: 141
Valleyview Provincial Park: 221
Victoria (Newfoundland): 373
Victoria (Prince Edward Island): 286–287
Victoria Park (Newfoundland): 360
Victoria Park (Nova Scotia): 171–172
Victoria Park (Prince Edward Island): 276
Victoria Park Craft Fair: 132
Victoria Provincial Park: 286
Vikings: 13

vineyards: Grand Pré 225; Jost 170; Sainte Famille Wines 225
visas: 45

## WX

Wabana: 373
Wabush: 416–417
waterfalls: Churchill Falls 416; Grand Falls (New Brunswick) 82; Grand Falls (Newfoundland) 390; Magaguadavic Falls 96; Margaret Bowater Park 400; Reversing Falls 105–106; Steady Brook Falls 402–403
water parks: Aquarena 367; Kensington Towers and Water Gardens 302; Magic Mountain 130; Rodd Mill River Aquaplex 311
water sports: 33; *see also specific place*
weather: 6–8
Weekday Tea: 189
weights and measures: 49
Western Nova Scotia Exhibition: 213
Westphal: 183
West Point: 311–312
West Point Lighthouse: 312
Whale Interpretive Centre: 247
what to take: 49
White Elephant Museum: 421
Whitman House: 236
Whycocomagh: 242
Whycocomagh Provincial Park: 242
wilderness areas, parks, and reserves: Avalon Wilderness Reserve 374; Bay Du Nord Wilderness Reserve 380; Daly Point Wildlife Reserve 144; Irving Eco-Centre 137; Liscomb Game Sanctuary 235; Shepody National Wildlife Area 117–119; Shubenacadie Wildlife Park & Environmental Centre 173;

Tintamarre Sanctuary 121; Upper Clements Wildlife Park 222; *see also ecological reserves*
wildflowers: 8–9, 54, 151
Wile Carding Mill Museum: 207
William E. deGarthe Memorial Provincial Park: 199
Windsor (Newfoundland): 389–390
Windsor (Nova Scotia): 225
windsurfing: 33; *see also specific place*
wine: 40; Grand Pré Vineyards 225; Jost Vineyards 170; New Brunswick 64; Sainte Famille Wines 225; Spring Wine Festival 265; World Wine Festival 132
Winter Carnival: 416
Winterhouses sweaters: 405
winter sports: 33
Witless Bay Ecological Reserve: 374
Wolfville: 222–224
Wooden Boat Festival: 201
Wood Islands: 288–289
Woodleigh Replicas & Gardens: 302
Woody Point: 396
World War I: 17
World Wine Festival: 132
work visas/regulations: 46

## YZ

Yarmouth: 211–214
Yarmouth County Museum: 212
Yarmouth Cup Ocean Races: 213
Yarmouth Lobster Sports: 213
Yeo House: 307
York Redoubt National Historic Site: 182
Youth Hostel Association: *see* Hostelling International
zoos: Cherry Brook Zoo 106; Magnetic Hill 129–130

## Whales/Whale-Watching

Cape Breton Highlands National Park: 247
Chéticamp: 245
Digby: 219
Lunenburg: 204
Newfoundland and Labrador: 333
Nova Scotia: 151–152
Saint John: 111–112
St. Andrews: 93
Terra Nova National Park: 386
Witless Bay: 374

TYPO'S
P 191

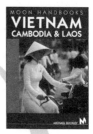

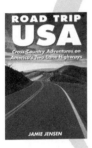

# U.S.~Metric Conversion

| | | |
|---:|---:|:---|
| 1 inch | = | 2.54 centimeters (cm) |
| 1 foot | = | .304 meters (m) |
| 1 yard | = | 0.914 meters |
| 1 mile | = | 1.6093 kilometers (km) |
| 1 km | = | .6214 miles |
| 1 fathom | = | 1.8288 m |
| 1 chain | = | 20.1168 m |
| 1 furlong | = | 201.168 m |
| 1 acre | = | .4047 hectares |
| 1 sq km | = | 100 hectares |
| 1 sq mile | = | 2.59 square km |
| 1 ounce | = | 28.35 grams |
| 1 pound | = | .4536 kilograms |
| 1 short ton | = | .90718 metric ton |
| 1 short ton | = | 2000 pounds |
| 1 long ton | = | 1.016 metric tons |
| 1 long ton | = | 2240 pounds |
| 1 metric ton | = | 1000 kilograms |
| 1 quart | = | .94635 liters |
| 1 US gallon | = | 3.7854 liters |
| 1 Imperial gallon | = | 4.5459 liters |
| 1 nautical mile | = | 1.852 km |

To compute celsius temperatures, subtract 32 from Fahrenheit and divide by 1.8. To go the other way, multiply celsius by 1.8 and add 32.

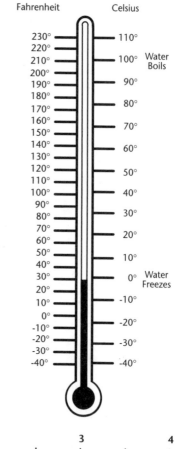

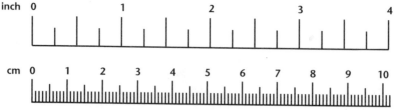